T0319799

Equity Valuation
and Portfolio
Management

The Frank J. Fabozzi Series

Fixed Income Securities, Second Edition by Frank J. Fabozzi
Focus on Value: A Corporate and Investor Guide to Wealth Creation by James L. Grant and James A. Abate
Handbook of Global Fixed Income Calculations by Dragomir Krgin
Managing a Corporate Bond Portfolio by Leland E. Crabbe and Frank J. Fabozzi
Real Options and Option-Embedded Securities by William T. Moore
Capital Budgeting: Theory and Practice by Pamela P. Peterson and Frank J. Fabozzi
The Exchange-Traded Funds Manual by Gary L. Gastineau
Professional Perspectives on Fixed Income Portfolio Management, Volume 3 edited by Frank J. Fabozzi
Investing in Emerging Fixed Income Markets edited by Frank J. Fabozzi and Efstathia Pilarinu
Handbook of Alternative Assets by Mark J. P. Anson
The Global Money Markets by Frank J. Fabozzi, Steven V. Mann, and Moorad Choudhry
The Handbook of Financial Instruments edited by Frank J. Fabozzi
Collateralized Debt Obligations: Structures and Analysis by Laurie S. Goodman and Frank J. Fabozzi
Interest Rate, Term Structure, and Valuation Modeling edited by Frank J. Fabozzi
Investment Performance Measurement by Bruce J. Feibel
The Handbook of Equity Style Management edited by T. Daniel Coggin and Frank J. Fabozzi
Foundations of Economic Value Added, Second Edition by James L. Grant
Financial Management and Analysis, Second Edition by Frank J. Fabozzi and Pamela P. Peterson
Measuring and Controlling Interest Rate and Credit Risk, Second Edition by Frank J. Fabozzi,
   Steven V. Mann, and Moorad Choudhry
Professional Perspectives on Fixed Income Portfolio Management, Volume 4 edited by Frank J. Fabozzi
The Handbook of European Fixed Income Securities edited by Frank J. Fabozzi and Moorad Choudhry
The Handbook of European Structured Financial Products edited by Frank J. Fabozzi and Moorad Choudhry
The Mathematics of Financial Modeling and Investment Management by Sergio M. Focardi and
   Frank J. Fabozzi
Short Selling: Strategies, Risks, and Rewards edited by Frank J. Fabozzi
The Real Estate Investment Handbook by G. Timothy Haight and Daniel Singer
Market Neutral Strategies edited by Bruce I. Jacobs and Kenneth N. Levy
Securities Finance: Securities Lending and Repurchase Agreements edited by Frank J. Fabozzi and Steven V. Mann
Fat-Tailed and Skewed Asset Return Distributions by Svetlozar T. Rachev, Christian Menn, and
   Frank J. Fabozzi
Financial Modeling of the Equity Market: From CAPM to Cointegration by Frank J. Fabozzi, Sergio M.
   Focardi, and Petter N. Kolm
Advanced Bond Portfolio Management: Best Practices in Modeling and Strategies edited by
   Frank J. Fabozzi, Lionel Martellini, and Philippe Priaulet
Analysis of Financial Statements, Second Edition by Pamela P. Peterson and Frank J. Fabozzi
Collateralized Debt Obligations: Structures and Analysis, Second Edition by Douglas J. Lucas, Laurie S.
   Goodman, and Frank J. Fabozzi
Handbook of Alternative Assets, Second Edition by Mark J. P. Anson
Introduction to Structured Finance by Frank J. Fabozzi, Henry A. Davis, and Moorad Choudhry
Financial Econometrics by Svetlozar T. Rachev, Stefan Mittnik, Frank J. Fabozzi, Sergio M. Focardi, and
   Teo Jasic
Developments in Collateralized Debt Obligations: New Products and Insights by Douglas J. Lucas,
   Laurie S. Goodman, Frank J. Fabozzi, and Rebecca J. Manning
Robust Portfolio Optimization and Management by Frank J. Fabozzi, Petter N. Kolm,
   Dessislava A. Pachamanova, and Sergio M. Focardi
Advanced Stochastic Models, Risk Assessment, and Portfolio Optimizations by Svetlozar T. Rachev,
   Stogan V. Stoyanov, and Frank J. Fabozzi
How to Select Investment Managers and Evaluate Performance by G. Timothy Haight,
   Stephen O. Morrell, and Glenn E. Ross
Bayesian Methods in Finance by Svetlozar T. Rachev, John S. J. Hsu, Biliana S. Bagasheva, and
   Frank J. Fabozzi
Structured Products and Related Credit Derivatives by Brian P. Lancaster, Glenn M. Schultz, and Frank J. Fabozzi
Quantitative Equity Investing: Techniques and Strategies by Frank J. Fabozzi, Sergio M. Focardi, and
   Petter N. Kolm
Introduction to Fixed Income Analytics, Second Edition by Frank J. Fabozzi and Steven V. Mann
The Handbook of Traditional and Alternative Investment Vehicles by Mark J. P. Anson, Frank J. Fabozzi,
   and Frank J. Jones
The Theory and Practice of Investment Management, Second Edition edited by Frank J. Fabozzi and
   Harry M. Markowitz

Equity Valuation and Portfolio Management

FRANK J. FABOZZI
HARRY M. MARKOWITZ
EDITORS

WILEY

John Wiley & Sons, Inc.

978-0-470-92991-9 (cloth); 978-1-118-15655-1 (ebk); 978-1-118-15653-7 (ebk);
978-1-118-15654-4 (ebk)

10 9 8 7 6 5 4 3 2 1

Contents

Preface xiii

About the Editors xxiii

Contributing Authors xxv

CHAPTER 1
An Introduction to Quantitative Equity Investing 1
Paul Bukowski
Equity Investing 1
Fundamental vs. Quantitative Investor 2
The Quantitative Stock Selection Model 7
The Overall Quantitative Investment Process 9
Research 9
Portfolio Construction 18
Monitoring 21
Current Trends 22
Key Points 23
Questions 24

CHAPTER 2
Equity Analysis Using Traditional and Value-Based Metrics 25
James L. Grant and Frank J. Fabozzi
Overview of Traditional Metrics 25
Price Multiples 32
Fundamental Stock Return 36
Traditional Caveats 38
Overview of Value-Based Metrics 39
Key Points 58
Appendix: Case Study 60
Questions 69

CHAPTER 3
A Franchise Factor Approach to Modeling P/E Orbits   71
Stanley Kogelman and Martin L. Leibowitz

Background   72
Historical Data Observations   75
Formulation of the Basic Model   81
P/E Myopia: The Fallacy of a Stable P/E   85
Two-Phase P/E Orbits   91
Franchise Valuation under Q-Type Competition   96
Franchise Labor   97
Key Points   101
Questions   102

CHAPTER 4
Relative Valuation Methods for Equity Analysis   105
Glen A. Larsen Jr., Frank J. Fabozzi, and Chris Gowlland

Basic Principles of Relative Valuation   106
Hypothetical Example   115
Key Points   123
Questions   124

CHAPTER 5
Valuation over the Cycle and the Distribution of Returns   125
Anders Ersbak Bang Nielsen and Peter C. Oppenheimer

The Link Between Earnings and Returns   126
The Phases Can Be Interpreted in Relationship to the Economy   132
Asset Class Performance Varies across the Phases   137
Incorporating Cyclicality into Valuations   139
Appendix: Dates and Returns of the Phases   142
Key Points   146
Questions   146

CHAPTER 6
An Architecture for Equity Portfolio Management   147
Bruce I. Jacobs and Kenneth N. Levy

Architectural Building Blocks   148
Traditional Active Management   151
Passive Management   156
Engineered Management   157

Expanding Opportunities   160
The Risk-Return Continuum   163
The Ultimate Objective   167
Key Points   168
Questions   169

CHAPTER 7
Equity Analysis in a Complex Market   **171**
Bruce I. Jacobs and Kenneth N. Levy

An Integrated Approach to a Segmented Market   172
Disentangling   176
Constructing, Trading, and Evaluating Portfolios   184
Profiting from Complexity   186
Key Points   187
Questions   188

CHAPTER 8
Survey Studies of the Use of Quantitative Equity Management **189**
Frank J. Fabozzi, Sergio M. Focardi, and Caroline L. Jonas

2003 Intertek European Study   189
2006 Intertek Study   197
2007 Intertek Study   205
Challenges for Quantitative Equity Investing   224
Modeling After the 2007–2009 Global Financial Crisis   226
Key Points   228
Questions   229

CHAPTER 9
Implementable Quantitative Equity Research   **231**
Frank J. Fabozzi, Sergio M. Focardi, and K. C. Ma

The Rise of Econophysics   233
A General Framework   235
Select a Sample Free from Survivorship Bias   238
Select a Methodology to Estimate the Model   239
Risk Control   246
Key Points   248
Questions   249

CHAPTER 10

Tracking Error and Common Stock Portfolio Management   **251**
Raman Vardharaj, Frank J. Fabozzi, and Frank J. Jones

Definition of Tracking Error   251
Components of Tracking Error   254
Forward-Looking vs. Backward-Looking Tracking Error   255
Information Ratio   256
Determinants of Tracking Error   257
Marginal Contribution to Tracking Error   261
Key Points   262
Questions   263

CHAPTER 11

Factor-Based Equity Portfolio Construction and Analysis   **265**
Petter N. Kolm, Joseph A. Cerniglia, and Frank J. Fabozzi

Factor-Based Trading   266
Developing Factor-Based Trading Strategies   269
Risk to Trading Strategies   271
Desirable Properties of Factors   273
Sources for Factors   273
Building Factors from Company Characteristics   274
Working with Data   275
Analysis of Factor Data   283
Key Points   287
Questions   289

CHAPTER 12

Cross-Sectional Factor-Based Models and Trading Strategies   **291**
Joseph A. Cerniglia, Petter N. Kolm, and Frank J. Fabozzi

Cross-Sectional Methods for Evaluation of Factor Premiums   292
Factor Models   300
Performance Evaluation of Factors   310
Model Construction Methodologies for a
  Factor-based Trading Strategy   317
Backtesting   328
Backtesting Our Factor Trading Strategy   330
Key Points   331
Appendix: The Compustat Point-in-Time,
  IBES Consensus Databases and Factor Definitions   333
Questions   337

CHAPTER 13

Multifactor Equity Risk Models and Their Applications   **339**
Anthony Lazanas, Antônio Baldaque da Silva,
Arne D. Staal, and Cenk Ural

Motivation   340
Equity Risk Factor Models   342
Applications of Equity Risk Models   350
Key Points   370
Questions   371

CHAPTER 14

Dynamic Factor Approaches to Equity Portfolio Management   **373**
Dorsey D. Farr

Methods of Active Management   376
Modeling   385
Implementation   392
Key Points   395
Questions   395

CHAPTER 15

A Factor Competition Approach to Stock Selection   **397**
Joseph Mezrich and Junbo Feng

The Problem   397
The Solution   403
Which Factors Get Picked?   407
Does the Alpha Repair Process Work?   408
Key Points   411
Questions   412

CHAPTER 16

Avoiding Unintended Country Bets in Global Equity Portfolios   **413**
Michele Aghassi, Cliff Asness,
Oktay Kurbanov, and Lars N. Nielsen

Country Membership and Individual Stock Returns   414
Ways to Build Active Global Portfolios   416
Studying the Naive Portfolio   419
Empirical Results   420
Why Does the Naive Stock Selection
Portfolio Make Country Noise Bets?   422
Key Points   423
Questions   424

CHAPTER 17
Modeling Market Impact Costs   **425**
Petter N. Kolm and Frank J. Fabozzi
  Market Impact Costs   426
  Liquidity and Transaction Costs   427
  Market Impact Measurements and Empirical Findings   430
  Forecasting and Modeling Market Impact   433
  Key Points   439
  Questions   440

CHAPTER 18
Equity Portfolio Selection in Practice   **441**
Dessislava A. Pachamanova and Frank J. Fabozzi
  Portfolio Constraints Commonly Used in Practice   442
  Benchmark Exposure and Tracking Error Minimization   450
  Incorporating Transaction Costs   454
  Incorporating Taxes   460
  Multi-Account Optimization   465
  Robust Parameter Estimation   469
  Portfolio Resampling   471
  Robust Portfolio Optimization   474
  Key Points   480
  Questions   481

CHAPTER 19
Portfolio Construction and Extreme Risk   **483**
Jennifer Bender, Jyh-Huei Lee, and Dan Stefek
  Measures of Extreme Loss   484
  Constraining Shortfall   485
  Performance   485
  Imposing Benchmark Neutrality   487
  Analysis   489
  Key Points   493
  Appendix: Constructing Out-of-Sample Shortfall Betas   494
  Questions   495

CHAPTER 20
Working with High-Frequency Data   **497**
Irene Aldridge
  What is High-Frequency Data?   497

How is High-Frequency Data Recorded? 499
Properties of High-Frequency Data 500
High-Frequency Data are Voluminous 501
High-Frequency Data are Subject to Bid-Ask Bounce 503
High-Frequency Data are Irregularly Spaced in Time 509
Equity Correlations Decay at High Frequencies 517
Key Points 519
Questions 520

CHAPTER 21
Statistical Arbitrage **521**
Brian J. Jacobsen

Pairs Trading 523
General Models 532
Key Points 534
Questions 534

About the Website **535**

Index **537**

Preface

In an editorial in the Winter 2011 issue of the *Journal of Portfolio Management*, Mark Kritzman notes the following regarding what is popularly referred to as *Markowitz portfolio theory:* "Mean-variance optimization is about to begin its 60th year and by all accounts it has aged extremely well."

He goes on to say, "As with many innovations, however, practitioners of the old technology resisted change and defended their resistance with a variety of excuses, which persist even today." There are several reasons why practitioners were reluctant or slow to adopt a more quantitative approach such as that offered by the mean-variance framework. The computing power needed to manipulate the databases used to obtain the required inputs for mean-variance analysis and then efficiently solve for the optimal portfolios was very limited in the years that followed its introduction in 1952. Major advances in computing power have taken care of this obstacle, as well as the availability of commercial software for solving large complex optimization problems.

A second reason for the reluctance or inability to adopt a more quantitative approach was simply practitioners' lack of the mathematical skill set necessary to appreciate the advantages of a quantitative approach. Since the late 1970s, however, university finance programs have armed their graduates with the mathematical and statistical skills needed to deal with quantitative models. In fact, over the past decade, a good number of universities have augmented their degree offerings beyond the traditional MBA with a specialization in finance to degree programs that bear titles such as "computational finance," "quantitative finance," "mathematical finance," and "financial engineering," in recognition of the need to equip students with strong quantitative skills.

Finally, the classical mean-variance model required refinements and extensions to deal with real-world institutional constraints and market frictions and allow it to be effectively implemented in the real world. In this book, the contributors provide the state-of-the-art methods for implementing equity valuation models, trading models, and portfolio management strategies. Both traditional equity management and quantitative equity management are covered. All of the contributors to this book have had experience as equity portfolio managers or equity strategists.

In the first chapter, Paul Bukowski reviews the fundamentals of quantitative equity investing, the core steps in the quantitative equity investment process, and the most common techniques used by quantitative equity managers. He contrasts quantitative equity investing with the traditional approaches and explains how the quantitative and traditional approaches differ in their creation of a repeatable process that utilizes several key criteria to find the most attractive companies—the stock selection model.

Chapters 2 and 3 cover relatively new and improved approaches for what would be classified as "traditional" approaches to equity selection. Fundamentals and valuation metrics are used in traditional and value-based approaches to equity valuation. James Grant and Frank Fabozzi explain and illustrate both approaches in Chapter 2 with the goal of showing their joint role in the valuation process. Liquidity, activity, debt (leverage), and profitability measures are used in the traditional approach, with growth rates and profitability measures often combined with relative valuation measures ("multiples") to assess the attractiveness or unattractiveness of a firm's common stock. Value-based metrics are financial measures that concentrate on metrics for discerning whether a company is pointing in the direction of wealth creation or wealth destruction. In this relatively new approach, the focus is on identifying firms that can consistently earn a return on capital that exceeds their weighted average cost of capital. A financial metric takes on a value-based metric character when there is an explicit recognition of and accounting for the overall cost of capital or the cost of equity. Hence, the most distinctive feature of the value-based metric analysis in contrast to traditional analysis is the formal recognition of the investor's required rate of return (cost of equity) and the overall cost of capital. The most often used value-based metrics—residual income, economic value added (EVA®), market value added (MVA), and cash flow return on investment (CFROI®)—are explained in the chapter. In the end, the objective of both the traditional and value-based approaches is to determine a target valuation for a company leading to a potential buy (or "overweight" relative to reference index), sell ("underweight" relative to index) or hold decision (benchmark weight) on a company's stock. After reviewing the relevant metrics, Grant and Fabozzi illustrate the benefits of using a synthesized approach to assess potential buy and sell (short) opportunities.

As Stanley Kogelman and Martin Leibowitz note in Chapter 3, although the standard dividend discount model is still often used as an equity valuation model, the model often masks the extreme variations in growth expectations, return on equity, and sustainable earnings that drive the change in valuations and move markets. These limitations of the dividend discount model are overcome by the franchise factor model developed by Kogelman and Leibowitz. This model offers greater clarity on how corporate and economic events impact the key components of a firm's value while still maintaining one of the major appeals of the dividend discount model—simplicity and intuitive appeal.

Relative valuation methods are a traditional approach for comparing several companies by using multiples or ratios (such as price–earnings, price–book, and price–free cash flow), implicitly assuming that the firms being analyzed are similar in their investment attributes and, therefore, on average, likely to trade at similar multiples. If so, relative valuation methods can be used by portfolio managers to identify companies that look "cheap" or "expensive" relative to their peers and thereby provide another tool for equity portfolio selection in long-only and long-short strategies. Relative valuation methods for equity analysis are covered in Chapter 4 by Glen Larsen Jr., Frank Fabozzi, and Chris Gowlland.

Empirical studies have found what intuition would suggest about stock behavior: Valuation is a good predictor of returns over the long run. Although today's valuations offer investors a good deal of information about future expected returns, they are silent regarding how these returns should be distributed over time. For example, investors would like to know whether future expected returns are evenly distributed over several years or whether returns cluster into short time periods. Moreover, investors want to know whether there is a process that determines how future expected returns are generated. In Chapter 5, Anders Ersbak Bang Nielsen and Peter Oppenheimer address this issue. As they point out, the empirical evidence based on historical observations suggests that there is a relationship between valuation, earnings, and the economic cycle that provides guidance to future expected returns. The practical implication of their findings that valuations and returns shift over the economic cycle is that valuation models should be adjusted to take into account this important relationship.

In Chapter 6, Bruce Jacobs and Kenneth Levy provide an architecture for equity portfolio management, outlining the fundamental relationships between stocks (the raw investment material), investment approaches (portfolio construction techniques), potential rewards, and possible risks. The basic building blocks for constructing portfolios is the equity core and its constituent style subsets that are comprised of stocks with similar price behaviors—large-cap growth, large-cap value, and small-cap stocks. Investors must also decide among possible investment approaches—traditional, passive, and engineered (quantitative) active—each of which can be characterized by an underlying investment philosophy and a general level of risk. Because investment performance reflects breadth of inquiry (the sheer number of investment opportunities) and depth of analysis (the strength of investment insights), the three investment approaches can be distinguished on that basis. Although the traditional management approach provides depth, it is characterized by a lack of breadth, susceptibility to cognitive errors, and lack of portfolio integrity. In contrast, there is no depth at all provided by the passive management approach but it does offer breadth, freedom from cognitive errors, and portfolio integrity. The advantage of the engineered management approach compared to the other two approaches is that it is capable of allowing a manager to construct portfolios that benefit from both breadth and depth of analysis, are free of cognitive errors, and have structural integrity. Breadth can be expanded with the use of short selling, either in market neutral long-short or 130–30 enhanced active long-short strategies.

Bruce Jacobs and Kenneth Levy describe in Chapter 7 their approach to investing and its application to the stock selection, portfolio construction, and performance evaluation problems in a complex system such as the equity market. They discuss the advantages and disadvantages of portfolio managers trying to cover the broadest possible range of stocks or realizing better analytical insights by allocating their limited resources so as to concentrate on a particular subset of the market or a limited number of stocks. They explain how combining the two may offer the best avenue for identifying investment opportunities. They also discuss what Harry Markowitz in his foreword to the 2000 Jacobs-Levy book (*Quantitative Analysis for Stock Selection*) has termed their "seminal work" on disentangling return-predictor relationships. This involves multivariate analysis of numerous individual stock fundamental and behavioral variables, industry affiliations, and macroeconomic conditions, to forecast "pure" returns to each predictor, independent of the effects of other factors. Disentangling return-predictor relationships can reveal hidden opportunities and distinguish real from spurious effects; the resulting return predictions are also additive and generally more persistent than "naïve" predictions obtained from simpler analyses using only one or a few factors at a time.

The balance of the book deals primarily with quantitative equity management. A review of three studies based on surveys and interviews of market participants about their use and experience with quantitative equity techniques is the subject of Chapter 8 coauthored by Frank Fabozzi, Sergio Focardi, and Caroline Jonas. They report that the primary methodology of financial modeling in investment management is factor models, which are used to forecast returns and to compute exposure to risk factors. Quantitative techniques that are also widely used are momentum and reversal models, cash flow–based models, and behavioral models. There is increased use of adaptive models capable of dealing with different market conditions and robust optimization models for portfolio optimization along with robust techniques for estimating inputs. It is expected that in the future there will see greater use of models for dealing with nonlinearities and fat-tailed distributions, the use of risk measures suitable for nonlinear distributions, and methods to measure the complexity of the financial system.

In the quantitative process, the identification of any persistent pattern in the data is sought and must then be converted it into implementable and profitable investment strategies. As explained by Frank Fabozzi, Sergio Focardi, and K. C. Ma in Chapter 9, how this is done requires the development of underlying economic theories, an explanation of actual returns, estimation of expected returns, and construction of corresponding portfolios. In evaluating models for potential implementation of investment strategies, two guiding principles are model simplicity and out-of-sample validation. A portfolio manager can place a higher level of confidence on a simple model validated on data different from those on which it has been built. The selection of a methodology for estimating a model should satisfy the same quality tests as developing economic theories and selecting samples. In the absence of strong intuition, the methodology that needs the least amount of human inputs should be employed for estimating a model. Even if the expected return is modeled properly at the individual stock level, the bottom line of implementable investment strategies is evaluated by an acceptable level of risk-adjusted portfolio excess returns. Because most institutional portfolios are benchmarked, the objective is to minimize tracking error given some level of portfolio excess return. For this purpose, risk control becomes technically much more complex than the conventional efficient portfolio concept.

The measure used to control equity portfolio risk relative to a specified benchmark, as well as for risk budgeting (i.e., allocation of risk) and assessing performance, is tracking error. This metric, also referred to as *tracking error risk*, is the dispersion of a portfolio's active returns (where the active return is the difference between a portfolio's return and a benchmark's return). In Chapter 10, Raman Vardharaj, Frank Fabozzi, and Frank Jones review the concepts of backward-looking and forward-looking tracking error and identify the major factors that affect tracking error.

In Chapters 11 and 12, companion chapters coauthored by Petter Kolm, Joseph Cerniglia, and Frank Fabozzi, a demonstration of how to employ factors to build equity forecasting models is provided. These models, also referred to as *alpha* or *stock selection models*, serve as mathematical representations of trading strategies. The eight main steps in the development of a factor-based trading strategy are defining a trading idea or investment strategy, developing factors, acquiring and processing data, analyzing the strategy, building the strategy, evaluating the strategy, backtesting the strategy, and implementing the strategy. The authors describe and illustrate with real-world examples these steps. In Chapter 11, the development of trading strategies based on factors constructed from common (cross-sectional) characteristics of stocks is provided. After providing a definition of factors, they examine the major sources of risk associated with trading strategies and demonstrate how factors are constructed from company characteristics and market data. Because the quality of the data used in this process is critical, several data scrubbing and adjustment techniques to deal with the problems arising from backfilling and restatements of data, missing data, inconsistently reported data, as well as survivorship and look-ahead biases are explained. Finally, they discuss the analysis of the statistical properties of factors. Basic statistical measures include the time-series and cross-sectional averages of the mean, standard deviations, and key percentiles.

In Chapter 12, Kolm, Cerniglia, and Fabozzi extend the analysis to include multiple factors with the goal of developing a dynamic multifactor trading strategy that incorporates a number of common institutional constraints, such as turnover, transaction costs, sector allocation, and tracking error. After reviewing several approaches for the evaluation of return premiums and risk characteristics to factors (the four most common being portfolio sorts, factor models, factor portfolios, and information coefficients), they describe four approaches (data driven, factor model, heuristic, and optimization) used to combine several factors into a single model—a trading strategy. To understand the performance and risk characteristics of a factor-based trading strategy, it is imperative to perform out-of-sample backtests. An out-of-sample methodology is a backtesting methodology where the researcher uses a subset of the sample to specify a model and then evaluates the forecasting ability of the model on a different subset of data. The authors explain the two approaches for implementing an out-of-sample methodology: the split-sample approach and the recursive out-of-sample test.

While Chapters 11 and 12 describe how to build and test factor-based models so that they can be used as the basis for trading strategies, in Chapter 13, Anthony Lazanas, Antonio Baldaque da Silva, Arne Staal, and Cenk Ural present an actual equity factor model—the Barclays Capital Global Risk Model—and demonstrate its applications to portfolio risk management, portfolio construction, portfolio rebalancing, scenario analysis, and performance attribution. Although the authors describe the structure of multifactor equity risk models, types of factors used in these models, and estimation techniques as in the prior two chapters, the applications are the focal point. In particular, they explain how an equity factor model provides portfolio managers with insight into the major sources of portfolio risk so that managers can control a portfolio's risk exposures and understand the contributions of different portfolio components to total risk. They also show how a factor model can be used in performance attribution analysis so as to (1) provide ex post insight into how the portfolio manager's views and corresponding investments can be translated into actual returns and (2) provide portfolio managers with a powerful tool to perform stress testing of portfolio positions and gain insight into the impact of specific market events on portfolio performance.

Portfolio managers use factor models to construct portfolios based on tactical exposure to factors such as equity style, industry, or geographic location, macroeconomic factors, or microeconomic factors while attempting to eliminate sources of security-specific risk. Dynamic factor approaches to portfolio management, the subject of Chapter 14, authored by Dorsey Farr, describes portfolio strategies based on dynamic factor methods, explores a variety of the modeling approaches used to govern the implementation of these strategies, reviews the increasing number of tools available for implementation of these strategies, and highlights how security selection is no longer necessary for an efficient implementation in many cases.

A dilemma facing managers employing factor models for stock selection is deciding when to abandon a factor that seems to have lost efficacy, and when to introduce one that appears to have become important. Joseph Mezrich and Junbo Feng describe an approach in Chapter 15, which they refer to as the "Alpha Repair" strategy, which deals with this issue. The objective of the proposed approach is to provide a systematic framework that removes failed strategies from the factor model until they prove worthy, while providing an opportunity for new strategies to be introduced into the factor model. They cast the problem as one of asset allocation for factors, with the important twist that a large set of factors always compete for a place in a small set of factors that are used for stock selection. The history of a factor return, volatility, and correlation with other factor returns in a given month is the criterion used to determine whether a factor remains in the model.

Although a good number of studies have analyzed the relative importance of stock-specific risk, sector risk, and country risk for global portfolios and find that country risk is a key driver of individual stock returns, there has been less focus on the impact of country membership on actively managed stock portfolios. For example, there is a question as to whether ignoring country membership in constructing global portfolios can hamper accurate risk allocation. This issue is addressed by Michele Aghassi, Cliff Asness, Oktay Kurbanov, and Lars Nielsen in Chapter 16, where they demonstrate that ignoring country membership in stock portfolio construction can yield sizeable country bets, which may in fact be dominated by unintended tilts. They show that these issues are especially pronounced in the context of emerging market countries. They then explain how a stock selection manager can (within a quantitative or qualitative process) adjust for country membership in order to achieve accurate risk allocation and thereby reduce the likelihood of "noise pollution" of alpha signals.

The transaction costs associated with trading adversely impact portfolio return. Therefore, efficient equity portfolio management requires a systematic integration of trading costs management, trading execution, and portfolio management. Petter Kolm and Frank Fabozzi address equity transaction costs in Chapter 17, first defining the different types of costs—explicit costs (which include brokerage and taxes) and implicit costs (which include market impact costs, price movement risk, and opportunity cost)—and then introducing several approaches for the modeling of transaction costs, in particular market impact costs. Typical forecasting models for market impact costs are based on a statistical factor approach.

Quantitative formulations of portfolio allocation problems used in equity portfolio management are presented in Chapters 18 and 19. As noted earlier, a quantitative equity portfolio selection often involves extending the classical mean-variance framework formulated by Harry Markowitz or modifying the framework to incorporate more advanced tail-risk portfolio allocation frameworks so as to include different constraints that take specific investment guidelines and institutional features into account. In Chapter 18, Dessislava Pachamanova and Frank Fabozzi discuss extensions—such as index tracking formulations, the incorporation of transaction costs, optimization of trades across multiple client accounts, and tax-aware strategies—and review methods for incorporating robustness into quantitative portfolio allocation procedures by applying robust statistics, simulation, and robust optimization techniques. In Chapter 19, Jennifer Bender, Jyh-Huei Lee, and Dan Stefek adapt mean-variance analysis so as to construct active equity portfolios with less exposure to extreme losses compared to normal optimized portfolio. They do so by introducing a measure of the sensitivity of a portfolio to periods of extreme stress that they refer to as shortfall beta and then constrain this measure in the optimization process. Their empirical evidence demonstrates the potential benefits of constraining shortfall beta.

The idiosyncrasies, opportunities, and pitfalls in equity portfolio management arising from the use of high-frequency data (i.e., bid and ask quotes, sizes and latest trade characteristics that are recorded sequentially at irregular time intervals) are covered in Chapter 20 by Irene Aldridge. She explains how and when the traditional methods of data analysis employed when low-frequency data (such as daily data) are used by equity managers must to be modified to deal with the unique nature of high-frequency data. Statistical arbitrage strategies seek to identify mispriced stocks using quantitative models of historical prices and then exploit the mispricings that have been identified. Investors employing such strategies are subject to a myriad of risks. The major risk is model risk, which is the risk that the quantitative model of the price process of stocks employed in the strategy to identify mispricing may not be valid. In Chapter 21, Brian Jacobsen explains two simple models of statistical arbitrage—pairs trading and correlation trading—and then presents a more general method based on modeling the long-run relationships and short-run dynamics of the pricing processes.

Frank J. Fabozzi
Harry M. Markowitz
May 2011

About the Editors

Frank J. Fabozzi is Professor of Finance at EDHEC Business School and a member of the EDHEC-Risk Institute. Prior to joining EDHEC in August 2011, he held various professorial positions in finance at Yale University's School of Management from 1994 to 2011 and from 1986 to 1992 was a visiting professor of finance and accounting at MIT's Sloan School of Management. Professor Fabozzi is the editor of the *Journal of Portfolio Management*, as well as an associate editor of the *Journal of Fixed Income* and on the editorial boards of the *Journal of Asset Management, Journal of Structured Finance, Quantitative Finance,* and *Review of Futures Markets.* He earned a doctorate in economics from the City University of New York in 1972. He is a trustee for the BlackRock family of closed-end funds. In 2002, he was inducted into the Fixed Income Analysts Society's Hall of Fame and is the 2007 recipient of the C. Stewart Sheppard Award given by the CFA Institute. He earned the designation of Chartered Financial Analyst and Certified Public Accountant. He has authored and edited numerous books in finance.

Harry M. Markowitz has applied computer and mathematical techniques to various practical decision making areas. In finance, in an article in 1952 and a book in 1959, he presented what is now referred to as MPT, "modern portfolio theory." This has become a standard topic in college courses and texts on investments and is widely used by institutional investors for tactical asset allocation, risk control, and attribution analysis. In other areas, Dr. Markowitz developed "sparse matrix" techniques for solving very large mathematical optimization problems. These techniques are now standard in production software for optimization programs. He also designed and supervised the development of the SIMSCRIPT programming language. SIMSCRIPT has been widely used for programming computer simulations of systems like factories, transportation systems, and communication networks. In 1989, Dr. Markowitz received the John von Neumann Award from the Operations Research Society of America for his work in portfolio theory, sparse matrix techniques, and SIMSCRIPT. In 1990, he shared the Nobel Prize in Economics for his work on portfolio theory.

Contributing Authors

Michele Aghassi	AQR Capital Management
Irene Aldridge	ABLE Alpha Trading
Cliff Asness	AQR Capital Management
António Baldaque da Silva	Barclays Capital
Jennifer Bender	MSCI
Paul Bukowski	Hartford Investment Management
Joseph A. Cerniglia	Courant Institute of Mathematical Sciences, New York University
Frank J. Fabozzi	EDHEC School of Business
Dorsey D. Farr	French Wolf & Farr
Junbo Feng	Nomura Securities International, Inc.
Sergio M. Focardi	EDHEC Business School and The Intertek Group
Chris Gowlland	Delaware Investments
James L. Grant	University of Massachusetts–Boston
Bruce I. Jacobs	Jacobs Levy Equity Management
Brian J. Jacobsen	Wells Fargo Funds Management and Wisconsin Lutheran College
Caroline L. Jonas	The Intertek Group
Frank J. Jones	San Jose State University
Stanley Kogelman	Delft Strategic Advisors, LLC
Petter N. Kolm	Courant Institute of Mathematical Sciences, New York University
Oktay Kurbanov	AQR Capital Management
Glen A. Larsen Jr.	Indiana University, Kelley School of Business–Indianapolis
Anthony Lazanas	Barclays Capital
Jyh-Huei Lee	MSCI
Martin L. Leibowitz	Morgan Stanley & Co.

Kenneth N. Levy	Jacobs Levy Equity Management
K. C. Ma	KCM Asset Management, Inc. and Stetson University
Joseph Mezrich	Nomura Securities International, Inc.
Lars N. Nielsen	AQR Capital Management
Anders Ersbak Bang Nielsen	Goldman Sachs International
Peter C. Oppenheimer	Goldman Sachs International
Dessislava A. Pachamanova	Babson College
Arne D. Staal	Barclays Capital
Dan Stefek	MSCI
Cenk Ural	Barclays Capital
Raman Vardharaj	OppenheimerFunds

CHAPTER 1

An Introduction to Quantitative Equity Investing

Paul Bukowski, CFA
Senior Vice President, Head of Equities
Hartford Investment Management

The goal of this chapter is to provide the reader a basic understanding of quantitative equity investing and to explain the quantitative investing process. We focus on the following three questions:

1. How do quantitative and fundamental equity investors differ?
2. What are the core steps in a quantitative equity investment process?
3. What are the basic building blocks used by quantitative equity investors?

In answering these questions, this chapter explores the quantitative equity investment process. We see how it is similar to many other approaches, all searching for the best stocks. Where it differs is in the creation of a repeatable process that uses several key criteria to find the most attractive companies—its stock selection model. Additionally, some of the most common techniques used by quantitative equity investors are covered.

It is important to understand that this chapter is dedicated to a traditional quantitative equity investing approach. There are many other types of investing that are quantitative in nature such as high-frequency trading, statistical arbitrage, and the like, however, these are not covered.

EQUITY INVESTING

Investing can take many forms, but it starts with an investor assigning a value to a security. Whether this value exceeds or is less than the current market price usually determines whether the investor will buy or sell the

EXHIBIT 1.1   The Value of a Stock Comes from Multiple Information Sources

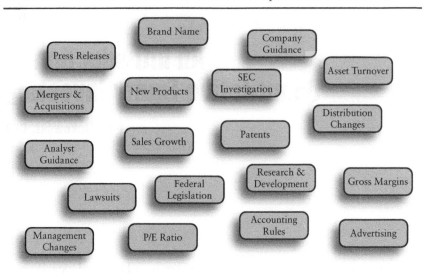

security. In the case of equities, the investor often seeks to understand the specific company under consideration, the broader economic environment, and the interplay between the two. This encompasses a wide range of information for the investor to consider as displayed in Exhibit 1.1. How this information is used differentiates the quantitative from the fundamental investor.

FUNDAMENTAL VS. QUANTITATIVE INVESTOR

Let's start with a basic question. How do portfolio managers select stocks from a broad universe of more than a thousand companies?

Fundamental managers start with a basic company screen. For instance, they may first look for companies that satisfy conditions such as a price-to-earnings (P/E) ratio that is less than 15, earnings growth greater than 10%, and profit margins in excess of 20%. Filtering by those characteristics may result in, say, 200 potential candidates. Next, portfolio managers in consultation with their group of stock analysts spend the majority of their time thoroughly reviewing each of the potential candidates to arrive at the best 50 to 100 stocks for their portfolio. A quantitative manager, in contrast, spends the bulk of their time determining the characteristics for the initial stock screen, their stock selection model. They will look for five or more unique characteristics that are good at identifying the most attractive 200 stocks of the universe. A quantitative manager will then purchase all 200 stocks for their portfolio.

So let's expand on how these two investors—fundamental and quantitative—differ? Exhibit 1.2 details the main attributes of the following two approaches:

1. *Focus: Company vs. characteristic.* The fundamental investor's primary analysis is on a single company at a time, while the quantitative investor's primary analysis is on a single characteristic at a time. For example, a fundamental investor may analyze a health care company to assess if a company's sales prospects look strong and whether this stronger sales growth is reflected in the company's current stock price. A quantitative investor may also invest in a company based on its sales growth, but will start by assessing the sales growth characteristic. The quantitative investor will determine whether stocks within the group, health care companies, with higher sales growth also have higher stock returns. If they do, then the quantitative investor will buy health care stocks with higher sales growth. In the end, both types of investors may buy a stock due to its good sales prospects, but both come at the decision from a different point of view.

2. *Narrow vs. broad.* Fundamental investors focus their attention narrowly on a small group of stocks. They cover fewer companies since

EXHIBIT 1.2 Fundamentals vs. Quantitative Investor: Viewing Information

Fundamental (Journalist)	Quantitative (Scientist)
Primary focus: company	Primary focus: characteristics
In-depth company analysis	Drivers of performance across companies Law of Large numbers
Targeted stock bets	Spread stock bets across companies
Qualitative assessment—story Forecast future earnings Predict company catalysts	Analyze company relative to broad peer group Disciplined—specific stock picking criteria (repeatable) Understanding what worked in the past
Know company specific risks	Know portfolio level risks
Narrow – Future - Story	Broad – Past - Disciplined

they make more in-depth reviews of each company. Fundamental investors immerse themselves in the company studying everything from financial information, to new products, to meeting management. Ideally, they are searching for exploitable differences between their detailed assessment of the company's value and the market's perception of that value. In contrast, quantitative investors focus more broadly. Rather than reviewing one company at a time, they look across a large group of companies. Quantitative investors' focus on what separates companies from one another; they search for pieces of information (characteristics) that they can use to exploit differences between securities. Since they are dealing with a great deal of data from a large number of companies, they employ quantitative techniques to quickly sift through the information.

3. *Position concentration/size of bets.* Another difference in the two approaches is the size of the positions within a portfolio; they tend to be larger for a fundamental investor and smaller for a quantitative investor. A fundamental investor performs in-depth company analysis so they will have greater conviction in taking larger positions in their selected stocks. A quantitative investor performs in-depth analysis across a group of companies, so they will tend to spread their bets across this larger group of companies.

4. *Risk perspective.* The fundamental investor sees risk at the company level while the quantitative investor is more focused at the portfolio level. The fundamental investor will review the risk to both their forecasts and catalysts for the company. They understand how a changing macro picture can impact their valuation of the company. In contrast, the quantitative investor's broader view relates to understanding the risks across their portfolio. They understand if there are risk characteristics in their portfolio that are different from their chosen stock selection model. For example, a quantitative investor who does not believe growth prospects matter to a company's stock performance would want to investigate if their model had them buying many very high- or low-growth companies.

5. *Past vs. future.* Finally, the fundamental investor often places greater emphasis on the future prospects of the company while the quantitative investor studies the company's past. Fundamental investors tend to paint a picture of the company's future, they will craft a story around the company and its prospects, and they will look for catalysts generating future growth for a company. They rely on their ability to predict

changes in a company. In contrast, the quantitative investor places more emphasis on the past, using what is known or has been reported by a company. Quantitative investors rely on historical accounting data as well as historical strategy simulations, or backtests, to search for the best company characteristics to select stocks. For instance, they will look at whether technology companies with stronger profitability have performed better than those without, or whether retail companies with stronger inventory controls have performed better than those without. Quantitative investors are looking for stock picking criteria, which can be tested and incorporated into a stock selection model.

In the end, we have two types of investors viewing information, often the same information, quite differently. The fundamental investor is a journalist focused on crafting a unique story of a company's future prospects and predicting the potential for gain in the company's stock. The quantitative investor is a scientist, broadly focused, relying on historical information to differentiate across all companies, testing large amounts of data and using statistical techniques to create a stock selection model.

These two investors can and often do create different portfolios based on their different approaches as shown in Exhibit 1.3. The fundamental investor is more focused, with higher conviction in their stocks resulting in fewer, larger positions in their portfolios. The quantitative investor, reviewing a large group of companies, generally takes a large number of smaller positions in their portfolio. The fundamental investor is investing in a stock (or sector) and therefore is most concerned with how much each of their stocks (or sectors) is contributing to performance. The quantitative investor is investing in a characteristic and how well it differentiates stocks. They want to know how each of their characteristics is contributing to performance. Finally, the fundamental investor's detailed view into the company allows them to understand the intrinsic risk of each investment they make—what are potential stumbling blocks for each company. The quantitative investor's goal is to understand specific characteristics across a broad uni-

EXHIBIT 1.3 Fundamental vs. Quantitative Investor: Process Differences

Fundamental	Quantitative
Small portfolio	Large portfolio
Larger positions	Smaller positions
Performance at sector/company level	Performance at characteristic level
Emphasize stock specific risk	Diversify stock specific risk

EXHIBIT 1.4   Benefits of a Combined Fundamental and Quantitative Approach

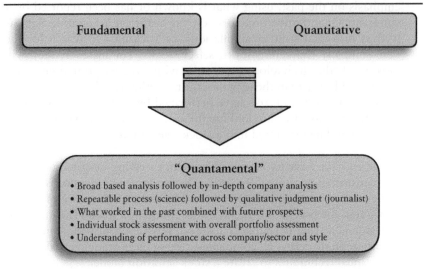

verse of stocks. They look at risks across their entire portfolio, attempting to diversify away any firm-specific risks ancillary to their strategy.

Now that you understand the basic differences between the two approaches, it might also be clear how using both investment styles can be very appealing. As Exhibit 1.4 shows, the two styles are quite complementary in nature and can provide a robust, well-rounded view of a company or portfolio. Combining the two approaches provides the following benefits:

- *Breadth and depth.* In-depth analysis across a large group of stocks selecting the best subset of companies, which is followed by in-depth review of the small subset of attractive companies.
- *Facts balanced with human insight.* The scientific approach reviewing large amounts of data across many companies complemented by personal judgment at the company level.
- *Past and future perspective.* A detailed historical review of companies combined with a review of future potential prospects of a company.
- *Full risk analysis.* A broad look at risk both within each company owned and across the entire portfolio.
- *Clear portfolio performance.* A thorough understanding of which companies, sectors, and characteristics are driving a portfolio's performance.

In fact, over the years, the defining line between the two approaches has been blurring. Some have coined the term for this joint process as *quanta-*

mental. Many investment managers are combining both approaches in one investment process, which is why whether you are a fundamental or quantitative investor, it is important to understand both perspectives.

Given our preceding discussion, the distinction between the quantitative and fundamental approaches should now be better appreciated. In the remainder of this chapter we restrict our focus to the quantitative equity investment process addressing the last two topics listed at the beginning of this chapter: the core steps in a quantitative equity investment process and some of the basic building blocks used by quantitative investors.

THE QUANTITATIVE STOCK SELECTION MODEL

Before diving into the details of the quantitative investment process, let's look at what is at its core—the stock selection model. As explained in the previous section, the quantitative investment approach is rooted in understanding what separates strong performing stocks from weak performing stocks.[1] The quantitative investor looks for sources of information or company characteristics (often referred to as factors or signals)[2] that help to explain why one stock outperforms another stock. They assemble these characteristics into a stock selection model that can be run daily to provide an updated view on every stock in their investment universe.

The stock selection model is at the heart of the quantitative process. To build their model, the quantitative investor will look throughout history and see what characteristics drive performance differences between stocks in a group such as a universe (i.e., small cap, small-cap value, and large-cap growth) or a sector (i.e., technology, financials, materials).

The quantitative investor's typical stock selection methodology is buying stocks with the most attractive attributes and not investing in (or shorting if permitted by investment guidelines) stocks with the least attractive attributes. For instance, let's suppose retail stocks that have the highest profitability tend to have higher stock returns than those with the lowest profitability. In this case, if a retail stock had strong profitability, there is a greater chance a portfolio manager would purchase it. Profitability is just one characteristic of a company. The quantitative investor will look at a

---

[1] Throughout the chapter, we discuss whether characteristics can separate a stock with strong future returns from one with weak future returns. Many times reference will be made to a "strong" characteristic that can differentiate the strong- from weak-performing stocks.

[2] In this chapter, "characteristic" means the attributes that differentiate companies. Quantitative investors often refer to these same characteristics as factors or signals, which they typically use in stock selection models and like models.

large number of characteristics, from 25 to over 100 to include in their stock selection model. In the end, they will narrow their final model to a few characteristics, which are best at locating performance differences among stocks in a particular universe or sector.

Exhibit 1.5 is an example of a stock selection model for the retail sector. If a stock has good margins, positive earnings growth, sell-side analyst like it, solid inventory management, and is attractively valued, especially as it pertains to earnings, then the quantitative investor would buy it. And if it did not have these characteristics, a quantitative investor would not own it, sell it, or short it. This example is for a retail sector; a quantitative investor could also have different models to select stocks in the bank sector or utilities sector or amongst small-cap value stocks.

So how does a quantitative investor create and use their stock selection model? A good analogy is a professional golfer. Like a quantitative investor, golfers create a model of their game. First, golfers analyze all elements of their basic swing from backswing to follow through. They then alter their swing to different conditions (high winds, rain, cold), and different courses types (links, woodlands, fast greens). Next golfers put their model into action. While they are golfing, they make mental notes about what is and isn't working to help enhance their game. Could they tweak their swing? What has been effective under the current weather conditions? How are they playing this type of course?

EXHIBIT 1.5 Sample Stock Selection Model for the Retail Sector

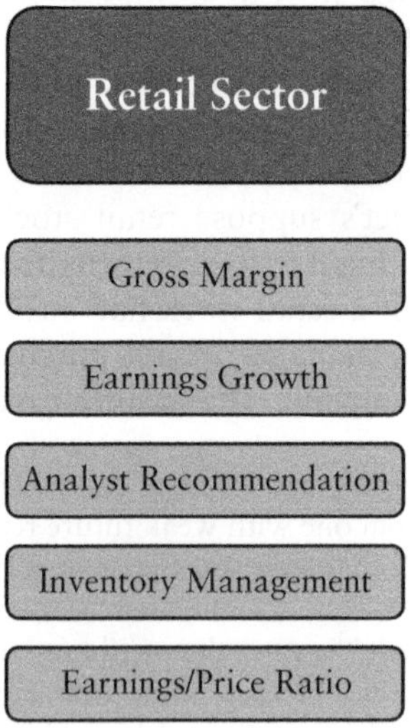

Overall, the golfers' process is much like a quantitative investors' process. They create a model, implement it, and then monitor it, assessing their ability to shoot below par. Like professional golfers who go to the driving range for countless hours to perfect their swing, quantitative investors will spend countless hours perfecting their model understanding how it works under many different market (weather/course) conditions.

With that analogy in mind, we now turn to the entire quantitative investment process.

THE OVERALL QUANTITATIVE INVESTMENT PROCESS

The quantitative process can be divided into the following three main phases (shown in Exhibit 1.6):

- Research
- Portfolio construction
- Monitoring

During the research phase, the stock selection model is created. During the portfolio construction phase, the quantitative investor "productionalizes" the stock selection model or gets it ready to invest in a live portfolio. Finally, during the monitoring phase, the quantitative investor makes sure the portfolio is performing as expected.

RESEARCH

Let's start with the research phase since it is the basic building block of the quantitative process. It is where the fact-finding mission begins. This is like when the golfer spends countless hours at the driving range perfecting his (or her) swing. In this phase, the quantitative investor determines what as-

EXHIBIT 1.6   Three Core Phases of the Quantitative Equity Investment Process

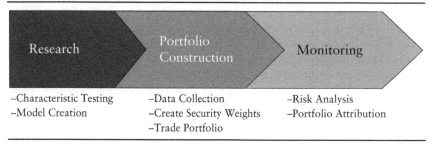

EXHIBIT 1.7   Two Core Steps in the Research Phase of the Quantitative Equity
Investment Process

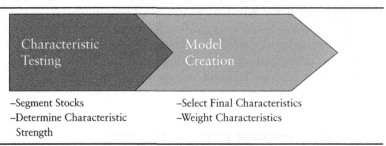

-Segment Stocks   -Select Final Characteristics
-Determine Characteristic   -Weight Characteristics
  Strength

pects of a company make its stock attractive or unattractive. The research
phase begins by the quantitative investors testing all the characteristics they
have at their disposal, and finishes with assembling the chosen characteristics into a stock selection model (see Exhibit 1.7).

1. *Characteristic testing.* First, quantitative investors determine which
   characteristics are good at differentiating strong performing from weak
   performing stocks. Initially, the quantitative investor segments the
   stocks, this could be by *sector*, such as consumer discretionary, *industry* such as consumer electronics or a *universe* such as small-cap value
   stocks. Once the stocks have been grouped, each of the characteristics is
   tested to see if they can delineate the strong performing stocks from the
   weak performing stocks.
2. *Model creation.* Second, quantitative investors select the final characteristics that are best at picking the most attractive stocks. Then they
   weight each characteristic in the stock selection model—determining
   which characteristics should be more relied upon when picking stocks,
   or if they all should be treated equally.

During the research phase, the quantitative investor tries to get a broad
picture of a characteristic making sure it performs well under a diverse set
of conditions and performance measures. For their testing, the quantitative
investor looks at historical information over 20 years or more in order to
cover multiple market cycles. While testing, many performance metrics are
reviewed to get an expansive view of a characteristic's ability to differentiate
stocks. These metrics span the return category, risk category and other metrics categories as outlined in Exhibit 1.8. Using an array of metrics, quantitative investors are better able to confirm a characteristic's consistency. They
make sure that the selected characteristics' score well on more than a single

EXHIBIT 1.8 Characteristic Testing in the Research Phase

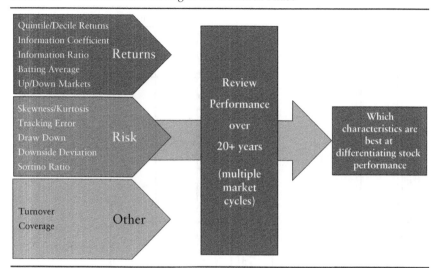

metric. Before continuing with the research process, let's review a few of the more commonly used metrics by quantitative investors.

Characteristic Testing: Key Quantitative Research Metrics

In this section, we review quintile returns and information coefficient that measure whether a characteristic can differentiate between winning and losing stocks. Although profitability was chosen for the examples, other characteristics such as sales growth, P/E ratio or asset turnover could have also been chosen.

Quintile Returns

The quintile return is already prevalent across most research publications, but is gaining popularity in more and more mainstream publications such as the *Wall Street Journal*, *Barron's*, and the like. Quintile returns measure how well a characteristic differentiates stocks. In essence, the stocks that are being reviewed are segmented into five groups (quintiles) and then are tested to determine if the companies in the group with the best attributes (top quintile) outperform the group with the least desirable attributes (bottom quintile).

Exhibit 1.9 provides an example. In this example, we start with 20 companies that we refer to as A through T. The first step—the left-hand side of the exhibit—is to order the 20 companies by profitability from highest to

EXHIBIT 1.9   Determining the Characteristic's Quintile Spread

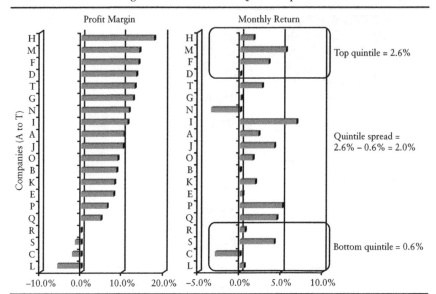

lowest. In the second step, this ordered list is divided into five groups, creating a most profitable group (top quintile) down to the least profitable group (bottom quintile). The top and bottom quintile groups are boxed on the right-hand chart of the exhibit. Finally, the performance of the top quintile is compared to the bottom quintile.

As Exhibit 1.9 shows, the stocks with highest profitability (top quintile) returned 2.6% on average while the stocks with the lowest profitability (bottom quintile) returned only 0.6% on average. So the top quintile stocks outperformed the bottom quintile stocks by 2.0% meaning for this month, the most profitable companies outperformed the least profitable companies by 2.0%. This is commonly referred to as the characteristic's *quintile return* or *quintile spread*. The higher the quintile spread, the more attractive the characteristic is.

Information Coefficient

Another common metric used for determining if a characteristic is good at separating the strong from the weak performing stocks is the *information coefficient* (IC). It does so by measuring the correlation between a stock's characteristic (i.e., profitability) and its return. The major difference between the IC and quintile return is that the IC looks across all of the stocks, while the quintile return only focuses on the best and worst stocks ignoring

EXHIBIT 1.10   Determining the Characteristic's Information Coefficient

	Company	Profit Margin Rank	Return Rank	
Profit Margin chart	H	1	11	
	M	2	2	
	F	3	7	
	D	4	17	
	T	5	8	Information
	G	6	16	coeeficient
	N	7	20	= Correlation
	I	8	1	= 11.0%
	A	9	9	
	J	10	5	
	O	11	12	
	B	12	18	
	K	13	10	
	E	14	15	
	P	15	3	
	Q	16	4	
	R	17	13	
	S	18	5	
	C	19	19	
	L	20	14	

those stocks in the middle. The IC is more concerned with differentiating performance across all stocks rather than the extremes.

The calculation of the IC is detailed in Exhibit 1.10. Similar to assessing the quintile return, the sort ordering of the companies based on profitability is done first. However, the next step is different. In the second step, each stock is ranked on both profitability and return. The most profitable company is assigned a rank of 1 all the way down to the least profitable company that is assigned a rank of 20. Likewise for stock returns, the highest returning stock is assigned a rank of 1 down to the lowest returning stock receiving a rank of 20. In the third step, the rank of the company's profitability is correlated with the rank of the company's return. The correlation of the two ranks is the IC that is 11% as shown in Exhibit 1.10. The higher the correlation (i.e., IC), the more likely companies with higher profitability also have higher returns and the more effective the characteristic.

When is it better to employ an IC over a quintile spread? IC is a better metric when a quantitative investor is considering owning a greater number of stocks in the portfolio. The reason is that the IC looks at the relationships across all of the stocks in the group. The quintile return is better suited for more concentrated bets in fewer stocks as it places a greater emphasis on measuring the few stocks at the extremes.

The last two examples reviewed how a characteristic (profitability) was able to explain the next month's return for a group of stocks. In both cases, it looked effective—a quintile return of 2.0% and an IC of 11%. However, in practice, it is also necessary to assess whether the characteristic was effective for not only one month, but over decades of investing encompassing multiple market cycles. To that end, during the research process a quantitative investor will look at the average quintile returns or ICs over an extended period of up to 20 years or more. When looking at these longer time series, quantitative investors use additional metrics to understand the characteristic's effectiveness.

Characteristic Testing: Key Measures of Consistency

Two commonly used measures of consistency are batting average and information ratio.

Batting Average

Batting average is a straightforward metric. In baseball a player's batting average is the number of hits divided by the number of times at bat. A similar metric is used in investing. Batting average is the number of positive performance months (hits) divided by the number of total months (at bats). The higher the batting average, the more consistently the characteristic generates positive performance.

As Exhibit 1.11 displays, to arrive at the batting average we take the number of months the quintile return was positive divided by the number of months tested. In our example, in 47 of the 72 months the profitability characteristic was effective, resulting in a positive return. This translates to a batting average of 65%, which is quite high. Imagine walking into a casino in Las Vegas where you have a 65% chance of winning every bet. That casino would not be in business very long with you at the table.

Information Ratio

Information ratio is also used to measure consistency. This measure is defined as the average return of a characteristic divided by its volatility—basically a measure of return per unit of risk or risk reward ratio. For volatility, quantitative investors use tracking error, which is the standard deviation of excess returns.

Exhibit 1.12 demonstrates the calculation of the information ratio. In this example, there are two characteristics. Which one should be selected? Based only on returns, we would choose Characteristic 2 since it has a higher excess return (3.0%) than Characteristic 1 (2.0%). However, as we can see in the exhibit, Characteristic 2 also has much larger swings in per-

EXHIBIT 1.11   Determining the Characteristic's Batting Average

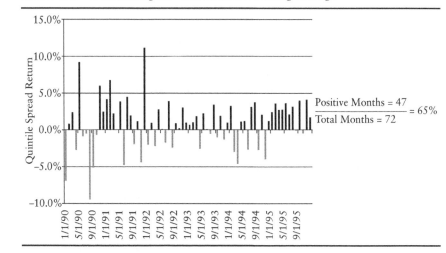

EXHIBIT 1.12   Determining the Characteristic's Information Ratio

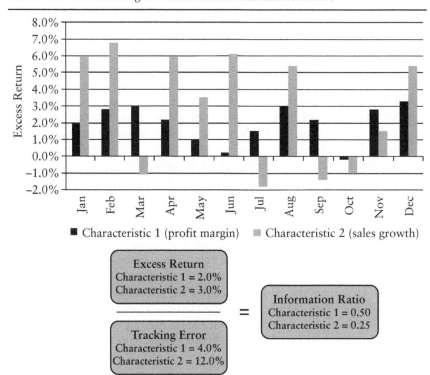

formance than Characteristic 1 and therefore more risk. The higher risk of Characteristic 2 is confirmed by its high tracking error of 12.0%, three times greater than Characteristic 1's tracking error of 4.0%. Characteristic 1 looks much better on a risk-adjusted basis with an information ratio of 0.50 (2.0%/4.0%) or twice Characteristic 2's information ratio of 0.25 (3.0%/12.0%). So even though Characteristic 1 has a lower return than Characteristic 2, it also has much less risk making it preferred since the investor is rewarded more for the risk she (or he) are taking.

Model Creation

After reviewing and selecting the best characteristics, the quantitative investor then needs to assemble them into a stock selection model. This step of the research process is called *model creation*. It usually involves two main components:

1. Ascertaining whether the characteristics selected are not measuring the same effect (i.e., are not highly correlated).
2. Assigning weights to the selected characteristics and potentially placing greater emphasis on those in which the quantitative investor has stronger convictions.

Let us begin by discussing the first component in model creation: measuring correlation. When including characteristics into a stock selection model, the quantitative investor does not want to include two characteristics that have very similar performance since they may be measuring similar aspects of the company. In these cases, the quantitative manager could be potentially doubling their position in a stock for the same reason. For instance, stocks with a historically high sales growth may perform similarly to stocks with high expected growth in the future or stocks with strong gross margins may perform similarly to stocks with strong profit margins. In either case, we would not include both similar characteristics.

An example is provided in Exhibit 1.13, which shows the cumulative quintile spread return over 10 years for three characteristics (which we have labeled A, B, and C). Characteristic A did the best at differentiating the winners from losers—the stocks it liked outperformed the stocks it did not like by almost 10% over the 10-year period. Characteristic B was next with a return slightly greater than 8% and characteristic C was the lowest with an almost 4% cumulative 10-year return. Given that all three characteristics have good performance, which two should the quantitative investor retain in the model?

EXHIBIT 1.13   Model Creation: Correlation Review

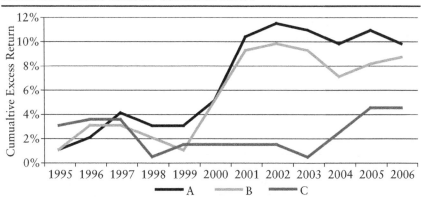

Characteristic Correlation Table

	A	B	C
A	1.00	0.80	0.12
B	0.80	1.00	0.04
C	0.12	0.04	1.00

Although characteristic A and B are better at differentiating winners from losers than characteristic C, A's return pattern looks very similar to B's. This is confirmed by the table in Exhibit 1.13 where characteristics A and B have a correlation of 0.80. Since a correlation of 1.00 means their returns move in lock step, a correlation of 0.80 indicates they are very similar. Rather than keeping both A and B and potentially doubling our positions from similar characteristics, it would be best to keep either A or B and combine the characteristic retained with C. Even though characteristic C is the worst performing of the three, for the stock selection model C provides a good uncorrelated source of performance.

Once the characteristics to select stocks are identified, the quantitative investor is ready to determine the importance or weight of each characteristic. They must decide whether all characteristics should have the same weight or whether better characteristics should have greater weight in the stock selection model.

There are many ways to determine the weights of the characteristics. We can simply equal weight them or use some other process such as create an algorithm, perform regressions, or optimize. Exhibit 1.14 shows how a typical stock selection model is created. In this step, the selected characteristics are combined to determine a target for each stock whether it be a return forecast, rank, or a position size.

EXHIBIT 1.14   Stock Selection Model: Characteristic Weightings

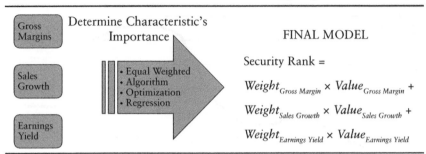

Once the combination of characteristics for the model is selected, the quantitative investor determines their weights and then reviews the model. Model review is similar to reviewing a single characteristic. The model is looked at from many perspectives, calculating all of the metrics described in Exhibit 1.8. The quantitative investor would look at how the top quintile stocks of the model perform versus the bottom and look at information coefficients of the stock selection model over time. In addition, how much trading or turnover the stock selection model creates is reviewed or if there are any biases in the stock selections (e.g., too many small-cap stocks, or a reliance on high- or low-beta stocks). In practice, the review is much more extensive covering many more metrics. If the stock selection model does not hold up under this final review, then the quantitative investor will need to change her stock selection model to eliminate the undesirable effects.

PORTFOLIO CONSTRUCTION

In the second phase of the investment process, the quantitative investor uses the stock selection model to buy stocks. It is in this phase that the quantitative investor puts the model into production. Returning to our golfer analogy, this is when he travels to the course to play a round of golf.

During the portfolio construction phase, the model is ready to create a daily portfolio. This phase consists of three main steps:

EXHIBIT 1.15   Three Main Steps of the Portfolio Construction Phase

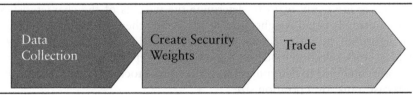

Step 1: Data collection. Data are collected on a nightly basis, making sure the data are correct and do not contain any errors.

Step 2: Create security weights. New, updated nightly, data are used to both select the stocks that should be purchased for the portfolio as well as how large its position should be.

Step 3: Trade. The stock selection model that has incorporated the most current information is used for trading.

Data Collection

As Exhibit 1.16 shows, data come from many different sources, such as company fundamental, pricing, economic, and other data (specialized data sources). All of these data are updated nightly so it is important to have robust systems and processes established to handle large amounts of data, clean the data (check for errors), and process it in a timely fashion. The quantitative investor seeks to have everything ready to trade at the market opening.

Creating Security Weights

After the data are collected and verified, the next step is running all of the updated company information through the stock selection model. This will

EXHIBIT 1.16   Data Collection Step of the Portfolio Construction Phase

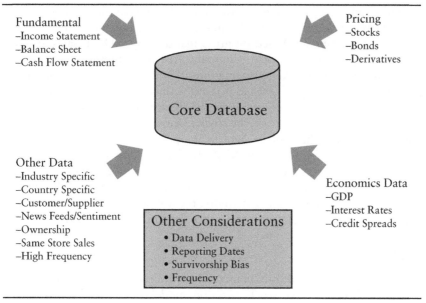

EXHIBIT 1.17   Creating Security Weights Step of the Portfolio Construction Phase

Overweight Position

Best Fundamentals

Worst Fundamentals

Underweight Position

	Company ABC		Company XYZ	
Gross margin	Top 10%	+	Top 20%	+
Sales growth	Top 30%	+	Bottom 20%	−
Earnings yield	Median	0	Bottom 10%	−
Active weight		+		−

Overweight   Underweight

Buy   Sell

create final positions for every stock in the screened universe. In this step, each stock is ranked using the stock selection model, with the better scoring companies making it into the portfolio.

Exhibit 1.17 provides a simplified example of this, showing a stock selection model with three characteristics: gross margins, sales growth, and earnings yield (i.e., earnings-to-price ratio, the higher the ratio the more attractively priced the stock is). From the example, Company ABC is in the top 10% of companies based on gross margin, top 30% in sales growth, and average on earnings yield. Company ABC may represent a company finding a profitable market, growing into it, and the rest of the market has not caught on to its prospects so it is still valued like an average stock. In this case, the stock rates favorably by the stock selection model and would be purchased. The other stock, the stock of Company XYZ, is not as favorable and would either not be held in the portfolio or if permitted could be shorted. Although Company XYZ also has good margins, its growth is slowing and it is relatively expensive compared to its earnings. The company could be one that had a profitable niche, but its niche may be shrinking as sales are dwindling. Furthermore, the investment community has not discounted the slowing growth and hence the stock is still expensive.

Trade

The final step in the portfolio construction process is to trade into the new positions chosen by the stock selection model. While many investment approaches trade regularly, even daily, quantitative investors tend not to. Quantitative investors tend to trade monthly or longer. They may wait for the views from their stock selection model to change significantly from their current portfolio before trading into the new views.

MONITORING

The third and final phase in the quantitative equity investment process is monitoring performance and risk. This step is important to check if any hidden biases are embedded in the portfolio and that the portfolio is performing in-line with expectations. Returning one last time to our golfer analogy, this is when the golfer is making mental notes as to what is and isn't working during the round to improve his game in the future. This step can be broken into two activities: risk management and performance attribution.

Risk Management

In risk management, the main emphasis is to make sure that the quantitative investor is buying companies consistent with her stock selection model. Returning to the retail model discussed earlier in this chapter, the model liked companies with good profit margins but had no view on the company's beta. So the quantitative investor would want to make sure that the companies included in her portfolio have high profit margins but average beta. If the portfolio started to include high-beta stocks, the quantitative investor would want to make adjustments to the process to eliminate this high-beta bias. There are many types of risk management software and techniques that can be used to detect any hidden risks embedded in the portfolio and ways to remedy those identified.

Another aspect of risk management is to make sure that the portfolio's risk level is consistent with the modeling phase. The quantitative investor wants to assure that there is not too high or low tracking error relative to expectations. Again, risk management techniques and software can be used to monitor tracking error, sources of tracking error, and remedy any deviations from expectations.

Performance Attribution

Performance attribution is critical in assuring the actual live portfolio's performance is coming from the characteristics in the stock selection model and is in-line with performance expected during the modeling stage. Performance attribution is like monitoring a car's gas mileage: If the gas mileage begins to dip below what the driver expects, or is known to be, then the driver would want to look under the car's hood. Similarly, if the stock selection model is not producing the desired results, or the results have changed, then the quantitative investor would need to look under the hood of the stock selection model. If performance is not being generated from the selected characteristics, then the quantitative manager would want to check out the model in more detail. One possibility is that another characteristic is cancelling the desired characteristics or perhaps there is something wrong with the model itself. Another possibility is that there are data issues.

The monitoring phase is critical in making sure that the stock selection model is being implemented as expected.

CURRENT TRENDS

Let's look at some recent trends in the quantitative investment industry.

Many quantitative equity investors are looking for additional sources of alpha by using alternative data sources to help select stocks. One notable source is industry-specific data (e.g., banking, airlines, and retail). Additionally, quantitative investors are turning to the Internet to better understand news flows for companies through Web-based search engines. Furthermore, quantitative investors are using more conditioning models. Conditioning occurs when two characteristics are combined together rather than choosing them side by side in a stock selection model. Traditional models would look for companies that have either attractive margins *or* growth. With conditioning models, companies that have both attractive margins *and* growth are sought.

Dynamic modeling is gaining a renewed popularity. It consists of timing characteristics, determining when they should enter or leave a stock selection model based on business cycle analysis, technical market indicators, or other information. For instance, during recessionary periods, a quantitative investor may want companies with strong profitability, while in expansionary periods companies with good growth prospects are sought. A stock selection model would contain profitability when the economy is entering a recession, and then include the growth characteristic once it felt that the economy is moving into an expansionary period. This is an example of how quantitative investors may be bringing more personal judgment to the process, similar to fundamental investors.

Finally, with the advent of high-frequency trading and more advanced trading analytics, many quantitative investors are reviewing how best they implement their stock selection models. Some characteristics such as earnings surprise may have short-lived alpha prospects, so quantitative investors would want to trade into these stocks more quickly. Other characteristics are longer-term in nature, such as valuation metrics, so investors would not have to trade into companies with attractive valuations as quickly. Furthermore, trading costs are being measured with greater granularity, allowing quantitative investors to measure transaction cost and incorporate these better estimates into their research modeling phase.

KEY POINTS

- Investing begins with processing many different types of information to find the most attractively priced assets. Fundamental and quantitative investors differ in their approach to the available information. The fundamental investor's primary focus is on a single company at a time, while the quantitative investor's primary focus is on a single characteristic at a time.
- Quantitative and fundamental approaches are complementary. By combining the two approaches, you can obtain a more well-rounded investment process including breadth and depth in analysis, facts based with human judgment, a past and future perspective of a company, and a more well-rounded view of risk and performance of the portfolio.
- The quantitative equity investment process is made up of three phases: research, portfolio construction, and monitoring. During the research phase, the stock selection model is created. During the portfolio construction phase, the quantitative investor "productionalizes" the stock selection model or gets it ready to invest in a live portfolio. Finally, during the monitoring phase, the quantitative investor makes sure the portfolio is performing as expected.
- At the heart of the quantitative equity investment process is the stock selection model. The model includes those characteristics that are best at delineating the highest from lowest returning stocks. Models can be created for industries, sectors, or styles.
- Two common metrics used to judge a characteristic's effectiveness are quintile returns and information coefficients. Two more metrics used to understand the consistency of a characteristic's performance over time are batting average and information ratio.
- During the portfolio construction phase, data is collected from multiple sources and run through the investor's stock selection model to arrive at a list of buy and sell candidates. The buy candidates will have the strongest characteristic values in the investor's stock selection model, and the sell candidates the weakest characteristic values.

■ The monitoring phase is where the investor assures that the performance in their portfolio is consistent with their expectations. During this phase, investors make sure there are no hidden bets in their portfolio and that the characteristics in their stock selection model are performing as expected.

QUESTIONS

1. Identify at least three ways that a quantitative investor's process may differ from a fundamental investor's process.

2. What are three ways in which the quantitative and fundamental approaches complement one another?

3. When would a quantitative investor use an information coefficient (IC) over a quintile return?

4. Why do quantitative investors create stock selection models for?

5. What types of data is used in traditional stock selection models?

CHAPTER 2

Equity Analysis Using Traditional and Value-Based Metrics

James L. Grant, Ph.D.
JLG Research and Professor of Finance
University of Massachusetts–Boston

Frank J. Fabozzi, Ph.D., CFA, CPA
Professor of Finance
EDHEC Business School

In this chapter, traditional metrics and value-based metrics are explained with the goal of showing their joint role in equity fundamental analysis and securities valuation. After reviewing the relevant metrics, we apply traditional and value-based metrics analyses to illustrate the benefits of using a synthesized approach to equity analysis in distinguishing "good" companies, which can be potential buy opportunities, from "bad," risky, or troubled companies, which can be potential sell or short-sell opportunities.

OVERVIEW OF TRADITIONAL METRICS

With numerous financial measures available, the investor is often left wondering which metrics are the most important to focus on. We address this metrics question by examining the information content of two well-known but seemingly distinct types of company and equity analyses—namely, traditional and *value-based metrics* (VBM) approaches to securities analysis. We begin our financial metrics journey with the traditional approach.

In the traditional approach to company analysis, there are several broad ratio categories. These categories include liquidity, activity, debt (leverage), and profitability measures. Within each category, there are several ratio choices. From the investor's perspective, *growth rates* and profitability measures are often combined with relative valuation measures ("multiples") to assess the attractiveness or unattractiveness of a firm's common stock. As with the value-based metrics approach (discussed later), the end result of a traditional fundamental analysis on a company is a target valuation leading to a potential buy (or "overweight" relative to reference index), sell ("underweight" relative to index), or hold decision (benchmark weight) on a company's stock. Some widely used traditional measures of growth and profitability include:

- Revenue growth
- Earnings and cash flow growth
- Book value and asset growth
- Dividend growth
- Return on equity (reflects profitability)
- Fundamental stock return

Likewise, some key valuation measures include:

- Price-to-revenue ratio
- Price-to-earnings ratio
- Price-to-cash flow ratio
- Price-to-book value ratio
- Dividend yield

While the names of these metrics are descriptive, we provide an overview of those measures that require formulas. Moreover, it is worth noting that some investors and analysts prefer a specific combination of traditional fundamentals and valuation measures when analyzing companies; for example, "tech" analysts may use a combination of revenue growth and price–revenue "multiple" to analyzing software and biotech companies, while other analysts may use an earnings (or book value) growth and price–earnings (or price–book) combination when evaluating the profitability and equity valuation characteristics of financial services companies.

Growth Rates

We begin the formulaic review of traditional metrics with annualized growth rates. Growth rates—variables expressed in terms of revenue, earnings, cash flow, book value, assets, or dividends—are calculated from the basic present value (PV) and future value (FV) relationship:

$$FV = PV \times (1 + g)''$$

Solving for the annualized growth rate, one obtains:

$$g = (FV/PV)^{1/n} - 1.0$$

This expression is used to calculate growth rates using the variables listed earlier. When growth rates are compared to a benchmark or industry standard, they can be used to distinguish companies having relatively favorable or unfavorable financial characteristics. Growth rates are also used in equity style analysis (value versus growth stocks) and they are a key input to pro forma forecasts of earnings and cash flows and, notably, in discounted cash flow (DCF) models (along with the required return).

Consider the revenue and earnings data shown in Exhibit 2.1 (among other financial data used later). Upon inserting the revenue figure at 2011 into FV, and the revenue figure at 2006 into PV, one obtains a five-year annualized growth rate, g_r, according to

$$g_r = (FV/PV)^{1/5} - 1.0$$
$$= (1.882 / 0.909)^{0.2} - 1.0 = 0.157 \text{ or } 15.7\%$$

The five-year *earnings per share* (EPS) growth rate, g_e, can be determined in a similar manner. At 13.9%, this annualized growth rate is calculated according to

$$g_e = (3.59/1.87)^{1/5} - 1.0 = 0.139 = 13.9\%$$

Other things the same, if the actual growth rate in either revenue, earnings, cash flows, book value, assets, or dividends is higher than benchmark, then based on growth rates alone the company is relatively attractive— meaning the stock is a potential buy opportunity. Otherwise, the company

EXHIBIT 2.1 Income and Balance Sheet Data (all figures USD billions except earnings per share)

Year	2006	2007	2008	2009	2010	2011
Revenue	0.909	1.052	1.212	1.423	1.575	1.882
Operating earnings (EBIT)	0.273	0.316	0.364	0.427	0.473	0.565
Pre-tax profit	0.232	0.262	0.291	0.338	0.380	0.451
Net income	0.151	0.170	0.189	0.220	0.247	0.293
Earnings per share	$1.87	$2.07	$2.30	$2.66	$2.98	$3.59
Equity	0.844	0.970	1.125	1.284	1.483	1.618
Assets	12.194	16.255	18.927	22.795	26.182	29.483

is relatively unattractive, which points to a potential sell or short-sell opportunity on the stock.

Return on Equity and Extended Dupont Formula

We now look at *return on equity* (ROE), which is perhaps the best-known traditional measure of corporate success. In accounting terms, ROE is simply net income over stockholders' equity. The classic *Dupont formula* (a pioneering formula developed by E. I. duPont de Nemours & Company in the early 1960s) expands this ratio by showing that ROE can be expressed as the product of other important ratios. For example, ROE can be measured by multiplying *return on assets* (ROA) by a corporate leverage ratio. The leverage ratio is commonly referred to as the "financial leverage multiplier," the "equity multiplier," or just plain "leverage." The leverage factor is measured by the ratio of total assets to stockholders' equity, while ROA in the Dupont formula is simply net income (NI) divided by total assets (A).

$$ROE = ROA \times Leverage = NI/A \times A/E$$

In turn, ROE is related to the *net profit margin* (NPM) and the asset turnover ratio according to

$$ROE = NPM \times Asset\ turnover \times Leverage$$
$$= NI/S \times S/A \times A/E$$

In this expression, ROA is expressed as the net profit margin (net income over revenue) times the asset turnover ratio—measured by the revenue-to-assets ratio. Investors can use this three-part ROE formula to measure the efficiency of management in generating (1) profit per dollar of sales, (2) sales per dollar of assets (via inventory and asset turns), and (3) assets per dollar of owners' or stockholders' equity (implicitly by using debt financing).

Moreover, to better assess the operating and efficiency aspects of a company as well as capital structure and tax issues, the above after-tax version of the Dupont formula can be extended to a five-part, pretax model. In the *extended Dupont formula*, the firm's ROE can be expressed as

$$ROE = Tax\ burden \times Interest\ burden$$
$$\times Operating\ profit\ margin \times Asset\ turnover \times Leverage$$
$$= NI/PBT \times PBT/EBIT \times EBIT/S \times S/A \times A/E$$

In the extended Dupont formula, the tax burden is measured by the ratio of (or conversion from) net income to pretax profit (PBT), the interest burden is measured by the ratio of profit before tax to operating earnings (EBIT), the *pretax operating margin* is measured by the ratio of operating earnings to sales, while the asset turnover and leverage ratios are the same as before. The obvious benefit of using the extended Dupont formula is that investors and analysts can focus more clearly on the operating profit and efficiency aspects of a business in the context of the operating profit margin and asset turnover ratio (or pretax ROA) as distinct from financing (capital structure) issues as reflected in the interest burden and leverage ratios, and tax issues as captured by the tax burden. Note that the tax burden in the extended ROE model is simply one minus the effective tax rate.

We use the income statement and balance sheet figures in Exhibit 2.1 to calculate the after-tax (three part) and pretax (five part) versions of the Dupont model for 2011. Based on these figures, the three-part ROE model yields

$$ROE = NI/E = 0.293/1.618 = 0.1811$$
$$= ROA \times A/E = 0.0099 \times 18.22$$
$$= NPM \times AT \times A/E = 0.1557 \times 0.0638 \times 18.22$$
$$= 0.1811$$

In turn, with a 35% tax rate $[1 - (0.293/0.451)]$ and a 30% operating profit margin $(0.565/1.882)$, the extended (five-part) ROE model yields:

$$ROE = NI/PBT \times PBT/EBIT \times EBIT/S \times S/A \times A/E$$
$$= 0.65 \times 0.798 \times 0.30 \times 0.0638 \times 18.22$$
$$= 0.1811$$

With a relatively high operating profit margin (30%), a low asset turnover ratio (0.0638), and a high equity multiplier (18.22), these are indicative of the ROE characteristics of a firm operating in the financial services sector, such as a profitable bank with a large amount of assets (i.e., creditworthy loans). A company operating in, say, the soft drink industry might have a similar ROE, but the "packaging" of the ROA and leverage components would be reversed. That is, beverage companies have relatively high pretax ROA and asset turnover ratios and are largely financed with equity, such that the values for the interest burden and the equity multiplier would be close to unity.

ROE and Leverage

Investors and analysts alike often look at corporate leverage ratios—such as debt-to-equity, debt-to-capital, and debt-to-asset ratios—when evaluating a firm's profit versus risk characteristics. In the traditional model, leverage can be value increasing because higher levels of corporate debt lead to both higher ROE and earnings per share. However, professional investors are keenly aware that excessive amounts of debt beyond some target level may be wealth destroying for the shareholders (investors). This negative side of debt is generally due to excessive earnings volatility associated with a rising probability of corporate default, leading to bankruptcy.

The traditional view that a larger proportion of debt in the firm's capital structure leads to higher profitability ratios can be seen in the Dupont formula. To emphasize the role of debt, a firm's ROE can be expressed in terms of its ROA and the inverse of one minus the corporate debt ratio according to

$$ROE = \frac{ROA}{1 - D/A}$$

In this expression, ROA is the after-tax return on assets (net income/assets), and D/A is the debt–asset ratio. The debt ratio in this version of the Dupont formula is the ratio of total liabilities (including current liabilities) to total assets, D/A.

Moreover, the "operating assets" approach[1] to ROE is yet another way to distinguish operating results from leverage, this time in the context of ROA' and the debt-to-equity ratio (D/E) according to

$$ROE = ROA' + (ROA' - \text{After-tax debt cost}) \times D/E$$

In this ROE expression, ROA' is the ratio of net operating profit after tax (NOPAT) to net assets or capital. In practice, NOPAT can be estimated as net income plus the after interest expense, while in a VBM context (shown later) NOPAT is often measured as tax-adjusted operating earnings (EBIT). Based on the previous formulations, it should be clear that with a higher degree of leverage, the Dupont formula shows that ROE goes up because the denominator in the former ROE expression falls as D/A rises; while in the latter or operating assets approach, ROE raises due to an increase in D/E. Conversely, as D/A declines relative to the firm's ROA, its ROE goes down because the denominator in the Dupont formula now goes up (equivalently, ROE goes down as D/E declines). In effect, when D/A (or D/E) rises relative to ROA, a smaller amount of equity capital is now generating the same amount of profit; thus, the return on shareholder equity goes up. A declining ROE results when a relatively larger equity base is generating the same amount of corporate earnings.

---

[1]Paul M. Healy and Krishna G. Palepu, *Business Analysis and Valuation: Using Financial Statements* (Mason, OH: Southwestern Thomson, 2007).

To illustrate the link between ROE and leverage (debt), assume that a firm's after-tax profit is $10 and its asset base is $100. Further, assume that the company is financed with all equity such that the D/A is zero. Not surprisingly, with 100% equity financing the firm's ROE is the same as its ROA, at 10%:

$$ROE = \frac{0.1}{1-0} = 0.1 \text{ or } 10\%$$

Now assume that the firm engages in financing that effectively swaps the equity shares for more debt, such that D/A rises to 40%. With this pure capital structure change, the firm's ROE rises from 10% to 16.7%:

$$ROE = \frac{0.10}{1-0.40} = 0.167 \text{ or } 16.7\%$$

As the company moves toward what it perceives to be its "optimal" (or target) capital structure, we see that ROE goes up. Hence, in the traditional view, it is argued that investors should be willing to pay more for the firm's now seemingly dearer shares as long as the firm does not violate its supposed optimal capital structure. We will say more on the firm's target capital structure as this is a key issue in the value-based metrics approach to equity analysis.

Financial Risk Considerations

The Dupont formula can also be used to illustrate the volatility of ROE at varying corporate debt levels. In this context, Exhibit 2.2 shows the projected ROE ratios with corporate debt levels ranging from 0% to 70% in the presence of ROA ratios varying from, say, 10% to –10%. As the economy expands or contracts with a 10% debt load, we see that ROE fluctuates from 11.1% on the high side to –11.1% on the downside.

EXHIBIT 2.2   ROE Impact of Corporate Debt Policy in a Changing Economy

ROE %	Corporate Debt Ratio[a]							
	0.0%	10%	20%	30%	40%	50%	60%	70%
Expansion: ROA = 10%	10.0	11.1	12.5	14.3	16.7	20.0	25.0	33.3
Contraction: ROA = –10%	–10.0	–11.1	–12.5	–14.3	–16.7	–20.0	–25.0	–33.3

[a]The "debt/cap" ratio for the market (S&P 500 companies) is around 40%.

Exhibit 2.2 also shows that with an economy-wide debt load of 40%, the ROE numbers vary from 16.7% down to –16.7%. Moreover, as the economy expands or contracts with a 60% debt ratio, the ROE is even more volatile, ranging from 25% to –25%. On balance, the table reveals that increasing leverage (or debt) in good times conveys a seemingly positive benefit to the shareholders, while rising corporate debt ratios in bad times are a source of investor concern due to heightened financial risk. If the traditional view of capital structure is correct, then investors may reap windfall capital gains or avoid losses by (1) buying the securities of companies having reasonable amounts of debt in anticipation of an expansionary economy, or (2) trading out of those companies with securities (e.g., the stocks of consumer durables and industrial cyclicals) that might be penalized by excessive amounts of debt in a slow-growth to recessionary economy.

PRICE MULTIPLES

Price multiples (or *price relatives*) are often used by investors and analysts to get a first impression of where a stock should be trading. Price multiples are typically based on the method of *comparables* or *forecasted fundamentals*, or may evolve from a statistical analysis of drivers or *common factors* that are likely to impact the price of a company's stock. With knowledge of a benchmark multiple of, say, revenue, earnings, cash flow, or book value, a company's stock price can be estimated by multiplying the appropriate price multiple by the relevant company fundamental (expressed per share). For example, if the selected earnings measure was EBITDA per share (earnings before interest, taxes, depreciation, and amortization), then a company's stock price could be estimated as

$$\text{Stock price} = \text{EBITDA multiple} \times \text{EBITDA}$$
$$= \text{P/EBITDA} \times \text{EBITDA}$$

The estimated stock price would then be compared to the actual price to see if the stock is either potentially *undervalued* (actual price or multiple is lower than estimated price or multiple) or overvalued (actual price or multiple is higher than estimated price or multiple). This type of equity valuation analysis, albeit simplistic, presumes that a company's stock price or actual multiple will return to an intrinsic value or target price multiple.

Stock Analysis Using Price Multiples

To illustrate the multiples approach to equity valuation, Exhibit 2.3 shows a graph of the price-to-earnings ratio (P/E) versus the earnings growth rate

EXHIBIT 2.3 P/E vs. Earnings Growth Rate: U.S. Equity Styles

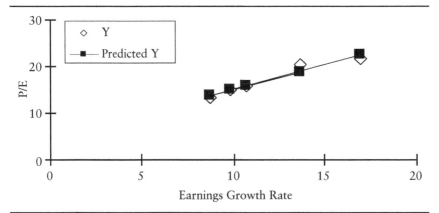

for U.S. equity "style" portfolios estimated at a point in time. The portfolios range from large- to small-capitalization companies, and they vary from value to growth stocks. The figure suggests a strong linear relationship between the P/E and the earnings growth rate for diversified portfolios of common stocks. In practice, an investor or analyst could plot a set of multiples and earnings growth rates (PEG ratios) around the line to see whether the stocks of individual companies are possibly undervalued or overvalued. Assuming a stationary relationship in Exhibit 2.3, those stocks that plot below the line would be potentially undervalued because for a given growth rate of earnings investors would be willing to pay a higher multiple of earnings. For example, if a company had a P/E of 12 and an earnings growth rate of 15%, then the stock would be considered undervalued as investors seem willing to pay a multiple of "20" for that growth rate.

Conversely, stocks falling above the line would be considered overvalued, as the underlying earnings growth rate is not sufficient to support the higher price multiple. This would happen if the price multiple were, say, 20 and the earnings growth rate were only 10%. In this case, investors will only pay a multiple of 15 for an earnings growth rate of 10%. As a word of caution, the estimated PEG relationship is relevant only within the estimated range of PEG points, and it is relevant only to the extent that the relationship is linear and stationary (that is, repeatable). Based on Exhibit 2.3 the estimated model would be relevant only for companies with a P/E range of about 13 to 22 and an earnings growth rate of about 8% to 17%.

In practice, price relatives can be a multiple of any number of accounting variables and include, the price–sales ratio, the price–cash flow ratio, the price-to-earnings ratio, and the price–book value per share ratio. As noted before, the specific price multiple used by investors is often dictated by the type of company or industry. For example, an investor or analyst might use a price–sales multiple to get a sense of where a tech stock should be trading, with high expectation of revenue growth in view of currently low to negative earnings and cash flows. A price–earnings or price–book multiple might be used in the equity valuation process for asset laden companies such as industrial companies as well as banks with a large loan base.

That said, it should be obvious that sole reliance on, say, a price-to-revenue multiple can be risky for the obvious reason that revenue is not profit. This simplistic approach to equity analysis was unfortunately commonplace in the valuation of Internet companies during the "dot-com" boom. During the tech bubble, it was thought by some investors and analysts that the mere expansion of sales or market share would ultimately lead to positive earnings and cash flows or rapid growth in these financial variables. If this thinking were correct, then it would have naturally justified higher market prices. Unfortunately, the bursting of the Nasdaq bubble during 2000 and first quarter of 2001 revealed the opposite price dynamics. On a more positive note, an investor or equity analyst might use a P/E multiple for consistent earnings growth companies in the health care sector (such as medical device firms as opposed to biotech companies), while, as noted before, another investor might obtain a first impression of a stock by using a price–book value ratio for companies (e.g., financial services and industrials) heavily laden with assets. However, the unadjusted P/E and P/BV approaches have limitations since they depend on accounting accruals as opposed to economic realities.

Price Multiples: Comparables vs. Forecasted Fundamentals

As mentioned previously, price multiples can be based on a method of comparables or a method of forecasted fundamentals. In the comparables approach, the investor compares the actual price multiple to a benchmark multiple for the sector or industry. This approach presumes that a high price relative will regress to the mean or median value (meaning that stock price will fall), while low-price-multiple companies would rise to the benchmark (meaning that stock price will go up). By contrast, the forecasted fundamentals approach to estimating a price multiple is a *discounted cash flow* (DCF) approach. In the DCF model, the investor estimates the fundamental (intrinsic) value of stock as the present value of estimated future cash flow. The investor then forms a ratio of estimated price to the relevant accounting measure-again, sales per share, earnings per share, cash flow per share, or book value per share.

If the actual price relative is higher than the price multiple based on forecasted fundamentals, then the stock is deemed overvalued; conversely, a stock would be considered undervalued if the estimated price relative were higher than the actual price multiple. Notably, the forecasted fundamentals approach to estimating a price relative can be used to show that the multiple is related to the required return (equity discount rate) and the long-term earnings (or cash flow) growth rate. In a simple constant-growth version of the DCF model, the price multiple is related to the inverse of the required return minus the expected growth rate, or the number one over the "equity cap rate."

Price Multiples Using Drivers or Common Factors

In Exhibit 2.3, we illustrated a single-factor model relationship between the P/E ratio and the earnings growth rate. In practice, investors and analysts might estimate a statistical relationship between a set of drivers or "common factors" that are likely to impact a company's price multiple. In this section, we illustrate how to interpret the results of a multiple regression approach to measuring a price relative. For example, consider the assumed P/E relationship from a cross-sectional regression of P/E on three well-known common factors, including the *dividend payout ratio* (DPR), risk (as measured by stock's beta or systematic risk), and the *earnings growth rate* (EGR):

$$\text{Predicted P/E} = 10 + 2 \times \text{DPR} - 0.5 \times \text{Beta} + 20 \times \text{EGR}$$

Let DPR = 0.25, Beta = 1.2, and EGR = 0.10 such that:

$$\text{Predicted P/E} = 10 + 0.50 - 0.6 + 2 = 11.90$$

$$\text{Actual P/E} = (\text{say})10$$

Given the regression parameters (or sensitivities) and assumed inputs, the regression model produces a predicted price multiple of 11.90. If the actual price multiple is higher than that predicted by the cross-sectional regression model, then the stock would be considered overvalued. In turn, a stock would be considered undervalued if the actual price relative were lower than that predicted by the assumed regression. With an actual price multiple of, say, 10, the common stock would be undervalued relative to the model.

The benefit of using a multifactor approach to measuring a price multiple is that the model can be estimated using readily available market and accounting data, such as size (equity capitalization), beta (a measure of macro risk), ROE components (as explained before), or growth rates in revenue, earnings, cash flow, dividends, and book value. However, a limitation of the statistical approach to estimating price multiples is that there is no predefined set of drivers or common factors that go into the model. Moreover, the regression drivers approach is not formally linked to financial theory via net present value or economic profit analysis. We describe the *value-based metrics* (VBM) approach to equity analysis following our discussion of the fundamental stock return (a traditional metric) and its link to the investor's required return (a key ingredient in the VBM approach).

FUNDAMENTAL STOCK RETURN

Another useful traditional measure of corporate success arises from the relationship between the fundamental return on a company's stock and its ROE. The *fundamental stock return* (FSR) is equal to the sum of the assessed dividend yield (DY) and the *internal capital generation rate* (ICGR). In formal terms, the FSR can be expressed as

$$FSR = DY + ICGR = DY + (1 - DPR) \times ROE$$
$$= D/P + PBR \times ROE$$

In this expression, DPR is the firm's dividend payout ratio, while D/P is the assessed dividend yield on its common stock. In turn, PBR is the "plowback ratio," measured by one minus DPR. Since PBR is the fraction of earnings that are retained by the firm for investment in real assets, the FSR shows how internal growth is related to financial happenings at the company level.

That is, the firm's internal capital generation rate (also called the *sustainable growth rate*) derives its value from the product of the fraction of earnings retained for future investment—which reflects additional equity capital resulting from reinvestment of a firm's profit—and the estimated return that the firm's managers can generate on those retained earnings. ROE in the traditional realm of financial analysis measures that likely return on stockholders' equity. As we argue below, the FSR should be compared to the investor's required return (or cost of equity) to see if the return that a company can deliver from its underlying fundamentals exceeds or falls short of the required return. Herein begins our first link to the VBM approach to company analysis, as a financial metric becomes a value-based metric when there is a formal recognition of and a link thereto the investor's required rate of return.

Required Return: The Missing Link

Up to this point, we have been long on traditional metrics but short on the notion of the investor's required rate of return. This observation points to a problem with the traditional model of company analysis—whether it is the extended Dupont model or otherwise. Unfortunately, in the traditional approach to equity analysis there is *no* direct link between metrics such as

ROE and FSR and the investor's return expectation for undertaking risk. This omission is important because the fundamental stock return is largely based on accounting data—such as the plowback ratio and ROE—while the investor's required return is (or should be) based on an equilibrium model of expected return and risk.

According to one widely used approach to estimating the required return on common stock, namely, the Capital Asset Pricing Model (CAPM), the required return is equal to

$$ER = R_f + MRP \times Beta$$

In the CAPM, R_f is the risk-free rate of interest, MRP is the expected market risk premium, and beta measures the systematic risk of a firm's common stock. In a nutshell, beta can be interpreted as a measure of macro risk, although beta also reflects other factors such as leverage via the debt–equity ratio. When beta is greater than unity—as is the case of growth stocks—the expected return on common stock is higher than that projected for the market portfolio. Conversely, when beta is less than one—typically for value stocks—the required or expected stock return (ER) is lower than the anticipated return on the market portfolio (M).

Note, too, that the CAPM provides a benchmark for determining whether the FSR on stock is attractive or unattractive. Exhibit 2.4 shows a graph of CAPM as measured by the expected return (as shown on the vertical axis) versus the expected risk (beta as shown on the horizontal axis). A plot of the CAPM is formally known as the *securities market line* (SML).

In principle, companies with FSRs that plot above the SML, such as value stocks B and C, and growth stocks F and G, are attractive because their ROE-induced growth prospects make an abnormally positive contribution to their fundamental stock return. Likewise, any company whose FSR falls below the CAPM benchmark, such as low-risk stock A and moderate-to-risky growth stocks E and H, would be considered unattractive in this security selection framework. This happens because the sum of the assessed dividend yield and internal capital generation rate is not high enough for the company's fundamental stock return to lie either above or on the SML.

In other words, the FSR-linked CAPM model indicates that investors should buy securities of firms having a fundamental stock return that lies above the CAPM line, as their prices seem low when evaluated in terms of the firm's underlying earnings capabilities. In contrast, they should sell or possibly short sell the shares of companies with FSRs that fall below the SML, because stock price appears high when measured relative to the firm's assessed dividend yield and anticipated growth opportunities. By inference, stocks that lie on the SML, such as market-risk stock D, are priced just right,

EXHIBIT 2.4   FSR vs. CAPM

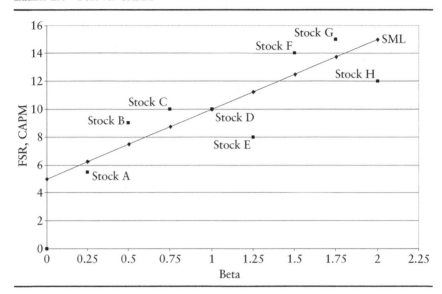

in the sense that their fundamental return could be synthetically replicated with an unlevered or levered index fund in combination with the risk-free asset (appropriate lending or borrowing points along the SML respectively).

TRADITIONAL CAVEATS

The link between FSR and CAPM provides a natural transition to the VBM approach to company analysis. We provide that discussion later in the chapter. However, as a cautionary word on the traditional role of corporate debt policy, it may seem odd that investors should somehow feel better off with higher amounts of leverage, even though the firm's return on assets (or capital) remains constant. This comment points to a hopefully obvious limitation of the traditional approach to company analysis. That is, unless the corporate debt change is associated with a rise in real profitability (due to cash-flow benefits received from a higher debt-interest-tax subsidy) or a perceived decline in equity risk (when a firm moves from a position of too much debt back to its presumed target level), then nothing of any real significance has changed for the shareholders. Without a meaningful change, investors have little incentive to pay a higher or lower price for the firm's shares due to corporate leverage changes per se.

Moreover, in a special case of the VBM approach to capital structure (namely, the original 1958 capital structure model developed by Modigliani and Miller[2]), the perceived stockholder benefits resulting from higher leverage are offset by a rise in the expected (required) rate of return on the firm's common stock. We discuss the comparative valuation effects of capital structure in the next section.

OVERVIEW OF VALUE-BASED METRICS

We now provide an overview of VBM. Value-based metrics are financial measures that largely evolve out of corporate finance. The focus here is on metrics that can assist managers and investors in discerning whether a company is pointing in the direction of wealth creation or, unfortunately, wealth destruction. In the VBM approach to fundamental analysis, the focus is on discovering firms that can consistently earn a return on capital (ROC) that exceeds the weighted average cost of capital (WACC).

A financial metric takes on a VBM character when there is an explicit recognition of and accounting for the overall cost of capital (WACC in the economic value added model described below) or the cost of equity (r in the residual income or abnormal earnings model also described below). Hence, the most distinctive feature of VBM analysis (in contrast to traditional analysis) is the formal recognition of the investor's required rate of return (cost of equity) and the overall cost of capital. Value-based metrics include:

- Residual income (abnormal earnings)
- Residual income spread
- Economic value added (EVA®)
- Economic value added spread
- Market value added (MVA)
- Cash flow return on investment (CFROI®)

Background

We'll begin the VBM approach to equity analysis with a metric called *economic value added* (EVA). EVA was developed commercially in the early 1980s by Joel Stern and G. Bennett Stewart III. This economic profit measure gained early acceptance in the corporate community because of its innovative way of looking at profit net of the overall dollar cost of capital,

---

[2]Franco Modigliani and Merton Miller, "The Cost of Capital, Corporation Finance and the Theory of Investment," *American Economic Review* 48, no. 3 (1958): 261–297.

including debt and equity capital costs. EVA principles have been used by many companies to design incentive compensation programs that provide value-based incentives for managers (agents) to make wealth-enhancing decisions for the shareholders (principals).

In turn, EVA gained popularity in the investment community with the establishment in 1996 of CS First Boston's annual conference on economic value added. In 1997, the U.S. Equity Research Group at Goldman Sachs developed an EVA platform to evaluate the performance of companies, industries, and sectors of the economy. On the buy side, Centre Asset Management LLC and EVA Advisors LLC are two examples of today's investment firms that use an EVA approach to select stocks and build long-short equity portfolios.

The financial significance of using EVA to evaluate company and stock performance is crystal clear: Wealth-creating firms have positive EVA because their NOPAT exceeds the dollar weighted average cost of capital. Wealth destroyers lose market value and incur share price decline because their corporate profitability falls short of the capital costs. This wealth loss can occur even though the firm's accounting profit is positive. This happens when pretax operating earnings (EBIT) are sufficient enough to cover debt-interest costs, but they are not high enough to cover the combined dollar costs of debt and equity financings. Herein lay a key distinction between accounting-based traditional metrics and value-based metrics.

Basic EVA

Central to the EVA calculation is the concept of levered and unlevered firms. A "levered" firm, like most real-world firms, is one that partly finances its growth opportunities with long-term debt. In contrast, an equivalent-risk "unlevered" firm is financed by 100% equity. This firm-type classification is helpful because EVA is calculated by subtracting the firm's dollar weighted average cost of debt and equity capital ($WACC) from its unlevered NOPAT.

$$EVA = NOPAT - \$WACC$$

NOPAT is used in the EVA formulation for two reasons. First, emphasis on this term serves as a reminder that the firm largely receives its profitability from the desirability of its products and services. Second, since most firms have some form of debt outstanding, they receive a yearly interest tax subsidy—measured by the corporate tax rate times the interest expense—that is already reflected in the dollar cost of capital.

This second point is important. An incorrect focus by managers or investors on the levered firm's net operating profit after taxes, LNOPAT, rather than its unlevered profit measure, NOPAT, would lead to an upward bias in the firm's economic value added. By avoiding the double counting of the firm's yearly interest tax subsidy, the investor avoids imparting a positive bias in not only the firm's profitability but also its enterprise value and underlying stock price.

In basic terms, NOPAT can be expressed as (1) tax-adjusted operating earnings (EBIT) or (2) net income (NI) plus after-tax interest expense according to

$$\text{NOPAT} = \text{EBIT} \times (1 - t)$$
$$= [S - \text{CGS} - \text{SGA} - D] \times (1 - t)$$
$$= \text{NI} + (1 - t) * \text{Interest expense}$$

In the first expression, NOPAT is shown as tax-adjusted operating earnings, EBIT $\times$ (1 - t). EBIT in the second expression is sales less cost of goods sold, selling, general, and administrative expenses, and depreciation. In principle, depreciation should be a charge that reflects the economic obsolescence of the firm's operating assets. In the third expression, the analyst or investor begins with accounting net income and adds back the after-tax interest expense to work back to tax-adjusted operating earnings, EBIT $\times$ (1 - t).

In turn, the firm's $WACC can be expressed as

$$\$\text{WACC} = [\%\text{WACC}/100] \times C$$

In this expression, %WACC is the firm's percentage weighted average cost of debt and equity capital, while the letter C is its operating capital. Note that capital can be expressed in terms of operating assets (such as net short-term operating assets plus net plant, property, and equipment) or financing capital (reflecting debt and equity financings). The cost of capital percentage is given by

$$\%\text{WACC} = \%\text{After-tax debt cost} \times \text{Target debt weight}$$
$$+ \%\text{Equity cost} \times \text{Target equity weight}$$

With NOPAT expressed as tax-adjusted operating earnings, we see that a firm's basic EVA can be expressed as

$$\text{EVA} = \text{NOPAT} - \$\text{WACC}$$
$$= \text{EBIT} \times (1 - t) - \text{WACC} \times C$$
$$= [S - \text{CGS} - \text{SGA} - D] \times (1 - t) - \text{WACC} \times C$$

This expression shows that the firm's EVA is equal to its NOPAT less the dollar cost of all capital employed in the business. Moreover, the EVA formula suggests at least five ways to increase a company's economic earnings. These include:

1. Increase revenue (growth).
2. Reduce operating expenses where prudent.
3. Use less capital to produce the same amount of goods and services (improved capital turnover ratios).
4. Use more capital in the presence of positive EVA growth opportunities.
5. Reduce WACC (via greater consistency of earnings and cash flows).

Exhibit 2.5 provides a three-part example on how to estimate basic EVA. The table shows how to estimate the three components of EVA, including NOPAT, WACC, and capital. In this illustration, the firm is pointing in the direction of value creation because its economic profit is positive. Likewise, in EVA spread terms, the firm is a potential wealth creator because its after-tax ROC is higher than its cost of capital.

In practice, there are numerous accounting adjustments that investors should be aware of when estimating EVA via NOPAT and capital. We cover some of the more popular ones at the end of our VBM survey. In the next few sections, we'll discuss related VBM metrics and concepts including (1) how to measure the EVA spread, (2) how to decompose ROC into profit *margins* and capital turns, (3) WACC issues, (4) cash flow return on investment, (5) residual income (abnormal earnings), and (6) the role of EVA and residual income momentum in discerning "good companies" from "bad" or risky-troubled companies and related stock valuation considerations. Finally, the appendix provides a case study on how to combine traditional and value-based metrics to come up with an integrated, overall stock rating.

EVA Spread

VBM can be expressed in either dollar or ratio terms. One of the more popular ratio (or percentage) forms is the EVA spread. This is also referred to as the *residual ROC* (or *surplus rate of return on capital*). The EVA spread is simply the return on capital less WACC. The EVA spread is obtained by dividing EVA by capital to obtain:

$$EVA/C = NOPAT/C - \$WACC/C$$
$$= ROC - WACC$$

EXHIBIT 2.5   Three-Part Calculation of EVA

1. *Calculate basic NOPAT.*

NOPAT = EBIT × $(1 - t)$ = $(S - CGS - SGA - D)$ × $(1 - t)$

Assume the following:

Sales = S = $140,000
Cost of goods sold = CGS = $80,000
Selling, general, and administrative expenses = SGA = $15,000
Depreciation = D = $2,000
Tax rate = t = 35%

Then,

NOPAT = ($140,000 - $80,000 - $15,000 - $2,000) × (1 - 0.35)
         = $43,000 × 0.65 = $27,950

Note that, in practice, NOPAT = Basic NOPAT (shown above) + VBM accounting adjustments (described later)

2. *Calculate the dollar weighted-average cost of capital, $WACC.*

WACC = After-tax debt cost × Target debt weight
           + Equity cost × Target equity weight
$WACC = WACC × C
After-tax debt cost = Pre-tax debt cost × $(1 - t)$
Cost of equity (using CAPM) = R_F + MRP × Beta

Assume the following:

Pretax debt cost = 6%
Risk-free rate = R_F = 3%
Market risk premium = MRP = 5%
Beta = 0.8
Target debt weight = 30%
Capital = $140,000 (Net working capital + Net PP&E; or Long-term debt + Equity)

Note that in practice, Capital = Basic capital (shown above) + Other debt and equity equivalents.
Then,

After-tax debt cost = 0.06% × (1 - 0.35) = 0.039 or 3.9%
CAPM = 0.03 + 0.05 × 0.80 = 0.07 or 7.0%
WACC = 0.039 × 0.3 + 0.07 × 0.70 = 0.0607 or 6.07%
$WACC = 0.0607 × $140,000 = $8,498

3. *Combine results to calculate economic value added, EVA.*

EVA = NOPAT − $WACC = $27,950 − $8,498 = $19,452 > 0 (potential wealth creator)

With this expression, an investor can assess whether a company is pointing in the direction of wealth creation, wealth neutrality, or wealth destruction. If the EVA spread is positive, the firm is a potential value creator, since ROC exceeds WACC. Conversely, if ROC is less than WACC, the firm points in the direction of value destruction, even though reported accounting earnings may be positive. While such a firm may meet its debt interest expense, it is unable to account for the opportunity cost of equity, whether measured in dollar or ratio terms. The EVA spread in the example given in Exhibit 2.5 is 13.89% as shown:

$$EVA/C = \$27,950/\$140,000 - \$8,498/\$140,000$$
$$= 0.1389 \text{ or } 13.89\%$$

The EVA spread is positive and attractive because the ROC, at 19.96%, is considerably higher than the WACC, at 6.07%.

Return on Capital Decomposition

Like ROA in the Dupont model, ROC can be expressed in terms of an operating profit margin and a capital turnover ratio:

$$ROC = NOPAT/C = NOPAT/S \times S/C$$

Moreover, since C (assets perspective) is equal to net short-term operating assets (NWC less short-term debt) plus net plant, property, and equipment, we can express ROC in terms of an operating margin and working capital and NPPE turns:

$$ROC = NOPAT/S \times S/[NWC + NPPE]$$

Not surprisingly, higher operating margins, higher net working capital, and net plant and equipment (including technology) turns lead to higher ROC. Assuming that WACC remains unchanged, the higher ROC leads to a higher EVA spread. This leads to higher EVA and, if sustainable, higher enterprise value—especially with capital expansion (role discussed shortly), assuming that this information is not already reflected in share price.

From Exhibit 2.5, the NOPAT margin (NOPAT/S) is coincidentally the same as ROC, at 19.96%. This happens because the capital turnover ratio (S/C) is unity:

$$ROC = \$27,950/\$140,000 \times \$140,000/\$140,000$$
$$= 0.1996 \text{ or } 19.96\%$$

WACC Issues

Central to the VBM model is the recognition that a firm is not truly profitable unless it earns a return on capital that exceeds the opportunity cost of capital. That being said, questions remain about the actual calculation of WACC. We provide an overview of two particular controversies that present real-world challenges to estimating WACC. These issues pertain to (1) the debt weight (and therefore equity weight) used in the EVA formulation and (2) how to estimate the investor's required rate of return (cost of equity).

Target Capital Structure

One of the major issues in the real-world application of EVA (or residual income) analysis is the question of capital structure. For our purposes, capital structure refers to the debt and equity weights that an investor or analyst should use in the EVA formulation. The question of a target capital structure—reflecting a presumed "optimal" mix of debt and equity financings—is a long-standing debate in the theory of corporate finance. Exhibit 2.6 provides a graphical depiction of the capital structure issue in terms of the traditional view of capital structure versus the Modigliani-Miller view (a celebrated theory proposed in 1958 with subsequent variation). The original theory by Modigliani and Miller (MM) can be interpreted as a special case of the VBM approach to capital structure.

EXHIBIT 2.6 Impact of Capital Structure Change on Enterprise Value

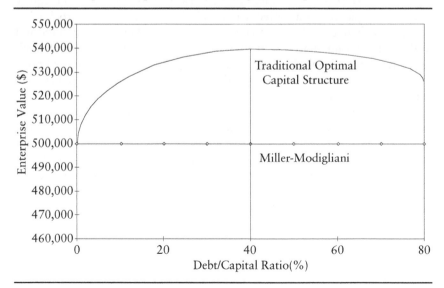

Exhibit 2.6 shows the pricing implications of the traditional versus MM views of capital structure, measured in terms of corporate value (vertical axis) and leverage (horizontal axis). In general, V_u is the market value of the unlevered firm—a firm having no long-term debt—while V_l denotes the market value of a levered firm—a firm with debt. In the traditional view, when the D/C (or D/A) rises from zero to the target level of, say, 40%, the market value of the firm and its outstanding shares goes up. In this debt range, stock price rises as the "good news" to the shareholders—resulting from positive ROE and EPS happenings net of a small change in perceived equity risk—causes investors to pay more for the firm's seemingly dearer shares.

However, if the D/C exceeds the 40% target (see Exhibit 2.6), then corporate value and stock price fall as the heightened financial risk—due to ever-rising fixed obligations that now place the firm in financial jeopardy—offsets the leverage-induced ROE and EPS benefits. With a 60% debt load, the firms' managers have pushed debt beyond the presumed optimal level; hence, they should engage in de-levering activities that effectively swap debt for more equity shares. Moreover, if the 40% debt level is in fact an optimal one, then stock price declines with any sizable movement to the left or right of this target capital structure position.

Exhibit 2.6 also illustrates the pricing implications of a special case of the VBM approach to capital structure—namely, the original MM model. In the MM model, the higher ROE and EPS generated by higher corporate leverage are entirely offset by a rise in the investor's required rate of return. In CAPM, for example, beta is linearly related to the debt–equity ratio. Consequently, in a perfect capital market, the company's stock price remains unchanged in the presence of the debt-induced rise in EPS and ROE. In their value-based framework, a firm's corporate value and stock price are impacted only by real investment opportunities (discounted positive EVA or positive NPV opportunities) as opposed to leverage policies (as in traditional realm) that give investors the illusion of value creation.

Investors and analysts alike must deal with the question of capital structure, since debt and equity weights are required inputs in the WACC (and therefore EVA) formulation. While in theory a capital structure controversy exists, we recommend that investors and analysts use a debt weight that is reflective of the target capital structure mix of debt and equity financings that a firm is likely to achieve over the long term. Moreover, we recommend that investors look "everywhere" for the debt when measuring corporate leverage and estimating stock price.

Estimating the Cost of Equity

In practice, the CAPM is perhaps the most popular approach to estimating the cost of equity. We used CAPM in the traditional approach to company analysis when we compared the FSR to the SML (see Exhibit 2.4). However, there are numerous empirical challenges to the CAPM that suggest that the model is not reflective of what actually happens in the real world regarding the relationship between average portfolio return and risk as specified by the beta factor. That is, numerous empirical studies suggest that over the long pull low-beta, "value"-style portfolios actually outperform high-beta, "growth"-style portfolios.

Given that there are significant challenges to the CAPM, the investor or analyst may prefer to use (1) an enhanced CAPM with other systematic, nondiversifiable risk factors (such as firm size to capture potential size effects and/or the price–book ratio to capture differential expected return effects between value and growth styles) or (2) a non-CAPM approach to measuring the cost of equity, that is, absent beta. Exhibit 2.7 illustrates the components of an equity risk buildup approach to estimating the required return on equity. This non-CAPM alternative was proposed by Abate, Grant, and Rowberry.[3]

EXHIBIT 2.7 Required Return on Equity: Equity-Risk Buildup Model

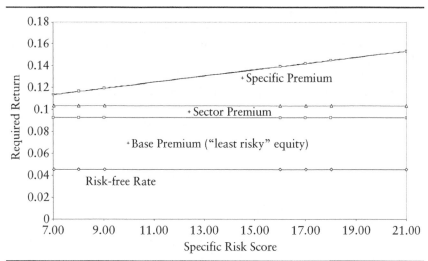

---

[3]James A. Abate, James L. Grant, and Chris Rowberry, "Understanding the Required Return Under New Uncertainty," *Journal of Portfolio Management* 32, no. 1 (2006): 93–102.

Here, the cost of equity is modeled in the context of four elements: (1) a risk-free rate of interest, (2) a base or *non*diversifiable risk premium to the "least risky" equity, (3) a sector-risk premium, and (4) a company-specific risk premium related to (say) abnormal firm size, leverage (debt–equity ratio), and EVA volatility. While we make no specific recommendation, the investor or analyst needs to decide on a particular approach to measuring the cost of equity, as the required ROE is a key component of the WACC used in the EVA formulation. The required return is also a key ingredient in the residual income or abnormal earnings approach, which we describe next.

Cash-Flow Return on Investment

Another widely used VBM is the cash-flow return on investment (CFROI®). CFROI is a commercial metric of Credit Suisse/HOLT. This metric is an internal rate of return (IRR)–based measure of company performance. CFROI takes on an economic profit perspective when it is compared to the cost of capital, WACC. Exhibit 2.8 shows a five-step process to calculate CFROI, although the actual calculation by CS/HOLT is much more complex with several value-based accounting adjustments. The exhibit also shows a simple example of how to estimate this widely known metric.

In Exhibit 2.8, the estimated CFROI is 16.26%. As a stand-alone figure, CFROI does not give the investor or analyst any indication of whether a company is pointing in the direction of wealth creation or destruction. However, CFROI takes on an economic profit perspective when the estimated IRR is compared to the cost of capital. Moreover, an economic profit relationship exists between the two VBMs because the spread between CFROI and WACC is similar to the economic profit or EVA spread.

Specifically, we know that EVA can be expressed in two ways:

$$EVA = NOPAT - WACC \times C$$

Or, in spread form,

$$EVA = [ROC - WACC] \times C$$

In principle, ROC is similar to CFROI, which is an IRR or rate of return on capital concept. While in theory the two value-based metrics (EVA and CFROI) are related in concept, there are notable differences in how these metrics are calculated in practice. A closer look at EVA and CFROI reveals that:

- EVA is a dollar-based measure of economic profit. CFROI is an IRR-like measure that takes on an economic profit perspective when compared to WACC.

■ EVA uses NOPAT and net invested capital, while CFROI is based on gross cash flows and gross investment.
■ EVA is measured in nominal terms, while CFROI is measured in real terms.
■ The accounting adjustments used to measure EVA and CFROI may differ in practice.

EXHIBIT 2.8   CFROI: A Five-Step Process to Calculate CFROI

Step 1. *Compute the average life of the firm's assets*

Note that average asset life equals gross depreciable assets/depreciation. Gross depreciable assets exclude land and construction in process.

Step 2. *Compute gross cash flow*

Gross cash flow equals net income adjusted for noncash operating expenses and financing expenses according to:

Net income before extraordinary items
+ Depreciation and amortization
+ Interest expense
+ Operating rental expense
+ Deferred taxes
= Gross cash flow

Step 3. *Compute gross cash investment*

Note that gross investment equals gross PP&E plus the present value of operating lease payments plus goodwill and accumulated intangibles amortization.

Step 4. *Compute the sum of all nondepreciating assets such as land, working capital, and other assets.*

Step 5. *Solve for the CFROI*

Calculator example:

Gross cash investment = PV = –$40,000
Gross cash flow = PMT = $12,000
Nondepreciating assets = FV = $2,000
Average life of assets = N = 5
CFROI = IRR = 16.26%

Residual Income

Another popular value-based metric is residual income (RI) or abnormal earnings. Residual income is simply accounting net income less the dollar cost of equity:

$$RI = \text{Net income} - \$\text{Cost of equity}$$
$$= [ROE - r] \times E$$

In this expression, the difference between ROE and the investor's required return (r) is the residual income (abnormal earnings) spread. While RI is analogous to EVA in that the measure of profit is net of the investor's dollar-based required return, the concept is somewhat less robust than EVA because ROE in the traditional realm of financial analysis reflects a mixing of operating and financing decisions.

Recall that in the Dupont formula ROE can be expressed as ROA times the equity multiplier (A/E). In contrast, in the EVA calculation the firm's operating and financing decisions are analyzed separately via NOPAT and $WACC. On the other hand, given the different reporting classifications on income and balance sheets for financial services versus nonfinancial services companies (e.g., loans are an asset for a bank while a liability for an industrial or technology firm), the RI (abnormal earnings) approach to equity analysis—with its focus on adjusted book value and the residual income spread—is particularly helpful in estimating and valuing the economic earnings of financial services companies.

Exhibit 2.9 provides an example of how to calculate expected future values of RI given (1) the current book value, (2) a consensus earnings growth estimate, (3) an assumed dividend payout ratio (or implied plowback ratio), and (4) the cost of equity.

Since the RI estimates in Exhibit 2.8 are positive, at $0.70 and $0.74 per share, the firm is expected to make a value-added contribution to shareholder equity. This happens because the estimated ROE (EPS/BV) figures for periods 1 and 2, at 22% and 20.58%, are higher than the investor's assumed required return of 8%.

Role of EVA Momentum

We now describe how the concept of *EVA momentum* (and, by extension, residual income or abnormal earnings momentum) can be used as a prism to discern *good company growth* characteristics from *bad company growth* characteristics. While the level of EVA is important in deciding whether a company is a value creator or value destroyer, this information may already be reflected in share price. Hence, investors need to assess whether the level

EXHIBIT 2.9   Forecasting Residual Income

Assume:
  Current book value per share = $5
  Current earnings = $1.00
  Earnings growth rate = 10%
  Dividend payout ratio = 20%
  Cost of equity = r = 8%

	Period 1	Period 2
Beginning BV per share	$5.00	$5.88
Earnings per share	1.10	1.21
Dividends per share	0.22	0.24
Retained earnings ($EPS - DPS$)	0.88	0.97
Ending BV per share	5.88	6.85
Net income per share (EPS)	1.10	1.21
Less equity charge [$r \times BV(t - 1)$]	0.40[a]	0.47[b]
Residual income	$0.70	0.74

[a]$0.08 \times \$5.00 = \$0.40$
[b]$0.08 \times \$5.88 = \$0.47$

of EVA is increasing or decreasing. A firm's EVA momentum can be assessed according to

$$\Delta EVA = EVA \text{ Spread} \times \Delta C$$
$$= [ROC - WACC] \times \Delta C$$

With EVA spread constancy, we see that the change in EVA is driven by the change in net invested capital; that is, capital investment beyond depreciation. We illustrate the importance of EVA momentum by placing companies into four quadrants. The EVA quadrants (or EVA "style") approach to equity analysis was developed by Grant and Abate[4] and applied in Abate, Grant, and Stewart[5] and Grant and Trahan.[6] As shown in Exhibit 2.10, the EVA quadrants are defined by the following characteristics:

- *Quadrant 1*: Stagnant company—ROC > WACC; $\Delta C \leq 0$
- *Quadrant 2*: Good company growth—ROC > WACC; $\Delta C > 0$

[4]James L. Grant and James A. Abate, *Focus on Value: A Corporate and Investor's Guide to Wealth Creation* (Hoboken, NJ: John Wiley & Sons, 2001).
[5]James A. Abate, James L. Grant, and G. Bennett Stewart III, "The EVA Style of Investing," *Journal of Portfolio Management* 30, no. 4 (2004): 61–72.
[6]James L. Grant and Emery Trahan, "Active Investing in Strategic Acquirers using an EVA Style Analysis," *Journal of Alternative Investments* 11, no. 4 (2009): 7–23.

- *Quadrant 3*: Bad company growth—ROC < WACC; ΔC > 0
- *Quadrant 4*: Positive Restructure—ROC < WACC; ΔC < 0

We apply this schematic to S&P Industrial stocks. In Exhibit 2.10, Quadrant 2 and 4 companies have positive EVA momentum. In contrast, Quadrant 1 and 3 companies are for differing reasons destroying economic value added. This is because the stagnant/mature companies in Quadrant 1 have limited future growth opportunities, while Quadrant 3 companies are expanding negative EVA spread businesses. Clearly, Quadrant 2 and 4 companies represent potential buy opportunities, while companies that populate Quadrants 1 and 3 are potential sell or short-sell candidates, assuming that market implied expectations of future EVA growth are not fully reflected in share price (see EVA valuation considerations in the next section). Grant and Abate emphasize the EVA spread and capital expansion term (or capital catalyst) in the screening of good companies from bad or risky-troubled companies.

Valuation Considerations

We now describe how to use EVA valuation concepts to identify potential buy opportunities (those we refer to as *good stocks*) and sell or short sell

EXHIBIT 2.10 EVA Spread vs. Capital Growth: S&P Industrials

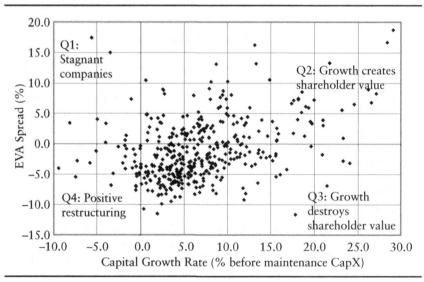

Source: Compustat and Centre Asset Management, LLC.

opportunities (those we identify as *bad stocks*). To illustrate the diversity of valuation approaches using VBM concepts, we also show how to estimate the intrinsic value of a share of common stock using the residual income or abnormal earnings valuation model. RI valuation is similar to EVA valuation, with the substitution of residual income for EVA, and the residual income (abnormal earnings) spread for the EVA spread.

Identifying Good Stocks

While EVA momentum can be used to distinguish good companies from bad companies, we still must see whether a stock is a potential buy or sell opportunity. That is, if the market is efficient, then market implied expectations of future economic profit growth will be consistent with actual growth expectations that a company can deliver. In this case, the stock would be fairly priced in the marketplace. However, if actual expectations of future economic profit growth are higher than market implied expectations, then a stock would be considered undervalued. In turn, if actual expectations of future EVA growth are lower than that embedded in share price, then a stock would be overvalued.

In theory, it can be shown that a firm's net present value (NPV) is equal to the present value of all future EVA. With constant growth, the firm's NPV—a measure of intrinsic value added in current dollars—can be expressed as

$$NPV = EVA/(WACC - g)$$

In this expression, EVA is a one-step-ahead forecast, WACC is the familiar cost of capital, and g is the expected long-run growth in economic earnings. Of course, this form of EVA valuation requires that WACC is greater than the growth rate. It follows that the intrinsic value of the firm can be expressed as:

$$V = C + NPV$$

From these relationships, we can calculate the value–capital ratio (V/C). This ratio is analogous to the price–book value ratio in the traditional realm of financial analysis:

$$V/C = 1 + NPV/C = 1 + [EVA/(WACC - g)]/C$$
$$= 1 + [ROC - WACC]/(WACC - g)$$

Since NPV (derived from EVA valuation) measures the value that a firm's management has added (albeit market and industry considerations) to the invested capital in their employ, the value–capital ratio is greater than unity if and only if the firm has discounted positive EVA; that is, NPV is positive, signifying a wealth creator. Equivalently, the V/C ratio is greater than one if the firm's management can sustainably generate a positive EVA spread [ROC > WACC, and WACC > g in the constant growth EVA valuation model].

In contrast, a firm's V/C ratio will be less than unity if discounted EVA is negative [ROC < WACC]; that is, NPV is negative, signifying a wealth destroyer. Note, too, that if the capital market is efficient, then the market's assessment of value added, denoted by MVA, will be equal to the firm's assessed NPV. From these relationships, we can identify the value-based conditions for discovering fairly priced stocks, undervalued stocks, and *overvalued stocks*; whereby MVA is equal to NPV, MVA is less than NPV, or MVA is higher than NPV, respectively. We summarize the security selection implications of these MVA and NPV conditions as:

Relationship	Condition
MVA = NPV	Stock is fairly priced
MVA < NPV	Stock is undervalued
MVA > NPV	Stock is overvalued

Exhibit 2.11 provides a graphical display of the EVA spread versus the V/C ratio for S&P Industrial stocks. The graph in this exhibit follows the EVA quadrants graph shown in Exhibit 2.10, and is based on the EVA style of investing approach developed by Grant and Abate.[7]

In Exhibit 2.11, the EVA spread is the y variable, while the V/C ratio is the x variable. Stocks that plot above the curve are deemed undervalued or good stocks as actual expectations of future economic profit growth, g, are higher than that reflected in share price; hence, the V/C ratio and stock price should rise. Stocks that plot below the curve are deemed overvalued or bad stocks since actual expectations of economic profit growth are lower than that embedded in share price; hence, V/C ratio and stock price should fall. In turn, stocks that plot on the curve are presumed to be efficiently priced as market implied expectations of future economic profit growth are equal to that which a company can realistically deliver. Moreover, a residual income (abnormal earnings) version of this EVA framework would show the residual income spread (ROE minus r) as the y variable and the price/book value ratio as the x variable.

---

[7]Grant and Abate, *Focus on Value: A Corporate and Investor's Guide to Wealth Creation.*

EXHIBIT 2.11   EVA Spread vs. Value/Capital Ratio: S&P Industrials

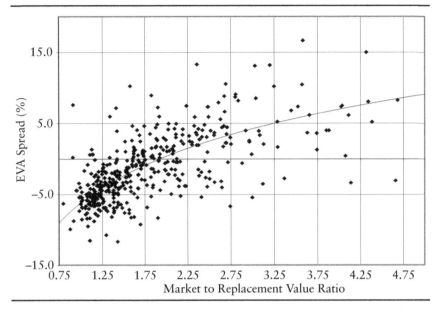

Source: Compustat and Centre Asset Management, LLC.

Residual Income (Abnormal Earnings) Valuation

We now illustrate how to calculate the intrinsic value of a share of stock using the residual income or abnormal earnings model. Specifically, Exhibit 2.12 shows how to calculate the intrinsic value of a share of common stock using a two-stage (or multistage) RI model. The valuation analysis assumes a required return (cost of equity) of 8%, along with forecasted EPS over a finite horizon period (we use the two years of RI estimates from Exhibit 2.8) and forecasted continuing residual earnings.

Like EVA, we can explain the relationship between residual income and the justified price–book ratio based on forecasted fundamentals. Since the forecasted fundamentals approach to multiples analysis is a *discounted cash flow* (DCF) or intrinsic value approach, we have

$$P = BV \text{ per share} + PV \text{ of RI per share}$$

such that

$$P/BV = 1 + [PV \text{ of RI}]/BV$$

EXHIBIT 2.12   Residual Income Valuation

Horizon Value Period: Years 1–2

   RI(1) = $0.70

   RI(2) = $0.74

   such that

   PV of RI per share = $0.70/(1.08) + $0.74/(1.08)^2 = $0.65 + $0.63 = $1.28

Continuing Value Period: Years 3 to ∞

   PV of RI (multistage)
   = PV of RI during forecast period + PV of RI during continuing period
   = $1.28 + PV(8%,2) × [RI(3) / (r – g)]

   Assume that long-term growth in RI = 0.02 (or 2%), such that

   RI(3) = RI(2) × (1 + g) = 0.74 × (1.02) = 0.75

   PV of RI (multistage)
   = $1.28 + PV(8%,2) × [$0.75/(0.08 – 0.02)]
   = $1.28 + PV(8%,2) × [$12.50] = $12.00

   such that,

   Estimated stock price
   = BV(t – 1) + PV of all future RI = $5.00 + $12.00
   = $17.00

Equity Strategy

   Compare estimated stock price (intrinsic value) to actual price to see if overvalued or undervalued.

where P/BV > 1.0 if the present value of residual income (abnormal earnings) is positive. In contrast, P/BV is less than unity when a company is perceived to have consistently negative residual income. Equivalently, P/BV ratio is greater than one if ROE is sustainably greater than r, while P/BV is less than unity when the firm is perceived to incur a negative residual income spread [ROE < r].

   Moreover, we could calculate the implied growth rate in residual income given the price–book ratio and an estimate of the required rate of return on equity. Using the constant growth assumption yields,

$$P = BV + PV \text{ of RI}$$
$$= BV + [ROE - r] \times BV/(r - g)$$

such that $P/BV = 1 + [ROE - r]/(r - g)$.

Hence, the investor or analyst could solve for market-implied growth in residual income, g, with knowledge of P/BV, ROE, and the investor's required rate of return. The investor could then compare market-implied g with the long-term growth in residual income that the analyst perceives the company could actually deliver to determine whether a stock is a potential buy or sell opportunity.

VBM Caveats

While value-based metrics such as EVA, CFROI, and RI are fundamentally linked to value creation (via NPV), there are numerous accounting adjustments that an investor or analyst must consider in practice. Indeed, the firm of Stern Stewart has discovered some 140 accounting adjustments to consider when moving from the traditional accounting concept of income to the VBM concept of economic earnings. At a minimum, we recommend that investors and analysts consider the following list of VBM accounting adjustments when measuring economic profit:

- Research and development (capitalized)
- Strategic investments (temporary suspension of capital charge)
- Intangibles (capitalized and not amortized)
- Deferred taxes (conversion to cash taxes)
- Operating leases (treated as debt equivalent)
- Last in, first out (LIFO) inventory costing-LIFO reserve add backs

It is important to note that there are income statement and balance sheet consequences for each VBM accounting adjustment. For instance, the year-over-year change in an unamortized research and development (R&D) account (that is, amortization expense) would get added back to NOPAT, while the accumulated unamortized R&D account would get added back to EVA capital. In this way, the capitalized value of each dollar of R&D has a capital cost as long as it remains on the EVA balance sheet. Also, the after-tax implied interest expense on operating leases would get added back to NOPAT, while the present value of operating leases would be treated as a debt equivalent on the EVA balance sheet. VBM accounting conventions apply to several other value-based accounting items.

Despite the caveats or limitations cited for both traditional and value-based approaches to equity analysis, we conclude this chapter by recommending that investors join the two approaches to securities analysis. In the process, investors and analysts must realize that a combination of traditional and VBM analyses will require an extra effort in terms of the acquisition of knowledge and skills in order to understand what these metrics have to say about the creation of shareholder value. That being said, we believe that the extra time spent will be worth the effort in terms of both educational value added and economic value added—a doubly winning EVA benefit!

Case Study: JLG Equity Analysis Template

We present in the appendix to this chapter a synthesized traditional and value-based analysis of Coca-Cola using financial software developed by JLG Research. The accompanying equity analysis includes growth rates, margins, multiples, ROE, and FSR on the traditional side and EVA, EVA spread, residual income (abnormal earnings), and EVA momentum on the value-based metrics side. The equity analysis template shown herewith can be used to distinguish good companies (potential buy opportunities) from average to risky-troubled companies (potential sell or short sell opportunities). The data inputs for the JLG Equity Analysis Template are drawn from a Value Line report.

We emphasize that the case study application is not meant to show that traditional metrics are better or worse than VBM, or that our stock recommendation is somehow better than that provided by Value Line. Rather, the goal of the case study application of Coca-Cola is to show that traditional and VBM analyses can in fact complement each other; noting that we give Coca-Cola a "Timeliness" rating of "2" and a "Safety" rating of unity. Based on the Value Line scaling of 1 to 5, these fundamental ratings represent high expected performance over the next 6 to 12 months and low expected risk (from the date of the analysis). Incidentally, Value Line gave the soft-drink company a Timeliness rating of "3" for average expected performance over the forward 6 to 12 months with their highest safety rating as of the report date. With respect to these comparative ratings, we realize that past performance is no guarantee of future performance and that investors should seek professional advice when buying or selling securities.

KEY POINTS

- Fundamentals and valuation metrics are used in traditional and value-based approaches to equity securities analysis.
- In the traditional realm, growth rates, margins, return on equity, multiples, and the fundamental stock return are at the heart of this well-known approach to company analysis.
- The extended Dupont formula goes a long way in showing how the multiplicative combination of operating margins, asset turns, interest burden, tax burden and the equity multiplier (leverage) at the company

level can impact—either positively or negatively—the shareholders' return on equity.

■ Valuation measures such as price-to-sales, price-to-earnings, and price-to-book ratios can be used by investors and analysts to assess whether a company's internal growth opportunities are correctly priced in the marketplace.

■ If the fundamental stock return (which includes the sustainable growth rate as measured by times return on equity) falls short of the required return—equivalently if the fundamental stock return lies below the securities market line—then the stock appears to be overvalued. Consequently, the investor should consider selling or short selling the presumably mispriced shares. In theory, the firm's common stock is priced "just right" when the fundamental stock return equals the investor's required return. In turn, a potential buy opportunity is present when the FSR exceeds the required rate. We also examined the traditional (and value-based) role of corporate debt policy.

■ Investors and analysts must determine whether a seemingly favorable change in return on equity is due to changes in a firm's real growth opportunities, or whether it is due to an illusionary benefit to shareholders resulting from a debt ratio that exceeds the presumed target or optimal level.

■ A value-based metric becomes a VBM when there is a direct recognition of and a formal link to the opportunity cost of capital (via WACC in the EVA formulation) or the investor's required rate of return (via r in the residual income or abnormal earnings model).

■ In the VBM approach to company and securities analysis, a firm is not truly profitable unless its return on capital is higher than the cost of capital, including the direct cost of debt and the indirect cost of equity financing. Moreover, the VBM approach emphasizes the concept of wealth creators and wealth destroyers. In this approach, the investor or analyst focuses on the fundamental ability of a firm to create shareholder value.

■ EVA momentum is crucial in determining whether or not a company is pointing in the direction of wealth creation or wealth destruction.

■ On balance, VBM and traditional metrics can (and should) be combined in a way that provides investors and analysts with a diversity of equity analysis tools to identify potential buy and sell opportunities in the marketplace.

APPENDIX: CASE STUDY

Coca-Cola: Integrated Traditional and VBM Analyses

In the appendix, we provide an integrated fundamental analysis of Coca-Cola Company (KO) using traditional and value-based metrics. Financial data for KO are drawn from the Value Line report shown in Exhibit 2.A1. An overall fundamental evaluation of the soft drink company is provided using the Timeliness (expected performance) and Safety (risk) rankings employed by Value Line. A Timeliness score of 1 means high expected stock performance, while a score of 5 means low expected stock performance over the next 6 to 12 months. A Safety score of 1 means high expected safety (low risk), while a score of 5 means low expected safety (high risk). A comparative rating using this system is also provided for a hypothetical analyst. The accompanying equity analysis of Coca-Cola is conducted using financial software developed by JLG Research and consists of three parts, shown in Exhibit 2.A2:

1. Evaluation of Expected Performance (timeliness)
2. Evaluation of Expected Risk (safety)
3. Equity Fundamental Summary and Rating

The usual caveat applies to the case study: Past performance is no guarantee of future performance, and investors should seek professional and legal guidance when buying and selling securities.

EXHIBIT 2.A1   The Value Line Report

COCA-COLA NYSE-KO	RECENT PRICE 53.24	P/E RATIO 15.9 (Trailing: 17.5 Median: 21.0)	RELATIVE P/E RATIO 1.03	DIV'D YLD 3.4%	VALUE LINE

TIMELINESS	3	Lowered 3/5/10
SAFETY	1	New 7/27/90
TECHNICAL	3	Lowered 5/28/10
BETA	.60	(1.00 = Market)

High: 70.9 66.9 62.2 57.9 50.9 53.5 45.3 49.3 64.3 65.6 59.4 57.8
Low: 47.3 42.9 42.4 42.9 37.0 38.3 40.3 39.4 45.6 40.3 37.4 49.5

LEGENDS
— 18.0 x "Cash Flow" p sh
···· Relative Price Strength
Options: Yes
Shaded area: prior recession
Latest recession began 12/07

2013-15 PROJECTIONS

	Price	Gain	Ann'l Total Return
High	105	(+95%)	21%
Low	85	(+60%)	15%

Insider Decisions

	S	O	N	D	J	F	M	A	M
to Buy	0	1	1	0	0	0	2	0	0
Options	0	0	3	0	0	0	0	1	
to Sell	0	2	0	3	0	0	0	0	1

Institutional Decisions

	3Q2009	4Q2009	1Q2010
to Buy	545	501	565
to Sell	612	647	601
Hld's(000)	1507749	1489243	1439743

Percent shares traded: 15 / 10 / 5

Target Price Range 2013 | 2014 | 2015

% TOT. RETURN 6/10
	THIS STOCK	VL ARITH. INDEX
1 yr.	7.8	29.6
3 yr.	4.9	-8.6
5 yr.	38.8	24.0

1994	1995	1996	1997	1998	1999	2000	2001	2002	2003E	2004	2005	2006	2007	2008	2009	2010	2011	© VALUE LINE PUB., INC.	13-15
6.34	7.19	7.48	7.64	7.63	8.01	8.23	7.06	7.92	8.62	9.12	9.75	10.39	12.45	13.82	13.46	14.00	15.85	Sales per sh	18.50
1.16	1.37	1.60	1.92	1.69	1.63	1.79	1.92	1.99	2.31	2.45	2.59	2.81	3.08	3.58	3.55	3.90	4.30	"Cash Flow" per sh	5.10
.99	1.19	1.40	1.64	1.42	1.30	1.48	1.60	1.65	1.95	2.06	2.17	2.37	2.57	3.02	2.93	3.35	3.70	Earnings per sh A	4.50
.39	.44	.50	.56	.60	.64	.68	.72	.80	.88	1.00	1.12	1.24	1.36	1.52	1.64	1.76	1.88	Div'ds Decl'd per sh B■	2.24
.34	.37	.40	.44	.35	.43	.30	.31	.34	.33	.31	.38	.61	.71	.85	.87	.85	.90	Cap'l Spending per sh	1.00
2.05	2.15	2.48	2.96	3.41	3.85	3.75	4.57	4.78	5.77	6.61	6.90	7.30	9.38	8.85	10.77	12.50	14.20	Book Value per sh C	19.80
2551.9	2504.6	2481.0	2470.6	2465.5	2471.6	2484.8	2486.2	2471.0	2441.5	2409.3	2369.0	2318.0	2318.0	2312.0	2303.0	2310	2305	Common Shs Outst'g D	2285
22.5	26.8	32.8	38.1	NMF	47.5	37.5	30.5	30.2	22.6	22.6	19.7	18.5	21.0	17.8	16.3	Bold figures are		Avg Ann'l P/E Ratio	21.0
1.48	1.79	2.05	2.20	NMF	2.71	2.44	1.56	1.65	1.29	1.19	1.05	1.00	1.11	1.07	1.09	Value Line estimates		Relative P/E Ratio	1.40
1.7%	1.4%	1.1%	.9%	.8%	1.0%	1.2%	1.5%	1.6%	2.0%	2.2%	2.6%	2.8%	2.5%	2.8%	3.4%			Avg Ann'l Div'd Yield	2.4%

CAPITAL STRUCTURE as of 7/2/10					
Total Debt $11709.0 mill. Due in 5 Yrs. $8616.0
LT Debt $4427.0 mill. Total Int. $265.0 mill.
(Total interest coverage: 15x)
(15% of Cap'l)
Pension Assets-12/09 $3.03 bill. Oblig. $3.99 bill.
Pfd Stock None
Common Stock 2,307,050,619 shs.
as of 4/26/10
MARKET CAP: $123 billion (Large Cap)

20458	17545	19564	21044	21962	23104	24088	28857	31944	30990	32375	36500	Sales ($mill)	42275
28.9%	35.1%	32.0%	31.6%	32.2%	30.8%	31.3%	30.0%	30.3%	30.7%	36.0%	35.0%	Operating Margin	37.0%
773.0	803.0	806.0	850.0	893.0	932.0	938.0	1163.0	1228.0	1236.0	1240	1250	Depreciation ($mill)	1275
3669.0	3979.0	4100.0	4790.0	5014.0	5196.0	5568.0	5981.0	7050.0	6940.0	7825	8625	Net Profit ($mill)	10400
27.1%	29.8%	27.0%	21.1%	24.5%	23.5%	22.4%	24.0%	22.2%	22.7%	23.5%	24.0%	Income Tax Rate	25.0%
17.9%	22.7%	21.0%	22.8%	22.8%	22.5%	23.1%	20.7%	22.1%	22.4%	24.2%	23.6%	Net Profit Margin	24.6%
d2701	d1258	11.0	510.0	1123.0	414.0	d449.0	d1120	d812.0	3830.0	4000	4000	Working Cap'l ($mill)	5000
835.0	1219.0	2701.0	2517.0	1157.0	1154.0	1314.0	3277.0	2781.0	5059.0	5000	4800	Long-Term Debt ($mill)	3500
9316.0	11366	11800	14090	15935	16355	16920	21744	20472	24799	28900	32800	Shr. Equity ($mill)	45200
36.4%	31.9%	28.8%	29.2%	29.5%	29.8%	30.7%	24.2%	30.6%	23.8%	23.5%	23.0%	Return on Total Cap'l	21.5%
39.4%	35.0%	34.7%	34.0%	31.5%	31.8%	32.9%	27.5%	34.4%	28.0%	27.0%	26.0%	Return on Shr. Equity	23.0%
21.3%	19.3%	17.9%	18.6%	16.2%	15.4%	15.7%	13.0%	17.2%	12.7%	13.0%	13.0%	Retained to Com Eq	11.5%
46%	45%	48%	45%	48%	52%	52%	53%	50%	55%	52%	50%	All Div'ds to Net Prof	49%

CURRENT POSITION (\$MILL.)

	2008	2009	7/2/10
Cash Assets	4979	9151	10099
Receivables	3090	3758	4001
Inventory (Avg Cst)	2187	2354	2363
Other	1920	2288	2111
Current Assets	12176	17551	18574
Accts Payable	6205	6657	6202
Debt Due	6531	6800	7282
Other	252	264	450
Current Liab.	12988	13721	13934

ANNUAL RATES

of change (per sh)	Past 10 Yrs.	Past 5 Yrs.	Est'd '07-'09 to '13-'15
Sales	5.5%	9.0%	5.5%
"Cash Flow"	7.0%	8.5%	7.0%
Earnings	7.0%	8.5%	8.0%
Dividends	9.5%	11.0%	7.0%
Book Value	11.0%	11.0%	12.5%

Cal-endar	QUARTERLY SALES ($ mill.)				Full Year
	Mar.Per	Jun.Per	Sep.Per	Dec.Per	
2007	6103	7733	7690	7331	28857
2008	7379	9046	8393	7126	31944
2009	7169	8267	8044	7510	30990
2010	7525	8674	8460	7716	32375
2011	7925	9500	10000	9075	36500

Cal-endar	EARNINGS PER SHARE A				Full Year
	Mar.Per	Jun.Per	Sep.Per	Dec.Per	
2007	.54	.80	.71	.52	2.57
2008	.64	.98	.81	.59	3.02
2009	.58	.88	.81	.66	2.93
2010	.69	1.02	.90	.74	3.35
2011	.76	1.10	.99	.85	3.70

Cal-endar	QUARTERLY DIVIDENDS PAID B ■				Full Year
	Mar.31	Jun.30	Sep.30	Dec.31	
2006	--	.31	.31	.62	1.24
2007	--	.34	.34	.68	1.36
2008	--	.38	.38	.76	1.52
2009	--	.41	.41	.82	1.64
2010	--	.44	.44		

BUSINESS: The Coca-Cola Company is the world's largest beverage company. It distributes major brands (Coca-Cola, diet Coke, Sprite, Barq's, Mr. Pibb Xtra, Fanta, Fresca, Dasani, Evian, Full Throttle, Powerade, Minute Maid, and others) through bottlers around the world. Business outside North America accounted for 74% of net sales in 2009. 2009 depreciation rate: 3.9%. Coca-Cola Enterprises (CCE) is a 36%-owned soft drink bottler. Advertising expenses, 9.0% of revenues. Has approximately 92,800 employees; Directors and Officers as a group own 5.4% of stock (3/10 Proxy). Chairman and C.E.O. Muhtar Kent. Incorporated: Delaware. Address: One Coca-Cola Plaza, Atlanta, Georgia 30313. Telephone: 404-676-2121. Internet: www.coca-cola.com.

Business at The Coca-Cola Company is improving. The beverage behemoth realized top- and bottom-line advances of 5% and 16%, compared to last year's second quarter. And we expect full-year sales to advance about 4.5%. The top line ought to stage a recovery, since the economy seems to be on the mend. Although consumer spending remains restrained, a more favorable pricing and product mix, and better consumer confidence, should bolster top-line results moving forward.

Earnings are set to progress at a faster pace. We expect KO to earn around $3.35 a share this year, representing an increase of some 14% from last year's tally, with another double-digit advance likely in 2011. An important factor affecting growth is KO's embarking on several efficiency initiatives at the onset of the recent recession. Perhaps the most significant shift in operations has been its move to acquire the North American operations of its largest bottler, Coca-Cola Enterprises. Although we have not yet incorporated this event into our estimates *(Value Line policy does not include acquisition figures until a deal is finalized)*, the purchase has significant cost savings potential for The Coca-Cola Company. And KO has not ruled out more small bolt-on acquisitions of other bottlers, as a means of dealing with a challenging operating landscape. Furthermore, hedging policies will likely remain intact.

The company has other expansion avenues. It recently augmented its still-drink lineup with the introduction of *Vitaminwater Zero* and the relaunch of *Dasani* flavored waters. As well, energy drinks are now included in its sparkling lineup. These drinks are gaining prominence, and KO's distribution partnership with Hansen Natural to distribute the latter company's popular *Monster* energy drink is positive. Too, KO is focused on geographic expansion, especially in emerging markets, like India and China.

This neutrally ranked stock may pique long-term investors' interest. Without considering the pending merger, the company still has decent appreciation potential for the 2013-2015 time frame. And a nice dividend payout sweetens incentives further.

Nira Maharaj   July 30, 2010

(A) Based on primary shs. through '96, diluted shs. thereafter. Next earnings report due late October. Excls. nonrec. losses: '99, (32¢); '00, (60¢); '01, (2¢); '02, (43¢); '03, (18¢); '04, (4¢); (B) Div'ds historically paid based on April 1, July 1, Oct. 1, Dec.1. ■ Div'd reinvestment plan avail. (C) Incl. intangibles. In '09: $12.8 bill., | 05, (13¢); '06, (21¢) '08 (53¢). $5.55/sh. (D) In millions. (E) Reflects reclassification of sales and expenses.

Company's Financial Strength	A++
Stock's Price Stability	100
Price Growth Persistence	30
Earnings Predictability	100

Source: Value Line Investment Survey, New York, NY. Reprinted with permission.

EXHIBIT 2.A2   JLG Equity Analysis Template*

JLG EQUITY ANALYSIS TEMPLATE

(Note disclaimer)

Description:

This template allows the user to conduct an integrated traditional and value-based metrics analysis of a company and its stock. The equity analysis goal is to rate the company on the basis of expected performance (timeliness) and expected risk (safety); Next, 6 to 12 months, score "1-to-5" each measure. Traditional measures of success and valuation include growth rates, margins, ROE and Dupont, multiples, PEG, and the fundamental stock return (FSR). Value-based measures include residual income (abnormal earnings), Economic Value Added (1), EVA spread, EVA Dupont, and EVA momentum. Equity risk measures include beta (macro risk), capital structure (leverage), and earnings consistency/predictability. Coded fields are shaded; open fields require user input.

FOCUS:

Part I: Evaluation of Expected Performance (timeliness), including:

Traditional metrics: growth rates, profit margins, multiples, 5-factor ROE Dupont analysis, and fundamental stock return.

Value-based metrics: Abnormal earnings (residual income), economic value added (EVA), ROC Dupont, and EVA momentum.

Part II: Evaluation of Expected Risk (safety), including:

Beta (macro risk), price growth persistence, earnings predictability, and capital structure.

Part III: Equity Fundamental Summary, including:

User assigned stock rating.

		Comments:
USER NAME:	Jane/Joe Analyst	User Name
Research Date	10/1/2010	User choice
Company:	COCA-COLA	User choice
Ticker	KO	Input ticker symbol
Data Source:	Value Line	VL or other data source
Date of source report	7/30/2010	Input report date

Ratings:	Timeliness	Safety
Value Line (or other source)	3	1
Jane/Joe Analyst	2	2

*The equity analysis template applied herewith is a financial product of JLG Research. All rights reserved worldwide. For more information, see www.jlgresearch.com.

EXHIBIT 2.A2   *(Continued)*

PART I: Evaluation of Expected Performance (timeliness)

TRADITIONAL METRICS:

A. *Expected Growth Rates*

		Enter Year: One-Step Ahead	
Year	2010	2011	2014
Year relative	*0*	*1*	*4*
Revenue/share	14.00	15.85	18.5
Cash flow/share	3.90	4.30	5.1
EPS	3.35	3.70	4.50
DPS	1.76	1.88	2.24
CapX/sh	0.85	0.90	1

	2010	2011	2014
Rev growth		0.1321	0.0529
CF growth		0.1026	0.0585
EPS growth		0.1045	0.0674
DPS growth		0.0682	0.0601
CapX/sh growth		0.0588	0.0357

Compare prospective growth rates
over time/industry/competitor

B. *Multiples and PEG*

Stock Price (at date of analysis):   53.24   **Input Stock Price**

	2010	2011	2014
Price-to-revenue ratio	3.803	3.359	2.878
Price-to-cash flow ratio	13.651	12.381	10.439
Price-to-earnings ratio	15.893	14.38919	11.831

PEG ratio	1.377	1.755

(P/E-to-EPS growth rate)

Compare PEG to comparable
company or industry benchmark

EXHIBIT 2.A2 *(Continued)*

C. Projected ROE	2011	
Basic Definition:		
Net profit (NP)	8625	Input "Net Profit"
Equity	32800	Input "Shareholders' Equity"
ROE (Net profit/Equity)	0.263	

Dupont Analysis:	2011	
ROE = ROA × A/E = NPM × AT × EM		

Net profit	8625	
Assets (= CL + LTD + Equity)	51534	Input "Assets"
ROA (NP/Assets)	0.167	
Equity multiplier (Assets/Equity)	1.571	
ROE	0.263	

Net profit	8625	
Sales (S)	36500	Input "Sales (revenue)"
Net profit margin (NP/S)	0.236	
Asset turnover (S/A)	0.708	
EM (A/E)	1.571	
ROE	0.263	

ROE: 5-Factor Dupont:

ROE = Tax burden × Interest burden × OPM × AT × EM

Reported income tax	0.24	Input "Income Tax Rate"
Pretax profit [NP/(1 − t)]	11348.68	
EBIT (from below)	11525.0	

Tax burden [NI/PBT= (1 − t)]	0.76
Interest burden[a] [PBT/EBIT]	0.98
OPM [EBIT/Sales]	0.316
Asset turnover	0.708
Equity multiplier	1.571
ROE: 5-factor Dupont	0.263

[a]*Interest burden net of nonoperating income/expense items.*

EXHIBIT 2.A2 *(Continued)*

D. Fundamental Stock Return | 2011

FSR = DY + PBR × ROE

Dividend yield (DPS/stock price)	0.035
Dividend payout ratio (DPS/EPS)	0.508
PRB (plowback ratio)	0.492

FSR	0.1647	
CAPM	0.08	See WACC calculation (below)
FSR spread	0.0847	
FSR > CAPM (?)	Yes	Good company if positive
		Stock plots above Securities Market Line (SML)

VALUE-BASED METRICS: Residual Income and EVA

A. Residual Income (abnormal earnings)

RI = Net Income − $Cost of Equity = RI Spread × Equity

ROE	0.263	
Required return (CAPM, etc.)	0.08	
Residual income spread	0.1830	Good company if positive
Residual income (RI)	6001	Good company if positive
RI spread × Equity		*Since ROE exceeds investor's required return*

EVA = NOPAT − $WACC

B. Estimating NOPAT (basic)

NOPAT = EBIT × (1 − T) = [S − COGS − SGA − Depr] × (1 − t) = [S × OM-Depr] × (1 − t)

where: OM = EBITD/Sales

Year	2011	
Sales	36500	
Operating margin (EBITD/Sales)	0.35	OM = (Sales − COGS − SGA)/Sales
EBITD	12775	
Depreciation	1250	
EBIT	11525	
Tax rate	0.35	Unlevered tax rate
NOPAT	7491	

EXHIBIT 2.A2 *(Continued)*

C. *Estimating $WACC (dollar cost of capital)*

Note: $WACC = WACC × Capital
  and
WACC = wd × AT debt cost + we × Cost of equity
WACC = wd × Pretax debt cost × $(1 - t)$ + we × CAPM

Debt Cost:

Pretax debt cost = Interest/LT debt

(Assumes bonds trading at "par")

$Interest	265	
LT debt	4427	

Pretax debt cost (5% default) 0.0599

AT debt cost = Pretax × $(1 - t)$

  0.0389

Equity Cost:

CAPM = RF + Beta × ERP

RF	0.0500	5-year Treasury
MRP	0.0500	Average market premium
Beta	0.6	
CAPM	0.08	

EVA Capital:

C = NWC + NPPE (assets approach)
C = Debt + Equity (financing approach)
(Can use EOY, BOY or average capital)

Year	2011	
LT debt	11709	Est. debt on balance sheet
Equity	32800	
Capital	44509	

WACC = wd × AT debt cost + we × CAPM

Debt wgt.	0.26307	Debt/Capital ratio
Equity wgt.	0.73693	
WACC	0.0692	Weighted average cost of debt and equity

$Capital cost = WACC × TC 3080

EXHIBIT 2.A2 *(Continued)*

D. *EVA and EVA Spread*

Year	2011	
EVA = NOPAT − $WACC	4412	Wealth creator if positive
Return on capital (ROC)	0.1683	ROC = NOPAT/Capital
WACC	0.0692	Cost of capital
EVA spread	0.0991	

E. *EVA Dupont: Breakdown of ROC*

ROC = NOPAT/C = NOPAT margin × Capital turnover

NOPAT	7491
Sales	36500
NOPAT margin	0.2052
Capital	44509
Capital turnover ratio	0.8201
ROC	0.1683

F. *EVA Momentum (determination of good/bad company growth)*

Delta EVA = EVA Spread × Delta CapX

EVA spread	0.0991		
CapX growth			
Year	*2010*	*2011*	*2014*
Year relative	*0*	*1*	*4*
CapX/Share	0.85	0.9	1
Shares	2310	2305	2285
Gross CapX	*1963.5*	*2074.5*	*2285*
Depreciation	1240	1250	1275
Net CapX	*723.5*	824.5	1010
Net CapX $ growth		101	186
Net CapX growth		0.1396	0.0700
(Annualized rate)			

EXHIBIT 2.A2 (*Continued*)

EVA Momentum (in $):	10.0110	18.3865

[*EVA spread* × *Net CapX $ growth*]   Good company growth if EVA momentum > 0
Growth creates shareholder value
(or positive restructure)

PART II: Evaluation of Expected Risk (safety)

Beta	0.6	Measures macro risk (*Beta < 1 = Good*)
Price growth persistence % (*Enter value*)	30	Measures consistency in price growth (*Scale 0 to 100; High = Good*)
Earnings predict % (*Enter value*)	100	Measures earnings consistency (*High = Good*)
Capital structure % (LT debt/Capital)	26.31%	Measures sebt capacity (*Low = Good: scale of 0% to 100%*)

Part III: Equity Fundamental Summary and Rating

Date:	10/1/2010
Company	COCA-COLA
Ticker	KO

Fundamentals:		Risk:		
(Traditional/VBM)		(Macro/Company specific)		
Growth rates (excluding CapX)	Good	Beta (macro risk)	Good	*User assigned (good, mixed, poor)*
FSR vs. CAPM	Good	Stock price growth	Poor	*User assigned*
EVA	Good	Earnings predictability	Good	*User assigned*
EVA & RI spread	Good	Capital structure	Good	*User assigned*
Net CapX growth	Mixed	Company's financial strength	Good	*User assigned*

Source:		"Timeliness"	"Safety"	
Value Line		3	1	
Analyst Rating:		2	2	User assigned (Scale of 1 to 5): *Ratings = (5 − Number of "good" + 1) for Number of "good" ≥ 1 Rating = 5 if number of "good" = 0*

Disclaimer: *JLG Research Templates are not provided to users with the intent of providing investment advice. Past performance is no guarantee of future performance.*
EVA® is a registered trademark of Stern Stewart & Co.

QUESTIONS

Use the Value Line report for IBM dated October 8, 2010, reproduced on the following page, to answer the questions regarding a traditional and value-based metrics analysis of this computers and peripherals company:

1. What are the estimated annualized growth rates in revenue, cash flow, and earnings per share for IBM over the period 2011 to 2014? Are these rates favorable or unfavorable?

2. What is the estimated ROE for IBM for 2011? Conduct a five-factor ROE Dupont analysis in answering this question. Is the estimated ROE for IBM attractive or unattractive?

3. What is the fundamental stock return for IBM for 2011? Does IBM plot above or below the Securities Market Line? Assume a risk-free rate of 5% and a market risk premium of 5% in answering this question.

4. What is estimated NOPAT, $WACC, and EVA of IBM for 2011? Based on the estimated EVA (economic value added), is IBM a potential wealth creator or wealth waster?

5. What is the prospective EVA style quadrant of IBM for 2011? Interpret the meaning of this quadrant.

6. Based on an integrated analysis of traditional and value-based metrics, do you agree with the Value Line ratings of Timeliness and Safety for IBM? Be sure to assign your own stock ratings and explain whether you think IBM is a potential buy or sell opportunity.

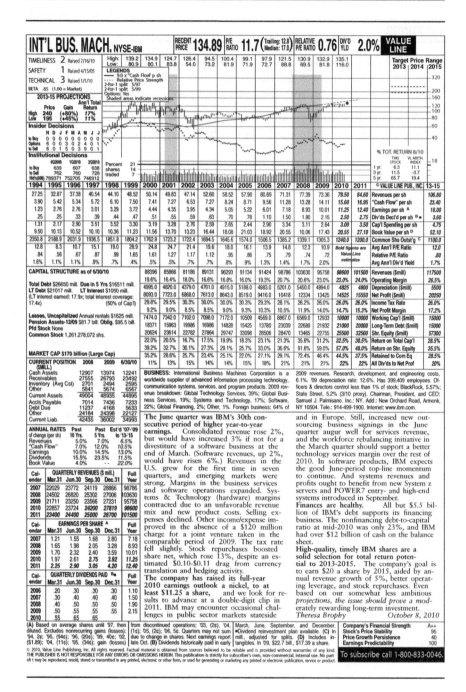

INT'L BUS. MACH. NYSE-IBM | RECENT PRICE **134.89** | P/E RATIO **11.7** (Trailing: 12.8 / Median: 17.0) | RELATIVE P/E RATIO **0.76** | DIV'D YLD **2.0%** | VALUE LINE

BUSINESS: International Business Machines Corporation is a worldwide supplier of advanced information processing technology, communication systems, services, and program products. 2009 revenue breakdown: Global Technology Services, 39%; Global Business Services, 19%; Systems and Technology, 17%; Software, 22%; Global Financing, 2%; Other, 1%. Foreign business: 64% of

2009 revenues. Research, development, and engineering costs, 6.1%. '09 depreciation rate: 12.6%. Has 399,409 employees. Officers & directors control less than 1% of stock; BlackRock, 5.57%; State Street, 5.2% (3/10 proxy). Chairman, President, and CEO: Samuel J. Palmisano. Inc.: NY. Add.: New Orchard Road, Armonk, NY 10504. Tele.: 914-499-1900. Internet: www.ibm.com.

The June quarter was IBM's 30th consecutive period of higher year-to-year earnings. Consolidated revenue rose 2%, but would have increased 3% if not for a divestiture of a software business at the end of March. (Software revenues, up 2%, would have risen 6%.) Revenues in the U.S. grew for the first time in seven quarters, and emerging markets were strong. Margins in the business services and software operations expanded. Systems & Technology (hardware) margins contracted due to an unfavorable revenue mix and new product costs. Selling expenses declined. Other income/expense improved in the absence of a $120 million charge for a joint venture taken in the comparable period of 2009. The tax rate fell slightly. Stock repurchases boosted share net, which rose 13%, despite an estimated $0.10-$0.11 drag from currency translation and hedging activity.

The company has raised its full-year 2010 earnings outlook a nickel, to at least $11.25 a share, and we look for results to advance at a double-digit clip in 2011. IBM may encounter occasional challenges in public sector markets stateside

and in Europe. Still, increased new outsourcing business signings in the June quarter augur well for services revenue, and the workforce rebalancing initiative in the March quarter should support a better technology services margin over the rest of 2010. In software products, IBM expects the good June-period top-line momentum to continue. And systems revenues and profits ought to benefit from new System z servers and POWER7 entry- and high-end systems introduced in September. Finances are healthy. All but $5.5 billion of IBM's debt supports its financing business. The nonfinancing debt-to-capital ratio at mid-2010 was only 23%, and IBM had over $12 billion of cash on the balance sheet.

High-quality, timely IBM shares are a solid selection for total return potential to 2013-2015. The company's goal is to earn $20 a share by 2015, aided by annual revenue growth of 5%, better operating leverage, and stock repurchases. Even based on our somewhat less ambitious projections, the issue should prove a moderately rewarding long-term investment.
Theresa Brophy   October 8, 2010

(A) Based on average shares until '97, then diluted. Excludes nonrecurring gains (losses): '94, 2¢; '95, (94¢); '96, (20¢); '99, 40¢; '02, ($1.89); '04, (11¢); '05, (34¢); gain (losses) from discontinued operations: '03, (2¢), '04, (1¢); '05, (2¢); '06, 5¢. Quarters may not sum due to change in shares. Next earnings report late Oct. (B) Dividends historically paid in early March, June, September, and December. ■Dividend reinvestment plan available. (C) In mill., adjusted for splits. (D) Includes intangibles. In '09, $22.7 bill., $17.39 a share.

Company's Financial Strength: A++
Stock's Price Stability: 95
Price Growth Persistence: 40
Earnings Predictability: 100

CHAPTER 3

A Franchise Factor Approach to Modeling P/E Orbits

Stanley Kogelman, Ph.D.
President and Founder
Delft Strategic Advisors, LLC

Martin L. Leibowitz, Ph.D.
Managing Director
Morgan Stanley & Co.

The standard *dividend discount model* (DDM) is still a commonly used equity valuation model. The DDM has the advantage of simplicity, intuitive appeal and broad generality, but these advantages often mute or disguise the extreme variations in growth expectations, return on equity and sustainable earnings that dramatically change valuations and move markets.[1]

The DDM provided the starting point for the development of the *franchise factor model* (FFM) that is the subject of this chapter. This model is based on a body of work that began as a series of papers that later were consolidated into two books on franchise value.[2]

In contrast to the DDM, the FFM provides a window through which we can peer more deeply into how variations in equity prices of companies or markets reflects the interplay between (1) optimistic and pessimistic growth projections, (2) return expectations on existing and potential businesses, and (3) long-term stable earnings. We find that competitive market forces,

---

[1] For further discussion see Zvi Bodie, Alex Kane, and Alan Marcus, *Investments* (New York: McGraw-Hill/Irwin, 2010) and Myron J. Gordon, *The Investment Financing and Valuation of the Corporation* (Homewood, IL: Richard D. Irwin, 1962).

[2] Martin L. Leibowitz and Stanley Kogelman, *Franchise Value and the Price/Earnings Ratio* (Charlottesville, VA: The Research Foundation of Chartered Financial Analysts, 1994); and Martin L. Leibowitz, *Franchise Value: A Modern Approach to Security Analysis* (Hoboken, NJ: John Wiley & Sons, 2004).

like magnetic attractors, tend to drive the P/Es of even the most outstanding companies toward equilibrium levels that fall well below current P/Es.

For the FFM, as with all models, the mathematics may be correct but the underlying assumptions will drive the results. When a model yields extremely optimistic price projections, you must look beneath the surface and evaluate the embedded underlying assumptions. In the DDM, for example, you typically find that continuous profitable growth is taken as a given, without any deeper examination of the fundamental sources of return or of the competitive forces that will, over time, likely drive P/Es toward lower equilibrium levels. When all visible future earnings are embedded in a model estimate, you should expect the firm's growth prospects and P/E ratio to gradually decline as prospective investments are executed and the firm's franchise is successfully consumed.

To mitigate this decline, firm management must uncover new, previously unknown and unanticipated investment opportunities of ever-increasing size. A $1 million investment is significant for a $1 million firm but, when that firm grows to a $10 billion firm, a $1 million investment becomes rather insignificant. To maintain a high P/E, a firm must continually reinvent itself by creating new products and identifying additional markets for both new and existing products. In a global market, the truly scarce resource will be the franchise opportunities themselves, not the capital required to exploit them. A firm will always be able to access funding needed to develop demonstrably productive opportunities through public and/or private markets.

Whenever the FFM leads to intrinsic value estimates that differ significantly from a security's market price, the model assumptions should be questioned first. If underlying flaws in the assumptions are uncovered, the assumptions should be adjusted to better reflect reality. Then the FFM-based P/E should be recalculated. If under a wide range of scenarios, the model results are stable, the model may be providing an important reality check relative to current valuations. This reality check is especially important when distinguishing between *hyper-franchise* firms with exceptional franchise value and growth prospects and *anti-franchise firms* with very limited growth prospects and negative franchise value.

BACKGROUND

At the heart of the FFM is the separation of firm value into two distinct parts: *tangible value* (TV) and *franchise value* (FV). Each of these value components separately contributes to the P/E. TV can be reasonably estimated because it reflects current businesses that produce steady earnings streams. From a valuation perspective, the TV makes a more predictable contribution to the firm's price-to-earnings ratio (P/E) than does the FV. The P/E contribution, P/E_{TV}, will be somewhat sensitive to inflation, to interest rates and to the equity market risk premium. Since these factors typically change more slowly than estimates of future opportunities, P/E_{TV} is relatively stable.

The total P/E is the sum of P/E_{TV} and P/E_{FV}. FV is dramatically different than TV and much more difficult to estimate accurately. This difficulty is related to the futuristic nature of FV. FV reflects businesses that a firm is *expected* to create at some (possibly indeterminate) point in the future by means of new, yet to be realized, investments. As investors, market analysts and corporate executives polish their crystal balls and peer into the future, their projections of a firm's growth opportunities will continually change along with estimates of FV.

Because of their prospective nature, FV estimates are more vulnerable to sudden changes in markets and in the global economy than TV estimates. Such changes can work in either a positive or negative direction. Long-term projections can just as easily under-estimate as overestimate future projects. As time passes and the fog of uncertainty clears, new markets may develop that earlier were inconceivable. Similarly, some perceived robust opportunities later may turn out to barely exist. Other previously anticipated projects, with uncertain prospects, may have a clearly improved likelihood of success and therefore make a more positive contribution to FV—or vice versa. In summary, P/E_{FV} inevitably will undergo more frequent and more dramatic changes than P/E_{TV}.

In our FFM, future investments that provide a return in excess of the cost of capital add to FV. Firms with global brands, unique products, and/ or substantial pricing power may even possess a hyper-franchise that, for long periods, enables them repeatedly to uncover significant new investment opportunities that provide returns that substantially exceed the cost of capital. In this case, P/E_{FV} will make a more substantial contribution to the total P/E than will P/E_{TV}. But, no franchise is unlimited and sooner or later P/E_{FV} will decline, leading to a corresponding decline in the total P/E.

At the other extreme, we find anti-franchise firms. Such firms may currently hold earlier investments that have become losers from which they cannot easily extricate themselves. For example, an anti-franchise firm may have reached a point where it is challenged to find big, new, high-return investments. The firm's CEO then may feel tempted to make new investments (rather than return money to shareholders) even in the face of, at best, an only modest probability that those investments will provide a long-term return that exceeds the cost of capital.

In the language of the FFM, all new investments that return less than the cost of capital will make a negative contribution to FV. If the overall FV is negative, the P/E_{FV} will also be negative. Thus, a negative FV will drag the total P/E down to a level below P/E_{TV} alone. In this respect, an anti-franchise firm is a value destroyer.

Some years ago, in a lunch conversation with Warren Buffett, Marty Leibowitz presented the anti-franchise concept. Buffett not only grasped the idea immediately, but provided an illustration of the concept in the form of story that Marty later used to open a keynote talk with a rather light touch:

> A man came to the United States and became a successful business- man. One day, he received a letter from a long-lost cousin in the old country informing him that an equally long-lost uncle had just passed away. The letter went on to talk of the poverty back home and requested some help to give the uncle a decent burial. Our busi- nessman quickly complied and sent the requested funds along with a brief note of consolation. A few weeks later, he received a second letter explaining that the uncle didn't have a suit to his name, and could some additional funds be sent over to cover the cost of a burial suit? Once again, a bit more warily, our businessman com- plied with this request, thinking that this should surely be the end of the saga. However, after a few weeks, a third letter came, again asking for more money to cover the expense of the suit. This time, our exasperated businessman, wondering why he should repeatedly pay for the same suit, dashed off an indignant response. Shortly thereafter, a reply came back from the cousin. It turns out that the suit they had used to bury the uncle was *rented*.

The moral of the story: Antifranchise firms throw good money after bad!

Unfortunately, we do not have to look too hard to find examples of anti-franchise firms. Such firms enthusiastically announce new projects with overstated forecasts and unrealizable returns. When anti-franchise firms seek earnings growth at any (capital) cost, they may be tempted to engage in imperialistic expansions that include overly optimistic acquisition pro- grams. Entrenched corporate executives may become wedded to pet projects while failing to jettison failing projects in a timely fashion.

Hyper- and antifranchise firms form the extremes between which most firms fall. A "typical" company is likely to take on a range of projects. Some projects will do very well while others, in hindsight, will turn out to be in error and yield poor results. Other projects will turn out to be value neutral, yielding returns that just equal the cost of capital. Value-neutral projects may create a positive cash flow and add to earnings, but their FV will be zero and such projects will not contribute to the firm's P/E, regardless of how large they may be. Value-neutral projects are simply part of the stable P/E_{TV}.

When firm value is primarily attributable to FV, as is the case for many growth firms, the more stable TV is a relatively small part of the firm's overall valuation. In this case, the market valuation is likely to respond dramatically to changing market conditions and to any doubts about future investment opportunities. P/E volatility is further exacerbated for newer firms with a small earnings base. A small change in earnings estimates will lead to a substantial change in the ratio of price to earnings.

For more mature *value* firms, TV often far exceeds FV. In this case, the relative stability of TV brings with it a more stable P/E_{TV} and lower price volatility.

HISTORICAL DATA OBSERVATIONS

Over the almost 25-year period from January 1, 1985, to June 30, 2010, an investment of $100 in the S&P 500 multiplied more than 11 times to $1,143, if no money was withdrawn and all dividends were reinvested. This growth represents a remarkable 10.0% annualized compound return over a period of dramatic market changes, upheavals and challenges.

The mid-1980s marked the beginning of an extraordinary bull market that accelerated through the Internet boom of the late 1990s. Prior to this time, value investing was viewed as the favored long-term strategy. But, during this period, value investing fell out of favor and growth dominated.

Between 2000 and 2002, the Internet bubble collapsed and the September 11, 2001, attacks on the World Trade Center brought further market declines. The weak markets of the early 2000s were followed by a new bull market in which value investing moved back into favor. But, all gains were erased with the so-called Great Recession that began in 2007.

Exhibit 3.1 plots the growth paths of hypothetical $100 investments in the S&P 500 Index and in the Russell 1000 Value Index. In a more subtle way, these paths underscore the challenges inherent in market forecasting. On January 1, 1985, no market observer could possibly have foreseen the unfolding of events that would rock the market. For reference, the exhibit also includes a smooth 10% growth path with the same beginning point and approximately the same end point as the market investments. The market does not follow this path! Rather the market lunges forward, corrects, lunges forward and then corrects, over and over again.

Note the interlacing of the growth paths of broad U.S. market index and the value index. Each crossing represents a point at which the cumulative investment value to date produces precisely the same result. For example, during the late 1990s an initial investment in the S&P500 raced ahead of a similar investment in the Russell 1000 Value Index. But, by the end

EXHIBIT 3.1   Growth of $100 Investment in S&P500 Index and Russell 1000 Value Index (including dividend reinvestment)

of 2001 a crossing point occurred as a consequence of the sudden rapid fall in the broad market and the steady rise in value stocks. Starting in late 2002, value stocks grew faster than the broad market and collapsed more quickly during the Great Recession. Once again, there was a crossing of the cumulative value graphs. Relevant investment results were dependent on an investor's ability to time the market, correctly switching between the broad market and value. But few if any investors have the forecasting skill required to consistently and accurately time markets. For truly long-term investors, the results of maintaining an investment in one index or the other were quite similar.

Rather than attempting to forecast the events that mark the beginning of major market corrections, we take a 60,000-foot view of both individual firms and broad regional markets. From this vantage point, we conceptualize market behavior as a reflection of a changing composite of views of inherent growth prospects. During periods of optimism and high expectations, it is hard to escape the feeling that companies have virtually unlimited opportunities to make new, profitable investments. Companies viewed as "undervalued" are expected to soon realize their "true" potential. Growth companies are projected to capitalize on seemingly boundless "franchise potential."

Growth potential is expressed in rising P/Es and a corresponding price escalation that may persist for years. Inevitably, boundless optimism is replaced by a dark pessimism and implicit revaluation of "franchise potential" is sudden, dramatic and relentless. Our Franchise Factor Model (FFM) does not make market forecasts. Rather, the FFM quantifies the return and investment assumptions that are implicit in a given P/E. In so doing, the FFM provides concrete and intuitive measures that the investment analyst can test against realizable return and investment prospects.

One of the great overestimates of market growth potential occurred in Japan in the late 1980s. Exhibit 3.2 shows how an investment of $100 in the Nikkei index more than tripled in value in the five years, beginning January 1, 1985. One analyst after another "capitulated" and began to join the bull market bandwagon. Going into 1989, Japan was widely viewed as an example of a new paradigm in which traditional valuation measures did not apply. We note that much of the same reasoning later applied during the Internet boom.

EXHIBIT 3.2   Cumulative Value of an Investment of $100 in the Nikkei Index

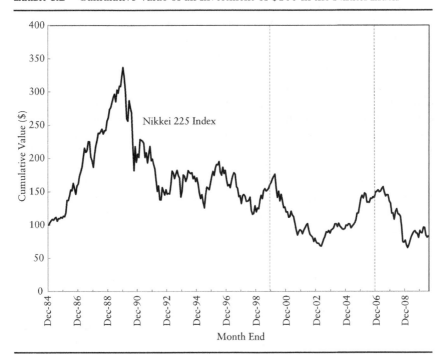

At the end of 1989, the Japanese market collapsed. In 1991, market observers began to take the view that the market could not get any worse and was about to turn. Instead, the market went nowhere. In 1998, the market began to rally along with the internet boom in the United States. But the market collapsed again in 1999. Finally, in 2003 signs seemed to appear that recovery was underway. Hopes were dashed again with the onset of the Great Recession. In mid-2010, the Nikkei 225 remained at only 24% of the peak realized more than 20 years earlier!

The Nikkei performance illustrates an inherent danger and warning signals in extreme peaking behavior. In a sense, the Japanese market was, for some time, viewed as having a hyper-franchise reflecting superior management, better work ethic, and manufacturing prowess. Even if these observations were to some extent correct, their macro valuation was unrealistic.

In the language of our model, over the course of time, hyper-franchise firms are likely to transition to no-growth, low-growth, or anti-franchise firms. Sometimes such firms eventually go out of business, although markets do not. In fairness, we do not mean to suggest that market observers and participants literally speak of franchise value. Rather, we argue that when application of our model to the market yields an implicit FV that is inconsistent with any reasonable assumptions, there should be an explicit questioning of the sustainability of valuations.

The phenomenon just observed for markets is equally apparent for some of America's greatest growth companies, as illustrated in the Exhibits 3.3 and 3.4. For an extended time, both of these Fortune 500 companies were viewed as holding a hyper-franchise, enabling the firm to make ever larger and more profitable investments. Firm A is a highly regarded well-diversified Fortune 50 company. Firm B is one of the great innovative megacap tech companies. The prices of both firms escalated for almost 15 years, with unprecedented acceleration occurring in the late 1990s. Early buyers who sold at the peak made fortunes. Long-term shareholders made modest or negative returns, depending on their entry point.

When market optimism came to an end in 2000, so did optimism regarding the FV of individual firms. The market could no longer foresee the investment opportunities required to justify sky-high valuations. During the run-up, the price of Firm A grew about 25 times. That remarkable growth pales in comparison to Firm B which grew about 120 times! As might have been expected, the correction in Firm B's price was far greater than for Firm A's price. But, both quickly returned to 1998 levels and then fell further.

Firm A bottomed in early 2003 when its price was only 40% of the peak. Then, prices began to escalate modestly, reflecting the view that the firm still had growth potential. Between 2003 and 2006, the firm provided a modest price return to investors. To raise the P/E the firm would have to

EXHIBIT 3.3   Firm A, Diversified Fortune 50 Company

reveal new unanticipated growth prospects that were large in comparison to the already enormous (Fortune 50!) firm size. Absent the discovery of such new opportunities (or improvement in the probability that previously envisioned projects would succeed), the firm's perceived FV would likely decrease and P/E declines would occur in lockstep with that decrease in FV. In the Great Recession, any such positive views of the firm collapsed and the price dropped even more sharply than during the burst of the Internet bubble. By mid-2010, the price was at 1996 levels!

From peak to trough, Firm B saw its price decline by 90%. Then, from 2002 to mid-2010, the price oscillated within a trading range and there remained no sign of a change in growth prospects. That is, FV was not about to change.

Firm size helps to some extent, but it also exacerbates the challenge an FV-driven firm faces in maintaining a high P/E (P/E_{FV}). On the one hand, big firms may dominate markets, have access to cheaper sources of production, achieve favorable pricing and realize lower capital costs. On the other hand, the dollar size of the investments that must be made to impact the P/E is enormous. A $1 billion investment is very meaningful to a $500 million company, but a mere "drop in the bucket" for a $30 billion company.

EXHIBIT 3.4   Firm B, Mega-Cap Tech Company

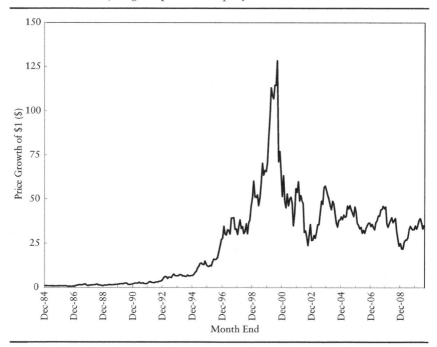

Successful companies like Firms A and B ultimately reach a point where few potential investments are large enough to significantly impact overall firm valuation. Is it possible that the same is also true for some broad markets?

The usual stable P/E assumption may not be realistic. In theory, there should be a *smooth* path of escalating and ultimately declining P/Es, reflecting the full cycle of future investment opportunities. In practice, P/E changes are often sudden and dramatic. In contrast to Firms A and B, the relatively unexciting midcap industrial Firm C in Exhibit 3.5 appears to be successfully navigating the FV challenge. This firm had a good but slower and less spectacular run-up from 1985 to 1998. Then there was a steep decline through 1997, with the trough being only 50% of the peak. But this drop was not as deep as it was for the other firms and we see a period of stability following the decline. In the terms of FFM, new unanticipated growth prospects began to emerge adding to FV and driving C's value to unprecedented levels. The 2007 price run up was too fast and the gains quickly evaporated in 2008. Through 2009–2010, the price continued to rise and the patient long-term investor saw price grow 10 times, along a path that was relatively stable.

EXHIBIT 3.5   Firm C, Midcap Industrial Firm

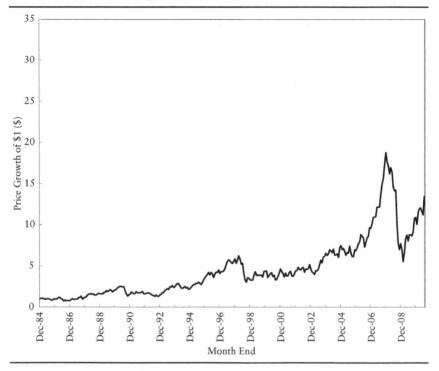

FORMULATION OF THE BASIC MODEL

Our basic FFM expresses a firm's theoretical value as the sum of two level payment annuities reflecting a current earnings stream (the tangible value, TV) and a flow of net profits from expected future investments (the franchise value, FV):

$$\text{Market value} = \text{Tangible value} + \text{Franchise value}$$

TV is the economic book value associated with annual earnings derived from current businesses without the addition of new capital. In the FFM, we obtain a valuable simplification by viewing this earnings stream as a perpetual annuity, with annual payments E. This model annuity is presumed to have the same present value as the actual projected earnings stream. Any pattern of projected earnings can be replicated, in present value terms, by an appropriately chosen perpetual earnings stream.

In actuality, analysts use either trailing or forward-looking earnings projections. Realized earnings exhibit considerable year-to-year variability and optimistic earnings projections are often "front-loaded" with rapid growth in the early years and more stable and possibly declining earnings in later years. The opposite path is also possible: slow earnings growth projected in the early years and more rapid growth later.

If k is the risk-adjusted discount rate (usually taken as equivalent to the cost of equity capital), then[3]

$$TV = \frac{E}{k}$$

The contribution of TV to the P/E ratio is obtained by dividing the above formula by E:

$$P/E_{TV} = \frac{1}{k}$$

From the above formula, we see that P/E_{TV} depends only on the equity capitalization rate k. Since k depends on inflation, real rates and the equity risk premium, so does P/E_{TV}. These variables change over time, but they do so rather slowly. Consequently, we conclude that the P/E_{TV} is relatively stable.

In order to simplify the discussion in this chapter, we do not address the impact of inflation on both current and future earnings. It should be noted that a firm that can, even partially, "pass-through" inflation into earnings will be intrinsically more valuable and command a higher P/E than a firm that lacks the pricing power to pass-through inflation. More detailed discussion of the impact of inflation flow through on both TV and FV can be found in our earlier works.

The remaining source of value stems from future prospects to invest capital and obtain a premium return. Evaluations of such prospects require peering into a proverbial crystal ball in order to see the future. As such, these evaluations are subject to continual revision and have higher volatility.

There seems to be an almost congenital human need to view all growth as smooth and consistent, but any forced smoothing of growth prospects is likely to lead to a number of fundamental evaluation errors. In fact, investments in new businesses can only be established as opportunities arise in some irregular pattern over time. At the outset, each new business will

---

[3]Modigliani and Miller showed that the theoretical total cost of capital is independent of both dividend policy and of the balance between debt and equity financing. See Franco Modigliani and Merton H. Miller, Dividend Policy, Growth, and the Valuation of Shares," *Journal of Business* 31, no. 4 (October 1958): 411–443.

require years of investment inflows, followed by subsequent years of (hopefully) positive returns. These returns will themselves vary from year to year. In the standard DDM, a fixed growth rate is chosen, and the size and timing of future projects are implicitly set by the level of earnings available for reinvestment.

In the FFM, we allow for a varying pattern of investments and returns. To do so, we model a project's investment and net return pattern as equivalent (in present value, PV) to a level annuity returning an appropriately chosen fixed rate R per dollar invested, year after year in perpetuity. The net new contribution to the firm's value is based on a fixed "franchise spread" $(R - k)$ over the cost of capital earned on dollars invested. In the standard DDM, the return on new investments, R, is implicitly assumed to be the same as the return on the current book of business r. This rather restrictive return equality is not required implicitly or explicitly in the FFM.

Since investment dollars are contributed at various points in the future, we normalize each of those investment dollars by measuring them in terms of today's dollars (the PV). We then compute the sum of all PVs of investment dollars. This sum is the single dollar amount that, if invested today, would act as a surrogate for all future investments. The concept of the PV equivalence of the totality of future growth prospects has the virtue of considerable generality. No longer are we restricted to smooth compounded growth at some fixed rate. Virtually any future pattern of future opportunities— no matter how erratic—can be modeled through PV equivalence.

The PV of all growth opportunities will generally sum to a massive dollar value. To make this term intuitive and estimable, we represent it as a multiple, G, of current book value, B. That is,

$$\text{PV of investable opportunities} = G \times B$$

or,

$$G = \frac{\text{PV of investment opportunities}}{B}$$

The totality of projected investments provides a perpetual stream of "net" profits with annual payments from the net spread earned by these investments:

$$\text{Annual net payments} = \text{Franchise spread} \times \text{PV of investible opportunities}$$
$$= (R - k) \cdot (G \times B)$$

FV is the present value of this perpetuity, which is calculated by dividing the above expression by k:

$$FV = \frac{(R-k)\cdot(G\times B)}{k}$$

The contribution of FV to the P/E ratio is obtained by dividing the above formula by E, which can be represented as the product of the book value B and the current return on equity r:

$$E = r \times B$$

$$P/E_{FV} = \frac{R-k}{rk}\cdot G$$

We call the first factor on the right side of the above equation, the franchise factor (FF),

$$FF = \frac{R-k}{rk}$$

The above formulation allows for any pattern of new investments and returns over time including returns on new investments, R, that may be vastly different from the current return on equity, r. By focusing on the net PV of new investments, we avoid having to consider whether the financing is internal or external. While the classic DDM requires self-financing via earnings retention, there is no such limitation in the FFM.

The FFM formulation enables us to see through potentially unrealizable growth assumptions. In essence, the formulas above provide a "sanity check" against future expectations that are, in fact, unreasonable and virtually impossible to justify. The following examples illustrate how this works.

Imagine a growth firm that is presumed capable of providing a perpetual annual return on equity of 15%. The firm has a unique franchise that gives it substantial pricing power. By exercising this franchise, the firm is projected to be able to make new investments that will provide an even more attractive 18% perpetual annual return. This is surely would be considered a terrific firm if the cost of capital was only 9%! Under these assumptions,

$$k = 9\%$$
$$r = 15\%$$
$$R = 18\%$$

and

$$P/E_{TV} = 11.1$$
$$FF = 6.7$$
$$P/E = 11.1 + 6.7G$$

We leave G unspecified because it is the most difficult number to estimate but G will be the key to analyzing the P/E that the market currently assigns to this firm. For example, suppose the market multiple is 25×. In order to justify that P/E, G would have to be about 2.1.

The G factor is a bit mysterious, but worth exploring. G is the PV of all future invested dollars, expressed as a percentage of the firm's current economic book value. If we are thinking of a $100 million Firm V, then a G of 2.1 means that the PV of all future investments would be about $210 million. If this firm possesses new technology that the market is likely to embrace, $210 million of additional high return investments might be a modest, achievable requirement. Taken to the extreme, such a firm might have far greater future possibilities if, as expected, the new the new technology is widely embraced. In that case, the P/E might be far greater than 25×.

Now suppose Firm W is already a $10 billion dollar firm. Proportionately, Firm W must do exactly the same as Firm V to justify the same P/E. Firm W's challenge is really formidable—the required PV of all future investments is $21 billion!

The $21 billion figure is even more imposing when we realize that it represents the present value dollars of investments that earn and maintain, in perpetuity, a 9% average excess spread over the cost of capital. For example, if the firm made $3.2 billion in new investments every year for the next 10 years, the PV would be $21 billion but the total dollars invested would be $32 billion. Even for extraordinary firms with market sector dominance, finding such investments is not easy.

By using the FFM in this way, investors and analysts are positioned to ask the right questions. Does Firm W have the ability to find and execute $21 billion (in PV) of new investments that, on average, will provide an 18% return on equity in perpetuity? Does Firm V have that ability? The market, by assigning a P/E of 25× is saying the answer to both questions is a resounding "yes."

This active questioning can be taken several steps further. What are the implications if the actual R is a little lower or higher than expected? How do the results change if the estimates of r are overly optimistic? What will happen if changing inflation expectations or changing equity risk premiums lead to changes in k?

P/E MYOPIA: THE FALLACY OF A STABLE P/E

To this point, we have utilized projections of future investments and returns to calculate the theoretical *prospective* P/E ratio at a single point in time. We now take a multiyear look at the time evolution of the relationship between *realized* earnings growth and *realized* P/E.

When estimating future earnings growth, historical earnings growth is the commonly used baseline around which an analyst will make some (typically modest) adjustments. Price appreciation is often assumed to follow the projected earnings growth with P/E remaining stable. In this way, investors tacitly elevate earnings growth to the central determinant of investment value.

Theoretically, stable P/Es are unlikely to be achieved, even under equilibrium conditions in which market returns and a company's long-term prospects remain stable. Rather there is a natural time-path of P/E evolution. This observation stands in stark contrast to the valuation methodology typically used to estimate the long-term potential of investment banking deals involving mergers, acquisitions and buyouts. In such valuations, growing earnings are projected along with a horizon P/E that is close to the current value. The combination of these growth and stability assumptions is likely to lead to excessively optimistic estimates of the IRR (internal rate of return) potential of such deals.

Given current P/E values, we ask how the P/E theoretically changes over subsequent years under varying earnings growth assumptions. By analogy to fixed income terminology, we label the equilibrium-implied future P/E, the *P/E forward*. We call the trace over time the *P/E orbit*. This seemingly straightforward approach leads to a number of striking implications. For example, it shows that high growth stocks can induce a P/E myopia, leading otherwise thoughtful analysts to an overestimation of holding-period returns.

In order to fruitfully discuss P/E orbits, we need to review a few basic relationships. The first of these relationships is the basic single-period return produced by an equity investment. The holding-period return is the sum of just two quantities, the dividend yield (DY), and price return (% price change):

$$\text{Holding period return} = \text{Dividend yield} + \text{Price return}$$

The dividend yield is usually fairly stable, so this component of return will provide a reliable, steady addition to return. Price return is more variable and is therefore the critical ingredient in return volatility. The price return can be shown mathematically to be the sum of the growth in earnings, g_E, and growth in P/E, $g_{P/E}$, over the holding period:

$$\text{Price return} = g_E + g_{P/E}$$

Armed with these basic formulas, we can compare the P/E orbit of a high growth stock with the P/E orbit of a low growth stock. We will use a numerical example, starting with k = 9% as the market discount rate for all stocks discussed in this chapter. In reality, of course, the discount rate varies from company to company, with changing market conditions, and should probably even be used to differentiate the risk prospects of the TV from the FV. If our hypothetical stock is fairly priced, it will provide a 9% holding period return. This equilibrium return assumption tells us a great deal about what theoretically should be happening to the P/E.

The discount rate k will actually change over time along with changes in interest rates and equity risk premiums. However, for simplicity and clarity we discount all earnings at a fixed k = 9%.

P/E Orbits for High-Growth Stocks

Suppose the stock of the high-growth Firm D trades at a P/E multiple of 25×. The expected earnings growth is 12.4% (the rationale for choosing this particular growth rate will become evident later) and the dividend yield is 1.6%.

Since the holding period return is the sum of the dividend yield and the price return, a 9% return and a 1.6% dividend yield implies that the price return must be 7.4% (9% – 1.6%). Repeating the formula above:

$$\text{Price return} = g_E + g_{P/E}$$
$$7.4\% = 12.4\% + g_{P/E}$$
$$g_{P/E} = -5\%$$

This result suggests that, over a one-year holding period, the P/E is implicitly expected to fall –5% from the current 25× to a forward P/E of 23.8×.

At first, this result is surprising. Why should the P/E register such a sharp decline over the course of a single year, especially after a 12.4% growth in earnings? The result is a direct consequence of our assumption that the initial P/E of 25× represents fair equilibrium pricing. The fair pricing assumption implies that, given the long-term prospects for the company, an appropriately specified valuation model would validate the P/E of 25× if the earnings discount rate was 9%. In this example, the first year of earnings growth was specified at 12.4%.

The P/E decline is also implicitly related to the assumption that, at the outset, the firm has a fixed FV that is consumed/utilized over time. High earnings growth in the early years can then be viewed as leading to rapid realization of the firm's potential.

We note that earnings growth rates can fluctuate widely from year-to-year and long-term growth forecasts are shrouded in more uncertainty short-term forecasts. In actuality, many future sequences of subsequent annual earnings growth rates can lead to the precisely the same initial fair value P/E of 25×.

Regardless of the future earnings growth path, an equilibrium 9% return assumption and 12.4% first year growth necessitates an expected 5% P/E decline and a new year-end fair value of 23.8×.

As long as Firm D's earnings growth rate remains at 12.4% and the market discount rate stays at 9%, the P/E should continue to decline by 5%. Thus, in the second year the P/E should decline from 23.8× to 22.6×. Continuing at this rate for 10 years brings the P/E down to 15×, as depicted in the curve that emanates from a P/E of 25× in Exhibit 3.6.

As an example, imagine a pharmaceutical company currently enjoying a healthy 12.4% earnings growth from sales of a proprietary drug. If the drug goes generic and the company's research pipeline is unpromising, the eroding franchise (i.e., the consumption of FV) will be reflected in a corresponding decline in P/E.

A few words of caution are needed so that Figure 3.6 is not misinterpreted. First, the descending P/E orbit does not imply a decline in the equity price. The 12.4% earnings growth brings investment gains that more than offset losses due to the P/E induced 5% price decline. The corresponding stock price trajectory will be one of 7.4% positive growth. When we add a 1.6% dividend to 7.4% price growth we achieve a 9% return, just as we

EXHIBIT 3.6 P/E Orbits with Constant Earnings Growth

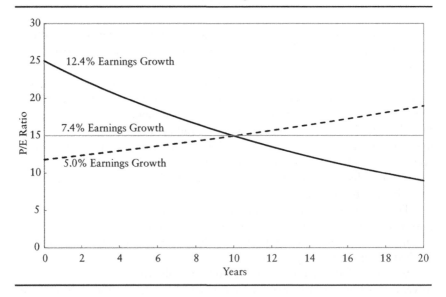

would expect with a 9% discount rate. Exhibit 3.7 illustrates how dividends, earnings growth and P/E decay combine to provide a 9% annual return.

The basic assumption is that the initial P/E of 25× represents fair-value discounting of the company's future earnings growth. But, the high 12.4% level of earnings growth cannot continue indefinitely. With a 9% discount rate, perpetual earnings growth at 12.4% would require an infinite starting P/E and necessarily violates the assumption that 25× represents fair pricing. The 12.4% curve in Exhibit 3.6 should be viewed as portraying the P/E descent for just so long as earnings growth remains at 12.4%.

The depicted P/E orbit does not depend on the choice of 25× as the starting P/E. As long as $k = 9\%$ and $g = 12.4\%$, the projected P/E "should" decline by 5% each and every year. Under these return and growth and assumptions, the same 5% year over year decline will apply for all initial P/E values!

There may be a myriad of reasons why a specific investor may hold to the belief that the P/E will not experience any such decline—improvement in the stock's prospects, the market's better appreciation of the stock's promise, the salutary effect of realized earnings growth (even if it only confirms the previously expected high 12.4% level), general market improvements, changes in required discount rates, and so on. All of these events constitute a departure, however, from the equilibrium conditions as they have been defined. Hence, excluding the P/E movements induced by such nonequilibrium

EXHIBIT 3.7 Growth of $100 Investment (1.6% dividend, 12.4% earnings growth, –5%. P/E decline

Time	Dividend Payment	Price Gain from Earnings Growth	Price Loss from P/E Decay	Total Value Including Dividend Reinvestment	Percent Return
0				100.0	
1	1.6	12.4	–5.0	109.0	9%
2	1.7	13.5	–5.5	118.8	9%
3	1.9	14.7	–5.9	129.5	9%
4	2.1	16.1	–6.5	141.2	9%
5	2.3	17.5	–7.1	153.9	9%
6	2.5	19.1	–7.7	167.7	9%
7	2.7	20.8	–8.4	182.8	9%
8	2.9	22.7	–9.1	199.3	9%
9	3.2	24.7	–10.0	217.2	9%
10	3.5	26.9	–10.9	236.7	9%

factors that result in unanticipated additions to FV, the stock's P/E should decline by 5%.

P/E Orbits for Low-Growth Stocks

For low-growth stocks, the same formulation as above also leads to continuous P/E change, but the change results in an ascending P/E orbit, as displayed in the 5% growth curve in Exhibit 3.6. If the starting P/E is 11.8× and the same 1.6% dividend yield and 9% market discount rate as in the previous example apply, the P/E will *grow* to 15× over 10 years.

Moving toward a higher P/E in the face of lower earnings growth seems contrary to basic intuition but it does make sense when we think in terms of FV consumption. High-growth firms rapidly consume their FV while low-growth firms consume FV slowly. In the equilibrium framework, the consensus investor *expects* a 9% total return. With a 1.6% dividend yield and *expected* 5% earnings growth, the only way we can reach that return is through *expected* P/E growth of 2.4%! Any P/E growth below this "required level" will be disappointing, and any greater increase will be a source of excess return.

The P/E orbit for $g = 5\%$ appears to rise without limit. Of course, this cannot be, either in practice or in any reasonable theory. Thus, the 5% P/E orbit must be viewed as the path for the early years for a company. In those years, new investments proceed slowly and FV is "under-consumed" but anticipated opportunities remain. At some later point in time, the firm is expected to invest more aggressively to take full advantage of its opportunities, thereby consuming FV and generating accelerated earnings growth.

An example of a low-growth company with a high and growing P/E might be a pharmaceutical company that has low current earnings but enjoys a pipeline of potentially blockbuster drug prototypes. The new drugs constitute a sizable franchise that will grow in value as their approval and launch times draw closer. At first, growth may accelerate, but eventually P/E will stabilize and then possibly decline.

The Stable P/E

The previous examples suggest that, under equilibrium assumptions the P/E will naturally change from year to year. There is one special case in which there is no change in P/E: when the earnings growth rate plus the dividend yield equals the 9% discount rate. In our example, that would be a 7.4% growth rate. We call this growth rate the "stabilizing" growth rate, g_S. With $g_S = 7.4\%$, the P/E will remain unchanged, providing an orbit that consists of a single horizontal line. This is illustrated by the middle line in Exhibit 3.6 where the P/E starts at 15× and remains at this level.

For growth rates that exceed g_s, the P/E orbit is descending. For growth rates below g_s the orbit is ascending. Neither continual ascent nor continual descent makes sense over the long term. Continual ascent would imply the P/E approaching infinity; continual descent would imply the P/E approaching zero. To achieve "sensible" orbits, the growth rate must undergo at least one future shift that is sufficient to change the orbit's basic direction. The simplest such orbital shift is a transition to a stabilizing growth rate that produces a horizontal orbit from the transition point forward. Such an orbit represents a going-forward version of the classic two-phase growth model.

TWO-PHASE P/E ORBITS

The examples of constant growth rates in Exhibit 3.6 illustrate the natural path of P/Es when the market provides the equilibrium 9% return and earnings growth and dividend yield are constant. To achieve "sensible" orbits, growth rates must undergo at least one future shift that changes the orbit's basic direction. The simplest such shift in growth rates is a transition to a stabilizing rate that produces a horizontal orbit from the transition point forward. Such an orbit represents a going-forward version of the classic two-phase DDM, in which one growth rate holds prior to a defined horizon and then a second growth rate prevails in perpetuity.[4]

In the most common situation, the first phase has a higher growth rate than the final phase. In such cases, the starting fair-value P/E is always higher than the final P/E. The P/E descends along its orbit until the horizon point, where it should match the stable P/E of the final phase.

As an illustration, we revisit the earlier example (Exhibit 3.6) of a firm with a dividend yield of 1.6%, initial P/E of 25× and 12.4% earnings growth, leading to a P/E decline to 15× after 10 years. Instead of maintaining a single growth rate, we now assume that earnings growth slows in year 10 and the company enters a final phase of perpetual 7.4% growth. The upper curve in Exhibit 3.8 illustrates this P/E orbit, including the stabilizing growth rate that leaves the P/E unchanged at 15× for the remainder of time. The two growth rates in this example totally determine that 25× is a fair value for the starting P/E and that 15× is the fair value for the terminal P/E.

This example clarifies why the P/E descent, which at first seems counterintuitive, makes sense in the context of fair valuation. The high growth rate in the first phase leads to the high starting P/E of 25×. From this height, FV

---

[4]Aswath Damodaran, *Damodaran on Valuation* (New York: John Wiley & Sons, 1994).

EXHIBIT 3.8   10-Year Two-Phase Growth with Various Starting P/Es and Required
Initial Growth Rates

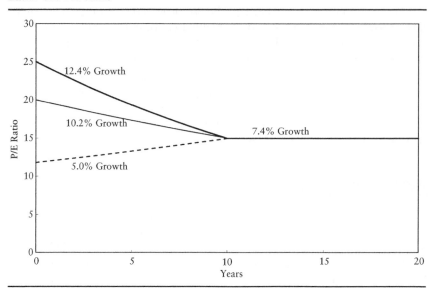

is consumed quickly and the P/E must move downward to its final-phase P/E
of 15× where FV is lower but sustainable.

Similarly, in the relatively unusual case in which a stock has a lower
growth rate in its first phase, the fair value for the starting P/E would be
expected to be lower, reflecting slower FV consumption, and then rise until
it ultimately reaches its final-phase level. This is illustrated in the lowest,
dotted curve in Exhibit 3.8 where after 10 years, the growth rate accelerates
from 5% to the 7.4% stabilizing rate.

For each starting P/E, there is one specific growth rate that will move
the P/E from its initial level to a final P/E of 15× after 10 years. For example,
a starting P/E of 20× would require a 10.2% initial growth rate to bring the
P/E down to 15×, as illustrated in the middle curve of Exhibit 3.8.

Tracing out these P/E orbits brings to the surface several of the problems inherent in standard valuation models. In many short- and interme-
diate-term models, earnings are assumed to grow at a specified rate until
some given horizon date—anywhere from 1 year to 10 years hence. Then,
the attained earnings level on the horizon date forms the basis for estimating
terminal price. Unfortunately, an all-too-common tendency is to determine
this terminal price by simply applying the current P/E to the horizon earnings level. In other words, the P/E is simply assumed to remain stable. But,
as the preceding examples show, this myopic assumption of P/E stability is

highly questionable—especially when a high rate of earnings growth prevails in the early years. To the extent that high growth rates and the dividend yield exceed the expected return, the baseline equilibrium estimate of forward P/Es should follow the orbital descent to lower values.

We now turn to our basic FFM to gain some further insights into the orbits we have just uncovered.

The Franchise Factor Model and P/E Orbits

The single- and multiphase P/E orbits in Exhibits 3.6 and 3.8 are related to how the balance between TV and FV evolves over time. FV always incorporates a consolidated market view of the totality of a firm's potential investments. Whenever some of that investment potential is realized through the execution of an anticipated investment, FV shrinks and TV grows. For example, FV depletion occurs when a pharmaceutical company brings an anticipated new drug to market or a when a restaurant chain opens a new restaurant. As such new products or businesses become valuable components of the firm's ongoing businesses, their related earnings streams become part of the TV. Thus, FV depletion equals TV expansion. But this equality does not hold for P/E_{TV} and P/E_{FV}.

Since $TV = E/k$, TV grows at exactly the same rate as E, provided all other parameters remain unchanged.

$$g_{TV} = g_E$$

Earnings growth may come from a variety of sources, many of which are unrelated to franchise consumption. For example, prospective investments with return, R, equal to the market rate, k, do not provide a net positive return to investors and make no contribution to FV, but they do add to TV. Since $TV = E/k$ grows with earnings, any investment with a positive return will add to TV as soon the investment begins to generate earnings. However, there is no addition to P/E_{TV} since the ratio $TV/E = 1/k$ remains unchanged.

Earlier in this chapter, we exhibited the following price return relationship:

$$\text{Price return} = g_E + g_{P/E} \qquad (3.1)$$

The second component of price return, $g_{P/E}$, mathematically can be shown to be

$$g_{P/E} = w(g_{FV} - g_E)$$

$$w = \frac{FV}{TV + FV} \qquad (3.2)$$

For growth firms, FV dominates TV and the price impact of any depletion in FV will be amplified in three ways. First, an FV decline means g_{FV}
is negative. Second, a drawdown in FV means new investments have been
made and add to earnings. Thus, g_E will increase, and the corresponding
term in equation (3.2) will become more negative. Since both terms within
the parentheses in equation (3.2) become more negative, the rate of decrease
in $g_{P/E}$ increases.

Finally, the dominance of FV (over TV) for growth firms implies that
the weight, w, will be relatively large. The combination of all three factors
leads to substantial theoretical P/E declines for growth firms, especially during periods of high earnings growth, as illustrated in Exhibit 3.6.

Unless growth comes from previously unexpected sources, the 5%
growth curve in Exhibit 3.6 illustrates a special situation in which firms
with high FV actually can experience positive P/E growth. When FV is utilized at a slow pace, earnings grow slowly and FV can grow with time. This
potential FV growth is related to the present value calculations embedded in
FV. FV includes the present value of future investments as well as the present
value of the returns they provide. In calculating FV, we discount future flows
to the present. If the first investment does not occur for several years, then
after the first year we will be discounting that flow as well as other future
flows for one period less. As a result, it will appear as if FV has grown at
the market rate. Ultimately, however, as the FV is "consumed" growth will
accelerate and the P/E will level off and eventually begin to decline.

In contrast to growth firms, for value firms where TV dominates FV, w
will be relatively small and the P/E impact of FV decay will be rather muted.

FV Growth, FV Decay and FV Bubbles

Equation (3.2) implicitly shows that, under our equilibrium assumptions,
the P/E will be stable (i.e., $g_{P/E} = 0$) if FV growth, g_{FV}, equals earnings growth,
g_E. This basic relationship underscores the challenge and tyranny of success.
Whenever a CEO succeeds in meeting investor expectations by appropriately and effectively bringing anticipated premium investments to fruition,
he is utilizing a portion of the firm's franchise value. As FV declines, so will
its contribution to the firm's P/E. That is, FV and P/E decay are natural consequences of the effective utilization of a firm's franchise.

We view FV as *consumed* whenever anticipated capital investments
are made in new businesses. If the P/E is to be maintained, the consumed
FV must be replenished. "Replenishment" is challenging because it means
adding more FV than was just consumed. This high replenishment follows
because the G factor in FV is measured relative to economic book value.

Business growth increases book value, so replenishment will be measured relative to a larger base.

In essence, each time a new business is added, the CEO must develop and convey a surprising new vision of business opportunities that are larger than the ones just built out. If this vision is not a surprise, the opportunities already would have been incorporated in previous business visions and in the existing FV.

To some extent, the market does reward high-octane CEOs with implicit votes of confidence in their ability to identify new opportunities. This confidence may even be expressed through a lowering of the discount rate as the perceived risk declines. But the challenge remains because each success will inevitably be met with ever greater expectations!

CEOs of hyper-franchise firms may for some time be able to uncover new opportunities at an increasing rate. In a global market place, the reach and brand of big firms may offer distinct advantages and facilitate the opening of unexpected new markets. Over time, the CEO may see possibilities that earlier were inconceivable. For example, the firm's market dominance may turn out to be an even greater advantage than anticipated, resulting in more pricing power and a higher franchise spread. When new, previously unimagined possibilities are announced, there is likely to be P/E growth or even a significant "jump" whenever a positive surprise is incorporated in the market's estimate of FV.

But the tyranny of size looms large. As a successful business transform a small firm into a big firm, only mega-investments can move the P/E dial. To some extent, a firm's size, expertise, and market dominance may be a major advantage that does, for a time, enable the firm's leadership to find precisely such investments. However, despite such advantages, big investments become harder and harder to find and to execute—even for the most talented executive.

The natural path of P/E decline may accelerate if a firm mistakenly engages in anti-franchise growth. For example, the FV might initially incorporate the expectation that large cash holdings would soon be used for investments or acquisitions yielding a positive franchise spread. If instead, it turns out that cash holdings turn out to become long-term investments with a bond-like return, then they will be P/E-depleting. From a shareholder perspective, it would be better to distribute cash through increased dividends or share repurchases. Shareholders then would have the opportunity to achieve the equity market rate (not the bond rate) through other investments.

A second example of anti-franchise growth stems from mega-mergers based on perceived but yet-to-be-attempted synergies. Unrealizable synergies may result in a negative franchise spread, thereby causing *FV decay*. Worse still, a change in market perceptions of a firm's franchise can lead to a sudden dramatic FV decay (and P/E collapse). Therefore, the pricing of mergers is critical. As the price increases, the probability of achieving a positive franchise spread declines.

Because FV estimation is an art rather than a science, FV estimates can easily reflect exaggerated euphoria or dismay as market conditions and perceptions wax and wane. When firms appear to be able to regularly rediscover and reinvent themselves, the opportunities seem boundless and momentum-driven FV estimates may be revised upward over and over again. In some cases, such optimism may be justified for years or even decades, as illustrated in Exhibit 3.3 and 3.4, possibly creating FV *bubbles*.

With the passage of time, in one way or another, a given level of uncertainty may slowly be transformed into greater certainty. Some former optimistic estimates may be realized, but others may turn out to have been wildly excessive. If doubts and negative sentiment grow, the FV bubble may burst via a precipitous drop in FV and P/E. Following such a decline, a company will be challenged to reinvent itself and show that it has a renewed franchise that will lead to an increasing estimate of FV. Some firms can do this; some cannot. As a result, many outstanding firms will see their P/Es gradually decline as they convert from growth to value firms.

FRANCHISE VALUATION UNDER Q-TYPE COMPETITION

In the two-phase growth model, we assumed that the firm with 12.4% growth (see Exhibit 3.8), transitioned after 10 years to a more stable 7.4% growth rate. This model is generally intended to reflect an initial span of growth and prosperity followed by a second-phase regression to a competitive equilibrium. This terminal stage can be construed as the period when sales growth stabilizes but the company's earnings continue to change as the pricing margin moves toward some competitive equilibrium. This margin-equilibrating process can usefully be described in terms of the ratio of asset replacement costs to the company's economic book value, B, and is related to Tobin's q.[5]

The valuation impact of this terminal-phase effect will depend totally on the nature of the company's business and its long-term competitive posture. Some companies will be positioned to gain from post-growth margin expansion. For some businesses, growth itself builds a relatively unassailable efficiency of scale with distinct organizational, distributional, and technological advantages. Patent protection and/or extraordinary brand acceptance may

---

[5]James Tobin, "A General Equilibrium Approach To Monetary Theory," *Journal of Money, Credit, and Banking* 1, no. 1 (1969): 15–29.

assure franchise-level margins for years to come. Leading-edge products may themselves act as germinators for subsequent generations of even more advanced products. For such fortunate companies, potential competitor's cost of building a new enterprise and comparable revenue stream might far exceed the existing firm's economic book value. In this case, the ratio, Q, of the competitive capital costs to B might be far greater than one. Investors in such companies may look forward to a future period of sustained high sales with margins that are maintained or even enhanced. At this point, the company begins to enjoy a "franchise ride" and the patient investor will finally be rewarded with the significant cash returns that formed the foundation for the value ascribed to the company at the outset.

For less fortunate growth companies, barriers to entry will indeed become porous over time. In this case, new technologies and efficiencies may offer competitors a Q value that is much less than one. In this case, the existing firm's high franchise margins will be vulnerable to erosion as the firm attempts to compete with lower prices. Earlier extraordinary earnings will be subject to the gravitational pull of commoditization and the P/E reduction will result from this "franchise slide."

Inevitably, large, technologically proficient, well-capitalized competitors lurk in the shadows of even the greatest franchise, even if the competitive Q is greater than one. Theoretically, such competitors will be eager to replicate a company's products and services provided their return offers a modest spread over their cost of capital. That is, the new business will be attractive if the competitor's cost of capital is Q times the original firm's cost of capital (that is, Qk) and the corresponding return on equity is greater than Qk. This *Q-type competition* implies that the original firm's premium pricing could be so adversely impacted that its initially high ROE would be eroded down towards the competitor's Qk. This situation raises questions about many two-phase growth models that assume the terminal earnings level can be sustained in perpetuity, even when high initial growth would elevate the ROEs to the point of attracting sufficient Q-type competition to lower all pricing margins.[6]

FRANCHISE LABOR

Many businesses are becoming ever more dependent on one key factor of production—the super-skilled or "franchise" employee. Exceptional managers have always been recognized as central to a company's success, but the new franchise cadre may reach far beyond the traditional managerial levels.

---

[6]For further discussion see Leibowitz, *Franchise Value: A Modern Approach to Security Analysis.*

Its ranks are certainly broader than the usual suspects—the sports star, the dynamic lawyer, the corporate deal maker, the software guru, the (currently) renowned media hero, and so on. The role of key individuals has been greatly enhanced by the growth of large enterprises—often highly knowledge based—that service global markets through extensive use of modern distribution and communication channels. In this environment, an incremental level of skill can be efficiently levered so as to have a major economic impact on a company's profitability.

We view *franchise labor* as comprising all employees who can effectively make an exceptional claim regarding their impact on the profitability of the business activities in which they are involved.[7] In any company, the franchise employee is *always* a scarce resource. The challenge is to accurately assess true current and *future* franchise labor. When a firm is doing well, franchise labor may be overestimated because of the firm's difficulty in discerning precisely which employees really are the key drivers of earnings. There is a certain temptation to assign franchise value to an overly large cohort of employees involved in an area that is generating an exceptional stream of profits. In such high profit areas, managers are reluctant to chance losing seemingly key employees and have to seek replacements. There is a natural tendency to doubt that any such replacements would actually turn out to be immediate and complete substitutes for lost on-board employees with their "right-on-point" experience.

The subject of franchise labor and identification of the truly "super-skilled" is further complicated by the fact that the composition of this critical group of employees is not stable. Rather, the critical group fluctuates along with changes in markets and changes in the firm's opportunities. It is also likely that management and employees have disparate views regarding who is super-skilled.

Of the employees who perceive themselves as "super-skilled" there are four possibilities:

- *These employees really are super-skilled and:*
  - The firm recognizes them as exceptional, critical to the firm's franchise, and reasonable in making a claim on excess earnings.
  - The firm does not perceive them as exceptional.
- *These employees are mistaken in their belief and:*
  - The firm knows they are not super-skilled.
  - The firm does not realize that, while these employees may be doing an excellent job, they are not critical to the firm's franchise.

---

[7]Gary S. Becker, *Human Capital* (Chicago: University of Chicago Press, 1993).

EXHIBIT 3.9   Effects of 10% Franchise Labor Claims

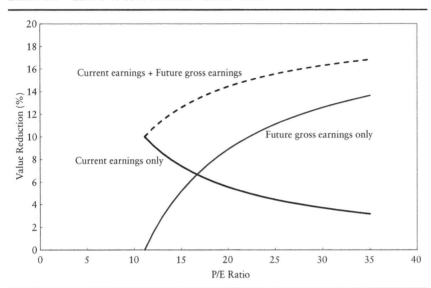

The ambiguity of franchise labor often leads to a certain moral hazard for management. Managers may find themselves being judged by their effectiveness in retaining the visible players on a winning team, which exacerbates the tendency to provide greater largesse, as a kind of retention "glue," to the presumptively super-skilled.

The accurate evaluation of franchise labor can have a material effect on company valuation in a number of ways. While public discussion has centered on ways in which stock options can distort the standard accounting statement of current earnings, relatively little attention has been given to the more subtle effects of franchise labor on *future* profits from brand new initiatives. These future franchise effects can be surprisingly large, depending on whether the claim is applied to the current book of earnings or to the incremental future earnings associated with new investment.

It can be shown that when an incremental claim of 10% is applied to current earnings (reflected in the TV portion of the firm's value), the valuation will be reduced by a percentage that depends critically on the stock's P/E.[8] This case is illustrated by the declining curve in Exhibit 3.9. At the base P/E of 11.1×, there is no FV and the impact of the claim applies directly to the TV, reducing the firm's value by 10%. At higher P/E multiples, the P/E impact is lower because the TV (on which the claim has

---

[8]Leibowitz, *Franchise Value: A Modern Approach to Security Analysis.*

been applied) forms a decreasing portion of the firm's value. For example, at a P/E of 25×, the value reduction is 4.4%. Note that in Exhibit 3.9, we make the same assumptions as we did earlier in this chapter: $k = 9\%$, $R = 18\%$. For each curve, the incremental franchise labor claim is 10%. That is, either current earnings, future net earnings or future gross earnings are reduced by 10%.

When a franchise labor situation exists, the likelihood is strong that the earnings from future growth will be subject to labor claims that can severely depress valuations. In this case, franchise employees act as if they were a kind of "super shareholder," extracting payments from gross revenues without consideration of appropriate returns to capital providers. The rising curve in Exhibit 3.9 shows the explosive effect of what might be called a "gross claim" of 10% on future profitability. This FV claim is modest for low P/Es where future investments contribute relatively little to overall firm value. As the P/E and FV become larger, however, the valuation impact of such claims rises rapidly. At a P/E of 25×, the gross claim grows to 11.1% of firm value. The combination of gross claims on future earnings and franchise claims on current earnings will erode firm value by 15.6%.

This leverage effect of FV claims is derived from the assumption that the 10% claim is applied to visible *gross* profit, ahead of any repayment to shareholders who supplied the fresh capital for the new initiatives. The key factor here is that the current shareholders begin to reap the rewards of any new initiative only after the suppliers of the new capital have been paid their due.

If the market rate for equity is 9%, suppliers of such equity capital will expect the newly issued stock to be priced so that it can provide a 9% annual return over time. Thus, in assessing the payoff from a new project with an 18% return on equity (ROE), the first 9% should be viewed as going to the new investors who supplied the needed capital, with the other 9% going to the earlier shareholders who, theoretically, owned the original "opportunity" for the high return investment. If a 10% franchise labor claim is now applied to the gross 18% ROE, then the available return declines to 16.2%. Consequently, the return reserved for current shareholders shrinks from 9% to 7.2%.

With so much at stake, the organization would be well advised to expend extraordinary effort to:

- Identify the true key employees and their respective contributions.
- Reward the real rainmakers in a way that is fair and aligns their interests with those of shareholders in terms of risk as well as reward.

- Properly assess the "net" payoff from new initiatives in a way that takes account of the legitimate claims of the employees needed to realize the company's promise.
- Assure that the management planning process, return estimates and investor's valuations incorporate consideration of such prospective franchise labor claims.
- Recognize that future gross franchise claims will have a much greater impact on valuation than claims based on current earnings.

KEY POINTS

- A "fundamental no-growth firm" with no prospects for productive investments will have the same intrinsic "tangible value" (TV) today, whether it pays out all its earnings or reinvests part or all of them at the market rate. The no-growth firm's "base" P/E will be the reciprocal of the market capitalization rate, k, for equities. A "growth firm" with significant "franchise value" (FV) must make future investments that provide a positive "franchise spread" (a return that exceeds the market-based cost of financing). For reasonable franchise spreads, high levels of future franchise investments (measured in today's dollars) are required to significantly raise the FV. Typically, the required magnitude of the future investments may be as much as two or more times the firm's current book value.
- The "natural orbit" of the P/E ratio is a decaying one. As anticipated investments are made and new businesses develop and grow, the firm's franchise value is "consumed" and converted into TV. Absent surprise opportunities, the balance between TV and FV shifts toward TV and the P/E inevitably declines. It is as if there is a natural gravitational pull toward the base P/E ratio.
- Hyper-franchise firms may experience bouts of "supercharged" growth from capitalizing on outsized returns on equity, especially in their early years. This growth is theoretically limited in scope and duration even though there are many examples where supercharged growth persists for 5, 10, or more years.
- The shorter-term, hyper-growth phase of exceptional franchise opportunities should be distinguished from longer-lasting, more stable, "mature" franchise opportunities. Such mature opportunities are likely to achieve a modest incremental return over the cost of capital that can be sustained for long periods of time.
- Ultimately, a firm's growth will stabilize to the growth rate of the market as a whole. Once the firm's franchise is consumed with new invest-

ment returns just meeting the cost of capital, the firm will have migrated into an almost pure TV firm with P/E close to the base value of $1/k$.

- The P/E impact of potential new investments depends on their size relative to the current firm. To maintain a high P/E, a firm must continue to uncover new and previously unforeseen investment opportunities of ever-greater magnitude. This tyranny of size reflects a kind of CEO paradox. A CEO who successfully fulfills a firm's initial promise will suffer a declining P/E as the firm's franchise is consumed.

- To maintain the firm's P/E, the CEO must continually uncover entirely new visions for the firm. For every anticipated investment that the CEO undertakes, that same CEO must identify future opportunities of ever greater magnitude. To the market, this newly revealed investment potential must be a complete surprise!

- Q-type competition can drive down profits because large, technologically proficient competitors lurk in the shadows of even the greatest franchise.

- Organizations should make every effort to accurately identify true key employees and to appropriately and effectively reward the real rainmakers.

QUESTIONS

1. Firm D and Firm E have the same performance characteristics. They both have a P/E of 20× and they also have the same cost of capital, return on equity, etc. The only difference is that Firm E's economic book value is $25 billion and Firm D's economic book value is $25 million. Explain why, in the language of the FFM, Firm E's P/E is more likely to decline than Firm D's.

2. Firm F is an excellent firm with superior management and a long history of steady earnings. After a long period of expansion, the Firm F has run out of opportunities to expand by building out new businesses. Toward what values are its TV, FV, and P/E likely to converge?

3. Why is it hard for CEOs of large successful companies to maintain the firm's P/E?

4. What is a reasonable level for the long-term P/E of a market under the following assumptions: economic book value = $500 billion, roe = 15%, cap rate = 9%, return on new investments = 18%, total investment in new businesses = $20 billion per year for the next 10 years? How does the projected P/E change if the cap rate is 8% or 10%? How does the projected P/E change if total investment is (a) $20 billion per

year for 20 years? (b) $300 billion per year for 20 years? (c) $400 billion per year for 20 years?

5. Explain the long term decline in value of an investment in Firm A or Firm B in terms of the FFM.

CHAPTER 4

Relative Valuation Methods for Equity Analysis

Glen A. Larsen Jr., Ph.D., CFA
Professor of Finance
Indiana University, Kelley School of Business–Indianapolis

Frank J. Fabozzi, Ph.D., CFA, CPA
Professor of Finance
EDHEC Business School

Chris Gowlland, CFA
Senior Quantitative Analyst
Delaware Investments*

Much research in corporate finance and similar academic disciplines is tilted toward the use of discounted cash flow (DCF) methods. However, many analysts also make use of relative valuation methods, which compare several firms by using multiples or ratios. Multiples that are commonly used for such purposes include price–earnings, price–book, and price–free cash flow.

Relative valuation methods implicitly assume that firms that are "similar" are likely to be receive "similar" valuations from investors. Therefore, on average, we would expect that firms that are generally comparable are likely to trade at similar multiples, in terms of price-to-earnings, price-to-book, or various other metrics. If this assumption is approximately correct, then relative valuation methods can be used to identify firms that look "cheap" or "expensive" relative to their peers. When a particular firm's multiples are extremely different from the rest of the universe, this may indicate

*The material discussed here does not necessarily represent the opinions, methods or views of Delaware Investments.

a potential investment opportunity—though further analysis will likely be required to determine whether there are reasons why such a firm is valued differently from other companies which otherwise appear comparable.

The basis of relative valuation methods is to use one or several ratios to determine whether a firm looks "cheap" or "expensive" by comparison with other firms that are generally similar. Relative valuation methods do not attempt to explain why a particular firm is trading at a particular price; instead, they seek to measure how the market is currently valuing a set of comparable companies, with the underlying assumption that the average multiple for a group of companies is probably a reasonable approximation to overall market sentiment toward that particular industry. In other words, relative valuation work assumes that on average, the share prices of companies in a particular universe are likely to trade at similar multiples relative to their own financial or operating performance. Baker and Ruback provide a more formal presentation of these concepts.[1] However, it is important to realize that at any particular time, some firms are likely to be trading at higher or lower multiples than would be justified under "fair value."

Making effective use of relative valuation methods does require careful selection of "similar" companies. Sometimes this is relatively simple, for instance when an analyst is dealing with industries where there are a large number of roughly homogeneous firms providing goods or services that are generally similar. However, sometimes there can be considerable difficulties in identifying "similar" companies, particularly if the firms under consideration are unusually idiosyncratic in terms of their product mix, geographical focus, or market position. In this chapter, we provide some tentative guidance about how to build a universe of comparable companies. However, ultimately this part of the process will depend on the skill and knowledge of the individual analyst; two different experts may pick different sets of "similar" firms, and thus generate different values from their relative valuation analysis.

BASIC PRINCIPLES OF RELATIVE VALUATION

Analysis based on relative valuation requires the analyst to choose a suitable universe of companies that are more or less comparable with each other. There is no standardized approach concerning how to choose such a universe of similar firms, and the process relies to some extent on an analyst's personal judgment concerning the particular industry and geography

---

[1]Malcolm Baker and Richard Ruback, *Estimating Industry Multiples* (Cambridge MA: Harvard Business School, 1999).

involved. However, it is possible to lay out some general principles that combine practitioners' insights with the results of academic inquiry.

Sources of Data

Relative valuation approaches can only be employed if there is sufficient information, produced on an approximately consistent footing, about the various companies that are the subjects of analysis. In most countries, companies that are publicly listed on stock exchanges are required by law and regulation to report their historical results publicly in a timely manner, or risk being delisted from the exchange. (There may be occasional exceptions to this general pattern, particularly for entities that are majority owned or controlled by their home country government. But such anomalies are not frequently observed except during crisis periods.) Consequently, it is almost always possible to obtain information about listed companies' historical results. However, multiples based solely on historical data may not provide a complete picture, as most analysts would probably agree that forward-looking estimates are likely to provide more useful insights into the market's opinion of a particular company.[2]

Investment banks, rating agencies, and other firms can provide estimates of a firm's future earnings, revenues, and other metrics, typically over the next two or three years. Various data providers, such as Bloomberg or Thomson Reuters, collect such information and use it as the basis for "consensus" estimates, which can be viewed as representing the market's general opinion of a company's future prospects. It is also possible to use a firm's own in-house estimates for the companies under coverage, as these may incorporate insights that are not yet reflected in current pricing. However, for precisely this reason, in-house estimates should be used as a supplement rather than as a replacement for consensus figures.

It is conventional to consider more than one year of data, as there may be disparities in how the market is valuing results in the immediate future and in the slightly longer term. However, it is often difficult or impossible to obtain consensus estimates more than two or three years into the future. Consequently, relative valuation approaches generally focus on relatively short periods into the future, rather than seeking to gauge how the market is valuing expected performance five or ten years hence. In this respect, relative valuation gives less attention to the distant future than is the case for DCF analysis. However, because expectations about firm value in the distant future are also presumably reflected in current multiples, the results

---

[2]See James J. Valentine, *Best Practices for Equity Research Analysts* (New York: McGraw-Hill, 2011), p. 271.

of analysis based on relative valuation analysis are arguably still compatible with those from DCF-based approaches.

Number of Comparable Firms

In general, an analyst would like to use data from other firms that are as similar as possible to each other. However, if the criteria for "similarity" are specified too stringently, then there may be too few firms included in the universe. And if the sample is too small, then the idiosyncrasies of individual firms may exert an excessive influence on the average multiple, even if the analyst focuses on the median rather than the mean when calculating the "average" multiple.

Generally speaking, we believe that it is desirable to have at least five or six comparable companies, in order to begin drawing conclusions about relative valuation for a particular industry. Conversely, there may be few benefits from considering more than twelve companies, particularly if the larger universe contains firms that resemble less closely the particular company that is the focus of the analyst's attention.[3] For most practical purposes, a group of between six and 12 comparable firms should be sufficiently large to produce usable results.

Basis for Selecting Comparable Firms

In an ideal situation, a universe of comparable companies would be similar in terms of level of risk. In order to create such a universe, it is common to rely on criteria such as size, industry focus, and geography. This tends to be easier when considering firms that are small or mid-sized—say, with market caps between $100 million and $10 billion (based on 2010 U.S. dollars). Firms that are below this size limit, in other words microcap stocks, may be more difficult to use for relative valuation purposes. Even if these firms are public, they may receive less coverage from research analysts, who typically are more interested in companies that are large, liquid, and already owned by institutional investors.[4]

---

[3]By contrast, in an example of how to assess a small wine producer, the proposed universe of comparables consisted of 15 "beverage firms," including both small and large caps, and covering specialists in beer, wine, and soft drink production. Arguably, some of these are unlikely to be very similar to the proposed target of analysis. (Aswath Damodaran, Chapter 7 in *Damodaran on Valuation: Security Analysis for Investment and Corporate Finance*, 2nd edition, New York: John Wiley & Sons, 2006.)

[4]Ravi Bhushan, "Firm Characteristics and Analyst Following," *Journal of Accounting and Economics* 11, nos. 2–3 (1989): 255–274.

Conversely, it can also be difficult to perform relative value analysis on companies with relatively high market capitalization. Many large firms are dominant players in their particular market niches, in which case they may be more likely to trade at a premium reflecting their higher degree of market power. Alternatively, large firms may be effectively a conglomerate of numerous smaller entities, each engaged in a specific activity, and there may be no other large or small firm that produces an approximately equivalent blend of goods and/or services.

When attempting to assess the relative value of firms that are large and/or complex, it can often be useful to assess "relative value" using two separate approaches. The first approach is to consider the firm as a complete entity, and trying to find other firms that are at least somewhat comparable in terms of size and complexity, even if their business mix is not precisely identical. In such cases, it can often be useful to consider similar firms that may be located in other countries, even though their different geographical positioning may affect their level of risk and thus the multiples at which they trade. The second approach, as already mentioned, is to use a sum-of-the-parts valuation method.

Geography and Clientele

Differences related to geographic location can affect the extent to which companies can be viewed as broadly similar. For instance, in the U.S. public utilities are predominantly regulated at the state level, and the public utility commissions in one state may operate quite differently from their counterparts elsewhere. Consequently, a public utility operating in one state may not be directly comparable with a public utility located in another state. In recent decades, there has been a wave of acquisition activity in the U.S. utility industry, so that there are now some utilities that have operations in multiple states. In such instances, the valuation placed on a utility will presumably incorporate investors' perceptions of the regulatory environment affecting each of its state-level operations. For relative value purposes, a group of multistate public utilities may not be very similar to a public utility that is operating in only one state.

Regional differences in regulatory regimes may only affect a subset of companies. However, firms in the same industry may well have quite different client bases and geographic exposures. For instance, one retailer may aim to sell a wide range of goods to a mass-market client base at the regional or national level, while another retailer might instead focus on selling a limited number of luxury products to the most affluent members of the global population. These two firms are likely to have substantially different product quality, cost bases, profit margins, and sensitivity to macroeconomic conditions. In particular, retailers of luxury goods to a global client base may have developed brands that transcend national borders, and a high proportion of their current and future revenues and profits may come from outside their home country. Under such conditions, it is possible that a suitable universe of comparable companies might include at least a few foreign firms, particularly if they have similarly broad geographic reach.

In past decades, analysts focusing on U.S. firms would probably have only rarely used foreign firms in their analysis of "comparable companies." However, as both U.S. and foreign firms have become increasingly globalized, and as accounting standards around the world have gradually started to become more similar, we believe that for some types of relative value analysis, there may be benefits to including firms that are generally comparable in terms of size and product mix, even if their legal headquarters are not located in the United States.[5]

Many companies have "depositary receipts" in other markets, such as ADRs. Consensus estimates may be available for a firm's local results and/or its depositary receipts. The estimates for the depositary receipts may be affected by actual or expected movements between the currencies of the two countries, which may bias the analysis. We therefore recommend that when calculating figures for companies that are listed in different countries, all multiples should be consistently calculated in terms of local currency throughout, in order to ensure that anticipated or historical currency fluctuations will not affect the results.

Sector and Industry Characteristics

Some academic research has examined different ways of selecting a universe of comparable firms. Bhojraj, Lee, and Oler compared the effect of using four different industry classification methods, and concluded that at least for a universe of U.S. securities, the Global Industry Classification Standard (jointly developed and maintained by Standard & Poor's and Morgan Stanley Capital International) appeared to do the best job of identifying firms with similar valuation multiples and stock price movements.[6] Chan, Lakonishok, and Swaminathan compared the effect of using industry classification schemes with statistically-based clustering approaches, and found that examining stocks in terms of industry membership seemed to give better

---

[5]For more insight into these issues, see Chapter 18 in Tom Copeland, Tim Koller, and Jack Murrin, *Valuation: Measuring and Managing the Value of Companies*, 3rd edition (New York: John Wiley & Sons, 2000).
[6]Sanjeev Bhojraj, Charles M.C. Lee, and Derek K. Oler, "What's My Line? A Comparison of Industry Classification Schemes for Capital Market Research," *Journal of Accounting Research* 41, no. 5 (2003): 745–774.

explanatory power than working in terms of either sectors or sub-industries.[7] To our knowledge, there have not been any parallel investigations into the effectiveness of different industry classification schemes for cross-national analysis. The results of Phylaktis and Xia suggest that the importance of sector-level effects has been increasing in recent years, while the influence of country-level effects has waned slightly.[8]

Technology and Intra-Industry Diversity

As discussed above, some academic research has suggested that firms from similar industries tend to trade at similar multiples, and to experience similar stock price movements. Industry membership therefore would seem to be a useful starting point for analysis. Thus, for instance, trucking companies and railroad companies both provide transportation services, but railroads will generally trade at different multiples from trucking companies because their cost structure and balance sheets tend to be quite different.

In some cases, there can be substantial variation even within a particular sub-industry. For instance, "publishing" covers a wide variety of different business models, including daily newspapers, weekly magazines, publishers of textbooks and professional journals, printers of fiction and nonfiction books, and suppliers of financial data. Each of these individual industries is likely to have different sources of revenue, different technological requirements, different cost structures, and different rates of expected growth. Admittedly, the larger publishing houses may have operations spanning several different fields, but the relative contributions of each division to the firm's overall revenues and profits may differ substantially. In such instances, relative value analysis may result in a wide range of valuation multiples, possibly with several different clusters reflecting each firm's competitive position. We consider such difficulties in the next section.

There are also some industries in which technological differences are the principal basis on which relative values are assigned. For instance, small companies in the field of biotechnology may have only a handful of products, each of which could potentially be a great success or a dismal failure. Some companies of this type may be still at the prerevenue stage when they go public, so that their valuation is entirely based on the market's expectations about the ultimate value of technology that has not yet generated

---

[7]Louis K. C. Chan, Josef Lakonishok, and Bhaskaran Swaminathan, "Industry Classifications and Return Comovement," *Financial Analysts Journal* 63, no. 6 (2007): 56–70.

[8]Kate Phylaktis and Lichuan Xia, "The Changing Roles of Industry and Country Effects in the Global Equity Markets," *European Journal of Finance* 12, no. 8 (2006): 627–648.

actual sales. In such instances, relative value analysis might require particularly careful selection of companies that are truly comparable in terms of the market's perception of their stage of development and the likelihood that their key products will ultimately be successful. Arguably, relative value analysis in such cases may not generate particularly useful results because the spread of potential outcomes is so broad.

Bimodal and Multimodal Patterns

Sometimes the outcome of a relative value analysis will show that the valuation multiples are not evenly spread between low and high, but instead are bimodal or multimodal—in other words, if there seem to be two or more clusters of results. We show an example of this in our hypothetical example below, which suggests that in a universe of seven firms, two are expected to achieve a return on equity (ROE) of 11% to 12% in FY0 and FY1, whereas the other companies are generally projected to deliver ROE of 8% to 9%. Such differences may appear relatively minor, but if the market really does expect these outcomes, then the two companies with higher profitability may legitimately be expected to trade at a premium to their peers.

When a relative valuation table appears to have bimodal or multimodal characteristics, an analyst will generally be well advised to investigate further. In any given sector or industry, there may well be some firms that are truly capable of producing higher returns than their peers, perhaps as a result of better management, a stronger market position, or a more supportive regulatory environment. Relative valuation methods can identify potential outliers of this type, but cannot test whether the estimates themselves are reasonable.

One potentially useful approach is to extend the analysis further back into the past, using historical prices for valuation purposes, and if possible also using as-was projections for the relevant period. Such projections are now widely available from various different data vendors, including Bloomberg, FactSet, and Thomson Reuters. Consider the companies that are currently trading at a premium or a discount to their peers—did they also trade at a discount to their peers in the past? A logical extension of relative value analysis based on a single period is to gauge whether a particular firm persistently tends to trade at a lower or higher multiple than its peers, and then assess whether its current multiple is above or below what would be expected on the basis of prior periods. Damodaran notes that relative valuations frequently have low persistence over time: for industries in which this is the case, then relative valuation methods may indeed provide useful investment signals.[9]

---

[9]Damodaran, *Damodaran on Valuation: Security Analysis for Investment and Corporate Finance*, p. 244.

Choice of Valuation Multiples

Many relative valuation methods compare a company's share price with some measure of its performance, such as earnings per share (EPS) or free cash flow per share. Other relative valuation methods compare a company's share price with some measure of its size, such as book value per share. Block has reported that the majority of practitioners consider that when analyzing securities, measures of earnings and cash flow are somewhat more important than measures of book value or dividends.[10] However, many practitioners will make use of various metrics in their work, in the expectation that the different multiples will provide varying perspectives. Liu, Nissim, and Thomas compared the efficacy of six different metrics for relative valuations of U.S. firms on a universe-wide basis.[11] They subsequently extended the analysis to seven different metrics applied to 10 different countries and multiple industries.[12] Hooke presents an example using eight different metrics applied to the single industry of temporary staffing companies.[13] In a hypothetical example below, we use three different metrics for relative valuation analysis, and we believe that most practitioners would consider that between three and six different metrics is probably justifiable. It is certainly possible to have a much larger number of metrics,[14] but the results may be harder to interpret.

A ratio such as price–earnings can be calculated in terms of share price or EPS, or alternatively can be interpreted as market cap or net income. For most purposes, these two ratios will be the same. However, share issuance or buyback activity may impair the comparability of figures expressed in terms of EPS. If there is any possibility of ambiguity, then we would generally recommend using market cap or net income.

For instance, a company may currently have 100 million shares outstanding, a current share price of $40, and expected earnings of $2 in FY0 and $3 in FY1. If the P/E ratio is calculated in terms of price or EPS, then the FY0 ratio is 20 and the FY1 ratio is 13.3. However, analysts may be expecting that the company will buy back and cancel 20% of its shares during FY1. If so, then the projected net income in FY1 would presumably be

---

[10]Stanley B. Block, "A Study of Financial Analysts: Practice and Theory," *Financial Analysts Journal 55*, no. 4 (1999): 86–95.

[11]Jing Liu, Doron Nissim, and Jacob Thomas, "Equity Valuation Using Multiples," *Journal of Accounting Research 40*, no. 1 (2002): 135–172.

[12]Jing Liu, Doron Nissim, and Jacob Thomas, "Is Cash Flow King in Valuations?" *Financial Analysts Journal 63*, no. 2 (2007): 56–68.

[13]See Chapter 15 in Jeffrey Hooke, *Security Analysis on Wall Street: A Comprehensive Guide to Today's Valuation Methods*, 2nd edition (Hoboken, NJ: John Wiley & Sons, 2010).

[14]Damodaran, *Damodaran on Valuation: Security Analysis for Investment and Corporate Finance*, p. 650.

$240 million rather than $300 million. If the P/E ratio is calculated using market cap and net income, then the FY1 ratio would be 16.7 rather than 13.3. This hypothetical example indicates the importance of ensuring that the denominator is being calculated on a basis that reflects the historical or projected situation for the relevant period. (An investor might consider that if a firm's management is indeed strongly committed to buying back its own shares, then this might indicate that the firm's management views the shares as being undervalued. However, such considerations would presumably be included as a qualitative overlay to the relative valuation analysis.)

Choice of Numerator: Market Cap vs. Firm Value

In some instances, the choice of numerator may have a significant impact on the multiple. For instance, many analysts will use price–sales ratios for valuation purposes. However, a firm's revenues are generated from the total of its capital base, comprising both equity and debt.

Consider two companies, A and B, which both have a current market cap of $300 million, and projected annual revenues of $600 million in FY0, so that they both have a current price/sales ratio of 2. But suppose that Company A has no outstanding borrowings, whereas Company B has net debt of $300 million. One could argue that Company B is actually rather less attractive than Company A, as apparently it requires twice as much capital to generate the same volume of sales. In effect, analyzing the company in terms of "firm value/sales" rather than price/sales would reveal that Company B is making less efficient use of its capital than Company A.

There is no single definition of "firm value" that is generally accepted by all practitioners. In an ideal world, one would want to have the market value of the firm's equity capital and of the firm's debt capital. However, because corporate bonds and bank loans typically are not traded in liquid markets, there may not be any reliable indicator of the market value of debt capital. Consequently, it is conventional to use market capitalization to estimate how investors are valuing the firm's equity capital, but then to use figures from the firm's most recent balance sheet together with the notes to the financial statements as a proxy for net debt. The broadest definition of which we are aware is the following:

$$\text{Net debt} = \text{Total short-term debt} + \text{Total long-term debt} \\ + \text{Minority interest} + \text{Unfunded pension liabilities} \\ - \text{Cash and equivalents}$$

In practice, for most firms, the biggest components of net debt are likely to be total short-term debt, total long-term debt, and cash and equivalents.

In most cases, using an alternative definition of firm value will often have only a small impact on the calculated multiple.

Conceptually, it is possible to divide the income statement between the line items that are generated on the basis of total capital, and those that pertain solely to equity capital. For most firms, the separator between these two categories is net interest expense or net interest income. Analyzing relative valuation for banks and insurance companies can be somewhat more complex, as discussed in Copeland, Koller, and Murrin.[15] Generally speaking, it is usually desirable that the numerator and denominator of a valuation metric should be consistent with each other.[16]

Industry-Specific Multiples

Analysts covering some industries may make use of information that is specific to that industry, such as paid miles flown for airlines, same-store sales for retailers, or revenue per available room for hotel chains. Such data can provide insights into how the market is valuing individual firms' historical or expected operating performance. However, we consider that they should be viewed as a supplement to other multiples, rather than as a replacement for them, because it can be difficult to reconcile a company's operating performance with its financial results, and also because there may be little or no intuition about what would be a "reasonable" estimate for long-run valuation levels.[17] Natural resource producers tend to be valued in terms of both their operating efficiency and the resources that they control, so it may be useful to include some measure of their reserves in the analysis.[18] Many practitioners make use of efficiency metrics when using relative valuation approaches to assess some types of banks and other lending institutions.[19]

HYPOTHETICAL EXAMPLE

Suppose that an analyst is seeking to gauge whether Company A is attractive or unattractive, on the basis of relative valuation methods. Suppose that the analyst has determined that there are six other listed companies in

---

[15]See Chapters 21 and 22 in Copeland, Koller, and Murrin, *Valuation: Measuring and Managing the Value of Companies.*

[16]Damodaran, *Damodaran on Valuation: Security Analysis for Investment and Corporate Finance,* pp. 239–240.

[17]Ibid., pp. 237–238.

[18]See Chapter 21 in Hooke, *Security Analysis on Wall Street: A Comprehensive Guide to Today's Valuation Methods.*

[19]See Chapter 22 in Hooke, *Security Analysis on Wall Street: A Comprehensive Guide to Today's Valuation Methods.*

EXHIBIT 4.1 Hypothetical Relative Valuation Results

Company	Share Price ($)	Market Cap ($m)	P/E FY0	P/E FY1	P/FCF FY0	P/FCF FY1	P/B FY0	P/B FY1
A	20.00	400	12.0	10.0	8.5	7.0	1.30	1.20
B	16.00	550	11.5	11.5	5.0	6.0	1.00	0.95
C	40.00	500	13.0	12.0	8.0	7.5	1.50	1.40
D	15.00	450	12.5	12.0	8.0	7.0	1.10	1.05
E	13.00	350	14.5	13.0	9.0	8.0	1.25	1.15
F	30.00	350	12.5	12.5	7.0	4.5	1.15	1.15
G	15.00	300	15.0	14.0	7.0	6.0	1.20	1.15
Median		400	12.75	12.25	7.50	6.50	1.18	1.15
Standard Deviation		98.3	1.33	0.89	1.37	1.26	0.17	0.15
A versus median		0%	−6%	−18%	13%	8%	11%	4%

Notes: P/E refers to price–earnings before extraordinary items; P/B refers to price–book value; P/FCF refers to price–free cash flow (defined as earnings before extraordinary items plus noncash items taken from the cash flow statement); FY0 refers to the current fiscal year; FY1 refers to the next fiscal year; figures for FY0 and FY1 could have been derived from consensus sell-side estimates or other sources.

the same industry that are approximately the same size and comparable in terms of product mix, client base, and geographical focus.[20] Based on this information, the analyst can calculate some potentially useful multiples for all seven companies. A hypothetical table of such results is shown in Exhibit 4.1. (For the purposes of this simple hypothetical example, we are assuming that all the firms have the same fiscal year. We consider calendarization later in this chapter.)

In this hypothetical scenario, Company A is being compared to companies B through G, and, therefore, Company A should be excluded from the calculation of median and standard deviation, to avoid double-counting. The median is used because it tends to be less influenced by outliers than the statistical mean, so it is likely to be a better estimate for the central tendency. (Similarly, the standard deviation can be strongly influenced by outliers, and it would be possible to use "median absolute deviation" as a more robust

---

[20]For further examples using real firms and actual figures, see Chapters 7 and 8 in Damodaran, *Damodaran on Valuation: Security Analysis for Investment and Corporate Finance*, and Chapter 15 in Hooke, *Security Analysis on Wall Street: A Comprehensive Guide to Today's Valuation Methods*.

way of gauging the spread around the central tendency. Such approaches may be particularly appropriate when the data contains one or a handful of extreme outliers for certain metrics, which might be associated with company-specific idiosyncrasies.) Exhibit 4.1 has been arranged in terms of market cap, from largest to smallest, which can sometimes reveal patterns associated with larger or smaller firms, though there don't appear to be any particularly obvious trends in this particular set of hypothetical numbers.

Exhibit 4.1 suggests that the chosen universe of comparable companies may be reasonably similar to Company A in several important respects. In terms of size, Companies B, C, and D are slightly larger, while Companies E, F, and G are slightly smaller, but the median market cap across the six firms is the same as Company A's current valuation. In terms of P/E ratios, Company A looks slightly cheap in terms of FY0 earnings and somewhat cheaper in terms of FY1 earnings. In terms of P/FCF ratios, Company A looks somewhat expensive in terms of FY0 free cash flow, but only slightly expensive in terms of FY1 free cash flow. And finally, in terms of P/B ratios, Company A looks somewhat expensive in terms of FY0 book value, but roughly in line with its peers in terms of FY1 book value.

Analysis of the Hypothetical Example

So what are the implications of these results? Firstly, Company A looks relatively cheap compared to its peer group in terms of P/E ratios, particularly in terms of its FY1 multiples. Secondly, Company A looks rather expensive compared to its peer group in terms of P/FCF and P/B ratios, particularly in terms of FY0 figures. If an analyst were focusing solely on P/E, then Company A would look cheap compared with the peer group, and this might suggest that Company A could be an attractive investment opportunity.

However, the analyst might be concerned that Company A looks comparatively cheap in terms of P/E, but somewhat expensive in terms of price–book value. One way to investigate this apparent anomaly is to focus on ROE, which is defined as earnings–book value. Using the data in Exhibit 4.1, it is possible to calculate the ROE for Company A and for the other six companies, by dividing the P/B ratio by the P/E ratio—because this effectively cancels out the "price" components, and thus will generate an estimated value for EPS divided by book value per share, which is one way to calculate ROE.

The results suggest that Company A is expected to deliver an ROE of 10.8% in FY0 and 12% in FY1, whereas the median ROE of the other six firms is 8.7% in FY0 and 8.8% in FY1. Most of the comparable companies are expected to achieve ROE of between 8% and 9% in both FY0 and FY1, though apparently Company C is expected to achieve ROE of 11.5% in FY0 and 11.7% in FY1. (A similar analysis can be conducted using "free cash flow to equity," which involves dividing the P/B ratio by the P/FCF ratio. This indicates that Company A is slightly below the median of Companies B through G in FY0, but in line with its six peers during FY1.)

These results suggest that Company A is expected to deliver an ROE that is substantially higher than most of its peers. Suppose that an analyst is skeptical that Company A really can deliver such a strong performance, and instead hypothesizes that Company A's ROE during FY0 and FY1 may only be in line with the median ROE for the peer group in each year. Based on the figures in Exhibit 4.1, Company A's book value in FY0 is expected to be $15.38, and the company is projected to deliver $1.67 of earnings. Now suppose that Company A's book value remains the same, but that its ROE during FY0 is only 8.7%, which is equal to the median for its peers. Then the implied earnings during FY0 would only be $1.35, and the "true" P/E for Company A in FY0 would be 14.9, well above the peer median of 12.75.

The analysis can be extended a little further, from FY0 to FY1. The figures in Exhibit 4.1 suggest that Company A's book value in FY1 will be $16.67, and that the company will generate $2.00 of earnings during FY1. But if Company A only produced $1.35 of earnings during FY0, rather than the table's expectation of $1.67, then the projected FY1 book value may be too high. A quick way to estimate Company A's book value in FY1 is to use a "clean surplus" analysis, using the following equation:

$$\text{Book}_{FY1} = \text{Book}_{FY0} + \text{Net income}_{FY1} - \text{Dividends}_{FY1}$$

Based on the figures in Exhibit 4.1, Company A is expected to have earnings of $1.67 during FY0, and $2.00 during FY1. The implied book value per share is $15.38 in FY0, and $16.67 during FY1. According to the clean surplus formula, Company A is expected to pay a dividend of $0.38 per share in FY1.

Assuming that the true earnings in FY0 are indeed $1.35 rather than $1.67, and that the dividend payable in FY1 is still $0.38, then the expected book value for Company A in FY1 would be $16.35 rather than $16.67. Taking this figure and applying the median FY1 peer ROE, the expected FY1 earnings for Company A would be $1.42 rather than $2.00, and consequently the "true" P/E for FY1 would be 13.9 instead of the figure of 10.0 shown in Exhibit 4.1. At those levels, the stock would presumably no longer appear cheap by comparison with its peer group. Indeed, Company A's FY1 P/E multiple would be roughly in line with Company G, which has the highest FY1 P/E multiple among the comparable companies.

This quick analysis therefore suggests that the analyst may want to focus on why Company A is expected to deliver FY0 and FY1 ROE, which is at or close to the top of its peer group. As noted previously, Company A and Company C are apparently expected to have ROE, which is substantially stronger than the other comparable companies. Is there something special about Companies A and C that would justify such an expectation? Conversely, is it possible that the estimates for Companies A and C are reasonable, but that the projected ROE for the other companies is too pessimistic? If the latter scenario is valid, then it's possible that the P/E ratios for some of the other companies in the comparable universe are too high, and thus that those firms could be attractively valued at current levels.

Other Potential Issues

Multiples Involving Low or Negative Numbers

It is conventional to calculate valuation multiples with the market valuation as the numerator, and the firms' financial or operating data as the denominator. If the denominator is close to zero, or negative, then the valuation multiple may be very large or negative. The simplest example of such problems might involve a company's earnings. Consider a company with a share price of $10 and projected earnings of $0.10 for next year. Such a company is effectively trading at a P/E of 100. If consensus estimates turn more bearish, and the company's earnings next year are expected to be minus $0.05, the company will now be trading at a P/E of –200.

It is also possible for a firm to have negative shareholders' equity, which would indicate that the total value of its liabilities exceeds the value of its assets. According to a normal understanding of accounting data, this would indicate that the company is insolvent. However, some companies have been able to continue operating under such circumstances, and even to retain a stock exchange listing. Firms with negative shareholders' equity will also have a negative price–book multiple. (In principle, a firm can even report negative net revenues during a particular period, though this would require some rather unusual circumstances. One would normally expect few firms to report negative revenues for more than a single quarter.)

As noted previously, averages and standard deviations tend to be rather sensitive to outliers, which is one reason to favor using the median and the median absolute deviation instead. But during economic recessions at the national or global level, many companies may have low or negative earnings. Similarly, firms in cyclical industries will often go through periods when sales or profits are unusually low, by comparison with their average levels through a complete business cycle. Under such circumstances, an analyst may prefer not to focus on conventional metrics such as price–earnings, but instead to use line items from higher up the income statement that will typically be less likely to generate negative numbers.

Calendarization

Some of the firms involved in the relative valuation analysis may have fiscal years that end on different months. Most analyst estimates are based on a firm's own reporting cycle. It is usually desirable to ensure that all valuation multiples are being calculated on a consistent basis, so that calendar-based effects are not driving the analysis.

One way to ensure that all valuation multiples are directly comparable is to calendarize the figures. Consider a situation where at the start of January, an analyst is creating a valuation analysis for one firm whose fiscal year ends in June, while the other firms in the universe have fiscal years that end in December. Calendarizing the results for the June-end firm will require taking half of the projected number for FY0, and adding half of the projected number for FY1. (If quarter-by-quarter estimates are available, then more precise adjustments can be implemented by combining 3QFY0, 4QFY0, 1QFY1, and 2QFY1.)

Calendarization is conceptually simple, but may require some care in implementation during the course of a year. One would expect that after a company has reported results for a full fiscal year, the year defined as "FY0" would immediately shift forward 12 months. However, analysts and data aggregators may not change the definitions of "FY0" and "FY1" for a few days or weeks. In case of doubt, it may be worth looking at individual estimates in order to double-check that the correct set of numbers is being used.

Sum-of-the-Parts Analysis

When attempting to use relative valuation methods on firms with multiple lines of business, the analyst may not be able to identify any company that is directly similar on all dimensions. In such instances, relative valuation methods can be extended to encompass "sum-of-the-parts" analysis, which considers each part of a business separately, and attempts to value them individually by reference to companies that are mainly or solely in one particular line of business.[21]

Relative valuation analysis based on sum-of-the-parts approaches will involve the same challenges as were described above—identifying a suitable universe of companies that are engaged in each particular industry, collecting and collating the necessary data, and then using the results to gauge what might be a "fair value" for each of the individual lines of business. But in addition to these considerations, there is an additional difficulty that is specific to sum-of-the-parts analysis. This problem is whether to apply a "conglomerate discount," and if so how much.

---

[21]See Chapter 18 in Hooke, *Security Analysis on Wall Street: A Comprehensive Guide to Today's Valuation Methods.*

Much financial theory assumes that all else equal, investors are likely to prefer to invest in companies that are engaged in a single line of business, rather than to invest in conglomerates that have operations across multiple industries. Investing in a conglomerate effectively means being exposed to all of that conglomerate's operations, and the overall mix of industry exposures might not mimic the portfolio that the investor would have chosen if it were possible instead to put money into individual companies.

A possible counterargument might be that a conglomerate with strong and decisive central control may achieve synergies with regard to revenues, costs or taxation would not be available to individual free-standing firms dealing at arms' length with each other. A skeptical investor might wonder, on the other hand, about whether the potential positive impact of such synergies may be partly or wholly undermined by the negative impacts of centralized decision making, transfer pricing, and regulatory or reputational risk.

For these reasons, an analyst might consider that it is reasonable to apply a discount to the overall value that emerges from the "sum of the parts." Some practitioners favor a discount of somewhere between 5% and 15%, for the reasons given earlier. Academic research on spinoffs has suggested that the combined value of the surviving entity and the spun-off firm tends to rise by an average of around 6%, though with a wide range of variation.[22] (Some analysts have suggested that in some particular contexts, for instance in markets where competent managers are very scarce, then investors should be willing to pay a premium for being able to invest in a conglomerate that is fortunate enough to have such executives. However, this appears not to be a mainstream view.)

Relative Valuation vs. DCF: A Comparison

Relative valuation methods can generally be implemented fairly fast, and the underlying information necessary to calculate can also be updated quickly. Even with the various complexities discussed above, an experienced analyst can usually create a relative valuation table within an hour or two. And the calculated valuation multiples can adjust as market conditions and relative prices change. In both respects, relative valuation methods have an advantage over DCF models, which may require hours or days of work to build or update, and that require the analyst to provide multiple judgment-based inputs about unknowable future events. Moreover, as noted by Baker and Ruback, if a DCF model is extended to encompass multiple possible scenarios, it may end up generating a range of "fair value" prices that is too wide

---

[22]See Timothy R. Burch and Vikram Nanda, "Divisional Diversity and the Conglomerate Discount: Evidence from Spinoffs," *Journal of Financial Economics*, 70, no. 1 (2003): 69–98.

to provide much insight into whether the potential investment is attractive at its current valuation.[23]

Relative valuation methods focus on how much a company is worth to a minority shareholder, in other words an investor who will have limited or zero ability to influence the company's management or its strategy. Such an approach is suitable for investors who intend to purchase only a small percentage of the company's shares, and to hold those shares until the valuation multiple moves from being "cheap" to being "in line" or "expensive" compared with the peer group. As noted above, relative valuation methods make no attempt to determine what is the "correct" price for a company's shares, but instead focuses on trying to determine whether a company looks attractive or unattractive by comparison with other firms that appear to be approximately similar in terms of size, geography, industry, and other parameters.

DCF methods attempt to determine how much a company is worth in terms of "fair value" over a long time horizon. DCF methods can readily incorporate a range of assumptions about decisions in the near future or the distant future, and therefore can provide a range of different scenarios. For this reason, most academics and practitioners consider that DCF methods are likely to produce greater insight than relative valuation methods into the various forces that may affect the fair value for a business. More specifically, DCF methods can be more applicable to situations where an investor will seek to influence a company's future direction—perhaps as an activist investor pushing management in new directions, or possibly as a bidder for a controlling stake in the firm. In such situations, relative valuation analysis is unlikely to provide much insight because the investor will actually be seeking to affect the company's valuation multiples directly, by affecting the value of the denominator.

Nevertheless, even where an analyst favors the use of DCF approaches, we consider that relative valuation methods can still be valuable as a "sanity check" on the output from a DCF-based valuation. An analyst can take the expected valuation from the DCF model, and compare it with the projected values for net income, shareholders' equity, operating cash flow, and similar metrics. These ratios drawn from the DCF modeling process can then be compared with the multiples for a universe of similar firms. If the multiples that are generated by the analyst's DCF model are approximately comparable with the multiples that can be derived for similar companies already being publicly traded, then the analyst may conclude that the DCF model's assumptions appear to be reasonable. However, if the multiples from the analyst's model appear to diverge considerably from the available information concerning valuation multiples for apparently similar firms,

---

[23]Baker and Ruback, *Estimating Industry Multiples*.

then it may be a good idea to reexamine the model, rechecking whether the underlying assumptions are truly justifiable.

Relative valuation methods can also be useful in another way when constructing DCF models. Most DCF models include a "terminal value" that represents the expected future value of the business, discounted back to the present, from all periods subsequent to the ones for which the analyst has developed explicit estimates. One way to calculate this terminal value is in terms of a perpetual growth rate, but the choice of a particular growth rate can be difficult to justify on the basis of the firm's current characteristics. An alternative approach is to take current valuation multiples for similar firms, and use those values as multiples for terminal value.[24]

KEY POINTS

- Relative valuation methods tend to receive less attention from academics than DCF approaches, but such methods are widely used by practitioners. If relative valuation approaches suggest that a company is cheap on some metrics but expensive on others, this may indicate that the market views that company as being an outlier for some reason, and an analyst will probably want to investigate further.
- Choosing an appropriate group of comparable companies is perhaps the most challenging aspect of relative valuation analysis. Where possible, an analyst should seek to identify 6 to 12 companies that are similar in terms of risk characteristics, perhaps with attention to criteria such as size, geography, and industry. If this is not possible, then an analyst should feel free to relax one or more of these parameters in order to obtain a usable universe.
- Determining an appropriate set of valuation multiples is also important. Calculating a single set of multiples is likely to provide fewer insights than using several different metrics that span multiple time periods. It is conventional to use consensus estimates of future financial and operating performance, as these presumably represent the market's collective opinion of each firm's prospects.
- Most relative valuation analysis is performed using standard multiples such as price–earnings or firm value–sales. Under some conditions, using industry-specific multiples can be valuable, though there may be fewer consensus estimates for such data, and there may also be less intuition about what is the "fair" price for such ratios.

---

[24]See Damodaran, *Damodaran on Valuation: Security Analysis for Investment and Corporate Finance*, pp. 143–144.

▪ Relative valuation methods are particularly useful for investors who aim to take minority stakes in individual companies when they are "cheap" relative to their peers, and then sell those stakes when the companies become "expensive." Such methods are likely to be less directly useful for investors who will seek to influence a company's management, or who aim to take a controlling stake in a company. For such investors, DCF methods are likely to be more applicable.

QUESTIONS

1. Applying relative valuation approaches is typically more challenging for very small or very large companies. Why?

2. Historical results for the financial and operating performance of listed companies are readily available. Getting reasonable numbers for forecast performance is typically more difficult, and sometimes impossible. Why not rely solely on historical numbers?

3. Consensus forecasts do not incorporate the unique insights into each company that are available from our in-house expert. Why not use our own internal estimates, rather than consensus numbers?

4. Many analysts favor the use of industry-specific multiples for relative valuation purposes. What are some notable examples, and what advantages or disadvantages might be associated with using such metrics?

5. Relative valuation approaches can be used for sum-of-the-parts analysis, but many practitioners will apply a "conglomerate discount" to the results of such analysis. Why do they do so, and what is the normal range applied?

CHAPTER 5

Valuation over the Cycle and the Distribution of Returns*

Anders Ersbak Bang Nielsen, Ph.D.
Portfolio Strategist
Goldman Sachs International

Peter C. Oppenheimer
Chief Global Equity Strategist
Goldman Sachs International

There is substantial empirical evidence that valuation is a good predictor of returns over the long run.[1] Put simply, as intuition would suggest, buying an equity market when the valuation multiples are low, and the dividend yield and required equity risk premium are high, typically generates much better future returns than if buying an equity market when the opposite holds. However, while valuation today provides a great deal of information about future expected returns, it tells us nothing about how these returns should be distributed over time. Are they evenly distributed over several years, or are the returns bunched into short periods of time? What, if anything, determines the way that these returns are generated?

Historical observation suggests that the answer to this questions can be found in the relationship between valuation, earnings, and the economic cycle. For example, during periods when investors are expecting the onset of recession and falling profits, returns to shareholders deteriorate as a result both of declining expectations about the near term prospects for profits as

---

[1]See the discussion in John Y. Campbell, "Estimating the Equity Premium," NBER Working Paper 13423 (2007), and the references therein for the arguments on both sides of this debate.

---

*We would like to thank Hanyi Lim and Matthieu Walterspiler for research assistance for the analysis used in this chapter.

well as a result of lower valuations attached to future expected cash flows. The opposite tends to occur at the peak of the cycle when investors are more confident. By contrast, at the trough of the equity market cycle, typically during recessions when profits remain depressed, the initial recovery is virtually always driven by rising valuations as investors anticipate future profit recovery. The observation that valuations and returns shift over the economic cycle suggests that any practical analysis of valuation should also take into account these important relationships.

In this chapter, we first show that the price–earnings (P/E) multiple exhibits both cyclical and lower frequency fluctuations. We then look at the theoretical drivers of the P/E multiple, how a typical equity market cycle evolves in terms of earnings growth, valuation and returns, and how this evolution is related to the economic cycle. In addition to looking at aggregated data through history, we also look at the performance of different asset classes and investment styles over the equity market cycle. Finally, we suggest how to adjust valuation analysis to take into account the cyclical fluctuations in valuation that we have documented.

THE LINK BETWEEN EARNINGS AND RETURNS

The P/E multiple that investors put on current earnings when valuing them, as well as other commonly used valuation metrics, shift significantly over time. Exhibit 5.1 shows the U.S. trailing P/E multiple since 1871. As can be seen, there is both a cyclical component to the changes in the multiple as well as movements at lower frequencies. The P/E multiple stayed below long term averages for most of the 1970s and above for a big part of the 1990s.

There are many potential reasons for these movements in the P/E ratio. One way to think about these drivers is to use a simple dividend discount model (DDM) with constant growth rates to measure the fair value of the market. In such a model, we have that

$$P = \sum_{i=1}^{\infty} \frac{PO \times E_0 \times (1+G)^t}{(1+R_f+ERP)^t} = \frac{PO \times E_1}{R_f+ERP-G} \tag{5.1}$$

where P is the theoretical market price, E_0 is the level of earnings over the last year, E_1 is the level of earnings over the next year, PO is the payout ratio, R_f is the nominal risk-free interest rate, ERP is the equity risk premium, and G is the nominal growth rate.

Dividing through by E gives

$$\frac{P}{E} = \frac{PO}{R_f+ERP-G}$$

EXHIBIT 5.1   The P/E Multiple has both Cyclical and Lower Frequency Movements

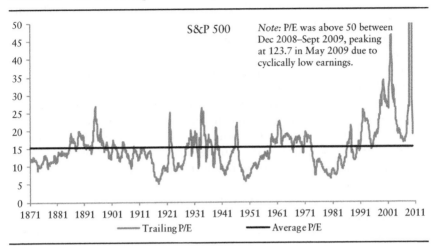

Source: Robert Shillers long run data series on the U.S. stock market.

Therefore, changes in the P/E multiple over time could arise from changes in payout ratios, interest rates, the equity risk premium and expectations of long-run growth. Changes in the equity risk premium and long-run growth assumptions are particularly hard to account for as they are not directly observable.

The cyclical fluctuations in the P/E multiple shown in Exhibit 5.1 means that there is not a direct translation from earnings growth into returns over shorter horizons, even though the mean reversion of the P/E multiple over longer horizons implies that earnings growth is the principal driver of equity market performance in the long run. In reality, earnings growth is only paid for to a very limited extent when it occurs.

To better understand the relationship between earnings and returns, we take a descriptive approach. We show that the equity market moves in cycles. Each of the five cycles from one peak of the market to the next since 1973 can be divided into four distinct phases, each with its own economic context and drivers of stock market returns.

The four phases are illustrated in Exhibit 5.2. We identify the phases of each cycle by determining the extent to which equity price performance is driven by actual profit growth and by "expectations" about future growth, measured as changes in the 12 month trailing P/E multiple. We look at broad market indexes for the United States, continental Europe, and the United Kingdom. The four phases we define are:

1. The *Despair phase* is defined as the period where the market moves from its peak to its trough. This correction is mainly driven by P/E multiple contraction as the market anticipates and reacts to a deteriorating macroeconomic environment and its implications in terms of lower future earnings.
2. The *Hope phase* is typically a short period (on average nine months in the United States), where the market rebounds from its trough through multiple expansion. This occurs in anticipation of a forthcoming trough in the economic cycle as well as future profit growth and is leading to a local peak in the trailing P/E multiple. We define the end of the Hope phase as this local peak of the trailing P/E multiple. It occurs when earnings are typically depressed or falling and often begins in the late stages of a recession.
3. The *"Growth phase"* is a typically longer period (on average 34 months), where earnings growth drives returns. We define the end of this period to be when multiple expansion again starts to provide a larger proportion of the returns than earnings growth.

EXHIBIT 5.2   Diagram of the Phases

Cycle of the Equity Market for the United States
(all growth rates are annualized averages)

1. Despair
Market moves from peak to trough
-Expectations are disappointed
-Worst return, –32.9%
-Poor earnings growth, –0.2%

4. Optimism
P/E multiple grows faster than earnings
-Expectation extrapolated
-Second best return, 24.9%
-Poor earnings growth, –1.9%

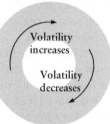

Volatility increases

Volatility decreases

2. Hope
P/E multiple expands
-Expectation of a better future
-Highest return, 50.9%
-Poor earnings growth, –6.0%

3. Growth
Earnings grow faster than the P/E multiple
-Reality catches up to expectations
-Second lowest return, –1.2%
-Strong earnings growth, 12.6%

4. The *Optimism phase* is the final part of the cycle, where returns driven by P/E multiple expansion outpace earnings growth, thereby setting the stage for the next market correction.

This pattern shows up in every single cycle in the United States, United Kingdom, and continental Europe since the early 1970s. As an example of how the phases in the market can be identified Exhibit 5.3 shows the performance of the U.S. market from its peak in March 2000 to its peak in October 2007.

The returns line shows the real price performance indexed to 100 at the peak of the market when the new cycle begins. The Despair phase starts at the peak and ends when the returns line troughs in October 2002. The end of the Hope phase is identified by the PE line, which measures the 12 month trailing PE, again indexed to 100 at the peak of the market. The PE rises during the Hope phase, and the end of the Hope phase is defined as the local peak in this line.

The Hope phase is followed by the Growth phase. The end of this phase is defined as the peak in the Earnings/(P/E) line. This is the ratio of the Earnings and the P/E line multiplied by 100. While this line is less intuitive at first glance, it is interesting because the change in the line over a period of time measures the contribution to returns from earnings growth compared to the contribution to returns from P/E expansion. If earnings contribute more to the return over this period of time than multiple expansion the line goes up.

EXHIBIT 5.3　Derivation of the Phases in the 2000–2007 Cycle in the United States

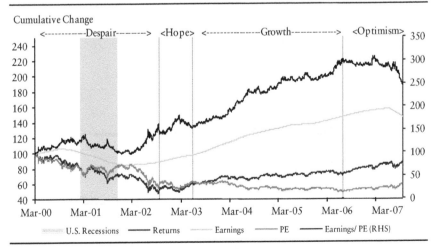

Data sources: Compustat and Haver Analytics.

Otherwise it goes down. We define the start of the Optimism phase as the point, where a larger part of the return starts to be due to multiple expansion rather than earnings growth and therefore as the point where the Earnings/(P/E) line peaks. Here we ignore the short "blip" up in the Earnings/PE line in March 2007, as it is above the levels reached in July 2006 for just five days, and there is a clear fall in the line both before and after those five days.

Nielsen and Oppenheimer[2] shows similar diagrams for all the cycles in the United States, continental Europe, and the United Kingdom. Here we just show the average return for each phase in the cycle for these three markets in Exhibit 5.4. Appendix A shows the dates and returns for each phase in the three markets used to calculate the averages.

The framework demonstrates that the relationship between earnings growth and price performance changes systematically over the cycle. While earnings growth is what fuels equity market performance over the very long run (because the P/E multiple tends to mean revert), most of the earnings growth is not paid for when it occurs but rather when it is correctly anticipated by investors in the Hope phase, and when investors get overly optimistic about the potential for future growth during the Optimism phase.

As can be seen from the exhibits, the situation is particularly extreme in the United States, where the quarterly reporting frequency of earnings makes it possible to make a more accurate separation of which part of

EXHIBIT 5.4 Average Earnings Growth, P/E Expansion, and Return by Phase United States

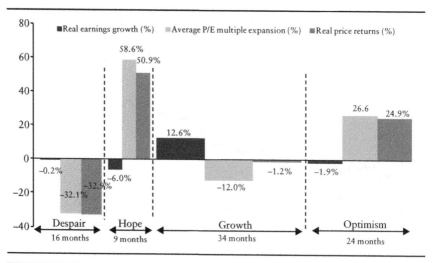

[2]Anders E. B. Nielsen and Peter Oppenheimer, "The Equity Cycle Part 1: Identifying the Phases," Goldman Sachs European Portfolio Strategy, 2009.

EXHIBIT 5.4 (Continued)
Europe (excluding United Kingdom)

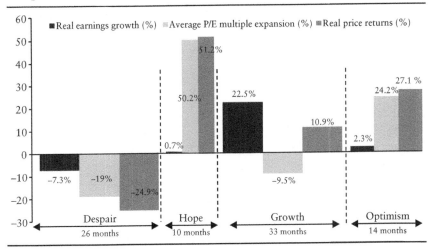

United Kingdom

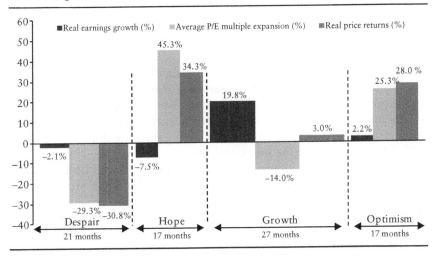

Data sources: Compustat, Worldscope, Datastream, and Haver Analytics.

the return is due to earnings growth and which part is due to P/E multiple expansion. Here, on average over the last five cycles, all the earnings growth has occurred during the growth phase, yet, the real price returns in that phase have been slightly negative.

EXHIBIT 5.5   The Market Rise from Through to Peak
(The proportion of total across the three phases that falls in each phase)

Phase	Hope	Growth	Optimism
United States			
Average length (in months)	9.3	34.1	24.1
Real earnings growth (%)	−5.3	109.7	−4.3
P/E expansion (%)	35.6	−5.7	70.1
Real price return (%)	32.3	−1.3	69.0
Europe (excluding United Kingdom)			
Average length (in months)	9.9	32.5	14.3
Real earnings growth (%)	0.2	98.8	1.0
P/E expansion (%)	69.9	−11.8	41.9
Real price return (%)	42.2	28.4	29.4
United Kingdom			
Average length (in months)	17.1	27.5	16.7
Real earnings growth (%)	−6.5	104.0	2.5
P/E expansion (%)	81.6	−5.1	23.5
Real price return (%)	58.8	3.3	37.9

Data sources: Compustat, Worldscope, Datastream, and Haver Analytics.

It is not surprising that the market rises in expectation of future earnings growth and that a part of the earnings growth in the Growth phase is therefore paid for during the Hope phase. But the degree to which price returns and earnings growth is separated is surprising. Almost the entire earnings growth for each region occurs during the growth phase, yet only −1%, 28%, and 3% of the index real price return from the trough to the peak of the market accumulates during that phase for the United States, Europe, and the United Kingdom respectively (Exhibit 5.5).

In terms of returns, the highest annualized returns occur during the Hope phase, followed by the Optimism phase, the Growth phase, and finally the Despair phase. This has been true in every cycle in the United States and holds in all regions on average.

THE PHASES CAN BE INTERPRETED IN RELATIONSHIP TO THE ECONOMY

The pattern in the way the equity market values earnings over the cycle documented in the previous section is far from arbitrary. The Nielsen and

Oppenheimer study mentioned earlier, shows that the phases in the equity market are linked to the underlying macroeconomy. This allows for a clearer interpretation of the phases and can help to identify when the market is moving from one phase to the next. This section covers these results.

We first look at investors real forward looking return requirements on investment. In the valuation model in equation (5.1), this would be the nominal risk free rate plus the equity risk premium minus expected inflation. This variable is interesting as it measures the real hurdle rate for investment in the stock market.

As mentioned above this is not directly observable, but we measure this Real Required Return (RRR) as the 10-year nominal government bond yield, plus a measure of the Equity Risk Premium that we will discuss further below, minus five-year average historical inflation as a measure of inflation expectations. This measure of the RRR generally increases in the Despair phase, decreases in the Hope and Optimism phases and is somewhat mixed in the Growth phase. Exhibit 5.6 shows the change in the RRR from the beginning to the end of each phase for each of the regions we consider.

EXHIBIT 5.6   Change in the RRR in Each Phase
United States

Cycles	Despair	Hope	Growth	Optimism
Nov. 1980–Aug. 1987	NA	−1.7	1.5	−2.8
Aug. 1987–Jun. 1990	1.6	−0.5	0.3	−0.9
Jun. 1990–Mar. 2000	0.8	−1.3	−0.3	−1.9
Mar. 2000–Oct. 2007	2.1	−0.5	0.2	−0.3
Average	1.5	−1.0	0.4	−1.4

Europe (excluding United Kingdom)

Cycles	Despair	Hope	Growth	Optimism
Oct. 1987–Jul. 1990	NA	NA	NA	0.1
Jul. 1990–Mar. 2000	2.5	−2.8	−1.2	−0.9
Mar. 2000–Jul. 2007	3.7	−0.9	−0.7	−0.3
Average	3.1	−1.9	−1.0	−0.3

United Kingdom

Cycles	Despair	Hope	Growth	Optimism
Jun. 1990–Mar. 2000	1.3	−2.0	0.5	−2.2
Mar. 2000–Oct. 2007	3.6	−0.6	−0.8	−0.2
Average	2.5	−1.3	−0.2	−1.2

We interpret the movements in investors' forward-looking return requirements across the phases as follows:

- During the Despair phase, investors get increasingly concerned about future prospects, and therefore require an increasingly high future expected return for holding equities. This reaction happens against a backdrop of an increase in volatility, an increase in the output gap and in four out of five cycles the start of a recession during this phase in the United States. This leads to lower P/E multiples and a falling market.
- In the Hope phase, an end to the crisis starts to be visible and this visibility caps the potential downside risk. Investors respond to the lower tail risk by accepting lower future expected returns. This drives up multiples and the market. While volatility is still high, it tends to fall towards the end of the Hope phase. In this phase investors essentially prepay for the expected recovery in earnings during the Growth phase.
- In the beginning of the Growth phase, investors have been through a period with high volatility. This is likely to make investors perceive equities as more risky and therefore less attractive. Investors have also already been paid for expected future earnings growth during the Hope phase, but the growth has yet to materialize. The output gap typically peaks some time during the Hope phase, but remains very high at the beginning of the Growth phase. The onset of the Growth phase is therefore a reasonable point in time for investors to question long-run growth expectations.

  These initial negatives tend to make investors less willing to pay for the earnings growth they see in the early stages of the Growth phase. This gives lower rates of return, which reinforces the negative picture of equities and makes investors less willing to pay for the improvements in fundamentals that they see on an ongoing basis. The result is that value in terms of expected future returns are rebuilt during the Growth phase in several cases, as earnings growth outpaces returns, and volatility declines.

  Another likely driver of the higher real return requirements in the equity market that are seen in many cases in this phase is the increase in the real yield which is seen in bond markets.
- Eventually, in the Optimism phase, the built-up value becomes large enough to attract investors and to reverse the dynamic of poor returns keeping away investors despite strengthening fundamentals. In the Optimism phase, returns outpace earnings and expected future returns consequently decline. Towards the end of the phase volatility picks up as the sustainability of the high returns are being tested by the market.

Next, we look at the broader macroeconomic backdrop. While there are few conclusions that hold up in every single cycle in every single region, the broad patterns which hold most of the time identified in the Nielsen and Oppenheimer study are:

■ *In the Despair phase, the economic environment deteriorates and the fall in the stock market is an early indicator of this:* The output gap first rises but then begins to fall, as the economy weakens. Unemployment rises as well as initial claims. The Institute for Supply Management manufacturing survey (ISM) and the Markit Economics Purchasing Managers Survey (PMI) indexes of manufacturing activity are falling. There are no robust patterns in the real bond yield. The RRR rises as investors demand higher compensation for future risk as described above.

■ *In the Hope phase, economic indicators tend to reach their worst levels and the stock market rebounds in expectation of future improvements:* The output gap continues to fall and normally troughs very close to the end of the Hope phase. Both unemployment and initial claims tend to peak in the Hope phase, but initial claims peak first. The ISM troughs. Volatility declines from the peak it reached at the initiation of the Hope phase. The real bond yield falls. The RRR falls as investors start to pay for expected future earnings growth.

■ *In the Growth phase, the economy recovers but stock market performance is weaker:* The output gap rises, often sharply as realized economic growth outpaces the long-run potential. The majority of the decline in the unemployment rate occurs in this phase and initial claims decline. The ISM normally peaks in this phase. Volatility continues its decline in the first part of the phase but starts to pick up again at the later stages of the phase. The real bond yield rises. The RRR often rises in the early parts of the phase but the results over the entire phase are mixed.

■ *In the Optimism phase, the limits of the economy are tested and stock market performance is strong until the limit is found with the initiation of the next Despair phase:* The behavior of the output gap is mixed. Unemployment continues to decline and initial claims level out. The ISM moderates from its peak in the Growth phase. Equity volatility continues the increase that began in the Growth phase. The real bond yield has a relatively flat profile and the RRR declines as stock market returns outpace earnings growth.

As an example of these developments the two charts in Exhibit 5.7 show the development of a number of macroeconomic indicators in the last cycle in the United States, which lasted from March 2000 to October

EXHIBIT 5.7   Macroeconomic Backdrop for the 2000–2007 Cycle in the United States

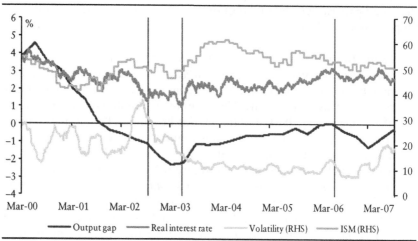

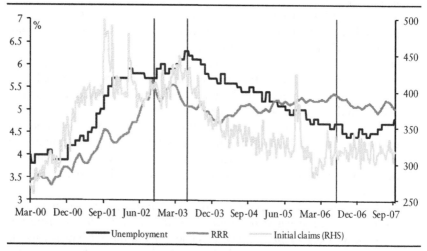

Data source: Haver Analytics.

2007. Nielsen and Oppenheimer show similar charts for all the cycles in the United States, Continental Europe and the United Kingdom since 1973 to support the conclusions above.

In line with the general patterns described above, equity volatility increased during the Despair phase, peaked around the end of that phase and then gradually declined until some time towards the end of the Growth phase at which point it started to pick up again. The output gap declined during the Despair phase, troughed close to the end of the Hope phase, improved dramatically during the Growth phase and remained flat from there. The ISM is less in line with the typical pattern, as it rises towards the end of the Despair phase. It does, however, have a local trough towards the end of the Hope phase, and its cycle peak in the Growth phase. The real bond yield falls a bit during the Hope phase and rises during the Growth phase after which it flattens out. Unemployment rose during the Despair and Hope phases, peaked at the end of the Hope phase, fell strongly during the Growth phase and was stable in the Optimism phase. Initial claims peaked before unemployment as is typically the case, but did so earlier than normal in the middle of the Despair phase. There was a second local peak in the Hope phase however, more in line with the typical experience. Finally the RRR was in line with the historical pattern.

ASSET CLASS PERFORMANCE VARIES ACROSS THE PHASES

The performance of other asset classes and investment styles also vary systematically with the phases. Exhibit 5.8 shows annualized real total return for U.S. equities, bonds, and the S&P GS Commodity Index for each of the phases in all of the five cycles. The general conclusions are:

- In the Despair phase a risk averse investor should own bonds, while a less risk averse investor should consider commodities. In this phase, bonds have always outperformed equities and commodities have outperformed equities in four out of five cases. The relative performance of bonds and commodities is more mixed, with commodities outperforming in three out of five cases. On a median basis, commodities have strongly outperformed bonds, but bonds are less risky with the worst annualized return being –3.7% as opposed to –20.2% for commodities. It is not surprising that equities are the poorest performer, since the Despair phase is marked by the move from the peak to the trough of the equity market, but the analysis shows how large the potential is for outperformance by diversifying into other asset classes at this point in the cycle.
- In the Hope phase, equities offer by far the best returns. In this phase there is a clear ranking of the asset classes. In all five cycles, equities outperform bonds and in four out of the five cycles, bonds in turn outperform commodities.
- In the Growth phase, commodities lead. Commodities outperformed both bonds and equities in four out of five cycles. On average commodities

outperformed bonds and equities by roughly 10% per annum whereas
on a median basis the outperformance was around 3.5% per annum.
Both equities and bonds perform poorly in this phase, with the relative
ranking being somewhat unstable.

EXHIBIT 5.8   Asset Class Returns by Phase
U.S. Equities

	Despair	Hope	Growth	Optimism
Jan. 1973–Nov. 1980	−34.8	65.2	−2.9	59.9
Nov. 1980–Aug. 1987	−18.6	83.7	−13.2	30.3
Aug. 1987–Jun. 1990	−77.7	93.4	−0.2	21.4
Jun. 1990–Mar. 2000	−48.7	32.2	9.1	27.6
Mar. 2000–Oct. 2007	−24.2	47.7	6.3	20.9
Average	−40.8	64.5	−0.2	32.0
Median	−34.8	65.2	−0.2	27.6

U.S. 10-year Treasuries

	Despair	Hope	Growth	Optimism
Jan. 1973–Nov. 1980	−3.7	0.2	−3.1	2.4
Nov. 1980–Aug. 1987	3.2	19.4	−0.3	10.4
Aug. 1987–Jun. 1990	1.6	13.1	0.2	5.9
Jun. 1990–Mar. 2000	−2.0	9.3	3.7	4.1
Mar. 2000–Oct. 2007	6.7	4.7	−0.3	3.9
Average	1.2	9.3	0.0	5.4
Median	1.6	9.3	−0.3	4.1

Commodities

	Despair	Hope	Growth	Optimism
Jan. 1973–Nov. 1980	−54.2	−27.7	1.5	41.0
Nov. 1980–Aug. 1987	−20.2	5.9	1.0	6.6
Aug. 1987–Jun. 1990	10.7	−1.5	25.8	17.5
Jun. 1990–Mar. 2000	221.1	−18.3	3.4	−1.9
Mar. 2000–Oct. 2007	2.6	18.2	17.8	−8.3
Average	53.7	−4.7	9.9	11.0
Median	10.7	−1.5	3.4	6.6

Data sources: Worldscope, Haver Analytics, and Datastream.

The general conclusions for asset classes together with the general conclusions for style performance from another study by Nielsen and Oppenheimer[3] are summarized in Exhibit 5.9. The conclusions are general in the sense that most patterns are not true in every single cycle in all markets but rather hold in most of the cases.

Typically cyclical stocks underperform defensive stocks in the Despair phase and outperform in the Hope phase. This speaks to the beta-driven environment of those two phases. Later in the cycle this is less important and results are more mixed on this dimension. Small caps outperform large caps in the Hope phase, whereas large caps historically have outperformed towards the end of the cycle in the Optimism phase. As noted in academic literature value stocks tend to outperform growth stocks.[4] This is particularly pronounced in the Growth phase, where it is true in every cycle and every market that were considered in the analysis. In line with the idea that investors in the Optimism phase extrapolate growth trends beyond what is sustainable, this is the only phase where growth stocks normally outperform.

INCORPORATING CYCLICALITY INTO VALUATIONS

The previous sections have described how valuations vary with the cycle and how those variations are tied to the macroeconomy. These variations imply that investors are not rewarded for most of the earnings growth when it occurs, but rather before it occurs during the Hope phase, and when investors get overly optimistic about the future during the Optimism phase.

This section describes how to adjust valuation analysis to take this cyclicality into account in a quantified way. In our view, the long run growth assumptions for company profits and payout ratios should remain relatively stable over time as long as there are no big structural shifts in the growth rate of the underlying economy. This has been a reasonable assumption for both the United States and Europe over the last few decades, and we think it still remains so. If long run growth assumptions are relatively stable, interest rates and the equity risk premium become key drivers of fluctuations in the P/E multiple over time as shown in equation (5.1).

Interest rates are observable but the ERP is not. The fact that the ERP cannot be directly observed is an even bigger challenge for valuation when

---

[3]Anders E. B. Nielsen and Peter Oppenheimer, "The Equity Cycle Part 2: Investing in the Phases," Goldman Sachs European Portfolio Strategy (2009).
[4]See, for example, Eugene F. Fama and Kenneth R. French, "The Cross-Section of Expected Stock Returns," *Journal of Finance* 47, no. 2 (1992): 427–465; and Eugene F. Fama and Kenneth R. French, "Common Risk Factors in the Returns on Stocks and Bonds," *Journal of Financial Economics* 33, no. 1 (1993): 3–56.

EXHIBIT 5.9 Asset Class and Style Performance Summary

	Despair	Hope	Growth	Optimism
Assets				
Outperformance	Commodities, bonds	Equities	Commodities	Equities
Underperformance	Equities	Bonds, commodities	Equities, bonds	Bonds, commodities
Styles				
Cyclicals vs. defensives	Underperformed	Outperformed	Mixed	Mixed
Industrial cyclicals vs. consumer cyclicals	Outperformed	Underperformed	Mixed	Mixed
Large cap vs. small cap	Mixed	Underperformed	Mixed	Outperformed
Value vs. growth	Outperformed	Outperformed	Outperformed	Underperformed

EXHIBIT 5.10   U.S. Market Implied and Macro-Benchmarked ERP

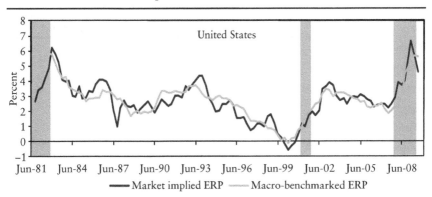

you accept that it is likely to change over time. Our recommended solution to this problem is to estimate the ERP by fixing the long run growth assumption and turning the Dividend Discount model on its head to calculate what risk premium is required at any given point in time, in order for the theoretical value from that model to equal the observed market price.

Taking this approach and using a slightly more advanced dividend discount model than the one in equation (5.1), Daly, Nielsen, and Oppenheimer[5] estimate the time series path of the ERP shown in Exhibit 5.10 as the Market implied ERP. The exhibit shows that the market implied ERP is mean reverting and clearly fluctuates with the economic cycle. It rises around the U.S. economic recessions and then declines during prolonged economic expansions.

This dependency is formalised in Exhibit 5.11, which shows *R*-squareds from univariate regressions of the market implied ERP on a number of macroeconomic variables. The U.S. output gap alone (as measured using the congressional budget offices measure of potential output) explains 74% of the variation over time of the market implied ERP.

The tight link between macroeconomic variables and the market implied ERP, can be used to estimate where the ERP "should" be at a given point in time given the macroeconomic environment. This normative measure of the ERP is the macro-benchmarked ERP in Exhibit 5.10. It is the fitted value from a regression of the market implied ERP on the one quarter ahead output gap in the United States, the two-quarter ahead output gap in Europe (since the European economy is often lagging the United States a bit, yet the

---

[5]Kevin Daly, Anders E. B. Nielsen and Peter Oppenheimer, "Finding Fair Value in Global Equities: Part II—Forecasting Returns," *Journal of Portfolio Management* 36, no. 3 (2010): 56–77.

EXHIBIT 5.11 R^2 from Univariate Regressions of the Market Implied ERP on Macro Variables

	Sign	R-Squared
Output gap	−	74%
Unemployment	+	58
Five-year core inflation	+	30
Ten-year bond	+	13
World GDP growth	−	9
Government debt/GDP	−	8
U.S. GDP growth	−	5
Two-year bond	+	5
Balance of payment	+	1
ERP 1 quarter ago	+	84
ERP 2 quarters ago	+	64
ERP 3 quarters ago	+	47
ERP 4 quarters ago	+	34

equity markets tend to trade together) and a four-quarter lag of the market implied ERP.

With the two measures of the ERP from Exhibit 5.10, it is possible to adjust valuation for the cycle. If the goal is to value a company relative to the market, it makes sense to use the market implied ERP and adjust it for the beta of the company when valuing the company. If, on the other hand, the goal is to value the company on an absolute basis, it makes more sense to use the macro-benchmarked ERP adjusted for beta, as that gives a measure of the appropriate compensation for risk, based upon the state of the economy rather than current market prices. Finally, if the goal is to get a long run equilibrium measure of value, one should use the long run average market implied equity risk premium of approximately 3% together with an equilibrium interest rate on government bonds.

APPENDIX: DATES AND RETURNS OF THE PHASES

Returns, P/E expansion, and earnings growth rates are measured as annualized geometrical averages in all regions.

United States

Phase	Despair	Hope	Growth	Optimism
1973–1980				
Start date	11-Jan-73	03-Oct-74	15-Jul-75	27-Mar-80
End date	03-Oct-74	15-Jul-75	27-Mar-80	20-Nov-80
Length (in months)	20.7	9.4	56.4	7.8
Real earnings growth (%)	11.9	−19.5	7.1	−12.1
P/E expansion (%)	−43.4	99.2	−13.3	78.6
Real price return (%)	−36.6	60.3	−7.1	56.9
1980–1987				
Start date	20-Nov-80	12-Aug-82	22-Jun-83	24-Jul-84
End date	12-Aug-82	22-Jun-83	24-Jul-84	25-Aug-87
Length (in months)	20.7	10.3	13.1	37.1
Real earnings growth (%)	−9.3	−3.9	18.9	−6.6
P/E expansion (%)	−15.7	83.9	−30.1	34.4
Real price return (%)	−23.5	76.6	−16.9	25.5
1987–1990				
Start date	25-Aug-87	04-Dec-87	17-Mar-88	03-Jan-89
End date	04-Dec-87	17-Mar-88	03-Jan-89	04-Jun-90
Length (in months)	3.3	3.4	9.6	17.0
Real earnings growth (%)	27.7	23.4	29.0	−10.8
P/E expansion (%)	−82.9	52.8	−24.6	31.3
Real price return (%)	−78.1	88.5	−2.7	17.1
1990–2000				
Start date	04-Jun-90	11-Oct-90	15-Jan-92	24-Jul-96
End date	11-Oct-90	15-Jan-92	24-Jul-96	23-Mar-00
Length (in months)	4.2	15.2	54.3	44.0
Real earnings growth (%)	5.1	−14.2	13.4	7.5
P/E expansion (%)	−51.5	47.7	−6.5	16.0
Real price return (%)	−49.1	26.8	6.0	24.7
2000–2007				
Start date	23-Mar-00	09-Oct-02	17-Jun-03	17-Jul-06
End date	09-Oct-02	17-Jun-03	17-Jul-06	09-Oct-07
Length (in months)	30.6	8.3	37.0	14.8
Real earnings growth (%)	−4.8	15.2	14.1	0.1
P/E expansion (%)	−21.4	26.0	−8.5	18.6
Real price return (%)	−25.2	45.1	4.4	18.7

Data sources: Compustat and Haver Analytics.

Europe (excluding United Kingdom)

Phase	Despair	Hope	Growth	Optimism
1973–1978				
Start date	22-Mar-73	07-Oct-74	15-Apr-75	15-Jul-77
End date	07-Oct-74	15-Apr-75	15-Jul-77	20-Oct-78
Length (in months)	18.5	6.2	27.0	15.2
Real earnings growth (%)	12.3	2.4	19.3	−7.0
P/E expansion (%)	−45.2	85.9	−11.5	18.4
Real price return (%)	−38.5	90.4	5.6	10.1
1978–1987				
Start date	20-Oct-78	17-Aug-82	01-Feb-84	01-Apr-85
End date	17-Aug-82	01-Feb-84	01-Apr-85	05-Oct-87
Length (in months)	45.9	17.5	14.0	30.1
Real earnings growth (%)	−10.0	−0.4	32.6	3.6
P/E expansion (%)	−3.0	36.6	−21.7	19.0
Real price return (%)	−12.7	36.1	3.7	23.3
1987–1990				
Start date	05-Oct-87	10-Nov-87	18-Mar-88	07-Nov-89
End date	10-Nov-87	18-Mar-88	07-Nov-89	18-Jul-90
Length (in months)	1.2	4.2	19.7	8.3
Real earnings growth (%)	2.9	−3.2	15.6	−12.0
P/E expansion (%)	−98.6	59.5	−0.6	36.7
Real price return (%)	−98.5	54.4	14.9	20.3
1990–2000				
Start date	18-Jul-90	05-Oct-92	31-Jan-94	18-Oct-99
End date	05-Oct-92	31-Jan-94	18-Oct-99	06-Mar-00
Length (in months)	26.6	15.9	68.6	4.6
Real earnings growth (%)	−11.5	−9.9	21.4	40.2
P/E expansion (%)	−6.8	56.1	−7.3	74.8
Real price return (%)	−17.6	40.7	12.4	145.1
2000–2007				
Start date	06-Mar-00	12-Mar-03	03-Sep-03	13-Jun-06
End date	12-Mar-03	03-Sep-03	13-Jun-06	16-Jul-07
Length (in months)	36.2	5.8	33.3	13.1
Real earnings growth (%)	−10.2	42.3	27.5	9.4
P/E expansion (%)	−18.9	36.8	−11.5	21.0
Real price return (%)	−27.1	94.8	12.8	32.4

Data sources: Worldscope, Datastream, and Haver Analytics.

United Kingdom

Phase	Despair	Hope	Growth	Optimism
1973–1979				
Start date	10-Jan-73	12-Dec-74	30-Jan-76	09-Mar-78
End date	12-Dec-74	30-Jan-76	09-Mar-78	04-May-79
Length (in months)	23.0	13.6	25.3	13.8
Real earnings growth (%)	30.2	−41.6	11.4	−7.8
P/E expansion (%)	−63.5	247.2	−16.2	36.1
Real price return (%)	−52.5	102.6	−6.6	25.4
1979–1987				
Start date	04-May-79	28-Sep-81	24-Jun-83	24-Sep-85
End date	28-Sep-81	24-Jun-83	24-Sep-85	16-Jul-87
Length (in months)	28.9	20.8	27.1	21.7
Real earnings growth (%)	−4.9	0.5	20.3	6.5
P/E expansion (%)	−9.1	27.1	−9.4	31.3
Real price return (%)	−13.5	27.8	9.0	39.9
1987–1989				
Start date	16-Jul-87	09-Nov-87	24-Jun-88	14-Dec-88
End date	09-Nov-87	24-Jun-88	14-Dec-88	05-Sep-89
Length (in months)	3.8	7.5	5.7	8.7
Real earnings growth (%)	1.0	3.9	35.1	−0.6
P/E expansion (%)	−76.3	19.8	−37.3	45.9
Real price return (%)	−76.1	24.5	−15.3	45.0
1989–1999				
Start date	05-Sep-89	28-Sep-90	02-Feb-94	17-Dec-96
End date	28-Sep-90	02-Feb-94	17-Dec-96	30-Dec-99
Length (in months)	12.8	40.2	34.5	36.4
Real earnings growth (%)	−6.7	−1.4	13.6	3.5
P/E expansion (%)	−18.5	17.3	−11.1	13.3
Real price return (%)	−23.9	15.7	1.0	17.3
1999–2007				
Start date	30-Dec-99	12-Mar-03	18-Jun-03	14-Mar-07
End date	12-Mar-03	18-Jun-03	14-Mar-07	15-Jun-07
Length (in months)	38.4	3.2	44.9	3.1
Real earnings growth (%)	−14.6	27.5	27.6	13.2
P/E expansion (%)	−7.6	98.0	−14.2	31.7
Real price return (%)	−21.1	152.5	9.5	49.2

Data sources: Worldscope, Datastream, and Haver Analytics.

KEY POINTS

- Valuation multiples exhibit both cyclical and lower frequency fluctuations.
- Some of the key drivers of the P/E multiple are interest rates, the equity risk premium, the payout ratio, and long term earnings growth.
- The equity markets in the United States, continental Europe, and the United Kingdom have historically moved in cycles, each consisting of four phases.
- On the path from the through to the peak of the market nearly all earnings growth occurs in the Growth phase on average, whereas only −1%, 28%, and 3% of the price return for the United States, continental Europe, and the United Kingdom respectively occurs in this phase.
- Between 32% and 59% of the return from through to peak occurs during the Hope phase despite its short duration and, typically declining earnings.
- There is variation in the performance of asset classes and investment styles across these phases.
- The market implied equity risk premium varies over time in a way that is tightly related to the output gaps of the economy at home and abroad.
- We recommend that valuation analysis should adjust for the state of the economic cycle.

QUESTIONS

1. Identify four key drivers of the P/E multiple.

2. What has historically been the key driver of equity prices in the very long run?

3. a. What are the ranking of the phases in terms of average real price returns?
   b. Which phase offers the highest average real earnings growth?

4. Which of the economic variables considered in the chapter explains most of the variation in the market implied equity risk premium?

5. What is the rational for adjusting valuation for the economic cycle?

CHAPTER 6

An Architecture for Equity Portfolio Management

Bruce I. Jacobs, Ph.D.
Principal
Jacobs Levy Equity Management

Kenneth N. Levy, CFA
Principal
Jacobs Levy Equity Management

Anyone who has ever built a house knows how important it is to start out with a sound architectural design. A sound design can help ensure that the end product will meet all the homeowner's expectations—material, aesthetic, and financial. A bad architectural design, or no design, offers no such assurance and is likely to lead to poor decision making, unintended results, and cost overruns.

It is equally important in building an equity portfolio to start out with some framework that relates the raw materials—stocks—and the basic construction techniques—investment approaches—to the end product. An architecture of equity management that outlines the basic relationships between the raw investment material, investment approaches, potential rewards, and possible risks can provide a blueprint for investment decision making.

We provide such a blueprint in this chapter. A quick tour of this blueprint reveals the following building blocks—an all-encompassing core comprising the whole investable universe (whether international or domestic) and its constituent style subsets of large-cap growth, large-cap value, and small-cap stocks. Investment approaches can also be roughly categorized into the following groups—passive, engineered (quantitative) active, or traditional active, with risk generally increasing as one moves from passive to traditional. These basic approaches may be extended by various means, including dynamic trading across market subsets or combining long positions with some degree of short selling. Understanding the market's building blocks and the advantages and disadvantages of each investment approach can improve overall investment results.

ARCHITECTURAL BUILDING BLOCKS

Exhibit 6.1 provides a simple but fairly comprehensive view of the *equity market*.[1] The heart of the structure, the core, represents the overall market. Theoretically, this would include all equity issues for the United States and other markets. In line with the practice of most equity managers, a broad-based equity index such as the S&P 500, or (even broader) the Russell 3000 or Wilshire 5000, may proxy for the aggregate U.S. market.

EXHIBIT 6.1   Equity Market Architectural Building Blocks

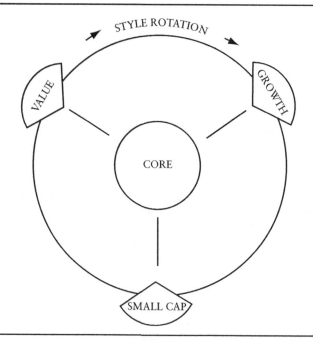

---

[1]See Bruce I. Jacobs and Kenneth N. Levy, "How to Build a Better Equity Portfolio," *Pension Management* (June 1996): 36–39.

For both equity managers and their clients, the overall market represents a natural and intuitive starting place. It is the ultimate selection pool for all equity strategies. Furthermore, the long-term returns offered by the U.S. equity market have historically outperformed alternative asset classes in the majority of multiyear periods. The aim of most institutional investors (even those that do not hold core investments per se) is to capture, or outdo, this equity return premium.

The core equity market can be broken down into subsets that comprise stocks with similar price behaviors—large-cap growth, large-cap value, and *small-cap stocks.* In Exhibit 6.1, the wedges circling the core represent these style subsets. The aggregate of the stocks forming the subsets equals the overall core market.

One advantage of viewing the market as a collection of subsets is the ability it confers upon the investor to mix and match. Instead of holding a core portfolio, for example, the investor can hold market subsets in market-like weights and receive returns and incur risks commensurate with those of the core. Alternatively, the investor can depart from core weights to pursue returns in excess of the core market return (at the expense, of course, of incremental risk). Investors who believe that small-cap stocks offer a higher return than the average market return, for example, can overweight that subset and underweight large-cap value and *growth stocks.*

Over time, different style subsets can offer differing relative payoffs as economic conditions change. As Exhibit 6.2 shows, small-cap stocks outperformed large-cap stocks by 60 percentage points or more in the rolling three-year periods ending in mid-1983 and by 45 to 55 percentage points in late 1993 and early 2006. But small-cap stocks underperformed by 20 to 40 percentage points in the rolling three-year periods between early 1986 and December 1991 and by as much as 80 percentage points in the first half of 1999. Exhibit 6.3 shows that large-cap growth stocks outperformed large-cap *value stocks* by over 90 percentage points in the rolling three-year period ending in March 2000 but underperformed by as much as 50 percentage points in mid-2003.

Just as some investors attempt to time the market by buying into and selling out of equities in line with their expectations of overall market trends, investors can attempt to exploit the dynamism of style subsets by rotating their investments across different styles over time, in pursuit of profit opportunities offered by one or another subset as market and economic conditions change.[2] The curved lines connecting the style wedges in Exhibit 6.1 represent this dynamic nature of the market.

---

[2]See Bruce I. Jacobs and Kenneth N. Levy, "High-Definition Style Rotation," *Journal of Investing* 5, no. 3 (1996): 14–23.

EXHIBIT 6.2   Small-Cap Stocks Outperform Large-Cap in Some Periods and Underperform in Others

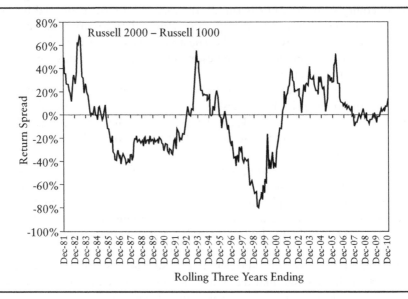

EXHIBIT 6.3   Large-Cap Growth Stocks Outperform Large-Cap Value in Some Periods and Underperform in Others

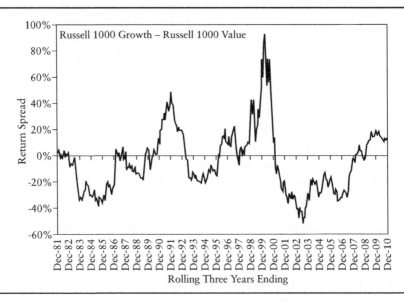

EXHIBIT 6.4   Equity Investment Approaches

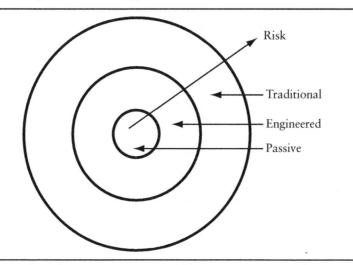

The *equity core* and its constituent style subsets constitute the basic building blocks—the equity selection universes—from which investors can construct their portfolios. Another important choice facing the investor, however, is the investment approach or approaches to apply to the selection universe. Exhibit 6.4 categorizes possible approaches into three groups—traditional, passive, and engineered. Each of these approaches can be characterized by an underlying investment philosophy and, very generally, by a level of risk relative to the underlying selection universe.

TRADITIONAL ACTIVE MANAGEMENT

Traditional investment managers focus on *stock picking*. In short, they hunt for individual securities that will perform well over the investment horizon. The search includes in-depth examinations of companies' financial statements and investigations of company managements, product lines, facilities, and the like. Based on the findings of these inquiries, traditional managers determine whether a particular firm is a good buy or a better sell.

The search area for traditional investing may be wide—the equivalent of the equity core—and may include market timing that exploits the dynamism of the overall market. Because in-depth analyses of large numbers of securities are just not practical for any one manager, however, traditional managers tend to focus on subsets of the equity market. Some may hunt for above-average earnings growth (growth stocks), while others look to buy future earnings streams cheaply (value stocks); still others beat the grasses off the trodden paths, in search of overlooked growth and/or value stocks (small-cap stocks). Traditional managers have thus fallen into the pursuit of growth, value, or small-cap styles.

Traditional managers often screen an initial universe of stocks based on some financial criteria, thereby selecting a relatively small list of stocks to be followed closely. Focusing on such a narrow list reduces the complexity of the analytical problem to human (that is, traditional) dimensions. Unfortunately, it may also introduce significant barriers to superior performance.

Exhibit 6.5 plots the combinations of breadth and depth of insights necessary to achieve a given investment return-risk level. Here, the breadth of insights may be understood as the number of independent insights—that is, the number of investment ideas or the number of stocks. The depth, or goodness, of insights is measured as the information coefficient—the correlation between the return forecasts made for stocks and their actual returns. Note that the goodness of the insights needed to produce the given return-risk ratio starts to increase dramatically as the number of insights falls below 100; the slope gets particularly steep as breadth falls below 50.

EXHIBIT 6.5 Combination of Breadth (Number) of Insights and Depth, or "Goodness," of Insights Needed to Produce a Given Investment Return-Risk Ratio[a]

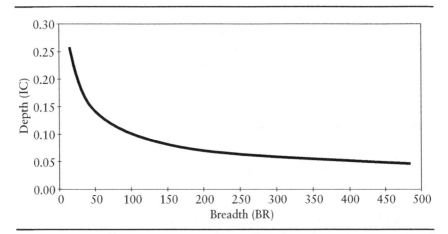

[a]The plot is based on the relationship $IR = IC\sqrt{BR}$, where IC is the information coefficient (the correlation between predicted and actual returns), BR is the number of independent insights, and IR is the ratio of annualized excess return to annualized residual risk (in this case, set equal to 1).
Source: Richard C. Grinold, "The Fundamental Law of Active Management," *Journal of Portfolio Management* 15, no. 3 (1989): 30–37.

Market timing strategies are particularly lacking in breadth, as an insight into the market's direction provides only one investment decision. Quarterly timing would produce four "bets" a year—a level of diversification few investors would find acceptable. Furthermore, unless timing is done on a daily basis or the timer is prodigiously skilled, it would take a lifetime to determine whether the results of timing reflect genuine skill or mere chance.

Traditional investing in effect relies on the ability of in-depth research to supply information coefficients that are high enough to overcome the lack of breadth imposed by the approach's fairly severe limitations on the number of securities that can be followed. As Exhibit 6.5 shows, however, the level of information coefficients required at such constricted breadth levels constitutes a considerable hurdle to superior performance. The insights from *traditional management* must be very, very good to overcome the commensurate lack of breadth.

Furthermore, lack of breadth may also have detrimental effects on the depth of traditional insights. While reducing the range of inquiry makes tractable the problem of stock selection via the labor-intensive methods of traditional *active management,* it is also bound to result in potentially relevant (and profitable) information being left out. Surely, for example, the behavior of the growth stocks not followed by traditional growth managers—even the behavior of value stocks outside the growth subset—may contain information relevant to the pricing of those stocks that do constitute the reduced traditional universe.

Another inherent weakness of traditional investment approaches is their heavy reliance on subjective human judgments. An ever-growing body of research suggests that stock prices, as well as being moved by fundamental information, are influenced by the psychology of investors. In particular, investors often appear to be under the influence of cognitive biases that cause them to err systematically in making investment decisions.[3]

Arrow, for example, finds that investors tend to overemphasize new information if it appears to be representative of a possible future event; thus, if investors perceive a firm's management to be good, and the firm has recently enjoyed high earnings, they will tend to place more reliance on the higher than the lower earnings estimates provided by analysts.[4] Shiller finds that investors are as susceptible as any other consumers to fads and fashions, bidding up prices of hot stocks and ignoring out-of-favor issues.[5] We describe below four common *cognitive errors* to which investors may fall prey.

---

[3]See Daniel Kahneman, and Amos Tversky, "Prospect Theory: An Analysis of Decisions Under Risk," *Econometrica* 47, no. 2 (1979): 263–292.
[4]See Kenneth J. Arrow, "Risk Perception in Psychology and Economics," *Economic Inquiry* 20, no. 1 (1982): 1–8.
[5]See Robert J. Shiller, "Stock Prices and Social Dynamics," *Brookings Papers on Economic Activity* 2 (1984): 457–510.

Cognitive Errors

Loss Aversion: The "Better Not Take the Chance/What the Heck" Paradox

Investors exhibit risk-averse behavior with respect to potential gains: faced with a choice between (1) a sure gain of $3,000 and (2) an 80% chance of gaining $4,000 or a 20% chance of gaining nothing, most people choose the sure thing, even though the $3,000 is less than the expected value of the gamble, which is $3,200 (80% of $4,000). But investors are generally risk seeking when it comes to avoiding certain loss: faced with a choice between (1) a sure loss of $3,000 and (2) an 80% chance of losing $4,000 or a 20% chance of losing nothing, most people will opt to take a chance. It's only human nature that the pain of loss exceeds the glee of gain, but putting human nature in charge of investment decision making may lead to suboptimal results. Shirking risk leads to forgone gains. Pursuing risk in avoidance of loss may have even direr consequences (digging a deeper hole).

Endowment Effect: The "Pride in Ownership" Syndrome

The price people are willing to pay to acquire an object or service is often less than the price they would be willing to sell the identical object or service for if they owned it. Say you bought a stock last year and it's quadrupled in price. If you won't buy more because "it's too expensive now," you should sell it. If you won't sell it because you were so brilliant when you bought it, you're sacrificing returns for pride in ownership.

The Gambler's Fallacy: "Hot Streaks, Empty Wallets"

Is it more likely that six tosses of a coin will come up HTTHTH or HHHTTT? Most people think the former sequence is more typical than the latter, but in truth both are equally likely products of randomness. In either case, the probability of the next flip of the coin turning up heads, or tails, is 50%. Market prices, too, will display patterns. It's easy to interpret such patterns as persistent trends and tempting to trade on them. But if the latest hot streak is merely a mirage thrown up by random price movements, it will prove an unreliable guide to future performance.

Confirmation Bias: "Don't Confuse Me with the Facts"

People search for and place more reliance upon evidence that confirms their preconceived notions, ignoring or devaluing evidence that refutes them. Four cards lie on a table, showing A, B, 2, and 3. What is the fewest number of cards you can turn over to confirm or refute that every card with a vowel on one side has an even number on the other side? Most people choose A, then 2. An odd number or a letter on the reverse of A would refute the conjecture. The 2, however, can merely confirm, not refute; the presence of a vowel on the reverse would confirm, but anything else would simply be immaterial. The correct choice is to turn A, 3, and B. A vowel on the reverse of 3 can refute, as can a vowel on the reverse of B. Investment approaches that do not have a method of systematically searching through all available evidence without prejudice, in order to find the exceptions that disprove their rules, may leave portfolios open to blindsiding and torpedo effects.

Investors who are susceptible to these biases will tend to take too little (or too much) risk, to hold on to an investment for too long, to see long-term trends where none exist, and to place too much reliance on information that confirms existing beliefs. As a result, the performances of their portfolios are likely to suffer.

The reliance of traditional *investment management* on the judgments of individual human minds makes for idiosyncrasies of habit that work to the detriment of investment discipline, and this is true at the level of the investment firm as well as the individual at the firm. It may be difficult to coordinate the individual mind-sets of all analysts, economists, investment officers, technicians, and traders, and this coordination is even harder to achieve when subjective standards for security analysis differ from individual to individual.

Constructing Portfolios

The qualitative nature of the outcome of the traditional security evaluation process, together with the absence of a unifying framework, can give rise to problems when individual insights into securities' performances are combined to construct a portfolio. However, on target an analyst's buy or sell recommendations may be, they are difficult to translate into guidelines for *portfolio construction*. Portfolio optimization procedures require quantitative estimates of relevant parameters, not mere recommendations to buy, hold, or sell.

The traditional manager's focus on stock picking and the resulting ad hoc nature of portfolio construction can lead to portfolios that are poorly defined in regard to their underlying selection universes. While any particular manager's portfolio return may be measured against the return on an index representative of an underlying equity core or style subset, that index does not serve as a benchmark in the sense of providing a guideline for portfolio risk. Traditional portfolios' risk-return profiles may thus vary greatly relative to those of the underlying selection universe.

As a result, traditional portfolios are not necessarily congruent with the equity market's basic building blocks. A traditional value manager, for example, may be averse to holding certain sectors, such as utilities. Not only will the portfolio's returns suffer when utilities perform well, but the portfolio will suffer from a lack of integrity, of wholeness. Such a portfolio will not be representative of the whole value subset. Nor could it be combined with growth and small-cap portfolios to create a corelike holding.

Because the relationship between the overall equity market and traditional managers' style portfolios may be ambiguous, value and growth, small-cap and large-cap may not be mutually exclusive. Value portfolios may hold some growth stocks, or growth portfolios some value stocks. There is no assurance that a combination of style portfolios can offer a market-like or above-market return at market-like risk levels.

Because of their heavy reliance on human mind power and subjective judgment, traditional approaches to investment management tend to suffer from a lack of breadth, a lack of discipline, and a resulting lack of portfolio integrity. Traditional management, while it may serve as well as any other approach for picking individual stocks, suffers from severe limitations when it comes to constructing portfolios of stocks. Perhaps it is for this reason that traditionally managed portfolios have often failed to live up to expectations.

PASSIVE MANAGEMENT

The generally poor performance of traditional investment management approaches helped to motivate the development, in the late 1960s and the 1970s, of new theories of stock price behavior. The efficient market hypothesis and random walk theory, the products of much research, offered a reason for the meager returns reaped by traditional investment managers: Stock prices effectively reflect all information in an efficient manner, rendering stock price movements random and unpredictable. Efficiency and randomness provided the motivation for passive investment management; advances in computing power provided the means.

Passive management aims to construct portfolios that will match the risk-return profiles of underlying market benchmarks. The benchmark may be core equity (as proxied by the S&P 500 or other broad index) or a style subset (as proxied by a large-cap growth, large-cap value, or small-cap index). Given the quantitative tools at its disposal, passive management can fine-tune the stock selection and portfolio construction problems in order to deliver portfolios that mimic very closely both the returns and risks of their chosen benchmarks.

Passive portfolios, unlike traditional portfolios, are disciplined. Any tendencies for passive managers to succumb to cognitive biases will be held in check by the exigencies of their stated goals—tracking the performances of their underlying benchmarks. Their success in this endeavor also means that the resulting portfolios will have integrity. A passive value portfolio will behave like its underlying selection universe, and a combination of passive style portfolios in market-like weights can be expected to offer a return close to the market's return at a risk level close to the market's. As the trading required to keep portfolios in line with underlying indexes is less than that required to beat the indexes, transaction costs for passive management are lower than those incurred by active investment approaches. As much of the stock selection and portfolio construction problem can be relegated to fast-acting computers, the management fees for passive management are also modest. For the same reason, the number of securities that can be covered by any given passive manager is virtually unlimited; all the stocks in the selection universe can be considered for portfolio inclusion.

Unlike traditional management, then, passive management offers great breadth. Breadth in this case doesn't count for much, however, because passive management is essentially insightless. Built on the premise that markets are efficient, hence market prices are random and unpredictable, passive management does not attempt to pursue or offer any return over the return on the relevant benchmark. Rather, its appeal lies in its ability to deliver the asset class return or to deliver the return of a style subset of the asset class. In practice, of course, trading costs and management fees, however modest, subtract from this performance.

An investor in pursuit of above-market returns may nevertheless be able to exploit passive management approaches via style subset selection and *style rotation.* That is, an investor who believes value stocks will outperform the overall market can choose to overweight a passive value portfolio in expectation of earning above-market (but not above-benchmark) returns. An investor with foresight into style performance can choose to rotate investments across different passive style portfolios as underlying economic and market conditions change.

ENGINEERED MANAGEMENT

Engineered management, based on quantitative techniques and methods, recognizes that markets are reasonably efficient in digesting information and that stock price movements in response to unanticipated news are largely random. It also recognizes, however, that significant, measurable pricing inefficiencies do exist, and it seeks to deliver incremental returns by modeling and exploiting these inefficiencies. In this endeavor, it applies to the same company fundamental and economic data used by traditional active management many of the tools that fostered the development of passive management, including modern computing power, finance theory, and statistical techniques, instruments that can extend the reaches (and discipline the vagaries) of the human mind.

Engineered approaches use quantitative methods to select stocks and construct portfolios that will have risk-return profiles similar to those of underlying equity benchmarks but offer incremental returns relative to those benchmarks, at appropriate incremental risk levels. The quantitative methods used may range from fairly straightforward to immensely intricate. In selecting stocks, for example, an engineered approach may use something as simple as a dividend discount model, or it may employ complex multivariate models that aim to capture the complexities of the equity market.

The engineered selection process can deal with and benefit from as wide a selection universe as passive management. It can thus approach the investment problem with an unbiased philosophy, unhampered, as is traditional management, by the need to reduce the equity universe to a tractable subset. At the same time, depending on the level of sophistication of the tools it chooses to use, engineered management can benefit from great depth of analysis, a depth similar to that of traditional approaches. Multivariate modeling, for example, can take into account the intricacies of stock price behavior, including variations in price responses across stocks of different industries, economic sectors, and styles.

Because engineered management affords both breadth and depth, the manager can choose a focal point from which to frame the equity market, without loss of important framing information. Analysis of a particular style subset, for example, can take advantage of information gleaned from the whole universe of securities, not just stocks of that particular style (or a subset of that style, as in traditional management). The increased breadth of inquiry should lead to improvements in portfolio performance compared with traditional style portfolios.

Engineering Portfolios

Engineered management utilizes all the information found relevant from an objective examination of the broad equity universe to arrive at numerical estimates for the expected returns and anticipated risks of the stocks in that universe. Unlike the subjective outcomes of traditional management, such numerical estimates are eminently suitable for portfolio construction via optimization techniques.[6]

---

[6]See Bruce I. Jacobs and Kenneth N. Levy, "Engineering Portfolios: A Unified Approach," *Journal of Investing* 4, no. 4 (1995): 8–14.

The goal of optimization is to maximize portfolio return while tying portfolio risk to that of the underlying benchmark. The portfolio's systematic risk should match the risk of the benchmark. The portfolio's *residual risk* should be no more than is justified by the expected incremental return. Risk control can be further refined by tailoring the optimization model so that it is consistent with the variables in the return estimation process.

The quantitative nature of the stock selection and portfolio construction processes imposes discipline on engineered portfolios. With individual stocks defined by expected performance parameters, and portfolios optimized along those parameters to provide desired patterns of expected risk and return, engineered portfolios can be defined in terms of preset performance goals. Engineered managers have little leeway to stray from these performance mandates, hence are less likely than traditional managers to fall under the sway of cognitive errors. In fact, engineered strategies may be designed to exploit such biases as investor overreaction (leading to price reversals) or investor herding (leading to price trends).

The discipline of engineered management also helps to ensure portfolio integrity. The style subset portfolios of a given firm, for example, should be non-overlapping, and the style subset benchmarks should in the aggregate be inclusive of all stocks in the investor's universe. Value portfolios should contain no growth stocks, nor growth portfolios any value stocks. The underlying benchmarks for value and growth portfolios, or large and small-cap portfolios, should aggregate to the equity core.

Engineering should reduce, relative to traditional management, portfolio return deviations from the underlying core or subset benchmark, while increasing expected returns relative to those available from passive approaches. While judicious stock selection can provide excess portfolio return over a passive benchmark, optimized portfolio construction offers control of portfolio risk.

Exhibit 6.6 compares the relative merits of traditional, passive, and engineered approaches to portfolio management. Traditional management offers depth, but strikes out with lack of breadth, susceptibility to cognitive errors, and lack of portfolio integrity. Passive management offers breadth,

EXHIBIT 6.6 Comparison of Equity Investment Approaches

	Traditional	Passive	Engineered
Depth of analysis	Yes	No	Simple: no Complex: yes
Breadth of analysis	No	Yes	Yes
Free of cognitive error	No	Yes	Yes
Portfolio integrity	No	Yes	Yes

freedom from cognitive error, and portfolio integrity, but no depth whatsoever. Only engineered management has the ability to construct portfolios that benefit from both breadth and depth of analysis, are free of cognitive errors, and have structural integrity.

Meeting Client Needs

A broad-based, engineered approach offers investment managers the means to tailor portfolios for a wide variety of client needs. Consider, for example, a client that has no opinion about style subset performance, but believes that the equity market will continue to offer its average historical premium over alternative cash and bond investments. This client may choose to hold the market in the form of an engineered core portfolio that can deliver the all-important equity market premium (at the market's risk level), plus the potential for some incremental return consistent with the residual risk incurred.

Alternatively, the client with a strong belief that value stocks will outperform can choose from among several engineered solutions. An engineered portfolio can be designed to deliver a value benchmark–like return at a comparable risk level or to offer, at the cost of incremental risk, a return increment above the value benchmark. Traditional value portfolios cannot be designed to offer the same level of assurance of meeting these goals.

With engineered portfolios, the client also has the ability to fine-tune bets. For example, the client can weight a portfolio toward value stocks while retaining exposure to the overall market by placing some portion of the portfolio in core equity and the remainder in a value portfolio, or by placing some percentage in a growth portfolio and a larger percentage in a value portfolio. Exposures to the market and to its various subsets can be engineered. Again, traditional management can offer no assurance that a combination of style portfolios will offer the desired risk-return profile.

EXPANDING OPPORTUNITIES

The advantages of an engineered approach are perhaps best exploited by strategies that are not constrained to deliver a benchmark-like performance. An engineered style rotation strategy, for example, seeks to deliver returns in excess of the market's return by forecasting style subset performance. Shifting investment weights aggressively among various style subsets as market and economic conditions evolve, style rotation takes advantage of the historical tendency of any given style to outperform the overall market in some periods and to underperform it in others. Such a strategy uses the entire selection universe and offers potentially high returns at commensurate risk levels.

Allowing short sales as an adjunct to an engineered strategy, whether that strategy utilizes core equity, a style subset, or style rotation, can further enhance return opportunities. While traditional management focuses on stock picking, the selection of "winning" securities, the breadth of engineered management allows for the consideration of "losers" as well as "winners." With an engineered portfolio that allows shorting of losers, the manager can pursue potential mispricings without constraint, going long underpriced stocks and selling short overpriced stocks.

In markets in which *short selling* is not widespread, there are reasons to believe that shorting stocks can offer more opportunity than buying stocks. This is because restrictions on short selling do not permit investor pessimism to be as fully represented in prices as investor optimism. In such a market, the potential candidates for short sale may be less efficiently priced, hence offer greater return potential, than the potential candidates for purchase.[7]

Even if all stocks are equally efficiently priced, however, shorting can enhance performance by eliminating constraints on the implementation of investment insights. Consider, for example, that a security with a median market capitalization has a weighting of approximately 0.01% of the market's capitalization. A manager who cannot short can underweight such a security by, at most, 0.01% relative to the market; this is achieved by not holding the security at all. Those who do not consider this unduly restrictive should consider that placing a like constraint on the maximum portfolio overweight would be equivalent to saying the manager could hold, at most, a 0.02% position in the stock, no matter how appetizing its expected return. Shorting allows the manager free rein in translating the insights gained from the stock selection process into portfolio performance.

Long-Short Portfolios

If security returns are symmetrically distributed about the underlying market return, there will be fully as many unattractive securities for short sale as there are attractive securities for purchase. Using optimization techniques, the manager can construct a portfolio that balances equal dollar amounts and equal systematic risks long and short. Such a long-short balance neutralizes the risk (and return) of the underlying market. The portfolio's return, which can be measured as the spread between the long and short returns, is solely reflective of the manager's skill at stock selection.[8]

---

[7]See Bruce I. Jacobs and Kenneth N. Levy, "20 Myths about Long-Short," *Financial Analysts Journal* 52, no. 5 (1996): 81–85.
[8]See Bruce I. Jacobs and Kenneth N. Levy, "The Long and Short on Long-Short," *Journal of Investing* 6, no. 1 (1997): 73–86.

Not only does such a market-neutral long-short portfolio neutralize underlying market risk, it offers improved control of residual risk relative even to an engineered long-only portfolio. For example, the long-only portfolio can control risk relative to the underlying benchmark only by converging toward the weightings of the benchmark's stocks; these weights constrain portfolio composition. Balancing securities' sensitivities long and short, however, eliminates risk relative to the underlying benchmark; benchmark weights are thus not constraining. Furthermore, the market-neutral long-short portfolio can use offsetting long and short positions to fine-tune the portfolio's residual risk.

In addition to enhanced return and improved risk control, an engineered long-short approach also offers clients added flexibility in asset allocation. A market-neutral long-short portfolio, for example, offers a return from security selection on top of a cash return (the interest received on the proceeds from the short sales). However, the long-short manager can also offer, or the client initiate, a market-neutral long-short portfolio combined with instruments (such as stock index futures) that provide exposure to the equity market as a whole. The resulting "equitized" portfolio will offer the market-neutral long-short portfolio's security selection return *and* the equity market return. Choice of other available overlays can provide the return from security selection in combination with exposure to other asset classes, including foreign equity and bonds. The transportability of the long-short portfolio's return offers clients the ability to take advantage of a manager's security selection skills while determining independently the plan's asset allocation mix.[9]

Enhanced active equity strategies such as 120-20 and 130-30 portfolios can provide investors with an even wider choice of *risk-return trade-offs* than long-only, market-neutral long-short, or equitized *long-short portfolios* can provide.[10] Enhanced active equity portfolios have short positions equal to some percentage of capital (generally 20% or 30%, but possibly 100% or more) and an equal amount of leveraged long positions. The

---

[9]See Bruce I. Jacobs and Kenneth N. Levy, "Alpha Transport with Derivatives," *Journal of Portfolio Management* 25, no. 5 (1999): 55–60.

[10]See Bruce I. Jacobs and Kenneth N. Levy, "Enhanced Active Equity Strategies: Relaxing the Long-Only Constraint in the Pursuit of Active Return," *Journal of Portfolio Management* 32, no. 3 (2006): 45–55; Bruce I. Jacobs and Kenneth N. Levy, "20 Myths About Enhanced Active 120-20 Strategies," *Financial Analysts Journal* 63, no. 4 (2007): 19–26; and Bruce I. Jacobs, Kenneth N. Levy, and David Starer, "On the Optimality of Long-Short Strategies," *Financial Analysts Journal* 54, no. 3 (1998): 40–51. For a comparison of enhanced active strategies with equitized long-short strategies, see Bruce I. Jacobs and Kenneth N. Levy, "Enhanced Active Equity Portfolios Are Trim Equitized Long-Short Portfolios," *Journal of Portfolio Management* 33, no. 4 (2007): 19–25.

enhanced active portfolio retains full sensitivity to underlying market movements, participating fully in the equity market return. If the securities held long outperform the underlying benchmark and the securities sold short underperform the benchmark, the enhanced active portfolio will achieve a return higher than the return on the underlying benchmark (at a higher risk level). It can also be expected to outperform a long-only portfolio based on comparable insights, because relaxation of the short-selling constraint allows the enhanced active portfolio to achieve security underweights that a long-only portfolio cannot attain, while the ability to invest the proceeds from short sales in additional long positions allows the portfolio to achieve security overweights that an unleveraged long-only portfolio cannot attain.

THE RISK-RETURN CONTINUUM

The various approaches to *investment management*, as well as the selection universes that are the targets of such approaches, can be characterized generally by distinct risk-return profiles. For example, in Exhibit 6.1, risk levels tend to increase as one moves from the core outward toward the dynamic view of the market; expected returns should also increase. Similarly, in Exhibit 6.4, risk can be perceived as increasing as one moves from passive investment management out toward traditional active management; expected returns should also increase.

Where should the investor be along this continuum? The answer depends in part on the investor's aversion to risk. The more risk-averse the investor, the closer to core/passive the portfolio should be, and the lower its risk and expected return. Investors who are totally averse to incurring residual risk (that is, departing from benchmark holdings and weights) should stick with passive approaches. They will thus be assured of receiving an equity market return at a market risk level. They will never beat the market.

Less risk-averse investors can make more use of style subsets (static or dynamic) and active (engineered or traditional) approaches. With the use of such subsets and such approaches, however, portfolio weights will shift away from overall equity market weights. The difference provides the opportunity for excess return, but it also creates residual risk. In this regard, engineered portfolios, which control risk relative to underlying benchmarks, have definite advantages over traditional portfolios.

The optimal level of residual risk for an investor will depend not only on the investor's level of aversion to residual risk, but also on the manager's skill. Skill can be measured as the manager's information ratio, or IR, the ratio of annualized excess return to annualized residual risk. For example,

EXHIBIT 6.7   Risk and Return Change with Investor Risk and Manager Skill

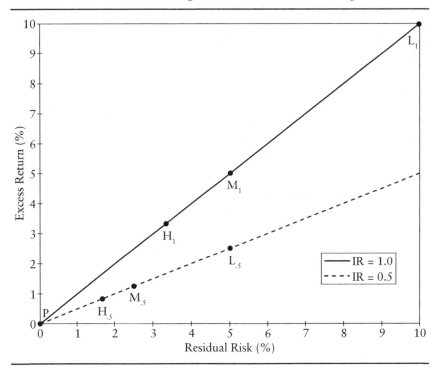

a manager that beats the benchmark by 2% per year, with 4% residual risk, has an IR of 2%/4%, or 0.5.

Grinold formulates the argument as follows:

$$\omega^* = \frac{IR}{2\lambda}$$

where ω^* equals the optimal level of portfolio residual risk given the manager's information ratio and the investor's level of risk aversion, λ.[11] Increases in the manager's IR will increase the investor's optimal level of residual risk and increases in the investor's risk-aversion level will reduce it.

Exhibit 6.7 illustrates some of the trade-offs between residual risk and excess return for three levels of investor aversion to residual risk and two levels of manager skill.[12] Here, the straight lines represent the hypothetical

[11]See Richard C. Grinold, "The Fundamental Law of Active Management," *Journal of Portfolio Management* 15, no. 3 (1989): 30–37.
[12]See Bruce I. Jacobs and Kenneth N. Levy, "Residual Risk: How Much is Too Much?" *Journal of Portfolio Management* 22, no. 3 (1996): 10–16.

continuum of portfolios (defined by their residual risks and excess returns) that could be offered by a highly skilled manager with an IR of 1.0 and a good manager with an IR of 0.5. (In reality, no manager will offer a strategy for each possible risk–return combination. Furthermore, although IR is a linear function of residual risk when liquidity is unlimited and short selling unrestricted, in the real world IR will begin to decline at high levels of residual risk.) The points H, M, and L represent the optimal portfolios for investors with high, medium, and low aversions to residual risk. The point at the origin, P, with zero excess return and zero residual risk, may be taken to be a passive strategy offering a return and a risk level identical to the benchmark's.

Several important observations can be made from Exhibit 6.7. First, it is apparent that greater tolerance for risk (a lower risk-aversion level) allows the investor to choose a portfolio with a higher risk level that can offer a higher expected return. Second, the more highly skilled the manager, the higher the optimal level of portfolio residual risk, and the higher the portfolio's expected excess return, whatever the investor's risk-aversion level. In short, higher excess returns accrue to higher-risk portfolios and to higher-IR managers.

Within this framework, an investor who takes less than the optimal level of residual risk or who selects less than the best manager will sacrifice return. Exhibit 6.8, for example, shows the decrease in return and utility (U) that results when an investor overestimates risk aversion. Here, an investor with a highly skilled manager, who actually has a medium level of risk aversion (M_1), chooses a portfolio suitable for an investor with a high level of risk aversion (H_1). The investor give-up in return can be measured as the vertical distance between M_1 and H_1. In somewhat more sophisticated terms, the higher-risk portfolio corresponds to a certainty-equivalent return of 2.500% and the less risky portfolio to a certainty-equivalent return of 2.221%, so the investor who overestimates his or her level of risk aversion and therefore chooses a suboptimal portfolio sacrifices 0.279 percentage points.

Exhibit 6.9 illustrates the return give-up that results when an investor with medium risk aversion uses a less skilled manager (IR of 0.5) rather than a higher-skill manager (IR of 1.0). Here the give-up in certainty-equivalent return between portfolio M_1 and portfolio $M_{.5}$ amounts to 1.875 percentage points. Choice of manager can significantly affect portfolio return.

Suppose an investor finds a highly skilled manager ($IR = 1$), but that manager does not offer a portfolio with a risk level low enough to suit the investor's high level of risk aversion. A less skilled ($IR = 0.5$) manager, however, offers portfolios $H_{.5}$ and $M_{.5}$, which do provide about the right level of residual risk for this investor.

EXHIBIT 6.8   Sacrifice in Return from Overestimating Investor Risk Aversion

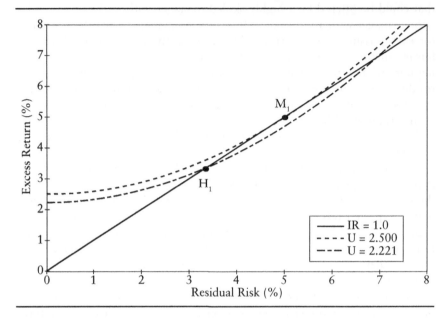

EXHIBIT 6.9   Sacrifice in Return from Using Less Skillful Manager

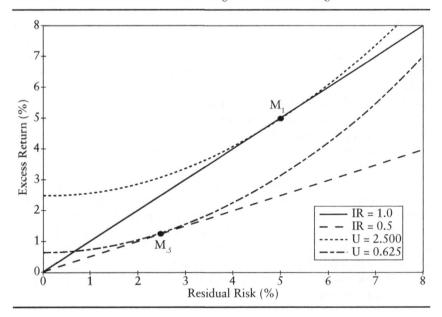

The investor might try to convince the $IR = 1$ manager to offer a lower-risk portfolio. If that fails, however, is the investor constrained to go with the less skilled manager? No. The investor can instead combine the highly skilled manager's H_1 portfolio with an investment in the passive benchmark portfolio P, reducing risk and return along the $IR = 1$ manager frontier. Such combination portfolios will offer a higher return than the portfolios of the less skilled manager, at a level of residual risk the investor can live with.

Finally, the manager's investment approach may affect the investor's optimal level of portfolio risk. Because engineered strategies control portfolio systematic and residual risk relative to the benchmark and take only compensated risks, they offer more assurance than traditional active strategies of achieving a return commensurate with the risk taken. Investors may feel more comfortable taking more risk with engineered portfolios, where risk and expected return are rigorously and explicitly assessed, than with traditional active portfolios.

THE ULTIMATE OBJECTIVE

The ultimate objective of investment management, of course, is to establish an investment structure that will, in the aggregate and over time, provide a return that compensates for the risk incurred, where the risk incurred is consistent with the investor's risk tolerance. The objective may be the equity market's return at the market's risk level or the market return plus incremental returns commensurate with incremental risks incurred.

This may be accomplished by focusing on the core universe and a passive representation or by mixing universes (core and static subsets, for example) and approaches (e.g., passive with traditional active or engineered). Whatever the selection universe and investment approach chosen, success is more likely when investors start off knowing their risk-tolerance levels and their potential managers' skill levels. The goal is to take no more risk than is compensated by expected return, but to take as much risk as risk-aversion level and manager skill allow.

Success is also more likely when *equity architecture* is taken into account. Without explicit ties between portfolios and the underlying market or market subsets (and thus between market subsets and the overall market), managers may be tempted to stray from their fold (core, value, or growth investing) in search of return. If value stocks are being punished, for example, an undisciplined value manager may be tempted to poach return from growth stock territory. An investor utilizing this manager cannot expect performance consistent with value stocks in general, nor can the investor combine this manager's "value" portfolio with a growth portfolio in the hopes of achieving an overall market return; the portfolio will instead be overweighted in growth stocks, and susceptible to the risk of growth stocks falling out of favor. The investor can mitigate the problem by balancing non-benchmark-constrained, traditional portfolios with engineered or passive portfolios that offer benchmark accountability.

When investors set goals in terms of return only, with no regard to equity architecture, similar problems can arise. Consider an investor who hires active managers and instructs them to make money, with no regard to market sector or investment approach. Manager holdings may overlap to an extent that the overall portfolio becomes overdiversified and individual manager efforts are diluted. The investor may end up paying active fees and active transaction costs for essentially passive results.

Equity architecture provides a basic blueprint for relating equity investment choices to their potential rewards and their risks. It can help investors construct portfolios that will meet their needs. First, however, the investor must determine what those needs are in terms of desire for return and tolerance for risk. Then the investor can choose managers whose investment approaches and market focuses offer, overall, the greatest assurance of fulfilling those needs.

We believe that engineered management can provide the best match between client risk-return goals and investment results. An engineered approach that combines range with depth of inquiry can increase both the number and goodness of investment insights. As a result, engineered management offers better control of risk exposure than traditional active management and incremental returns relative to passive management, whether the selection universe is core equity, static style subsets, or dynamic style subsets.

KEY POINTS

- The equity core and its constituent style subsets constitute the basic building blocks from which investors can construct their portfolios.
- Investors must also decide between possible investment approaches—traditional, passive, and engineered—each of which can be characterized by an underlying investment philosophy and a general level of risk.
- Investment performance reflects both breadth of inquiry, the sheer number of investment opportunities, and depth of analysis, the strength of investment insights.
- Traditional management offers depth, but strikes out with lack of breadth, susceptibility to cognitive errors, and lack of portfolio integrity.
- Passive management offers breadth, freedom from cognitive errors, and portfolio integrity, but no depth whatsoever.

- Engineered management has the ability to construct portfolios that benefit from both breadth and depth of analysis, are free of cognitive errors, and have structural integrity.
- Breadth can be expanded with the use of short selling, either in market-neutral long-short or 120-20/130-30 enhanced active strategies.
- The optimal level of residual risk for any investor will depend both on the investor's level of risk aversion and on the given manager's level of skill.
- An investor who takes less than the optimal level of residual risk or who selects less than the best manager will needlessly sacrifice return.

QUESTIONS

1. What is one advantage of viewing the market as an equity core comprised of various style subsets?

2. What are the advantages and disadvantages of a traditional active approach to investing?

3. What are the advantages and disadvantages of a passive approach?

4. What are the advantages and disadvantages of engineered approaches?

5. Name some ways in which an engineered approach can be expanded.

6. What factors might influence the optimal level of residual risk an investor should take?

CHAPTER 7

Equity Analysis in a Complex Market

Bruce I. Jacobs, Ph.D.
Principal
Jacobs Levy Equity Management

Kenneth N. Levy, CFA
Principal
Jacobs Levy Equity Management

S cientists classify systems into three types—ordered, random, and complex. Ordered systems, such as the structure of diamond crystals or the dynamics of pendulums, are definable and predictable by relatively simple rules and can be modeled using a relatively small number of variables. Random systems like the Brownian motion of gas molecules or white noise (static) are unordered; they are the product of a large number of variables. Their behavior cannot be modeled and is inherently unpredictable.

Complex systems like the weather and the workings of DNA fall somewhere between the domains of order and randomness. Their behavior can be at least partly comprehended and modeled, but only with great difficulty. The number of variables that must be modeled and their interactions are beyond the capacity of the human mind alone. Only with the aid of advanced computational science can the mysteries of complex systems be unraveled.[1]

The stock market is a complex system.[2] Stock prices are not completely random, as the efficient market hypothesis and random walk theory would have it. Some price movements can be predicted, and with some consistency. But stock price behavior is not ordered. It cannot be successfully modeled

---

[1]See Heinz R. Pagels, *The Dreams of Reason: The Computer and the Rise of the Sciences of Complexity* (New York: Simon & Schuster, 1988); and Stephen Wolfram, *A New Kind of Science* (Champaign, IL: Wolfram Media Inc., 2002).

[2]See Bruce I. Jacobs and Kenneth N. Levy, "The Complexity of the Stock Market," *Journal of Portfolio Management* 16, no. 1 (1989): 19–27.

by simple rules or screens such as low price–earnings ratios (P/Es) or even by elegant theories such as the capital asset pricing model or arbitrage pricing theory. Rather, stock price behavior is permeated by a complex web of interrelated return effects. A model of the market that is complex enough to disentangle these effects provides opportunities for modeling price behavior and predicting returns.

This chapter describes our approach to investing and its application to the stock selection, portfolio construction, and performance evaluation problems. We begin with the very basic question of how one should approach the equity market. Should one attempt to cover the broadest possible range of stocks, or can greater analytical insights be garnered by focusing on a particular subset of the market or a limited number of stocks? Each approach has its advantages and disadvantages. However, combining the two may offer the best promise of finding the key to unlocking investment opportunity in a complex market.

While covering the broadest possible range of stocks, a complex approach recognizes that there are significant differences in the ways different types of stocks respond to changes in both fundamentals and investor behavior. This requires taking into account the interrelationships between numerous potential sources of price behavior. Multivariate analysis disentangles the web of return-predictor relationships that constitutes a complex market and provides independent, additive return predictions that are more robust than the predictions from univariate analyses.

AN INTEGRATED APPROACH TO A SEGMENTED MARKET

While one might think that U.S. equity markets are fluid and fully integrated, in reality there are barriers to the free flow of capital. Some of these barriers are self-imposed by investors. Others are imposed by regulatory and tax authorities or by client guidelines.

Some funds, for example, are prohibited by regulation or internal policy guidelines from buying certain types of stock—nondividend-paying stock, or stock below a given capitalization level. Tax laws, too, may effectively lock investors into positions they would otherwise trade. Such barriers to the free flow of capital foster market segmentation.

Other barriers are self-imposed. Traditionally, for example, managers have focused (whether by design or default) on distinct approaches to stock selection. Value managers have concentrated on buying stocks selling at prices perceived to be low relative to the company's assets or earnings. Growth managers have sought stocks with above-average earnings growth not fully reflected in price. Small-capitalization managers have searched for opportunity in stocks that have been overlooked by most investors. The stocks that constitute the natural selection pools for these managers tend to group into distinct market segments.

Client preferences encourage this balkanization of the market. Some investors, for example, prefer to buy *value stocks*, while others seek *growth stocks;* some invest in both, but hire separate managers for each segment. Both institutional and individual investors generally demonstrate a reluctance to upset the apple cart by changing allocations to previously selected style managers. Several periods of underperformance, however, may undermine this loyalty and motivate a flow of capital from one segment of the market to another (often just as the out-of-favor segment begins to benefit from a reversion of returns back up to their historical mean).

The actions of investment consultants have formalized a market segmented into style groupings. Consultants design style indexes that define the constituent stocks of these segments and define managers in terms of their proclivity for one segment or another. As a manager's performance is measured against the given style index, managers who stray too far from index territory are taking on extra risk. Consequently, managers tend to stick close to their style homes, reinforcing market segmentation.

An investment approach that focuses on individual market segments can have its advantages. Such an approach recognizes, for example, that the U.S. equity market is neither entirely homogeneous nor entirely heterogeneous. All stocks do not react alike to a given impetus, but nor does each stock exhibit its own, totally idiosyncratic price behavior. Rather, stocks within a given style, or sector, or industry tend to behave similarly to each other and somewhat differently from stocks outside their group.

An approach to stock selection that specializes in one market segment can optimize the application of talent and maximize the potential for outperformance. This is most likely true for traditional, fundamental analysis. The in-depth, labor-intensive research undertaken by traditional analysts can become positively ungainly without some focusing lens.

An investment approach that focuses on the individual segments of the market, however, presents some theoretical and practical problems. Such an approach may be especially disadvantaged when it ignores the many forces that work to integrate, rather than segment, the market.

Many managers, for example, do not specialize in a particular market segment but are free to choose the most attractive securities from a broad universe of stocks. Others, such as style rotators, may focus on a particular type of stock, given current economic conditions, but be poised to change their focus should conditions change. Such managers make for capital flows and price arbitrage across the boundaries of particular segments.

Furthermore, all stocks can be defined by the same fundamental parameters—by market capitalization, P/E, dividend discount model ranking, and so on. All stocks can be found at some level on the continuum of values for each parameter. Thus, growth and value stocks inhabit the opposite ends of the continuums of P/E and dividend yield, and small and large stocks the opposite ends of the continuums of firm capitalization and analyst coverage.

As the values of the parameters for any individual stock change, so too does the stock's position on the continuum. An out-of-favor growth stock may slip into value territory. A small-cap company may grow into the large-cap range.

Finally, while the values of these parameters vary across stocks belonging to different market segments—different styles, sectors, and industries—and while investors may favor certain values—low P/E, say, in preference to high P/E—arbitrage tends to counterbalance too pronounced a predilection on the part of investors for any one set of values. In equilibrium, all stocks must be owned. If too many investors want low P/E, low-P/E stocks will be bid up to higher P/E levels, and some investors will step in to sell them and buy other stocks deserving of higher P/Es. Arbitrage works toward market integration and a single pricing mechanism.

A market that is neither completely segmented nor completely integrated is a complex market. A complex market calls for an investment approach that is 180 degrees removed from the narrow, segment-oriented focus of traditional management. It requires a *complex, unified approach* that takes into account the behavior of stocks across the broadest possible selection universe, without losing sight of the significant differences in price behavior that distinguish particular market segments.

Such an approach offers three major advantages. First, it provides a coherent evaluation framework. Second, it can benefit from all the insights to be garnered from a wide and diverse range of securities. Third, because it has both breadth of coverage and depth of analysis, it is poised to take advantage of more profit opportunities than a more narrowly defined, segmented approach proffers.

A Coherent Framework

To the extent that the market is integrated, an investment approach that models each industry or style segment as if it were a universe unto itself is not the best approach. Consider, for example, a firm that offers both core and value strategies. Suppose the firm runs a model on its total universe of, say, 3,000 stocks. It then runs the same model or a different, segment-specific model on a 500-stock subset of large-cap value stocks.

If different models are used for each strategy, the results will differ. Even if the same model is estimated separately for each strategy, its results will differ because the model coefficients are bound to differ between the broader universe and the narrower segment. What if the core model predicts GM will outperform Ford, while the value model shows the reverse? Should the investor start the day with multiple estimates of one stock's alpha? This would violate what we call the *law of one alpha*.[3]

Of course, the firm could ensure coherence by using separate models for each market segment—growth, value, small-cap, linking the results via a single, overarching model that relates all the subsets. But the firm then runs into a second problem with segmented investment approaches: To the extent that the market is integrated, the pricing of securities in one segment may contain information relevant to pricing in other segments.

For example, within a generally well-integrated national economy, labor market conditions in the United States differ region by region. An economist attempting to model employment in the Northeast would probably consider economic expansion in the Southeast. Similarly, the investor who wants to model growth stocks should not ignore value stocks. The effects of inflation, say, on value stocks may have repercussions for growth stocks; after all, the two segments represent opposite ends of the same P/E continuum.

An investment approach that concentrates on a single market segment does not make use of all available information. A complex, unified approach considers all the stocks in the universe, value and growth, large and small. It thus benefits from all the information to be gleaned from a broad range of stock price behavior.

Of course, an increase in breadth of inquiry will not benefit the investor if it comes at the sacrifice of depth of inquiry. A complex approach does not ignore the significant differences across different types of stock, differences exploitable by specialized investing. What's more, in examining similarities and differences across market segments, it considers numerous variables that may be considered to be defining.

For value, say, a complex approach does not confine itself to a dividend discount model measure of value, but examines also earnings, cash flow, sales, and yield value, among other attributes. Growth measurements to be considered include historical, expected, and sustainable growth, as well as the momentum and stability of earnings. Share price, volatility, and analyst coverage are among the elements to be considered along with market capitalization as measures of size.

At a deeper level of analysis, one must also consider alternative ways of specifying such fundamental variables as earnings or cash flow. Over what

---

[3]See Bruce I. Jacobs and Kenneth N. Levy, "The Law of One Alpha," *Journal of Portfolio Management* 21, no. 4 (1995): 78–79.

period does one measure earnings? If using analyst earnings expectations, which measure provides the best estimate of future real earnings? The consensus of all available estimates made over the past six months, or only the very latest earnings estimates? Are some analysts more accurate or more influential? What if a recent estimate is not available for a given company?[4]

Predictor variables are often closely correlated with each other. *Small-cap stocks,* for example, tend to have low P/Es; low P/E is correlated with high yield; both low P/E and high yield are correlated with dividend discount model (DDM) estimates of value. Furthermore, they may be correlated with a stock's industry affiliation. A simple low-P/E screen, for example, will tend to select a large number of bank and utility stocks. Such correlations can distort naive attempts to relate returns to potentially relevant predictors. A true picture of the return-predictor relationship emerges only after *disentangling* the predictors.

DISENTANGLING

The effects of different sources of stock return can overlap. In Exhibit 7.1, the lines represent connections documented by academic studies; they may appear like a ball of yarn after the cat got to it. To unravel the connections between predictor variables and return, it is necessary to examine all the variables simultaneously.

For instance, the low P/E effect is widely recognized, as is the small-size effect. But stocks with low P/Es also tend to be of small size. Are P/E and size merely two ways of looking at the same effect? Or does each variable matter? Perhaps the excess returns to small-cap stocks are merely a January effect, reflecting the tendency of taxable investors to sell depressed stocks at year-end. Answering these questions requires disentangling return effects via multivariate regression.[5]

Common methods of measuring return effects (such as quintiling or univariate, single-variable, regression) are naive because they assume, naively, that prices are responding only to the single variable under consideration, low P/E, say. But a number of related variables may be affecting returns. As we have noted, small-cap stocks and banking and utility industry stocks tend to have low P/Es. A univariate regression of return on low P/E will capture,

[4]See Bruce I. Jacobs, Kenneth N. Levy, and Mitchell C. Krask, "Earnings Estimates, Predictor Specification, and Measurement Error," *Journal of Investing* 6, no. 2 (1997): 29–46.
[5]See Bruce I. Jacobs and Kenneth N. Levy, "Disentangling Equity Return Regularities: New Insights and Investment Opportunities," *Financial Analysts Journal* 44, no. 3 (1988): 18–44.

EXHIBIT 7.1   Return Effects Form a Tangled Web

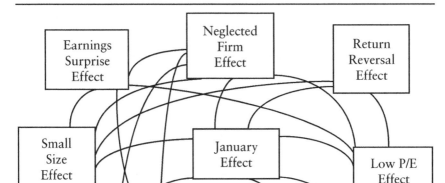

along with the effect of P/E, a great deal of noise related to firm size, industry affiliation, and other variables.

Simultaneous analysis of all relevant variables via multivariate regression takes into account and adjusts for such interrelationships. The result is the return to each variable separately, controlling for all related variables. A multivariate analysis for low P/E, for example, will provide a measure of the excess return to a portfolio that is market-like in all respects except for having a lower-than-average P/E ratio. Disentangled returns are *pure returns*.

Noise Reduction

Exhibit 7.2 plots naive and pure cumulative monthly excess (relative to a 3,000-stock universe) returns to high book–price ratio (B/P). (Conceptually, naive and pure returns come from a portfolio having a B/P that is one standard deviation above the universe mean B/P; for the pure returns, the portfolio is also constrained to have universe-average exposures to all the other variables in the model, including fundamental characteristics and industry affiliations.) The *naive returns* show a great deal of volatility; the pure returns,

EXHIBIT 7.2   Naive and Pure Returns to High Book-to-Price Ratio

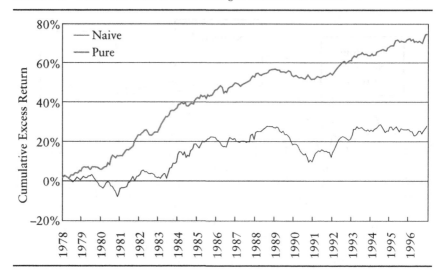

by contrast, follow a much smoother path. There is a lot of noise in the naive returns. What causes it?

Notice the divergence between the naive and pure return series for the 12 months starting in March 1979. This date coincides with the crisis at Three Mile Island nuclear power plant. Utilities such as GPU, operator of the Three Mile Island power plant, tend to have high B/Ps, and naive B/P measures will reflect the performance of these utilities along with the performance of other high-B/P stocks. Electric utility prices plummeted 24% after the Three Mile Island crisis. The naive B/P measure reflects this decline.

But industry-related events such as Three Mile Island have no necessary bearing on the B/P variable. An investor could, for example, hold a high-B/P portfolio that does not overweight utilities, and such a portfolio would not have experienced the decline reflected in the naive B/P measure in Exhibit 7.2. The naive returns to B/P reflect noise from the inclusion of a utility industry effect. A pure B/P measure is not contaminated by such irrelevant variables.

Disentangling distinguishes real effects from mere proxies and thereby distinguishes between real and spurious investment opportunities. As it separates high B/P and industry affiliation, for example, it can also separate the effects of firm size from the effects of related variables. Disentangling shows that returns to small firms in January are not abnormal; the apparent January seasonal merely proxies for year-end tax-loss selling.[6] Not all small firms will benefit from a January rebound; indiscriminately buying small firms at the turn of the year is not an optimal investment strategy. Ascertaining true causation leads to more profitable strategies.

Return Revelation

Disentangling can reveal hidden opportunities. Exhibit 7.3 plots the naively measured cumulative monthly excess returns (relative to the 3,000-stock universe) to portfolios that rank lower than average in market capitalization and price per share and higher than average in terms of analyst neglect. These results derive from monthly univariate regressions. The small-cap line thus represents the cumulative excess returns to a portfolio of stocks naively chosen on the basis of their size, with no attempt made to control for other variables.

All three return series move together. The similarity between the small-cap and neglect series is particularly striking. This is confirmed by the correlation coefficients in the first column of Exhibit 7.4. Furthermore, all series show a great deal of volatility within a broader up, down, up pattern.

EXHIBIT 7.3 Naive Returns Can Hide Opportunities: Three Size-Related Variables

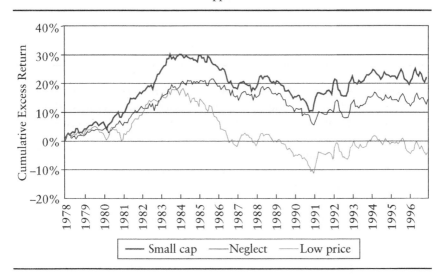

[6]See Bruce I. Jacobs and Kenneth N. Levy, "Calendar Anomalies: Abnormal Returns at Calendar Turning Points," *Financial Analysts Journal* 44, no. 6 (1988): 28–39.

EXHIBIT 7.4 Correlations Between Monthly Returns to Size-Related Variables[a]

Variable	Naive	Pure
Small cap/low price	0.82	–0.12
Small cap/neglect	0.87	–0.22
Neglect/low price	0.66	–0.11

[a]A coefficient of 0.14 is significant at the 5% level.

EXHIBIT 7.5 Pure Returns Can Reveal Opportunities: Three Size-Related Variables

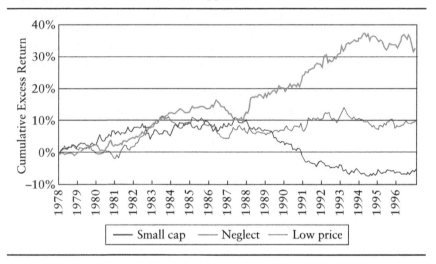

Exhibit 7.5 shows the pure cumulative monthly excess returns to each size-related attribute over the period. These disentangled returns adjust for correlations not only between the three size variables, but also between each size variable and industry affiliations and each variable and growth and value characteristics. Two findings are immediately apparent from Exhibit 7.5.

First, pure returns to the size variables do not appear to be nearly as closely correlated as the naive returns displayed in Exhibit 7.3. In fact, over the second half of the period, the three return series diverge substantially. This is confirmed by the correlation coefficients in the second column of Exhibit 7.4.

In particular, pure returns to small capitalization accumulate quite a gain over the period; they are up 30%, versus an only 20% gain for the naive returns to small cap. Purifying returns reveals a profit opportunity not apparent in the naive returns. Furthermore, pure returns to analyst neglect amount to a substantial loss over the period. Because disentangling controls

EXHIBIT 7.6　Pure Returns Are Less Volatile, More Predictable:
Standard Deviations of Monthly Returns to Size-Related Variables[a]

Variable	Naive	Pure
Small cap	0.87	0.60
Neglect	0.87	0.67
Low price	1.03	0.58

[a]All differences between naive and pure return standard deviations are significant at the 1% level.

for proxy effects, and thereby avoids redundancies, these pure return effects are additive. A portfolio could have aimed for superior returns by selecting small-cap stocks with a higher-than-average analyst following (that is, a negative exposure to analyst neglect).

Second, the pure returns appear to be much less volatile than the naive returns. The naive returns in Exhibit 7.3 display much month-to-month volatility within their more general trends. By contrast, the pure series in Exhibit 7.5 are much smoother and more consistent. This is confirmed by the standard deviations given in Exhibit 7.6.

The pure returns in Exhibit 7.5 are smoother and more consistent than the naive return responses in Exhibit 7.3 because the pure returns capture more signal and less noise. And because they are smoother and more consistent than naive returns, pure returns are also more predictive.

Predictive Power

Disentangling improves the predictive power of estimated returns by providing a clearer picture of the relationships between investor behavior, fundamental variables, and macroeconomic conditions. For example, investors often prefer value stocks in bearish market environments, because growth stocks are priced more on the basis of high expectations, which get dashed in more pessimistic eras. But the success of such a strategy will depend on the variables one has chosen to define value.

Exhibit 7.7 displays the results of regressing both naive and pure monthly returns to various value-related variables on market (S&P 500) returns over the 1978–1996 period. The results indicate that DDM value is a poor indicator of a stock's ability to withstand a tide of receding market prices. The regression coefficient in the first column indicates that a portfolio with a one-standard-deviation exposure to DDM value will tend to outperform by 0.06% when the market rises by 1.00% and to underperform by a similar margin when the market falls by 1.00%. The coefficient for

EXHIBIT 7.7 Market Sensitivities of Monthly Returns to Value-Related Variables

Variable	Naive	(t-stat.)	Pure	(t-stat.)
DDM	0.06	(5.4)	0.04	(5.6)
B/P	−0.10	(−6.2)	−0.01	(−0.8)
Yield	−0.08	(−7.4)	−0.03	(−3.5)

pure returns to DDM is similar. Whether their returns are measured in pure or naive form, stocks with high DDM values tend to behave procyclically.

High B/P appears to be a better indicator of a defensive stock. It has a regression coefficient of −0.10 in naive form. In pure form, however, B/P is virtually uncorrelated with market movements; pure B/P signals neither an aggressive nor a defensive stock. B/P as naively measured apparently picks up the effects of truly defensive variables, such as high yield.

The value investor in search of a defensive posture in uncertain market climates should consider moving toward high yield. The regression coefficients for both naive and pure returns to high yield indicate significant negative market sensitivities. Stocks with high yields may be expected to lag in up markets but to hold up relatively well during general market declines.

These results make broad intuitive sense. DDM is forward-looking, relying on estimates of future earnings. In bull markets, investors take a long-term outlook, so DDM explains security pricing behavior. In bear markets, however, investors become myopic; they prefer today's tangible income to tomorrow's promise. Current yield is rewarded.

Pure returns respond in intuitively satisfying ways to macroeconomic events. Exhibit 7.8 illustrates, as an example, the estimated effects of changes in various macroeconomic variables on the pure returns to small size (as measured by market capitalization). Consistent with the capital constraints on small firms and their relatively greater sensitivity to the economy, pure returns to small size may be expected to be negative in the first four months following an unexpected increase in the Baa corporate rate and positive in the first month following an unexpected increase in industrial production.[7] Investors can exploit such predictable behavior by moving into and out of the small-cap market segment as economic conditions evolve.[8]

These examples serve to illustrate that the use of numerous, finely defined fundamental variables can provide a rich representation of the complexity of security pricing. The model can be even more finely tuned, however, by including variables that capture such subtleties as the effects of

---

[7]See Bruce I. Jacobs and Kenneth N. Levy, "Forecasting the Size Effect," *Financial Analysts Journal* 45, no. 3 (1989): 38–54.
[8]See Bruce I. Jacobs and Kenneth N. Levy, "High-Definition Style Rotation," *Journal of Investing* 6, no. 1 (1996): 14–23.

EXHIBIT 7.8   Forecast Response of Small Size to Macroeconomic Shocks

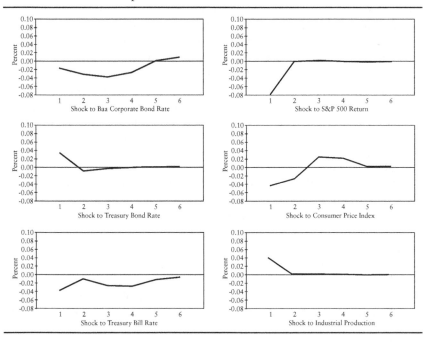

investor psychology, possible nonlinearities in variable-return relationships, and security transaction costs.

Additional Complexities

In considering possible variables for inclusion in a model of stock price behavior, the investor should recognize that pure stock returns are driven by a combination of economic fundamentals and investor psychology. That is, economic fundamentals such as interest rates, industrial production, and inflation can explain much, but by no means all, of the systematic variation in returns. Psychology, including investors' tendency to overreact, their desire to seek safety in numbers, and their selective memories, also plays a role in security pricing.

What's more, the modeler should realize that the effects of different variables, fundamental and otherwise, can differ across different types of stocks. The value sector, for example, includes more financial stocks than the growth sector. Investors may thus expect value stocks in general to be more sensitive than growth stocks to changes in interest rate spreads.

Psychologically based variables such as short-term overreaction and price correction also seem to have a stronger effect on value than on growth stocks. Earnings surprises and earnings estimate revisions, by contrast, appear to be more important for growth than for value stocks. Thus, Google shares can take a nosedive when earnings come in a penny under expectations, whereas Duke Energy shares remain unmoved even by fairly substantial departures of actual earnings from expectations.

The relationship between stock returns and relevant variables may not be linear. The effects of positive earnings surprises, for instance, tend to be arbitraged away quickly; thus positive earnings surprises offer less opportunity for the investor. The effects of negative earnings surprises, however, appear to be more long-lasting. This nonlinearity may reflect the fact that sales of stock are limited to those investors who already own the stock (and to a relatively small number of short sellers).[9]

Risk-variable relationships may also differ across different types of stock. In particular, small-cap stocks generally have more idiosyncratic risk than large-cap stocks. Diversification is thus more important for small-stock than for large-stock portfolios.

Return-variable relationships can also change over time. Recall the difference between DDM and yield value measures: high-DDM stocks tend to have high returns in bull markets and low returns in bear markets; high-yield stocks experience the reverse. For consistency of performance, return modeling must consider the effects of market dynamics, the changing nature of the overall market.

The investor may also want to decipher the informational signals generated by informed agents. Corporate decisions to issue or buy back shares, split stock, or initiate or suspend dividends, for example, may contain valuable information about company prospects. So, too, may insiders' (legal) trading in their own firms' shares.

Finally, a complex model containing multiple variables is likely to turn up a number of promising return-variable relationships. But are these perceived profit opportunities translatable into real economic opportunities? Are some too ephemeral? Too small to survive frictions such as trading costs? Estimates of expected returns must be combined with estimates of the costs of trading to arrive at realistic returns net of trading costs.

CONSTRUCTING, TRADING, AND EVALUATING PORTFOLIOS

To maximize implementation of the model's insights, the portfolio construction process should consider exactly the same dimensions found relevant by

---

[9]See Bruce I. Jacobs and Kenneth N. Levy, "Long/Short Equity Investing," *Journal of Portfolio Management* 20, no. 1 (1993): 52–63.

the stock selection model. Failure to do so can lead to mismatches between model insights and portfolio exposures.

Consider a commercially available portfolio optimizer that recognizes only a subset of the variables in the valuation model. Risk reduction using such an optimizer will reduce the portfolio's exposures only along the dimensions the optimizer recognizes. As a result, the portfolio is likely to wind up more exposed to those variables recognized by the model, but not the optimizer, and less exposed to those variables common to both the model and the optimizer.

Imagine an investor who seeks low-P/E stocks that analysts are recommending for purchase, but who uses a commercial optimizer that incorporates a P/E factor but not analyst recommendations. The investor is likely to wind up with a portfolio that has a less-than-optimal level of exposure to low P/E and a greater-than-optimal level of exposure to analyst purchase recommendations. *Optimization* using all relevant variables ensures a portfolio whose risk and return opportunities are balanced in accordance with the model's insights. Furthermore, the use of more numerous variables allows portfolio risk to be more finely tuned.

Insofar as the investment process, both stock selection and portfolio construction, is model-driven, it is more adaptable to electronic trading venues. This should benefit the investor in several ways. First, electronic trading is generally less costly, with lower commissions, market impact, and opportunity costs. Second, it allows real-time monitoring, which can further reduce trading costs. Third, an automated trading system can take account of more factors, including the urgency of a particular trade and market conditions, than individual traders can be expected to bear in mind.

Finally, the *performance attribution* process should be congruent with the dimensions of the selection model (and portfolio optimizer). Insofar as performance attribution identifies sources of return, a process that considers all the sources identified by the selection model will be more insightful than a commercial performance attribution system applied in a one-size-fits-all manner. Our investor who has sought exposure to low P/E and positive analyst recommendations, for example, will want to know how each of these factors has paid off and will be less interested in the returns to factors that are not a part of the stock selection process.

A performance evaluation process tailored to the model also functions as a monitor of the model's reliability. Has portfolio performance supported the model's insights? Should some be reexamined? Equally important, does the model's reliability hold up over time? A model that performs well in today's economic and market environments may not necessarily perform well in the future. A feedback loop between the evaluation and the research or modeling processes can help ensure that the model retains robustness over time.

PROFITING FROM COMPLEXITY

H. L. Mencken is supposed to have noted, "For every complex problem, there is a simple solution, and it is almost always wrong." Complex problems more often than not require complex solutions.

A complex approach to stock selection, portfolio construction, and performance evaluation is needed to capture the complexities of the stock market. Such an approach combines the breadth of coverage and the depth of analysis needed to maximize investment opportunity and potential reward.

Grinold presents a formula that identifies the relationships between the depth and breadth of investment insights and investment performance:[10]

$$IR = IC\sqrt{BR}$$

IR is the manager's information ratio, a measure of the success of the investment process. *IR* equals annualized excess return over annualized residual risk (e.g., 2% excess return with 4% tracking error provides 0.5 *IR*). *IC*, the information coefficient, or correlation between predicted and actual security returns, measures the goodness of the manager's insights, or the manager's skill. *BR* is the breadth of the strategy, measurable as the number of independent insights upon which investment decisions are made.

One can increase *IR* by increasing *IC* or *BR*. Increasing IC means coming up with some means of improving predictive accuracy. Increasing *BR* means coming up with more "investable" insights. A casino analogy may be apt even if it is anathema to prudent investors.

A gambler can seek to increase *IC* by card counting in blackjack or by building a computer model to predict probable roulette outcomes. Similarly, some investors seek to outperform by concentrating their research efforts on a few stocks: by learning all there is to know about Microsoft, for example, one may be able to outperform all the other investors who follow this stock. But a strategy that makes a few concentrated stock bets is likely to produce consistent performance only if it is based on a very high level of skill, or if it benefits from extraordinary luck.

Alternatively, an investor can place a larger number of smaller stock bets and settle for more modest returns from a greater number of investment decisions. That is, rather than behaving like a gambler in a casino, the investor can behave like the casino. A casino has only a slight edge on any spin of the roulette wheel or roll of the dice, but many spins of many roulette wheels can result in a very consistent profit for the house. Over time, the odds will strongly favor the casino over the gambler.

[10]See Richard C. Grinold, "The Fundamental Law of Active Management," *Journal of Portfolio Management* 15, no. 3 (1989): 30–37.

A complex approach to the equity market, one that has both breadth of inquiry and depth of focus, can enhance the number and the goodness of investment insights. A complex approach to the equity market requires more time, effort, and ability, but it will be better positioned to capture the complexities of security pricing. The rewards are worth the effort.

KEY POINTS

- Ordered systems are definable and predictable by relatively simple rules; random systems cannot be modeled and are inherently unpredictable; complex systems can be at least partly comprehended and modeled, but only with difficulty.
- Stock price behavior is permeated by a complex web of interrelated return effects, and it requires a complex approach to stock selection, portfolio construction, and performance evaluation to capture this complexity.
- A complex approach combines the breadth of coverage and the depth of analysis needed to maximize investment opportunity and potential reward.
- Simple methods of measuring return effects (such as quintiling or univariate, single-variable regression) are naive because they assume that prices are responding only to the single variable under consideration.
- Simultaneous analysis of all relevant variables via multivariate regression takes into account and adjusts for interrelationships between effects, giving the return to each variable separately.
- Disentangling distinguishes real effects from mere proxies and thereby distinguishes between real and spurious investment opportunities.
- Because disentangling controls for proxy effects, pure return effects are additive, each having the potential to improve portfolio performance.
- In general, disentangling enhances the predictive power of estimated returns by providing a clearer picture of the relationships between investor behavior, fundamental variables, and macroeconomic conditions.
- To maximize implementation of insights gained from disentangling the market's complexity, the portfolio construction process should consider exactly the same dimensions found relevant by the stock selection process.
- Performance attribution should be congruent with the stock selection and portfolio construction processes so that it can be used to monitor the reliability of the stock selection process and provide input for research.

QUESTIONS

1. In what ways is the stock market a complex system?

2. Is the stock market segmented or integrated?

3. What advantages does a complex, unified approach offer?

4. a. What is "disentangling"?
   b. What advantages does disentangling offer over simpler, univariate analysis of return-related variables?
   c. Give an example of disentangling at work.

5. Why is it important to have portfolio construction and performance measurement processes that are congruent with the stock selection process?

6. How do the breadth of coverage and depth of analysis provided by a complex, unified approach improve the likelihood of successful investment results?

CHAPTER 8

Survey Studies of the Use of Quantitative Equity Management

Frank J. Fabozzi, Ph.D., CFA, CPA
Professor of Finance
EDHEC Business School

Sergio M. Focardi, Ph.D.
Professor of Finance
EDHEC Business School
and
Partner, The Intertek Group

Caroline L. Jonas
Partner
The Intertek Group

In the other chapters of this book, the motivation for quantitative equity investing and actual quantitative equity models are covered. In this chapter, we discuss three studies on the use of quantitative equity management conducted by The Intertek Group. The studies are based on surveys and interviews of market participants.[1] We conclude the chapter with a discussion of the challenges ahead.

2003 INTERTEK EUROPEAN STUDY

The 2003 Intertek European study deals with the use of financial modeling at European asset management firms.[2] It is based on studies conducted by

---

[1]In the quotes from sources in these studies, we omit the usual practice of identifying the reference and page number. The study where the quote is obtained will be clear.
[2]The results of this study are reported in Frank J. Fabozzi, Sergio M. Focardi, and Caroline L. Jonas, "Trends in Quantitative Asset Management in Europe," *Journal of Portfolio Management* 31, no. 4 (2004): 125–132 (Special European Section).

The Intertek Group to evaluate model performance following the fall of the markets from their peak in March 2000, and explores changes that have occurred since then. In total, 61 managers at European asset management firms in the Benelux countries, France, Germany, Italy, Scandinavia, Switzerland, and the United Kingdom were interviewed. (The study does not cover alternative investment firms such as hedge funds.) At least half of the firms interviewed are among the major players in their respective markets, with assets under management ranging from €50 to €300 billion.

The major findings are summarized next.

Greater Role for Models

In the two years following the March 2000 market highs, quantitative methods in the investment decision-making process began to play a greater role. Almost 75% of the firms interviewed reported this to be the case, while roughly 15% reported that the role of models had remained stable. The remaining 10% noted that their processes were already essentially quantitative. The role of models had also grown in another sense; a higher percentage of assets were being managed by funds run quantitatively. One firm reported that over the past two years assets in funds managed quantitatively grew by 50%.

Large European firms had been steadily catching up with their U.S. counterparts in terms of the breadth and depth of use of models. As the price of computers and computer software dropped, even small firms reported that they were beginning to adopt quantitative models. There were still differences between American and European firms, though. American firms tended to use relatively simple technology but on a large scale; Europeans tended to adopt sophisticated statistical methods but on a smaller scale.

Demand pull and management push were among the reasons cited for the growing role of models. On the demand side, asset managers were under pressure to produce returns while controlling risk; they were beginning to explore the potential of quantitative methods. On the push side, several sources remarked that, after tracking performance for several years, their management has made a positive evaluation of a model-driven approach against a judgment-driven decision-making process. In some cases, this led to a corporate switch to a quantitative decision-making process; in other instances, it led to shifting more assets into quantitatively managed funds.

Modeling was reported to have been extended over an ever greater universe of assets under management. Besides bringing greater structure and discipline to the process, participants in the study remarked that models helped contain costs. Unable to increase revenues in the period immediately following the March 2000 market decline, many firms were cutting costs.

Modeling budgets, however, were reported as being largely spared. About 68% of the participants said that their investment in modeling had grown over the prior two years, while 50% expected their investments in modeling to continue to grow over the next year.

Client demand for risk control was another factor that drove the increased use of modeling. Pressure from institutional investors and consultants in particular continued to work in favor of modeling.

More generally, risk management was widely believed to be the key driving force behind the use of models.

Some firms mentioned they had recast the role of models in portfolio management. Rather than using models to screen and rank assets—which has been a typical application in Europe—they applied them after the asset manager had acted in order to measure the pertinence of fundamental analysis, characterize the portfolio style, eventually transform products through derivatives, optimize the portfolio, and track risk and performance.

Performance of Models Improves

Over one-half of the study's participants responded that models performed better in 2002 than two years before. Some 20% evaluated 2002 model performance as stable with respect to two years ago, while another 20% considered that performance had worsened. Participants often noted that it was not models in general but specific models that had performed better or more poorly.

There are several explanations for the improved performance of models. Every model is, ultimately, a statistical device trained and estimated on past data. When markets began to fall from their peak in March 2000, models had not been trained on data that would have allowed them to capture the downturn—hence, the temporary poor performance of some models. Even risk estimates, more stable than expected return estimates, were problematic. In many cases, it was difficult to distinguish between volatility and model risk. Models have since been trained on new sets of data and are reportedly performing better.

From a strictly scientific and economic theory point of view, the question of model performance overall is not easy to address. The basic question is how well a theory describes reality, with the additional complication that in economics uncertainty is part of the theory. We cannot object to financial modeling but we cannot pretend a priori that model performance be good. Modeling should reflect the objective amount of uncertainty present in a financial process. The statement that "models perform better" implies that the level of uncertainty has changed. To make this discussion meaningful, clearly somehow we have to restrict the universe of models under consideration.

In general, the uncertainty associated with forecasting within a given class of models is equated to market volatility. And as market volatility is not an observable quantity but a hidden one, it is model-dependent.[3] In other words, the amount of uncertainty in financial markets depends on the accuracy of models. For instance, an ARCH-GARCH model will give an estimate of volatility different from that of a model based on constant volatility. On top of volatility, however, there is another source of uncertainty, which is the risk that the model is misspecified. The latter uncertainty is generally referred to as *model risk*.

The problem experienced when markets began to fall was that models could not forecast volatility simply because they were grossly misspecified. A common belief is that markets are now highly volatile, which is another way of saying that models do not do a good job of predicting returns. Yet models are now more coherent; fluctuations of returns are synchronized with expectations regarding volatility. Model risk has been reduced substantially.

Overall, the global perception of European market participants who participated in the study was that models are now more dependable. This meant that model risk had been reduced; although their ability to predict returns had not substantially improved, models were better at predicting risk. Practitioners' evaluation of model performance can be summarized as follows: (1) models will bring more and more insight to risk management; (2) in stock selection, we will see some improvement due essentially to better data, not better models; and (3) in asset allocation, the use of models will remain difficult as markets remain difficult to predict.

Despite the improved performance of models, the perception European market participants shared was one of uncertainty as regards the macroeconomic trends of the markets. Volatility, structural change, and unforecastable events continue to challenge models. In addition to facing uncertainty related to a stream of unpleasant surprises as regards corporate accounting at large public firms, participants voiced the concern that there is considerable fundamental uncertainty on the direction of financial flows.

A widely shared evaluation was that, independent of models themselves, the understanding of models and their limits had improved. Most traders and portfolio managers had at least some training in statistics and finance theory; computer literacy was greatly increased. As a consequence, the majority of market participants understand at least elementary statistical analyses of markets.

---

[3]This statement is not strictly true. With the availability of high-frequency data, there is a new strain of financial econometrics that considers volatility as an observable realized volatility.

Use of Multiple Models on the Rise

According to the 2003 study's findings, three major trends had emerged in Europe over the prior few years: (1) a greater use of multiple models, (2) the modeling of additional new factors, and (3) an increased use of value-based models.

Let's first comment on the use of multiple models from the point of view of modern financial econometrics and, in particular, from the point of view of the mitigation of model risk. The present landscape of financial modeling applied to investment management is vast and well articulated.[4] Financial models are typically econometric models, they do not follow laws of nature but are approximate models with limited validity. Every model has an associated model risk, which can be roughly defined as the probability that the model does not forecast correctly. Note that it does not make sense to consider model risk in abstract terms and against every possible assumption; model risk can be meaningfully defined only by restricting the set of alternative assumptions. For instance, we might compute measures of the errors made by an option pricing model if the underlying follows a distribution different from the one on which the model is based. Clearly, what must be specified are the families of alternative distributions.

Essentially every model is based on some assumption about the functional form of dependencies between variables and on the distribution of noise. Given the assumptions, models are estimated, and decisions made. The idea of estimating model risk is to estimate the distribution of errors that will be made if the model assumptions are violated. For instance, are there correlations or autocorrelations when it is assumed there are none? Are innovations fat-tailed when it is assumed that noise is white and normal? From an econometric point of view, combining different models in this way means constructing a mixture of distributions. The result of this process is one single model that weights the individual models.

Some managers interviewed for the 2003 study reported they were using judgment on top of statistical analysis. This entails that models be reviewed when they begin to produce results that are below expectations. In practice, quantitative teams constantly evaluate the performance of different families of models and adopt those that perform better. Criteria for switching from one family of models to another are called for, though. This, in turn, requires large data samples.

Despite these difficulties, application of multiple models has gained wide acceptance in finance. In asset management, the main driver is the uncertainty related to estimating returns.

---

[4]For a discussion of the different families of financial models and modeling issues, see Sergio M. Focardi and Frank J. Fabozzi, *The Mathematics of Financial Modeling and Investment Management* (Hoboken, NJ: John Wiley & Sons, 2004).

Focus on Factors, Correlation, Sentiment, and Momentum

Participants in the 2003 study also reported efforts to determine new factors that might help predict expected returns. Momentum and sentiment were the two most cited phenomena modeled in equities. Market sentiment, in particular, was receiving more attention.

The use of factor models is in itself a well-established practice in financial modeling. Many different families of models are available, from the widely used classic static return factor analysis models to dynamic factor models. What remains a challenge is determination of the factors. Considerable resources have been devoted to studying market correlations. Advanced techniques for the robust estimation of correlations are being applied at large firms as well as at boutiques.

According to study respondents, over the three years prior to 2001, quantitative teams at many asset management firms were working on determining which factors are the best indicators of price movements. Sentiment was often cited as a major innovation in terms of modeling strategies. Asset management firms typically modeled stock-specific sentiment, while sentiment as measured by business or consumer confidence was often the responsibility of the macroeconomic teams at the mother bank, at least in continental Europe. Market sentiment is generally defined by the distribution of analyst revisions in earnings estimates. Other indicators of market confidence are flows, volume, turnover, and trading by corporate officers.

Factors that represent market momentum were also increasingly adopted according to the study. *Momentum* means that the entire market is moving in one direction with relatively little uncertainty. There are different ways to represent momentum phenomena. One might identify a specific factor that defines momentum, that is, a variable that gauges the state of the market in terms of momentum. This momentum variable then changes the form of models. There are models for trending markets and models for uncertain markets.

Momentum can also be represented as a specific feature of models. A random walk model does not have any momentum, but an autoregressive model might have an intrinsic momentum feature.

Some participants also reported using market-timing models and style rotation for the active management of funds. Producing accurate timing signals is complex, given that financial markets are difficult to predict. One source of predictability is the presence of mean reversion and cointegration phenomena.

Back to Value-Based Models

At the time of the 2003 study, there was a widespread perception that value-based models were performing better in post-2000 markets. It was believed that markets were doing a better job valuing companies as a function of the value of the firm rather than price trends, notwithstanding our remarks on the growing use of factors such as market sentiment. From a methodological point of view, methodologies based on cash analysis had increased in popularity in Europe. A robust positive operating cash flow is considered to be a better indication of the health of a firm than earnings estimates, which can be more easily massaged.

Fundamental analysis was becoming highly quantitative and automated. Several firms mentioned that they were developing proprietary methodologies for the automatic analysis of balance sheets. For these firms, with the information available on the Internet, fundamental analysis could be performed without actually going to visit firms. Some participants remarked that caution might be called for in attributing the good performance of value-tilted models to markets. One of the assumptions of value-based models is that there is no mechanism that conveys a large flow of funds through preferred channels, but this was the case in the telecommunications, media, and technology (TMT) bubble, when value-based models performed so poorly. In the last bull run prior to the study, the major preoccupation was to not miss out on rising markets; investors who continued to focus on value suffered poor performance. European market participants reported that they are now watching both trend and value.

Risk Management

Much of the attention paid to quantitative methods in asset management prior to the study had been focused on risk management. According to 83% of the participants, the role of risk management had evolved significantly over the prior two years to extend across portfolios and across processes.

One topic that has received a lot of attention, both in academia and at financial institutions, is the application of *extreme value theory* (EVT) to financial risk management. The RiskLab in Zurich, headed by Paul Embrechts, advanced the use of EVT and copula functions in risk management. At the corporate level, universal banks such as HSBC CCF have produced theoretical and empirical work on the applicability of EVT to risk management.[5] European firms were also paying considerable attention to risk measures.

For participants in the Intertek study, risk management was the area where quantitative methods had made their biggest contribution. Since the pioneering work of Harry Markowitz in the 1950s, the objective of investment management has been defined as determining the optimal risk-return trade-off in an investor's profile. Prior to the diffusion of modeling techniques,

---

[5]François Longin, "Stock Market Crashes: Some Quantitative Results Based on Extreme Value Theory." *Derivatives Use, Trading and Regulation* 7, no. 3 (2001): 197–205.

though, evaluation of the risk-return trade-off was left to the judgment of individual asset managers. Modeling brought to the forefront the question of ex ante risk-return optimization. An asset management firm that uses quantitative methods and optimization techniques manages risk at the source. In this case, the only risk that needs to be monitored and managed is model risk.[6]

Purely quantitative managers with a fully automated management process were still rare according to the study. Most managers, although quantitatively oriented, used a hybrid approach calling for models to give evaluations that managers translate into decisions. In such situations, risk is not completely controlled at the origin.

Most firms interviewed for the study had created a separate risk management unit as a supervisory entity that controls the risk of different portfolios and eventually—although still only rarely—aggregated risk at the firm-wide level. In most cases, the tools of choice for controlling risk were multifactor models. Models of this type have become standard when it comes to making risk evaluations for institutional investors. For internal use, however, many firms reported that they made risk evaluations based on proprietary models, EVT, and scenario analysis.

Integrating Qualitative and Quantitative Information

More than 60% of the firms interviewed for the 2003 Intertek study reported they had formalized procedures for integrating quantitative and qualitative input, although half of these mentioned that the process had not gone very far; 30% of the participants reported no formalization at all. Some firms mentioned they had developed a theoretical framework to integrate results from quantitative models and fundamental views. Assigning weights to the various inputs was handled differently from firm to firm; some firms reported establishing a weight limit in the range of 50% to 80% for quantitative input.

A few quantitative-oriented firms reported that they completely formalized the integration of qualitative and quantitative information. In these cases, everything relevant was built into the system. Firms that both quantitatively managed and traditionally managed funds typically reported that formalization was implemented in the former but not in the latter.

Virtually all firms reported at least a partial automation in the handling of qualitative information. For the most part, a first level of automation—including automatic screening and delivery, classification, and search—is provided by suppliers of sell-side research, consensus data, and news. These suppliers are automating the delivery of news, research reports, and other information.

---

[6]Asset management firms are subject to other risks, namely, the risk of not fulfilling a client mandate or operational risk. Although important, these risks were outside the scope of the survey.

About 30% of the respondents note they have added functionality over and above that provided by third-party information suppliers, typically starting with areas easy to quantify such as earnings announcements or analysts' recommendations. Some have coupled this with quantitative signals that alert recipients to changes or programs that automatically perform an initial analysis.

Only the braver will be tackling difficult tasks such as automated news summary and analysis. For the most part, news analysis was still considered the domain of judgment. A few firms interviewed for this study reported that they attempted to tackle the problem of automatic news analysis, but abandoned their efforts. The difficulty of forecasting price movements related to new information was cited as a motivation.

2006 INTERTEK STUDY

The next study we discuss is based on survey responses and conversations with industry representatives in 2006.[7] Although this predates the subprime mortgage crisis and the resulting impact on the performance of quantitative asset managers, the insights provided by this study are still useful. In all, managers at 38 asset management firms managing a total of $4.3 trillion in equities participated in the study. Participants included individuals responsible for quantitative equity management and quantitative equity research at large- and medium-sized firms in North America and Europe.[8] Sixty-three percent of the participating firms were among the largest asset managers in their respective countries; they clearly represented the way a large part of the industry was going with respect to the use of quantitative methods in equity portfolio management.[9]

The findings of the 2006 study suggested that the skepticism relative to the future of quantitative management at the end of the 1990s had given way by 2006 and quantitative methods were playing a large role in equity portfolio management. Of the 38 survey participants, 11 (29%) reported that more than 75% of their equity assets were being managed quantitatively. This includes a wide spectrum of firms, with from $6.5 billion to over

---

[7]The results of this study are reported in Frank J. Fabozzi, Sergio M. Focardi, and Caroline Jonas, "Trends in Quantitative Equity Management: Survey Results," *Quantitative Finance* 7, no. 2 (2007): 115–122.

[8]The home market of participating firms was a follows: 15 from North America (14 from the United States, 1 from Canada) and 23 from Europe (7 from United Kingdom, 5 from Germany, 4 from Switzerland, 3 from Benelux, 2 from France, and 2 from Italy).

[9]Of the 38 participants in this survey, two responded only partially to the questionnaire. Therefore, for some questions, there are 36 (not 38) responses.

$650 billion in equity assets under management. Another 22 firms (58%) reported that they have some equities under quantitative management, though for 15 of these 22 firms the percentage of equities under quantitative management was less than 25%—often under 5%—of total equities under management. Five of the 38 participants in the survey (13%) reported no equities under quantitative management.

Relative to the period 2004–2005, the amount of equities under quantitative management was reported to have grown at most firms participating in the survey (84%). One reason given by respondents to explain the growth in equity assets under quantitative management was the flows into existing quantitative funds. A source at a large U.S. asset management firm with more than half of its equities under quantitative management said in 2006 "The firm has three distinct equity products: value, growth, and quant. Quant is the biggest and is growing the fastest."

According to survey respondents, the most important factor contributing to a wider use of quantitative methods in equity portfolio management was the positive result obtained with these methods. Half of the participants rated positive results as the single most important factor contributing to the widespread use of quantitative methods. Other factors contributing to a wider use of quantitative methods in equity portfolio management were, in order of importance attributed to them by participants, (1) the computational power now available on the desk top, (2) more and better data, and (3) the availability of third-party analytical software and visualization tools.

Survey participants identified the prevailing in-house culture as the most important factor holding back a wider use of quantitative methods (this evaluation obviously does not hold for firms that can be described as quantitative): more than one third (10/27) of the respondents at other than quant-oriented firms considered this the major blocking factor. This positive evaluation of models in equity portfolio management in 2006 was in contrast with the skepticism of some 10 years early. A number of changes have occurred. First, expectations at the time of the study had become more realistic. In the 1980s and 1990s, traders were experimenting with methodologies from advanced science in the hope of making huge excess returns. Experience of the prior 10 years has shown that models were capable of delivering but that their performance must be compatible with a well-functioning market.

More realistic expectations have brought more perseverance in model testing and design and have favored the adoption of intrinsically safer models. Funds that were using hundred fold leverage had become unpalatable following the collapse of LTCM (Long-Term Capital Management). This, per se, has reduced the number of headline failures and had a beneficial impact on the perception of performance results. We can say that models worked better in 2006 because model risk had been reduced: simpler, more robust models delivered what was expected. Other technical reasons that explained improved model performance included a manifold increase in computing power and more and better data. Modelers by 2006 had available on their desk top computing power that, at the end of the 1980s, could be got only from multimillion-dollar supercomputers. Cleaner, more complete data, including intraday data and data on corporate actions and dividends, could be obtained. In addition, investment firms (and institutional clients) have learned how to use models throughout the investment management process. Models had become part of an articulated process that, especially in the case of institutional investors, involved satisfying a number of different objectives, such as superior information ratios.

Changing Role for Models in Equity Portfolio

The 2006 study revealed that quantitative models were now used in active management to find sources of excess returns (i.e., alphas), either relative to a benchmark or absolute. This was a considerable change with respect to the 2003 Intertek European study where quantitative models were reported as being used primarily to manage risk and to select parsimonious portfolios for passive management.

Another finding of the study was the growing amount of funds managed automatically by computer programs. The once futuristic vision of machines running funds automatically without the intervention of a portfolio manager was becoming a reality on a large scale: 55% (21/38) of the respondents reported that at least part of their equity assets were being managed automatically with quantitative methods; another three planned to automate at least a portion of their equity portfolios within the next 12 months. The growing automation of the equity investment process suggests that there was no missing link in the technology chain that leads to automatic quantitative management. From return forecasting to portfolio formation and optimization, all the needed elements were in place. Until recently, optimization represented the missing technology link in the automation of portfolio engineering. Considered too brittle to be safely deployed, many firms eschewed optimization, limiting the use of modeling to stock ranking or risk control functions. Advances in robust estimation methodologies and in optimization now allow an asset manager to construct portfolios of hundreds of stocks chosen in universes of thousands of stocks with little or no human intervention outside of supervising the models.

Modeling Methodologies and the Industry's Evaluation

At the end of the 1980s, academics and researchers at specialized quant boutiques experimented with many sophisticated modeling methodologies including chaos theory, fractals and multifractals, adaptive programming, learning theory, complexity theory, complex nonlinear stochastic models, data mining, and artificial intelligence. Most of these efforts failed to live up to expectations. Perhaps expectations were too high. Or perhaps the resources or commitment required were lacking. Emanuel Derman provides a lucid analysis of the difficulties that a quantitative analyst has to overcome. As he observed, though modern quantitative finance uses some of the techniques of physics, a wide gap remains between the two disciplines.[10]

The modeling landscape revealed by the 2006 study is simpler and more uniform. Regression analysis and momentum modeling are the most widely used techniques: respectively, 100% and 78% of the survey respondents said that these techniques were being used at their firms. With respect to regression models used today, the survey suggests that they have undergone a substantial change since the first multifactor models such as Arbitrage Pricing Theory (APT) were introduced. Classical multifactor models such as APT are static models embodied in linear regression between returns and factors at the same time. Static models are forecasting models insofar as the factors at time t are predictors of returns at time behavior $t + 1$. In these static models, individual return processes might exhibit zero autocorrelation but still be forecastable from other variables. Predictors might include financial and macroeconomic factors as well as company specific parameters such as financial ratios. Predictors might also include human judgment, for example, analyst estimates, or technical factors that capture phenomena such as momentum. A source at a quant shop using regression to forecast returns said,

> Regression on factors is the foundation of our model building. Ratios derived from financial statements serve as one of the most important components for predicting future stock returns. We use these ratios extensively in our bottom-up equity model and categorize them into five general categories: operating efficiency, financial strength, earnings quality (accruals), capital expenditures, and external financing activities.

Momentum and reversals were the second most widely diffused modeling technique among survey participants. In general, momentum and reversals were being used as a strategy, not as a model of asset returns. Momentum strategies are based on forming portfolios choosing the highest or lowest

---

[10]Emanuel Derman, "A Guide for the Perplexed Quant," *Quantitative Finance* 1, no. 5 (2001): 476–480.

returns, where returns are estimated on specific time windows. Survey participants gave these strategies overall good marks but noted that (1) they do not always perform so well; (2) they can result in high turnover (though some were using constraints/penalties to deal with this problem); and (3) identifying the timing of reversals was tricky.

Momentum was first reported in 1993 by Jegadeesh and Titman in the U.S. market.[11] Nine years later, they confirmed that momentum continued to exist in the 1990s in the U.S. market.[12] Two years later, Karolyi and Kho examined different models for explaining momentum and concluded that no random walk or autoregressive model is able to explain the magnitude of momentum empirically found[13]; they suggested that models with time varying expected returns come closer to explaining empirical magnitude of momentum. Momentum and reversals are presently explained in the context of local models updated in real time. For example, momentum as described in the original Jegadeesh and Titman study is based on the fact that stock prices can be represented as independent random walks when considering periods of the length of one year. However, it is fair to say that there is no complete agreement on the econometrics of asset returns that justifies momentum and reversals and stylized facts on a global scale, and not as local models. It would be beneficial to know more about the econometrics of asset returns that sustain momentum and reversals.

Other modeling methods that were widely used by participants in the 2006 study included cash flow analysis and behavioral modeling. Seventeen of the 36 participating firms said that they modeled cash flows; behavioral modeling was reported as being used by 16 of the 36 participating firms.[14] Considered to play an important role in asset predictability, 44% of the

[11]Narasimhan Jegadeesh and Sheridan Titman, "Returns to Buying Winners and Selling Losers: Implications for Stock Market Efficiency," *Journal of Finance* 48, no. 1 (1993): 65–92.

[12]Narasimhan Jegadeesh and Sheridan Titman, "Cross-Sectional and Time-Series Determinants of Momentum Returns," *Review of Financial Studies* 15, no. 1 (2002): 143–158.

[13]George A. Karolyi and Bong-Chan Kho, "Momentum Strategies: Some Bootstrap Tests," *Journal of Empirical Finance* 11 (2004): 509–536.

[14]The term behavioral modeling is often used rather loosely. Full-fledged behavioral modeling exploits a knowledge of human psychology to identify situations where investors are prone to show behavior that leads to market inefficiencies. The tendency now is to call *behavioral* any model that exploits market inefficiency. However, implementing true behavioral modeling is a serious challenge; even firms with very large, powerful quant teams who participated in the survey reported that there is considerable work needed to translate departures from rationality into a set of rules for identifying stocks as well as entry and exit points for a quantitative stock selection process.

survey respondents said that they use behavioral modeling to try to capture phenomena such as departures from rationality on the part of investors (e.g., belief persistence), patterns in analyst estimates, and corporate executive investment/disinvestment behavior. Behavioral finance is related to momentum in that the latter is often attributed to various phenomena of persistence in analyst estimates and investor perceptions. A source at a large investment firm that has incorporated behavioral modeling into its active equity strategies commented,

> The attraction of behavioral finance is now much stronger than it was just five years ago. Everyone now acknowledges that markets are not efficient, that there are behavioral anomalies. In the past, there was the theory that was saying that markets are efficient while market participants such as the proprietary trading desks ignored the theory and tried to profit from the anomalies. We are now seeing a fusion of theory and practice.

As for other methodologies used in return forecasting, sources cited nonlinear methods and cointegration. Nonlinear methods are being used to model return processes at 19% (7/36) of the responding firms. The nonlinear method most widely used among survey participants is classification and regression trees (CART). The advantage of CART is its simplicity and the ability of CART methods to be cast in an intuitive framework. A source in the survey that reported using CART as a central part of the portfolio construction process in enhanced index and longer-term value-based portfolios said,

> CART compresses a large volume of data into a form that identifies its essential characteristics, so the output is easy to understand. CART is nonparametric—which means that it can handle an infinitely wide range of statistical distributions—and nonlinear—so as a variable selection technique it is particularly good at handling higher-order interactions between variables.

Only 11% (4/36) of the respondents reported using nonlinear regime-shifting models; at most firms, judgment was being used to assess regime change. Participants identified the difficulty in detecting the precise timing of a regime switch and the very long time series required to estimate shifts as obstacles to modeling regime shifts. A survey participant at a firm where regime-shifting models have been experimented with commented,

Everyone knows that returns are conditioned by market regimes, but the potential for overfitting when implementing regime-switching models is great. If you could go back with fifty years of data—but we have only some ten years of data and this is not enough to build a decent model.

Cointegration was being used by 19% (7/36) of the respondents. Cointegration models the short-term dynamics (direction) and long-run equilibrium (fair value). A perceived plus of cointegration is the transparency that it provides: The models are based on economic and finance theory and calculated from economic data.

Optimization

Another area where much change was revealed by the 2006 study was optimization. According to sources, optimization was being performed at 92% (33/36) of the participating firms, albeit in some cases only rarely. Mean variance was the most widely used technique among survey participants: it was being used by 83% (30/36) of the respondents. It was followed by utility optimization (42% or 15/36) and, robust optimization (25% or 9/36). Only one firm mentioned that it is using stochastic optimization.

The wider use of optimization was a significant development compared to the 2003 study when many sources had reported that they eschewed optimization: The difficulty of identifying the forecasting error was behind the then widely held opinion that optimization techniques were too brittle and prone to error maximization. The greater use of optimization was attributed to advances in large-scale optimization coupled with the ability to include constraints and robust methods for both estimation and optimization. This result is significant as portfolio formation strategies rely on optimization. With optimization feasible, the door was open to a fully automated investment process. In this context, it is noteworthy that 55% of the survey respondents in the 2006 study reported that at least a portion of their equity assets is being managed by a fully automated process.

Optimization is the engineering part of portfolio construction. Most portfolio construction problems can be cast in an optimization framework, where optimization is applied to obtain the desired optimal risk-return profile. Optimization is the technology behind the current offering of products with specially engineered returns, such as guaranteed returns. However, the offering of products with particular risk-return profiles requires optimization methodologies that go well beyond classical mean-variance optimization. In particular, one must be able to (1) work with real-world utility functions and (2) apply constraints to the optimization process.

Challenges

The growing diffusion of models is not without challenges. The 2006 survey participants noted three: (1) increasing difficulty in differentiating products; (2) difficulty in marketing quant funds, especially to noninstitutional investors; and (3) performance decay.

Quantitative equity management has now become so wide spread that a source at a long-established quantitative investment firm remarked:

> There is now a lot of competition from new firms entering the space [of quantitative investment management]. The challenge is to continue to distinguish ourselves from competition in the minds of clients.

With quantitative funds based on the same methodologies and using the same data, the risk is to construct products with the same risk-return profile. The head of active equities at a large quantitative firm with more than a decade of experience in quantitative management remarked in the survey, "Everyone is using the same data and reading the same articles: It's tough to differentiate."

While sources in the survey reported that client demand was behind the growth of (new) pure quantitative funds, some mentioned that quantitative funds might be something of a hard sell. A source at a medium-sized asset management firm servicing both institutional clients and high-net worth individuals said:

> Though clearly the trend towards quantitative funds is up, quant approaches remain difficult to sell to private clients: They remain too complex to explain, there are too few stories to tell, and they often have low alpha. Private clients do not care about high information ratios.

Markets are also affecting the performance of quantitative strategies. A 2006 report by the Bank for International Settlements noted that this is a period of historically low volatility. What is exceptional about this period, observes the report, is the simultaneous drop in volatility in all variables: stock returns, bond spreads, rates, and so on. While the role of models in reducing volatility is unclear, what is clear is that models immediately translate this situation into a rather uniform behavior. Quantitative funds try to differentiate themselves either finding new unexploited sources of return forecastability, for example, novel ways of looking at financial statements, or using optimization creatively to engineer special risk-return profiles.

A potentially more serious problem is performance decay. Survey participants remarked that model performance was not so stable. Firms are tackling these problems in two ways. First, they are protecting themselves from model breakdown with model risk mitigation techniques, namely by averaging results obtained with different models. It is unlikely that all models break down in the same way in the same moment, so that averaging with different models allows asset managers to diversify risk. Second, there is an ongoing quest for new factors, new predictors, and new aggregations of factors and predictors. In the long run, however, something more substantial might be required.

2007 INTERTEK STUDY

The 2007 Intertek study, sponsored by the Research Foundation of the CFA Institute (now the Chartered Financial Analysts Institute), is based on conversations with asset managers, investment consultants, and fund-rating agencies as well as survey responses from 31 asset managers in the United States and Europe.[15] In total, 12 asset managers and eight consultants and fund-rating agencies were interviewed and 31 managers with a total of $2.2 trillion in equities under management participated in the survey. Half of the participating firms were based in the United States; half of the participating firms were among the largest asset managers in their countries. Survey participants included chief investment officers of equities and heads of quantitative management and/or quantitative research.

A major question in asset management that this study focused on was if the diffusion of quantitative strategies was making markets more efficient, thereby reducing profit opportunities. The events of the summer of 2007, which saw many quantitatively managed funds realize large losses, brought an immediacy to the question. The classical view of financial markets holds that market speculators make markets efficient, hence the absence of profit opportunities after compensating for risk. This view had formed the basis of academic thinking for several decades starting from the 1960s. However, practitioners had long held the more pragmatic view that a market formed by fallible human agents (as market speculators also are) offers profit opportunities due to the many small residual imperfections that ultimately result in delayed or distorted responses to news.

---

[15]The results of this study are reported in Frank J. Fabozzi, Sergio M. Focardi, and Caroline Jonas, *Challenges in Quantitative Equity Management* (Charlottesville, VA: CFA Institute Research Foundation, 2008); and Frank J. Fabozzi, Sergio M. Focardi, and Caroline L. Jonas, "On the Challenges in Quantitative Equity Management." *Quantitative Finance* 8, no. 7 (2008): 649–655.

A summary of the findings of this study are provided next.

Are Model-Driven Investment Strategies Impacting Market Efficiency and Price Processes?

The empirical question of the changing nature of markets is now receiving much academic attention. For example, using empirical data from 1927 to 2005, Hwang and Rubesam[16] argued that momentum phenomena disappeared during the period 2000–2005, while Figelman,[17] analyzing the S&P 500 over the period 1970–2004, found new evidence of momentum and reversal phenomena previously not described. Khandani and Lo[18] show how a mean-reversion strategy that they used to analyze market behavior lost profitability in the 12-year period from 1995 to 2007.

Intuition suggests that models will have an impact on price processes but whether models will make markets more efficient or less efficient will depend on the type of models widely adopted. Consider that there are two categories of models, those based on fundamentals and those based on the analysis of time series of past prices and returns. Models based on fundamentals make forecasts based on fundamental characteristics of firms and, at least in principle, tend to make markets more efficient. Models based on time series of prices and returns are subject to self-referentiality and might actually lead to mispricings. A source at a large financial firm that has both fundamental and quant processes said:

> The impact of models on markets and price processes is asymmetrical. [Technical] model-driven strategies have a less good impact than fundamental-driven strategies as the former are often based on trend following.

Another source commented:

> Overall quants have brought greater efficiency to the market, but there are poor models out there that people get sucked into. Take momentum. I believe in earnings momentum, not in price momentum: It is a fool buying under the assumption that a bigger fool will buy in the future. Anyone who uses price momentum assumes that

[16]Soosung Hwang and Alexandre Rubesam, "The Disappearance of Momentum" (November 7, 2008). Available at SSRN: http://ssrn.com/abstract=968176.
[17]Ilya Figelman, "Stock Return Momentum and Reversal," *Journal of Portfolio Management* 34, no. 1 (2007): 51–69.
[18]Amir E. Khandani and Andrew W. Lo, "What Happened to the Quants in August 2007," *Journal of Investment Management* 5, no. 4 (2007): 29–78.

there will always be someone to take the asset off your hands—a fool's theory. Studies have shown how it is possible to get into a momentum-type market in which asset prices get bid up, with everyone on the collective belief wagon.

The question of how models impact the markets—making them more or less efficient—depends on the population of specific models. As long as models based on past time series of prices and returns (i.e., models that are trend followers) are being used, it will not be possible to assume that models make markets more efficient. Consider that it is not only a question of how models compete with each other but also how models react to exogenous events and how models themselves evolve. For example, a prolonged period of growth will produce a breed of models different from models used in low-growth periods.

Performance Issues

When the 2006 Intertek study was conducted on equity portfolio modeling in early 2006, quantitative managers were very heady about performance. By mid-2007, much of that headiness was gone. By July–August 2007, there was much perplexity.

Many participants in the 2007 Intertek study attributed the recent poor performance of many quant equity funds to structural changes in the market. A source at a large financial firm with both fundamental and quantitative processes said:

> The problem with the performance of quant funds [since 2006] is that there was rotation in the marketplace. Most quants have a strong value bias so they do better in a value market. The period 1998–1999 was not so good for quants as it was a growth market; in 2001–2005, we had a value market so value-tilted styles such as the quants were doing very well. In 2006, we were back to a growth market. In addition, in 2007, spreads compressed. The edge quants had has eroded.

One might conclude that if markets are cyclical, quant outperformance will also be cyclical. A leading investment consultant who participated in the survey remarked:

> What is most successful in terms of producing returns—quant or fundamental—is highly contextual: there is no best process, quant or fundamental. Quants are looking for an earnings-quality component

that has dissipated in time. I hate to say it, but any manager has to have the wind behind its strategies, favoring the factors.

Speaking in August 2007, the head of active quantitative research at a large international firm said:

> It has been challenging since the beginning of the year. The problem is that fundamental quants are stressing some quality—be it value or growth—but at the beginning of the year there was a lot of activity of hedge funds, much junk value, much froth. In addition, there was a lot of value-growth style rotation, which is typical when there is macro insecurity and interest rates go up and down. The growth factor is better when rates are down, the value factor better when rates are up. Fundamental quants could not get a consistent exposure to factors they wanted to be exposed to.

Another source said, "We tried to be balanced value-growth but the biggest danger is rotation risk. One needs a longer-term view to get through market cycles." The CIO of equities at a large asset management firm added, "Growth and value markets are cyclical and it is hard to get the timing right."

The problem of style rotation (e.g., value versus growth) is part of the global problem of adapting models to changing market conditions. Value and growth represent two sets of factors, both of which are captured, for example, in the Fama-French three-factor model.[19] But arguably there are many more factors. So factor rotation is more than just a question of value and growth markets. Other factors, such as momentum, are subject to the same problem; that is to say, one factor prevails in one market situation and loses importance in another and is replaced by yet another factor(s).

Other reasons were cited to explain why the performance of quantitative products as a group has been down since 2006. Among these is the fact that there were now more quantitative managers using the same data, similar models, and implementing similar strategies. A source at a firm that has both quant and fundamental processes said:

> Why is performance down? One reason is because many more people are using quant today than three, five years ago. Ten years ago the obstacles to entry were higher: data were more difficult to obtain, models were proprietary. Now we have third-party suppliers of data feeds, analytics, and backtesting capability.

---

[19]Eugene F. Fama and Kenneth R. French, "Common Risk Factors and the Returns on Stocks and Bonds," *Journal of Financial Economics*, 47, no. 2 (1993): 427–465.

A consultant concurred:

> The next 12 to 24 months will be tough for quants for several reasons. One problem is...the ease with which people can now buy and manipulate data. The problem is too many people are running similar models so performance decays and it becomes hard to stay ahead. Performance is a genuine concern.

Still another source said:

> Quant performance depends on cycles and the secular trend but success breeds its own problems. By some estimates there are $4 trillion in quantitative equity management if we include passive, active, hedge funds, and proprietary desks. There is a downside to the success of quants. Because quants have been so successful, if a proprietary desk or a hedge fund needs to get out of a risk, they can't. Then you get trampled on as others have more to sell than you have to buy. The business is more erratic because of the sheer size and needs of proprietary desks and hedge funds whose clients hold 6 to 12 months against six years for asset managers.

However, not all sources agreed that quantitative managers using the same data or similar models entails a loss of performance. One source said:

> Though all quants use the same data sources, I believe that there is a difference in models and in signals. There are details behind the signals and in how you put them together. Portfolio construction is one very big thing.

Another source added:

> All quants use similar data but even minor differences can lead to nontrivial changes in valuation. If you have 15 pieces of information, different sums are not trivial. Plus if you combine small differences in analytics and optimization, the end result can be large differences. There is not one metric but many metrics and all are noisy.

Investment consultants identified risk management as among the biggest pluses for a quantitative process. According to one source:

> Quantitative managers have a much greater awareness of risk. They are attuned to risk in relation to the benchmark as well as to systemic

risk. Fundamental managers are often not aware of concentration in, for example, factors or exposure.

In view of the performance issues, survey participants were asked if they believed that quantitative managers were finding it increasingly difficult to generate excess returns as market inefficiencies were exploited. Just over half agreed, while 32% disagreed and 16% expressed no opinion. When the question was turned around, 73% of the survey participants agreed that, though profit opportunities would not disappear, quantitative managers would find it increasingly hard to exploit them. One source remarked:

> Performance is getting harder to wring out not because everyone is using the same data and similar models, but because markets are more efficient. So we will see Sharpe ratios shrink for active returns. Managers will have to use more leverage to get returns. The problem is more acute for quant managers as all quant positions are highly correlated as they all use book to price; fundamental managers, on the other hand, differ on the evaluation of future returns.

When asked what market conditions were posing the most serious challenge to a quantitative approach in equity portfolio management, survey respondents ranked in order of importance on a scale from one to five the rising correlation level, style rotation, and insufficient liquidity. Other market conditions rated important were a fundamental market shift, high (cross sector) volatility and low (cross) volatility. Felt less important were the impact of the dissipation of earnings and nontrending markets.

In their paper on the likely causes of the summer 2007 events, Khandani and Lo[20] note the sharp rise in correlations over the period 1998–2007. They observe that this rise in correlations reflects a much higher level of interdependence in financial markets. This interdependence is one of the factors responsible for the contagion from the subprime mortgage crisis to the equity markets in July–August 2007. When problems began to affect equity markets, the liquidity crisis started. Note that liquidity is a word that assumes different meanings in different contexts. In the study, liquidity refers to the possibility of finding buyers and thus to the possibility of deleveraging without sustaining heavy losses. One CIO commented:

> Everyone in the quant industry is using the same factors [thus creating highly correlated portfolios prone to severe contagion effects]. When you need to unwind, there is no one there to take the trade:

---

[20]Khandani and Lo, "What Happened to the Quants in August 2007?"

Quants are all children of Fama and French. Lots of people are using earnings revision models.

Another source remarked, "Because quants have been so successful, if you need to get out of a risk for whatever reason, you can't get out. This leads to a liquidity sell-off."

Specific to recent market turmoil, participants identified the unwinding of long-short positions by hedge funds as by far the most important factor contributing to the losses incurred by some quant equity finds in the summer of 2007. One source said wryly, "Everyone is blaming the quants; they should be blaming the leverage."

Improving Performance

As it was becoming increasingly difficult to deliver excess returns, many quant managers had turned to using leverage in an attempt to boost performance—a strategy most sources agreed was quite risky. The events of the summer of 2007 were to prove them right. Given the performance issues, survey participants were asked what they were likely to do to try to improve performance.

The search to identify new and unique factors was the most frequently cited strategy and complementary to it, the intention to employ new models. A CIO of equities said:

> Through the crisis of July–August 2007, quant managers have learned which of their factors are unique and will be focusing on what is unique. There will be a drive towards using more proprietary models, doing more unique conceptual work. But it will be hard to get away from fundamental concepts: you want to hold companies that are doing well and do not want to pay too much for them.

As for the need to employ new models, the global head of quantitative strategies at a large financial group remarked:

> Regression is the art of today's tool kit. To get better performance, we will have to enlarge the tool kit and add information and dynamic and static models. People are always changing things; maybe we will be changing things just a bit quicker.

Other strategies to improve performance given by the 2007 survey participants included attempts to diversify sources of business information and data. As one investment consultant said:

> All quant managers rely on the same set of data but one cannot rely on the same data and have an analytical edge; it is a tough sell. Quant managers need an informational edge, information no one else has or uses. It might be coming out of academia or might be information in the footnotes of balance sheet data or other information in the marketplace that no one else is using.

Just over 60% of the survey participants agreed that, given that everyone is using the same data and similar models, quantitative managers need a proprietary informational edge to outperform. Sources mentioned that some hedge fund managers now have people in-house on the phone, doing proprietary market research on firms.

Opinions among survey respondents diverged as to the benefits to be derived from using high-frequency (up to tick-by-tick) data. Thirty-eight percent of the participants believed that high-frequency data can give an informational edge in equity portfolio management while 27% disagreed and 35% expressed no opinion. It is true that there was still only limited experience with using high-frequency data in equity portfolio management at the time of the survey. One source remarked, "Asset managers now have more frequent updates, what was once monthly is now daily with services such as WorldScope, Compustat, Market QA, Bloomberg, or Factset. But the use of intraday data is still limited to the trading desk."

Fund Flows

Estimates of how much was under management in active quant strategies in 2007 vary from a few hundred million dollars to over $1 trillion. In a study that compared cumulative net flows in U.S. large-cap quantitative and "other" products as a percentage of total assets during the 36-month period that coincided with the 2001–2005 value market, Casey, Quirk and Associates[21] found that assets grew 25% at quantitative funds and remained almost flat for other funds. A coauthor of that study commented:

> What we have seen in our studies, which looked at U.S. large-cap funds, is that since 2004 investors have withdrawn money from

---

[21]Casey, Quirk and Associates, "The Geeks Shall Inherit the Earth?" November 2005.

the U.S. large-cap segment under fundamental managers but active quants have held on to their assets or seen them go up slightly.

Addressing the question of net flows into quantitatively managed equity funds before July–August 2007, a source at a leading investment consultancy said:

> There has been secular growth for quant equity funds over the past 20 or so years, first into passive quant and, over the past 12–36 months, into active quant given their success in the past value market. Right now there is about an 80/20 market split between fundamental and active quant management. If active quants can continue their strong performance in a growth market that I think we are now in, I can see the percentage shift over the next three years to 75/25 with active quant gaining a few points every year.

Despite the high-profile problems at some long-short quantitative managed funds during the summer of 2007, 63% of the respondents indicated that they were optimistic that, overall, quantitatively managed equity funds will continue to increase their market share relative to traditionally managed funds, as more firms introduce quantitative products and exchange-traded funds (ETFs) give the retail investor access to active quant products. However, when the question was reformulated, that optimism was somewhat dampened. Thirty-nine percent of the survey participants agreed that overall quantitatively managed funds would not be able to increase their market share relative to traditionally managed funds for the year 2007 while 42% disagreed.

Many consultants who were interviewed for the study just before the July–August 2007 market turmoil were skeptical that quantitative managers could continue their strong performance. These sources cited performance problems dating back to the year 2006.

Lipper tracks flows of quantitative and nonquantitative funds in four equity universes: large cap, enhanced index funds, market neutral, and long-short funds. The Lipper data covering the performance of quantitatively and nonquantitatively driven funds in the three-year period 2005–2007 showed that quant funds underperformed in 2007 in all categories except large cap—a reversal of performance from 2005 and 2006 when quant managers were outperforming nonquantitative managers in all four categories. However, Lipper data are neither risk adjusted nor fee adjusted and the sampling of quant funds in some categories is small. For the period January 2005–June 2008, according to the Lipper data, long-only funds—both quant and nonquant—experienced a net outflow while all other categories experienced net inflows—albeit at different rates—with the exception of nonquant market neutral funds. The differences (as percentages) between quant and nonquant funds were not very large but quant funds exhibited more negative results.

In view of the preceding, the survey participants were asked if, given the poor performance of some quant funds in the year 2007, they thought that traditional asset management firms that have diversified into quantitative management would be reexamining their commitment. Nearly one third agreed while 52% disagreed (16% expressed no opinion). Those that agreed tended to come from firms at which equity assets under management represent less than 5% of all equities under management or where there is a substantial fundamental overlay to the quantitative process.

The head of quantitative equity at a large traditional manager said:

> When the firm decided back in the year 2000 to build a quant business as a diversifier, quant was not seen as a competitor to fundamental analysis. The initial role of quant managers was one of being a problem solver, for 130-30-like strategies or whereever there is complexity in portfolio construction. If quant performance is down, the firm might reconsider its quant products. Should they do so, I would expect that the firm would keep on board some quants as a support to their fundamental business.

Quantitative Processes, Oversight, and Overlay

Let's define what we mean by a quantitative process. Many traditionally managed asset management firms now use some computer-based, statistical decision-support tool and do some risk modeling. The study referred to an investment process as fundamental (or traditional) if it is performed by a human asset manager using information and judgment, and quantitative if the value-added decisions are made primarily in terms of quantitative outputs generated by computer-driven models following fixed rules. The study referred to a process as being *hybrid* if it uses a combination of the two. An example of the latter is a fundamental manager using a computer-driven stock-screening system to narrow his or her portfolio choices.

Among participants in the study, two-thirds had model-driven processes allowing only minimum (5%–10%) discretion or oversight, typically to make sure that numbers made sense and that buy orders were not issued for firms that were the subject of news or rumors not accounted for by the models. Model oversight was considered a control function. This oversight was typically exercised when large positions were involved. A head of quantitative equity said, "Decision making is 95% model-driven, but we will look at a trader's list and do a sanity check to pull a trade if necessary."

Some firms indicated that they had automated the process of checking if there are exogenous events that might affect the investment decisions. One source said:

> Our process is model driven with about 5% oversight. We ask ourselves: "Do the numbers make sense?" and do news scanning and flagging using in-house software as well as software from a provider of business information.

This comment underlines one of the key functions of judgmental overlays: the consideration of information with a bearing on forecasts that does not appear yet in the predictors. This information might include, for example, rumors about important events that are not yet confirmed, or facts hidden in reporting or news releases that escape the attention of most investors.

Fundamental analysts and managers might have sources of information that can add to the information that is publicly available. However, there are drawbacks to a judgmental approach to information gathering. As one source said, "An analyst might fall in love with the Chief Financial Officer of a firm, and lose his objectivity."

Other sources mentioned using oversight in the case of rare events such as those of July–August 2007. The head of quantitative management at a large firm said:

> In situations of extreme market events, portfolio managers talk more to traders. We use Bayesian learning to learn from past events but, in general, dislocations in the market are hard to model.

Bayesian priors are a disciplined way to integrate historical data and a manager's judgment in the model.

Another instance of exercising oversight is in the area of risk. One source said, "The only overlay we exercise is on risk, where we allow ourselves a small degree of freedom, not on the model."

The key question is: Is there a best way to comingle judgment and models? Each of these presents pitfalls. Opinions among participants in the 2007 Intertek study differed as to the advantage of commingling models and judgment and ways that it might be done. More than two-thirds of the survey participants (68%) disagreed with the statement that the most effective equity portfolio management process combines quantitative tools and a fundamental overlay; only 26% considered that a fundamental overlay adds value. Interestingly, most investment consultants and fund-rating firms interviewed for the study shared the appraisal that adding a fundamental overlay to a quantitative investment process did not add value.

A source at a large consultancy said:

> Once you believe that a model is stable, effective over a long time, it is preferable not to use human overlay as it introduces emotion, judgment. The better alternative to human intervention is to arrive at an understanding of how to improve model performance and implement changes to the model.

Some sources believed that a fundamental overlay had value in extreme situations, but not everyone agreed. One source said:

> Overlay is additive and can be detrimental, oversight is neither. It does not alter the quantitative forecast but implements a reality check. In market situations such as of July–August 2007, overlay would have been disastrous. The market goes too fast and takes on a crisis aspect. It is a question of intervals.

Among the 26% who believed that a fundamental overlay does add value, sources cited the difficulty of putting all information in the models. A source that used models for asset managers said:

> In using quant models, there can be data issues. With a fundamental overlay, you get more information. It is difficult to convert all fundamental data, especially macro information such as the yen/dollar exchange rate, into quant models.

A source at a firm that is using a fundamental overlay systematically said:

> The question is how you interpret quantitative outputs. We do a fundamental overlay, reading the 10-Qs and the 10-Ks and the footnotes, plus looking at, for example, increases in daily sales invoices. I expect that we will continue to use a fundamental overlay: it provides a common-sense check. You cannot ignore real-world situations.

In summary, overlays and human oversight in model-driven strategies can be implemented in different ways. First, as a control function, oversight allows managers to exercise judgment in specific situations. Second, human judgment might be commingled with a model's forecasts.

Implementing a Quant Process

The 2007 survey participants were asked how they managed the model building and backtesting process. One-fourth of the participants said that their firms admitted several processes. For example, at 65% of the sources, quantitative models are personally built and backtested by the asset manager; at 39%, quantitative models are built and backtested by the firm's central research center. More rarely, at 23% models might also be built by the corporate research center to the specifications of the asset manager, while at 16% models might also be built by the asset manager but are backtested by the research center. (The percentages do not add to 100 because events overlap.)

Some sources also cited a coming together of quantitative research and portfolio management. Certainly this is already the case at some of the largest quantitative players that began in the passive quantitative arena, where, as one source put it, "the portfolio manager has Unix programming skills as a second nature."

The need to continuously update models was identified by sources as one of the major challenges to a quantitative investment process. A consultant to the industry remarked:

The specifics of which model each manager uses is not so important as long as management has a process to ensure that the model is always current, that as a prism for looking at the universe the model is relevant, that it is not missing anything. One problem in the U.S. in the 1980s–'90s was that models produced spectacular results for a short period of time and then results decayed. The math behind the models was static, simplistic, able to capture only one trend. Today, quants have learned their lesson; they are paranoid about the need to do a constant evaluation to understand what's working this year and might not work next year. The problem is one of capturing the right signals and correctly weighting them when things are constantly changing.

The need to sustain an ongoing effort in research was cited by investment consultants as determinant in manager choices. One consultant said:

When quant performance decays it is often because the manager has grown complacent and then things stop working. When we look at a quant manager, we ask: Can they continue to keep doing research?

One way to ensure that models adapt to the changing environment is to use adaptive modeling techniques. One quantitative manager said:

You cannot use one situation, one data set in perpetuity. For consistently good performance, you need new strategies, new factors. We use various processes in our organization, including regime-shifting adaptive models. The adaptive model draws factors from a pool and selects variables that change over time.

The use of adaptive models and of strategies that can self-adapt to changing market conditions is an important research topic. From a mathematical point of view, there are many tools that can be used to adapt models. Among these is a class of well-known models with hidden variables, including state-space models, hidden Markov models, or regime-shifting models. These models have one or more variables that represent different market conditions. The key challenge is estimation: the ability to identify regime shifts sufficiently early calls for a rich regime structure. Estimating a rich regime shifting model, however, calls for a very large data sample—something we rarely have in finance.

The survey participants were asked if they thought that quantitative-driven equity investment processes were moving towards full automation. By a fully automated quant investment process we intend a process where investment decisions are made by computers with little or no human intervention. An automated process includes the input of data, production of forecasts, optimization and portfolio formation, oversight, and trading. Among those expressing an opinion, as many believed that quantitative managers are moving toward full automation (38%) as not (38%). Industry observers and consultants also had difficulty identifying a trend. One source remarked, "There are all degrees of automation among quants and we see no obvious trend either towards or away from automation." It would appear that we will continue to see a diversity in management models. This diversity is due to the fact that there is no hard science behind quantitative equity investment management; business models reflect the personalities and skill sets inside an organization.

Obstacles to full automation are not due to technical shortcomings. As noted earlier, there are presently no missing links in the automation chain going from forecasting to optimization. Full automation is doable, but successful implementation depends on the ability to link seamlessly a return forecasting tool with a portfolio formation strategy. Portfolio formation strategies can take the form of full optimization or be based on some heuristics with constraints.

The progress of full automation will ultimately depend on performance and investor acceptance. Consultants that interviewed for this study were divided in their evaluation of the advisability of full automation. One source said, "All things being equal, I actually prefer a fully automated process once you believe that a model is stable, effective over a long time." However, in a divergent view, another consultant said, "I am not keen on fully automated processes. I like to see human intervention, interaction before and after optimization, and especially before trading."

Risk Management

The events of July–August 2007 highlighted once more that quantitatively managed funds can be exposed to the risk of extreme events (i.e., rare large—often adverse—events). Fundamentally, managed funds are also exposed to the risk of extreme events, typically of a more familiar nature, such as a market crash or a large drop in value of single firms or sectors. A head of quantitative management remarked, "There are idiosyncratic risks and systemic risks. Fundamental managers take idiosyncratic risk while the quants look at the marginal moves, sometimes adding leverage."

There seems to be a gap between state-of-the-art risk management and the practice of finance. At least, this is what appears in a number of statements made after the summer of 2007 that attributed losses to multisigma events in a Gaussian world. It is now well known that financial phenomena do not follow normal distributions and that the likelihood of extreme events is much larger than if they were normally distributed. Financial phenomena are governed by fat-tailed distributions. The fat-tailed nature of financial phenomena has been at the forefront of research in financial econometrics since the 1990s. Empirical research has shown that returns are not normal and most likely can be represented as fat-tailed processes.

Facts like this have an important bearing on the distribution of returns of dynamic portfolios. Consequently, the 2007 study asked survey participants if they believed that the current generation of risk models had pitfalls that do not allow one to properly anticipate risks such as those of July–August 2007. Just over two-thirds of the survey respondents evaluated agreed that, because today's risk models do not take into consideration global systemic risk factors, they cannot predict events such as those of July–August 2007. One source commented:

> Risk management models work only under benign conditions and are useless when needed. We use two risk methods, principal component analysis and rare (six-sigma) events, and risk models from MSCI Barra and Northfield. But the risk models are misspecified: most pairs of stocks have high correlations.

Another source added:

There are estimation errors in everything, including in risk models. You know that they will fail, so we add heuristics to our models. Risk models do not cover downside risk but they do help control it. Studies have shown that risk models do improve the information ratio.

The growing use of derivatives in equity portfolio management is adding a new type of risk. One source commented:

> The derivatives markets are susceptible to chaos; they overheat compared to normal markets. Derivatives contracts are complex and no one knows how they will behave in various scenarios. In addition, there is credit risk or counterparty risk dealing with entities such as Sentinel—not a Wall Street firm—that can go with a puff of smoke. Their going under was blamed on the subprime crisis but it was fraud.

Sixty-three percent of the survey participants agreed that the derivative market is a market driven by its own supply and demand schedule and might present risk that is not entirely explained in terms of the underlying.

Why Implement a Quant Process?

According to survey respondents, three main objectives were behind the decision to adopt (at least partially) a quantitative-based equity investment process: tighter risk control, more stable returns, and better overall performance. The profile of a firm's founder(s) and/or the prevailing in-house culture were correlated in that they provided the requisite environment.

Other major objectives reported behind the decision to implement a quantitative equity investment process include diversification in general or in terms of new products such as 130-30-type strategies and scalability, including the ability to scale to different universes. Relative to the diversification in a global sense, a source at a large asset management firm with a small quant group said:

> An important motivating factor is diversification of the overall product lineup performance. Management believes that quant and fundamental products will not move in synch.

As for the ability to offer new products such as the long-short strategies, a source at a sell-side firm modeling for the buy side remarked:

We are seeing a lot of interest by firms known for being fundamental and that now want to introduce quant processes in the form of screens or other. These firms are trying to get into the quant space and it is the 130-30-type product that is pushing into this direction.

It was generally believed that quantitatively managed funds outperform fundamental managers in the 130-30-type arena. The ability to backtest the strategy was cited as giving quantitatively managed funds the edge. A manager at a firm that offers both fundamental and quantitative products said, "Potential clients have told us that new products such as the 130-30 strategies are more believable with extensive quant processes and testing behind them."

More generally, sources believed that quantitative processes give an edge whenever there is a complex problem to solve. An investment consultant remarked:

Quant has an advantage when there is an element of financial engineering. The investment process is the same but quant adds value when it comes to picking components and coming up with products such as the 130-30.

Another source added:

A quant process brings the ability to create structured products. In the U.S., institutional investors are using structured products in especially fixed income and hedge funds. Given the problem of aging, I would expect more demand in the future from private investors who want a product that will give them an income plus act as an investment vehicle, such as a combination of an insurance-type payout and the ability to decompose and build up.

As for scalability, a consultant to the industry remarked:

One benefit a quantitative process brings to the management firms is the ability to apply a model quickly to a different set of stocks. For example, a firm that had been applying quant models to U.S. large cap also tested these models on 12–15 other major markets in the backroom. Once they saw that the models had a successful in-house track record in different universes, they began to commercialize these funds.

Among survey participants, the desire to stabilize costs, revenues, and performance or to improve the cost–revenues ratio were rated relatively low as motivating factors to introduce quantitative processes. But one source at a large asset management firm said that stabilizing costs, revenues, and performance was an important factor in the firm's decision to embrace a quantitative process. According to this source, "Over the years, the firm has seen great consistency in a quant process: Fees, revenues, and costs are all more stable, more consistent than with a fundamental process."

Bringing management costs down was rated by participants as the weakest factor behind the drive to implement a quantitative-driven equity investment process. A source at a large asset management firm with a small quantitative group said:

> Has management done a cost–benefit analysis of quant versus fundamental equity investment management process? Not to my knowledge. I was hired a few years ago to start up a quant process. But even if management had done a cost–benefit analysis and found quant attractive, it would not have been able to move into a quant process quickly. The average institutional investor has a seven-man team on the fund. If you were to switch to a two-man quant team, 80% of the clients would go away. Management has to be very careful; clients do not like to see change.

Barriers to Entry

The 2007 study concluded with an investigation of the barriers to entry in the business. Seventy-seven percent of the survey respondents believed that the active quantitative arena will continue to be characterized by the dominance of a few large players and a large number of small quant boutiques. Only 10% disagreed.

Participants were asked to rate a number of factors as barriers to new entrants into the quant equity investment space. The most important barrier remained the prevailing in-house culture. While one source at a fundamental-oriented firm said that very few firms are seriously opposed to trying to add discipline and improve performance by applying some quant techniques, the problem is that it is not so easy to change an organization.

A source at a large international investment consultancy commented:

> For a firm that is not quant-endowed, it is difficult to make the shift from individual judgment to a quant process. Those that have been most successful in terms of size in the active quant arena are those that began in passive quant. They chose passive because they

understood it would be easier for a quantitative process to perform well in passive as opposed to active management. Most of these firms have been successful in their move to active quant management.

A source at a large firm with fundamental and quant management styles said:

> Can a firm with a fundamental culture go quant? It is doable but the odds of success are slim. Fundamental managers have a different outlook and these are difficult times for quants.

Difficulty in recruiting qualified persons was rated the second most important barrier while the cost of qualified persons was considered less of a barrier. Next was the difficulty in gaining investor confidence and the entrenched position of market leaders. An industry observer remarked:

> What matters most is the investment culture and market credibility. If an investor does not believe that the manager has quant as a core skill, the manager will not be credible in the arena of quant products. There is the risk that the effort is perceived by the investor as a backroom effort with three persons, understaffed, and undercommitted.

Among the selling points, participants (unsurprisingly) identified alpha generation as the strongest selling point for quant funds, followed by the disciplined approach and better risk management. Lower management and trading costs and a statistics-based stock selection process were rated lowest among the suggested selling points.

Survey participants were also asked to rate factors holding back investment in active quant equity products. A lack of understanding of quant processes by investors and consultants was perceived to be the most important factor holding back investments in active quant products. As one quantitative manager at an essentially fundamental firm noted, "Quant products are unglamorous. There are no 'story' stocks to tell, so it makes it a hard sell for consultants to their clients."

The need to educate consultants and investors alike, in an effort to gain their confidence, was cited by several sources as a major challenge going forward. Educating investors might require more disclosure about quant processes. At least that was what just under half of the survey participants believed, while one-fourth disagree and one-fourth have no opinion.

One CIO of equities who believes that greater disclosure will be required remarked:

Following events of this summer [i.e., July–August 2007], quants will need to be better on explaining what they do and why it ought to work. They will need to come up with a rationale for what they are doing. They will have to provide more proof-of-concept statements.

However, among the sources that disagreed, the CIO of equities at another firm said:

One lesson from the events of July–August 2007 is that we will be more circumspect when describing what we are doing. Disclosing what one is doing can lead to others replicating the process and thus a reduction of profit opportunities.

Lack of stellar performance was rated a moderately important factor in holding back investments in quantitative funds. Lack of stellar performance is balanced by a greater consistency in performance. A source at a fund rating service said, "Because quant funds are broadly diversified, returns are watered down. Quants do not hit the ball out of the park, but they deliver stable performance." The ability to deliver stable if not stellar performance can, of course, be turned into a major selling point.

Quantitative managers cite how Oakland Athletics' manager Billy Beane improved his team's performance using sabermetrics, the analysis of baseball through objective (i.e., statistical) evidence. Beane's analysis led him to shifting the accent from acquiring players who hit the most home runs to acquiring players with the most consistent records of getting on base.[22] Interestingly, Beane is credited with having made the Oakland Athletics the most cost-effective team in baseball though winning the American League Championship Series has proved more elusive.

CHALLENGES FOR QUANTITATIVE EQUITY INVESTING

The studies we have just discussed suggested challenges that participants see in implementing quantitative strategies. We can see a number of additional challenges. Robust optimization, robust estimation, and the integration of the two are probably on the research agenda of many firms. As asset management firms strive to propose innovative products, robust and flexible optimization methods will be high on the R&D agenda. In addition, as asset management firms try to offer investment strategies to meet a stream of liabilities (i.e., measured against liability benchmarking),

---

[22]As reported in Michael Lewis, *Moneyball: The Art of Winning an Unfair Game* (New York: Norton, 2003).

multistage stochastic optimization methods will become a priority for firms wanting to compete in this arena. Pan, Sornette, and Kortanek call "Intelligent Finance" the new field of theoretical finance at the confluence of different scientific disciplines.[23] According to them, the theoretical framework of intelligent finance consists of four major components: (1) financial information fusion, (2) multilevel stochastic dynamic process models, (3) active portfolio and total risk management, and (4) financial strategic analysis.

Modelers are facing the problem of performance decay that is the consequence of a wider use of models. Classical financial theory assumes that agents are perfect forecasters in the sense that they know the stochastic processes of prices and returns. Agents do not make systematic predictable mistakes: their action keeps the market efficient. This is the basic idea underlying rational expectations and the intertemporal models of Merton.[24]

Practitioners (and now also academics) have relaxed the hypothesis of the universal validity of market efficiency; indeed, practitioners have always been looking for asset mispricings that could produce alpha. As we have seen, it is widely believed that mispricings are due to behavioral phenomena, such as belief persistence. This behavior creates biases in agent evaluations— biases that models attempt to exploit in applications such as momentum strategies. However, the action of models tends to destroy the same sources of profit that they are trying to exploit. This fact receives specific attention in applications such as measuring the impact of trades. In almost all current implementations, measuring the impact of trades means measuring the speed at which models constrain markets to return to an unprofitable efficiency. To our knowledge, no market impact model attempts to measure the opposite effect, that is, the eventual momentum induced by a trade.

It is reasonable to assume that the diffusion of models will reduce the mispricings due to behavioral phenomena. However, one might reasonably ask whether the impact of models on prices will ultimately make markets more efficient, destroying any residual profitability in excess of market returns, or if the action of implementing models will create new opportunities that can be exploited by other models, eventually by a new generation of models based on an accurate analysis of model biases. It is far from being obvious that markets populated by agents embodied in computerized programs tend to be efficient. In fact, models might create biases of their own. For example, momentum strategies (buy winners, sell losers) are a catalyst for increased momentum, further increasing the price of winners and depressing the price of losers.

---

[23]Heping Pan, Dider Sornette, and Kenneth Kortanek, "Intelligent Finance—An Emerging Direction." *Quantitative Finance* 6, no. 4 (2006): 273–277.
[24]Robert C. Merton, "An Intertemporal Capital Asset Pricing Model," *Econometrica* 41, no. 5 (1973): 867–887.

This subject has received much attention in the past as researchers studied the behavior of markets populated by boundedly rational agents. While it is basically impossible, or at least impractical, to code the behavior of human agents, models belong to a number of well-defined categories that process past data to form forecasts. Several studies, based either on theory or on simulation, have attempted to analyze the behavior of markets populated by agents that have bounded rationality, that is, filter past data to form forecasts.[25] One challenge going forward is to study what type of inefficiencies are produced by markets populated by automated decision-makers whose decisions are based on past data. It is foreseeable that simulation and artificial markets will play a greater role as discovery devices.

MODELING AFTER THE 2007–2009 GLOBAL FINANCIAL CRISIS

The period following the 2007–2009 global financial crisis has witnessed the acceleration of a number of modeling trends identified in previous research by Fabozzi, Focardi, and Jonas. In particular, the growing awareness of the nonnormal nature of returns is fueling efforts to adopt models and risk measures able to cope with nonlinearity. Among these are conditional value-at-risk (CVaR) to measure risk and copula functions to measure comovements. Regime shifting models, which are in principle able to capture transitions from one regime to another, for example from stable to volatile market states, are increasingly being considered as a modeling option. Modelers also sought to find new factors and new predictors (hopefully unique), using new data sources, in particular from the derivatives market. However, as equity markets began to rebound in 2010, modeling strategies that essentially work in growth markets were back in favor. This includes strategies such as equal-weighted portfolios that benefit from both mean reversion and upward market valuations.

The 2007–2009 global financial crisis underlined the importance of asset allocation in explaining returns. The renewed awareness of the overwhelming

---

[25]For the theoretical underpinning of bounded rationality from a statistical point of view, see Thomas J. Sargent, *Bounded Rationality in Macroeconomics* (New York: Oxford University Press, 1994). For the theoretical underpinning of bounded rationality from a behavioral finance perspective, see Daniel Kahneman, "Maps of Bounded Rationality: Psychology for Behavioral Economics," *American Economic Review* 93, no. 5 (2003): 1449–1475. For a survey of research on computational finance with boundedly rational agents, see Blake LeBaron, "Agent-Based Computational Finance," in *Handbook of Computational Economics*, edited by Leigh Tesfatsion and Kenneth L. Judd (Amsterdam: North-Holland, 2006).

importance of asset allocation, compared to, for example, stock selection or execution, has accelerated the adoption of dynamic asset allocation. According to the paradigm of dynamic asset allocation, investors switch into and out of asset classes, or at least dynamically change the weighting of different asset classes, as a function of the their forecast of the average return of each class. While traditional asset allocation is reviewed at time horizons of one to three years, the time horizon of dynamic asset allocation is typically of the order of months.

The execution process has also undergone important changes since about 2004. The increasing availability of intraday (or high frequency) data and modeling techniques based on optimizing the market impact of trades are behind the diffusion of program trading and high-frequency trading. Program trading, which utilizes computer programs to reduce the market impact of large trades by subdividing a large trade into many small trades with optimal rules, created a flow of high-frequency trades that has, in turn, created trading opportunities for those able to make, at a very low cost, many small trades with very short holding periods. Holding periods for high-frequency trades are generally less than one day and can be as short as a few milliseconds.

The diffusion of high-frequency trading, which is now estimated to represent more than half of all trading activity on major U.S and European exchanges, has fundamentally changed the characteristics of exchanges and created a new generation of models. High-frequency trading is a form of trading that leverages high-speed computing, high-speed communications, tick-by-tick data, and technological advances to execute trades in as little as milliseconds. A typical objective of high-frequency trading is to identify and capture (small) price discrepancies present in the market. This is done using computer algorithms to automatically capture and read market data in real-time, transmit thousands of order messages per second to an exchange, and execute, cancel or replace orders based on new information on prices or demand.[26]

Lastly, awareness of systemic risk has created a new area of research whose objective is to measure market connectivity. This research is based on a fundamental property of all random networks, namely that random networks exhibit connectivity thresholds. Below the connectivity thresholds, clusters remain small, with an exponential distribution; however, when approaching the connectivity threshold, very large clusters can be formed. This fact has an important bearing on risk management because connected

---

[26]For a review of the issues and opportunities associated with high-frequency trading, see Frank J. Fabozzi, Sergio M. Focardi, and Caroline Jonas, "High-Frequency Trading: Methodologies and Market Impact," *Review of Futures Markets*, 19 (2011): 7–38.

clusters might propagate large losses. An example from the 2007–2009 crisis is the propagation of losses due to the subprime mortgage crisis. Focardi and Fabozzi suggest the use of a connectivity parameter based on percolation theory to improve the measurement of credit risk.[27] More recently, and in the wake of the 2007–2009 global financial crisis, the Bank of England's executive director of financial stability Andrew Haldane, suggested the use of connectivity parameters to measure the risk of widespread contagion and propagation of losses.[28]

KEY POINTS

- The first decade of the twentieth century witnessed an increasing use of quantitative models in investment management.
- Initially used primarily in passive management and risk management, models are increasingly used in active management and to engineer innovative investment strategies such as the use of optimized indexes and dynamic asset allocation. One reason many investment firms built up quantitative teams was to have the ability to extend the product offering to new products for which there is demand, such as exchange-traded funds.
- The performance of models has improved; this improved performance has been particularly effective in active strategies, where it has helped reduce risk.
- Factor models are the primary methodology of financial modeling in investment management; they are used to forecast returns and to compute exposure to risk factors. Momentum and reversal models, cash flow-based models, and behavioral models are also widely used. It is likely that multiple models suitable for different market conditions are needed and we begin to see the deployment of adaptive models able to adapt to changing market conditions.
- Thanks to progress in robust estimation techniques and robust optimization methods, portfolio optimization is now being used in asset management.
- Execution has been impacted by the availability of tick-by-tick data and fast computer and communications technology, making program trading and subsequently high-speed trading the new "best execution."

---

[27]Sergio M. Focardi and Frank J. Fabozzi, "A Percolation Approach to Modeling Credit Loss Distribution Under Contagion," *Journal of Risk* 7, no. 1 (2004): 75–94.
[28]Andrew G. Haldane, "Rethinking the Financial Network," Speech to the Financial Student Association in Amsterdam (April 28, 2009).

- While much progress has been made in modeling, many economic and financial phenomena are still being handled by humans. Macroeconomic issues, such as the understanding of what conditions lead to a crisis are an example. However, new modeling techniques such as Markov switching models are beginning to tackle these areas.
- Looking forward a major use of methods to handle nonlinearities and fat-tailed distributions, the use of risk measures suitable for nonlinear distributions such as conditional VaR, and methods to measure the complexity of the financial system is expected.

QUESTIONS

1. What is the purpose of estimating model risk?

2. How is behavioral modeling used?

3. What are some of the reasons for the greater use of optimization techniques?

4. What are meant by a fundamental, quantitative, and hybrid investment processes?

5. a. Why are adaptive modeling techniques used by quantitative equity managers?
   b. Describe several examples of adaptive modeling techniques and the challenge in using them.

6. What is meant by "performance decay"?

7. How has the execution process undergone important changes in recent years?

CHAPTER 9

Implementable Quantitative Equity Research*

Frank J. Fabozzi, Ph.D., CFA, CPA
Professor of Finance
EDHEC Business School

Sergio M. Focardi, Ph.D.
Professor of Finance
EDHEC Business School
and
Partner, The Intertek Group

K. C. Ma, Ph.D., CFA
KCM Asset Management, Inc.
and
Roland George Chair of Applied Investments
Stetson University

Finance is by nature quantitative like economics but it is subject to a large level of risk. It is the measurement of risk and the implementation of decision-making processes based on risk that makes finance a quantitative science and not simply accounting. Equity investing is one of the most fundamental processes of finance. With the diffusion of affordable fast computers and with progress made in understanding financial processes, financial modeling has become a determinant of investment decision-making processes. Despite the growing diffusion of financial modeling, objections to its use are often raised.

---

*Parts of this chapter are adapted from Frank J. Fabozzi, Sergio M. Focardi, and K. C. Ma, "Implementable Quantitative Research and Investment Strategies," *Journal of Alternative Investments* 8, no. 2 (2005): 71–79.

In the second half of the 1990s, there was so much skepticism about quantitative equity investing that David Leinweber, a pioneer in applying advanced techniques borrowed from the world of physics to fund management, wrote an article entitled: "Is quantitative investment dead?"[1] In the article, Leinweber defended quantitative fund management and maintained that in an era of ever faster computers and ever larger databases, quantitative investment was here to stay. The skepticism toward quantitative fund management, provoked by the failure of some high-profile quantitative funds at that time, was related to the fact that investment professionals felt that capturing market inefficiencies could best be done by exercising human judgment.

Despite mainstream academic opinion that held that equity markets are efficient and unpredictable, the asset managers' job is to capture market inefficiencies and translate them into enhanced returns for their clients. At the academic level, the notion of efficient markets has been progressively relaxed. Empirical evidence led to the acceptance of the notion that financial markets are somewhat predictable and that systematic market inefficiencies can be detected. There has been a growing body of evidence that there are market anomalies that can be systematically exploited to earn excess profits after considering risk and transaction costs.[2] In the face of this evidence, Andrew Lo proposed replacing the efficient market hypothesis with the *adaptive market hypothesis* as market inefficiencies appear as the market adapts to changes in a competitive environment.[3]

In this scenario, a quantitative equity investment management process is characterized by the use of computerized rules as the primary source of decisions. In a quantitative process, human intervention is limited to a control function that intervenes only exceptionally to modify decisions made by computers. We can say that a quantitative process is a process that quantifies things. The notion of quantifying things is central to any modern science, including the dismal science of economics. Note that everything related to accounting—balance sheet/income statement data, and even accounting at the national level—is by nature quantitative. So, in a narrow sense, finance has always been quantitative. The novelty is that we are now quantifying things that are not directly observed, such as risk, or things that are not quantitative per se, such as market sentiment and that we seek simple rules to link these quantities.

[1]David Leinweber, "Is Quantitative Investing Dead?" *Pensions & Investments*, February 8, 1999.

[2]For a modern presentation of the status of market efficiency, see M. Hashem Pesaran, "Market Efficiency Today," Working Paper 05.41, Institute of Economic Policy Research, 2005.

[3]Andrew Lo, "The Adaptive Markets Hypothesis: Market Efficiency from an Evolutionary Perspective," *Journal of Portfolio Management* 30 (2004): 15–29.

The gradual move of replacing traditional human judgments with machine calculations is based on the assumption that computers outperform most humans. Since a quantitative process is capable of systematically handling a large amount of information quickly and consistently, ambiguity and unpredictability that are often associated with subjective choices during decision making can be kept to a minimum. For fact or fancy, most modern portfolio managers include some form of quantitative approach in their overall investment process.

However, "quants" are often too anxious and overzealous to prove their points. This attitude leads to several side effects that offset some of the advantages of quantitative analysis. First, cards can be unintentionally stacked toward locating some significant pattern that they are eager to show. Finding a way to do this is much easier than conventional subjective reasoning, due to fast computing power that allows numerous trials and errors. Second, using the conventional criterion of significance at some statistical level, researchers who are superstitious of its power often quickly jump to the wrong conclusion. What they sometimes fail to realize is that statistical significance is neither a necessary nor sufficient condition for implementable excess returns because trading strategies often work only on portions of the data. For example, a return reversal strategy might be profitable even if the information coefficient is very low at a good confidence level. Third, humans have a tendency to only look at the unusual. Do you notice an event because it is interesting or is it interesting because you notice it? The resulting bias is that theories are established or tests are performed more easily on extraordinary events, and seemingly correlations are easily mistaken for causalities. This bias is further reinforced by high-speed computing, since quantitative tools are very efficient in locating outliers and finding correlations.

In this chapter, we explain the process of performing quantitative equity research and converting that research into implementable trading strategies. We begin by comparing the discovery process in the physical sciences and in economics.

THE RISE OF ECONOPHYSICS

Before outlining a general framework for quantitative equity research, let's briefly compare the discovery process in the physical sciences and in economics. The classical view of scientific discovery (albeit grossly oversimplified) is one of empirical observations plus human genius. Vast amounts of data are collected and then a theoretical synthesis is made. The end result is a mathematical model that explains the data and allows accurate predictions. In modern science, this process forces us to make model revisions when even very small discrepancies occur between prediction and observation.

Let's mention a few points that have become pivotal to modern scientific methodology and that are important as well to economics:

1. "Observation" is far from being an obvious term. Any observation presupposes some theory. In the parlance of the modern philosophy of science, we say that observations are "theory laden." Thus we see a stratification of science, where advanced theories live on the back of simpler theories. For example, the so called "stylized facts" are an example of first level theories. They are empirical observations that presuppose a significant amount of theory.
2. There is an ongoing debate as to whether science actually "describes" an objective reality or simply provides recipes for predicting the outcome of observations without any descriptive pretension. In economics, the latter point of view was forcefully made by Milton Friedman.[4]
3. In general, different (infinite) models can explain the same data. The criterion of choice between different theories is often "aesthetic" in the sense of mathematical simplicity and elegance. Theories can always be mended to accommodate new facts: eventually they are replaced by simpler and more elegant theories.
4. It is questionable whether the process of discovery is an unexplicable product of human genius or if there is some compelling logic that inevitably leads to discoveries.

We do not want to discuss these points here, but only to point out that the above considerations have become important in economics and financial theories. There is one point of departure from economics and the physical sciences: in the physical sciences theories are constructed and validated on empirical data with a high level of accuracy. One makes experiments and tests different empirical settings. However, the level of statistical significance of theories in the physical sciences is extremely high

Methodologies used in economics[5] are different from those used in the physical sciences in three key ways:

1. Economic laws are never validated with a high level of precision: There is ample room for ambiguity.
2. The economy is a human artifact as well as an intelligent processor of information: One cannot think of the economy as a permanent physical

---

[4]Milton Friedman, *Essays in Positive Economics* (Chicago: University of Chicago Press, 1953).
[5]The same considerations apply to other scientific domains ranging from biology, medicine, ecological studies, and so on. Our focus here is economics.

object. In today's parlance, economies are evolving, self-reflecting, complex systems.

3. With the advent of computers, human creativity is complemented and even replaced by a learning approach based on statistics and data mining.

The field of "econophysics," a term used by Mantegna and Stanley,[6] has tried to bridge the gap between the two worlds, drawing attention to the need for strict scientific validation of laws and results. Still it is important to realize that true differences exist, to avoid the forcing upon economics of an impossible scientific paradigm. We have to ask on what genuine knowledge implementable strategies are based.

The level of significance of economic theories is low: No economic model fits data with a very high level of significance. Many different models fit data and it is often impossible to distinguish them on the basis of significance. The financial literature is full of bona fide defenses of contradictory facts. As a consequence, in economics it is very difficult to generalize and integrate theories. This happens because every theory or model is somehow misspecified and passes tests only within a given level of approximations and significance. When different models are integrated and generalized, approximations no longer hold.

For these reasons, two principles are fundamental in economic analysis: (1) model simplicity and (2) out-of-sample validation. We can place a higher level of confidence on a simple model validated on data different from those on which it has been built. These principles apply in particular when a "learning" approach is deployed. A learning approach is based on models of unbounded complexity able to perfectly fit any set of data. For example, an autoregressive model can have an arbitrary number of lags, a neural network can have an arbitrary number of nodes, and so on. Models of this type can describe any set of data with arbitrary precision. For example, provided that a sufficient number of lags is allowed, an autoregressive model can describe *any* time series with zero error. Forecasting performance, however, would be extremely bad as the model fits noise.

A GENERAL FRAMEWORK

The common objective of a quantitative process is to identify any persistent pattern in the data and, in finance, convert it into implementable

[6]Rosario N. Mantegna and H. Eugene Stanley, *An Introduction to Econophysics: Correlations and Complexity in Finance* (Cambridge: Cambridge University Press, 2000).

and profitable investment strategies. Given the relatively young life of its application to investment management, we find that there is a need to explore the general process of a quantitative procedure, and identify some of the commonly induced biases in this process. Specifically, in Exhibit 9.1, we provide a flowchart that demonstrates the process of how quantitative research is performed and converted into implementable trading strategies. Generally, it includes developing underlying economic theories, explaining actual returns, estimating expected returns, and formulating corresponding portfolios. We discuss each step in the following sections.

EXHIBIT 9.1   Process of Quantitative Research and Investment Strategy

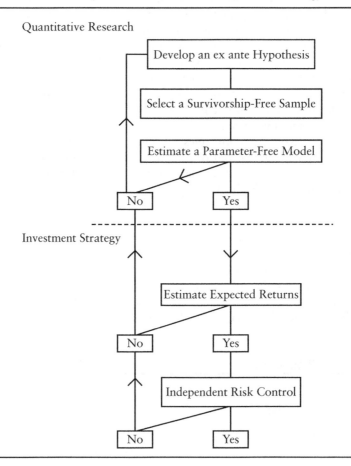

Develop a Truly Ex Ante Economic Justification

Sound economic hypothesis is a necessary condition for the birth of an implementable and replicable investment strategy. True economics, however, can only be motivated with creative intuitions and scrutinized by strict logical reasoning, but it does not come from hindsight or prior experience. This requirement is critical since scientific conclusions can easily be contaminated by the process of *data snooping*, especially when a truly independent economic theory is not established first.

Data snooping (or data mining) is identifying seemingly significant but in fact spurious patterns in the data.[7] All empirical tests are at risk for this problem, especially if a large number of studies have been performed on the same data sets. Given enough time and trials, people who are convinced of the existence of a pattern will eventually manage to find that pattern, real or imagined. Furthermore, there is an identical life cycle of experience in data snooping. Researchers are often confronted with exactly the same issues and will have to make the same types of choices in the process.

The process of data snooping comes in several forms. At some basic but subtle level, an economic hypothesis is founded by the knowledge of past patterns in data. Researchers may establish their "prior" from their knowledge, learning, experience, or simply what others have said. A good example for a classic yet wrong way to model the excess return is "market capitalization should be included in the model because there is evidence of a size effect."

From then on, the problem can only get worse as long as there is more room for choices. A researcher may choose to design the same statistical tests because of what others have done using similar data. The choices in these tests include, but are not limited to, the selection of explanatory variables, how to measure them, the functional form of the model, the length of the time period, the underlying probability distribution, and test statistics. The difference in each of these artificial choices by itself may be small, but its resulting investment performance impact is often significant.

Ideally, there should be no need to make artificial selections since all of the tests should have been dictated by the underlying economic theories. However, even the best economic concept, being abstract and simplified, does not always fully specify its application in reality. There are ample opportunities that decision makers have to find proxies and instruments to complete the process.

---

[7]See, for example, Stephen A. Ross, "Survivorship Bias in Performance Studies," and Andrew Lo, "Data-Snooping Biases in Financial Analysis," both appearing in *Proceedings of Blending Quantitative and Traditional Equity Analysis* (Charlottesville, VA: Association for Investment Management and Research, 1994).

Always Start from the Beginning!

A common fallacy, however, is that researchers tend to go back to the most immediate prior step in searching for solutions when the result is not what they expect to see. Of course, this attitude reflects the general human tendency to overweight the information in the most recent period in their decision making. This could easily lead to the mindless trial of numerous alternatives, which are most likely not justified.

Therefore, a direct way to control for data snooping at all levels is that the entire process will have to be reconstructed right from the beginning whenever the output at any step cannot pass the quality test. If the estimated model cannot explain the variation of excess returns to some satisfactory degree, the process needs to be stopped and abandoned. We need to go back to Step 1 and develop a new theory. If the predicted model does not produce acceptable excess returns, go back to Step 1. Finally, if the level of the actual risk-adjusted excess return found from following the strategy "does not cut the muster"—go back to Step 1. This "trial-and-error" process may correct for most, but not all, of the data snooping problem. As we throw away the obvious, "bad" models through testing, we learn from the experience of trial and error. This experience itself inevitably affects the seemingly "independent" creation of the economic intuition of next generation.

Of course, most of us would agree that there is almost no way to completely eliminate some form of data snooping since even the most rigorous scientific process is no more than a sequence of choices, subjective or not. As suggested by Andrew Lo,[8] like someone suffering from substance abuse, the first sign of recovery is the recognition of the problem. The next step is to facilitate a research environment that avoids the temptations of making choices. (This reluctance is probably the single most important reason for the recently developed machine learning techniques.) What this conclusion also means is that researchers should be extremely disciplined at every step of the process in making choices, with the explicit understanding of the problem and bias induced from data snooping.

SELECT A SAMPLE FREE FROM SURVIVORSHIP BIAS

Since all backtest research is performed on a data set that looks back in time, the entire history of an observation will not be available if it does not survive the present. The sample that researchers can work with is a set of observations that have been preselected through time by some common denominators. A sample of a sample should not pose a problem if the subset

---

[8]Lo, "Data-Snooping Biases in Financial Analysis."

is selected randomly. But this is not the case for most samples, which suffer from survivorship bias. The bias becomes relevant if the common bond to survive the observation is related to the pattern for which we are looking. A finding of a statistically significant pattern merely reflects the underlying common bond that was used to construct the testing sample.

One typical point of interest, which is severely affected by the survivorship bias, is performance comparison. By only looking at the portfolios currently outstanding, it is obvious that portfolios that did not survive through time due to poor performance are excluded from the sample. By design, the sample only contains good portfolios. How can the true factors that have caused the bad performance ever be identified?

Commercial data vendors are not helping on this issue. Because of cost consideration, most data sets are only provided on a live basis. That is, for a currently non-existent sample observation, the common practice is to delete its entire history from the data set. To simulate the true historical situation, it is the researchers' responsibility to bring these observations back to the sample. The sample collection procedure should be reversed in time. Cases that existed at the beginning of the sample period should be included and tracked through time.

SELECT A METHODOLOGY TO ESTIMATE THE MODEL

The selection of a certain methodology should pass the same quality tests as developing economic theories and selecting samples. Without strong intuition, researchers should choose the methodology that needs the least amount of human inputs. A good example is the machine-learning method that uses computerized algorithms to discover the knowledge (pattern or rule) inherent in data. Advances in modeling technology such as artificial intelligence, neural network, and genetic algorithms fit in this category. The beauty of this approach is its vast degree of freedom. There are none of the restrictions, which are often explicitly specified in traditional, linear, stationary models.

Of course, researchers should not rely excessively on the power of the method itself. Learning is impossible without knowledge. Even if you want to simply throw data into an algorithm and expect it to spit out the answer, you need to provide some background knowledge, such as the justification and types of input variables. There are still numerous occasions that require researchers to make justifiable decisions. For example, a typical way of modeling stock returns is using the following linear form,

$$ER_{it} = a + b_{1t}F1_{it-1} + b_{2t}F2_{it-1} + \dots b_{nt}Fn_{it-1} \tag{9.1}$$

where

ER_{it} = excess return for the ith security in period t

Fj_{it-1} = jth factor value for the ith security at the beginning of period t

b_{kt} = the market-wide payoff for factor k in period t

Trade-Off between Better Estimations and Prediction Errors

Undoubtedly, in testing and estimating equation (9.1), the first task is to decide which and how many explanatory variables should be included. This decision should not be a question whether the test is justified by a truly ex ante economic hypothesis. Economic theories, however, are often developed with abstract concepts that need to be measured by alternative proxies. The choice of proper proxies, while getting dangerously close to data snooping, makes the determination of both the type and the number of explanatory variables an art rather than a science. The choice of a particular proxy based on the rationale "Because it works!" is not sufficient unless it is first backed up by the theory.

One rule of thumb is to be parsimonious. A big model is not necessarily better, especially in the context of predictable risk-adjusted excess return. While the total power of explanation increases with the number of variables (size) in the model, the marginal increase of explanatory power drops quickly after some threshold. Whenever a new variable is introduced, what comes with the benefit of the additional description is the increase of estimation error of an additional parameter. In Exhibit 9.2, we demonstrate the explanatory power of a typical multifactor model for stock returns by including one additional variable at a time from a study conducted by Ma in 2010.[9] The second and the third columns clearly show that although by design the R-square increases with the number of the variables, the adjusted R-square, which also reflects the impact of the additional estimation error, levels off and starts decreasing after some point. This example suggests that in the process of estimation, the cost of estimation error is even compounded when new prediction is further extended into the forecast period. In Exhibit 9.2, we also perform out-of-sample prediction based on the estimated multifactor model in each stage. Columns 4 and 5 in the exhibit show a more striking pattern that the risk-adjusted excess return, in the form of information ratio, deteriorates even more quickly when the model becomes large.

---

[9]Christopher K. Ma, "How Many Factors Do You Need?" Research Paper #96-4, KCM Asset Management, Inc. (2005 and 2010).

EXHIBIT 9.2 Marginal Contribution of Additional Explanatory Variables

Additional Explanatory Variable	In Sample		Out of Sample		
	Explanatory Power (R^2)	Explanatory Power (Adj. R^2)	Annualized Excess Return (%)	Annualized Standard Deviation (%)	Information Ratio
1st	0.086	0.082	2.52	7.15	0.352
2nd	0.132	0.105	2.98	7.10	0.420
3rd	0.175	0.117	3.61	6.97	0.518
4th	0.188	0.165	3.82	6.82	0.560
5th	0.202	0.174	4.05	6.12	0.662
6th	0.251	0.239	3.99	6.08	0.656
7th	0.272	0.221	3.76	6.19	0.607
8th	0.282	0.217	3.71	6.22	0.596
9th	0.291	0.209	3.64	6.37	0.571
10th	0.292	0.177	3.53	6.58	0.536

Source: K. C. Ma, "How Many Factors Do You Need?" Research Paper #96-4, KCM Asset Management, Inc. (2010).

Animal Spirits

It is the exact same objectivity that quantitative analysts are proud of regarding their procedures that often leads to the question, "If everyone has the algorithms, will they not get the same answers?" The "overmining" on the same data set using simple linear models almost eliminates the possibility of gaining economic profit.

Pessimism resulting from the competition of quantitative research also justifies the need to include some form of "animal spirit" in the decision process. Being able to do so is also probably the single most important advantage that traditional security analysis can claim over quantitative approach. Casual observations provide ample examples that investor behavior determining market pricing follows neither symmetric nor linear patterns: investors tend to react to bad news much differently than to good news;[10] information in more recent periods is overweighed in the decision

---

[10]See Keith Brown, W. Van Harlow, and Seha.M. Tinic, "Risk Aversion, Uncertain Information, and Market Efficiency," *Journal of Financial Economics* 22, no. 2 (1988): 355–386.

process;[11] investors ignore the probability of the event but emphasize the magnitude of the event;[12] stocks are purchased for their glamour but not for intrinsic value;[13] and, low PE stocks paying high returns do not imply that high price–earnings stocks pay low returns.[14] We are not proposing that a quantitative model should include all these phenomenon, but the modeling methodology should be flexible enough to entertain such possibilities if they are warranted by the theory.

Statistical Significance Does Not Guarantee Economic Profits

As a result, staunch defenders of quantitative research argue that profitable strategies cannot be commercialized by quantitative analysis;[15] the production of excess returns will stay idiosyncratic and proprietary. Profits will originate in those proprietary algorithms that outperform commercially standardized packages for data analysis. In other words, researchers will have to learn to gain confidence even if there is no statistical significance, while statistical significance does not guarantee economic profit.

Since quantitative market strategists often start with the identification of a pattern that is defined by statistical standards, it is easy to assume economic profit from conventional statistical significance. To show that there is not necessarily a link, we perform a typical momentum trading strategy that is solely based on the predictability of future returns from past returns. A simplified version of the return-generating process under this framework follows:

$$E_{t-1}(R_t) = a + b_{t-1}R_{t-1}$$

where $E_{t-1}(R_t)$ is the expected return for the period t, estimated at point $t - 1$, a is time-invariant return, and b_{t-1} is the momentum coefficient observed at time t-1. When b_{t-1} is (statistically) significantly positive, the time-series returns are said to exhibit persistence and positive momentum. To implement the trading strategy using the information in correlations, stocks with

---

[11]See Werner F. DeBondt and Richard Thaler," Does the Stock Market Overreact?" *Journal of Finance* 40, no. 1 (1985): 793–805.

[12]See K. C. Ma, "Preference Reversal in Futures Markets," working paper, Stetson University, 2010.

[13]See Josef Lakonishok, Andrei Shleifer, and Robert W. Vishny, "Contrarian Investment, Extrapolation, and Risk," *Journal of Finance* 49, no. 5 (1994): 1541–1578.

[14]See K. C. Ma, "How Many Factors Do You Need?" Stetson University, 2005 and 2010.

[15]See, for example, Russell H. Fogler, "Investment Analysis and New Quantitative Tools," *Journal of Portfolio Management* (1995): 39–47.

EXHIBIT 9.3   Statistical Significance and Economic Profits

Correlation Coefficient[a]	t-Value[b]	Annual Excess Return (%)	Annual Standard Deviation (%)	Information Ratio
0.10	2.10[b]	0.50	2.17	0.230
0.25	3.78[b]	1.82	4.06	0.448
0.50	7.15[b]	3.71	4.25	0.873
0.15	1.20	0.58	1.10	0.527
0.35	2.93[b]	1.98	4.55	0.435
0.60	2.75[b]	3.80	4.55	0.835

[a]Significant at the 1% level.
[b]t-value is for the significance of correlation coefficient.
Source: K. C. Ma, "How Many Factors Do You Need?" Research Paper #96-4, KCM Asset Management, Inc., 2010.

at least a certain level of correlation are included in portfolios at the beginning of each month, and their returns are tracked. The performance of these portfolios apparently reflects the statistical significance (or lack of) in correlation between successive returns. In Exhibit 9.3, we summarize the performance of some of the representative portfolios from a study conducted and updated by Ma in 2005 and 2010.[16]

It is not surprising that higher excess returns are generally associated with higher correlation between successive returns. More importantly, higher risk seems to be also related to higher statistical significance of the relationship (correlation). The bottom line is that an acceptable level of risk-adjusted excess return, in the form of information ratio (e.g., 1), cannot always be achieved by statistical significance alone. A more striking observation, however, is that, sometime without conventional statistical significance, the portfolio was able to deliver superior risk-adjusted economic profit. While the driving force may yet be known, evidence is provided for the disconnection between statistical significance and economic profit.

A Model to Estimate Expected Returns

The estimation for the model to explain past returns from Step 3, by itself, is not enough, since the objective of the process is to predict future returns. A good model for expected return is much harder to come by since we simply don't have enough data. As pointed out by Fischer Black, people are often confused between a model to explain average returns and a model to predict

---

[16]Ma, "How Many Factors Do You Need?" 2005 and 2010.

expected returns.[17] While the former can be tested on a large number of historical data points, the latter requires such a long time period (sometimes decades) to cover various conditions to predict the expected return. Since we do not have that time to wait, one common shortcut is to simply assume that the model to explain average returns will be the model to predict expected returns. Of course, such prediction is highly inaccurate, given the assumption of constant expected returns.

We can easily find evidence to show it is a bad assumption. For example, if one can look at the actual model that explains the cross-sections of short-term stock returns, even the most naive researcher can easily conclude that there is little resemblance between the models from one period to the next. This would in turn suggest, at least in the short term, the model to explain past returns cannot be used to predict expected returns.

We are calling for brand new efforts to establish an ex ante expected return model. The process has to pass the same strict tests for quality that are required for any good modeling, as discussed earlier. These tests would include the independent formulation of the hypothesis for expected return and a methodology and sample period free from data snooping and survivorship bias. While they are not necessarily related, the process of developing hypotheses for conditional expected return models can greatly benefit from the insights from numerous models of past returns estimated over a long time period.

Largest Value Added

Apparently, the final risk-adjusted returns from a strategy can be attributed to the proper execution of each step described in Exhibit 9.1. The entire process can be generally described in a three-step procedure consisting of economic hypothesis, model estimation, and prediction. It is only natural for researchers to ask how to allocate their efforts among the three steps to maximize the return contribution.

To answer this question, we examine the return contribution from model estimation and prediction. For this purpose, we use a typical multifactor model to explain the return for all stocks in the Standard & Poor's 500 Index. Assume that at the beginning of each period, the best model actually describing the return in the period is known to the portfolio manager. Using this information, a portfolio consisting of the predicted top quartile is formed. The excess return from this portfolio generated with perfect information would suggest the extent of return contribution from

---

[17]Fischer Black, "Estimating Expected Return," *Financial Analysts Journal* 49, no. 5 (1993): 36–38.

EXHIBIT 9.4   Potential Returns for Perfect Estimation and Prediction:
S&P 500 Stocks, 1975–2010

| | Annualized Excess Returns if Perfect Foresight | | | |
| | Best Model[a] for S&P 500 | | Actual[b] S&P 500 Quartiles | |
	Top Quartile	Bottom Quartile	Top Quartile	Bottom Quartile
Monthly period[c]	19.3%	–21.4%	121.7%	–97.5%
Quarterly period	25.7	–26.1	91.2	–82.1
Annual period	11.8	–13.6	42.5	–26.7

[a]The parameters of the actual model to explain S&P 500 performance is known beforehand.
[b]The performance of each stock, in terms of the actual quartile, is known beforehand.
[c]The length of investment horizon for each portfolio is rebalanced based on the perfect information.
Source: K. C. Ma, "Nonlinear Factor Payoffs?" Research Paper #97-5, KCM Asset Management, Inc., 2010.

model estimation. Accordingly, based on a 2010 study by Ma[18] reported in Exhibit 9.4, the annual mean excess return of the top predicted quartile is between 12% and 26%, depending on the length of the investment horizon.

In contrast, the annual mean excess return of the actual top quartile in the S&P 500 Index is between 42% and 121%. The difference in excess return between the actual top quartile portfolio and the predicted top quartile portfolio, between 30% and 95%, would suggest the extent of the return contribution from model prediction. It is clear then that for all investment horizons, the return contribution from model prediction is on average two to five times the excess returns from model estimation.

Therefore, for all practical purposes, the step of identifying a predictable model is responsible for the largest potential value added in generating predictable excess returns. The implication is that resources allocated to research should be placed disproportionately toward the effort of out-of-sample prediction.

Test the Prediction Again!

Another safeguard against data snooping is to scrutinize the model once more through time. That is, the conditional model to estimate expected return needs to be tested again in a "fresh" data period. As it requires multiple

[18]K. C. Ma, "Nonlinear Factor Payoffs?" Research Paper #97-5, KCM Asset Management, Inc., 2010.

EXHIBIT 9.5   The Sample Period

Estimation	Testing	Forecast	Estimation	Testing	Forecast	
Period I	Period I	Period I	Period II	Period II	Period II	...Now

time periods to observe the conditional model for expected returns, the prediction model derived under a single condition has to be confirmed again. In Exhibit 9.5, we specify the relationship in time periods among estimation, testing, and confirmation.

The sequential testing of the prediction model in the forecast period would affirm the condition that converts the model of actual returns to the model of expected returns still produces an acceptable level of performance. As the conditioning factor varies from one period to anther, the consistent performance of the three-period process suggests that it is not driven by a constant set of artificial rules introduced by data snooping.

Test against a Random Walk

After completing the modeling exercise it is always wise to test the model against an artificial data set formed from independent and identically distributed returns. Any trading strategy applied to purely random data should yield no average profit. Of course, purely random fluctuations will produce profits and losses. However, because we can simulate very long sequences of data, we can test with high accuracy that our models do not actually introduce artefacts that will not live up to a real life test.

RISK CONTROL

Even if the expected return is modeled properly at the individual stock level, the bottom line of implementable investment strategies is evaluated by an acceptable level of risk-adjusted portfolio excess returns. As most institutional portfolios are benchmarked, the goal is to minimize tracking error (standard deviation of excess returns), given some level of portfolio excess return. Consequently, risk control becomes technically much more complex than the conventional efficient portfolio concept. As shown by Richard Roll, an optimal portfolio that minimizes tracking error subject to a level of excess return is not a mean-variance efficient portfolio.[19] It should be noted that, due to the objective and competitive nature of the quantitative approach in its strong form, most models produce similar rankings in

---

[19]Richard R. Roll, "A Mean/Variance Analysis of Tracking Error," *Journal of Portfolio Management* 18, no. 4 (1992): 13–23.

expected returns. The variation in performance among quantitative portfolios is mainly attributed to a superior risk control technology.

One commonly used, but less preferred practice in risk management is often performed right at the stage of identifying the model for expected returns. It involves revising the estimates from the model to explain the actual return. The purpose is to control the risk by attempting to reduce the estimation error for the model of expected returns. This approach has several flaws. First, in most cases, the procedure of revising the parameter estimates (from the model of actual returns) so they can be used in the model of expected returns is often performed on an ad hoc basis, and vulnerable to data snooping. Second, in revising the parameter estimates, the task of building a relevant expected model with low prediction errors is mistaken for risk control on portfolio returns. Finally, there is a lesser degree of freedom in that estimates are made based on the estimates of previous steps. The "risk control" procedure becomes dependent to the process of estimating expected returns. Consequently, an independent risk control procedure, usually through an optimization process, should be performed as an overlay on the stock selections that are determined initially by the predicted expected returns.

For computing efficiency, the iterations can be significantly reduced if several other conditions are simultaneously imposed. For example, it has been shown that the largest source of tracking error is the deviation of portfolio sector weights from its benchmark sector weights.[20] Consequently, most optimal benchmarked portfolios are "sector neutral," that is, portfolios do not make sector bets against the benchmark. This consideration would indicate the need to include a constraint that sets maximum acceptable deviations of portfolio sector weights from benchmark sector weights.

Along the same line, tracking error can be further controlled when the individual stock weight is constrained to conform to its corresponding weight in the benchmark. It is also accomplished by setting a maximum allowed deviation of stock weight in the portfolio from the weight in the benchmark.

Additional realistic portfolio constraints may be considered. Examples would include specification of a (1) minimum level of market liquidity for individual stocks, (2) maximum absolute weight in which any stock is allowed to invest, (3) minimum total number of stocks held, (4) minimum number of stocks held in each sector, and (5) maximum level of portfolio turnover allowed.

---

[20]See Ma, "Nonlinear Factor Payoffs?"

KEY POINTS

- Despite mainstream academic opinion equity markets are efficient, there is a growing body of evidence that there are market anomalies that can be systematically exploited to earn excess profits after considering risk and transaction costs.
- The technological advances in computing power have tempted investors to use machines to make investment decisions. In the process of doing so, it is easy to lose sight of the essence of human knowledge required in any good decision making process.
- In evaluating models for potential implementation of investment strategies, two guiding principles are model simplicity and out-of-sample validation. We can place a higher level of confidence on a simple model validated on data different from those on which it has been built.
- In the quantitative process the identification of any persistent pattern in the data is sought and must then be converted it into implementable and profitable investment strategies. How this is done requires the development of underlying economic theories, an explanation of actual returns, estimation of expected returns, and construction of corresponding portfolios.
- For backtesting proposed strategies, the sample used can be a set of observations that have been preselected through time by some common denominators. Although a sample of a sample should not pose a problem in backtesting if the subset is selected randomly, this is not the case for most samples that suffer from survivorship bias. A statistically significant pattern found for a strategy may merely reflect the underlying common bond that was used to construct the testing sample.
- The selection of a methodology for estimating a model should satisfy the same quality tests as developing economic theories and selecting samples. In the absence of strong intuition, the methodology that needs the least amount of human inputs should be employed for estimating a model.
- For both testing and model estimation, the first task is to decide which and how many explanatory variables should be included. Economic theories underlying a model typically involve abstract concepts that need to be measured by alternative proxies. Selection of the appropriate proxies, while getting dangerously close to data snooping, makes the determination of both the type and the number of explanatory variables an art rather than a science. One rule of thumb is to be parsimonious.
- To safeguard against data snooping there should be a sequential testing of the prediction model in the forecast period in order to affirm that the condition that converts the model of actual returns to the model of expected returns still produces an acceptable level of performance.

■ Even if the expected return is modeled properly at the individual stock level, the bottom line of implementable investment strategies is evaluated by an acceptable level of risk-adjusted portfolio excess returns. Because most institutional portfolios are benchmarked, the objective is to minimize tracking error given some level of portfolio excess return. For this purpose, risk control becomes technically much more complex than the conventional efficient portfolio concept.

QUESTIONS

1. What is the extent and purpose of human intervention in a quantitative investment management process?

2. How are the methodologies utilized in economics different from those employed in the physical sciences?

3. What is the common objective of all quantitative processes?

4. What are the steps in the process for converting quantitative research into an implementable trading process?

5. What is meant by "data snooping"?

6. Why would it be prudent to test a quantitative model before it is implemented against an artificial data set formed from independent and identically distributed returns?

Tracking Error and Common Stock Portfolio Management

Raman Vardharaj, CFA
Portfolio Manager
OppenheimerFunds

Frank J. Fabozzi, Ph.D., CFA, CPA
Professor of Finance
EDHEC Business School

Frank J. Jones, Ph.D.
Professor of Finance
San Jose State University

In this chapter, we describe the concept of tracking error, how it is computed, and identify some of the factors that affect tracking error for an equity portfolio.

DEFINITION OF TRACKING ERROR

The risk of a portfolio can be measured by the standard deviation of portfolio returns. This statistical measure provides a range around the average return of a portfolio within which the actual return over a period is likely to fall with some specific probability. The mean return and standard deviation (or volatility) of a portfolio can be calculated over a period of time.

The standard deviation or volatility of a portfolio or a market index is an absolute number. A portfolio manager or client can also ask what the variation of the return of a portfolio is relative to a specified benchmark. Such variation is called the portfolio's *tracking error*.

Specifically, tracking error measures the dispersion of a portfolio's returns relative to the returns of its benchmark. That is, tracking error is the standard deviation of the portfolio's *active return* where active return is defined as:

Active return = Portfolio actual return − Benchmark actual return

A portfolio created to match the benchmark index (i.e., an index fund) that regularly has zero active returns (i.e., always matches its benchmark's actual return) would have a tracking error of zero. But a portfolio that is actively managed that takes positions substantially different from the benchmark would likely have large active returns, both positive and negative, and thus would have an annual tracking error of, say, 5% to 10%.

To find the tracking error of a portfolio, it is first necessary to specify the benchmark. The tracking error of a portfolio, as indicated, is its standard deviation relative to the benchmark, not its total standard deviation. Exhibit 10.1 presents the information used to calculate the tracking error for a hypothetical portfolio and benchmark using 30 weekly observations. The fourth column in the exhibit shows the active return for the week. It is from the data in this column that the tracking error is computed. As reported in the exhibit, the standard deviation of the weekly active returns is 0.54%. This value is then annualized by multiplying by the square root of 52—52 representing the number of weeks in a year. This gives a value of 3.89%. If the observations were monthly rather than weekly, the monthly tracking error would be annualized by multiplying by the square root of 12.

Given the tracking error, a range for the possible portfolio active return and corresponding range for the portfolio can be estimated assuming that the active returns are normally distributed. For example, assume the following:

Benchmark = S&P 500
Expected return on S&P 500 = 20%
Tracking error relative to S&P 500 = 2%

Then, the range for portfolio returns and associated probabilities are as follows:

Number of Standard Deviations	Range for Portfolio Active Return	Corresponding Range for Portfolio Return	Probability
1	±2%	18%–22%	67%
2	±4%	16%–24%	95%
3	±6%	14%–26%	99%

EXHIBIT 10.1 Data and Calculation for Active Return, Alpha, and Information Ratio

Week	Weekly Returns (%) Portfolio	Benchmark	Active
1	3.69%	3.72%	−0.03%
2	−0.56	−1.09	0.53
3	−1.41	−1.35	−0.06
4	0.96	0.34	0.62
5	−4.07	−4.00	−0.07
6	1.27	0.91	0.37
7	−0.39	−0.08	−0.31
8	−3.31	−2.76	−0.55
9	2.19	2.11	0.09
10	−0.02	−0.40	0.37
11	−0.46	−0.42	−0.05
12	0.09	0.71	−0.62
13	−1.93	−1.99	0.06
14	−1.91	−2.37	0.46
15	1.89	1.98	−0.09
16	−3.75	−4.33	0.58
17	−3.38	−4.22	0.84
18	0.60	0.62	−0.02
19	−10.81	−11.60	0.79
20	6.63	7.78	−1.15
21	3.52	2.92	0.59
22	1.24	1.89	−0.66
23	−0.63	−1.66	1.03
24	3.04	2.90	0.14
25	−1.73	−1.58	−0.15
26	2.81	3.05	−0.23
27	0.40	1.64	−1.23
28	1.03	1.03	0.01
29	−0.94	−0.95	0.00
30	1.45	1.66	−0.21

Average of active returns = 0.04%
Standard deviation of active returns = 0.54%

Annualizing:
  Annual average = Weekly average × 52
  Annual variance = Weekly variance × 52
  Annual std dev = Weekly std dev × ($52^{0.5}$)

Therefore, on an annual basis:
Alpha = 1.83% (= 0.04% × 52 = Annualized average of weekly active returns)
Tracking error = 3.89% (= 0.54% × [$52^{0.5}$] = Annualized std dev of weekly active returns)
Information ratio = Alpha/Tracking error = 1.83%/3.89%= 0.47

Tracking Error for an Active/Passive Portfolio

A manager can pursue a blend of an active and a passive (i.e., indexing) strategy. That is, a manager can construct a portfolio such that a certain percentage of the portfolio is indexed to some benchmark index and the balance actively managed. Assume that the passively managed portion (i.e., the indexed portion) has a zero tracking error relative to the index. For such a strategy, we can show (after some algebraic manipulation) that the tracking error for the overall portfolio would be as follows:

> Portfolio tracking error relative to index
> = (Percent of portfolio actively managed)
>   × (Tracking error of the actively managed portion relative to index)

An enhanced index fund differs from an index fund in that it deviates from the index holdings in small amounts and hopes to slightly outperform the index through those small deviations. In terms of an active/passive strategy, the manager allocates a small percentage of the portfolio to be actively managed. The reason is that in case the bets prove detrimental, then the underperformance would be small. Thus, realized returns would always deviate from index returns only by small amounts. There are many enhancing strategies. Suppose that a manager whose benchmark is the S&P 500 pursues an enhanced indexing strategy allocating only 5% of the portfolio to be actively managed and 95% indexed. Assume further that the tracking error of the actively managed portion is 15% with respect to the S&P 500. The portfolio would then have a tracking error calculated as follows:

> Percent of portfolio actively managed relative to S&P 500 = 5%
> Tracking error relative to S&P 500 = 15%
> Portfolio's tracking error relative to S&P 500 = 5% × 15% = 0.75%

COMPONENTS OF TRACKING ERROR

There are two distinct approaches to portfolio selection. The first is a top-down approach. Here the manager tries to pick broad economic themes, such as sectors, style, size, and the like, which are likely to outperform in the coming periods and holds stocks that are consistent with the chosen theme. The second is a bottom-up approach, where the manager picks each individual stock in the portfolio on its own merit.

Insofar as the themes or stocks emphasized in the portfolio differ from those in the benchmark (through overweights and underweights), there will be a tracking error. We can then view the tracking error as arising partly from the theme-picking and partly from the stock-picking.

Since top-down managers believe they can add value mainly through discerning trends in returns associated with broad themes, they may want to reduce the portion of their portfolio's tracking error that arises from stock-specific reasons.

Bottom-up managers believe it is difficult, if not impossible, to forecast trends in themes. Returns associated with such broad themes tend to be volatile and this can amplify mistakes. Such managers believe it is more prudent to place a lot of small bets via stock selection than to place a few large bets via theme selection. Bottom-up managers would, therefore, seek to reduce the portion of the tracking error of their portfolios that comes from theme-specific reasons.

To answer the needs of these two types of managers, it would be useful to decompose a portfolio's tracking error along these lines. Fortunately, this can be done using multifactor risk models.

FORWARD-LOOKING VS. BACKWARD-LOOKING TRACKING ERROR

In Exhibit 10.1 the tracking error of the hypothetical portfolio is shown based on the active returns reported. However, the performance shown is the result of the portfolio manager's decisions during those 30 weeks with respect to portfolio positioning issues such as beta, sector allocations, style tilt (that is, value versus growth), stock selections, and the like. Hence, we can call the tracking error calculated from these trailing active returns a *backward-looking tracking error*. It is also called the ex post tracking error.

One problem with a backward-looking tracking error is that it does not reflect the effect of current decisions by the portfolio manager on the future active returns and hence the future tracking error that may be realized. If, for example, the manager significantly changes the portfolio beta or sector allocations today, then the backward-looking tracking error that is calculated using data from prior periods would not accurately reflect the current portfolio risks going forward. That is, the backward-looking tracking error will have little predictive value and can be misleading regarding portfolio risks going forward.

The portfolio manager needs a forward-looking estimate of tracking error to accurately reflect the portfolio risk going forward. The way this is done in practice is by using the services of a commercial vendor that has a model, called a multifactor risk model, that has defined the risks associated with a benchmark index. Statistical analysis of the historical return data of the stocks in the benchmark index are used to obtain the factors and quantify their risks. (This involves the use of variances and correlations.) Using the manager's current portfolio holdings, the portfolio's current exposure to the various factors can be calculated and compared to the benchmark's exposures to the factors. Using the differential factor exposures and the risks of the factors, a *forward-looking tracking error* for the portfolio can be computed. This tracking error is also referred to as the *predicted tracking error* or *ex ante tracking error*.

There is no guarantee that the forward-looking tracking error at the start of, say, a year would exactly match the backward-looking tracking error calculated at the end of the year. There are two reasons for this. The first is that as the year progresses and changes are made to the portfolio, the forward-looking tracking error estimate would change to reflect the new exposures. The second is that the accuracy of the forward-looking tracking error depends on the extent of the stability in the variances and correlations that were used in the analysis. These problems notwithstanding, the average of forward-looking tracking error estimates obtained at different times during the year will be reasonably close to the backward-looking tracking error estimate obtained at the end of the year.

Each of these estimates has its use. The forward-looking tracking error is useful in risk control and portfolio construction. The manager can immediately see the likely effect on tracking error of any intended change in the portfolio. Thus, she can do a what-if analysis of various portfolio strategies and eliminate those that would result in tracking errors beyond her tolerance for risk. The backward-looking tracking error can be useful for assessing actual performance analysis, such as the information ratio discussed next. Evaluating the factors that caused past portfolio performance, called *attribution analysis*, is an important use.

INFORMATION RATIO

Alpha is the average active return over a time period. Since backward-looking tracking error measures the standard deviation of a portfolio's active return, it is different from alpha. A portfolio does not have backward-looking tracking error simply because of outperformance or underperformance. For instance, consider a portfolio that outperforms (or underperforms) its benchmark by exactly 10 basis points every month. This portfolio would have a backward-looking tracking error of zero and a positive (negative) alpha of 10 basis points. In contrast, consider a portfolio that outperforms its benchmark by 10 basis points during half the months and underperforms by 10 basis points during the other months. This portfolio would have a backward-looking tracking error that is positive but an alpha equal to zero.

(Note that in some texts, alpha and tracking error are calculated respectively as the average and the standard deviation of the beta-adjusted active return, instead of the total active return.)

The *information ratio* combines alpha and tracking error as follows:

$$\text{Information ratio} = \frac{\text{Alpha}}{\text{Backward-looking tracking error}}$$

The information ratio is essentially a reward-to-risk ratio. The reward is the average of the active return, that is, alpha. The risk is the standard deviation of the active return, the tracking error, and, more specifically, backward-looking tracking error. The higher the information ratio, the better the manager performed relative to the risk assumed.

To illustrate the calculation of the information ratio, consider the active returns for the hypothetical portfolio shown in Exhibit 10.1. The weekly average active return is 0.04%. Annualizing the weekly average active return by multiplying by 52 gives an alpha of 1.83%. Since the backward-tracking error is 3.89%, the information ratio is 0.47 (1.83%/3.89%).

DETERMINANTS OF TRACKING ERROR

Several factors affect the level of tracking error. The major factors include:

- Number of stocks in the portfolio
- Portfolio market capitalization and style difference relative to the benchmark
- Sector deviation from the benchmark
- Market volatility
- Portfolio beta

The impact of each of these factors is investigated in Vardharaj, Fabozzi, and Jones.[1]

Number of Stocks in the Portfolio

Tracking error decreases as the portfolio progressively includes more of the stocks that are in the benchmark index. This general effect is illustrated in Exhibit 10.2 that shows the effect of portfolio size for a large-cap portfolio benchmarked to the S&P 500. Notice that an optimally chosen portfolio of just 50 stocks can track the S&P 500 within 1.6%. For midcap and

---

[1]Raman Vardharaj, Frank J. Fabozzi, and Frank J. Jones, "Determinants of Tracking Error For Equity Portfolios," *Journal of Investing* 13, no. 2 (2004): 37–47.

EXHIBIT 10.2 Typical Tracking Error vs. the Number of Benchmark Stocks in the Portfolio for the S&P 500

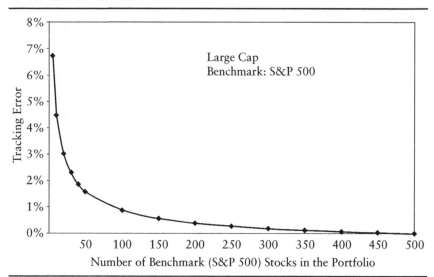

small-cap stocks, Vardharaj, Fabozzi, and Jones found that the tracking errors are 3.5% and 4.3%, respectively.[2] In contrast, tracking error increases as the portfolio progressively includes more stocks that are not in the benchmark. This effect is illustrated in Exhibit 10.3. In this case, the benchmark index is the S&P 100 and the portfolio progressively includes more and more stocks from the S&P 500 that are not in the S&P 100. The result is that the tracking error with respect to the S&P 100 rises.

Portfolio Market Cap and Style Difference Relative to the Benchmark

Vardharaj, Fabozzi, and Jones found tracking error increases as the average market cap of the portfolio deviates from that of the benchmark index.[3] Tracking error also increases as the overall style (growth/value) of the portfolio deviates from that of the benchmark index. First, holding style constant, they find that tracking error rises when the cap size difference increases. For example, a midcap blend portfolio has a tracking error of 7.07% while a small-cap blend portfolio has a tracking error of 8.55% with respect to the S&P 500, which is a large-cap blend portfolio. Second, for a given cap size, tracking error is greater when the style is either growth or value than when it is the blend.

---

[2]Ibid.
[3]Ibid.

EXHIBIT 10.3 Tracking Error vs. the Number of Nonbenchmark Stocks in the Portfolio

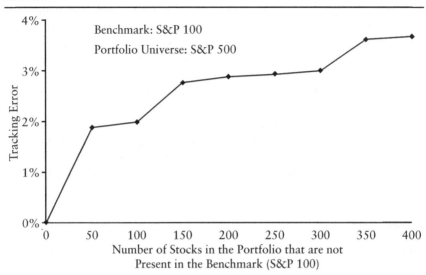

Vardharaj, Fabozzi, and Jones examine portfolios that deviate from the S&P 500 either in cap size or in style and have the same tracking error. They find that the farther a portfolio is from the center of the Morningstar equity fund box for large-cap blend stocks (proxied by S&P 500), the greater is its tracking error.

Sector Deviation from the Benchmark

When a portfolio's allocations to various economic sectors differ from those of its benchmark, it results in tracking error. In general, when the differences in sector allocation increase, the tracking error increases. Vardharaj, Fabozzi, and Jones found that in general, the tracking error increased as the level of sector bets increased.

Market Volatility

Managed portfolios generally hold only a fraction of the assets in their benchmark. Given this, a highly volatile benchmark index (as measured in terms of standard deviation) would be harder to track closely than a generally less volatile benchmark index. As market volatility rises, the portfolio tracking error increases. This correspondingly increases the probability of "dramatic underperformance," by which we mean an underperformance of 10% or more. This can be seen in Exhibit 10.4. On the horizontal axis of the exhibit is the tracking error and on the vertical axis is the probability of a shortfall of 10% or more from the benchmark index. (In this calculation, we assumed normal distribution of active returns and an alpha of zero.)

As the tracking error rises, the probability of dramatic outperformance increases just as much as the probability of dramatic underperformance. But, the portfolio management consequences of these two types of extreme relative performances are not symmetric—dramatic underperformance can cause a manager to be terminated. Another implication is that since an increase in market volatility increases tracking error and, thereby, the chances of dramatic underperformance, there is an increased need for managers to monitor the portfolio tracking error more frequently and closely during periods of high market volatility.

Portfolio Beta

The beta for the market portfolio is 1 and beta for the risk-free portfolio (cash) is zero. Suppose an investor holds a combination of cash and the market portfolio. Then, the portfolio beta falls below 1. The managed portfolio is less sensitive to systematic risk than the market, and is therefore less risky than the market. Conversely, when the investor holds a leveraged market portfolio, by borrowing at the risk-free rate and investing in the market portfolio, the beta is above 1, and the portfolio is more risky than the market.

EXHIBIT 10.4   Tracking Error and Dramatic Shortfall

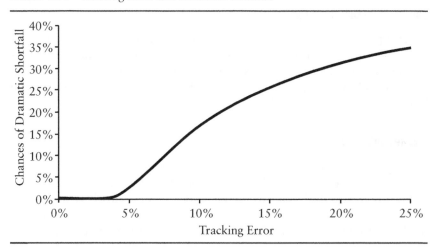

EXHIBIT 10.5   Tracking Error and Beta

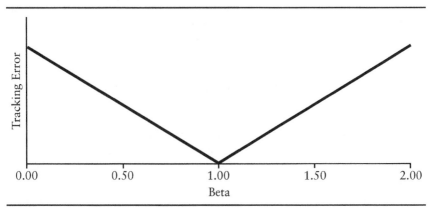

It can be demonstrated that the portfolio tracking error with respect to the market portfolio, increases both when the beta falls below 1 and when the beta rises above 1. So, as the portfolio increases the proportion of cash held, even though its absolute risk falls, its tracking error risk rises. As shown in Exhibit 10.5, tracking error rises linearly as the beta deviates from 1.

In the above example, we make the simplistic assumption that the manager only chooses between holding the market portfolio and cash when making changes to its beta. In the more general case where the fund can hold any number of stocks in any proportion, its beta can differ from 1 due to other reasons. But, even in this general case, the tracking error increases when the portfolio beta deviates from the market beta.

MARGINAL CONTRIBUTION TO TRACKING ERROR

Since tracking error arises from various bets (some intentional and some unintentional) placed by the manager through overweights and underweights relative to the benchmark index, it would be useful to understand how sensitive the tracking error is to small changes in each of these bets.

Suppose, for example, a portfolio initially has an overweight of 3% in the semiconductor industry relative to its benchmark index, and that the tracking error is 6%. Suppose that the tracking error subsequently increases to 6.1% due to the semiconductor industry weight in the portfolio increasing by 1% (and hence the overweight goes to 4%). Then, it can be said that this industry adds 0.1% to tracking error for every 1% increase in its weight. That is, its *marginal contribution to tracking error* is 0.1%. This would hold only at the margin, that is, for a small change, and not for large changes.

Marginal contributions can be also calculated for individual stocks. If the risk analysis employs a multifactor risk model, then similar marginal contribution estimates can be obtained for the risk factors also.

Generally, marginal contributions would be positive for overweighted industries (or stocks) and negative for underweighted ones. The reason is as follows. If a portfolio already holds an excess weight in an industry, then increasing this weight would cause the portfolio to diverge further from the benchmark index. This increased divergence adds to tracking error, leading to a positive marginal contribution for this industry. Suppose, however, the portfolio has an underweight in an industry. Then, increasing the portfolio weight in this industry would make the portfolio converge towards the benchmark, thus reducing tracking error. This leads to a negative marginal contribution for this industry.

An analysis of the marginal contributions can be useful for a manager who seeks to alter the portfolio tracking error. Suppose a manager wishes to reduce the tracking error, then she should reduce portfolio overweights in industries (or stocks) with the highest positive marginal contributions. Alternatively, she can reduce the underweights (that is, increase the overall weights) in industries (or stocks) with the most negative marginal contributions. Such changes would be most effective in reducing the tracking error while minimizing the necessary turnover and the associated expenses.

KEY POINTS

- Tracking error is a key concept in understanding the potential performance of a common stock portfolio relative to a benchmark index and the actual performance of a common stock portfolio relative to a benchmark index.
- Tracking error can be used to measure the degree of active management by a portfolio manager.
- Tracking error measures the variation of a portfolio's active return (i.e., the difference between the portfolio return and the benchmark return).
- Backward-looking tracking error or ex post tracking error is tracking error calculated from historical active returns; it will have little predictive value and can be misleading regarding portfolio risks going forward.
- A portfolio manager used forward-looking tracking error to estimate portfolio risk going forward.
- The information ratio, found by dividing alpha (i.e., the average active return over a time period) by the backward tracking error, is a reward-to-risk ratio.

- As the portfolio differs from its benchmark index in terms of the number of stocks held, their average market caps, sector allocations, and beta, its tracking error rises. Tracking error also rises in volatile markets.
- For a portfolio manager, the risk of heavily underperforming or outperforming the benchmark rises as the tracking error increases. Thus tracking error is an important indicator of portfolio performance and should be monitored frequently.

QUESTIONS

1. Calculate the annualized alpha, tracking error, and information ratio based on the 12 monthly returns below:

Month	Active Return (%)
1	0.37
2	−0.31
3	−0.55
4	0.09
5	0.37
6	−0.05
7	−0.62
8	0.06
9	0.46
10	−0.09
11	0.58
12	0.84

2. Assuming active returns are normally distributed, calculate the expected returns about the benchmark at various at the 67%, 95%, and 99% confidence levels assuming the following data:

Expected active return (%)	2%
Tracking error (%)	3%
Benchmark expected return	8%

3. Suppose that a manager whose benchmark is the S&P 500 pursues an enhanced indexing strategy allocating 10% of the portfolio to be actively managed and 90% indexed. Assume further that the tracking

error of the actively managed portion is 12% with respect to the S&P 500. What is the portfolio's tracking error?

4. Why is backward-looking tracking error not a good indicator of future risk?

5. In practice, how is forward-looking tracking error calculated?

6. Why is there no guarantee that the forward-looking tracking error at the start of a quarter will exactly match the backward-looking tracking error calculated at the end of that quarter?

7. a. What does the marginal contribution to tracking error mean?
   b. Suppose that the marginal contribution to tracking error for some factor is negative. What does that mean?
   c. Why is the marginal contribution to tracking error a useful measure for a portfolio manager?

CHAPTER 11

Factor-Based Equity Portfolio Construction and Analysis

Petter N. Kolm, Ph.D.
Deputy Director of the Mathematics in Finance Masters Program
and Clinical Associate Professor
Courant Institute of Mathematical Sciences, New York University

Joseph A. Cerniglia
Visiting Researcher
Courant Institute of Mathematical Sciences, New York University

Frank J. Fabozzi, Ph.D., CFA, CPA
Professor of Finance
EDHEC Business School

Common stock investment strategies can be broadly classified into the following categories: (1) factor-based trading strategies (also called stock selection or alpha models), (2) statistical arbitrage, (3) high-frequency strategies, and (4) event studies. Factors and factor-based models form the core of a major part of today's quantitative trading strategies. The focus of this and the companion chapter that follows is on developing trading strategies based on factors constructed from common (cross-sectional) characteristics of stocks. For this purpose, first we provide a definition of factors. We then examine the major sources of risk associated with trading strategies, and demonstrate how factors are constructed from company characteristics and market data. The quality of the data used in this process is critical. We examine several data cleaning and adjustment techniques to account for problems occurring with backfilling and restatements of data, missing data, inconsistently reported data, as well as survivorship and look-ahead biases. In the last section of this chapter, we discuss the analysis of the statistical properties of factors. In the companion chapter, we extend this analysis to include multiple factors and cover techniques used to implement multifactor trading strategies.

In a series of examples throughout both chapters, we show the individual steps for developing a basic trading strategy. The purpose of these examples is not to provide yet another profitable trading strategy, but rather to illustrate the process an analyst may follow when performing research. In fact, the factors that we use for this purpose are well known and have for years been exploited by industry practitioners. We think that the value added of these examples is in the concrete illustration of the research and development process of a factor-based trading model.

FACTOR-BASED TRADING

Since the first version of the classic text on security analysis by Benjamin Graham and David Dodd[1]—considered to be the Bible on the fundamental approach to security analysis—was published in 1934, equity portfolio management and trading strategies have developed considerably. Graham and Dodd were early contributors to factor-based strategies because they extended traditional valuation approaches by using information throughout the financial statements[2] and by presenting concrete rules of thumb to be used to determine the attractiveness of securities.[3]

Today's quantitative managers use factors as fundamental building blocks for trading strategies. Within a trading strategy, factors determine when to buy and sell securities. We define a factor as a common characteristic among a group of assets. In the equities market, it could be a particular financial ratio such as the price–earnings (P/E) or the book–price (B/P) ratios. Some of the most well-known factors and their underlying basic economic rationale references are provided in Exhibit 11.1.

Most often this basic definition is expanded to include additional objectives. First, factors frequently are intended to capture some economic intuition. For instance, a factor may help understand the prices of assets by reference to their exposure to sources of macroeconomic risk, fundamental characteristics, or basic market behavior. Second, we should recognize that assets with similar factors (characteristics) tend to behave in similar ways. This attribute is critical to the success of a factor. Third, we would like

---

[1] Benjamin Graham and David Dodd, *Security Analysis* (New York: McGraw-Hill, 1962).
[2] Benjamin Graham, *The Intelligent Investor* (1949; reprint New York: Harper & Row, 1973).
[3] Peter L. Bernstein, *Capital Ideas: The Improbable Origins of Modern Wall Street* (New York: The Free Press, 1992).

EXHIBIT 11.1 Summary of Well-Known Factors and Their Underlying Economic Rationale

Factor	Economic Rationale
Dividend yield	Investors prefer to immediately receive receipt of their investment returns.
Value	Investors prefer stocks with low valuations.
Size (market capitalization)	Smaller companies tend to outperform larger companies.
Asset turnover	This measure evaluates the productivity of assets employed by a firm. Investors believe higher turnover correlates with higher future return.
Earnings revisions	Positive analysts' revisions indicate stronger business prospects and earnings for a firm.
Growth of fiscal year 1 and fiscal year 2 earnings estimates	Investors are attracted to companies with growing earnings.
Momentum	Investors prefer stocks that have had good past performance.
Return reversal	Investors overreact to information, that is, stocks with the highest returns in the current month tend to earn lower returns the following month.
Idiosyncratic risk	Stocks with high idiosyncratic risk in the current month tend to have lower returns the following month.
Earnings surprises	Investors like positive earnings surprises and dislike negative earnings surprises
Accounting accruals	Companies with earnings that have a large cash component tend to have higher future returns.
Corporate governance	Firms with better corporate governance tend to have higher firm value, higher profits, higher sales growth, lower capital expenditures, and fewer corporate acquisitions.
Executive compensation factors	Firms that align compensation with shareholders interest tend to outperform.
Accounting risk factors	Companies with lower accounting risk tend to have higher future returns.

our factor to be able to differentiate across different markets and samples. Fourth, we want our factor to be robust across different time periods.

Factors fall into three categories—macroeconomic influences, cross-sectional characteristics, and statistical factors. Macroeconomic influences are time series that measure observable economic activity. Examples include interest rate levels, gross domestic production, and industrial production. Cross-sectional characteristics are observable asset specifics or firm characteristics. Examples include, dividend yield, book value, and volatility. Statistical factors are unobservable or latent factors common across a group of assets. These factors make no explicit assumptions about the asset characteristics that drive commonality in returns. Statistical factors, also referred to as latent factors, are not derived using exogenous data but are extracted from other variables such as returns. These factors are calculated using various statistical techniques such as principal components analysis or factor analysis.

Within asset management firms, factors and forecasting models are used for a number of purposes. Those purposes could be central to managing portfolios. For example, a portfolio manager can directly send the model output to the trading desk to be executed. In other uses, models provide analytical support to analysts and portfolio management teams. For instance, models are used as a way to reduce the investable universe to a manageable number of securities so that a team of analysts can perform fundamental analysis on a smaller group of securities.

Factors are employed in other areas of financial theory, such as asset pricing, risk management, and performance attribution. In asset pricing, researchers use factors as proxies for common, undiversifiable sources of risk in the economy to understand the prices or values of securities to uncertain payments. Examples include the dividend yield of the market or the yield spread between a long-term bond yield and a short-term bond yield.[4] In risk management, risk managers use factors in risk models to explain and to decompose variability of returns from securities, while portfolio managers rely on risk models for covariance construction, portfolio construction, and risk measurement. In performance attribution, portfolio managers explain past portfolio returns based on the portfolio's exposure to various factors. Within these areas, the role of factors continues to expand. Recent research presents a methodology for attributing active return, tracking error, and the information ratio to a set of custom factors.[5]

The focus in this and the companion chapter is on using factors to build equity forecasting models, also referred to as *alpha* or *stock selection models*.

---

[4]Eugene F. Fama and Kenneth R. French, "Dividend Yields and Expected Stock Returns," *Journal of Financial Economics* 22, no. 1 (1988): 3–25.

[5]Jose Menchero and Vijay Poduri, "Custom Factor Attribution," *Financial Analysts Journal* 62, no. 2 (2008): 81–92.

The models serve as mathematical representations of trading strategies. The mathematical representation uses future returns as dependent variables and factors as independent variables.

DEVELOPING FACTOR-BASED TRADING STRATEGIES

The development of a trading strategy has many similarities with an engineering project. We begin by designing a framework that is flexible enough so that the components can be easily modified, yet structured enough that we remain focused on our end goal of designing a profitable trading strategy.

Basic Framework and Building Blocks

The typical steps in the development of a trading strategy are:

- Defining a trading idea or investment strategy.
- Developing factors.
- Acquiring and processing data.
- Analyzing the factors.
- Building the strategy.
- Evaluating the strategy.
- Backtesting the strategy.
- Implementing the strategy.

In what follows, we take a closer look at each step.

Defining a Trading Idea or Investment Strategy

A successful trading strategy often starts as an idea based on sound economic intuition, market insight, or the discovery of an anomaly. Background research can be helpful in order to understand what others have tried or implemented in the past.

We distinguish between a trading idea and trading strategy based on the underlying economic motivation. A trading idea has a more short-term horizon often associated with an event or mispricing. A trading strategy has a longer horizon and is frequently based on the exploitation of a premium associated with an anomaly or a characteristic.

Developing Factors

Factors provide building blocks of the model used to build an investment strategy. We introduced a general definition of factors earlier in this chapter.

After having established the trading strategy, we move from the economic concepts to the construction of factors that may be able to capture our intuition. In this chapter, we provide a number of examples of factors based on the cross-sectional characteristics of stocks.

Acquiring and Processing Data

A trading strategy relies on accurate and clean data to build factors. There are a number of third-party solutions and databases available for this purpose such as Thomson MarketQA,[6] Factset Research Systems,[7] and Compustat Xpressfeed.[8]

Analyzing the Factors

A variety of statistical and econometric techniques must be performed on the data to evaluate the empirical properties of factors. This empirical research is used to understand the risk and return potential of a factor. The analysis is the starting point for building a model of a trading strategy.

Building the Strategy

The model represents a mathematical specification of the trading strategy. There are two important considerations in this specification: The selection of which factors and how these factors are combined. Both considerations need to be motivated by the economic intuition behind the trading strategy. We advise against model specification being strictly data driven because that approach often results in overfitting the model and consequently overestimating forecasting quality of the model.

Evaluating, Backtesting, and Implementing the Strategy

The final step involves assessing the estimation, specification, and forecast quality of the model. This analysis includes examining the goodness of fit (often done in sample), forecasting ability (often done out of sample), and sensitivity and risk characteristics of the model.

We cover the last two steps in greater detail in the companion chapter that follows.

---

[6]Thomson MarketQA, http://thomsonreuters.com/products_services/financial/financial_products/quantitative_analysis/quantitative_analytics.

[7]Factset Research Systems, http://www.factset.com.

[8]Compustat Xpressfeed, http://www.compustat.com.

RISK TO TRADING STRATEGIES

In investment management, risk is a primary concern. The majority of trading strategies are not risk free but rather subject to various risks. It is important to be familiar with the most common risks in trading strategies. By understanding the risks in advance, we can structure our empirical research to identify how risks will affect our strategies. Also, we can develop techniques to avoid these risks in the model construction stage when building the strategy.

We describe the various risks that are common to factor trading strategies as well as other trading strategies such as risk arbitrage. Many of these risks have been categorized in the behavioral finance literature.[9] The risks discussed include fundamental risk, noise trader risk, horizon risk, model risk, implementation risk, and liquidity risk.

Fundamental risk is the risk of suffering adverse fundamental news. For example, say our trading strategy focuses on purchasing stocks with high earnings-to-price ratios. Suppose that the model shows a pharmaceutical stock maintains a high score. After purchasing the stock, the company releases a news report that states it faces class-action litigation because one of its drugs has undocumented adverse side effects. While during this period other stocks with high earnings-to-price ratio may perform well, this particular pharmaceutical stock will perform poorly despite its attractive characteristic. We can minimize the exposure to fundamental risk within a trading strategy by diversifying across many companies. Fundamental risk may not always be company specific, sometimes this risk can be systemic. Some examples include the exogenous market shocks of the stock market crash in 1987, the Asian financial crisis in 1997, and the tech bubble in 2000. In these cases, diversification was not that helpful. Instead, portfolio managers that were sector or market neutral in general fared better.

Noise trader risk is the risk that a mispricing may worsen in the short run. The typical example includes companies that clearly are undervalued (and should therefore trade at a higher price). However, because noise traders may trade in the opposite direction, this mispricing can persist for a long time. Closely related to noise trader risk is *horizon risk*. The idea here is that the premium or value takes too long to be realized, resulting in a realized return lower than a target rate of return.

Model risk, also referred to as *misspecification risk*, refers to the risk associated with making wrong modeling assumptions and decisions. This includes the choice of variables, methodology, and context the model operates in.

---

[9] See Nicholas Barberis and Richard Thaler, "A Survey of Behavioral Finance," in *Handbook of the Economics of Finance*, edited by George M. Constantinides, M. Harris, and Rene M. Stulz (Amsterdam: Elsevier Science, 2003).

There are different sources that may result in model misspecification and there are several remedies based on information theory, Bayesian methods, shrinkage, and random coefficient models.[10]

Implementation risk is another risk faced by investors implementing trading strategies. This risk category includes transaction costs and funding risk. Transaction costs such as commissions, bid-ask spreads and market impact can adversely affect the results from a trading strategy. If the strategy involves shorting, other implementation costs arise such as the ability to locate securities to short and the costs to borrow the securities. *Funding risk* occurs when the portfolio manager is no longer able to get the funding necessary to implement a trading strategy. For example, many statistical arbitrage funds use leverage to increase the returns of their funds. If the amount of leverage is constrained then the strategy will not earn attractive returns. Khandani and Lo confirm this example by showing that greater competition and reduced profitability of quantitative strategies today require more leverage to maintain the same level of expected return.[11]

Liquidity risk is a concern for investors. Liquidity is defined as the ability to (1) trade quickly without significant price changes, and (2) the ability to trade large volumes without significant price changes. Cerniglia and Kolm discuss the effects of liquidity risk during the "quant crisis" in August 2007. [12] They show how the rapid liquidation of quantitative funds affected the trading characteristics and price impact of trading individual securities as well as various factor-based trading strategies.

These risks can detract or contribute to the success of a trading strategy. It is obvious how these risks can detract from a strategy. What is not always clear is when any one of these unintentional risks contributes to a strategy. That is, sometimes when we build a trading strategy we take on a bias that is not obvious. If there is a premium associated with this unintended risk then a strategy will earn additional return. Later the premium to this unintended risk may disappear. For example, a trading strategy that focuses on price momentum performed strongly in the calendar years of 1998 and 1999. What an investor might not notice is that during this period the portfolio became increasingly weighted toward technology stocks, particularly Internet-related stocks. During 2000, these stocks severely underperformed.

---

[10]For a discussion of the sources of model misspecification and remedies, see Frank J. Fabozzi, Sergio Focardi, and Petter N. Kolm, *Quantitative Equity Investing* (Hoboken, NJ: John Wiley & Sons, 2010).

[11]Amir E. Khandani and Andrew W. Lo, "What Happened to the Quants in August 2007?" *Journal of Investment Management* 5, no. 4 (2007): 5–54.

[12]Joseph A. Cerniglia and Petter N. Kolm,"The Information Content of Order Imbalances: A Tick-by-Tick Analysis of the Equity Market in August 2007," working paper, Courant Institute, New York University, 2009.

DESIRABLE PROPERTIES OF FACTORS

Factors should be founded on sound economic intuition, market insight, or an anomaly. In addition to the underlying economic reasoning, factors should have other properties that make them effective for forecasting.

It is an advantage if factors are intuitive to investors. Many investors will only invest in a particular fund if they understand and agree with the basic ideas behind the trading strategies. Factors give portfolio managers a tool in communicating to investors what *themes* they are investing in.

The search for the economic meaningful factors should avoid strictly relying on pure historical analysis. Factors used in a model should not emerge from a sequential process of evaluating successful factors while removing less favorable ones.

Most importantly, a group of factors should be parsimonious in its description of the trading strategy. This requires careful evaluation of the interaction between the different factors. For example, highly correlated factors will cause the inferences made in a multivariate approach to be less reliable. Another possible problem when using multiple factors is the possibility of overfitting in the modeling process.

Any data set contains outliers, that is, observations that deviate from the average properties of the data. Outliers are not always trivial to handle and sometimes we may want to exclude them and other times not. For example, they could be erroneously reported or legitimate abnormal values. Later in this chapter we discuss a few standard techniques to perform data cleaning. The success or failure of factors selected should not depend on a few outliers. In most cases, it is desirable to construct factors that are reasonably robust to outliers.

SOURCES FOR FACTORS

How do we find factors? The sources are widespread with no one source clearly dominating. Employing a variety of sources seems to provide the best opportunity to uncover factors that will be valuable for developing a new model.

There are a number of ways to develop factors based on economic foundations. It may start with thoughtful observation or study of how market participants act. For example, we may ask ourselves how other market participants will evaluate the prospects of the earnings or business of a firm. We may also want to consider what stock characteristics investors will reward in the future. Another common approach is to look for inefficiencies in the way that investors process information. For instance, research may discover that consensus expectations of earnings estimates are biased.

A good source for factors is the various reports released by the management of companies. Many reports contain valuable information and may provide additional context on how management interprets the company results and financial characteristics. For example, quarterly earning reports (10-Qs) may highlight particular financial metrics relevant to the company and the competitive space they are operating within. Other company financial statements and SEC filings, such as the 10-K or 8-K, also provide a source of information to develop factors. It is often useful to look at the financial measures that management emphasize in their comments.

Factors can be found through discussions with market participants such as portfolio managers and traders. Factors are uncovered by understanding the heuristics experienced investors have used successfully. These heuristics can be translated into factors and models.

Wall Street analyst reports—also called sell-side reports or equity research reports—may contain valuable information. The reader is often not interested in the final conclusions, but rather in the methodology or metrics the analysts use to forecast the future performance of a company. It may also be useful to study the large quantity of books written by portfolio managers and traders that describe the process they use in stock selection.

Academic literature in finance, accounting, and economics provides evidence of numerous factors and trading strategies that earn abnormal returns. Not all strategies will earn abnormal profits when implemented by practitioners, for example, because of institutional constraints and transaction costs. Bushee and Raedy[13] find that trading strategy returns are significantly decreased due to issues such as price pressure, restrictions against short sales, incentives to maintain an adequately diversified portfolio, and restrictions to hold no more than 5% ownership in a firm.

In uncovering factors, we should put economic intuition first and data analysis second. This avoids performing pure data mining or simply overfitting our models to past history. Research and innovation is the key to finding new factors. Today, analyzing and testing new factors and improving upon existing ones, is itself a big industry.

BUILDING FACTORS FROM COMPANY CHARACTERISTICS

The following sections focus on the techniques for building factors from company characteristics. Often we desire our factors to relate the financial data provided by a company to metrics that investors use when making

---

[13]Brian J. Bushee and Jana Smith Raedy, "Factors Affecting the Implementability of Stock Market Trading Strategies," working paper, University of Pennsylvania and University of North Carolina, 2006.

decisions about the attractiveness of a stock such as valuation ratios, operating efficiency ratios, profitability ratios, and solvency ratios. Factors should also relate to the market data such as analysts' forecasts, prices and returns, and trading volume.

WORKING WITH DATA

In this section, we discuss how to work with data and data quality issues, including some well-probed techniques used to improve the quality of the data. Though the role of getting and analyzing data can be mundane and tedious, we need not forget that high-quality data are critical to the success of a trading strategy. It is important to realize model output is only as good as the data used to calibrate it. As the saying goes: "Garbage in, garbage out."

Understanding the structure of financial data is important. We distinguish three different categories of financial data: time series, cross-sectional, and panel data. Time series data consist of information and variables collected over multiple time periods. Cross-sectional data consist of data collected at one point in time for many different companies (the cross-section of companies of interest). A panel data set consists of cross-sectional data collected at different points in time. We note that a panel data set may not be homogeneous. For instance, the cross-section of companies may change from one point in time to another.

Data Integrity

Quality data maintain several attributes such as providing a consistent view of history, maintaining good data availability, containing no survivorship, and avoiding look-ahead bias. As all data sets have their limitations, it is important for the quantitative researcher to be able to recognize the limitations and adjust the data accordingly.[14]

Data used in research should provide a consistent view of history. Two common problems that distort the consistency of financial data are backfilling and restatements of data. *Backfilling of data* happens when a company

---

[14]Many years ago one of the coauthors met Marcus C. Bogue, founder of Charter Oak Investment Systems. His firm created a Compustat Add-On Database to address the needs of the more quantitatively oriented, longer-term backtesting researchers by storing all data from current Compustat data before it gets overwritten (updated). Mr. Bogue works with most of the quantitative investment management industry. In the conversion with him the question of what distinguishes the most successful quantitative managers came up. Mr Bogue suggested that their familiarity with the data is the differentiator. Familiarity entails understanding quality, definitions, measurement, and sample characteristics of the data sets used in the investment process.

is first entered into a database at the current period and its historical data are also added. This process of backfilling data creates a selection bias because we now find historical data on this recently added company when previously it was not available. Restatements of data are prevalent in distorting consistency of data. For example, if a company revises its earnings per share numbers after the initial earnings release, then many database companies will overwrite the number originally recorded in the database with the newly released figure.

A frequent and common concern with financial databases is data availability. First, data items may only be available for a short period of time. For example, there were many years when stock options were granted to employees but the expense associated with the option grant was not required to be disclosed in financial statements. It was not until 2005 that accounting standards required companies to recognize directly stock options as an expense on the income statement. Second, data items may be available for only a subset of the cross-section of firms. Some firms, depending on the business they operate in, have research and development expenses while others do not. For example, many pharmaceutical companies have research and development expenses while utilities companies do not. A third issue is that a data item may simply not be available because it was not recorded at certain points in time. Sometimes this happens for just a few observations, other times it is the case for the whole time-series for a specific data item for a company. Fourth, different data items are sometimes combined. For example, sometimes depreciation and amortization expenses are not a separate line item on an income statement. Instead it is included in cost of goods sold. Fifth, certain data items are only available at certain periodicities. For instance, some companies provide more detailed financial reports quarterly while others report more details annually. Sixth, data items may be inconsistently reported across different companies, sectors, or industries. This may happen as the financial data provider translates financial measures from company reports to the specific database items (incomplete mapping), thereby ignoring or not correctly making the right adjustments.

For these issues some databases provide specific codes to identify the causes of missing data. It is important to have procedures in place that can distinguish among the different reasons for the missing data and be able to make adjustments and corrections.

Two other common problems with databases are survivorship and look-ahead bias. *Survivorship bias* occurs when companies are removed from the database when they no longer exist. For example, companies can be removed because of a merger or bankruptcy. This bias skews the results because only successful firms are included in the entire sample. *Look-ahead bias* occurs when data are used in a study that would not have been available during the actual period analyzed. For example, the use of year-end earnings data immediately at the end of the reporting period is incorrect because the data is not released by the firm until several days or weeks after the end of the reporting period.

Data alignment is another concern when working with multiple databases. Many databases have different identifiers used to identify a firm. Some databases have vendor specific identifiers, others have common identifiers such as CUSIPs or ticker symbols. Unfortunately, CUSIPs and ticker symbols change over time and are often reused. This practice makes it difficult to link an individual security across multiple databases across time.

Example: The EBITDA/EV Factor

This example illustrates how the nuances of data handling can influence the results of a particular study. We use data from the Compustat Point-In-Time database and calculate the EBITA/EV factor.[15] This factor is defined as earnings before interest, taxes, depreciation, and amortization divided by enterprise value (EBITDA/EV). Our universe of stocks is the Russell 1000 from December 1989 to December 2008, excluding financial companies. We calculate EBITDA /EV by two equivalent but different approaches. Each approach differs by the data items used in calculating the numerator (*EBITDA*):

1. EBITDA = Sales (Compustat data item 2) – Cost of goods sold (Compustat data item 30) – Selling and general administrative expenses (Compustat data item 1).
2. EBITDA = Operating income before depreciation (Compustat data item 21).

According to the Compustat manual, the following identity holds:

Operating income before depreciation
= Sales – Cost of goods sold – Selling and general administrative expenses

However, while this mathematical identity is true, this is not what we discover in the data. After we calculate the two factors, we form quintile portfolios of each factor and compare the individual holding rankings between the portfolio. Exhibit 11.2 displays the percentage differences in

---

[15]The ability of EBITDA/EV to forecast future returns is discussed in, for example, Patricia M. Dechow, S. P. Kothari, and Ross L. Watts, "The Relation Between Earnings and Cash Flows," *Journal of Accounting and Economics* 25, no. 2 (1998): 133–168.

EXHIBIT 11.2 Percentage of Companies in Russell 1000 with Different Ranking According to the EBITDA/EV Factor

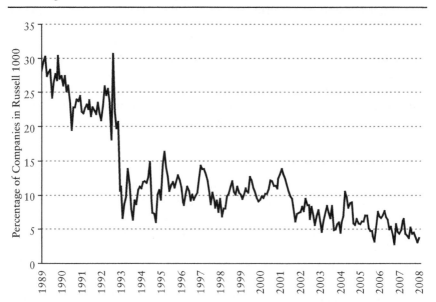

rankings for individual companies between the two portfolios. We observe that the results are not identical. As a matter of fact, there are large differences, particularly in the early period. In other words, the two mathematically equivalent approaches do not deliver the same empirical results.

Potential Biases from Data

There are numerous potential biases that may arise from data quality issues. It is important to recognize the direct effects of these data issues are not apparent a priori. We emphasize three important effects:[16]

1. *Effect on average stock characteristics.* When calculating cross-sectional averages of various metrics such as book-to-price or market capitalization, data issues can skew statistics and lead to incorrect inference about the population characteristics used in the study.
2. *Effect on portfolio returns.* The portfolio return implications of data issues are not always clear. For example, survivor bias results in firms

[16]Stefan Nagel, "Accounting Information Free of Selection Bias: A New UK Database 1953–1999," working paper, Stanford Graduate School of Business, 2001.

being removed from the sample. Typically firms are removed from the sample for one of two reasons—mergers and acquisitions or failure. In most cases firms are acquired at a premium from the prevailing stock price. Leaving these firms out of the sample would have a downward bias on returns. In cases where companies fail, the stock price falls dramatically and removing these firms from the sample will have an upward bias on returns.

3. *Effects on estimated moments of returns.* A study by Kothari, Sabino, and Zach[17] found that nonsurviving firms tend to be either extremely bad or extremely good performers. Survivor bias implies truncation of such extreme observations. The authors of the study show that even a small degree of such nonrandom truncation can have a strong impact on the sample moments of stock returns.

Dealing with Common Data Issues

Most data sets are subject to some quality issues. To work effectively, we need to be familiar with data definitions and database design. We also need to use processes to reduce the potential impact of data problems as they could cause incorrect conclusions.

The first step is to become familiar with the data standardization process vendors use to collect and process data. For example, many vendors use different templates to store data. Specifically, the Compustat US database has one template for reporting income statement data, while the Worldscope Global database has four different templates depending on whether a firm is classified as a bank, insurance company, industrial company, or other financial company. Other questions related to standardization a user should be familiar with include:

- What are the sources of the data—publicly available financial statements, regulatory filings, newswire services, or other sources?
- Is there a uniform reporting template?
- What is the delay between publication of information and its availability in the database?
- Is the data adjusted for stock splits?
- Is history available for extinct or inactive companies?
- How is data handled for companies with multiple share classes?
- What is the process used to aggregate the data?

---

[17]S. P. Kothari, Jowell S. Sabino, and Tzachi Zach, "Implications of Survival and Data Trimming for Tests of Market Efficiency," *Journal of Accounting and Economics* 39, no. 1 (2005): 129–161.

Understanding of the accounting principles underlying the data is critical. Here, two principles of importance are the valuation methodology and data disclosure or presentation. For the valuation, we should understand the type of cost basis used for the various accounting items. Specifically, are assets calculated using historical cost basis, fair value accounting, or another type? For accounting principles regarding disclosure and presentation, we need to know the definition of accounting terms, the format of the accounts, and the depth of detail provided.

Researchers creating factors that use financial statements should review the history of the underlying accounting principles. For example, the cash flow statement reported by companies has changed over the years. Effective for fiscal years ending July 15, 1988, Statement of Financial Accounting Standards No. 85 (SFAS No. 85) requires companies to report the Statement of Cash Flows. Prior to the adoption of that accounting standard, companies could report one of three statements: Working Capital Statement, Cash Statement by Source and Use of Funds, or Cash Statement by Activity. Historical analysis of any factor that uses cash flow items will require adjustments to the definition of the factor to account for the different statements used by companies.

Preferably, automated processes should be used to reduce the potential impact of data problems. We start by checking the data for consistency and accuracy. We can perform time series analysis on individual factors looking at outliers and for missing data. We can use magnitude tests to compare current data items with the same items for prior periods, looking for data that are larger than a predetermined variance. When suspicious cases are identified, the cause of the error should be researched and any necessary changes made.

Methods to Adjust Factors

At first, factors consist of raw data from a database combined in an economically meaningful way. After the initial setup, a factor may be adjusted using analytical or statistical techniques to be more useful for modeling. The following three adjustments are common.

Standardization

Standardization rescales a variable while preserving its order. Typically, we choose the standardized variable to have a mean of zero and a standard deviation of one by using the transformation

$$x_i^{new} = \frac{x_i - \bar{x}}{\sigma_x}$$

where x_i is the stock's factor score, $\bar{x}$ is the universe average, and σ_x is the universe standard deviation. There are several reasons to scale a variable in this way. First, it allows one to determine a stock's position relative to the universe average. Second, it allows better comparison across a set of factors since means and standard deviations are the same. Third, it can be useful in combining multiple variables.

Orthogonalization

Sometimes the performance of our factor might be related to another factor. Orthogonalizing a factor for other specified factor(s) removes this relationship. We can orthogonalize by using averages or running regressions.

To orthogonalize the factor using averages according to industries or sectors, we can proceed as follows. First, for each industry we calculate the industry scores

$$s_k = \frac{\sum_{i=1}^{n} x_i \cdot \text{ind}_{i,k}}{\sum_{i=1}^{n} \text{ind}_{i,k}}$$

where x_i is a factor and $\text{ind}_{i,k}$ represent the weight of stock i in industry k. Next, we subtract the industry average of the industry scores, s_k, from each stock. We compute

$$x_i^{\text{new}} = x_i - \sum_{k \in \text{Industries}} \text{ind}_{i,k} \cdot s_k$$

where x_i^{new} is the new industry neutral factor.

We can use linear regression to orthogonalize a factor. We first determine the coefficients in the equation

$$x_i = a + b \cdot f_i + \varepsilon_i$$

where f_i is the factor to orthogonalize the factor x_i by, b is the contribution of f_i to x_i, and ε_i is the component of the factor x_i not related to f_i. ε_i is orthogonal to f_i (that is, ε_i is independent of f_i) and represents the neutralized factor

$$x_i^{\text{new}} = \varepsilon_i$$

In the same fashion, we can orthogonalize our variable relative to a set of factors by using the multivariate linear regression

$$x_i = a + \sum_j b_j \cdot f_j + \varepsilon_i$$

and then setting $x_i^{new} = \varepsilon_i$.

Often portfolio managers use a risk model to forecast risk and an alpha model to forecast returns. The interaction between factors in a risk model and an alpha model often concerns portfolio managers. One possible approach to address this concern is to orthogonalize the factors or final scores from the alpha model against the factors used in the risk model. Later in the chapter, we discuss this issue in more detail.

Transformation

It is common practice to apply transformations to data used in statistical and econometric models. In particular, factors are often transformed such that the resulting series is symmetric or close to being normally distributed. Frequently used transformations include natural logarithms, exponentials, and square roots. For example, a factor such as market capitalization has a large skew because a sample of large-cap stocks typically includes mega-capitalization stocks. To reduce the influence of mega-capitalization companies, we may instead use the natural logarithm of market capitalization in a linear regression model.

Outlier Detection and Management

Outliers are observations that seem to be inconsistent with the other values in a data set. Financial data contain outliers for a number of reasons including data errors, measurement errors, or unusual events. Interpretation of data containing outliers may therefore be misleading. For example, our estimates could be biased or distorted, resulting in incorrect conclusions.

Outliers can be detected by several methods. Graphs such as boxplots, scatter plots, or histograms can be useful to visually identify them. Alternatively, there are a number of numerical techniques available. One common method is to compute the interquartile-range and then identify outliers as those values that are some multiple of the range. The interquartile-range is a measure of dispersion and is calculated as the difference between the third and first quartiles of a sample. This measure represents the middle 50% of the data, removing the influence of outliers.

After outliers have been identified, we need to reduce their influence in our analysis. Trimming and winsorization are common procedures for this purpose. Trimming discards extreme values in the data set. This transformation requires the researcher to determine the direction (symmetric or asymmetric) and the amount of trimming to occur.

Winsorization is the process of transforming extreme values in the data. First, we calculate percentiles of the data. Next we define outliers by referencing a certain percentile ranking. For example, any data observation that is greater than the 97.5 percentile or less than the 2.5 percentile could be considered an outlier. Finally, we set all values greater or less than the reference percentile ranking to particular values. In our example, we may set all values greater than the 97.5 percentile to the 97.5 percentile value and all values less than 2.5 percentile set to the 2.5 percentile value. It is important to fully investigate the practical consequences of using either one of these procedures. In the companion chapter to follow, we apply what we learn from the following statistical summaries of the factors to build a model and implement our trading strategy.

ANALYSIS OF FACTOR DATA

After constructing factors for all securities in the investable universe, each factor is analyzed individually. Presenting the time-series and cross-sectional averages of the mean, standard deviations, and key percentiles of the distribution provide useful information for understanding the behavior of the chosen factors.

Although we often rely on techniques that assume the underlying data generating process is normally distributed, or at least approximately, most financial data is not. The underlying data generating processes that embody aggregate investor behavior and characterize the financial markets are unknown and exhibit significant uncertainty. Investor behavior is uncertain because not all investors make rational decisions or have the same goals. Analyzing the properties of data may help us better understand how uncertainty affects our choice and calibration of a model.

Below we provide some examples of the cross-sectional characteristics of various factors. For ease of exposition we use histograms to evaluate the data rather than formal statistical tests. We let particular patterns or properties of the histograms guide us in the choice of the appropriate technique to model the factor. We recommend that an intuitive exploration should be followed by a more formal statistical testing procedure. Our approach here is to analyze the entire sample, all positive values, all negative values, and zero values. Although omitted here, a thorough analysis should also include separate subsample analysis.

Example 1: EBITDA/EV

The first factor we discuss is the earnings before interest taxes and amortization to enterprise value (EBITDA/EV) factor. Enterprise value is calculated as the market value of the capital structure. This factor measures the price (enterprise value) investors pays to receive the cash flows (EBITDA) of a company. The economic intuition underlying this factor is that the valuation of a company's cash flow determines the attractiveness of companies to an investor.

Exhibit 11.3(A) presents a histogram of all cross-sectional values of the EBITDA/EV factor throughout the entire history of the study. The distribution is close to normal, showing there is a fairly symmetric dispersion among the valuations companies receive. Exhibit 11.3(B) shows that the distribution of all the positive values of the factor is also almost normally distributed. On the other hand, Exhibit 11.3(C) shows that the distribution of the negative values is skewed to the left. However, because there are only a small number of negative values, it is likely that they will not greatly influence our model.

Example 2: Revisions

We evaluate the cross-sectional distribution of the earnings revisions factor.[18] The revisions factor we use is derived from sell-side analyst earnings forecasts from the IBES database. The factor is calculated as the number of analysts who revise their earnings forecast upward minus the number of downward forecasts, divided by the total number of forecasts. The economic intuition underlying this factor is that there should be a positive relation to changes in forecasts of earnings and subsequent returns.

In Exhibit 11.4(A) we see that the distribution of revisions is symmetric and leptokurtic around a mean of about zero. This distribution ties with the economic intuition behind the revisions. Since business prospects of companies typically do not change from month-to-month, sell-side analysts will not revise their earnings forecast every month. Consequently, we expect and find the cross-sectional range to be peaked at zero. Exhibit 11.4(B) and (C), respectively, show there is a smaller number of both positive and negative earnings revisions and each one of these distributions are skewed.

Example 3: Share Repurchase

We evaluate the cross-sectional distribution of the shares repurchases factor. This factor is calculated as the difference of the current number of common

---

[18]For a representative study see, for example, Anthony Bercel, "Consensus Expectations and International Equity Returns," *Financial Analysts Journal* 50, no. 4 (1994): 76–80.

EXHIBIT 11.3   Histograms of the Cross-Sectional Values for the EBITDA/EV Factor

A. All Factor Values

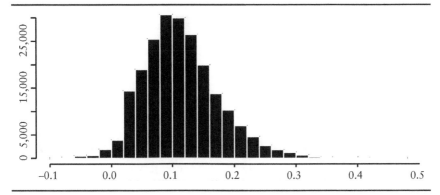

B. Positive Factor Values

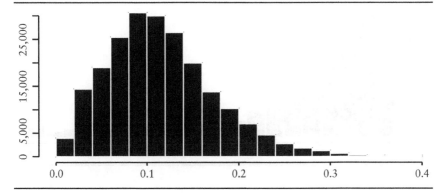

C. Negative Factor Values

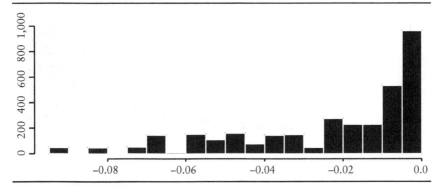

EXHIBIT 11.4 Histograms of the Cross-Sectional Values for the Revisions Factor

A. All Factor Values

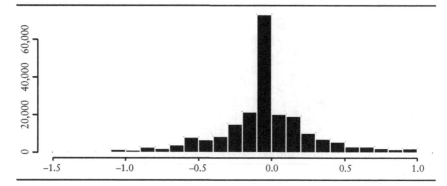

B. Positive Factor Values

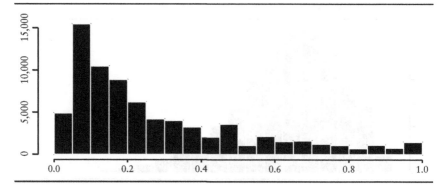

C. Negative Factor Values

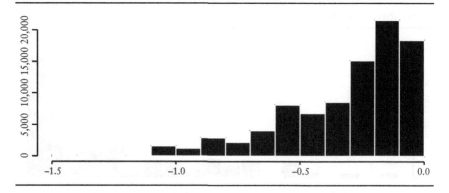

shares outstanding and the number of shares outstanding 12 months ago, divided by the number of shares outstanding 12 months ago. The economic intuition underlying this factor is that share repurchase provides information to investors about future earnings and valuation of the company's stock.[19] We expect there to be a positive relationship between a reduction in shares outstanding and subsequent returns.

We see in Exhibit 11.5(A) that the distribution is leptokurtic. The positive values (see Exhibit 11.5(B)) are skewed to the right and the negative values (see Exhibit 11.5(C)) are clustered in a small band. The economic intuition underlying share repurchases is the following. Firms with increasing share count indicate they require additional sources of cash. This need could be an early sign that the firm is experiencing higher operating risks or financial distress. We would expect these firms to have lower future returns. Firms with decreasing share count have excess cash and are returning value back to shareholders. Decreasing share count could result because management believes the shares are undervalued. As expected, we find the cross-sectional range to be peaked at zero (see Exhibit 11.5(D)) since not all firms issue or repurchase shares on a regular basis.

KEY POINTS

- A factor is a common characteristic among a group of assets. Factors should be founded on sound economic intuition, market insight, or an anomaly.
- Factors fall into three categories—macroeconomic, cross-sectional, and statistical factors.
- The main steps in the development of a factor-based trading strategy are (1) defining a trading idea or investment strategy, (2) developing factors, (3) acquiring and processing data, (4) analyzing the factors, (5) building the strategy, (6) evaluating the strategy, (7) backtesting the strategy, and (8) implementing the strategy.
- Most trading strategies are exposed to risk. The main sources of risk are fundamental risk, noise trader risk, horizon risk, model risk, implementation risk, and liquidity risk.
- Factors are often derived from company characteristics and metrics, and market data. Examples of company characteristics and metrics include valuation ratios, operating efficiency ratios, profitability ratios, and solvency ratios. Example of useful market data include analysts forecasts, prices and returns, and trading volume.

---

[19]Gustavo Grullon and Roni Michaely, "The Information Content of Share Repurchase Programs," *Journal of Finance* 59, no. 2 (2004): 651–680.

EXHIBIT 11.5 Histograms of the Cross-Sectional Values for the Share Repurchase Factor
A. Positive Factor Values

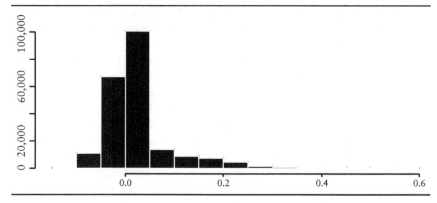

Panel B: Positive Factor Values

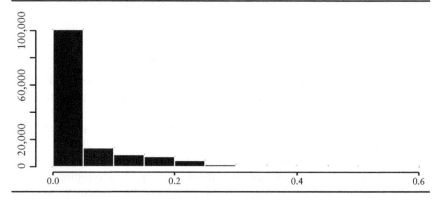

- High-quality data are critical to the success of a trading strategy. Model output is only as good as the data used to calibrate it.
- Some common data problems and biases are backfilling and restatements of data, missing data, inconsistently reported data, and survivorship and look-ahead biases.
- The ability to detect and adjust outliers is crucial to a quantitative investment process.
- Common methods used for adjusting data are standardization, orthogonalization, transformation, trimming, and winsorization.
- The statistical properties of factors need to be carefully analyzed. Basic statistical measures include the time-series and cross-sectional averages of the mean, standard deviations, and key percentiles.

EXHIBIT 11.5 (Continued)
C. Negative Factor Values

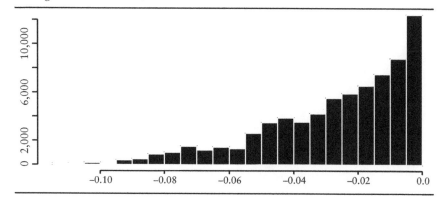

D. Zero Factor Values

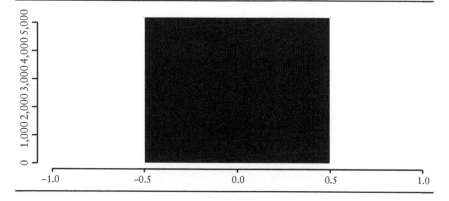

QUESTIONS

1. List and define the typical risks of an investment strategy.

2. What areas of finance use factor models?

3. Explain some of the major data issues encountered when working with financial data.

4. How are financial data organized?

5. a. What are outliers?
   b. Why do outliers occur in financial data?

QUESTIONS

CHAPTER 12

Cross-Sectional Factor-Based Models and Trading Strategies

Joseph A. Cerniglia
Visiting Researcher
Courant Institute of Mathematical Sciences, New York University

Petter N. Kolm, Ph.D.
Director of the Mathematics in Finance Masters Program
and Clinical Associate Professor
Courant Institute of Mathematical Sciences, New York University

Frank J. Fabozzi, Ph.D., CFA, CPA
Professor of Finance
EDHEC Business School

In the previous chapter, we demonstrated how factors are constructed from company characteristics and market data. Subsequently, we discussed the analysis of the statistical properties of the factors. In this chapter, we extend the analysis to include multiple factors with the purpose of developing a dynamic multifactor trading strategy that incorporates a number of common institutional constraints such as turnover, transaction costs, sector, and tracking error. For this purpose, we use a combination of growth, value, quality, and momentum factors. Our universe of stocks is the Russell 1000 from December 1989 to December 2008, and we construct our factors by using the Compustat Point-In-Time and IBES databases. A complete list of the factors and data sets used in this chapter is provided in the appendix.

We begin by reviewing several approaches for the evaluation of return premiums and risk characteristics to factors, including portfolio sorts, factor models, factor portfolios, and information coefficients. We then turn to techniques that are used to combine several factors into a single model—a trading strategy. In particular, we discuss the data driven, factor model, heuristic, and optimization approaches. It is critical to perform out-of-sample backtests of a trading strategy to understand its performance and risk characteristics. We cover the split-sample and recursive out-of-sample tests.

Throughout this chapter, we provide a series of examples, including backtests of a multifactor trading strategy. As noted in the previous chapter, the purpose of these examples is not to provide yet another profitable trading strategy, but rather to illustrate the process an analyst may follow when performing research. We emphasize that the factors that we use are well known and have for years been exploited by industry practitioners. We think that the value added of these examples is in the concrete illustration of the research and development process of a factor-based trading model.

CROSS-SECTIONAL METHODS FOR EVALUATION OF FACTOR PREMIUMS

There are several approaches used for the evaluation of return premiums and risk characteristics to factors. In this section, we discuss the four most commonly used approaches: portfolio sorts, factor models, factor portfolios, and information coefficients. We examine the methodology of each approach and summarize its advantages and disadvantages.

In practice, to determine the right approach for a given situation there are several issues to consider. One determinant is the structure of the financial data. A second determinant is the economic intuition underlying the factor. For example, sometimes we are looking for a monotonic relationship between returns and factors while at other times we care only about extreme values. A third determinant is whether the underlying assumptions of each approach are valid for the data generating process at hand.

Portfolio Sorts

In the asset pricing literature, the use of portfolio sorts can be traced back to the earliest tests of the capital asset pricing model (CAPM). The goal of this particular test is to determine whether a factor earns a systematic premium. The portfolios are constructed by grouping together securities with similar characteristics (factors). For example, we can group stocks by market capitalization into 10 portfolios—from smallest to largest—such that each portfolio contains stocks with similar market capitalization. The next step is to calculate and evaluate the returns of these portfolios.

The return for each portfolio is calculated by equally weighting the individual stock returns. The portfolios provide a representation of how returns vary across the different values of a factor. By studying the return behavior of the factor portfolios, we may assess the return and risk profile of the factor. In some cases, we may identify a monotonic relationship of the returns across the portfolios. In other cases, we may identify a large difference in returns between the extreme portfolios. Still in other cases, there may be no relationship between the portfolio returns. Overall, the return behavior of the portfolios will help us conclude whether there is a premium associated with a factor and describe its properties.

One application of the portfolio sort is the construction of a *factor mimicking portfolio* (FMP). An FMP is a long-short portfolio that goes long stocks with high values of a factor and short stocks with low values of a factor, in equal dollar amounts. An FMP is a zero-cost factor trading strategy.

Portfolio sorts have become so widespread among practitioners and academics alike that they elicit few econometric queries, and often no econometric justification for the technique is offered. While a detailed discussion of these topics are beyond the scope of this book, we would like to point out that asset pricing tests used on sorted portfolios may exhibit a bias that favors rejecting the asset pricing model under consideration.[1]

The construction of portfolios sorted on a factor is straightforward:

- Choose an appropriate sorting methodology.
- Sort the assets according to the factor.
- Group the sorted assets into N portfolios (usually $N = 5$, or $N = 10$).
- Compute average returns (and other statistics) of the assets in each portfolio over subsequent periods.

The standard statistical testing procedure for portfolios sorts is to use a Student's t-test to evaluate the significance of the mean return differential between the portfolios of stocks with the highest and lowest values of the factor.

Choosing the Sorting Methodology

The sorting methodology should be consistent with the characteristics of the distribution of the factor and the economic motivation underlying its premium. We list six ways to sort factors:

Method 1
- Sort stocks with factor values from the highest to lowest.

Method 2
- Sort stocks with factor values from the lowest to highest.

---

[1]For a good overview of the most common issues, see Jonathan B. Berk, "Sorting out Sorts," *Journal of Finance* 55, no. 1 (2000): 407–427 and references therein.

Method 3
- First allocate stocks with zero factor values into the bottom portfolio.
- Sort the remaining stocks with nonzero factor values into the remaining portfolios.

For example, the dividend yield factor would be suitable for this sorting approach. This approach aligns the factor's distributional characteristics of dividend and nondividend-paying stocks with the economic rationale. Typically, nondividend-paying stocks maintain characteristics that are different from dividend paying stocks. So we group nondividend-paying stocks into one portfolio. The remaining stocks are then grouped into portfolios depending on the size of their nonzero dividend yields. We differentiate among stocks with dividend yield because of two reasons: (1) the size of the dividend yield is related to the maturity of the company, and (2) some investors prefer to receive their investment return as dividends.

Method 4
- Allocate stocks with zero factor values into the middle portfolio.
- Sort stocks with positive factor values into the remaining higher portfolios (greater than the middle portfolio).
- Sort stocks with negative factor values into the remaining lower portfolios (less than the middle portfolio).

Method 5
- Sort stocks into partitions.
- Rank assets within each partition.
- Combine assets with the same ranking from the different partitions into portfolios.

An example will clarify this procedure. Suppose we want to rank stocks according to earnings growth on a sector neutral basis. First, we separate stocks into groups corresponding to their sector. Within each sector, we rank the stocks according to their earnings growth. Lastly, we group all stocks with the same rankings of earning growth into the final portfolio. This process ensures that each portfolio will contain an equal number of stocks from every sector, thereby the resulting portfolios are sector neutral.

Method 6
- Separate all the stocks with negative factors values. Split the group of stocks with negative values into two portfolios using the median value as the break point.
- Allocate stocks with zero factor values into one portfolio.

■ Sort the remaining stocks with nonzero factor values into portfolios based on their factor values.

For an example of method 6, recall the discussion of the share repurchase factor from the prior companion chapter. We are interested in the extreme positive and negative values of this factor. As we see in Exhibit 12.5(A), the distribution of this factors is leptokurtic with the positive values skewed to the right and the negative values clustered in a small range. By choosing method 6 to sort this variable, we can distinguish between those values we view as extreme. The negative values are clustered so we want to distinguish among the magnitudes of those values. We accomplish this because our sorting method separates the negative values by the median of the negative values. The largest negative values form the extreme negative portfolio. The positive values are skewed to the right, so we want to differentiate between the larger from smaller positive values. When implementing portfolio method 6, we would also separate the zero values from the positive values.

The portfolio sort methodology has several advantages. The approach is easy to implement and can easily handle stocks that drop out or enter into the sample. The resulting portfolios diversify away idiosyncratic risk of individual assets and provide a way of assessing how average returns differ across different magnitudes of a factor.

The portfolio sort methodology has several disadvantages. The resulting portfolios may be exposed to different risks beyond the factor the portfolio was sorted on. In those instances, it is difficult to know which risk characteristics have an impact on the portfolio returns. Because portfolio sorts are nonparametric, they do not give insight as to the functional form of the relation between the average portfolio returns and the factor.

Next we provide three examples to illustrate how the economic intuition of the factor and cross sectional statistics can help determine the sorting methodology.

Example 1: Portfolio Sorts Based on the EBITDA/EV Factor

In the previous chapter, we introduced the EBITDA/EV factor. Panel A of Exhibit 12.1 contains the cross-sectional distribution of the EBITDA/EV factor. This distribution is approximately normally distributed around a mean of 0.1, with a slight right skew. We use method 1 to sort the variables into five portfolios (denoted by q1, ..., q5) because this sorting method aligns the cross-sectional distribution of factor returns with our economic intuition that there is a linear relationship between the factor and subsequent return. In Exhibit 12.1(B), we see that there is a large difference between the equally

EXHIBIT 12.1 Portfolio Sorts Based on the EBITDA/EV Factor

A. All Factor Values

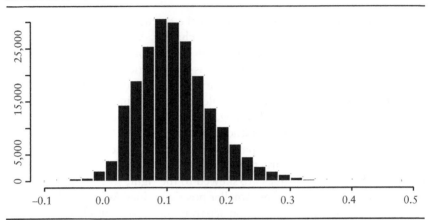

B. Monthly Average Returns for the Sorted Portfolios

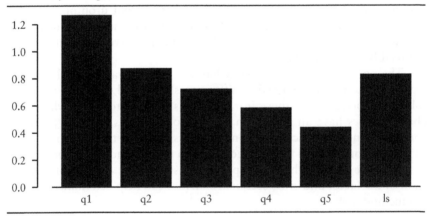

weighted monthly returns of portfolio 1 (q1) and portfolio 5 (q5). Therefore, a trading strategy (denoted by ls in the graph) that goes long portfolio 1 and short portfolio 5 appears to produce abnormal returns.

Example 2: Portfolios Sorts Based on the Revisions Factor

In Exhibit 12.2(A), we see that the distribution of earnings revisions is leptokurtic around a mean of about zero, with the remaining values symmetrically distributed around the peak. The pattern in this cross-sectional distribution provides insight on how we should sort this factor. We use method

EXHIBIT 12.2 The Revisions Factor
A. All Factor Values

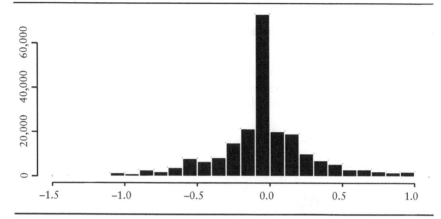

B. Monthly Average Returns for the Sorted Portfolios

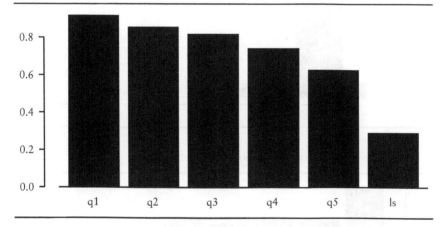

3 to sort the variables into five portfolios. The firms with no change in revisions we allocate to the middle portfolio (portfolio 3). The stocks with positive revisions we sort into portfolios 1 and 2, according to the size of the revisions—while we sort stocks with negative revisions into portfolios 4 and 5, according to the size of the revisions. In Exhibit 12.2(B), we see there is the relationship between the portfolios and subsequent monthly returns. The positive relationship between revisions and subsequent returns agrees with the factor's underlying economic intuition: We expect that firms with improving earnings should outperform. The trading strategy that goes long

portfolio 1 and short portfolio 5 (denoted by ls in the graph) appears to produce abnormal returns.

Example 3: Portfolio Sorts Based on the Share Repurchase Factor

In Exhibit 12.3(A), we see the distribution of share repurchase is asymmetric and leptokurtic around a mean of zero. The pattern in this cross-sectional distribution provides insight on how we should sort this factor. We use method 6 to sort the variables into seven portfolios. We group stocks

EXHIBIT 12.3   The Share Repurchase Factor
A. All Factor Values

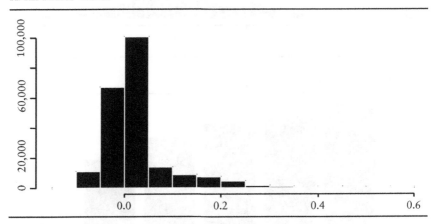

B. Monthly Average Returns for the Sorted Portfolios

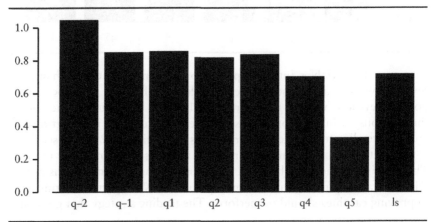

with positive revisions into portfolios 1 through 5 (denoted by q_1, ..., q_5 in the graph) according to the magnitude of the share repurchase factor. We allocate stocks with negative repurchases into portfolios q–2 and q–1 where the median of the negative values determines their membership. We split the negative numbers because we are interested in large changes in the shares outstanding. In Exhibit 12.3(B), unlike the other previous factors, we see that there is *not* a linear relationship between the portfolios. However, there is a large difference in return between the extreme portfolios (denoted by ls in the graph). This large difference agrees with the economic intuition of this factor. Changes in the number of shares outstanding is a potential signal for the future value and prospects of a firm. On the one hand, a large increase in shares outstanding may (1) signal to investors the need for additional cash because of financial distress, or (2) that the firm may be overvalued. On the other hand, a large decrease in the number of shares outstanding may indicate that management believes the shares are undervalued. Finally, small changes in shares outstanding, positive or negative, typically do not have an impact on stock price and therefore are not significant.

Information Ratios for Portfolio Sorts

The *information ratio* (IR) is a statistic for summarizing the risk-adjusted performance of an investment strategy. It is defined as the ratio of the average excess return to the standard deviation of return. For actively managed equity long portfolios, the IR measures the risk-adjusted value a portfolio manager is adding relative to a benchmark.[2] IR can also be used to capture the risk-adjusted performance of long-short portfolios from a portfolio sorts. When comparing portfolios built using different factors, the IR is an effective measure for differentiating the performance between the strategies.

New Research on Portfolio Sorts

As we mentioned earlier in this section, the standard statistical testing procedure for portfolios sorts is to use a Student's t-test to evaluate the mean return differential between the two portfolios containing stocks with the

---

[2]See Richard C. Grinold and Ronald N. Kahn, *Active Portfolio Management: A Quantitative Approach for Providing Superior Returns and Controlling Risk* (New York: McGraw-Hill, 1999), the authors discuss the differences between the t-statistic and the information ratio. Both measures are closely related in their calculation. The t-statistic is the ratio of mean return of a strategy to its standard error. Grinold and Kahn state the related calculations should not obscure the distinction between the two ratios. The t-statistic measures the statistical significance of returns while the IR measures the risk-reward trade-off and the value added by an investment strategy.

highest and lowest values of the sorting factor. However, evaluating the return between these two portfolios ignores important information about the overall pattern of returns among the remaining portfolios.

Recent research by Patton and Timmermann[3] provides new analytical techniques to increase the robustness of inference from portfolios sorts. The technique tests for the presence of a monotonic relationship between the portfolios and their expected returns. To find out if there is a systematic relationship between a factor and portfolio returns, they use the *monotonic relation* (MR) test to reveal whether the null hypothesis of no systematic relationship can be rejected in favor of a monotonic relationship predicted by economic theory. By MR it is meant that the expected returns of a factor should rise or decline monotonically in one direction as one goes from one portfolio to another. Moreover, Patton and Timmermann develop separate tests to determine the direction of deviations in support of or against the theory.

The authors emphasize several advantages in using this approach. The test is nonparametric and applicable to other cases of portfolios such as two-way and three-way sorts. This test is easy to implement via bootstrap methods. Furthermore, this test does not require specifying the functional form (e.g., linear) in relating the sorting variable to expected returns.

FACTOR MODELS

Classical financial theory states that the average return of a stock is the payoff to investors for taking on risk. One way of expressing this risk-reward relationship is through a factor model. A factor model can be used to decompose the returns of a security into factor-specific and asset-specific returns,

$$r_{i,t} = \alpha_i + \beta_{i,1}f_{1,t} + \ldots + \beta_{i,K}f_{K,t} + \varepsilon_{i,t}$$

where $\beta_{i,1}, \beta_{i,2}, \ldots, \beta_{i,K}$ are the factor exposures of stock i, $f_{1,t}, f_{2,t}, \ldots, f_{K,t}$ are the factor returns, α_i is the average abnormal return of stock i, and $\varepsilon_{i,t}$ is the residual.

This factor model specification is *contemporaneous*, that is, both left- and right-hand side variables (returns and factors) have the same time subscript, t. For trading strategies one generally applies a *forecasting* specification where the time subscript of the return and the factors are $t + h$ ($h \geq 1$) and t, respectively. In this case, the econometric specification becomes

---

[3]Andrew J. Patton and Allan Timmermann, "Monotonicity in Asset Returns: New Tests with Applications to the Term Structure, the CAPM and Portfolio Sorts," working paper, University of California–San Diego, 2009.

$$r_{i,t+b} = \alpha_i + \beta_{i,1}f_{1,t} + \ldots + \beta_{i,K}f_{K,t} + \varepsilon_{i,t+b}$$

How do we interpret a trading strategy based on a factor model? The explanatory variables represent different factors that forecast security returns, each factor has an associated factor premium. Therefore, future security returns are proportional to the stock's exposure to the factor premium,

$$E(r_{i,t+b} \mid f_{1,t}, \ldots, f_{K,t}) = \alpha_i + \beta_i' f_t$$

and the variance of future stock return is given by

$$\mathrm{Var}(r_{i,t+b} \mid f_{1,t}, \ldots, f_{K,t}) = \beta_i' E(f_t f_t') \beta_i$$

where $\beta_i = (\beta_{i,1}, \beta_{i,2}, \ldots, \beta_{i,K})'$ and $f_t = (f_{1,t}, f_{2,t}, \ldots, f_{K,t})'$.

In the next section we discuss some specific econometric issues regarding cross-sectional regressions and factor models.

Econometric Considerations for Cross-Sectional Factor Models

In cross-sectional regressions, where the dependent variable[4] is a stock's return and the independent variables are factors, inference problems may arise that are the result of violations of classical linear regression theory. The three most common problems are measurement problems, common variations in residuals, and multicollinearity.

Measurement Problems

Some factors are not explicitly given, but need to be estimated. These factors are estimated with an error. This error can have an impact on the inference from a factor model. This problem is commonly referred to as the "errors in variables problem." For example, a factor that is comprised of a stock's beta is estimated with an error because beta is determined from a regression of stock excess returns on the excess returns of a market index. While beyond the scope of this book, several approaches have been suggested to deal with this problem.[5]

---

[4]See, for example, Eugene F. Fama and Kenneth R. French, "The Capital Asset Pricing Model: Theory and Evidence," *Journal of Economic Perspectives* 18, no. 3 (2004): 25–46.

[5]One approach is to use the Bayesian or model averaging techniques. For more details on the Bayesian approach, see, for example, Svetlozar T. Rachev, John S. J. Hsu, Biliana S. Bagasheva, and Frank J. Fabozzi, *Baysian Methods in Finance* (Hoboken, NJ: John Wiley & Sons, 2008).

Common Variation in Residuals

The residuals from a regression often contain a source of common variation. Sources of common variation in the residuals are heteroskedasticity and serial correlation.[6] We note that when the form of heteroskedasticity and serial correlation is known, we can apply *generalized least squares* (GLS). If the form is not known, it has to be estimated, for example as part of *feasible generalized least squares* (FGLS). We summarize some additional possibilities next.

Heteroskedasticity occurs when the variance of the residual differs across observations and affects the statistical inference in a linear regression. In particular, the estimated standard errors will be underestimated and the *t*-statistics will therefore be inflated. Ignoring heteroskedasticity may lead the researcher to find significant relationships where none actually exist. Several procedures have been developed to calculate standard errors that are robust to heteroskedasticity, also known as *heteroskedasticity-consistent standard errors*.

Serial correlation occurs when residuals terms in a linear regression are correlated, violating the assumptions of regression theory. If the serial correlation is positive, then the standard errors are underestimated and the *t*-statistics will be inflated. Cochrane[7] suggests that the errors in cross-sectional regressions using financial data are often off by a factor of 10. Procedures are available to correct for serial correlation when calculating standard errors.

When the residuals from a regression are both heteroskedastic and serially correlated, procedures are available to correct them. One commonly used procedure is the one proposed by Newey and West referred to as the "Newey-West corrections,"[8] and its extension by Andrews.[9]

Petersen[10] provides guidance on choosing the appropriate method to use for correctly calculating standard errors in panel data regressions when the residuals are correlated. He shows the relative accuracy of the different methods depends on the structure of the data. In the presence of firm effects, where the residuals of a given firm may be correlated across years, *ordinary*

---

[6]For a discussion of dealing with these econometric problems, see Chapter 2 in Frank J. Fabozzi, Sergio Focardi, and Petter N. Kolm, *Quantitative Equity Investing* (Hoboken, NJ: John Wiley & Sons, 2010).

[7]John H. Cochrane, *Asset Pricing* (Princeton, NJ: Princeton University Press, 2005).

[8]Whitney K. Newey and Kenneth D. West, "A Simple, Positive Semidefinite Heteroskedasticity and Autocorrelation Consistent Covariance Matrix," *Econometrica* 56, no. 3 (1987): 703–708.

[9]Donald W. K. Andrews, "Heteroskedasticity and Autocorrelation Consistent Covariance Matrix Estimation," *Econometrica* 59, no. 3 (1991): 817–858.

[10]Mitchell A. Petersen, "Estimating Standard Errors in Finance Panel Sets: Comparing Approached," *Review of Financial Studies* 22, no. 1 (2009): 435–480.

least squares (OLS), Newey-West (modified for panel data sets), or Fama-MacBeth,[11] corrected for first-order autocorrelation, all produce biased standard errors. To correct for this, Petersen recommends using standard errors clustered by firms. If the firm effect is permanent, the fixed effects and random effects models produce unbiased standard errors. In the presence of time effects, where the residuals of a given period may be correlated across difference firms (cross-sectional dependence), Fama-MacBeth produces unbiased standard errors. Furthermore, standard errors clustered by time are unbiased when there are a sufficient number of clusters. To select the correct approach he recommends determining the form of dependence in the data and comparing the results from several methods.

Gow, Ormazabal, and Taylor[12] evaluate empirical methods used in accounting research to correct for cross-sectional and time-series dependence. They review each of the methods, including several methods from the accounting literature that have not previously been formally evaluated, and discuss when each methods produces valid inferences.

Multicollinearity

Multicollinearity occurs when two or more independent variables are highly correlated. We may encounter several problems when this happens. First, it is difficult to determine which factors influence the dependent variable. Second, the individual p values can be misleading—a p value can be high even if the variable is important. Third, the confidence intervals for the regression coefficients will be wide. They may even include zero. This implies that, we cannot determine whether an increase in the independent variable is associated with an increase—or a decrease—in the dependent variable. There is no formal solution based on theory to correct for multicollinearity. The best way to correct for multicollinearity is by removing one or more of the correlated independent variables. It can also be reduced by increasing the sample size.

Fama-MacBeth Regression

To address the inference problem caused by the correlation of the residuals, Fama and MacBeth[13] proposed the following methodology for estimating

---

[11]We cover Fama-MacBeth regression in this section.

[12]Ian D. Gow, Gaizka Ormazabal, and Daniel J. Taylor, "Correcting for Cross-Sectional and Time-Series Dependence in Accounting Research," working paper, Kellogg School of Business and Stanford Graduate School, 2009.

[13]Eugene F. Fama and James D. MacBeth, "Risk, Return, and Equilibrium: Empirical Tests," *Journal of Political Economy* 81, no. 3 (1973): 607–636.

cross-sectional regressions of returns on factors. For notational simplicity, we describe the procedure for one factor. The multifactor generalization is straightforward.

First, for each point in time t we perform a cross-sectional regression:

$$r_{i,t} = \beta_{i,t} f_t + \varepsilon_{i,t}, \quad i = 1, 2, \ldots, N$$

In the academic literature, the regressions are typically performed using monthly or quarterly data, but the procedure could be used at any frequency.

The mean and standard errors of the time series of slopes and residuals are evaluated to determine the significance of the cross-sectional regression. We estimate f and ε_i as the average of their cross-sectional estimates, therefore,

$$\hat{f} = \frac{1}{T} \sum_{t=1}^{T} \hat{f}_t, \quad \hat{\varepsilon}_i = \frac{1}{T} \sum_{t=1}^{T} \hat{\varepsilon}_{i,t}$$

The variations in the estimates determine the standard error and capture the effects of residual correlation without actually estimating the correlations.[14] We use the standard deviations of the cross-sectional regression estimates to calculate the sampling errors for these estimates,

$$\sigma_{\hat{f}}^2 = \frac{1}{T^2} \sum_{t=1}^{T} \left(\hat{f}_t - \hat{f} \right)^2, \quad \sigma_{\hat{\varepsilon}_i}^2 = \frac{1}{T^2} \sum_{t=1}^{T} \left(\hat{\varepsilon}_{i,t} - \hat{\varepsilon}_i \right)^2$$

Cochrane[15] provides a detailed analysis of this procedure and compares it to cross-sectional OLS and pooled time-series cross-sectional OLS. He shows that when the factors do not vary over time and the residuals are cross-sectionally correlated, but not correlated over time, then these procedures are all equivalent.

Information Coefficients

To determine the forecast ability of a model, practitioners commonly use a statistics called the *information coefficient* (IC). The IC is a linear statistic that measures the cross-sectional correlation between a factor and its subsequent realized return:[16]

---

[14]Fama and French, "The Capital Asset Pricing Model: Theory and Evidence."
[15]Cochrane, *Asset Pricing*.
[16]See, for example, Grinold and Kahn, *Active Portfolio Management A Quantitative Approach for Providing Superior Returns and Controlling Risk*; and Edward E. Qian, Ronald H. Hua, and Eric H. Sorensen, *Quantitative Portfolio Management: Modern Techniques and Applications* (New York: Chapman & Hall/CRC, 2007).

$$IC_{t,t+k} = \text{corr}(\mathbf{f}_t, \mathbf{r}_{t,t+k})$$

where $\mathbf{f}_t$ is a vector of cross sectional factor values at time t and $\mathbf{r}_{t,t+k}$ is a vector of returns over the time period t to $t + k$.

Just like the standard correlation coefficient, the values of the IC range from -1 to $+1$. A positive IC indicates a positive relation between the factor and return. A negative IC indicates a negative relation between the factor and return. ICs are usually calculated over an interval, for example, daily or monthly. We can evaluate how a factor has performed by examining the time series behavior of the ICs. Looking at the mean IC tells how predictive the factor has been over time.

An alternate specification of this measure is to make $\mathbf{f}_t$ the rank of a cross-sectional factor. This calculation is similar to the Spearman rank coefficient. By using the rank of the factor, we focus on the ordering of the factor instead of its value. Ranking the factor value reduces the unduly influence of outliers and reduces the influence of variables with unequal variances. For the same reasons, we may also choose to rank the returns instead of using their numerical value.

Sorensen, Qian, and Hua[17] present a framework for factor analysis based on ICs. Their measure of IC is the correlation between the factor ranks, where the ranks are the normalized z-score of the factor,[18] and subsequent return. Intuitively, this IC calculation measures the return associated with a one standard deviation exposure to the factor. Their IC calculation is further refined by risk adjusting the value. To risk adjust, the authors remove systematic risks from the IC and accommodate the IC for specific risk. By removing these risks, Qian and Hua[19] show that the resulting ICs provide a more accurate measure of the return forecasting ability of the factor.

The subsequent realized returns to a factor typically vary over different time horizons. For example, the return to a factor based on price reversal is realized over short horizons, while valuation metrics such as EBITDA/EV are realized over longer periods. It therefore makes sense to calculate multiple ICs for a set of factor forecasts whereby each calculation varies the horizon over which the returns are measured.

---

[17] Eric H. Sorensen, Ronald Hua, and Edward Qian, "Contextual Fundamentals, Models, and Active Management," *Journal of Portfolio Management* 32, no. 1 (2005): 23–36.

[18] A factor normalized z-score is given by the formula z-score $= (\mathbf{f} - \bar{\mathbf{f}}) / \text{std}(\mathbf{f})$ where $\mathbf{f}$ is the factor, $\bar{\mathbf{f}}$ is the mean and $\text{std}(\mathbf{f})$ is the standard deviation of the factor.

[19] Ronald Hua and Edward Qian, "Active Risk and Information Ratio," *Journal of Investment Management* 2, no. 3 (2004): 1–15.

The IC methodology has many of the same advantages as regression models. The procedure is easy to implement. The functional relationship between factor and subsequent returns is known (linear).

ICs can also be used to assess the risk of factors and trading strategies. The standard deviation of the time series (with respect to t) of ICs for a particular factor $(std(IC_{t,t+k}))$ can be interpreted as the strategy risk of a factor. Examining the time series behavior of $std(IC_{t,t+k})$ over different time periods may give a better understanding of how often a particular factor may fail. Qian and Hua show that $std(IC_{t,t+k})$ can be used to more effectively understand the active risk of investment portfolios. Their research demonstrates that ex post tracking error often exceeds the ex ante tracking provided by risk models. The difference in tracking error occurs because tracking error is a function of both ex ante tracking error from a risk model and the variability of information coefficients, $std(IC_{t,t+k})$. They define the expected tracking error as

$$\sigma_{TE} = std(IC_{t.t+k})\sqrt{N}\sigma_{model}dis(\mathbf{R}_t)$$

where N is the number of stocks in the universe (breath), σ_{model} is the risk model tracking error, and $dis(\mathbf{R}_t)$ is dispersion of returns[20] defined by

$$dis(\mathbf{R}_t) = std(r_{1,t}, r_{2,t}, ..., r_{N,t})$$

Example: Information Coefficients

Exhibit 12.4 displays the time-varying behavior of ICs for each one of the factors EBITDA/EV, growth of fiscal year 1 and fiscal year 2 earnings estimates, revisions, and momentum. The graph shows the time series average of information coefficients:

$$\overline{IC}_k = mean(\mathbf{IC}_{t,t+k})$$

The graph depicts the information horizons for each factor, showing how subsequent return is realized over time. The vertical axis shows the size of the average information coefficient $\overline{IC}_k$ for $k = 1, 2, ..., 15$.

Specifically, the EBITDA/EV factor starts at almost 0.03 and monotonically increases as the investment horizon lengthens from one month to 15 months. At 15 months, the EBITDA/EV factor has an IC of 0.09, the highest value among all the factors presented in the graph. This relationship

---

[20]We are conforming to the notation used in Qian and Hua, "Active Risk and Information Ratio." To avoid confusion, Qian and Hua use dis() to describe the cross-sectional standard deviation and std() to describe the time series standard deviation.

EXHIBIT 12.4 Information Coefficients over Various Horizons for EBITDA/EV, Growth of Fiscal Year 1 and Fiscal Year 2 Earnings Estimates, Revisions, and Momentum Factors

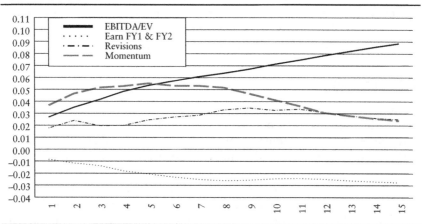

suggests that the EBITDA/EV factor earns higher returns as the holding period lengthens.

The other ICs of the factors in the graph are also interesting. The growth of fiscal year 1 and fiscal year 2 earnings estimates factor is defined as the growth in current fiscal year (fy1) earnings estimates to the next fiscal year (fy2) earnings estimates provided by sell-side analysts.[21] We call the growth of fiscal year 1 and fiscal year 2 earnings estimates factor the *earnings growth factor* throughout the remainder of the chapter. The IC is negative and decreases as the investment horizon lengthens. The momentum factor starts with a positive IC of 0.02 and increases to approximately 0.055 in the fifth month. After the fifth month, the IC decreases. The revisions factor starts with a positive IC and increases slightly until approximately the eleventh month at which time the factor begins to decay.

Looking at the overall patterns in the graph, we see that the return realization pattern to different factors varies. One notable observation is that the returns to factors don't necessarily decay but sometimes grow with the holding period. Understanding the multiperiod effects of each factor is important when we want to combine several factors. This information may influence how one builds a model. For example, we can explicitly incorporate this information about information horizons into our model by using a function that describes the decay or growth of a factor as a parameter to be calibrated. Implicitly, we could incorporate this information by changing

---

[21]The earnings estimates come from the IBES database. See Appendix A for a more detailed description of the data.

the holding period for a security traded for our trading strategy. Specifically, Sneddon[22] discusses an example that combines one signal that has short-range predictive power with another that has long-range power. Incorporating this information about the information horizon often improves the return potential of a model. Kolm[23] describes a general multiperiod model that combines information decay, market impact costs, and real world constraints.

Factor Portfolios

Factor portfolios are constructed to measure the information content of a factor. The objective is to mimic the return behavior of a factor and minimize the residual risk. Similar to portfolio sorts, we evaluate the behavior of these factor portfolios to determine whether a factor earns a systematic premium.

Typically, a factor portfolio has a unit exposure to a factor and zero exposure to other factors. Construction of factor portfolios requires holding both long and short positions. We can also build a factor portfolio that has exposure to multiple attributes, such as beta, sectors, or other characteristics. For example, we could build a portfolio that has a unit exposure to book-to-price and small size stocks. Portfolios with exposures to multiple factors provide the opportunity to analyze the interaction of different factors.

A Factor Model Approach

By using a multifactor model, we can build factor portfolios that control for different risks.[24] We decompose return and risk at a point in time into a systematic and specific component using the regression:

$$r = Xb + u$$

where r is an N vector of excess returns of the stocks considered, X is an N by K matrix of factor loadings, b is a K vector of factor returns, and u is a N vector of firm specific returns (residual returns). Here, we assume that factor returns are uncorrelated with the firm specific return. Further assuming

[22]Leigh Sneddon, "The Tortoise and the Hare: Portfolio Dynamics for Active Managers," *Journal of Investing* 17, no. 4 (2008): 106–111.
[23]Petter N. Kolm, "Multi-Period Portfolio Optimization with Transaction Costs, Alpha Decay, and Constraints," working paper, Courant Institute of Mathematical Sciences, New York University, 2010.
[24]This derivation of factor portfolios is presented in Grinold and Kahn, *Active Portfolio Management A Quantitative Approach for Providing Superior Returns and Controlling Risk.*

that firm specific returns of different companies are uncorrelated, the N by N covariance matrix of stock returns $\mathbf{V}$ is given by

$$\mathbf{V} = \mathbf{XFX}' + \mathbf{\Delta}$$

where $\mathbf{F}$ is the K by K factor return covariance matrix and $\mathbf{\Delta}$ is the N by N diagonal matrix of variances of the specific returns.

We can use the Fama-MacBeth procedure discussed earlier to estimate the factor returns over time. Each month, we perform a GLS regression to obtain

$$\mathbf{b} = (\mathbf{X}'\mathbf{\Delta}^{-1}\mathbf{X})^{-1}\mathbf{X}'\mathbf{\Delta}^{-1}\mathbf{r}$$

OLS would give us an unbiased estimate, but since the residuals are heteroskedastic the GLS methodology is preferred and will deliver a more efficient estimate. The resulting holdings for each factor portfolio are given by the rows of $(\mathbf{X}'\mathbf{\Delta}^{-1}\mathbf{X})^{-1}\mathbf{X}\mathbf{\Delta}^{-1}$.

An Optimization-Based Approach

A second approach to build factor portfolios uses mean-variance optimization. Using optimization techniques provide a flexible approach for implementing additional objectives and constraints.[25]

Using the notation from the previous subsection, we denote by $\mathbf{X}$ the set of factors. We would like to construct a portfolio that has maximum exposure to one target factor from $\mathbf{X}$ (the *alpha* factor), zero exposure to all other factors, and minimum portfolio risk. Let us denote the alpha factor by $\mathbf{X}_\alpha$ and all the remaining ones by $\mathbf{X}_\sigma$. Then the resulting optimization problem takes the form

$$\max_{\mathbf{w}} \left\{ \mathbf{w}'\mathbf{X}_a - \frac{1}{2}\lambda \mathbf{w}'\mathbf{V}\mathbf{w} \right\}$$
$$\text{s.t.} \quad \mathbf{w}'\mathbf{X}_\sigma = 0$$

The analytical solution to this optimization problem is given by

$$h^* = \frac{1}{\lambda}\mathbf{V}^{-1}\left[\mathbf{I} - \mathbf{X}_\sigma \left(\mathbf{X}_\sigma'\mathbf{V}^{-1}\mathbf{X}_\sigma \right)^{-1} \mathbf{X}_\sigma'\mathbf{V}^{-1} \right]\mathbf{X}_\alpha$$

---

[25]Dimitris Melas, Raghu Suryanarayanan, and Stefano Cavaglia, "Efficient Replication of Factor Returns," *MSCI Barra Research Insight*, June 2009.

We may want to add additional constraints to the problem. Constraints are added to make factor portfolios easier to implement and meet additional objectives. Some common constraints include limitations on turnover, transaction costs, the number of assets, and liquidity preferences. These constraints[26] are typically implemented as linear inequality constraints. When no analytical solution is available to solve the optimization with linear inequality constraints, we have to resort to quadratic programming (QP).[27]

PERFORMANCE EVALUATION OF FACTORS

Analyzing the performance of different factors is an important part of the development of a factor-based trading strategy. A researcher may construct and analyze over a hundred different factors, so a process to evaluate and compare these factors is needed. Most often this process starts by trying to understand the time-series properties of each factor in isolation and then study how they interact with each other.

To give a basic idea of how this process may be performed, we use the five factors introduced earlier in this chapter: EBITDA/EV, revisions, share repurchase, momentum, and earnings growth. These are a subset of the factors that we use in the factor trading strategy model discussed later in the chapter. We choose a limited number of factors for ease of exposition. In particular, we emphasize those factors that possess more interesting empirical characteristics.

Exhibit 12.5(A) presents summary statistics of monthly returns of long-short portfolios constructed from these factors. We observe that the average monthly return ranges from –0.05% for the earnings growth to 0.90% for the momentum factor. The t-statistics for the mean return are significant at the 95% level for the EBITDA/EV, share repurchase, and momentum factors. The monthly volatility ranges from 3.77% for the revisions factor to 7.13% for the momentum factor. In other words, the return and risk characteristics among factors vary significantly. We note that the greatest monthly drawdown has been large to very large for all of the factors, implying significant downside risk. Overall, the results suggest that there is a systematic premium associated with the EBITDA/EV, share repurchase, and momentum factors.

---

[26]An exception is the constraint on the number of assets that results in integer constraints.

[27]For a more detailed discussion on portfolio optimization problems and optimization software see, for example, Frank J. Fabozzi, Petter N. Kolm, Dessislava Pachamanova, and Sergio M. Focardi, *Robust Portfolio Optimization and Management* (Hoboken, NJ: John Wiley & Sons, 2007).

EXHIBIT 12.5 Results from Portfolio Sorts

A. Summary Statistics of Monthly Returns of Long-short Portfolios

	Mean	Stdev	Median	t-stat	Max	Min	pctPos	pctNeg
Revisions	0.29	3.77	0.77	1.17	10.43	−19.49	0.55	0.45
EBITDA/EV	0.83	5.80	0.72	2.16	31.61	−30.72	0.55	0.45
Share repurchase	0.72	3.89	0.43	2.78	22.01	−14.06	0.61	0.39
Momentum	0.90	7.13	0.97	1.90	25.43	−42.71	0.61	0.39
Earning growth	−0.05	4.34	0.25	−0.18	14.03	−23.10	0.53	0.47

B. Correlations between Long-Short Portfolios

	Revisions	EBITDA/EV	Share Repurchase	Momentum	Earnings Growth
Revisions	1.00	−0.28	0.01	0.79	0.25
EBITDA/EV	−0.28	1.00	0.78	−0.12	0.01
Share repurchase	0.01	0.78	1.00	0.20	0.12
Momentum	0.79	−0.12	0.20	1.00	0.28
Earnings growth	0.25	0.01	0.12	0.28	1.00

Let pctPos and pctNeg denote the fraction of positive and negative returns over time, respectively. These measures offer another way of interpreting the strength and consistency of the returns to a factor. For example, EBITDA/EV and momentum have t-statistics of 2.16 and 1.90, respectively, indicating that the former is stronger. However, pctPos (pctNeg) are 0.55 versus 0.61 (0.45 versus 0.39) showing that positive returns to momentum occur more frequently. This may provide reassurance of the usefulness of the momentum factor, despite the fact that its t-statistic is below the 95% level.

Exhibit 12.5(B) presents unconditional correlation coefficients of monthly returns for long-short portfolios. The comovement of factor returns varies among the factors. The lowest correlation is –0.28 between EBITDA/EV and revisions. The highest correlation is 0.79 between momentum and revisions. In addition, we observe that the correlation between revisions and share repurchase, and between EBITDA/EV and earnings growth are close to zero. The broad range of correlations provides evidence that combining uncorrelated factors could produce a successful strategy.

Exhibit 12.6 presents the cumulative returns for the long-short portfolios. The returns of the long-short factor portfolios experience substantial

EXHIBIT 12.6   Cumulative Returns of Long-Short Portfolios

volatility. We highlight the following patterns of cumulative returns for the different factors:

- The cumulative return of the revisions factor is positive in the early periods (12/1989 to 6/1998). While it is volatile, its cumulative return is higher in the next period (7/1998 to 7/2000). It deteriorates sharply in the following period (8/2000 to 6/2003), and levels out in the later periods (7/2003 to 12/2008).
- The performance of the EBITDA/EV factor is consistently positive in the early periods (12/1989 to 9/1998), deteriorates in the next period (10/1998 to 1/2000) and rebounds sharply (2/2000 to 7/2002), grows at slower but more historically consistent rate in the later periods (8/2002 to 4/2007), deteriorates in the next period (5/2007 to 9/2007), and returns to more historically consistent returns in last period (10/2007 to 12/2008).
- The cumulative return of the share repurchase factor grows at a slower pace in the early years (12/1989 to 5/1999), falls slightly in the middle periods (6/1999 to 1/2000), rebounds sharply (2/2000 to 7/2002), falls then flattens out in the next period (8/2002 to 4/2008), and increases at a large rate late in the graph (5/2008 to 12/2008).
- The momentum factor experiences the largest volatility. This factor performs consistently well in the early period (12/1989 to 12/1998), experiences sharp volatility in the middle period (1/1999 to 5/2003), flattens out (6/2003 to 6/2007), and grows at an accelerating rate from (7/2007 to 12/2008).
- The performance of the earnings growth factor is flat or negative throughout the entire period.

The overall pattern of the cumulative returns among the factors clearly illustrate that factor returns and correlations are time varying.

In Exhibit 12.7(A), we present summary statistics of the monthly information coefficients of the factors. The average monthly information coefficients range from 0.03 for EBITDA/EV and momentum, to 0.01 for the share repurchase factor. The t-statistics for the mean ICs are significant at the 95% level for all factors except earnings growth. With the exception of share repurchase and earnings growth, the fraction of positive returns of the factors are significantly greater than that of the negative returns.

The share repurchase factor requires some comments. The information coefficient is negative, in contrast to the positive return in the long-short portfolio sorts, because negative share repurchases are correlated with subsequent return. The information coefficient is lower than we would expect because there is not a strong linear relation between the return and the

EXHIBIT 12.7 Summary of Monthly Factor Information Coefficients

A. Basic Statistics for Monthly Information Coefficients

	Mean	Stdev	Median	t-stat	Max	Min	pctPos	pctNeg
Revisions	0.02	0.10	0.02	2.51	0.31	−0.29	0.58	0.42
EBITDA/EV	0.03	0.13	0.02	3.13	0.48	−0.41	0.59	0.41
Share repurchase	−0.01	0.10	−0.00	−2.13	0.20	−0.45	0.48	0.52
Momentum	0.03	0.18	0.05	2.86	0.50	−0.57	0.59	0.41
Earnings growth	−0.00	0.13	0.00	−0.56	0.26	−0.28	0.51	0.49

B. Correlations for Monthly Average Information Coefficients

	Revisions	EBITDA/EV	Share Repurchase	Momentum	Earnings Growth
Revisions	1.00	−0.31	0.13	0.79	−0.14
EBITDA/EV	−0.31	1.00	−0.66	−0.26	−0.49
Share repurchase	0.13	−0.66	1.00	0.02	0.58
Momentum	0.79	−0.26	0.02	1.00	−0.05
Earnings growth	−0.14	−0.49	0.58	−0.05	1.00

measures. As the results from the portfolio sorts indicate, the extreme values of this factor provide the highest returns.

Exhibit 12.7(B) displays unconditional correlation coefficients of the monthly information coefficients. The comovement of the ICs factor returns varies among the factors. The lowest correlation is –0.66 between EBITDA/EV and share repurchases. But again this should be interpreted with caution because it is negative repurchases that we view as attractive. The highest correlation reported in the exhibit is 0.79 between momentum and revisions. Similar to the correlation of long-short factor portfolio returns, the diverse set of correlations provides evidence that combining uncorrelated factors may produce a successful strategy.

In Exhibit 12.8(A), we present summary statistics of the time series average of the monthly coefficients from the Fama-MacBeth (FM) regressions of the factors. The information provided by the FM coefficients differs from the information provided by portfolio sorts. The FM coefficients show the linear relationship between the factor and subsequent returns, while the results from the portfolio sorts provide information on the extreme values of the factors and subsequent returns. The difference in the size of the mean returns between the FM coefficients and portfolio sorts exits partially because the intercept terms from the FM regressions are not reported in the exhibit.

The average monthly FM coefficient ranges from –0.18 for share repurchase to 0.31 for the momentum factor. Again the share repurchase results should be interpreted with caution because it is negative repurchases that we view as attractive. The t-statistics are significant at the 95% level for the EBITDA/EV and share repurchase factors.

Also, we compare the results of portfolio sorts in Exhibit 12.7(A) with the FM coefficients in Exhibit 12.8(A). The rank ordering of the magnitude of factor returns is similar between the two panels. The t-statistics are slightly higher in the FM regressions than the portfolio sorts. The correlation coefficients for the portfolio sorts in Exhibit 12.7(B) are consistent with the FM coefficients in Exhibit 12.8(B) for all the factors except for shares repurchases. The results for share repurchases needs to be interpreted with caution because it is negative repurchases that we view as attractive. The portfolio sorts take that into account while FM regressions do not.

To better understand the time variation of the performance of these factors, we calculate rolling 24-month mean returns and correlations of the factors. The results are presented in Exhibit 12.9. We see that the returns and correlations to all factors are time varying. A few of the time series experience large volatility in the rolling 24-month returns. The EBITDA/EV factor shows the largest variation followed by the momentum and share

EXHIBIT 12.8 Summary of Monthly Fama-MacBeth Regression Coefficients

A. Basic Statistics for Fama-MacBeth Regression Coefficients

	Mean	Stdev	Median	t-stat	Max	Min	pctPos	pctNeg
Revisions	0.09	1.11	0.22	1.22	3.36	-5.26	0.59	0.41
EBITDA/EV	0.27	1.61	0.14	2.50	8.69	-7.81	0.59	0.41
Share repurchase	-0.18	0.96	-0.06	-2.90	3.21	-5.91	0.44	0.56
Momentum	0.31	2.42	0.29	1.94	9.97	-12.37	0.60	0.40
Earnings growth	-0.08	0.99	-0.04	-1.20	2.83	-4.13	0.48	0.52

B. Correlations for Fama-MacBeth Regression Coefficients

	Revisions	EBITDA/EV	Share Repurchase	Momentum	Earnings Growth
Revisions	1.00	-0.27	0.05	0.77	-0.26
EBITDA/EV	-0.27	1.00	-0.75	-0.18	-0.58
Share repurchase	0.05	-0.75	1.00	-0.04	0.64
Momentum	0.77	-0.18	-0.04	1.00	-0.18
Earnings growth	-0.26	-0.58	0.64	-0.18	1.00

EXHIBIT 12.9   Rolling 24-Month Mean Returns for the Factors

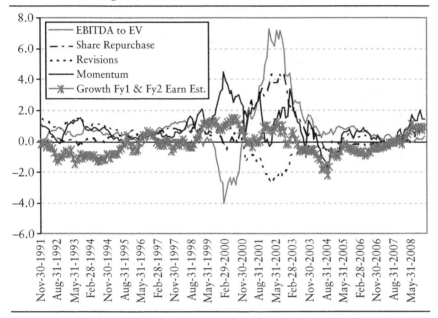

repurchase factors. All factors experience periods where the rolling average returns are both positive and negative.

Exhibit 12.10 presents the rolling correlation between pairs of the factors. There is substantial variability in many of the pairs. In most cases the correlation moves in a wave-like pattern. This pattern highlights the time-varying property of the correlations among the factors. This property will be important to incorporate in a factor trading model. The most consistent correlation is between momentum and revisions factors and this correlation is, in general, fairly high.

MODEL CONSTRUCTION METHODOLOGIES FOR A FACTOR-BASED TRADING STRATEGY

In the previous section, we analyzed the performance of each factor. The next step in building our trading strategy is to determine how to combine the factors into one model. The key aspect of building this model is to (1) determine what factors to use out of the universe of factors that we have, and (2) how to weight them.

EXHIBIT 12.10   Rolling 24-Month Correlations of Monthly Returns for the Factors

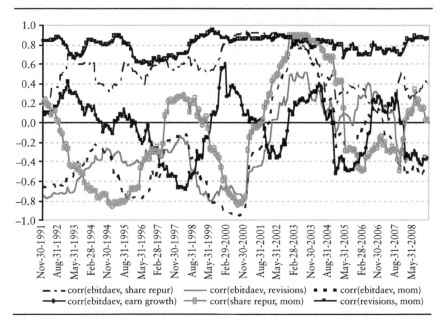

We describe four methodologies to combine and weight factors to build a model for a trading strategy. These methodologies are used to translate the empirical work on factors into a working model. Most of the methodologies are flexible in their specification and there is some overlap between them. Though the list is not exhaustive, we highlight those processes frequently used by quantitative portfolio managers and researchers today. The four methodologies are the data driven, the factor model, the heuristic, and the optimization approaches.

It is important to be careful how each methodology is implemented. In particular, it is critical to balance the iterative process of finding a robust model with good forecasting ability versus finding a model that is a result of data mining.

The Data Driven Approach

A *data driven approach* uses statistical methods to select and weight factors in a forecasting model. This approach uses returns as the independent variables and factors as the dependent variables. There are a variety of estimation procedures, such as neural nets, classification trees, and principal components, that can be used to estimate these models. Usually a statistic is established to determine the criteria for a successful model. The algorithm of the statistical method evaluates the data and compares the results against the criteria.

Many data driven approaches have no structural assumptions on potential relationships the statistical method finds. Therefore, it is sometimes difficult to understand or even explain the relationship among the dependent variables used in the model.

Deistler and Hamann[28] provide an example of a data driven approach to model development. The model they develop is used for forecasting the returns to financial stocks. To start, they split their data sample into two parts—an in-sample part for building the model, and out-of-sample part to validate the model. They use three different types of factor models for forecasting stocks returns: quasistatic principal components, quasistatic factor models with idiosyncratic noise, and reduced rank regression. For model selection Deistler and Hamann use an iterative approach where they find the optimal mix of factors based on the Akaike's information criterion and the Bayesian information criterion. A large number of different models are compared using the out-of-sample data. They find that the reduced rank model provides the best performance. This model produced the highest out-of-sample R^2s, hit rates,[29] and Diebold Mariano test statistic[30] among the different models evaluated.

The Factor Model Approach

In this section, we briefly address the use of factor models for forecasting. The goal of the factor model is to develop a parsimonious model that forecast returns accurately. One approach is for the researcher to predetermine the variables to be used in the factor model based on economic intuition. The model is estimated and then the estimated coefficients are used to produce the forecasts.

A second approach is to use statistical tools for model selection. In this approach we construct several models—often by varying the factors and the

---

[28]Manfred Deistler and Eva Hamann, "Identification of Factor Models for Forecasting Returns," *Journal of Financial Econometrics* 3, no. 2 (2005): 256–281.

[29]The hit rate is calculated as

$$h = \frac{1}{T_2 - T_1} \sum_{t=T_1+1}^{T_2} \text{sign}(y_t^i \hat{y}_{t|t-1}^i)$$

where y_t^i is one-step ahead realized value and $\hat{y}_{t|t-1}^i$ is the one-step ahead predicted value.

[30]For calculation of this measure, see Francis X. Diebold and Roberto S. Mariano, "Comparing Predictive Accuracy," *Journal of Business and Economic Statistics* 13, no. 3 (2005): 253–263.

number of factors used—and have them compete against each other, just like in a horse race. We then choose the best performing model.

Factor model performance can be evaluated in three ways. We can evaluate the fit, forecast ability, and economic significance of the model. The measure to evaluate the fit of a model is based on statistical measures including the model's R^2 and adjusted R^2, and F- and t-statistics of the model coefficients.

There are several methods to evaluate how well a model will forecast. West[31] discusses the theory and conventions of several measures of relative model quality. These methods use the resulting time series of predictions and prediction errors from a model. In the case where we want to compare models, West suggests ratios or differences of mean; mean-square or mean-absolute prediction errors; correlation between one model's prediction and another model's realization (also know as forecast encompassing); or comparison of utility or profit-based measures of predictive ability. In other cases where we want to assess a single model, he suggests measuring the correlation between prediction and realization, the serial correlation in one step ahead prediction errors, the ability to predict direction of change, and the model prediction bias.

We can evaluate economic significance by using the model to predict values and using the predicted values to build portfolios. The profitability of the portfolios is evaluated by examining statistics such as mean returns, information ratios, dollar profits, and drawdown.

The Heuristic Approach

The heuristic approach is another technique used to build trading models. Heuristics are based on common sense, intuition, and market insight and are not formal statistical or mathematical techniques designed to meet a given set of requirements. Heuristic-based models result from the judgment of the researcher. The researcher decides the factors to use, creates rules in order to evaluate the factors, and chooses how to combine the factors and implement the model.

Piotroski[32] applies a heuristic approach in developing an investment strategy for high value stocks (high book-to-market firms). He selects nine

[31]Kenneth D. West, "Forecast Evaluation," in *Handbook of Economic Forecasting*, vol. 1, edited by Graham Elliot, Clive W. J. Granger, and Allan G. Timmermann (Amsterdam: Elsevier, 2006).
[32]Joseph D. Piotroski, "Value Investing: The Use of Historical Financial Statement Information to Separate Winners from Losers," *Journal of Accounting Research* 38, no. 3 supplement (2000): 1–41.

fundamental factors[33] to measure three areas of the firm's financial condition: profitability, financial leverage and liquidity, and operating efficiency. Depending on the factor's implication for future prices and profitability, each factor is classified as either "good" or "bad." An indicator variable for the factor is equal to one (zero) if the factor's realization is good (bad). The sum of the nine binary factors the F_SCORE. This aggregate score measures the overall quality, or strength, of the firm's financial position. According to the historical results provided by Piotroski, this trading strategy is very profitable. Specifically, a trading strategy that buys expected winners and shorts expected losers would have generated a 23% annual return between 1976 and 1996.

There are different approaches to evaluate a heuristic approach. Statistical analysis can be used to estimate the probability of incorrect outcomes. Another approach is to evaluate economic significance. For example, Piotroski determines economic significance by forming portfolios based on the firm's aggregate score (F_SCORE) and then evaluates the size of the subsequent portfolio returns.

There is no theory that can provide guidance when making modeling choices in the heuristic approach. Consequently, the researcher has to be careful not to fall into the data-mining trap.

The Optimization Approach

In this approach, we use optimization to select and weight factors in a forecasting model. An optimization approach allows us flexibility in calibrating the model and simultaneously optimize an objective function specifying a desirable investment criteria.

There is substantial overlap between optimization use in forecast modeling and portfolio construction. There is frequently an advantage in working with the factors directly, as opposed to all individual stocks. The factors provide a lower dimensional representation of the complete universe of the stocks considered. Besides the dimensionality reduction, which reduces computational time, the resulting optimization problem is typically more robust to changes in the inputs.

Sorensen, Hua, Qian, and Schoen[34] present a process that uses an optimization framework to combine a diverse set of factors (alpha sources) into

---

[33]The nine factors are return on assets, change in return on assets, cash flow from operations scaled by total assets, cash compared to net income scaled by total assets, change in long-term debt/assets, change in current ratio, change in shares outstanding, change in gross margin, and change in asset turnover.

[34]Eric H. Sorensen, Ronald Hua, Edward Qian, and Robert Schoen, "Multiple Alpha Sources and Active Management," *Journal of Portfolio Management* 30, no. 2 (2004): 39–45.

a multifactor model. Their procedure assigns optimal weights across the factors to achieve the highest information ratio. They show that the optimal weights are a function of average ICs and IC covariances. Specifically,

$$\mathbf{w} \propto \text{cov}(\mathbf{IC})^{-1} \times \overline{\mathbf{IC}}$$

where $\mathbf{w}$ is the vector of factor weights, $\overline{\mathbf{IC}}$ is the vector of the average of the risk-adjusted ICs, and $\text{cov}(\mathbf{IC})^{-1}$ is the inverse of the covariance matrix of the ICs.

In a subsequent paper, Sorensen, Hua, and Qian[35] apply this optimization technique to capture the idiosyncratic return behavior of different security contexts. The contexts are determined as a function of stock risk characteristics (value, growth, or earnings variability). They build a multifactor model using the historical risk-adjusted IC of the factors, determining the weights of the multifactor model by maximizing the IR of the combined factors. Their research demonstrates that the weights to factors of an alpha model (trading strategy) differ depending on the security contexts (risk dimensions). The approach improves the ex post information ratio compared to a model that uses a one-size-fits-all approach.

Importance of Model Construction and Factor Choice

Empirical research shows that the factors and the weighting scheme of the factors are important in determining the efficacy of a trading strategy model. Using data from the stock selection models of 21 major quantitative funds, the quantitative research group at Sanford Bernstein analyzed the degree of overlap in rankings and factors.[36] They found that the models maintained similar exposures to many of the same factors. Most models showed high exposure to cash flow–based valuations (e.g., EV/EBITDA) and price momentum, and less exposure to capital use, revisions, and normalized valuation factors. Although they found commonality in factor exposures, the stock rankings and performance of the models were substantially different. This surprising finding indicates that model construction differs among the various stock selection models and provides evidence that the efficacy of common signals has not been completely arbitraged away.

---

[35]Eric H. Sorensen, Ronald Hua, and Edward Qian, "Contextual Fundamentals, Models, and Active Management," *Journal of Portfolio Management* 32, no. 1 (2005): 23–36.
[36]Vadim Zlotnikov, Ann Marie Larson, Wally Cheung, Serdar Kalaycioglu, Ronna D. Lao, and Zachary A. Apoian, "Quantitative Research—January 2007: Survey of Quantitative Models—Vastly Different Rankings and Performance, Despite Similarity in Factor Exposures," Bernstein Research, January 16, 2007.

A second study by the same group showed commonality across models among cash flow and price momentum factors, while stock rankings and realized performance were vastly different.[37] They hypothesize that the difference between good and poor performing models may be related to a few unique factors identified by portfolio managers, better methodologies for model construction (e.g., static, dynamic, or contextual models), or good old-fashioned luck.

Example: A Factor-Based Trading Strategy

In building this model, we hope to accomplish the following objectives: identify stocks that will outperform and underperform in the future, maintain good diversification with regard to alpha sources, and be robust to changing market conditions such as time varying returns, volatilities, and correlations.

We have identified 10 factors that have an ability to forecast stock returns.[38] Of the four model construction methodologies discussed previously, we use the optimization framework to build the model as it offers the greatest flexibility.

We determine the allocation to specific factors by solving the following optimization problem:

$$\min_{\mathbf{w}} \mathbf{w}' \Sigma \mathbf{w}, \quad \mathbf{w} \geq 0$$

$$\sum_{v \in \text{Value}} w_v \geq 0.35$$

$$\sum_{g \in \text{Growth}} w_g \geq 0.20$$

$$3 \leq \sum_{i=1}^{10} \delta_i \leq 7$$

with the budget constraint

$$\mathbf{w}'\mathbf{e} = 1, \quad \mathbf{e} = (1, ..., 1)'$$

---

[37]Vadim Zlotnikov, Ann Marie Larson, Serdar Kalaycioglu, Ronna D. Lao, and Zachary A. Apoian, "Quantitative Research: Survey of Quantitative Models—Continued Emphasis on EV/EBIT, Momentum, Increased Focus on Capital Use; Some Evidence on Non-linear Factor Implementation; Low Return Consistency," Bernstein Research, November 21, 2007.

[38]We use a combination of growth, value, quality, and momentum factors. The appendix to this chapter contains definitions of all of them.

where Σ is the covariance matrix of factor returns, Value and Growth are the sets of value and growth factors, and δ_i is equal to one if $w_i > 0$ or zero otherwise.

We constrain the minimum exposure to values factors to be greater than or equal to 35% of the weight in the model based on the belief that there is a systematic long-term premium to value.

Using the returns of our factors, we perform this optimization monthly to determine which factors to hold and in what proportions. Exhibit 12.11 displays how the factor weights change over time.

In the next step, we use the factor weights to determine the attractiveness of the stocks in our universe. We score each stock in the universe by multiplying the standardized values of the factors by the weights provided by the optimization of our factors. Stocks with high scores are deemed attractive and stocks with low scores are deemed unattractive.

To evaluate how the model performs, we sort the scores of stocks into five equally weighted portfolios and evaluate the returns of these portfolios. Exhibit 12.12(A) provides summary statistics of the returns for each portfolio. Note that there is a monotonic increasing relationship among the portfolios with portfolio 1 (q1) earning the highest return and portfolio 5 (q5) earning the lowest return. Over the entire period, the long-short portfolio (LS) that is long portfolio 1 and short portfolio 5 averages about 1% per month with a monthly Sharpe ratio of 0.33. Its return is statistically significant at the 97.5% level.

Exhibit 12.12(B) shows the monthly average stock turnover of portfolio 1 (q1) and portfolio 5 (q5). Understanding how turnover varies from month to month for a trading strategy is important. If turnover is too high then it might be prohibitive to implement because of execution costs. While beyond the scope of this chapter, we could explicitly incorporate transaction costs in this trading strategy using a market impact model.[39] Due to the dynamic nature of our trading strategy—where active factors may change from month to month—our turnover of 20% is a bit higher than what would be expected using a static approach.

We evaluate the monthly information coefficient between the model scores and subsequent return. This analysis provides information on how well the model forecasts return. The monthly mean information coefficient of the model score is 0.03 and is statistically significant at the 99% level. The monthly standard deviation is 0.08. We note that both the information coefficients and returns were stronger and more consistent in the earlier periods.

---

[39]See Joseph A. Cerniglia and Petter N. Kolm, "Factor-Based Trading Strategies and Market Impact Costs," working paper, Courant Institute of Mathematical Sciences, New York University, 2010.

EXHIBIT 12.11 Factor Weights of the Trading Strategy

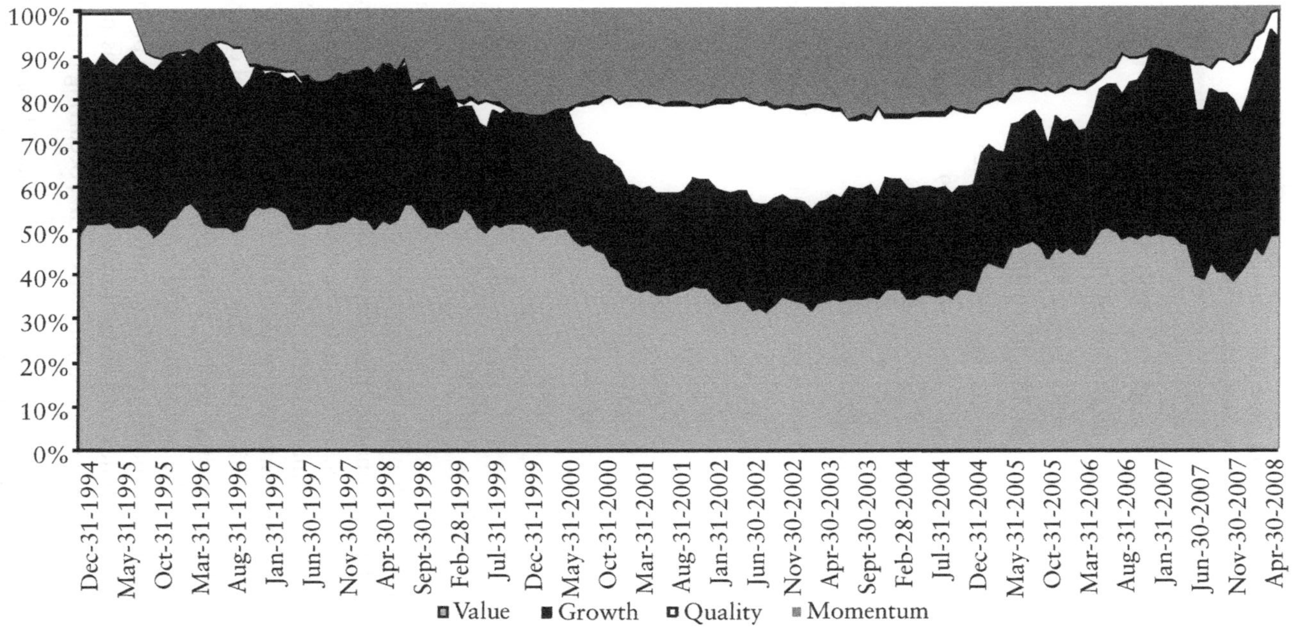

□ Value ■ Growth □ Quality ■ Quality ■ Momentum

EXHIBIT 12.12 Summary of Model Results

A. Summary Statistics of the Model Returns

	q1	q2	q3	q4	q5	LS
Mean	1.06	0.98	0.83	0.65	0.12	0.94
Stdev	5.64	5.18	4.98	5.31	5.88	2.82
Median	1.61	1.61	1.58	1.55	1.11	0.71
Max	15.79	11.18	10.92	13.26	13.01	12.84
Min	−23.59	−23.32	−19.45	−21.25	−24.51	−6.87
Num	169	169	169	169	169	169
t-statistic	2.44	2.45	2.17	1.59	0.27	4.33
IR	0.19	0.19	0.17	0.12	0.02	0.33

B. Summary Statistics of Turnover for Portfolio 1 (q1) and Portfolio 5 (q5)

	q1	q5
Mean	0.20	0.17
Stdev	0.07	0.06
Median	0.19	0.16
Max	0.53	0.39
Min	0.07	0.05
Num	169	169
t-statistic	36.74	39.17

Exhibit 12.13 displays the cumulative return to portfolio 1 through portfolio 5. Throughout the entire period there is a monotonic relationship between the portfolios. To evaluate the overall performance of the model, we analyze the performance of the long-short portfolio returns. We observe that the model performs well in December 1994 to May 2007 and April 2008 to June 2008. This is due to the fact that our model correctly picked the factors that performed well in those periods. We note that the model performs poorly in the period July 2007–April 2008, losing an average of 1.09% a month. The model appears to suffer from the same problems many quantitative equity funds and hedge funds faced during this period.[40] The worst performance in a single month was −6.87, occurring in January 2001,

---

[40]Matthew S. Rothman, "Turbulent Times in Quant Land," Lehman Brothers Equity Research, August 9, 2007; and Kent Daniel, "The Liquidity Crunch in Quant Equities Analysis and Implications," Goldman Sachs Asset Management, December 13, 2007 presentation from The Second New York Fed-Princeton Liquidity Conference.

EXHIBIT 12.13 Cumulative Return of the Model

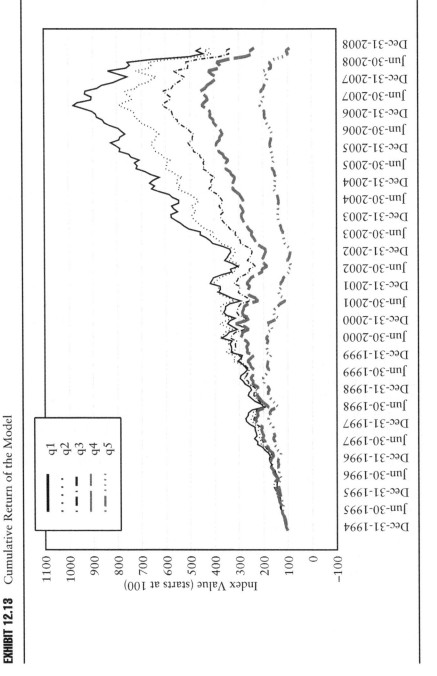

and the maximum drawdown of the model was –13.7%, occurring during the period from May 2006 (peak) to June 2008 (trough).[41]

To more completely understand the return and risk characteristic of the strategy, we would have to perform a more detailed analysis, including risk and performance attribution, and model sensitivity analysis over the full period as well as over subperiods. As the turnover is on the higher side, we may also want to introduce turnover constraints or use a market impact model.

Periods of poor performance of a strategy should be disconcerting to any analyst. The poor performance of the model during the period June 2007–March 2008 indicates that many of the factors we use were not working. We need to go back to each individual factor and analyze them in isolation over this time frame. In addition, this highlights the importance of research to improve existing factors and develop new ones using unique data sources.

BACKTESTING

In the research phase of the trading strategy, model scores are converted into portfolios and then examined to assess how these portfolios perform over time. This process is referred to as *backtesting a strategy*. The backtest should mirror as closely as possible the actual investing environment incorporating both the investment's objectives and the trading environment.

When it comes to mimicking the trading environment in backtests, special attention needs to be given to transaction costs and liquidity considerations. The inclusion of transaction costs is important because they may have a major impact on the total return. Realistic market impact and trading costs estimates affect what securities are chosen during portfolio construction. Liquidity is another attribute that needs to be evaluated. The investable universe of stocks should be limited to stocks where there is enough liquidity to be able to get in and out of positions.

Portfolio managers may use a number of constraints during portfolio construction. Frequently these constraints are derived from the portfolio policy of the firm, risk management policy, or investor objectives. Common constraints include upper and lower bounds for each stock, industry, or risk factor—as well as holding size limits, trading size limits, turnover, and the number of assets long or short.

---

[41]We ran additional analysis on the model by extending the holding period of the model from 1 to 3 months. The results were much stronger as returns increased to 1.6% per month for a two-month holding period and 1.9% per month for a three-month holding period. The risk as measured by drawdown was higher at –17.4% for a two-month holding period and –29.5% for the three-month holding period.

To ensure the portfolio construction process is robust we use sensitivity analysis to evaluate our results. In sensitivity analysis we vary the different input parameters and study their impact on the output parameters. If small changes in inputs give rise to large changes in outputs, our process may not be robust enough. For example, we may eliminate the five best and worst performing stocks from the model, rerun the optimization, and evaluate the performance. The results should be similar as the success of a trading strategy should not depend on a handful of stocks.

We may want to determine the effect of small changes in one or more parameters used in the optimization. The performance of the optimal portfolio should in general not differ significantly after we have made these small changes.

Another useful test is to evaluate a model by varying the investment objective. For example, we may evaluate a model by building a low-tracking-error portfolio, a high-tracking-error portfolio, and a market-neutral portfolio. If the returns from each of these portfolios are decent, the underlying trading strategy is more likely to be robust.

Understanding In-Sample and Out-of-Sample Methodologies

There are two basic backtesting methodologies: in-sample and out-of-sample. It is important is to understand the nuances of each.

We refer to a backtesting methodology as an in-sample methodology when the researcher uses the same data sample to specify, calibrate, and evaluate a model.

An out-of-sample methodology is a backtesting methodology where the researcher uses a subset of the sample to specify and calibrate a model, and then evaluates the forecasting ability of the model on a different subset of data. There are two approaches for implementing an out-of-sample methodology. One approach is the *split-sample method*. This method splits the data into two subsets of data where one subset is used to build the model while the remaining subset is used to evaluate the model.

A second method is the *recursive out-of-sample test*. This approach uses a sequence of recursive or rolling *windows* of past history to forecast a future value and then evaluates that value against the realized value. For example, in a rolling regression–based model we will use data up to time t to calculate the coefficients in the regression model. The regression model forecasts the $t + h$ dependent values, where $h > 0$. The prediction error is the difference between the realized value at $t + h$ and the predicted value from the regression model. At $t + 1$ we recalculate the regression model and evaluate the predicted value of $t + 1 + h$ against realized value. We continue this process throughout the sample.

The conventional thinking among econometricians is that in-sample tests tend to reject the null hypotheses of no predictability more often than out-of-sample tests. This view is supported by many researchers because they reason that in-sample tests are unreliable, often finding spurious predictability. Two reasons given to support this view is the presence of unmodeled structural changes in the data and the use of techniques that result in data mining and model overfitting.

Inoune and Kilian[42] question this conventional thinking. They use asymptotic theory to evaluate the "trade-offs between in-sample tests and out-of-sample tests of predictability in terms of their size and power." They argue strong in-sample results and weak out-of-sample results are not necessarily evidence that in-sample tests are not reliable. Out-of-sample tests using sample-splitting result in a loss of information and lower power for small samples. As a result, an out-of-sample test may fail to detect predictability while the in-sample test will correctly identify predictability. They also show that out-of-sample tests are not more robust to parameter instability that results from unmodeled structural changes.

A Comment on the Interaction between Factor-Based Strategies and Risk Models

Frequently, different factor models are used to calculate the risk inputs and the expected return forecasts in a portfolio optimization. A common concern is the interaction between factors in the models for risk and expected returns. Lee and Stefek[43] evaluate the consequences of using different factor models, and conclude that (1) using different models for risk and alpha can lead to unintended portfolio exposures that may worsen performance; (2) aligning risk factors with alpha factors may improve information ratios; and (3) modifying the risk model by including some of the alpha factors may mitigate the problem.

BACKTESTING OUR FACTOR TRADING STRATEGY

Using the model scores from the trading strategy example, we build two optimized portfolios and evaluate their performance. Unlike the five equally weighted portfolios built only from model scores, the models we now discuss

---

[42]Atsushi Inoune and Lutz Kilian, "In-Sample or Out-of-Sample Tests of Predictability: Which One Should We Use?" working paper, North Carolina State University and University of Michigan, 2002.

[43]Jyh-Huei Lee and Dan Stefek, "Do Risk Factors Eat Alphas?" *Journal of Portfolio Management* 34, no. 4 (2008): 12–24.

were built to mirror as close as possible tradable portfolios a portfolio manager would build in real time. Our investable universe is the Russell 1000. We assign alphas for all stock in the Russell 1000 with our dynamic factor model. The portfolios are long only and benchmarked to the S&P 500. The difference between the portfolios is in their benchmark tracking error. For the low-tracking error portfolio the risk aversion in the optimizer is set to a high value, sectors are constrained to plus or minus 10% of the sector weightings in the benchmark, and portfolio beta is constrained to 1.00. For the high-tracking error portfolio, the risk aversion is set to a low value, the sectors are constrained to plus or minus 25% of the sector weightings in the benchmark, and portfolio beta is constrained to 1.00. Rebalancing is performed once a month. Monthly turnover is limited to 10% of the portfolio value for the low-tracking error portfolio and 15% of the portfolio value for the high-tracking error portfolio.

Exhibit 12.14 presents the results of our backtest. The performance numbers are gross of fees and transaction costs. Performance over the entire period is good and consistent throughout. The portfolios outperform the benchmark over the various time periods. The resulting annualized Sharpe ratios over the full period are 0.66 for the low-tracking error portfolio, 0.72 for the high-tracking error portfolio, and 0.45 for the S&P 500.[44]

KEY POINTS

- The four most commonly used approaches for the evaluation of return premiums and risk characteristics to factors are portfolio sorts, factor models, factor portfolios, and information coefficients.
- The portfolio sorts approach ranks stocks by a particular factor into a number of portfolios. The sorting methodology should be consistent with the characteristics of the distribution of the factor and the economic motivation underlying its premium.
- The information ratio (IR) is a statistic for summarizing the risk-adjusted performance of an investment strategy and is defined as the ratio of average excess return to the standard deviation of return.
- We distinguish between contemporaneous and forecasting factor models, dependent on whether both left- and right-hand side variables (returns and factors) have the same time subscript, or the time subscript of the left-hand side variable is greater.
- The three most common violations of classical regression theory that occur in cross-sectional factor models are (1) the errors in variables

---

[44]Here we calculate the Sharpe ratio as portfolio excess return (over the risk-free rate) divided by the standard deviation of the portfolio excess return.

EXHIBIT 12.14 Total Return Report (annualized)

From 01/1995 to 06/2008	QTD	YTD	1 Year	2 Year	3 Year	5 Year	10 Year	Since Inception
Portfolio: Low-tracking error	−0.86	−10.46	−11.86	4.64	7.73	11.47	6.22	13.30
Portfolio: High-tracking error	−1.43	−10.47	−11.78	4.15	8.29	13.24	7.16	14.35
S&P 500: Total return	−2.73	−11.91	−13.12	2.36	4.41	7.58	2.88	9.79

problem, (2) common variation in residuals such as heteroskedasticity and serial correlation, and (3) multicollinearity. There are statistical techniques that address the first two. The third issue is best dealt with by removing collinear variables from the regression, or by increasing the sample size.

- The Fama-MacBeth regression addresses the inference problem caused by the correlation of the residuals in cross-sectional regressions.
- The information coefficient (IC) is used to evaluate the return forecast ability of a factor. It measures the cross-sectional correlation between a factor and its subsequent realized return.
- Factor portfolios are used to measure the information content of a factor. The objective is to mimic the return behavior of a factor and minimize the residual risk. We can build factor portfolios using a factor model or an optimization. An optimization is more flexible as it is able to incorporate constraints.
- Analyzing the performance of different factors is an important part of the development of a factor-based trading strategy. This process begins with understanding the time-series properties of each factor in isolation and then studying how they interact with each other.
- Techniques used to combine and weight factors to build a trading strategy model include the data driven, the factor model, the heuristic, and the optimization approaches.
- An out-of-sample methodology is a backtesting methodology where the researcher uses a subset of the sample to specify a model and then evaluates the forecasting ability of the model on a different subset of data. There are two approaches for implementing an out-of-sample methodology: the split-sample approach and the recursive out-of-sample test.
- Caution should be exercised if different factor models are used to calculate the risk inputs and the expected return forecasts in a portfolio optimization.

APPENDIX: THE COMPUSTAT POINT-IN-TIME, IBES CONSENSUS DATABASES AND FACTOR DEFINITIONS

The factors used in this chapter and Chapter 11 were constructed on a monthly basis with data from the Compustat Point-In-Time and IBES Consensus databases. Our sample includes all stocks contained in the Russell 1000 index over the period December 31, 1989, to December 31, 2008.

The Compustat Point-In-Time database[45] contains quarterly financial data from the income, balance sheet, and cash flow statements for active

---

[45]Capital IQ, Compustat, http://www.compustat.com.

and inactive companies. This database provides a consistent view of historical financial data, both reported data and subsequent restatements, the way
it appeared at the end of any month. Using this data allows the researcher
to avoid common data issues such as survivorship and look-ahead bias. The
data is available from March 1987.

The Institutional Brokers Estimate System (IBES) database[46] provides
actual earnings from companies and estimates of various financial measures
from sell-side analysts. The estimated financial measures include estimates
of earnings, revenue and sales, operating profit, analyst recommendations,
and other measures. The data is offered on a summary (consensus) level or
detailed (analyst-by-analyst) basis. The U.S. data covers reported earnings
estimates and results since January 1976.

The factors used in this chapter and the prior one are defined as follows.[47]

Value Factors

Operating income before depreciation to enterprise value = EBITDA/EV

where

$$EBITDA = Sales\ LTM\ (Compustat\ Item\ 2)$$
$$- Cost\ of\ goods\ Sales\ LTM\ (Compustat\ Item\ 30)$$
$$- SG\&A\ Exp\ (Compustat\ Item\ 1)$$

and

$$EV = [Long\text{-}term\ debt\ (Compustat\ Item\ 51)$$
$$+ Common\ shares\ outstanding\ (Computstat\ Item\ 61)$$
$$\times Price\ (PRCCM) - Cash\ (Compustat\ Item\ 36)]$$

$$Book\ to\ price = Stockholders'\ equity\ total\ (Computstat\ Item\ 60)$$
$$\div [Common\ shares\ outstanding\ (Computstat\ Item\ 59)$$
$$\times Price\ (PRCCM)]$$

$$Sales\ to\ price = Sales\ LTM\ (Computstat\ Item\ 2)$$
$$\div [Common\ shares\ outstanding\ (Computstat\ Item\ 61)$$
$$\times Price\ (PRCCM)]$$

---

[46]Thomson Reuters, http://www.thomsonreuters.com.
[47]LTM refers to the last four reported quarters.

Quality Factors

Share repurchase = [Common shares outstanding (Computstat Item 61)
– Common shares outstanding (Computstat Item 61) from 12 months ago]
÷ Common shares outstanding (Computstat Item 61) from 12 months ago

Asset turnover = Sales LTM (Computstat Item 2)/[(Assets (Computstat Item 44)
– Assets (Computstat Item 44) from 12 months ago)/ 2]

Return on invested capital = Income/Invested capital

where

> Income = Income before extra items LTM (Computstat Item 8)
> + Interest expense LTM (Computstat Item 22)
> + Minority interest expense LTM (Computstat Item 3)

and

> Invested capital = Common equity (Computstat Item 59)
> + Long-term debt (Computstat Item 51)
> + Minority interest (Computstat Item 53)
> + Preferred stock (Computstat Item 55)

Debt to equity = Total debt/Stockholder's equity

where

> Total debt = [Debt in current liabilities (Computstat Item 45)
> + Long-term debt – Total (Computstat Item 51)]

and

> Stockholder's equity = Stockholder's equity (Computstat Item 60)

Chg. debt to equity = (Total debt – Total debt from 12 months ago)
÷ [(Stockholder's equity
+ Stockholder's equity from 12 months ago)/2]

Growth

Revisions = [Number of up revisions (IBES item NUMUP)
            − Number of down revisions (IBES item NUMDOWN)]
            ÷ Number of estimates revisions (IBES item NUMEST)

Growth of fiscal Year 1 and fiscal Year 2 earnings estimates
= Consensus mean of FY2 (IBES item MEAN FY2)
     ÷ Consensus mean of FY1 (IBES item MEAN FY1) − 1

Momentum

Momentum = Total return of last 11 months excluding
                 the most returns from the most recent month

Summary Statistics

Exhibit 12.A1 contains monthly summary statistics of the factors defined previously. Factor values greater than the 97.5 percentile or less than the 2.5 percentile are considered outliers. We set factor values greater than the 97.5 percentile value to the 97.5 percentile value, and factor values less than the 2.5 percentile value to the 2.5 percentile value, respectively.

EXHIBIT 12.A1   Summary Statistics

	Mean	Standard Deviation	Median	25 Percentile	75 Percentile
EBITDA/EV	0.11	0.06	0.11	0.07	0.15
Book to price	0.46	0.30	0.40	0.24	0.62
Sales to price	0.98	0.91	0.69	0.36	1.25
Share repurchase	0.03	0.09	0.00	−0.01	0.03
Asset turnover	1.83	1.89	1.46	0.64	2.56
Return on invested capital	0.13	0.11	0.11	0.07	0.17
Debt to equity	0.97	1.08	0.62	0.22	1.26
Change in debt to equity	0.10	0.31	0.01	−0.04	0.17
Revisions	−0.02	0.33	0.00	−0.17	0.11
Growth of fiscal year 1 and fiscal year 2 earnings estimates	0.37	3.46	0.15	0.09	0.24
Momentum	13.86	36.03	11.00	−7.96	31.25

QUESTIONS

1. a. Why is the portfolio sorts methodology used?
   b. What is an application of the portfolio sort methodology?

2. How is the interpretation of a factor model using stock returns influenced by the specification of time lag of the (or no time lag) dependent variable?

3. Explain some of the common inference problems that arise in cross-sectional regressions where the dependent variable is a stock's return.

4. a. What are factor portfolios?
   b. What methodologies can be used to build these portfolios?

5. What is the difference between in-sample and out-of-sample testing?

CHAPTER 13

Multifactor Equity Risk Models and Their Applications*

Anthony Lazanas, Ph.D.
Managing Director
Barclays Capital

António Baldaque da Silva, Ph.D.
Director
Barclays Capital

Arne D. Staal, Ph.D.
Director
Barclays Capital

Cenk Ural, Ph.D.
Vice President
Barclays Capital

Risk management is an integral part of the portfolio management process. Risk models are central to this practice, allowing managers to quantify and analyze the risk embedded in their portfolios. Risk models provide managers insight into the major sources of risk in a portfolio, helping them to control their exposures and understand the contributions of different portfolio components to total risk. They help portfolio managers in their decision-making process by providing answers to important questions such as: How does my small-cap exposure affect portfolio risk? Does my underweight in diversified financials hedge my overweight in banks? Risk models are also widely used in various other areas such as in portfolio construction, performance attribution, and scenario analysis.

*The authors would like to thank Andy Sparks, Anuj Kumar, and Chris Sturhahn of Barclays Capital for their help and comments.

In this chapter, we discuss the structure of multifactor equity risk models, types of factors used in these models, and describe certain estimation techniques. We also illustrate the use of equity risk factor models in various applications, namely the analysis of portfolio risk, portfolio construction, scenario analysis, and performance attribution.

Throughout this chapter, we will be using the Barclays Capital Global Risk Model[1] for illustration purposes. For completeness, we also refer to other approaches one can take to construct such a model.

MOTIVATION

In this section, we discuss the motivation behind the multifactor equity risk models. Let's assume that a portfolio manager wants to estimate and analyze the volatility of a large portfolio of stocks. A straightforward idea would be to compute the volatility of the historical returns of the portfolio and use this measure to forecast future volatility. However this framework does not provide any insight into the relationships between different securities in the portfolio or the major sources of risk. For instance it does not assist a portfolio manager interested in diversifying her portfolio or constructing a portfolio that has better risk adjusted performance.

Instead of estimating the portfolio volatility using historical portfolio returns, one could utilize a different strategy. The portfolio return is a function of stock returns and the market weights of these stocks in the portfolio. Using this, the forecasted volatility of the portfolio (σ_p) can be computed as a function of the weights (w) and the covariance matrix (Σ_s) of stock returns in the portfolio:

$$\sigma_p^2 = w^T \cdot \Sigma_s \cdot w$$

This covariance matrix can be decomposed into individual stock volatilities and the correlations between stock returns. Volatilities measure the riskiness of individual stock returns and correlations represent the relationships between the returns of different stocks. Looking into these correlations

---

[1]The Barclays Capital Global Risk Model is available through POINT®, Barclays Capital portfolio management tool. It is a multicurrency cross-asset model that covers many different asset classes across the fixed income and equity markets, including derivatives in these markets. At the heart of the model is a covariance matrix of risk factors. The model has more than 500 factors, many specific to a particular asset class. The asset class models are periodically reviewed. Structure is imposed to increase the robustness of the estimation of such large covariance matrix. The model is estimated from historical data. It is calibrated using extensive security-level historical data and is updated on a monthly basis.

and volatilities, the portfolio manager can gain insight into her portfolio, namely the riskiness of different parts of the portfolio or how the portfolio can be diversified. As we outlined above, to estimate the portfolio volatility we need to estimate the correlation between each pair of stocks. Unfortunately, this means that the number of parameters to be estimated grows quadratically with the number of stocks in the portfolio.[2] For most practical portfolios, the relatively large number of stocks makes it difficult to estimate the relationship between stock returns in a robust way. Moreover, this framework uses the history of individual stock returns to forecast future stock volatility. However stocks characteristics are dynamic and hence using returns from different time periods may not produce good forecasts.[3] Finally, the analysis does not provide much insight regarding the broad factors influencing the portfolio. These drawbacks constitute the motivation for the multifactor risk models, detailed in this chapter.

One of the major goals of multifactor risk models is to describe the return of a portfolio using a smaller set of variables, called factors. These factors should be designed to capture broad (systematic) market fluctuations, but should also be able to capture specific nuances of individual portfolios. For instance, a broad U.S. market factor would capture the general movement in the equity market, but not the varying behavior across industries. If our portfolio is heavily biased toward particular industries, the broad U.S. market factor may not allow for a good representation of our portfolio's return.

In the context of factor models, the total return of a stock is decomposed into a systematic and an idiosyncratic component. Systematic return is the component of total return due to movements in common risk factors, such as industry or size. On the other hand, idiosyncratic return can be described as the residual component that cannot be explained by the systematic factors. Under these models, the idiosyncratic return is uncorrelated across issuers. Therefore, correlations across securities are driven by their exposures to the systematic risk factors and the correlation between those factors.

The following equation demonstrates the systematic and the idiosyncratic components of total stock return:

$$r_s = L_s \cdot F + \varepsilon_s$$

The systematic return for security s is the product of the loadings of that security (L_s, also called sensitivities) to the systematic risk factors and the

---

[2]As an example, if the portfolio has 10 stocks, we need to estimate 45 parameters, with 100 stocks we would need to estimate 4,950 parameters.

[3]This is especially the case over crisis periods where stock characteristics can change dramatically over very short periods of time.

returns of these factors (F). The idiosyncratic return is given by ε_s. Under these models, the portfolio volatility can be estimated as

$$\sigma_p^2 = L_p^T \cdot \Sigma_F \cdot L_p + w^T \cdot \Omega \cdot w$$

Models represented by equations of this form are called *linear factor models.* Here L_p represents the loadings of the portfolio to the risk factors (determined as the weighted average of individual stock loadings) and Σ_F is the covariance matrix of factor returns. w is the vector of security weights in the portfolio and Ω is the covariance matrix of idiosyncratic stock returns. Due to the uncorrelated nature of these returns, this covariance matrix is diagonal, with all elements outside its diagonal being zero. As a result, the idiosyncratic risk of the portfolio is diversified away as the number of securities in the portfolio increases. This is the diversification benefit attained when combining uncorrelated exposures.

For most practical portfolios, the number of factors is significantly smaller than the number of stocks in the portfolio. Therefore, the number of parameters in Σ_F is much smaller than in Σ_S, leading to a generally more robust estimation. Moreover, the factors can be designed in a way that they are relatively more stable than individual stock returns, leading to models with potentially better predictability.

Another important advantage of using linear factor models is the detailed insight they provide into the structure and properties of portfolios. These models characterize stock returns in terms of systematic factors that (can) have intuitive economic interpretations. Linear factor models can provide important insights regarding the major systematic and idiosyncratic sources of risk and return. This analysis can help managers to better understand their portfolios and can guide them through the different tasks they perform, such as rebalancing, hedging or the tilting of their portfolios. The Barclays Capital Global Risk Model—the model used for illustration throughout this chapter—is an example of such a linear factor model.

EQUITY RISK FACTOR MODELS

The design of a linear factor model usually starts with the identification of the major sources of risk embedded in the portfolios of interest. For an equity portfolio manager who invests in various markets across the globe, the major sources of risk are typically country, industry membership, and other fundamental or technical exposures such as size, value, and momentum. The relative significance of these components varies across different regions. For instance, for regional equity risk models in developed markets, industry factors tend to be more important than country factors, although in periods of financial distress country factors become more significant. On the other hand, for emerging markets models the country factor is still considered to be the most important source of risk. For regional models, the relative significance of industry factors depends on the level of financial integration across different local markets in that region. The importance of these factors is also time-varying, depending on the particular time period of the analysis. For instance, country risk used to be a large component of total risk for European equity portfolios. However, country factors have been losing their significance in this context due to financial integration in the region as a result of the European Union and a common currency, the euro. This is particularly true for larger European countries. Similarly, the relative importance of industry factors is higher over the course of certain industry-led crises, such as the dot-com bubble burst (2000–2002) and the 2007–2009 banking and credit crisis. As we will see, the relative importance of different risk factors varies also with the particular design and the estimation process chosen to calibrate the model.

A typical global or regional equity risk model has the following structure:

$$r_i = \beta_i^{MKT} \cdot F^{MKT} + \beta_i^{IND} \cdot F^{IND} + \beta_i^{CNT} \cdot F^{CNT} + \sum_{j=1}^{n} \ell_{ij} \cdot F_j^{FT} + \varepsilon_i$$

where

r_i = the rate of return for stock i
F^{MKT} = the market factor
F^{IND} = the industry factor corresponding to stock i
F^{CNT} = the country factor corresponding to stock i
β_i = the exposure (beta) of the stock to the corresponding factor
F^{FT} = the set of fundamental and technical factors
ℓ_{ij} = the loading of stock i to factor F_j^{FT}
ε_i = the residual return for stock i

There are different ways in which these factors can be incorporated into an equity risk model. The choice of a particular model affects the interpretation of the factors. For instance, consider a model that has only market and industry factors. Industry factors in such a model would represent industry-specific moves net of the market return. On the other hand, if we remove the market factor from the equation, the industry factors now incorporate the overall market effect. Their interpretation would change, with their returns now being close to market value-weighted industry indexes. Country-specific risk models are a special case of the previous representation where the country factor disappears and the market factor is represented by the returns of the countrywide market. Macroeconomic factors are also used in some equity risk models, as discussed later.

The choice of estimation process also influences the interpretation of the factors. As an example, consider a model that has only industry and country factors. These factors can be estimated jointly in one step. In this case, both factors represent their own effect net of the other one. On the other hand, these factors can be estimated in a multistep process—e.g., industry factors estimated in the first step and then the country factors estimated in the second step, using residual returns from the first step. In this case, the industry factors have an interpretation close to the market value-weighted industry index returns, while the country factors would now represent a residual country average effect, net of industry returns. We discuss this issue in more detail in the following section.

Model Estimation

In terms of the estimation methodology, there are three major types of multi-factor equity risk models: cross-sectional, time series, and statistical. All three of these methodologies are widely used to construct linear factor models in the equity space.[4] In cross-sectional models, loadings are known and factors are estimated. Examples of loadings used in these models are industry membership variables and fundamental security characteristics (e.g., the book-to-price ratio). Individual stock returns are regressed against these security-level loadings in every period, delivering estimation of factor returns for that period. The interpretation of these estimated factors is usually intuitive, although dependent on the estimation procedure and on the quality of the loadings. In time-series models, factors are known and loadings are estimated. Examples of factors in these models are financial or macroeconomic variables, such as market returns or industrial production. Time series of individual equity returns are regressed against the factor returns, delivering empirical sensitivities (loadings or betas) of each stock to the risk factors. In these models, factors are constructed and not estimated, therefore, their interpretation is straightforward. In statistical models (e.g., principal component analysis), both factors and loadings are estimated jointly in an iterative fashion. The resulting factors are statistical in nature, not designed to be intuitive. That being said, a small set of the statistical factors can be (and usually are) correlated with broad economic factors, such as the market. Exhibit 13.1 summarizes some of the characteristics of these models.

An important advantage of cross-sectional models is that the number of parameters to be estimated is generally significantly smaller as compared to the other two types of models. On the other hand, cross-sectional models

---

[4]Fixed income managers typically use cross-sectional type of models.

EXHIBIT 13.1 Cross-Sectional, Time-Series, and Statistical Factor Models

Model	Cross-Sectional	Time-Series	Statistical
Input set	Security-specific loadings and returns	Factor and security returns	Security returns
Factors and loadings	Factors are estimated using the known loadings (e.g., industry beta or momentum score)	Factors are known (e.g., market or industrial production) and loadings are estimated (e.g., industry or momentum betas)	Both factors and loadings are estimated
Interpretation	Clean interpretation of loadings; generally intuitive interpretation of factors	Straightforward interpretation of factors	Factors may have no intuitive interpretation
Number of parameters	(No. of factors) × (No. of time periods)	(No. of securities) × (No. of factors)	(No. of securities) × (No. of factors)

require a much larger set of input data (company-specific loadings). Cross-sectional models tend to be relatively more responsive as loadings can adjust faster to changing market conditions. There are also hybrid models, which combine cross-sectional and time-series estimation in an iterative fashion; these models allow the combination of observed and estimated factors. Statistical models on the other hand require only a history of security returns as input to the process. They tend to work better when economic sources of risk are hard to identify and are primarily used in high-frequency applications.

As we mentioned in the previous section, the estimation process is a major determinant in the interpretation of factors. Estimating all factors jointly in one-step regression allows for a natural decomposition of total variance in stock returns. However it also complicates the interpretation of factors as each factor now represents its own effect net of all other factors. Moreover, multicollinearity problems arise naturally in this set-up, potentially delivering lack of robustness to the estimation procedure and leading to unintuitive factor realizations. This problem can be serious when using factors that are highly correlated.

An alternative in this case is to use a multistep estimation process where different sets of factors are estimated sequentially, in separate regressions. In the first step, stock returns are used in a regression to estimate a certain set of factors and then residual returns from this step are used to estimate the second step factors and so on. The choice of the order of factors in such estimation influences the nature of the factors and their realizations. This choice should be guided by the significance and the desired interpretation of the resulting factors. The first-step factors have the most straightforward interpretation as they are estimated in isolation from all other factors using raw stock returns. For instance in a country-specific equity risk model where there are only industry and fundamental or technical factors, the return series of industry factors would be close to the industry index returns if they are estimated in isolation in the first step. This would not be the case if all industry, fundamental, and technical factors are estimated in the same step.

An important input to the model estimation is the security weights used in the regressions. There is a variety of techniques employed in practice but generally more weight is assigned to less volatile stocks (usually represented by larger companies). This enhances the robustness of the factor estimates as stocks from these companies tend to have relatively more stable return distributions.

Types of Factors

In this section, we analyze in more detail the different types of factors typically used in equity risk models. These can be classified under five major categories: market factors, classification variables, firm characteristics, macroeconomic variables, and statistical factors.

Market Factors

A market factor can be used as an observed factor in a time-series setting (e.g., in the capital asset pricing model, the market factor is the only systematic factor driving returns). As an example, for a U.S. equity factor model, S&P 500 can be used as a market factor and the loading to this factor—market beta—can be estimated by regressing individual stock returns to the S&P 500. On the other hand, in a cross-sectional setting, the market factor can be estimated by regressing stock returns to the market beta for each time period (this beta can be empirical—estimated via statistical techniques—or set as a dummy loading, usually 1). When incorporated into a cross-sectional regression with other factors, it generally works as an intercept, capturing the broad average return for that period. This changes the interpretation of all other factors to returns relative to that average (e.g. industry factor returns would now represent industry-specific moves net of market).

Classification Variables

Industry and country are the most widely used classification variables in equity risk models. They can be used as observed factors in time-series models via country/industry indexes (e.g. return series of GICS indexes[5] can be used as observed industry factors). In a cross-sectional setting, these factors are estimated by regressing stock returns to industry/country betas (either estimated or represented as a 0/1 dummy loading). These factors constitute a significant part of total risk for a majority of equity portfolios, especially for portfolios tilted toward specific industries or countries.

Firm Characteristics

Factors that represent firm characteristics can be classified as either fundamental or technical factors. These factors are extensively used in equity risk models; exposures to these factors represent tilts towards major investment themes such as size, value, and momentum. Fundamental factors generally employ a mix of accounting and market variables (e.g., accounting ratios) and technical factors commonly use return and volume data (e.g., price momentum or average daily volume traded).

In a time-series setting, these factors can be constructed as representative long-short portfolios (e.g., Fama-French factors). As an example, the value factor can be constructed by taking a long position in stocks that have a large book to price ratio and a short position in the stocks that have a small book to price ratio. On the other hand, in a cross-sectional setup, these factors can be estimated by regressing the stock returns to observed firm characteristics. For instance, a book to price factor can be estimated by regressing stock returns to the book to price ratios of the companies. In practice, fundamental and technical factors are generally estimated jointly in a multivariate setting.

A popular technique in the cross-sectional setting is the standardization of the characteristic used as loading such that it has a mean of zero and a standard deviation of one. This implies that the loading to the corresponding factor is expressed in relative terms, making the exposures more comparable across the different fundamental/technical factors. Also, similar characteristics can be combined to form a risk index and then this index can be used to estimate the relevant factor (e.g., different value ratios such as earnings to price and book to price can be combined to construct a value index, which would be the exposure to the value factor). The construction of an index from similar characteristics can help reduce the problem of multicollinearity referred to above. Unfortunately, it can also dilute the signal each characteristic has, potentially reducing its explanatory power. This trade-off should be taken into account while constructing the model. The construction of fundamental factors and their loadings requires careful handling

---

[5]GICS is the Global Industry Classification Standard by Standard & Poor's, a widely used classification scheme by equity portfolio managers.

of accounting data. These factors tend to become more significant for portfolios that are hedged with respect to the market or industry exposures.

Macroeconomic Variables

Macroeconomic factors, representing the state of the economy, are generally used as observed factors in time-series models. Widely used examples include interest rates, commodity indexes, and market volatility (e.g., the VIX index). These factors tend to be better suited for models with a long horizon. For short to medium horizons, they tend to be relatively insignificant when included in a model that incorporates other standard factors such as industry. The opposite is not true, suggesting that macro factors are relatively less important for these horizons. This does not mean that the macroeconomic variables are not relevant in explaining stock returns; it means that a large majority of macroeconomic effects can be captured through the industry factors. Moreover, it is difficult to directly estimate stock sensitivities to slow-moving macroeconomic variables. These considerations lead to the relatively infrequent use of macro variables in short to medium horizon risk models.[6]

Statistical Factors

Statistical factors are very different in nature than all the aforementioned factors as they do not have direct economic interpretation. They are estimated using statistical techniques such as principal component analysis where both factors and loadings are estimated jointly in an iterative fashion. Their interpretation can be difficult, yet in certain cases they can be re-mapped to well-known factors. For instance, in a principal component analysis model for the U.S. equity market, the first principal component would represent the U.S. market factor. These models tend to have a relatively high in-sample explanatory power with a small set of factors and the marginal contribution of each factor tends to diminish significantly after the first few factors. Statistical factors can also be used to capture the residual risk in a model

---

[6]An application of macro variables in the context of risk factor models is as follows. First, we get the sensitivities of the portfolio to the model's risk factors. Then we project the risk factors into the macro variables. We then combine the results from these two steps to get the indirect loadings of the portfolio to the macro factors. Therefore, instead of calculating the portfolio sensitivities to macro factors by aggregating individual stock macro sensitivities—that are always hard to estimate—we work with the portfolio's macro loadings, estimated indirectly from the portfolio's risk factor loadings as described above. This indirect approach may lead to statistically more robust relationships between portfolio returns and macro variables.

with economic factors. These factors tend to work better when there are unidentified sources of risk such as in the case of high frequency models.

Other Considerations in Factor Models

Various quantitative and qualitative measures can be employed to evaluate the relative performance of different model designs. Generically, better risk models are able to forecast more accurately the risk of different types of portfolios, across different economic environments. Moreover, a better model allows for an intuitive analysis of the portfolio risk along the directions used to construct and manage the portfolio. The relative importance of these considerations should frame how we evaluate different models.

A particular model is defined by its estimation framework and the selection of its factors and loadings. Typically, these choices are evaluated jointly, as the contributions of specific components are difficult to measure in practice. Moreover, decisions on one of these components (partially) determine the choice of the others. For instance, if a model uses fundamental firm characteristics as loadings, it also uses estimated factors—more generally, decisions on the nature of the factors determine the nature of the loadings and vice-versa.

Quantitative measures of factor selection include the explanatory power or significance of the factor, predictability of the distribution of the factor and correlations between factors. On a more qualitative perspective, portfolio managers usually look for models with factors and loadings that have clean and intuitive interpretation, factors that correspond to the way they think about the asset class, and models that reflect their investment characteristics (e.g., short vs. long horizon, local vs. global investors).

Idiosyncratic Risk

Once all systematic factors and loadings are estimated, the residual return can be computed as the component of total stock return that cannot be explained by the systematic factors. Idiosyncratic return—also called residual, nonsystematic or name-specific return—can be a significant component of total return for individual stocks, but tends to become smaller for portfolios of stocks as the number of stocks increases and concentration decreases (the aforementioned diversification effect). The major input to the computation of idiosyncratic risk is the set of historical idiosyncratic returns of the stock. Because the nature of the company may change fast, a good idiosyncratic risk model should use only recent and relevant idiosyncratic returns. Moreover, recent research suggests that there are other conditional variables that may help improving the accuracy of idiosyncratic risk estimates. For instance, there is substantial evidence that the market value of a company is highly correlated with its idiosyncratic risk, where larger companies exhibit smaller idiosyncratic risk. The use of such variables as an extra adjustment factor can improve the accuracy of idiosyncratic risk estimates.

As mentioned before, idiosyncratic returns of different issuers are assumed to be uncorrelated. However different securities from the same issuer can show a certain level of comovement, as they are all exposed to specific events affecting their common issuer.

Interestingly, this comovement is not perfect or static. Certain news can potentially affect the different securities issued by the same company (e.g., equity, bonds, or equity options) in different ways. Moreover, this relationship changes with the particular circumstances of the firm. For instance, returns from securities with claims to the assets of the firm should be more highly correlated if the firm is in distress. A good risk model should be able to capture these phenomena.

APPLICATIONS OF EQUITY RISK MODELS

Multifactor equity risk models are employed in various applications such as the quantitative analysis of portfolio risk, hedging unwanted exposures, portfolio construction, scenario analysis, and performance attribution. In this section we discuss and illustrate some of these applications.

Portfolio managers can be divided broadly into indexers (those that measure their returns relative to a benchmark index) and absolute return managers (typically hedge fund managers). In between stand the enhanced indexers, those that are allowed to deviate from the benchmark index in order to express views, presumably leading to superior returns. All are typically subject to a risk budget that prescribes how much risk they are allowed to take to achieve their objectives: minimize transaction costs and match the index return for the pure indexers, maximize the net return for the enhanced indexers, or maximize absolute return for absolute return managers. In all of these cases, the manager has to merge all her views and constraints into a final portfolio.

The investment process of a typical portfolio manager involves several steps. Given the investment universe and objective, the steps usually consist of portfolio construction, risk prediction, and performance evaluation. These steps are iterated throughout the investment cycle over each rebalancing period. The examples in this section are constructed following these steps. In particular, we start with a discussion on the portfolio construction process for three equity portfolio managers with different goals: The first aims to track a benchmark, the second to build a momentum portfolio, and the third to implement sector views in a portfolio. We conduct these exercises through a risk-based portfolio optimization approach at a monthly rebalancing frequency. For the index-tracking portfolio example, we then conduct a careful evaluation of its risk exposures and contributions to ensure that the portfolio manager's views and intuition coincide with the actual portfolio exposures. Once comfortable with the positions and the associated risk, the portfolio is implemented. At the end of the monthly investment cycle, the performance of the portfolio and return contributions of its different components can be evaluated using performance attribution.

Scenario analysis can be employed in both the portfolio construction and the risk evaluation phases of the portfolio process. This exercise allows the manager to gain additional intuition regarding the exposures of her portfolio and how it may behave under particular economic circumstances. It usually takes the form of stress testing the portfolio under historical or hypothetical scenarios. It can also reveal the sensitivity of the portfolio to particular movements in economic and financial variables not explicitly considered during the portfolio construction process. The last application in this chapter illustrates this kind of analysis.

Throughout our discussion, we use a suite of global cash equity risk models available through POINT®, the Barclays Capital portfolio analytics and modeling platform.[7]

Portfolio Construction

Broadly speaking there are two main approaches to portfolio construction: a formal quantitative optimization-based approach and a qualitative approach that is based primarily on manager intuition and skill. There are many variations within and between these two approaches. In this section, we focus on risk-based optimization using a linear factor model. We do not discuss other more qualitative or nonrisk-based approaches (e.g., a stratified sampling). A common objective in a risk-based optimization exercise is the minimization of volatility of the portfolio, either in isolation or when evaluated against a benchmark. In the context of multifactor risk models, total volatility is composed of a systematic and an idiosyncratic component, as described above. Typically, both of these components are used in the objective function of the optimization problems. We demonstrate three

---

[7]The equity risk model suite in POINT consists of six separate models across the globe: the United States, United Kingdom, Continental Europe, Japan, Asia (excluding Japan), and global emerging markets equity risk models (for details see Antonio B. Silva, Arne D. Staal, and Cenk Ural, "The U.S. Equity Risk Model," *Barclays Capital Publication*, July 2009). It incorporates many unique features related to factor choice, industry and fundamental exposures, and risk prediction.

different portfolio construction exercises and discuss how equity factor models are employed in this endeavor. The examples were constructed using the POINT® Optimizer.[8]

Tracking an Index

In our first example, we study the case of a portfolio manager whose goal is to create a portfolio that tracks a benchmark equity index as closely as possible, using a limited number of stocks. This is a very common problem in the investment industry since most assets under management are benchmarked to broad market indexes. Creating a benchmark-tracking portfolio provides a good starting point for implementing strategic views relative to that benchmark. For example, a portfolio manager might have a mandate to outperform a benchmark under particular risk constraints. One way to implement this mandate is to dynamically tilt the tracking portfolio towards certain investment styles based on views on the future performance of those styles at a particular point in the business cycle.

Consider a portfolio manager who is benchmarked to the S&P 500 index and aims to build a tracking portfolio composed of long-only positions from the set of S&P 500 stocks. Because of transaction cost and position management limitations, the portfolio manager is restricted to a maximum number of 50 stocks in the tracking portfolio. Her objective is to minimize the *tracking error volatility* (TEV) between her portfolio and the benchmark. Tracking error volatility can be described as the volatility of the return differential between the portfolio and the benchmark (i.e. measures a typical movement in this net position). A portfolio's TEV is commonly referred to as the risk or the (net) volatility of the portfolio.

As mentioned before, the total TEV is decomposed into a systematic TEV and an idiosyncratic TEV. Moreover, because these two components are assumed to be independent,

$$\text{Total } TEV = \sqrt{\text{Systematic } TEV^2 + \text{Idiosyncratic } TEV^2}$$

The minimization of systematic TEV is achieved by setting the portfolio's factor exposures (net of benchmark) as close to zero as possible, while respecting other potential constraints of the problem (e.g., maximum number of 50 securities in the portfolio). The minimization of idiosyncratic volatility is achieved through the diversification of the portfolio holdings.

Exhibit 13.2 illustrates the total risk for portfolio versus benchmark that comes out of the optimization problem. We see that total TEV of the

---

[8]See Anuj Kumar, "The POINT Optimizer," *Barclays Capital Publication*, June 2010. All optimization problems were run as of July 30, 2010.

EXHIBIT 13.2 Total Risk of Index-Tracking Portfolio vs. the Benchmark (bps/month)

Attribute	Realized Value
Total TEV	39.6
Idiosyncratic TEV	35.8
Systematic TEV	16.9

EXHIBIT 13.3 Position Amount of Individual Stocks in the Optimal Tracking Portfolio

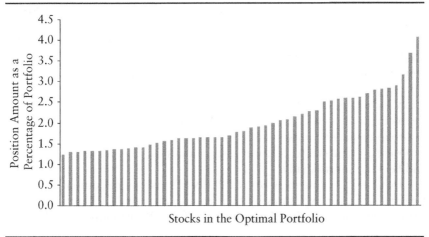

net position is 39.6 bps/month with 16.9 bps/month of systematic TEV and 35.8 bps/month of idiosyncratic TEV. If the portfolio manager wants to reduce her exposure to name-specific risk, she can increase the upper bound on the number of securities picked by the optimizer to construct the optimal portfolio (increasing the diversification effect). Another option would be to increase the relative weight of idiosyncratic TEV compared to the systematic TEV in the objective function. The portfolio resulting from this exercise would have smaller idiosyncratic risk but, unfortunately, would also have higher systematic risk. This trade-off can be managed based on the portfolio manager's preferences.

Exhibit 13.3 depicts the distribution of the position amount for individual stocks in the portfolio. We can see that the portfolio is well diversified across the 50 constituent stocks with no significant concentrations in any of the individual positions. The largest stock position is 4.1%, about three times larger than the smallest holding. Later in this chapter, we analyze the risk of this particular portfolio in more detail.

Constructing a Factor-Mimicking Portfolio

Factor-mimicking portfolios allow portfolio managers to capitalize on their views on various investment themes. For instance, the portfolio manager may forecast that small-cap stocks will outperform large-cap stocks or that value stocks will outperform growth stocks in the near future. By constructing long-short factor-mimicking portfolios, managers can place positions in line with their views on these investment themes without taking explicit directional views on the broader market.

Considering another example, suppose our portfolio manager forecasts that recent winner (high momentum) stocks will outperform recent losers (low momentum). To implement her views, she constructs two portfolios, one with winner stocks and one with loser stocks (100 stocks from the S&P 500 universe in each portfolio). She then takes a long position in the winners portfolio and a short position in the losers portfolio. While a sensible approach, a long-short portfolio constructed in this way would certainly have exposures to risk factors other than momentum. For instance, the momentum view might implicitly lead to unintended sector bets. If the portfolio manager wants to understand and potentially limit or avoid these exposures, she needs to perform further analysis. The use of a risk model will help her substantially.

Exhibit 13.4 illustrates one of POINT®'s risk model outputs—the 10 largest risk factor exposures by their contribution to TEV (last column in the exhibit) for this initial long-short portfolio. While momentum has the

EXHIBIT 13.4 Largest Risk Factor Exposures for the Momentum Winners/Losers Portfolio (bps/month)

Factor Name	Sensitivity/ Exposure	Net Exposure	Factor Volatility	Contribution to TEV
EQUITIES DEVELOPED MARKETS				
U.S. Equity Energy	Empirical beta	−0.094	651	25.3
U.S. Equity Materials	Empirical beta	−0.045	808	15.9
U.S. Equity CYC Media	Empirical beta	0.027	759	−9.9
U.S. Equity FIN Banks	Empirical beta	0.088	900	13.0
U.S. Equity FIN Diversified Financials	Empirical beta	−0.108	839	39.6
U.S. Equity FIN Real Estate	Empirical beta	0.100	956	−19.0
U.S. Equity TEC Software	Empirical beta	−0.057	577	17.2
U.S. Equity TEC Semiconductors	Empirical beta	−0.029	809	9.9
U.S. Equity Corporate Default Probability	CDP	−0.440	76	23.2
U.S. Equity Momentum (9m)	Momentum	1.491	73	74.9

largest contribution to volatility, other risk factors also play a significant role. As a result, major moves in risk factors other than momentum can have a significant—and potentially unintended—impact on the portfolio's return.

Given this information, suppose our portfolio manager decides to avoid these exposures to the extent possible. She can do that by setting all exposures to factors other than momentum to zero (these type of constraints may not always be feasible and one may need to relax them to achieve a solution). Moreover, because she wants the portfolio to represent a pure systematic momentum effect, she seeks to minimize idiosyncratic risk. There are many ways to implement these goals, but increasingly portfolio managers are turning to risk models (using an optimization engine) to construct their portfolios in a robust and convenient way. She decides to setup an optimization problem where the objective function is the minimization of idiosyncratic risk. The tradable universe is the set of S&P 500 stocks and the portfolio is constructed to be dollar-neutral. This problem also incorporates the aforementioned factor exposure constraints.

The resulting portfolio has exactly the risk factor exposures that were specified in the problem constraints. It exhibits a relatively low idiosyncratic TEV as a result of being well diversified with no significant concentrations in individual positions. Exhibit 13.5 depicts the largest 10 positions on the long and short sides of the momentum factor-mimicking portfolio; we see that there are no significant individual stock concentrations.

EXHIBIT 13.5 Largest 10 Positions on Long and Short Sides for the Momentum Portfolio

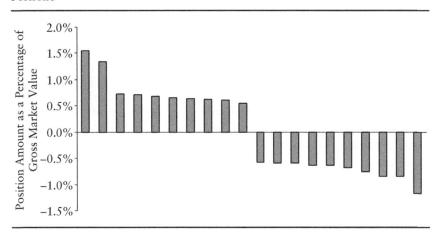

Implementing Sector Views

For our final portfolio construction example, let's assume we are entering a recessionary environment. An equity portfolio manager forecasts that the consumer staples sector will outperform the consumer discretionary sector in the near future, so she wants to create a portfolio to capitalize on this view. One simple idea would be to take a long position in the consumer staples sector (NCY: noncyclical) and a short position in the consumer discretionary sector (CYC: cyclical) by using, for example, sector ETFs. Similar to the previous example, this could result in exposures to risk factors other than the industry factors. Exhibit 13.6 illustrates the exposure of this long-short portfolio to the risk factors in the POINT® U.S. equity risk model. As we can see in the table, the portfolio has significant net exposures to certain

EXHIBIT 13.6 Factor Exposures and Contributions for Consumer Staples vs. Consumer Discretionary Portfolio (bps/month)

Factor Name	Sensitivity/ Exposure	Net Exposure	Factor Volatility	Contribution to TEV
CURRENCY				
USD (U.S. dollar)	Market weight (%)	0.00	0	0.0
EQUITIES DEVELOPED MARKETS				
U.S. Equity CYC Automobiles	Empirical beta	−0.069	1,086	60.3
U.S. Equity CYC Consumer Durables	Empirical beta	−0.093	822	59.1
U.S. Equity CYC Consumer Services	Empirical beta	−0.140	690	71.1
U.S. Equity CYC Media	Empirical beta	−0.292	759	172.8
U.S. Equity CYC Retailing	Empirical beta	−0.317	745	185.1
U.S. Equity NCY Retailing	Empirical beta	0.226	404	−44.9
U.S. Equity NCY Food	Empirical beta	0.546	418	−96.4
U.S. Equity NCY Household	Empirical beta	0.236	415	−55.3
U.S. Equity Total Yield	Total yield	0.269	36	−3.7
U.S. Equity Corporate Default Probability	CDP	−0.201	76	9.0
U.S. Equity Share Turnover Rate	Share turnover	−0.668	59	−10.3
U.S. Equity Momentum (9m)	Momentum	−0.144	73	−5.6
U.S. Equity Discretionary Accruals	Accruals	−0.020	31	−0.2
U.S. Equity Market Value	Size	0.193	111	1.7
U.S. Equity Realized Volatility	Realized volatility	−0.619	97	5.5
U.S. Equity Earnings to Price	Earnings–Price	0.024	44	0.0
U.S. Equity Book to Price	Book–Price	−0.253	40	5.8
U.S. Equity Earnings Forecast	Earnings forecast	0.038	67	−0.4

fundamental and technical factors, especially realized volatility and share turnover.

Suppose the portfolio manager decides to limit exposures to fundamental and technical factors. We can again use the optimizer to construct a long-short portfolio, with an exposure (beta) of 1 to the consumer staples sector and a beta of –1 to the consumer discretionary sector. To limit the exposure to fundamental and technical risk factors, we further impose the exposure to each of these factors to be between –0.2 and 0.2.[9] We also restrict the portfolio to be dollar neutral, and allow for only long positions in the consumer staples stocks and for only short positions in consumer discretionary stocks. Finally, we restrict the investment universe to the members of the S&P 500 index[10].

The resulting portfolio consists of 69 securities (approximately half of discretionary and staples stocks in S&P 500) with 31 long positions in the consumer staples stocks and 38 short positions in consumer discretionary stocks. Exhibit 13.7 depicts the factor exposures for this portfolio. As we can see in the table, the sum of the exposures to the industry factors is 1 for the consumer staples stocks and –1 for the consumer discretionary stocks. Exposures to fundamental and technical factors are generally significantly smaller when compared to the previous table, limiting the adverse effects of potential moves in these factors. Interestingly, no stocks from the automobiles industry are selected in the optimal portfolio, potentially due to excessive idiosyncratic risk of firms in that particular industry. The contribution to volatility from the discretionary sector is higher than that from the staples sector, due to higher volatility of industry factors in the discretionary sector.

The bounds used for the fundamental and technical factor exposures in the portfolio construction process were set to force a reduction in the exposure to these factors. However, there is a trade-off between having smaller exposures and having smaller idiosyncratic risk in the final portfolio. The resolution of this trade-off depends on the preferences of the portfolio manager. When the bounds are more restrictive, we are also decreasing the feasible set of solutions available to the problem and therefore potentially achieving a higher idiosyncratic risk (remember that the objective is the minimization of idiosyncratic risk). In our example, the idiosyncratic TEV of the portfolio increases from 119 bps/month (for staples—discretionary portfolio before the optimization) to 158 bps/month on the optimized portfolio.

---

[9]The setting of these exposures and its trade-offs are discussed later in this chapter.
[10]As POINT® U.S. equity risk model incorporates industry level factors, a unit exposure to a sector is implemented by restricting exposures to different industries within that sector to sum up to 1. Also, note that as before, the objective in the optimization problem is the minimization of idiosyncratic TEV to ensure that the resulting portfolio represents systematic—not idiosyncratic—effects.

EXHIBIT 13.7 Factor Exposures and Contributions for the Optimal Sector View Portfolio (bps/month)

Factor Name	Sensitivity/ Exposure	Net Exposure	Factor Volatility	Contribution to TEV
CURRENCY				
USD (U.S. dollar)	Market weight (%)	0.00	0.00	0.00
EQUITIES DEVELOPED MARKETS				
U.S. Equity CYC Consumer Durables	Empirical beta	−0.118	822	80.6
U.S. Equity CYC Consumer Services	Empirical beta	−0.222	690	124.9
U.S. Equity CYC Media	Empirical beta	−0.242	759	151.0
U.S. Equity CYC Retailing	Empirical beta	−0.417	745	264.2
U.S. Equity NCY Retailing	Empirical beta	0.287	404	−67.9
U.S. Equity NCY Food	Empirical beta	0.497	418	−112.6
U.S. Equity NCY Household	Empirical beta	0.216	415	−56.2
U.S. Equity Total Yield	Total yield	−0.059	36	0.8
U.S. Equity Corporate Default Probability	CDP	−0.042	76	1.7
U.S. Equity Share Turnover Rate	Share turnover	−0.196	59	−3.9
U.S. Equity Momentum (9m)	Momentum	−0.138	73	−4.7
U.S. Equity Discretionary Accruals	Accruals	−0.014	31	−0.1
U.S. Equity Market Value	Size	−0.011	111	−0.1
U.S. Equity Realized Volatility	Realized volatility	−0.199	97	−0.1
U.S. Equity Earnings to Price	Earnings–Price	0.027	44	0.0
U.S. Equity Book to Price	Book–Price	−0.070	40	1.4
U.S. Equity Earnings Forecast	Earnings forecast	0.085	67	−1.1

This change is the price paid for the ability to limit certain systematic risk factor exposures.

Analyzing Portfolio Risk Using Multifactor Models

Now that we have seen examples of using multifactor equity models for portfolio construction and briefly discussed their risk outcomes, we take a more in-depth look at portfolio risk. Risk analysis based on multifactor models can take many forms; from a relatively high-level aggregate approach, to an in-depth analysis of the risk properties of individual stocks and groups of stocks. Multifactor equity risk models provide the tools to perform the analysis of portfolio risk in many different dimensions, including exposures to risk factors, security factor contributions to total risk, analysis at the ticker level, and scenario analysis. In this section, we provide an overview of such detailed analysis using the S&P 500 index tracker example we created in the previous section.

Recall from Exhibit 13.2 that the TEV of the optimized S&P 500 tracking portfolio was 39.6 bps/month, composed mostly of idiosyncratic risk (35.8 bps/month) and a relatively small amount of systematic risk (16.9 bps/month). To analyze further the source of these numbers, we first compare the holdings of the portfolio with those of the benchmark and then study the impact of the mismatch to the risk of the net position (Portfolio – Benchmark). The first column in Exhibit 13.8 shows the net market weights (NMW) of the portfolio at the sector level (GICS level 1). Our portfolio appears to be well balanced with respect to the benchmark both from a market value and from a risk contribution perspective. The largest market value discrepancies are an overweight in information technology and an underweight in consumer discretionary and health care companies. However, the sector with the largest contribution to overall risk (contribution to TEV, or CTEV) is financials (7.5 bps/month). This may seem unexpected, given the small NMW of this sector (only 0.1%). This result is explained by the fact that contributions to risk (CTEV) are dependent on the net market weight, the risk of the underlying positions and also the correlation between the different exposures. Looking into the decomposition of the CTEV, the exhibit also shows that most of the total contribution to risk from financials is idiosyncratic (7.0 bps/month). This result is due to the small number of

EXHIBIT 13.8 Net Market Weights and Risk Contributions by Sector (bps/month)

	Net Market Weight (%)	Contribution to TEV (CTEV)		
		Systematic	Idiosyncratic	Total
Total	0.0	7.2	32.7	39.8
Energy	1.4	1.3	4.4	5.7
Materials	–2.1	1.0	1.3	2.3
Industrials	2.1	0.3	3.8	4.1
Consumer discretionary	–3.6	1.7	4.7	6.3
Consumer staples	–0.5	0.5	2.2	2.6
Health care	–3.3	1.3	2.2	3.4
Financials	0.1	0.6	7.0	7.5
Information tech	5.2	0.6	5.5	6.1
Telecom services	2.4	0.2	0.8	1.0
Utilities	–1.7	–0.1	0.9	0.8

securities our portfolio has in this sector and the underlying high volatility
of these stocks. In short, the diversification benefits across financial stocks
are small in our portfolio: we could potentially significantly reduce total risk
by constructing our financials exposure using more names. Note that this
analysis is only possible with a risk model.

Exhibit 13.9 highlights additional risk measures by sector. What we see
in the first column is the isolated TEV, that is, the risk associated with the
stocks in that particular sector only. On an isolated basis, the information
technology sector has the highest risk in the portfolio. This top position
in terms of isolated risk does not translate into the highest contribution to
overall portfolio risk, as we saw in Exhibit 13.8. The discrepancy between
isolated risk numbers and contributions to risk is explained by the correlation between the exposures and allows us to understand the potential hedging effects present across our portfolio. The liquidation effect reported in the
table represents the change in TEV when we completely hedge that particular position, that is, enforce zero net exposure to any stock in that particular sector. Interestingly, eliminating our exposure to information technology
stocks would actually increase our overall portfolio risk by 6.2 bps/month.
This happens because the overweight in this sector is effectively hedging
out risk contributions from other sectors. If we eliminate this exposure,
the portfolio balance is compromised. The TEV elasticity reported gives
an additional perspective regarding how the TEV in the portfolio changes
when we change the exposure to that sector. Specifically, it tells us the

EXHIBIT 13.9 Additional Risk Measures by Sector

	Isolated TEV (bps/month)	Liquidation Effect on TEV (bps/month)	TEV Elasticity (x100) (bps)	Systematic Beta (bps)
Total	39.64	−39.64	100.00	1.00
Energy	13.94	−3.38	14.25	0.89
Materials	16.94	1.29	5.74	1.25
Industrials	20.99	1.41	10.27	1.20
Consumer discretionary	29.34	4.25	15.89	1.11
Consumer Staples	10.70	−1.20	6.59	0.70
Health Care	17.37	0.37	8.56	0.65
Financials	20.77	−2.19	18.93	1.34
Information Tech	31.90	6.20	15.30	0.99
Telecom Services	11.58	0.67	2.53	0.76
Utilities	10.30	0.56	1.93	0.79

percentage change in TEV for each 1% change in our exposure to that particular sector. For example, if we double our exposure to the energy sector, our TEV would increase by 14.25% (from 39.6 bps/month to 45.2 bps/month). Finally, the report estimates the portfolio to have a beta of 1.00 to the benchmark, which is, of course, in line with our index tracking objective. The beta statistic measures the comovement between the systematic risk drivers of the portfolio and the benchmark and should be interpreted only as that. In particular, a low portfolio beta (relative to the benchmark) does not imply low portfolio risk. It signals relatively low systematic comovement between the two universes or a relatively high idiosyncratic risk for the portfolio. For example, if the sources of systematic risk from the portfolio and the benchmark are distinct, the portfolio beta is close to zero. The report also provides the systematic beta associated with each sector. For instance, we see that a movement of 1% in the benchmark leads to a 1.34% return in the financials component of our portfolio. As expected, consumer staples and health care are two low beta industries, as they tend to be more stable through the business cycle.[11]

Although important, the information we examined so far is still quite aggregated. For instance, we know from Exhibit 13.8 that a large component of idiosyncratic risk comes from financials. But what names are contributing most? What are the most volatile sectors? How are systematic exposures distributed within each sector? Risk models should be able to provide answers to all these questions, allowing for a detailed view of the portfolio's risk exposures and contributions. As an example, Exhibit 13.10 displays all systematic risk factors the portfolio or the benchmark loads onto. It also provides the portfolio, benchmark, and net exposures for each risk factor, the volatility of each of these factors, and their contributions to total TEV. The table shows that the net exposures to the risk factors are generally low, meaning that the tracking portfolio has small active exposures. This finding is in line with the evidence from Exhibit 13.2, where we see that the systematic risk is small (16.9 bps/month). If we look into the contributions of individual factors to total TEV, the exhibit shows that the top contributors are the size, share turnover, and realized volatility factors. The optimal index tracking portfolio tends to be composed of very large-cap names within the specified universe, and that explains the net positive loading to the market value (size) factor. This portfolio tilt is due to the generally low idiosyncratic risk large companies have. This is seen favorably by the optimization engine, as it tries to minimize idiosyncratic risk. This same tilt would explain our net exposure to both the share turnover and realized volatility factors, as larger companies tend to have lower realized volatility

---

[11]Note that we can sum the sector betas into the portfolio beta, using portfolio sector weights (not net weights) as weights in the summation.

EXHIBIT 13.10 Factor Exposures and Contributions for the Tracking Portfolio vs. S&P 500 (bps/month)

Factor Name	Sensitivity/Exposure	Portfolio Exposure	Benchmark Exposure	Net Exposure	Factor Volatility	Contribution to TEV
CURRENCY						
USD (U.S. dollar)	Market weight (%)	100.00	100.00	0.00	0	0.00
EQUITIES DEVELOPED MARKETS						
U.S. Equity Energy	Empirical beta	0.10	0.10	0.00	651	0.17
U.S. Equity Materials	Empirical beta	0.01	0.03	-0.02	808	0.59
U.S. Equity IND Capital Goods	Empirical beta	0.11	0.08	0.03	723	-0.66
U.S. Equity IND Commercial	Empirical beta	0.00	0.01	-0.01	640	0.13
U.S. Equity IND Transportation	Empirical beta	0.01	0.02	-0.01	739	0.12
U.S. Equity CYC Automobiles	Empirical beta	0.00	0.01	-0.01	1,086	0.35
U.S. Equity CYC Consumer Durables	Empirical beta	0.01	0.01	0.00	822	-0.09
U.S. Equity CYC Consumer Services	Empirical beta	0.00	0.01	-0.01	690	0.47
U.S. Equity CYC Media	Empirical beta	0.02	0.03	-0.01	759	0.42
U.S. Equity CYC Retailing	Empirical beta	0.03	0.03	-0.01	745	0.28
U.S. Equity NCY Retailing	Empirical beta	0.02	0.03	-0.01	404	0.11
U.S. Equity NCY Food	Empirical beta	0.04	0.06	-0.02	418	0.32
U.S. Equity NCY Household	Empirical beta	0.05	0.03	0.02	415	-0.25
U.S. Equity HLT Health Care	Empirical beta	0.02	0.04	-0.02	518	0.82
U.S. Equity HLT Pharmaceuticals	Empirical beta	0.06	0.07	-0.02	386	0.31
U.S. Equity FIN Banks	Empirical beta	0.03	0.03	0.00	900	-0.01
U.S. Equity FIN Diversified Financials	Empirical beta	0.08	0.08	0.01	839	-0.16

EXHIBIT 13.10 (Continued)

Factor Name	Sensitivity/Exposure	Portfolio Exposure	Benchmark Exposure	Net Exposure	Factor Volatility	Contribution to TEV
U.S. Equity FIN Insurance	Empirical beta	0.02	0.04	-0.02	712	0.54
U.S. Equity FIN Real Estate	Empirical beta	0.03	0.01	0.02	956	-0.19
U.S. Equity TEC Software	Empirical beta	0.10	0.09	0.02	577	-0.61
U.S. Equity TEC Hardware	Empirical beta	0.08	0.07	0.00	645	-0.08
U.S. Equity TEC Semiconductors	Empirical beta	0.05	0.02	0.02	809	-0.49
U.S. Equity Telecommunication	Empirical beta	0.05	0.03	0.02	458	-0.37
U.S. Equity Utilities	Empirical beta	0.02	0.04	-0.01	554	0.17
U.S. Equity Total Yield	Total yield	0.12	0.05	0.07	36	0.04
U.S. Equity Corporate Default Probability	CDP	-0.15	-0.07	-0.08	76	0.22
U.S. Equity Share Turnover Rate	Share turnover	-0.20	0.01	-0.21	59	1.28
U.S. Equity Momentum (9m)	Momentum	-0.02	-0.03	0.01	73	0.02
U.S. Equity Discretionary Accruals	Accruals	-0.03	0.02	-0.05	31	-0.14
U.S. Equity Market Value	Size	0.29	0.20	0.09	111	1.16
U.S. Equity Realized Volatility	Realized volatility	-0.21	-0.08	-0.13	97	2.38
U.S. Equity Earnings to Price	Earnings–Price	0.09	0.04	0.05	44	0.19
U.S. Equity Book to Price	Book–Price	-0.06	-0.03	-0.03	40	0.02
U.S. Equity Earnings Forecast	Earnings forecast	0.08	0.05	0.03	67	0.12
U.S. Equity Other Market Volatility	Market weight	1.00	1.00	0.00	17	0.00

EXHIBIT 13.11   Individual Securities and Idiosyncratic Risk Exposures

Company Name	Portfolio Weight (%)	Benchmark Weight (%)	Net Weight (%)	Idiosyncratic TEV (bps/month)
Vornado Realty Trust	2.80	0.13	2.67	7.42
Kohls Corp	1.41	0.15	1.26	6.58
Bank of America Corp	2.71	1.41	1.29	6.16
Conocophillips	2.29	0.82	1.47	6.03
Roper Industries Inc	1.62	0.06	1.56	5.98
Walt Disney Co	2.26	0.66	1.60	5.48
Honeywell International Inc.	2.58	0.33	2.25	5.48
Cincinnati Financial Corp	1.88	0.05	1.83	5.35
Goldman Sachs	0.00	0.78	−0.78	5.25

and share turnover too. Interestingly, industry factors have relatively small contributions to TEV, even though they exhibit significantly higher volatilities. This results from the fact that the optimization engine specifically targets these factors because of their high volatility and is successful in minimizing net exposure to industry factors in the final portfolio.

Finally, remember from Exhibit 13.2 that the largest component of the portfolio risk comes from name-specific exposures. Therefore, it is important to be aware of which individual stocks in our portfolio contribute the most to overall risk. Exhibit 13.11 shows the set of stocks in our portfolio with the largest idiosyncratic risk. The portfolio manager can use this information as a screening device to filter out undesirable positions with high idiosyncratic risk and to make sure her views on individual firms translate into risk as expected. In particular, the list in the exhibit should only include names about which the portfolio manager has strong views, either positive—expressed with positive NMW—or negative—in which case we would expect a short net position.

It should be clear from the above examples that although the factors used to measure risk are predetermined in a linear factor model, there is a large amount of flexibility on the way the risk numbers can be aggregated and reported. Instead of sectors, we could have grouped risk by any other classification of individual stocks, for example, by regions or market capitalization. This allows the risk to be reported using the same investment philosophy underlying the portfolio construction process[12] regardless of the

---

[12]For a detailed methodology on how to perform this customized analysis, see Antonio Silva, "Risk Attribution with Custom-Defined Risk Factors," *Barclays Capital Publication*, August 2009.

underlying factor model. There are also many other risk analytics available not mentioned in this example that give additional detail about specific risk properties of the portfolio and the constituents. We have only discussed total, systematic, and idiosyncratic risk (which can be decomposed into risk contributions on a flexible basis), and referred to isolated and liquidation TEV, TEV elasticity, and portfolio beta. Most users of multifactor risk models will find their own preferred approach to risk analysis through experience.

Performance Attribution

Now that we discussed portfolio construction and risk analysis as the first steps of the investment process, we give a brief overview of performance attribution, an ex post analysis of performance typically conducted at the end of the investment horizon. Performance attribution analysis provides an evaluation of the portfolio manager's performance with respect to various decisions made throughout the investment process. The underperformance or outperformance of the portfolio manager, when compared to the benchmark can be due to different reasons including effective sector allocation, security selection, or tilting the portfolio towards certain risk factors. Attribution analysis aims to unravel the major sources of this performance differential. The exercise allows the portfolio manager to understand how her particular views—translated into net exposures—performed during the period and reveals whether some of the portfolio's performance was the result of unintended bets.

There are three basic forms of attribution analysis used for equity portfolios. These are return decomposition, factor model–based attribution, and style analysis. In the return decomposition approach, the performance of the portfolio manager is generally attributed to top-down allocation (e.g., currency, country, or sector allocation) in a first step, followed by a bottom-up security selection performance analysis. This is a widely used technique among equity portfolio managers.

Factor model–based analysis attributes performance to exposures to risk factors such as industry, size, and financial ratios. It is relatively more complicated than the previous approach and is based on a particular risk model that needs to be well understood. For example, let's assume that a portfolio manager forecasts that value stocks will outperform growth stocks in the near future. As a result, the manager tilts the portfolio toward value stocks as compared to the benchmark, creating an active exposure to the value factor. In an attribution framework without systematic factors, such sources of performance cannot be identified and hence may be inadvertently attributed to other reasons. Factor model–based attribution analysis adds value by incorporating these factors (representing major investment themes) explicitly into the return decomposition process and by identifying additional sources of performance represented as active exposures to systematic risk factors.

Style analysis on the other hand is based on a regression of the portfolio return to a set of style benchmarks. It requires very little information (e.g., we do not need to know the contents of the portfolio) but the outcome depends significantly on the selection of style benchmarks. It also assumes constant loadings to these styles across the regression period, which may be unrealistic for managers with somewhat dynamic allocations.

Factor—Based Scenario Analysis

The last application we review in this chapter goes over the use of equity risk factor models in the context of scenario analysis. Many investment professionals utilize scenario analysis in different shapes and forms for both risk and portfolio construction purposes. Factor-based scenario analysis is a tool that helps portfolio managers in their decision making process by providing additional intuition on the behavior of their portfolio under a specified scenario. A scenario can be a historical episode, such as the equity market crash of 1987, the war in Iraq, or the 2008 credit crisis. Alternatively, scenarios can be defined as a collection of hypothetical views (e.g., user-defined scenarios) in a variety of forms such as a view on a given portfolio or index (e.g., S&P 500 drops by 20%) or a factor (e.g., U.S. equity–size factor moves by 3 standard deviations) or correlation between factors (e.g., increasing correlations across markets in episodes of flight to quality). In this section, we use the POINT® Factor-Based Scenario Analysis Tool to illustrate how we can utilize factor models to perform scenario analysis.

Before we start describing the example, let's take an overview of the mechanics of the model. It allows for the specification of user views on returns of portfolios, indexes, or risk factors. When the user specifies a view on a portfolio or index, this is translated into a view on risk factor realizations, through the linear factor model framework.[13] These views are combined with ones that are directly specified in terms of risk factors. It is important to note that the portfolio manager does not need to specify views on all risk factors, and typically has views only on a small subset of them. Once the manager specifies this subset of original views, the next step is to expand these views to the whole set of factors. The scenario analysis engine achieves this by estimating the most likely realization of all other factors—given the factor realizations on which views are specified—using the risk model covariance matrix. Once all factors realizations are populated, the

---

[13]Specifically, we can back out factor realizations from the portfolio or index returns by using their risk factor loadings.

EXHIBIT 13.12 Index Returns under Scenario 1 (VIX jumps by 50%)

Universe	Type	Measure	Unit	Result
S&P 500	Equity index	Return	%	−7.97
FTSE U.K. 100	Equity index	Return	%	−9.34
DJ EURO STOXX 50	Equity index	Return	%	−11.63
NIKKEI 225	Equity index	Return	%	−4.99
MSCI-AC ASIA PACIFIC EX JAPAN	Equity index	Return	%	−10.33
MSCI-EMERGING MARKETS	Equity index	Return	%	−9.25

scenario outcome for any portfolio or index can be computed by multiplying their specific exposures to the risk factors by the factor realizations under the scenario. The tool provides a detailed analysis of the portfolio behavior under the specified scenario.

We illustrate this tool using two different scenarios: a 50% shift in the U.S. equity market volatility—represented by the VIX index—(scenario 1) and a 50% jump in the European credit spreads (scenario 2).[14] We use a set of equity indexes from across the globe to illustrate the impact of these two scenarios. We run the scenarios as of July 30, 2010, which specifies the date both for the index loadings and the covariance matrix used. Base currency is set to U.S. dollars (USD) and hence index returns presented below are in USD.

Exhibit 13.12 shows the returns of the chosen equity indexes under the first scenario. We see that all indexes experience significant negative returns with Euro Stoxx plummeting the most and Nikkei experiencing the smallest drop. To understand these numbers better, let's look into the contributions of different factors to these index returns.

Exhibit 13.13 illustrates return contributions for four of these equity indexes under scenario 1. Specifically, for each index, it decomposes the total scenario return into return coming from different factors each index has exposure to. In this example, all currency factors are defined with respect to USD. Moreover, equity factors are expressed in their corresponding local currencies and can be described as broad market factors for their respective regions.

Not surprisingly, Exhibit 13.13 shows that the majority of the return contributions for selected indexes come from the reaction of equity market factors to the scenario. However, foreign exchange (FX) can also be a significant portion of total return for some indexes, such as in the case of the Euro Stoxx (−4.8%). Nikkei experiences a relatively smaller drop in USD terms,

---

[14]For reference, as of July 30, 2010, scenario 1 would imply the VIX to move from 23.5 to 35.3 and scenario 2 would imply that the credit spread for the Barclays Capital European Credit Index to change from 174 bps to 261 bps.

EXHIBIT 13.13 Return Contributions for Equity Indexes under Scenario 1 (in %)

Group	Factor	S&P 500	FTSE U.K. 100	DJ EURO STOXX 50	NIKKEI 225
FX	GBP		-1.77		
FX	JPY				1.21
FX	EUR		-0.38	-4.80	
Equity	U.S. equity	-7.97			
Equity	U.K. equity		-6.67		
Equity	Japan equity				-6.20
Equity	EMG equity		-0.09		
Equity	Continental Europe equity		-0.43	-6.83	
Total		-7.97	-9.34	-11.63	-4.99

EXHIBIT 13.14 Factor Returns and Z-Scores under Scenario 1

Group	Name	Measure	Unit	Value	Std. Dev.	Z-Score
Equity	U.K. equity	Return	%	-7.85	4.99	-1.57
Equity	U.S. equity	Return	%	-8.61	6.06	-1.42
Equity	Continental Europe equity	Return	%	-7.12	5.04	-1.41
Equity	Japan equity	Return	%	-5.96	4.73	-1.26
Equity	EMG equity	Return	%	-8.50	6.88	-1.24
FX	EUR	Return	%	-4.80	3.93	-1.22
FX	GBP	Return	%	-1.93	3.42	-0.56
FX	JPY	Return	%	1.21	3.39	0.36

majorly due to a positive contribution coming from the JPY FX factor. This positive contribution is due to the safe haven nature of Japanese yen in case of flight to quality under increased risk aversion in global markets.

Exhibit 13.14 demonstrates the scenario implied factor realizations (value), factor volatilities, and the Z-scores for the risk factors given in Exhibit 13.13. The Z-score of the factor quantifies the effect of the scenario on that specific factor. It is computed as

$$z = \frac{r}{\sigma_r}$$

where r is the return of the factor in the scenario and σ_r is the standard deviation of the factor. Hence, the Z-score measures how many standard de-

EXHIBIT 13.15   Index Returns under Scenario 2 (EUR Credit Spread Jumps by 50%)

Universe	Type	Measure	Unit	Result
S&P 500	Equity index	Return	%	−13.03
FTSE U.K. 100	Equity index	Return	%	−18.62
DJ EURO STOXX 50	Equity index	Return	%	−19.68
NIKKEI 225	Equity index	Return	%	−8.92
MSCI-AC ASIA PACIFIC EX JAPAN	Equity index	Return	%	−18.40
MSCI-EMERGING MARKETS	Equity index	Return	%	−16.83

EXHIBIT 13.16   Factor Returns and Z-Scores under Scenario 2

Group	Name	Measure	Unit	Value	Std. Dev.	Z-Score
Equity	Continental Europe equity	Return	%	−14.02	5.04	−2.78
Equity	U.K. equity	Return	%	−13.05	4.99	−2.62
Equity	Japan equity	Return	%	−11.53	4.73	−2.44
Equity	U.S. equity	Return	%	−14.09	6.06	−2.33
Equity	EMG equity	Return	%	−15.93	6.88	−2.32
FX	GBP	Return	%	−6.54	3.42	−1.91
FX	EUR	Return	%	−6.23	3.93	−1.59
FX	JPY	Return	%	3.07	3.39	0.90

viations a factor moves in a given scenario. Exhibit 13.14 lists the factors by increasing Z-score under scenario 1. The U.K. equity factor experiences the largest negative move, at −1.57 standard deviations. FX factors experience relatively smaller movements. JPY is the only factor with a positive realization due to the aforementioned characteristic of the currency.

In the second scenario, we shift European credit spreads by 50% (a 3.5-sigma event) and explore the effect of credit market swings on the equity markets. As we can see in Exhibit 13.15, all equity indexes experience significant returns, in line with the severity of the scenario.[15] The result also underpins the strong recent co-movement between the credit and equity markets. The exception is again the Nikkei that realizes a relatively smaller return.

Exhibit 13.16 provides the return, volatility, and the Z-score of certain relevant factors under scenario 2. As expected, the major mover on the equity side is the continental Europe equity factor, followed by the United Kingdom. Given the recent strong correlations between equity and credit

---

[15]The same scenario results in a −8.12% move in the Barclays Capital Euro Credit Index.

markets across the globe, the exhibit suggests that a 3.5 standard deviation shift in the European spread factor results in 2 to 3 standard deviation movement of global equity factors.

The two examples above illustrate the use of factor models in performing scenario analysis to achieve a clear understanding of how a portfolio may react under different circumstances.

KEY POINTS

- Multifactor equity risk models provide detailed insight into the structure and properties of portfolios. These models characterize stock returns in terms of systematic factors and an idiosyncratic component. Systematic factors are generally designed to have intuitive economic interpretation and they represent common movements across securities. On the other hand, the idiosyncratic component represents the residual return due to stock-specific events.
- Systematic factors used in equity risk models can be broadly classified under five categories: market factors, classification variables, firm characteristics, macroeconomic variables, and statistical factors.
- Relative significance of systematic risk factors depends on various parameters such as the model horizon, region/country for which the model is designed, existence of other factors, and the particular time period of the analysis. For instance, in the presence of industry factors, macroeconomic factors tend to be insignificant for short to medium horizon equity risk models whereas they tend to be more significant for long-horizon models. On the other hand, for developed equity markets, industry factors are more significant as compared to the country factors. The latter are still the dominant effect for emerging markets.
- Choice of the model and the estimation technique affect the interpretation of factors. For instance, in the existence of a market factor, industry factors represent industry-specific movements net of market. If there is no market factor, their interpretation is very close to market value-weighted industry indexes.
- Multifactor equity risk models can be classified according to how their loadings and factors are specified. The most common equity factor models specify loadings based on classification (e.g., industry) and fundamental or technical information, and estimate factor realizations every period. Certain other models take factors as known (e.g., returns on industry indexes) and estimate loadings based on time-series information. A third class of models is based purely on statistical approaches without concern for economic interpretation of factors and loadings.

Finally, it is possible to combine these approaches and construct hybrid models. Each of these approaches has its own specific strengths and weaknesses.

- A good multifactor equity risk model provides detailed information regarding the exposures of a complex portfolio and can be a valuable tool for portfolio construction and risk management. It can help managers construct portfolios tracking a particular benchmark, express views subject to a given risk budget, and rebalance a portfolio while avoiding excessive transaction costs. Further, by identifying the exposures where the portfolio has the highest risk sensitivity it can help a portfolio manager reduce (or increase) risk in the most effective way.
- Performance attribution based on multifactor equity risk models can give ex post insight into how the portfolio manager's views and corresponding investments translated into actual returns.
- Factor-based scenario analysis provides portfolio managers with a powerful tool to perform stress testing of portfolio positions and gain insight into the impact of specific market events on portfolio performance.

QUESTIONS

Questions 1 through 5 pertain to the following information:

Assume that a portfolio managers constructs an equally-weighted portfolio of two stocks from different industries and wants to analyze the risk of this portfolio using a two-factor model in the following form:

$$r = \beta \cdot F^{IND} + \ell \cdot F^{SIZE} + \varepsilon$$

where F^{IND} is the industry factor and F^{SIZE} is the size factor return, β and ℓ are the security loadings to these two factors respectively and ε is the idiosyncratic return.

Using statistical techniques, the portfolio manager finds that the first stock has an industry beta of $\beta_1 = 1.4$ and the second stock has an industry beta of $\beta_2 = 0.8$. This means that the first stock moves more than average when its industry moves in a certain direction and the opposite is true for the second stock. The loading to the size factor (ℓ) is a function of the market value of the company and is standardized such that it has a mean of 0 and a standard deviation of 1. Using this formulation, the portfolio manager finds that the first stock has a size loading of $\ell_1 = -1$. This means that the market value of this stock is 1 standard deviation smaller than the market average. The second stock has a size loading of $\ell_2 = 2$, which tells us that it belongs to a large-cap company.

The industry factor corresponding to the first stock has a monthly volatility of $\sigma_{IND1} = 5\%$ while the industry factor of the second stock has a volatility of $\sigma_{IND2} = 10\%$. The volatility of the size factor is $\sigma_{SIZE} = 1\%$. The correlation between the two industry factors is $\rho_{IND1,IND2} = 0.5$, while the size factor has a correlation of $\rho_{IND1,SIZE} = -0.3$ with the first industry and $\rho_{IND2,SIZE} = -0.5$ with the second industry. Generally speaking, correlations between industry factors tend to be significant and positive in such a model as industry factors incorporate the market effect. On the other hand, the correlation between the size factor and a given industry factor tends to be negative as large-cap stocks tend to be less volatile than small caps. Finally, the monthly idiosyncratic volatility of the first stock is $\sigma_{1,IDIO} = 12\%$ and the one of the second stock is $\sigma_{2,IDIO} = 5\%$.

1. What is the systematic risk of each stock?

2. What is the total risk of each stock?

3. What is the isolated risk of the portfolio coming from each systematic factor?

4. What are the systematic risk, idiosyncratic risk, and the total risk of the portfolio?

5. What is the correlation between the total return of the two stocks?

6. What is the contribution of each stock to total portfolio risk?

CHAPTER 14

Dynamic Factor Approaches to Equity Portfolio Management

Dorsey D. Farr, Ph.D., CFA
Principal
French Wolf & Farr

The term *portfolio management* evokes an image of a security selector—preferably a skilled one—who, like a scavenger in search of hidden treasure, dons a green eyeshade, scours the universe of securities in search of those with the most attractive prospects based on detailed financial statement analysis, and combines them together into a portfolio that will collectively provide a superior risk-adjusted return relative to some passive benchmark. For many years, this was the characteristic image of the portfolio manager and an accurate description of the practice of portfolio management. However, in response to several unique developments, the image of a portfolio manager and the practice of portfolio management have changed dramatically over the past two decades.

First, a growing body of empirical research on the success of active investment strategies employed by professional money managers has generally revealed that active management fails to live up to its promise of superior returns. The mounting acceptance of the *efficient markets hypothesis*—at least in its weaker forms as described by Fama[1]—and the understanding that active management is a zero-sum game—as articulated by Sharpe[2]—helped to promote the use of passive (index-based) portfolio management strategies.

Additionally, a separate literature evolved that mistakenly cast doubt on the importance of security selection for portfolio performance. The landmark

---

[1]Eugene F. Fama, "Efficient Capital Markets: A Review of Theory and Empirical Work," *Journal of Finance* 25, no. 2 (1970): 383–417.
[2]William F. Sharpe, "The Arithmetic of Active Management," *Financial Analysts Journal* 47, no 1 (1976): 7–9.

studies by Brinson, Beebower, and Hood[3] and Brinson, Beebower, and Singer[4] demonstrated that, on average, asset allocation accounted for the vast majority of the variation in portfolio return over time. However, the most common interpretation of these studies held that asset allocation decisions—the distribution of a portfolio's assets among stocks, bonds, and cash—was the primary determinant of the level of a portfolio's return, implying a hierarchy among investment decisions that does not necessarily exist.

Unfortunately, the widespread misinterpretation of these studies popularized the notion that asset allocation is more important that security selection, even though these studies, which merely describe behavior, say nothing about the fundamental importance of asset allocation relative to security selection. Although subsequent studies[5] either called into question the interpretation that asset allocation decisions are paramount in determining the level of returns or demonstrated that it is not possible to unequivocally state that either asset allocation or security selection decisions are more important than the other, asset allocation had been forever elevated in importance, and the perceived importance of security selection had been diminished. The introduction of returns-based style analysis as presented by Sharpe further reduced the perceived importance of individual security selection and ultimately cast more doubt on the role of traditional security selection as the fundamental element of active portfolio management, leading to the view that portfolios should be interpreted as collections of asset classes, factors, or style exposures rather than collections of individual securities.[6]

The growth in popularity and use of Sharpe's technique as a portfolio attribution tool coincided with the proliferation of various types of indexes. Index providers such as Russell, Standard & Poor's, Dow Jones, Wilshire, MSCI, and others began increasing the availability of macro data and produced a greater emphasis on macro factors and a corresponding reduction in the emphasis on individual security selection. In turn, these newly

---

[3]Gary P. Brinson, G. Randolph Hood, and Gilbert L. Beebower, "Determinants of Portfolio Performance," *Financial Analysts Journal* 42, no. 4 (1986): 39–44.

[4]Gary P. Brinson, Gilbert L. Beebower, and Brain D. Singer, "Determinants of Portfolio Performance II: An update," *Financial Analysts Journal* 47, no. 3 (1991): 40–48.

[5]See, for examples, Roger G. Ibbotson and Paul D. Kaplan, "Does Asset Allocation Policy Explain 40, 90, or 100 Percent of Performance?" *Financial Analysts Journal* 56, no. 3 (2000): 26–33; Mark Kritzman and Sebastian Page, "The Hierarchy of Investment Choice," *Journal of Portfolio Management* 29, no. 4 (2003): 11–24; and Kodjovi Assoe, Jean-François L'Her, and Jean-François Plante, "The Relative Performance of Asset Allocation and Security Selection," *Journal of Portfolio Management* 33, no. 1 (2006): 46–55.

[6]William F. Sharpe, "Asset Allocation: Management Style and Performance Measurement," *Journal of Portfolio Management* 18, no. 2 (1992): 7–19.

available indexes increased the popularity of portfolio management strategies based on macro factors rather than traditional security selection.

Moreover, the increase in the availability of macro data corresponded with a rapid decline in the cost of computing power. The combination of these factors and the corresponding adoption of quantitative methods by professional investors resulted in the development of new approaches to portfolio management that represented a dramatic departure from the ways of yesterday's stock picker who spent his time visiting with corporate management, sifting through research reports, and estimating price targets.

This chapter discusses a variety of approaches to portfolio management that are based on determining whether some broadly defined group of securities will outperform a larger group of securities that constitute a benchmark. We broadly classify the methods described herein as *dynamic factor approache*s to portfolio management, since these portfolio management strategies generally involve a dynamic allocation process across or among a number of factors such as equity style (e.g., value, growth, etc.), geographic location, industry or sector, macroeconomic factors such as the term structure of interest rates, credit spreads, inflation, and GDP growth, or microeconomic factors such as beta, liquidity, profitability, or leverage. Grant was perhaps the first to label such dynamic allocation strategies as legitimate styles of portfolio management.[7] However, in recent years, these strategies have taken on new dimensions and their use has greatly expanded.

The methods discussed herein are not necessarily mutually exclusive with traditional forms of portfolio management based on individual security selection. Indeed, security selection may be complementary with or based upon dynamic factor methods. However, as we will discuss, many portfolio management strategies based on dynamic factor methods can be implemented in the absence of any security selection decisions.

The remainder of this chapter is organized as follows. We begin with a theoretical discussion of the methods of active management and describe several of the common portfolio management strategies based on dynamic factor methods. We then explore a variety of the modeling approaches used to govern the implementation of these strategies. Finally, we review the growing array of tools available for implementation of these strategies and highlight how security selection is no longer necessary for an efficient implementation in many cases.

---

[7]Dwight Grant, "Market Timing and Portfolio Management," *Journal of Finance* 33, no. 4 (1978): 1119–1131.

METHODS OF ACTIVE MANAGEMENT

The goal of all forms of active portfolio management is to produce a return in excess of a benchmark without incurring an excessive degree of risk. Traditional portfolio managers endeavor to achieve excess return by weighting the securities in their portfolio differently from the weightings of the securities in the benchmark. However, these weights are determined and whatever their values may be, one can generally think of any portfolio as a linear combination of the benchmark-replicating portfolio and a pure active portfolio:

$$r_t = \lambda r_t^B + (1 - \lambda) r_t^A \qquad (14.1)$$

where r_t is the portfolio return, λ is a weighting parameter, r_t^B is the return of the benchmark-replicating portfolio, and r_t^A is the return of the active portfolio. Although many active managers might argue that the weighting parameter λ is equal to zero—that is, they provide purely an active return, most actually provide some blend of benchmark exposure and active exposure. Without loss of generality, one can view all active portfolio management strategies relative to some benchmark, and thus any portfolio can be decomposed into an active and passive component.[8] Regardless of the particular value of the parameter λ or the process employed by a manager, the return decomposition implied in equation (14.1) applies to any portfolio.

Both the benchmark-replicating portfolio and the active portfolio are linear combinations of their constituent securities:

$$r_t^j = \sum_i \omega_i^j r_{i,t}, \, j = A, B \qquad (14.2)$$

where ω_i^j is the weight of security i in portfolio j, and r_t^j is the return of portfolio j, and $r_{i,t}$ is the return of security i.

While portfolios generally consist of a collection of securities, one may also think of both the active portfolio and the benchmark in aggregate as a collection of exposures to various factors. A factor model decomposes a portfolio's return according to its factor content. These factors could be equity style (e.g., value, growth, etc.), geographic location, industry, or sector, macroeconomic factors such as the term structure of interest rates, credit spreads, inflation, and GDP growth, or microeconomic factors such as beta, liquidity, profitability, leverage, industry, or liquidity.

---

[8]M. Barton Waring and Laurence B. Siegel, "The Myth of the Absolute Return Investor," *Financial Analysts Journal* 62, no. 2 (2006): 14–21.

Factor models have a close relationship with theoretical asset pricing models. The capital asset pricing model of Sharpe[9] suggests that the expected return of any security is driven by a single factor—the expected market risk premium—and its empirical analogue depicts the risk premium on any stock as a linear function of the observed market risk premium:

$$\left(r_t^i - r_t^{rf}\right) = \beta^i \left(r_t^{\text{market}} - r_t^{rf}\right) \tag{14.3}$$

In equation (14.3), r_t^i is the return on security i, r_t^{rf} is the risk-free return, β^i is a parameter measuring the exposure of security i to the market risk premium, and r_t^{market} is the market return. The arbitrage pricing theory of Ross[10] is also closely related to factor models. In the APT model, the expected return on any asset i relative to the risk-free return $\left(r_t^i - r_t^{rf}\right)$ is a function of its exposure ($\beta_{j,t}^i$) to each of the j APT factors and each of their returns relative to the risk-free return $\left(F_{j,t} - r_t^{rf}\right)$:

$$\left(r_t^i - r_t^{rf}\right) = \beta_{1,t}^i \left(F_{1,t} - r_t^{rf}\right) + \beta_{2,t}^i \left(F_{2,t} - r_t^{rf}\right) + \ldots + \beta_{H,t}^i \left(F_{H,t} - r_t^{rf}\right) \tag{14.4}$$

The difference between the APT model and the empirical factor models used by practitioners is that the APT factors are unobserved and theory does not explicitly identify the list of relevant factors. However, in either of these theoretical asset pricing models and many others, the (excess) return of any security is a linear function of one or more factors, and there is an observational equivalence between the reduced form of a general asset pricing model and a factor model of the following form:

$$\left(r_t^i - r_t^{rf}\right) = \sum_{h=1\ldots H} \beta_{h,t}^i (F_{h,t} - r_t^{rf}) \tag{14.5}$$

Combining equations (14.2) and (14.5), it is clear that traditional active management, which is based on individual security selection and decomposes a portfolio into its constituent securities, is nested in the concept of a factor based view of the portfolio. Moreover, factor based approaches to portfolio management are not necessarily at odds with individual security selection. Because any security can be written as a linear combination of factors, whether it is a single factor as in the case of the CAPM or a host of factors as in the APT, any portfolio of securities (which is a linear combination of the securities) may likewise be written as a linear combination of the factors.

---

[9]William F. Sharpe, "Capital Asset Prices: A Theory of Market Equilibrium under Conditions of Risk," *Journal of Finance* 19, no. 3 (1964): 425–442.
[10]Stephen F. Ross, "The Arbitrage Theory of Capital Asset Pricing," *Journal of Economic Theory* 13, no. 3 (1976): 343–362.

$$\left(r_t^p - r_t^{rf} \right) = \sum_i \omega_i \left(r_t^i - r_t^{rf} \right) = \sum_i \omega_i \sum_j \beta_t^{i,j} \left(F_t^j - r_t^{rf} \right) \qquad (14.6)$$

What the foregoing detour into the algebra of portfolio return highlights is that there are many ways to skin a cat. Dynamic factor strategies are not entirely different from traditional portfolio management strategies. The difference arises in the rationale behind any particular holding. As we will discuss later, the primary difference with a dynamic factor strategy is that securities are selected because of the exposure they provide to various factors, rather than their idiosyncratic characteristics. Indeed, most dynamic factor strategies attempt to eliminate sources of security-specific risk.

Security Selection

Traditionally, most active portfolio management has focused on security selection and has often attempted (or claimed to) neutralize the exposures to various factors relative to a benchmark index. In other words, these portfolios are designed to reflect the best securities of the benchmark, while maintaining benchmark neutrality with respect to beta, size, style, and sector exposure.

Exhibit 14.1 depicts a typical portfolio management procedure. A portfolio manager begins with a universe of securities, which may be assigned to him by his client. He then employs a series of initial screens to narrow the universe down to a manageable number. This subuniverse is then put through an additional set of screens in order to identify the most interesting prospects. Finally, an even smaller group is put through the portfolio manager's rigorous analysis, which may include onsite visits with corporate management. The result of this process is typically a buy list—a list of securities that the portfolio manager is willing to buy at a certain price for any of his portfolios. Not every security will find its way into each portfolio, since any given portfolio may contain legacy holdings due to variations in portfolio start date, limitations on sector allocations or benchmark deviation, or client-specific restrictions. Security weightings in the portfolio are not generally scientifically derived; weightings typically follow a $1/n$ approach, implying that the weight given to each security in the portfolio is not based on the prospective return and volatility characteristics of each security but in a manner that is proportional to the number of securities (n) in the portfolio. This process is, in general, continuous, which is implied by the arrows in Exhibit 14.1.

An often overlooked result in the early studies on the importance of asset allocation[11] is the finding that—despite all of this screening and corporate

---

[11]See, for instance, Brinson, Hood, and. Beebower, "Determinants of Portfolio Performance."

EXHIBIT 14.1   Traditional Portfolio Management Funnel Chart

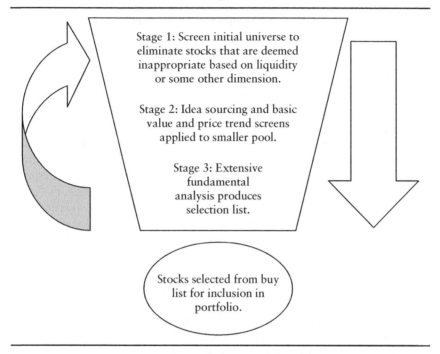

Stage 1: Screen initial universe to eliminate stocks that are deemed inappropriate based on liquidity or some other dimension.

Stage 2: Idea sourcing and basic value and price trend screens applied to smaller pool.

Stage 3: Extensive fundamental analysis produces selection list.

Stocks selected from buy list for inclusion in portfolio.

visitation—very little active management finds its way into most portfolios. In the language of the mathematical presentation of equation (14.1), λ is close to unity. As noted by Waring and Siegel,[12] the fact that asset allocation decisions account for approximately 90% of the variance of portfolio return, combined with the fact that the typical institutional portfolio has a target total risk budget of about 10% in standard deviation, suggests that the average active risk budget is only about 3%. That is, very little return variation comes from selecting security weights that deviate from benchmark weightings.

In general, the focus of the traditional portfolio management process is the companies issuing the securities. Often, a portfolio manager will develop stories about the securities they own. Far less attention is given to the factors driving the returns of each security or the factor characteristics of the overall portfolio. Factor exposure is present, but it is a by-product of the procedure outlined in Exhibit 14.1.

---

[12]M. Barton Waring and Laurence B. Siegel, "The Dimensions of Active Management," *Journal of Portfolio Management* 29, no. 3 (2003): 35–51.

Examples of Factor Exposure

In this subsection, we provide examples of factor exposure.

Style and Size

The vast majority of dynamic factor strategies incorporate tactical variation in equity style and size. While the literature generally suggests that value stocks earn a premium return relative to growth stocks and small capitalization stocks earn a premium return relative to large capitalization stocks,[13] these premiums exhibit considerable variation in both size and sign over time. Because strategies emphasizing value stocks and small capitalization stocks often entail a substantial degree of short-term risk, many active equity portfolio managers have sought to find the equivalent of the investor's "holy grail"—an algorithm to guide them toward the right end of the style and size spectrum at the right time, even if—on average —one is rewarded more over the long run for owning value stocks and small capitalization stocks.

Kao and Shumaker report a substantial potential benefit from style timing and size timing in the United States based on simulated long-short portfolios with perfect foresight and either monthly or annual rebalancing.[14] Levis and Liodakis employ models with less than perfect foresight and find that strategies seeking to exploit cycles in equity style and size offer substantial promise even with modest forecasting ability.[15] Ahmed, Lockwood, and Nanda demonstrate that the potential benefits of so-called "multistyle" rotation strategies substantially outweigh those of style strategies or size strategies alone.[16]

A typical dynamic factor model designed to time the cycles in style and size can be written as follows:

$$(r_t - r_t^{rf}) = \beta_t^{style}(r_t^{value} - r_t^{growth}) + \beta_t^{size}(r_t^{small} - r_t^{big}) + \beta_t(r_t^{market} - r_t^{rf}) \qquad (14.7)$$

where $(r_t - r_t^{rf})$ is the portfolio return relative to the risk-free return, $(r_t^{value} - r_t^{growth})$ is a measure of the spread between the return on value stocks

[13]See Eugene F. Fama and Kenneth R. French, "The Cross Section of Expected Stock Returns," *Journal of Finance* 47, no. 2 (1992): 427–65; and Eugene F. Fama and Kenneth R. French, Value versus Growth: The International Evidence," *Journal of Finance* 53, no. 6 (1998): 1975–1999.

[14]Duen-Li Kao and Robert D. Shumaker, "Equity Style Timing," *Financial Analysts Journal* 55, no. 1 (1999): 37–48.

[15]Mario Levis and Manolis Liodakis, "The Profitability of Style Rotation Strategies in the United Kingdom," *Journal of Portfolio Management* 26, no. 1 (1999): 73–86.

[16]Parvez Ahmed, Larry J . Lockwood, and Sudhir Nanda, "Multistyle Rotation Strategies," *Journal of Portfolio Management* 28, no. 3 (2002): 17–29.

and growth stocks, $(r_t^{small} - r_t^{big})$ is a measure of the spread between the return on small stocks are large stocks, and $(r_t^{market} - r_t^{rf})$ is the market risk premium. The parameters $[\beta_t^{style}, \beta_t^{size}, \beta_t]$ measure the sensitivity of the portfolio return at date t to the value premium, the size premium and the market risk premium, respectively. As can be seen from equation (14.7), all style timing models are essentially time-varying parameter variations on the three-factor model presented by Fama and French.[17] However, the modeling strategies vary greatly, and we discuss some of the methods employed to govern the time variation in the parameters β_t^{style} and β_t^{size} later in this chapter.

Regions, Countries, Industries, and Sectors

In all dynamic factor strategies, the primary focus is on factors rather than individual securities. Rather than pick stocks for their unique characteristics, one seeks to find stocks that provide exposure to the underlying phenomena that are driving their returns. Global portfolio managers face a unique situation in that they can choose to emphasize tactical exposure to regions, countries, industries and sectors in their portfolio management process, offering them more degrees of freedom than many equity portfolio managers.

Often these broad categories of geographic or industry location explain a significant degree of the variation in equity returns. As noted by Malkiel, anything with "tron" or "onics" in its name seemed to soar in price during the early 1960s.[18] Following the Arab oil embargo of 1973, seven of the top 15 companies in the Fortune 500 were energy-related and these stocks represented one of the few groups that produced positive real returns during the 1970s. Emerging markets stocks performed extremely well as the Asian tiger economies grew faster than the developed world during the early 1990s; however, when the Asian currency crisis of 1997–1998 hit, emerging markets—particularly those in Asia—were among the worst performing of all equity categories. Japan was truly thought to be the land of the rising sun during the late 1980s, and Japanese stocks outperformed the equity markets in most other developed countries. Technology, media, and telecomm dominated the equity markets during the 1990s, leading to one of the greatest asset pricing bubbles of all time. These are just a few of the major examples of industry or geographic segments of the market that have made

---

[17]See, Eugene F. Fama and Kenneth R. French, "Common Risk Factors in the Returns on Stocks and Bonds," *Journal of Financial Economics* 33, no. 1 (1993): 3–56; and Eugene F. Fama and Kenneth R. French, "Multifactor Explanations of Asset Pricing Anomalies," *Journal of Finance* 51, no. 1 (1996): 55–84.
[18]Burton G. Malkiel, *A Random Walk Down Wall Street* (New York: W. W. Norton, 1990).

abnormally large contributions—good and bad—to the performance of the global equity markets.

While individual countries and sectors are often important drivers of global equity performance, broad country and sector allocations provide important diversification benefits. This is especially the case for country allocations, since macroeconomic aggregates—such as productivity and output—which are important determinants of long-run stock returns, are generally more highly correlated across industries within a country than across countries within a given industry.[19] These established correlation patterns highlight the presence of important border effects and suggest that country effects are at least as large as industry and sector effects. However, despite the empirical evidence highlighting the importance of border effects and evidence suggesting that country diversification is more powerful than industry diversification,[20] a growing consensus has emerged around the idea that country effects have declined in importance, while the importance of industry and sector effects has been enhanced. Del Negro and Brooks argue that the apparent shift in the relative importance of industries versus countries is likely to be transitory, given that it is largely attributable to the rise of the technology, media, and telecommunication sectors during the equity bubble of the late 1990s, when these three sectors dominated the behavior of the global equity markets.[21]

In the same way that the decomposition of a portfolio's return can be based on style or other factors, it is possible to write a return decomposition model in terms of industry and geographic exposures:

$$\left(r_t - r_t^{rf}\right) = \sum_j \delta_j (\text{INDUSTRY}_j - r_t^{rf}) + \sum_k \gamma_k (\text{COUNTRY}_k - r_t^{rf}) \qquad (14.8)$$

where $\left(r_t - r_t^{rf}\right)$ is the return of stock or portfolio relative to the risk-free return, $(\text{INDUSTRY}_{j,t} - r_t^{rf})$ is the risk premium associated with industry j, $(\text{COUNTRY}_{k,t} - r_t^{rf})$ is the risk premium associated with country k, and the parameters $[\delta_1, \delta_2, ..., \delta_J, \gamma_1, \gamma_2, ..., \gamma_K]$ measure the sensitivity of the portfolio or security to each industry or country-level risk premium. Generally, a model of the form in equation (14.8) would not be used in isolation as a portfolio management tool. It would often be used as an overlay in concert with a security selection model for each individual industry and country.

---

[19]Donna Costello, "A Cross-Country, Cross-Industry Comparison of Productivity Growth," *Journal of Political Economy* 101, no. 2 (1993): 207–222.

[20]Steven L. Heston and K. Geert Rouwenhorst, "Does Industrial Structure Explain the Benefits of International Diversification?" *Journal of Financial Economics* 36 (1994): 3–27.

[21]Marco Del Negro and Robin Brooks, "The Rise in Comovement Across National Stock Markets: Market Integration or IT Bubble?" *Journal of Empirical Finance* 11, no. 5 (2004): 659–680.

However, country-level equity market timing strategies have been shown to be fruitful.

Asness, Krail, and Liew study a country-level timing strategy based on a measure of the value spread for 17 developed equity markets and highlight the potential importance of country timing for global equity managers.[22] Farr examines the impact of timing the cycles between the United States and the EAFE (Europe, Australasia, and the Far East) countries on a global equity portfolio and finds that such country timing offers substantial benefit;[23] the perfect foresight portfolio with monthly rebalancing produces a return that is 3.5 times as large as either index in isolation or a benchmark with a constant 50% weighting to each index.

Timing of countries or sectors may also be driven by a model based on country-specific fundamental factors or country-specific exposures to a global risk premium. Hardy finds that tactical variations among country weightings based on global short-term interest rates and country-specific interest rate term structure and dividend yields can—without any security selection within countries—produce substantial gains over a portfolio with passive international diversification.[24] Ferson and Harvey study a model with global risk premia and time-varying, country-specific betas in 18 national equity markets.[25] Their model captures a large portion of the predictable variation in country returns, and they find that the country-specific information is statistically important.

Macroeconomic Factors

It is widely accepted that the macroeconomic environment is important for asset prices. The stage of the business cycle and the behavior of inflation are both viewed as particularly important for equity returns.

Chen, Roll, and Ross study an empirical version of the APT using the unexpected component of industrial production, credit spreads, the term structure of interest rates, and inflation as predictive factors.[26] They find

---

[22]Clifford S. Asness, Robert J. Krail, and John M. Liew, "Country-Level Equity Style Timing," Chapter 17 in *The Handbook of Equity Style Management*, edited by T. Daniel Coggin and Frank J. Fabozzi (Hoboken, NJ: John Wiley & Sons, 2003).

[23]Dorsey D. Farr, "Tactical Asset Allocation in a Global Equity Portfolio," Chapter 39 in *The Handbook of Finance*, edited by Frank J. Fabozzi (Hoboken, NJ: John Wiley & Sons, 2008).

[24]Daniel C. Hardy, "Market Timing and International Diversification," *Journal of Portfolio Management* 16, no. 4 (1990): 23–27.

[25]Wayne E. Ferson and Campbell R. Harvey, "The Risk and Predictability of International Equity Returns," *Review of Financial Studies* 6, no. 3 (1993): 527–566.

[26]Nai-Fu Chen, Richard Roll, and Stephen A. Ross, "Economic Forces and the Stock Market," *Journal of Business* 59, no. 3 (1986): 383–403.

that innovations in each of these macroeconomic variables are priced by the market. Dahlquist and Harvey demonstrate how macroeconomic variables such as the term structure of interest rates and the business cycle (which affects firm cash flows and profitability) are not only important for financial market returns, but are somewhat predictable because of their persistence.[27]

Kao and Shumaker study the relationship between style return spreads and macroeconomic factors in the United States.[28] Using a single-variable framework, they show that style return spreads—measured by the 12-month return of value relative to growth—are positively related to the steepness of the yield curve, the level of real interest rates, and estimated GDP growth, and negatively related to the spread between the equity market earnings yield and the long-term bond yield.

The responsiveness of asset prices to macroeconomic variables and the predictability of these variables suggest that portfolio management strategies based on exposure to macroeconomic factors may produce excess returns relative to passive strategies, even though a straightforward macro implementation is not always readily available.

Microeconomic Factors

Factor models based on microeconomic variables such as leverage, profitability, beta, and liquidity are most closely related to the techniques and practice of traditional security selection. Most traditional stock pickers generally think in terms of these microeconomic variables as they identify the desired characteristics of companies in a portfolio. However, whereas most traditional portfolio managers have a specific viewpoint on the sign and magnitude of the payoff associated with a particular variable, a portfolio manager using a factor model based on these microeconomic variables may or may not take a position on the signs of the coefficients (or payoffs) associated with each variable.

Haugen argues that the most important factors are those that are related to risk, liquidity, price level, growth potential, and price history (trends).[29] Specifically, he identifies the following variables as predictive of stock returns: the one-month price change, the 12-month price change, the current earnings yield, the return on equity, and the volume as a share of market capitalization. Dahlquist and Harvey identify firm risk exposure as one of

[27]Magnus Dahlquist and Campbell Harvey, "Global Tactical Asset Allocation," *Emerging Markets Quarterly 5, no. 1* (2001): 6–14.
[28]Kao and Shumaker, "Equity Style Timing."
[29]Robert A. Haugen, *The Inefficient Stock Market: What Ways off and Why* (Upper Saddle River, NJ: Prentice Hall, 1999).

four key determinants of equity value.[30] While risk evolves with the business cycle, firm-specific variables such as capital structure (leverage), cash flow volatility, and beta are important drivers of stock returns. Vuolteenaho[31] describes an active strategy—based on Black[32]—driven by tactical variation in the exposure to low-beta stocks and high-beta stocks (which generally earn market returns despite greater than market risk). All of these models have an element of traditional security selection models imbedded in them in that they are based upon security selection rules rather aggregate exposures; however, the security selection itself is driven by a small number of factors.

MODELING

All active management strategies—whether they are based on stocks, factors or markets—rely on forecasts, and all active managers employ some forecasting methodology. The quest to predict financial market returns and the debate over the futility of this endeavor will likely endure forever.

Samuelson argues that stock markets are efficient at the micro level, but inefficient at the macro level.[33] Although equity prices are known to exhibit an excessive degree of volatility relative to their fundamentals,[34] equity markets do appear very efficient at the micro level in the sense that individual stock dividend yields forecast future dividend growth rates in a manner consistent with the simple efficient markets model. That is, high dividend yields indicate low future dividend growth and low dividend yields signify high future dividend growth. Shiller and Jung find that evidence supportive of Samuelson's apparent paradox;[35] their empirical tests reveal that the dividend yield has significant predictive power for forecasting future dividend growth rates for individual firms, although measures of an aggregate dividend yield exhibits no significant relationship with future aggregate dividend growth and the coefficient is often of the wrong sign. They interpret these results as evidence in favor of Samuelson's thesis. Campbell

---

[30]Dahlquist and Harvey, "Global Tactical Asset Allocation."

[31]Tuomo Vuolteenaho, "Beta Arbitrage as an Alpha Opportunity," working paper, Arrowstreet Capital, 2006.

[32]Fisher Black, "Beta and Return," *Journal of Portfolio Management* 20, no. 1 (1993): 8–18.

[33]Paul Samuleson, "Summing up on Business Cycles: Opening Address," in *Beyond Shocks: What Causes Business Cycles*, edited by Jeffrey C. Fuhrer and Scott Schuh (Boston: Federal Reserve Bank of Boston, 1998).

[34]Robert J. Shiller, "Do Stock Prices Move too Much to be Justified by Subsequent Changes in Dividends?" *American Economic Review* 71, no. 1 (1981): 421–436.

[35]Robert J. Shiller and Jeeman Jung, "Samuelson's Dictum and the Stock Market," Cowles Foundation Paper No. 1183, 2006.

and Shiller demonstrate that aggregate stock market returns are forecastable using various valuation metrics and show that the dividend yield for the aggregate U.S. stock market does not forecast dividend growth in a manner consistent with theory.[36]

Whatever the forecasting technique, the seemingly paradoxical combination of macro inefficiency and micro efficiency suggests that portfolio management strategies based on selective exposure to various macro factors may be more effective than those based purely on bottom-up security selection techniques. While individual security selection may present more opportunity to enhance returns due to greater breadth[37]—the number of securities in the global market is much larger than the number of countries, industries, or asset classes—there is plenty of evidence highlighting the difficulty associated with achieving excess returns via traditional security.

Fundamental Valuation–Based Methods

A large literature examines the use of valuation ratios (e.g., book-to-price, dividend yield, earnings yield, etc.) in forecasting future stock returns. Most of this research suggests that valuation ratios are extremely useful forecasting metrics, especially at the aggregate level.[38]

The most basic model of stock valuation is the dividend discount model, which is commonly attributed to Gordon.[39] The derivation of this model begins with the representation of the price (P) of a stock in any period as the sum of the discounted value of the sum of the expected dividend (D) received at the end of the current period plus the expected stock price in the following period:

---

[36]John Y. Campbell and Robert J. Shiller, "Valuation Ratios and the Long-Run Stock Market Outlook," *Journal of Portfolio Management* 24, no. 2 (1998): 11–26.

[37]Mark Kritzman and Sebastian Page, "The Hierarch of Investment Choice," *Journal of Portfolio Management* 29, no. 4 (2003): 11–23.

[38]See, for examples, Robert J. Shiller, "Price–Earnings Ratios as Forecasters of Returns: The Stock Market Outlook in 1996," mimeo, 1996; Robert J. Shiller, *Irrational Exuberance* (Princeton, NJ: Princeton University Press, 2000); John Y. Campbell and Robert J. Shiller, "The Dividend-Price Ratio and Expectations of Future Dividends and Discount Factors," *Review of Financial Studies* 1, no. 3 (1988): 195–228; John Y. Campbell and Robert J. Shiller, "Valuation Ratios and the Long-Run Stock Market Outlook," *Journal of Portfolio Management* 24 (1998): 11–26; John Y. Campbell and Robert J. Shiller, "Valuation Ratios and the Long-Run Stock Market Outlook: An Update," NBER Working Paper no. 8221, 2001; and John Cochrane, "Explaining the Variance of Price-Dividend Ratios," *Review of Financial Studies* 5, no. 2 (1992): 243–280.

[39]Myron J. Gordon, *The Investment, Financing, and Valuation of the Corporation* (Homewood, IL: Irwin, 1962).

$$P_t = D_t + \frac{P_{t+1}}{(1+r)} \tag{14.9}$$

A close inspection of equation (14.9) reveals that it is nothing more than the definition of return. Assuming that (P_{t+K}) is bounded, then the recursive substitution for (P_{t+1}) reveals that the current stock price is equal to the present discounted value of all future dividends:

$$P_t = \sum_{j=0}^{\infty} \frac{D_{t+j}}{(1+r)^j} \tag{14.10}$$

With a constant dividend growth rate, the expected return of a stock $(E(r))$ may be written as the sum of the current dividend yield and the expected growth rate (g):

$$E(r) = \frac{D}{P} + E(g) \tag{14.11}$$

Often, an aggregate version of the Gordon model is used to model the return spread between two categories or indexes of stocks. For instance, it is possible to use this approach to model relative expected returns for two stocks, styles, or asset categories by writing the expected return spread as the sum of the difference in dividend yields and the difference in expected growth rates:

$$E(r^i - r^j) = \left(\frac{D^i}{P^i} - \frac{D^j}{P^j} \right) + E(g^i - g^j) \tag{14.12}$$

Using an aggregated version of equation (14.12) based on stock-level data and a composite value metric based on earnings, sales, and dividends, Asness, Friedman, Krail, and Liew examine the usefulness of this type of methodology for forecasting style return spreads in the United States and find that both fundamental value spreads—$(D^i/P^i - D^j/P^j)$—and growth spreads—$E(g^i - g^j)$—are important determinants of the future return spread between value and growth stocks.[40] They find that these metrics jointly account for almost 40% of the variability in the following year's style return spread. Periods when value stocks offer larger than average yield premiums relative to growth stocks and growth stocks offer lower than average premiums in terms of expected growth are particularly good for value. In their study of country-level timing based on value factors, Asness, Krail, and Liew find that the value spread for country equity indexes identifies

---

[40] Clifford S. Asness, Jacques A. Friedman, Robert J. Krail, and John M. Liew, "Style Timing: Value versus Growth," *Journal of Portfolio Management* 26, no. 3 (2000): 50–60.

opportunities to earn above average expected returns by focusing on countries with lower than normal book-to-market values.[41] Cohen, Polk, and Vuolteenahoalso find that the times series variation in the spread between the average return on growth stocks and value stocks is related to the so-called value spread;[42] abnormally high value spreads are predictive of higher expected returns from value strategies relative to growth strategies.

Momentum-Based and Trend-Sensitive Methods

Although valuation-based trading strategies offer some promise and fit well with the fundamental theoretical model of Gordon and the mental framework of many investors, there remains a great deal of interest in momentum strategies. Why might financial markets exhibit momentum and why might momentum strategies work? Two primary reasons to expect the presence of momentum and the success of trend-based strategies are the possibility that market participants systematically underreact to news—good or bad—or the possibility that market participants are subject to a herd mentality of some sort. While there is some evidence suggesting that market participants systematically overreact to new information, leading to mean reversion in stock market returns,[43] many believe these results are driven by systematic risk factors such as style and size premiums, and there is now widespread agreement among financial economists and practitioners on the existence of momentum effects exist in financial markets and the efficacy of momentum strategies.

Jegadeesh and Titman find that momentum strategies—that is, strategies that buy stocks past winners (those that have performed well in the recent past) and sell past losers (that have performed poorly in the recent past)—generate significant positive returns over 3- to 12-month holding periods.[44] Chan, Jegadeesh, and Lakonishok also study momentum effects and find that past returns and earnings surprise are both predictive of future returns and that these effects are not explained by market risk, size, or style effects.[45] Rouwenhorst studies international equity markets and finds evidence

[41]Cliff S. Asness, Robert J. Krail, and John M. Liew, "Country-Level Equity Style Timing," Chapter 17 in *The Handbook of Equity Style Management*, edited by T. Daniel Coggin and Frank J. Fabozzi (Hoboken, NJ: John Wiley & Sons, 2003).
[42]Randolph B. Cohen, Christopher Polk and Tuomo Vuolteenaho, "The Value Spread," *Journal of Finance* 58, no. 2 (2003): 609–642.
[43]Werner F. M. De Bondt and Richard Thaler, "Does the Stock Market Overreact?" *Journal of Finance* 40, no. 3 (1985): 793–808.
[44]Narasimham Jegadeesh and Sheridan Titman, "Returns to Buying Winners and Selling Losers: Implications for Stock Market Efficiency," *Journal of Finance* 48, no. 1 (1993): 65–91.
[45]Louis K. C. Chan, Narasimham Jegadeesh, and Josef Lakonishok, "The Profitability of Momentum Strategies," *Financial Analysts Journal* 55, no. 6 (1999): 80–90.

of momentum, showing that an internationally diversified portfolio of recent winners outperforms recent losers by more than one percent per month.[46] While momentum is related to firm size, Rouwenhorst finds evidence of momentum across the size spectrum, indicating that momentum is not entirely explained by the size effect.

Momentum models differ in the forecast horizon and the time lags used to measure trends. They can be built at the individual stock level or on some aggregate basis. However, at the heart of any momentum model, there is a relationship of the following form:

$$(r^i_{t,t+k} - r^j_{t,t+k})$$
$$= f(r^i_{t-k-1,t-1} - r^j_{t-k-1,t-1}, r^i_{t-k-2,t-2} - r^j_{t-k-2,t-2}, ..., r^i_{t-k-n,t-n} - r^j_{t-k-n,t-n}, Z_{t-1}) \quad (14.13)$$

In equation (14.13), $f(.)$ is assumed to be increasing in past values of $(r^i - r^j)$, suggesting that future return spreads are a positively related to past return spreads. Generally, momentum models are designed to forecast returns a reasonably high frequency (e.g., days, weeks, or months) since value (or mean-reversion) appears to dominate over long time periods.

Momentum and trend-based strategies are attractive because of their simplicity. Indeed, the ability to forecast future returns based on nothing more than past returns is appealing—if for nothing else because of its absurdity. These models are similar to mathematical or statistical versions of technical analysis, which basically attempts to forecast future prices based on charts of past prices behavior. When employing these techniques, care must be taken to avoid data mining, spurious correlations, and chasing after cycles that are merely artifacts of a particular smoothing process.[47]

Combined Methods

Value strategies tend to trade early because financial market prices often exhibit a pattern of overshooting their fundamental value. This pattern implies that value strategies often appear foolish in the short run due to their tendency to purchase unloved securities that continue to fall in price and sell glamour securities that continue to increase in price. Momentum and trend-driven strategies by definition must trade late, and, if market cycles are characterized by the largest return spreads near the beginning of a regime shift, slow-moving momentum strategies may fail to deliver superior returns.

---

[46]K. Geert Rouwenhorst, "International Momentum Strategies," *Journal of Finance* 53, no. 1 (1998): 267–284.
[47]Charles R. Nelson and Heejoon Kang, "Spurious Periodicity in Inappropriately Detrended Time Series," *Econometrica* 49, no. 3 (1981): 741–751.

EXHIBIT 14.2 The Timing of Value and Momentum Strategies

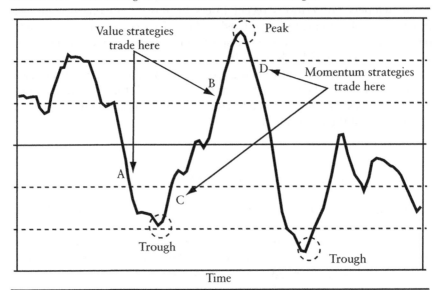

Exhibit 14.2 illustrates these points. The line in the figure depicts both the relative value and relative return of two assets. When asset X is cheap relative to asset Y (and vice versa) value strategies sell asset $Y(X)$ in order to buy asset $X(Y)$. These instances are depicted in points A and B. When momentum shifts in favor asset X at the expense of asset Y, momentum strategies sell asset Y in order to buy asset X; conversely, when momentum shifts in favor of asset Y at the expense of asset X, momentum strategies sell asset X in order to buy asset Y. These instances are depicted in points C and D. Neither strategy is a perfect timing device. That is, neither the value strategy nor the momentum strategy precisely identifies the local peaks and troughs in the relative returns of the two assets. The value strategy is generally early, and the momentum strategy is—by definition—always late.

Grantham argues that an appropriate balance between momentum effects and value effects is one of the central aspects of successful portfolio management.[48]

Models incorporating a combination of valuation and momentum strategies are designed to remedy these problems, by allowing momentum to dominate when valuations have not yet reached an extreme position and

[48]Jeremy Grantham, "Everything I Know About the Market in 15 Minutes," *GMO, Quarterly Letter*, Special Topic, July 2006, pp. 1–3. Originally published in 1991. http://www.fullermoney.com/content/2006-08-02/Grantham-CMSAttachment-Download.pdf>

valuations to dominate when momentum breaks down. Although it is rare in practice, the concurrence of valuation signals and momentum signals is a powerful indicator, since both momentum and valuation have been shown to be predictive of future returns.

There is some empirical evidence suggesting that valuation approaches and momentum approaches may be complementary. Asness argues that the interaction of value and momentum strategies is important for understanding the success of both value and momentum strategies.[49] He shows that the efficacy of value strategies is greatest for low momentum stocks and the success of momentum strategies is greatest among expensive stocks. Because of the instability in the forecasting content of valuation ratios and the presence of serial correlation in country-level and regional stock returns, Farr advocates the use of a combination of valuation and momentum methods.[50]

Other Techniques

During the 1980s and 1990s, quantitative portfolio managers began to employ models to forecast portfolio risk and tracking error (the volatility of a portfolio's excess return relative to its benchmark). These risk models are basically multifactor regression models used to isolate the past determinants of volatility and project future volatility.

Haugen and Baker turn a return attribution model into a return forecasting model by assuming investors have a form of adaptive preferences and expectations which are influenced by the recent past.[51] This type of model is truly agnostic in the sense that it does not reflect any belief about the elemental importance of fundamental or technical factors. While it does rely on the assumption that investors have a form of adaptive expectations (and hence the presence of momentum in factor payoffs)—it lets the data do the talking as to which factors are most important at any given time.

Haugen and Baker begin with a return decomposition of the following form, which depicts the return for stock i at date t is a function of a set of factors and the payoffs to each factor:

$$r_{j,t} = \sum_i \text{PAYOFF}_{i,t} * \text{FACTOR}_{j,i,t-1} + u_{j,t} \qquad (14.14)$$

In (14.14) $\text{PAYOFF}_{i,t}$ is the estimated regression coefficient for factor i at date t, and $\text{FACTOR}_{j,i,t-1}$ is the exposure to factor i for stock j at date $t - 1$.

[49]Cliff S. Asness, "The Interaction of Value and Momentum Strategies," *Financial Analysts Journal* 53, no. 2 (1997): 29–36.
[50]Farr, "Tactical Asset Allocation in a Global Equity Portfolio."
[51]Robert A. Haugen and Nardin L. Baker, "Commonality in the Determinants of Expected Stock Returns," *Journal of Financial Economics* 41, no. 3 (1996): 401–439.

The model is a standard multifactor return attribution model incorporating time-varying payoffs. A version of this type of model is commonly used as a portfolio attribution model or as a portfolio risk model (used to forecast the active risk of a portfolio relative to a passive benchmark).

If one can forecast the date t payoff values at date $t - 1$, then it is possible to transform equation (14.14) from a return attribution model into a return forecasting model. Haugen and Baker use a simple 12-month smoothing to project the next period's payoff values,

$$\left(E_{t-1}(\text{PAYOFF}_{i,t}) = \frac{1}{12} \Sigma_{j=1}^{12} \text{PAYOFF}_{i,t-j} \right)$$

so that the expected return for stock i at date t is projected as

$$r_{j,t} = \sum_{i} E_{t-1}(\text{PAYOFF}_{i,t}) * \text{FACTOR}_{j,i,t-1} \qquad (14.15)$$

The model in equation (14.15) is closely related to the investor preference theory of Stevens, Borger, and Reynolds.[52] They argue that since broadly recognized factor returns—e.g., value and size—are likely to be arbitraged away and investor preferences evolve slowly over time with changes in market conditions, a dynamic model of investor preferences (and hence expected returns) is necessary. The primary drawback of these models is their lack of parsimony, and thus their tendency to fall victim to the criticism of data mining.

IMPLEMENTATION

Building portfolios based on views about a small number of individual securities is relatively straightforward. After ranking the universe of securities and deciding upon which ones to own, the portfolio manager simply buys shares of those securities. Part of the challenge associated with dynamic factor approaches to portfolio management rests in the implementation. Because the returns associated with individual securities contain an element of idiosyncratic risk, imperfect exposure to various factors is generally unavoidable. As such, the implementation of portfolio management strategies based on dynamic factor allocations is fraught with error. However, the problem of implementation error has been alleviated in recent years by several developments facilitating the implementation of factor-based strategies.

[52]Thomas D. Stevens, David R. Borger, and Hal W. Reynolds, "Investor Preference Theory," working paper, Los Angeles Capital Management, 2004.

Physical Securities

The implementation of dynamic factor strategies with individual stocks requires a portfolio with a large number of holdings in order to achieve suitable factor exposure and avoid an excessive degree of security-specific risk. A portfolio of securities can be constructed in order to provide exposure to a specific set of factors. With a large enough number of holdings, the idiosyncratic return is minimized and the overall portfolio will reflect its factor content rather than the constituent securities. The securities are included in the portfolio in order to capture the returns associated with the characteristics they exhibit. Much like an insurance company manages risk by relying on a law of large numbers, a factor-based equity portfolio built with a large enough number of individual securities will perform in a manner driven the factor content rather than the individual stocks in the portfolio.

The decline in the cost of computing power over the past two decades has not only improved the modeling side of portfolio management, but it has also improved the ability to implement macro strategies through the use of portfolios of individual securities. First, access to inexpensive computing power is central to the modeling and construction of portfolios of large numbers of individual securities. Equally as important, technology has dramatically reduced trading costs and introduced efficiencies into the portfolio management process that allow for the implementation of strategies that were impractical in the past.

Trading in Aggregates

Some dynamic factor strategies may be implemented at the macro level through direct (or semidirect) exposure to a particular set of factors. Many index providers have created benchmarks designed to proxy one or more of the various factors discussed earlier in this chapter. For example, S&P, Russell, Wilshire, MSCI, and Morningstar all have developed indexes to proxy the performance of value stocks and growth stocks, as well as various segments of the capitalization spectrum. While these benchmarks are far from flawless (e.g., the definition of value in some indexes results in excessive turnover that has little to do with changes in equity style), they are useful for categorizing segments of the equity market, and the number of indexes appears to be mushrooming. Recently, in response to Arnott, Hsu, and Moore[53] and Siegel,[54] a host of new *active* or *fundamental* indexes have

---

[53]Robert D. Arnott, Jason Hsu, and Philip Moore, "Fundamental Indexation," *Financial Analysts Journal* 61, no. 2 (2005): 83–99.
[54]Jeremy Siegel, *The Future for Investors: Why the Tried and True Triumph Over the Bold and New* (New York: Crown Business, 2005).

been developed, opening the door for an endless array of factor-based indexes that can be used to model, benchmark and implement dynamic factor approaches to portfolio management.

Investable versions of these indexes are increasingly available to implement style tilts and gain exposure to other factors. Futures contracts are available for various equity size and style exposures. However, the use of futures in equity style management has been plagued by a lack of liquidity in the underlying futures contracts.[55] Futures contracts are often used to implement global tactical asset allocation strategies, which trade country-level exposure to various equity and fixed income markets and currencies.

Swap contracts can also be used for various factor exposures. Indeed, because of the ability for customization, swap contracts are one of the most flexible tools available for implementing factor modeling strategies. Swaps are especially attractive for taxable investors, since gains on futures are generally realized frequently and are taxed unfavorably, while swaps allow deferment of capital gains through the term of the contract, as well as loss harvesting by terminating a contract prior to its intended settlement.

Exchange-traded funds (ETFs) represent a basket of securities that are traded on an exchange, and they are typically designed to replicate an index or benchmark. Along with the proliferation of indexes based on various factors and segments of the equity market, an increasing number of ETFs designed to replicate these indexes has emerged.

ETFs have provided portfolio managers the ability to gain exposure to a particular style, industry, sector, country, market capitalization segment or other factor for an indefinite period at extremely low cost in a single trade. As a result of their advantages over traditional mutual funds (e.g., low-costs, intraday trading and high tax efficiency) and their lack of the regulatory burdens associated with trading futures contracts, these funds have experienced explosive growth in number and total assets since their introduction. As the ETF market grows, it appears that an increasing number of factor-like exposures will become easily tradeable on equity exchanges. A comprehensive treatment of ETFs can be found in Gastineau.[56]

---

[55]Joanne M. Hill, "Trading (and investing) in "Style" using Futures and Exchange-Traded Funds," Chapter 20 in *The Handbook of Equity Style Management*, edited by T. Daniel Coggin and Frank J. Fabozzi (Hoboken, NJ: John Wiley & Sons, 2003).
[56]Gary L. Gatineau, *The Exchange-Traded Funds Manual* (Hoboken, NJ: John Wiley & Sons, 2002).

KEY POINTS

■ Advances in computational technology, introduction of new benchmarks and trading tools, and a decline in the cost of computing power have all driven changes in the techniques of portfolio management over the past decade.

■ All active portfolios can be decomposed into an active component and a passive (benchmark replicating) component.

■ Dynamic factor models are used to build portfolios based on tactical exposure to factors such as equity style, industry or geographic location, macroeconomic factors, or microeconomic factors.

■ Factor models have a close relationship with theoretical asset pricing models.

■ Dynamic factor strategies attempt to eliminate sources of security-specific risk.

■ Portfolio managers use a variety of methods for modeling the time series variation in factor exposure, including relative value spreads, momentum and trends, as well as other combinations.

■ Both value and momentum strategies have been shown to be effective for security selection within particular markets as well as selection across markets (e.g., sectors or countries).

■ Implementation of dynamic factor approaches to portfolio management has been facilitated by new developments in modeling, benchmarking, computing power, and trading technology.

■ Many dynamic factor models may be implemented at the macro level—via direct exposure to one or more factors—or at the micro level through factor-based security selection models.

QUESTIONS

1. Discuss some of the developments that led to the rise of dynamic factor models and their growing role in portfolio management.

2. Explain how traditional approaches to portfolio management based on individual security selection are nested in the concept of a factor-based view of the portfolio.

3. Discuss how individual stocks may be of less importance to a portfolio manager employing a factor-based approach.

4. Describe the empirical evidence on value and momentum strategies and explain how value and momentum may be used as complementary factors in portfolio management.

5. How have financial innovations such as altered the way in which portfolio managers can express views in a portfolio?

CHAPTER 15

A Factor Competition Approach to Stock Selection

Joseph Mezrich, Ph.D.
Managing Director
Nomura Securities International, Inc.

Junbo Feng, Ph.D.
Vice President
Nomura Securities International, Inc.

Successful investing is difficult because of the rarity of durable investment strategies. The plain fact is that strategies fail despite the support of logic or history. The approach we introduce in this chapter confronts the problem of strategy failure as an expected feature of investing. Every investment strategy has three core properties: (1) the return that the strategy generates, (2) the volatility of that return, and (3) the correlation of that return with alternate strategies. The problem we address is the fragility of the first property, the source of reward uncertainty. Our solution is derived by exploiting the second and third properties, the more persistent risk features of investment strategy. Mainly we exploit the persistence of correlation of investment strategies to counter the lack of persistence of the return to investment strategies.

The goal of our approach is to provide a systematic framework that removes failed strategies from the playing field until they prove worthy, while providing an opportunity for new strategies to join the team.

THE PROBLEM

We created a set of factors within the Russell 1000 to understand the relationships that drive stock prices. For the most part, our factors are derived from the familiar concepts employed by fundamental analysts when they evaluate stocks. For all Russell 1000 stocks, each score on a particular factor is calculated from several sources (CompuStat, I/B/E/S, and IDC pricing databases) and then ranked cross-sectionally at a point in time. Factor returns are generated by calculating the subsequent performance of a portfolio that is long the highest scores (i.e., the top decile containing approximately 100 stocks) and short the decile with the lowest scores (rebalanced monthly).

The complete set of 45 factors is defined in Exhibit 15.1. The historical returns to these factors are shown in Exhibit 15.2 and they are sorted by their 2006 to August 2010 returns and ranks. A subset of the 45 factors is shown in Exhibit 15.3 to illustrate how some popular strategies have failed while others have emerged as winners. Consider the cumulative factor returns for the five strategies displayed in the Exhibit 15.3:

- Dividend yield (dividend per share divided by price).
- Estimate dispersion (standard deviation of I/B/E/S fiscal year (FY) 1 EPS estimates divided by ABS (mean of I/B/E/S FY1 estimates)).
- Earnings quality (accruals).
- Up to down revisions (number of FY1 up revisions minus number of FY1 down revisions divided by total number of estimates).
- One-year price momentum (12-month total return less the last one-month return).

EXHIBIT 15.1   Factor Definitions

Factor	Definition
1-month price reversal	Last-month total return
1-year dividend growth	1-year dividends per share growth
1-year EPS growth	1-year earnings per share growth
1-year price momentum	12-month total return excluding the most recent month
Analyst coverage	Number of IBES FY1 estimates/Log (market cap)
Asset turnover	Sales/Total average assets
B/P	Book value/Market cap
B/P (excluding goodwill)	Book value excluding Goodwill/Market cap
Beta	60 month beta to Russell 1000 Index
CapEx/Sales	Capital expenditures/Total average assets
Capex/Assets	Capital expenditures/Average sales
Cash Flow/EV	(Operating income × (1 − Tax rate) + Depreciation − Change in net operating accruals − Capital Expenditures − Preferred dividends)/EV
Cash/Assets	Cash and equivalents/Total assets
Default risk	Merton type default probability
Dividend payout ratio	Dividend per share/Earnings per share
Dividend yield	Dividend per share/Price

EXHIBIT 15.1   (Continued)

Factor	Definition
Dividend yield + Share buy backs	Dividend yield + Share buyback yield
E/P	EPS (excluding extraordinary items)/Price
EBIT/EV	Earnings before interest and taxes/EV
EBIT/Price	Earnings before interest and taxes/Market cap
EBIT/WCPPE	Earnings before interest and taxes/(Net working capital + Net property, plant and equipment)
EBITDA/EV	Earnings before interest, taxes, depreciation and amortization/EV
EBITDA/Price	Earnings before interest, taxes, depreciation and amortization/Market cap
EPS variability	Standard deviation of trailing 5-Year EPS/ABS(mean of trailing 5-Year EPS)
Earnings quality (accruals)	3-month percentage change in total net operating accruals (operating assets − operating liabilities)
Estimate dispersion	Standard deviation of IBES FY1 estimates/ABS(mean of IBES FY1 estimates)
Gross margin	(Sales − Cost of goods sold)/Sales
Market cap	(Small − Large)Market cap
Operating income variability	Standard deviation of trailing 5-year EBIT/Mean of trailing 5-year EBIT
Operating leverage	5-year percentage change in EBIT/5-year percentage change in sales
PEG	(EPS/Price) × IBES 5-year growth
PEGY	(EPS/Price) × (IBES 5-year growth + Dividend yield)
Predicted E/P	Fiscal year–weighted sum of FY1, FY2, FY3 IBES mean EPS estimate/Price
R&D/EV	5-year weighted sum of R&D expense/EV
R&D/Sales	R&D expense/Sales
ROA	Earnings before interest and taxes/Average total assets
ROE	Net income excluding extraordinary items/Average common equity
ROIC	Earnings before interest and taxes/Invested capital
ROIC × B/P	ROIC × B/P
Sales growth	Weighted average of annual sales growth for trailing 5 years. More weight given to recent periods
Sales variability	Standard deviation of trailing 5-year sales/Mean of trailing 5-year sales
Sales/Employee	Sales/Employees
Sales/Price	Sales/Market cap
Share buybacks	12-month percentage change in shares outstanding
Up-to-down revisions	(IBES FY1 up estimates − IBES FY1 down estimates)/IBES FY1 estimates

Notes: Table shows definitions of factors used in this chapter.
Data sources: Nomura Securities International, Inc., from CompuStat, I/B/E/S, Russell, and IDC data.

EXHIBIT 15.2 History of Factor Returns (as of August 31, 2010)

	Annualized Returns					Ranks				
Factor	1986–1990	1991–1995	1996–2000	2001–2005	2006–Aug. 2010	1986–1990	1991–1995	1996–2000	2001–2005	2006–Aug. 2010
1 Market cap (Small – Large)	0.4	8.5	-7.1	22.2	18.2	33	11	45	7	1
2 Beta	-5.1	13.8	10.7	-0.9	13.9	40	3	16	39	2
3 EBITDA/Price	8.0	0.8	4.4	25.3	11.3	12	32	35	5	3
4 Sales/Price	-4.5	4.2	-3.6	28.1	8.5	39	20	43	2	4
5 Dividend yield	-0.9	0.2	-2.7	6.1	7.9	35	35	42	28	5
6 EBIT/Price	9.6	-0.4	11.1	21.4	7.3	4	38	13	8	6
7 B/P (excluding goodwill)	-3.7	2.6	10.8	15.6	6.5	38	27	15	17	7
8 EPS variability	0.3	7.7	2.9	-0.6	6.4	34	13	39	37	8
9 B/P	-6.0	6.5	-4.0	18.6	5.3	42	18	44	13	9
10 EBITDA/EV	9.0	1.4	9.8	33.8	4.4	7	31	20	1	10
11 Operating income variability	-2.7	3.7	4.6	10.0	4.0	37	22	33	23	11
12 Earnings quality (accruals)	4.0	7.1	19.6	11.6	4.0	20	14	5	20	12
13 Cash flow/EV	6.0	10.0	12.5	20.9	3.8	16	7	11	9	13
14 ROIC x B/P	8.7	5.2	10.9	25.6	3.2	9	19	14	4	14
15 ROA	13.4	-9.0	4.3	9.4	3.1	3	45	36	27	15
16 R&D/EV	-8.1	20.7	22.3	17.1	2.9	43	1	3	15	16
17 Dividend yield + Share buybacks	7.9	0.7	21.4	9.9	2.7	13	33	4	24	17
18 Sales growth	3.4	-2.3	10.0	12.7	2.6	22	42	18	19	18
19 Share buybacks	8.0	-0.4	18.3	9.8	2.4	11	37	6	25	19
20 ROIC	9.0	-2.0	7.9	10.8	1.9	6	41	22	21	20
21 Analyst coverage	-2.1	0.6	15.6	-7.5	1.8	36	34	8	43	21
22 Sales variability	6.2	-4.0	4.5	4.8	1.6	15	44	34	31	22
23 EBIT/EV	9.3	2.0	13.2	26.9	1.3	5	29	10	3	23
24 Gross margin	8.8	6.6	13.2	4.1	1.1	8	17	9	32	24
25 Default risk	8.8	6.6	7.8	-3.3	1.1		16	23	41	25

EXHIBIT 15.2 (Continued)

	Annualized Returns							Ranks					
Factor	1986–1990	1991–1995	1996–2000	2001–2005	2006–Aug. 2010	1986–1990	1991–1995	1996–2000	2001–2005	2006–Aug. 2010
26 Capex/Assets	0.4	9.4	6.1	3.5	0.7	32	9	26	33	26
27 Cash/Assets	1.2	8.4	16.1	−5.1	0.2	28	12	7	42	27
28 CapEx/Sales	1.1	6.7	5.0	16.0	−0.4	29	15	31	16	28
29 R&D/Sales	−12.9	17.1	24.0	−14.0	−0.5	44	2	2	45	29
30 Operating leverage	4.4	2.5	4.8	0.2	−1.1	19	28	32	36	30
31 PEGY	2.3	9.9	5.8	18.5	−1.5	26	8	27	14	31
32 Asset turnover	3.3	3.2	10.0	19.9	−1.8	23	25	17	11	32
33 EBIT/WCPPE	3.5	3.7	6.5	5.1	−2.3	21	21	25	30	33
34 Dividend payout ratio	3.1	3.1	7.1	0.9	−2.3	24	26	24	35	34
35 1-year dividend growth	7.6	−2.4	3.6	−1.5	−2.4	14	43	37	40	35
36 1-year EPS growth	5.1	3.4	5.3	3.4	−2.5	18	24	29	34	36
37 PEG	2.6	12.1	5.0	20.2	−3.2	25	4	30	10	37
38 Estimate dispersion	−5.6	2.0	3.3	9.6	−3.4	41	30	38	26	38
39 Sales/Employee	1.5	−0.3	9.8	5.7	−3.6	27	36	19	29	39
40 ROE	5.6	−0.4	8.2	10.4	−3.8	17	39	21	22	40
41 Up-to-down revisions	17.9	10.9	2.7	−9.8	−5.6	1	5	40	44	41
42 E/P	0.5	3.6	11.7	18.9	−8.3	31	23	12	12	42
43 Predicted E/P	0.7	10.8	5.3	22.2	−8.9	30	6	28	6	43
44 1-month price reversal	8.5	−0.7	0.7	13.6	−9.3	10	40	41	18	44
45 1-year price momentum	13.7	9.1	24.1	−0.9	−15.9	2	10	1	38	45

Notes: Table shows history of factor returns. The Russell 1000 stocks are ranked according to a particular factor. Factor returns are generated by calculating the subsequent performance of an equal-weighted portfolio that is long the decile with the highest scores and short the decile with the lowest scores (rebalanced monthly).

Data sources: Nomura Securities International, Inc, Russell, CompuStat, I/B/E/S, and IDC.

EXHIBIT 15.3 Rarity of Durability (as of August 31, 2010)

Russell 1000 Factor	Average Annual Returns						Ranks*					
	1986–1990	1991–1995	1996–2000	2001–2005	2006–8/2010		1986–1990	1991–1995	1996–2000	2001–2005	2006–8/2010	
Dividend yield	−0.9	0.2	−2.7	6.1	7.9		35	35	42	28	5	
Estimate dispersion	−5.6	2.0	3.3	9.6	−3.4		41	30	38	26	38	
Earnings quality (accruals)	4.0	7.1	19.6	11.6	4.0		20	14	5	20	12	
Up-to-down revisions	17.9	10.9	2.7	−9.8	−5.6		1	5	40	44	41	
1-year price momentum	13.7	9.1	24.1	−0.9	−15.9		2	10	1	38	45	

Notes: Highest returns receive lowest rank (Rank 1 is best). Please refer to Exhibit 15.2 for description of factors.
Data sources: Nomura Securities International, Inc., from CompuStat, I/B/E/S, Russell, IDC data.

The ranks in Exhibit 15.3 are for the particular time period shown and are relative to the 45-factor set. In each period, the top strategy is ranked number 1 and the bottom strategy is ranked number 45.

Note how former winners became losers and how former losers became winners. Dividend yield, for example, recently touted as the thing to bet on was the top five strategy since 2006. But the exhibit shows that dividend yield's record prior to 2006 was very poor. Will dividend yield's recent success last?

Let's consider some previously celebrated strategies that have become disappointments. One-year price momentum was dead last since 2006, even though it was in the top 10 for 15 years in the period 1986–2000. Earnings quality (accruals) was a mediocre factor since 2001, while it was in the top five in the period 1996–2000. The best way to pick stocks in the period 1986–1990 was up to down revisions. This was also the fifth-best strategy in the period 1991–1995, but it was in the bottom 10 since 1996. As Exhibit 15.2 shows, of the top 10 strategies for the period 2006–August 2010, only five were in the top 10 in the period 2001–2005, only one in the top 10 in the period 1991–2000, and only two were in the top 10 in the period 1986–1990.

The changing nature of factor efficacy is illustrated graphically in Exhibit 15.4, which shows the cumulative returns to dividend yield, a recent winner, and the long-ago winner, estimate revisions. The reader is invited to peruse Exhibit 15.2 for more examples demonstrating the rarity of durable strategies.

THE SOLUTION

If we think of each factor as an asset to own, we can frame the decision of how to weight the factors as an asset allocation problem. The objective is to own the portfolio of factors weighted to produce the highest Sharpe ratio. In this context, the uncertainty of future factor success is mitigated by taking advantage of the power of diversification defined by the historical factor returns. But that doesn't tell us how many factors to include in the portfolio. There are 45 factors in our database (described in Exhibit 15.1). Should all be used? Should we add to this list? While more factors could improve the Sharpe ratio by reducing risk, a diversified portfolio of many factors would likely produce lower returns than a concentrated portfolio of good factors.

Factor Competition

There is another consideration that suggests keeping the number of factors (assets) at a fixed small number. The goal of our approach is to provide a

EXHIBIT 15.4   Past Performance Does Not Guarantee a Winner (as of August 31, 2010)

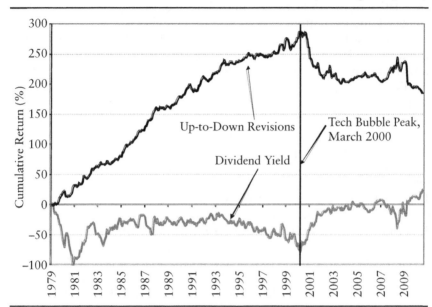

Note: Refer to Exhibit 15.1 for definitions of factors.
Data sources: Nomura Securities International, Inc., Russell 1000, I/B/E/S, Compu-Stat, and IDC data.

systematic framework that removes failed strategies from the playing field until they prove worthy, while providing an opportunity for new strategies to join the team. If we have a large pool of factors, that should be good enough to use for stock selection. And if we use a formal objective every month to decide which factors will be "on the team," then we can have a systematic approach to weeding out poor "players" and allowing fresh talent to get into the game. The Sharpe ratio makes sense to use as the objective function in this process partly because of the asset allocation role mentioned and the way correlation gets used.

Assume, for example, that the price-to-earnings ratio (P/E) is a factor that is good enough to use for stock selection. Which earnings should be used, the realized historical earnings or analysts' estimate of future earnings? Returns to these two P/Es, based on different measures of earnings, should be correlated but would not be identical. Perhaps one of these is typically better, but the best P/E might change with market or macro conditions. The returns and rankings of these two factors in Exhibit 15.2 suggested exactly that they are highly correlated, but can be very different sometimes. For instance, in the period 1991–1995, E/P was the 23rd ranked factor with an annualized return of 3.6% while predicted E/P ranked sixth with a much superior return of 10.8%. However, in most of the other periods from 1986 to 1990 and 2006 to August 2010, they are very similar in both returns and ranks.

By restricting the strategy to a small number of factors, and by requiring weights on factors to be positive, the correlated factors will compete with each other. The larger contributor to maximizing the Sharpe ratio will get into the factor portfolio, and the other factors will be rejected. Furthermore, since the number of factors is fixed, a new factor gets into the factor portfolio only if one that was already in the portfolio is ejected. Hence, the "better" P/E factor would enter the portfolio by replacing a correlated but newly inferior factor such as operating income divided by price.

In this approach, factors not in the portfolio for a particular month constitute a pool of contenders for membership in the factor portfolio for the subsequent month. All factors compete for a spot on the team; those in the portfolio can be replaced by factors in the pool of contenders. The potential loss of alpha due to decay of factor efficacy is repaired by this process of factor competition.

How Many Factors Should Be Used?

Empirical results help this choice. Using our historical database of factor returns (see Exhibit 15.1), we calculate the historical mean, volatility, and correlations of a set of factor returns under consideration. Five years of trailing data are used to forecast one-month-ahead values. Since recent returns are not predictive of future returns (think of the hazard of forecasting the return to price momentum at the end of February 2000 based on performance of price momentum in the prior months), the trailing five-year mean was used as the forecast for the subsequent month's factor return. However, recent volatility and correlation are good near-term predictors of volatility and correlation.[1] So, in order to forecast the future month's covariance, we emphasize recent trailing data by imposing a linear time decay of weights on the trailing data.

Every month we run an optimization to find the set of factors and their weights (positive weights summing to one) that give the highest ratio of return to volatility for the weighted portfolio of factors. This optimization

---

[1]The persistence of volatility and correlation are well documented, and are at the heart of generalized autoregressive conditional heteroscedasticity (GARCH) forecasting models. See, for example: Robert Engle and Joseph Mezrich, "Grappling with GARCH," *Risk* 8, no. 8 (1995): 112–117; and Robert Engle and Joseph Mezrich "GARCH for Groups," *Risk* 9, no. 8 (1996): 35–40. We do not use GARCH forecasting models here, but we do rely on the persistence of covariance.

finds the factor portfolio that is expected to achieve the highest month-ahead return-to-volatility ratio. In this report we use the return-to-volatility ratio as a zero interest rate version of the Sharpe ratio. We can repeat the optimization to create separate monthly weighted factor portfolios for factor sets of size 2 through 10. For example, for the factor set of size 5, the optimizer determines the particular five factors and their weights (positive values summing to one) that achieve the highest return-to-volatility ratio expected for the subsequent (out-of-sample) month based on prior historical data. The five factors selected and the weights are free to change month-to-month. The weighted factor portfolio created at the end of each month produces an out-of-sample expected return for the subsequent month. This data enable us to calculate the average annual return and average annual return-to-volatility that would have been realized for each of the set sizes. Exhibit 15.5 shows the results of this optimization process using our database for the Russell 1000 in the 25-year period from 1982 to 2006.

The annualized return-to-volatility increases with the number of factors used. But the annual return progressively declines from factor portfolios of size greater than three. The more factors used, the better the diversification and risk-adjusted return. The fewer factors used, the higher the annualized

EXHIBIT 15.5   How Many Factors Should Be Used? (as of December 31, 2006)

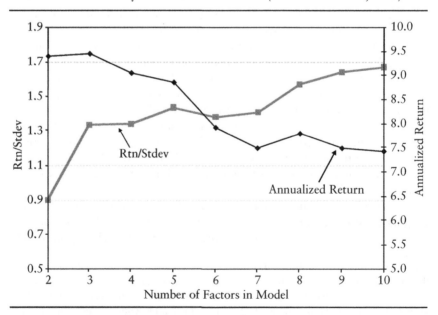

Data sources: Nomura Securities International, Inc., Compustat, I/B/E/S, IDC, and Russell.

return. Three factors is a good compromise between these competing features.[2] An obvious question is this: If only three factors are to be used, why do we need a large pool of contenders? Our database has over 40 strategies. Why so many? Since markets change, what works will change, and we find it best to have a large opportunity set for the process to choose from. It is important to note that there is nothing in this process that precludes using more than three factors if the risk matters more. We focus on the particular choice of three factors here to show what can be achieved.

WHICH FACTORS GET PICKED?

Our proposed remedy for failed factors is to use a three-factor portfolio each month that is derived using the optimization process described in the previous section. Exhibit 15.6 gives a visualization of the history of which factors get picked for the 29-year period from 1982 through 2010. Factors that can be picked are labeled on the right and left vertical axes, with time along the horizontal axis. For each date on the horizontal axis, there are three points on the chart signifying what was selected for that date. The length of the line segments in the exhibit indicates the length of time that factors remained in the model. The bottom of the exhibit shows, for example, that up-to-down revisions was in the model from 1982 until 1996 but has not been in the model since then. P/E was in the model for a few years in the 1990s, where earnings was analyst forecast; see the label PREDICTED_EP in the middle of the exhibit. P/E where earnings represents historical earnings has not yet been in the model.

Exhibit 15.6 shows, in broad terms, that some structural changes occurred in the persistence of factors in the model. The horizontal line segments on the right side of the exhibit are somewhat shorter and more dispersed among the pool of contenders than those in the middle of the exhibit. This pattern suggests that in recent years factors need to be changed more frequently for the process of alpha repair to be effective. That does not necessarily mean that the process demands higher stock turnover. There are two reasons. First, the objective function will tend to swap factors that are correlated. The inferior factor in the portfolio will get replaced by a correlated contender that produces a superior result for the objective function. Consequently, the alpha of stocks (which we describe in more detail) is not dramatically affected. Second, we constrain stock turnover in the portfolio construction process as described in the next section.

---

[2]The surprisingly low number of factors is basically consistent with an observation from our principal components analysis that 80% of the variance in our set of factors (excluding beta and one-month return) is produced by three principal components.

EXHIBIT 15.6   The Evolution of Factors in the Model (as of August 31, 2010)

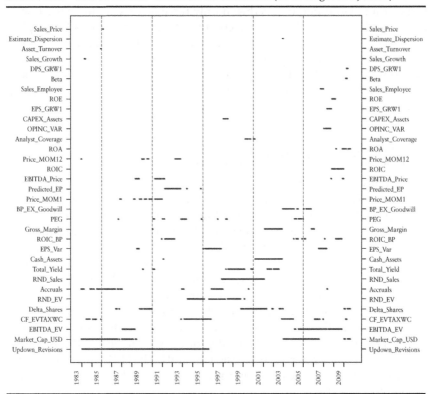

Note: See Exhibit 15.2 for definitions of factors.
Data sources: Nomura Securities International, Inc., CompuStat, I/B/E/S, Russell, and IDC.

DOES THE ALPHA REPAIR PROCESS WORK?

The process of alpha repair is tested by using this approach to create portfolios of stocks. First, the factors selected each month are used to create stock scores, which are taken as expected returns (aside from a linear transformation) for the stock portfolio construction process.

The scoring process for January 2007 is illustrated in Exhibit 15.7 using IBM. The three factors picked for January 2007 are market cap (Small – Big) at 35.6% weight, EBITDA/EV at 35.2% weight, and gross margin at 29.2% weight. Given the level of EBITDA/EV for every stock in the Russell 1000 on December 31, 2006, the Z-score is calculated (using the value of EBITDA/EV minus the average for the universe, divided by the standard deviation of

EXHIBIT 15.7　Example of How Stocks Get Scored: IBM on December 31, 2006

Optimal Factors	Optimized Factor Weights		Stock Exposure to Factor (Z-score)		Product of Weights and Scores
Market cap	0.36	×	−3.92	=	−1.41
EBITDA/EV	0.35	×	0.02	=	0.01
Gross margin	0.29	×	0.28	=	0.08
Score	1.00				−1.32

Notes: A cross-sectional mean and standard deviation of the raw scores for the selected factors are calculated. This mean is subtracted from IBM's raw score and the difference is divided by the standard deviation to generate the company's Z-score on the factor. IBM's overall score is then the weighted sum of the Z-scores.
Data sources: Nomura Securities International, Inc., CompuStat, I/B/E/S, Russell, and IDC.

EXHIBIT 15.8　Alpha Repair Portfolio Excess Returns over Russell 1000 (as of August 31, 2010)

	Jan. 2010– Aug. 2010	Sep. 2007– Aug. 2010	Sep. 2005– Aug. 2010	Sep. 2000– Aug. 2010	Since Inception, 1997
Excess return	4.8%	3.2%	4.2%	4.1%	3.9%

Notes: Backtest assumes 100% turnover.
Data sources: Nomura Securities International, Inc., from Compustat, I/B/E/S, IDC, and Russell.

the EBITDA/EV levels for the universe). That Z-score is multiplied by the weight for that factor, 0.35. Similar calculations for IBM are done for market cap and gross margin. The net score for IBM based on end-of-December data is −1.32, which is a below average score. The score for every stock in the Russell 1000 is calculated in this fashion, and that score is used as the measure of expected return for January.

Using the monthly scores, portfolios are constructed to maximize alpha subject to a target 600 basis point tracking error relative to universe. The example we use here selects stock portfolios from the Russell 1000 universe, targeted to 100% per year turnover. Our portfolio construction apparatus lets us start the out-of-sample tests at the beginning of 1997.

The annualized excess return over Russell 1000 of the portfolios generated for almost 14 years was about 4% per year, with similar recent 10-year, 5-year, 3-year, and 1-year performances. Exhibit 15.8 summarizes the results of Alpha Repair portfolios' excess returns over Russell 1000.

Exhibit 15.9 shows the portfolio's cumulative outperformance. This highlights the consistency of the added value. The vertical line indicates

EXHIBIT 15.9   Outperformance of Alpha Repair Portfolio (as of August 31, 2010)

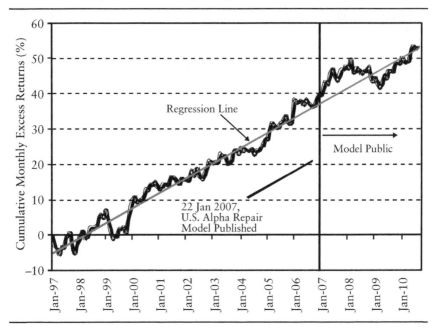

U.S. Alpha Repair model outperformed Russell 1000 by:
  4.8% in Jan.–Aug. 2010
  4.2% annually past 5 years
  4.1% annually past 10 years

Data sources: Nomura Securities International, Inc., Compustat, I/B/E/S, IDC, and Russell.

the time when Alpha Repair model was first published in January 2007.[3] Even though we separate the backtest and public portfolio periods, we have throughout implemented an out-of-sample strategy. Each month-end we select three factors using optimization to give us the best Sharpe ratio. A composite score is given to each stock in the universe (Russell 1000 in this case) and used to construct a long-only portfolio. The portfolio has an ex ante 6% tracking error. The targeted annual turnover is 100% per year. We then monitor the performance of the portfolio for the next month. The performance thus is always out of sample. As indicated by the regression line, throughout the whole time, the Alpha Repair strategy has outperformed the benchmark Russell 1000 in a consistently linear fashion.

---

[3]See Joseph J. Mezrich and Junbo Feng, "Alpha Repair," Nomura Securities International Inc., January 22, 2007.

EXHIBIT 15.10   Dynamic Nature of Factor Weighting Strategy

April 1, 2000		January 1, 2007	
Factor	Optimal Weights	Factor	Optimal Weights
R&D/Sales	24.9	Market cap (small – large)	35.5
Analyst coverage	25.2	EBITDA/EV	35.2
Share buybacks	49.9	Gross margin	29.3

Note: See Exhibit 15.1 for description of factors. Optimal weights are percent.
Data sources: Nomura Securities International, Inc., Compustat, I/B/E/S, IDC, and Russell.

Exhibit 15.10 exemplifies the dynamic nature of the factor weighting strategy. Note how the factors selected at April 2000 for the stocks, when the tech bubble was at its peak, differ from those selected at January 2007. The factors selected back in 2000 had roughly 25% in the "research spending divided by sales" (R&D/sales) and analyst coverage. These two factors performed extremely well in the tech bubble—but they were in a danger of falling over the cliff at the time. Yet the largest weight of share buybacks was almost 50%. In the next two years, until August 2002, share buybacks as a factor had returns of more than 140%. This set of strategies was well diversified to offset the effect of the tech bubble crash.

Still referring to Exhibit 15.10, the factors for January 2007 are entirely different from those selected for April 2000. The January 2007 set has roughly equal weights on a value factor EBITDA/EV (earnings before interest, taxes and depreciation divided enterprise value), a profitability factor "Gross margin" and a size factor "Market cap (Small – Large)." It is important to note that in the period 2001–2005, "Market cap (Small – Large)," EBITDA/EV, and gross margin ranked seventh, first, and thirty-second, respectively. Clearly, our strategy for factor selection is not based simply on what has worked lately. Even though this set of factors is totally different from April 2000, they are also well diversified.

KEY POINTS

- Failed factors are a frustrating reality of investing. The dilemma investors constantly face is determining when to discard a factor that seems to have lost efficacy, and when to embrace one that seems to have become important. The Alpha Repair strategy we have described focuses on this issue.

■ The goal is to provide a systematic framework that removes failed strategies from the playing field until they prove worthy, while providing an opportunity for new strategies to join the team.

■ The problem is framed as one of asset allocation for factors, with the important twist that a large set of factors always compete for a place in a small set of factors that are used for stock selection.

■ The criterion for making the team of selected factors in a given month depends on the history of factor return, volatility, and correlation with other factor returns. The size of the team of factors is kept small so that as similar factors compete for a spot, only the best ones survive the process.

■ The success of this factor competition criterion exploits the persistence of correlation to counter the lack of persistence in the return to investment strategies. The process is dynamic, yet it does not demand high turnover of stocks. This approach is an algorithm applied to a database of factor returns.

QUESTIONS

1. What is the motivation of using the Alpha Repair investment process?

2. What's the objective function used to select factors in the Alpha Repair strategy?

3. Why should a relatively small number of factors such as three factors be selected?

4. Does the more frequent change of factors selected in recent years mean higher stock turnovers?

5. Are stock portfolios simply a basket of the top ranked stocks?

CHAPTER 16

Avoiding Unintended Country Bets in Global Equity Portfolios*

Michele Aghassi, Ph.D., CFA
Vice President
AQR Capital Management

Cliff Asness, Ph.D.
Managing and Founding Principal
AQR Capital Management

Oktay Kurbanov
Principal
AQR Capital Management

Lars N. Nielsen
Principal
AQR Capital Management

The diversification benefit of investing internationally has led to a signifi-cant shift in assets from domestic to global portfolios over time. However, investing internationally involves taking on risks that are not present when investing domestically. For example, a U.S.-based investor investing in a Japanese car manufacturer not only gains exposure to that specific stock but also to the overall Japanese market. The academic literature has exten-sively analyzed the relative importance of stock-specific risk, sector risk, and country risk for global stocks. Specifically, it is well documented that

---

*We thank Michael Katz, John Liew, Lasse Pedersen, and Prasad Ramanan for help-ful comments. The views and opinions expressed herein are those of the authors and do not necessarily reflect the views of AQR Capital Management, LLC, its affiliates, or its employees.

country risk is an important driver of individual stock returns, especially in emerging markets.[1]

In contrast, the literature has devoted less attention to the impact of country membership on actively managed stock portfolios. For instance, it is an open question whether ignoring country membership can yield negative side effects in portfolio construction. We address this question by showing that failing to explicitly control for country membership can lead to significant misallocation of risk. In particular, country bets can dominate a portfolio that aims to represent skill in selecting individual stocks. Worse, the country bets can be completely unrelated to the underlying investment signals and can thereby potentially reduce risk-adjusted returns. While the issues we present are relevant for all global investors, we further show that they are markedly more pronounced in emerging markets compared to developed markets.

We begin by presenting empirical evidence on the importance of country membership in explaining stock returns. We then present several approaches to constructing active global stock portfolios. In particular, we compare an approach that ignores each stock's country to an approach that explicitly accounts for this information.

COUNTRY MEMBERSHIP AND INDIVIDUAL STOCK RETURNS

Let's start by examining the importance, in both developed and emerging markets, of country membership in determining a stock's return. In order to measure this importance, we run a series of cross-sectional regressions where the dependent variable is a stock's return in a given month and the explanatory variables are dummies for the country membership of that stock. We run these regressions each month from 1995 to 2009. A high regression R-squared means that country membership explained a lot of the cross-sectional variation in stock returns in that month. In the extreme, an R-squared

---

[1]See Jianguo Chen, Ting Zheng, and Andrea Bennett, "Sector Effects in Developed vs. Emerging Markets," *Financial Analysts Journal* 62, no. 6 (2006): 40–51; Steven L. Heston and K. Geert Rouwenhorst, "Industry and Country Effects in International Stock Returns," *Journal of Portfolio Management* 21, no. 3 (1995): 53–58; Kate Phylaktis and Lichuan Xia, "Sources of Firms' Industry and Country Effects in Emerging Markets," *Journal of International Money and Finance* 25, no. 3 (2006): 459–475; Ana Paula Serra, "Country and Industry Factors in Returns: Evidence from Emerging Markets' Stocks," *Emerging Markets Review* 1, no. 1 (2000): 127–151; Frank Nielsen, "Emerging Markets: A 2009 Update," MSCI Barra webinar, August 13, 2009; and MSCI Barra, "Country and Industry Effects in Global Equities," *MSCI Barra Research Bulletin*, October 2008, http://www.mscibarra.com/products/analytics/models/RB_Country_Global_Effects_Global_Equities.pdf.

EXHIBIT 16.1 Explanatory Power of Country Membership for Monthly Stock Returns, 1995–2009

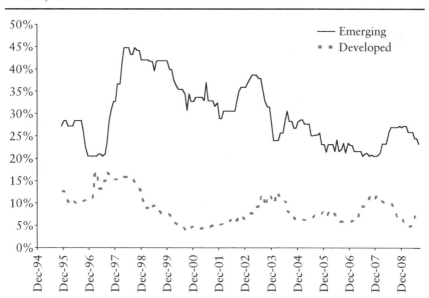

Note: One-year moving median *R*-squared from monthly regressions of stock returns on country dummies for emerging and developed markets.

of 100% indicates that every stock in a country had the same return (i.e., country membership fully determined returns in that month).

Exhibit 16.1 shows the rolling 12-month moving median *R*-squared from these regressions, run separately for developed and emerging markets. Country membership explained on average 11% of the cross-sectional variation of individual stock returns within developed markets. In emerging markets, the equivalent number was a remarkable 30%.[2] As shown in Exhibit 16.1, the importance of country membership in emerging markets has fluctuated dramatically over time, ranging from as little as 20% to as much as 45%. Although these numbers have generally trended downward over time, as recently as 2009, country membership still explained 24% of the cross-sectional variation of emerging markets stock returns.[3]

---

[2]As an interesting comparison, sector membership explained on average 13% of returns in developed markets but only 5% in emerging markets.

[3]All statistics cited in this paragraph, as well as the results shown in Exhibit 16.1, are based on AQR internal analysis, using Barra, MSCI, and XpressFeed data for stock returns and country and sector classifications.

These numbers demonstrate a striking difference between emerging and developed markets. But what does that mean for active investors?

WAYS TO BUILD ACTIVE GLOBAL PORTFOLIOS

In order to answer this question, we examine alternative approaches to constructing global stock portfolios. However, we first need an investment strategy as the context in which to compare these different methods. For robustness purposes, we will use two such canonical investment strategies, value and momentum. Value says that, all else equal, we like stocks that are cheap versus stocks that are expensive. Momentum says that, all else equal, we like stocks that have been doing well, that is, "improving," recently. To measure how cheap a stock is we look at its book-to-price ratio, and to measure momentum we look at a stock's prior one-year performance.[4] Given these indicators, we next construct three long-short portfolios at each point in time, using techniques detailed in the rest of this section.

Naive Stock Selection

Naive stock selection is our straw man, representing a pure stock picker looking for cheap stocks or stocks with good momentum, without any regard to country membership. This approach may perhaps be overly naive, but it allows us to quantify the negative side-effects of not adequately considering country membership when constructing global stock portfolios.

With that said, let's go on to the portfolio construction methodology for this investor. Without an additional adjustment, choosing stocks based on the above value and momentum measures may yield large sector bets (i.e., stock valuations and returns within the same sector tend to cluster). Since we want to focus this discussion on country bets, we neutralize overall sector

---

[4]We perform our analysis using emerging and developed markets large-cap universes and monthly data from 1995 to 2009. Financial statement data are from Worldscope, and market capitalization and returns are from Barra, MSCI, and XpressFeed. We calculate all quantities (book value, market capitalization, and 1-year returns) in units of USD, using currency exchange rate data provided by Factset. As is typical in the academic literature, when measuring one-year performance for the momentum strategy, we exclude the most recent month. See, for example, Cliff S. Asness, Tobias J. Moskowitz, and Lasse H. Pedersen, "Value and Momentum Everywhere," working paper, AQR Capital Management, 2008. This exclusion allows us to avoid the effect of short-term price reversions that often occur after large price moves. To control for outliers, we Winsorize the stock data, at each month in the sample, to the 1st and 99th percentiles.

bets by adjusting our signals.[5] Specifically, at each month t, we run the following cross-sectional regressions across all stocks j:

$$B/P(j,t) = \sum_{i \in \text{Industry}} a(i,t)D(j,i) + e(j,t)$$

$$Mom(j,t) = \sum_{i \in \text{Industry}} b(i,t)D(j,i) + u(j,t)$$

In the first regression, the dependent variable is stock j's book-to-price ratio at time t, $B/P(j,t)$, and the explanatory variables are dummies for sector membership ($D(j,i) = 1$ if stock j is in sector i). The resulting residuals, $e(j,t)$, from this regression are the stocks' sector-adjusted book-to-price ratios. We run the same regression for our momentum signals, $Mom(j,t)$, in order to compute each stock's sector-adjusted momentum, $u(j,t)$.

Because these adjusted signals have zero net exposure to each sector, they also have zero net market exposure. We form constant volatility, long-short portfolios by scaling the sector-adjusted signals to target 7% annualized volatility, using BARRA's estimate of the covariance matrix at time t.[6] This scaling yields portfolio weights which we denote by $W_{naive}(j,t)$. Note that the choice of 7% is arbitrary, but we want to scale all of the candidate portfolios to the same level of ex ante risk to ensure comparability.

By construction, the resulting portfolios will take long and short positions in stocks around the world. For the purposes of interpretation, in the context of a traditional global portfolio, one can think of these long and short positions as overweight and underweight positions in stocks versus a benchmark. Obviously, we are ignoring any investment constraints such as no net short-selling restrictions.

Country-Neutral Stock Selection

Country-neutral stock selection represents an approach to picking stocks that is neutral to both sector and country exposures. We believe that this approach is the cleanest way to construct a global portfolio that seeks to add value from only security selection, and not from sector or country selection.

In order to construct country- and sector-neutral signals for value and momentum, we run the following cross-sectional regressions at each time t, across all stocks j:

$$B/P(j,t) = \sum_{i \in \text{Industry}} a(i,t)D(j,i) + \sum_{K \in \text{Country}} a(K,t)D(j,K) + v(j,t)$$

$$Mom(j,t) = \sum_{i \in \text{Industry}} b(i,t)D(j,i) + \sum_{K \in \text{Country}} b(K,t)D(j,K) + w(j,t)$$

---

[5]We use GIC sectors, based on data from MSCI and XpressFeed.
[6]We use BARRA's GEM risk model.

As with the regressions in the naive stock selection strategy, we run cross-sectional regressions of B/P and Mom on dummies for sectors, but here, we further add dummy variables for countries ($D(j,K) = 1$ if stock j is in country K).[7] The resulting residuals $v(j,t)$ and $w(j,t)$ from these regressions are stock j's sector- and country-adjusted book-to-price and momentum signals, respectively, at time t. By construction, each set of residuals will sum to zero across all stocks. To obtain long-short portfolio weights, $W_{\text{country-neutral}}(j,t)$, we scale the portfolios resulting from each set of residuals—one for value and one for momentum—to 7% annualized volatility using BARRA's estimate of the covariance matrix at time t.

Country Selection

Finally, we introduce a country selection portfolio as a tool to analyze the composition of country bets that arise under the naive stock selection approach. Country selection is different from the above stock selection strategies, in that it evaluates and takes positions in countries using baskets of stocks within each country. We use equal-weighted stock baskets, and thus, within each country, every stock will have the same weight.

For country K, the signals are

$$\overline{B/P}(K,t) = \sum_{j \in \text{Country}K} \frac{B/P(j,t)}{n(K)}$$

$$\overline{Mom}(K,t) = \sum_{j \in \text{Country}K} \frac{Mom(j,t)}{n(K)}$$

where $\overline{B/P}(K,t)$ represents the average book-to-price ratio at time t over all stocks j in country K, $\overline{Mom}(K,t)$ represents the average momentum at time t over all stocks j in country K, and $n(K)$ represents the number of stocks in country K. We do not sector adjust these country selection signals. The reason is that a positive or negative bet on a country necessarily translates to the same bet on that country's underlying sectors. To the extent that sector composition differs by country, these implicit sector bets may not net out to zero overall.

From each set of country averages—one for value and one for momentum—we form a set of standardized country scores by computing cross-sectional z-scores. We then divide each country's Z-score by the number of stocks within that country and assign the resulting number to each stock in that country. To transform these stock scores into a set of portfolio weights, $W_{\text{country}}(j,t)$, we scale the stock scores to target 7% annualized volatility

---

[7]To avoid multicollinearity, we omit one dummy variable corresponding to the sector, or country, having the smallest number of stocks.

using BARRA's estimate of the covariance matrix at time t. By construction, each stock j within a country K always has the same weight in the resulting portfolio.

We argue that the cleanest way to bet on both stocks and countries is to combine the country-neutral stock selection and country selection portfolios that we present above. This approach enables precise risk allocation between stock bets and country bets. In contrast, we demonstrate that the naive stock selection approach prevents clean risk allocation, and worse, may yield unintended but significant country exposures.

STUDYING THE NAIVE PORTFOLIO

We next examine what kinds of country bets result from the naive stock selection strategy. Specifically, we measure the extent to which the resulting country exposures are consistent (i.e., line up) with the country selection portfolio. We obtain these measures by decomposing the portfolio's holdings into three components: country selection, country noise, and pure stock selection.

For each of the two investment strategies, value, and momentum, we perform the decomposition by a two-stage regression. In the first stage, at each month t, we run a cross-sectional regression of the stock selection portfolio's holdings on the holdings of the country selection portfolio, across all stocks j:

$$W_{naive}(j,t) = b_{naive}(t) W_{country}(j,t) + e_{naive}(j,t)$$

The intercepts are all zero since the weights are constructed to sum to zero. In this regression, $b_{naive}(t)$ measures the degree to which the portfolio makes country bets that are correlated with those of the country selection portfolio.

The residuals, $e_{naive}(j,t)$, represent the positions in the portfolio that are not correlated with the country selection portfolio. If we assume that the country selection portfolio represents the bets that are most consistent with the investment approach (i.e., choosing country baskets based on value and momentum), then any other country bets may be regarded as "unintended."

The second step of the decomposition isolates these unintended country bets by running cross-sectional regressions of these residuals on country dummies at each month t, across all stocks j:

$$e_{naive}(j,t) = \sum_{K \in \text{Country}} c_{naive}(K,t)D(j,K) + u_{naive}(j,t)$$

The loadings $c_{\text{naive}}(K,t)$ represent country bets that the portfolio is making at time t and that are uncorrelated with the bets in the country selection strategy. These are what we consider unintended country bets or "country noise."

By plugging the second regression back into the first, we get our decomposition of the portfolio weights into the three components of (1) country selection, (2) country noise, and (3) pure stock selection.

$$W_{\text{naive}}(j,t) = \underbrace{b_{\text{naive}}(t)W_{\text{country}}(j,t)}_{\substack{\text{Country} \\ \text{selection}}} + \underbrace{\sum_{K \in \text{Country}} c_{\text{naive}}(K,t)D(j,K)}_{\substack{\text{Country} \\ \text{noise}}} + \underbrace{u_{\text{naive}}(j,t)}_{\substack{\text{Pure stock} \\ \text{selection}}}$$

The country selection component captures the country exposures consistent with the country selection portfolio's views. The country noise component captures any country bets that are inconsistent with the country selection portfolio. Finally, the pure stock selection component captures the stock-specific bets that are unrelated to and unexplainable by country exposures.

One could perform this decomposition for any portfolio. However, in the absence of country bets, as in the case of the country-neutral stock selection portfolio, the country selection and country noise components in the decomposition will be zero.

EMPIRICAL RESULTS

In Exhibit 16.2, we quantify how much each of the three components—country selection, country noise, and pure stock selection—explains the stock portfolio's holdings. To do this, we rewrite the above decomposition as a weighted average of "equal" parts, given by the components scaled to a constant level of expected risk, using BARRA's estimate of the covariance matrix. The weights in this weighted average indicate the relative importance of the components in the composition of the stock selection portfolio's cross-section of holdings. Any portfolio can be decomposed in this way, and the weights in the decomposition indicate the extent to which each of the components explains the portfolio's positions. The numbers in this exhibit show median values of the component weights over time.

Before we discuss the implications of the results shown in Exhibit 16.2, let us give an intuitive interpretation of these numbers. Consider, for example, the case of the naive stock portfolio based on value in emerging markets. This portfolio's stock weights are 41% explained by a country selection component, 25% explained by a country noise component, and only 34% explained by a pure stock selection component. This breakdown means that investing $100 in this naive stock selection portfolio is equivalent to allocating

EXHIBIT 16.2 Weights of Underlying Components in Stock Selection Portfolios

	Emerging		Developed	
	Country-Neutral Stock Selection	Naive Stock Selection	Country-Neutral Stock Selection	Naive Stock Selection
Value				
Country selection	0%	41%	0%	15%
Country noise	0%	25%	0%	33%
Pure stock selection	100%	34%	100%	52%
Momentum				
Country selection	0%	37%	0%	11%
Country noise	0%	25%	0%	21%
Pure stock selection	100%	36%	100%	67%

Note: Statistics from the decomposition of the naive and country-neutral stock selection portfolios into country selection, country noise, and pure stock selection components. The numbers shown indicate the weight of each component in the stock selection portfolio.

$41 to a country selection manager, $25 to a country noise "manager," and only $34 to a pure stock selection manager.[8] Note that, by construction, all country-neutral stock selection portfolios are 100% explained by pure stock selection, since they make no country bets of any kind.

The results in Exhibit 16.2 are striking. It is clear that, in both emerging and developed markets, the naive stock selection portfolio makes significant country bets. For example, for value in developed markets, only 52% of the portfolio composition is driven by pure stock bets, while the corresponding emerging markets number is a remarkably low 34%. The analogous emerging versus developed markets comparison for momentum is as extreme. In developed markets, 67% of the portfolio composition is explained by pure stock bets, while the corresponding emerging markets number is only 36%.

For the naive stock selection strategy, both the country selection and country noise exposures are problematic. The loading on country selection, while potentially a source of alpha, represents a possible deviation from the targeted risk allocation and an obstacle for transparent and accurate risk allocation in general. The loading on country noise is worse, in the following sense. While it is reasonable for an investor to allocate risk to both stock selection and country selection, it is neither intuitive nor optimal to make

---

[8]We view each manager in this interpretation as targeting the same level of expected risk.

country bets unless they are supported by the underlying investment signals. Since the country selection portfolio is designed to fully capture country selection alpha, we may regard any residual country bets as having zero expected alpha, hence our use of the term "noise."

In this way, another striking result in Exhibit 16.2 is that a very substantial portion of the naive stock selection portfolio is coming from country noise bets, which represent a pure opportunity cost. For instance, in the developed markets value portfolio, 33% of the stock portfolio's stock weights are composed of country bets that cannot be explained by country selection decisions. Remarkably, the noise component is significant in both developed and emerging markets. These results indicate that letting country bets "fall out" from the underlying stock positions introduces exposures not associated with alpha.

WHY DOES THE NAIVE STOCK SELECTION PORTFOLIO MAKE COUNTRY NOISE BETS?

Having explained how to detect and measure the extent of country noise bets, let us now explain how and why they arise in the naive stock selection portfolio. Both naive stock selection and country-neutral stock selection are intended to compare stocks, while country selection is intended to compare countries. Any comparison is naturally relative to some notion of what is typical within the sample of reference. Crucially, what is typical for a stock is not necessarily the same as what is typical for a country. Naive stock selection falls into the trap of not recognizing this distinction and therefore makes accidental, i.e., noisy, country bets. The primary reason for the difference in what is typical is simply that various countries are not equally represented in the cross-section of stocks. Countries that are over-represented in the cross-section of stocks will dominate a country-agnostic stock average.

This inconsistency in the definition of "typical" is what yields country noise. Let us present a simple example to make these issues more concrete. Consider a hypothetical global market of 90 U.S. stocks, five U.K. stocks, and five Japanese stocks, with book-to-price ratios randomly distributed around a mean of 0.50 for the United States, 0.75 for the United Kingdom, and 1.00 for Japan, respectively. The average country score, taken over the cross-section of countries, is 0.75 (= $1/3 \times 0.50 + 1/3 \times 0.75 + 1/3 \times 1.00$). In contrast, the average stock score, taken over the cross-section of stocks, is 0.54 (= $(90 \times 0.50 + 5 \times 0.75 + 5 \times 1.00)/100$). By design, the average in the space of countries treats the three countries equally, whereas the average over the cross-section of stocks treats the 100 stocks equally. Because there are more U.S. stocks, the stock-based average places greater importance on the United States when determining the typical value for a stock.

The difference in these averages drives the misalignment of resulting country bets in the country selection and naive stock selection portfolios. Continuing our example, country selection makes relative comparisons versus the average of 0.75. Accordingly, the country selection portfolio will deem the United Kingdom to be average and will take a neutral active weight in the United Kingdom. In contrast, naive stock selection makes comparisons versus the average of 0.54. As a result, at the country level, the naive stock selection portfolio will consider the United Kingdom stocks to be cheaper than average and will overweight this country. Consequently, the resulting country bets in the two portfolios will be misaligned.

As our choice of the label "naive" indicates, one can do a lot better than the country-agnostic stock selection approach. However, as our discussion in this section illustrates, to fix this weakness inherently requires a country-aware methodology, such as, a country-neutral portfolio construction framework. In other words, it is impossible to avoid country noise in a stock selection process that ignores country membership.[9]

KEY POINTS

- The academic literature has focused on the explanatory power of country membership with respect to the cross-section of individual stock returns. The literature has devoted less attention to the impact in an active portfolio management context.
- Understanding unintended bets that can arise when ignoring country membership in stock portfolio construction is important for active investors.
- In any active management strategy, accurate risk allocation is crucial. In particular, not allocating risk to unintended bets is first order. We demonstrate that avoiding unintended country exposures in stock portfolios requires careful portfolio construction.
- These issues arise in any global stock investment context, but are especially challenging in emerging markets. In emerging markets, lack of country neutralization can yield stock selection portfolios as little as one-third attributable to stock-specific bets and as much as two-thirds driven by country exposures. In developed markets, that decomposition can be as off-target as half stock bets and half country bets.

---

[9]Importantly, this conclusion holds regardless of how the country selection portfolios are expressed through stocks (i.e., regardless of the weighting scheme used to distribute country bets to the underlying stocks).

- Importantly, in both regions, a significant portion of the resulting country exposures may represent "noise" (i.e., bets that bear no relation to the underlying investment idea and that are thus a zero-alpha, pure opportunity cost).
- By properly adjusting stock selection portfolios for country membership, a manager can achieve accurate risk allocation and can prevent "noise pollution" of alpha signals. As a practical matter, this means separating the security selection decision from the country selection decision.
- While this can be done naturally within a quantitative investment process, it can also be done conceptually in a qualitative investment process by evaluating the relative attractiveness of stocks within a country and then separately evaluating the country as a whole.

QUESTIONS

1. When constructing stock portfolios, what negative side effects can result from ignoring country membership?

2. What are the two types of country bets that may arise in stock portfolios and what are the drawbacks of each?

3. Why do "country noise" bets arise and why is it impossible to avoid them without directly considering country membership?

4. How do these issues differ between developed and emerging markets?

5. What approach do we recommend for avoiding unintended country bets in stock portfolios?

CHAPTER 17

Modeling Market Impact Costs

Petter N. Kolm, Ph.D.
Director of the Mathematics in Finance Masters Program
and Clinical Associate Professor
Courant Institute of Mathematical Sciences, New York University

Frank J. Fabozzi, Ph.D., CFA, CPA
Professor of Finance
EDHEC Business School

Trading is an integral component of the equity investment process. A poorly executed trade can eat directly into portfolio returns. This is because equity markets are not frictionless and transactions have a cost associated to them. Costs are incurred when buying or selling stocks in the form of, for example, brokerage commissions, bid-ask spreads, taxes, and market impact costs.

In recent years, portfolio managers have started to more carefully consider transaction costs. The literature on market microstructure, analysis and measurement of transaction costs, and market impact costs on institutional trades is rapidly expanding.[1] One way of describing transaction costs is to categorize them in terms of *explicit costs* such as brokerage and taxes, and implicit costs, which include market impact costs, price movement risk, and opportunity cost. *Market impact cost* is, broadly speaking, the price an investor has to pay for obtaining liquidity in the market, whereas *price movement risk* is the risk that the price of an asset increases or decreases from the time the investor decides to transact in the asset until the transaction

---

[1] See, for example, Ian Domowitz, Jack Glen, and Ananth Madhavan, "Liquidity, Volatility, and Equity Trading Costs Across Countries and Over Time," *International Finance* 4, no. 2 (2001): 221–255; and Donald B. Keim and Ananth Madhavan, "The Costs of Institutional Equity Trades," *Financial Analysts Journal* 54, no. 4 (1998): 50–69.

actually takes place. *Opportunity cost* is the cost suffered when a trade is not executed. Another way of seeing transaction costs is in terms of *fixed costs* versus *variable costs*. Whereas commissions and trading fees are fixed—bid-ask spreads, taxes, and all implicit transaction costs are variable.

Portfolio managers and traders need to be able to effectively model the impact of trading costs on their portfolios and trades. In this chapter, we introduce several approaches for the modeling of transaction costs, in particular market impact costs.

MARKET IMPACT COSTS

The *market impact cost* of a transaction is the deviation of the transaction price from the market (mid) price[2] that would have prevailed had the trade not occurred. The price movement is the cost, the market impact cost, for liquidity. Market impact of a trade can be negative if, for example, a trader buys at a price below the no-trade price (i.e., the price that would have prevailed had the trade not taken place). In general, liquidity providers experience negative costs while liquidity demanders will face positive costs.

We distinguish between two different kinds of market impact costs, temporary and permanent. Total market impact cost is computed as the sum of the two. The temporary market impact cost is of transitory nature and can be seen as the additional *liquidity concession* necessary for the liquidity provider (e.g., the market maker) to take the order, *inventory effects* (price effects due to broker/dealer inventory imbalances), or *imperfect substitution* (for example, price incentives to induce market participants to absorb the additional shares).

The permanent market impact cost, however, reflects the persistent price change that results as the market adjusts to the information content of the trade. Intuitively, a sell transaction reveals to the market that the security may be overvalued, whereas a buy transaction signals that the security may be undervalued. Security prices change when market participants adjust their views and perceptions as they observe news and the information contained in new trades during the trading day.

Traders can decrease the temporary market impact by extending the trading horizon of an order. For example, a trader executing a less urgent order can buy or sell his position in smaller portions over a period and make sure that each portion only constitutes a small percentage of the average volume. However, this comes at the price of increased opportunity costs, delay costs, and price movement risk.

---

[2]Since the buyer buys at the ask and the seller sells at the bid, this definition of market impact cost ignores the bid–ask spread which is an explicit cost.

Market impact costs are often *asymmetric*; that is, they are different for buy and sell orders. Several empirical studies suggest that market impact costs are generally higher for buy orders. Nevertheless, while buying costs might be higher than selling costs, this empirical fact is most likely due to observations during rising/falling markets, rather than any *true* market microstructure effects. For example, a study by Hu shows that the difference in market impact costs between buys and sells is an artifact of the trade benchmark.[3] (We discuss trade benchmarks later in this chapter.) When a pre-trade measure is used, buys (sells) have higher implicit trading costs during rising (falling) markets. Conversely, if a post-trade measure is used, sells (buys) have higher implicit trading costs during rising (falling) markets. In fact, both pre-trade and post-trade measures are highly influenced by market movement, whereas during- or average-trade measures are neutral to market movement.

Despite the enormous global size of equity markets, the impact of trading is important even for relatively small funds. In fact, a sizable fraction of the stocks that compose an index might have to be excluded or their trading severely limited. For example, RAS Asset Management, which is the asset manager arm of the large Italian insurance company RAS, has determined that single trades exceeding 10% of the daily trading volume of a stock cause an excessive market impact and have to be excluded, while trades between 5% and 10% need execution strategies distributed over several days.[4] According to RAS Asset Management estimates, in practice funds managed actively with quantitative techniques and with market capitalization in excess of €100 million can operate only on the fraction of the market above the €5 million, splitting trades over several days for stocks with average daily trading volume in the range from €5 million to €10 million. They can freely operate only on two-thirds of the stocks in the MSCI Europe.

LIQUIDITY AND TRANSACTION COSTS

Liquidity is created by agents transacting in the financial markets when they buy and sell securities. Market makers and brokers–dealers do not create liquidity; they are intermediaries who facilitate trade execution and maintain an orderly market.

Liquidity and transaction costs are interrelated. A highly liquid market is one were large transactions can be immediately executed without incurring high transaction costs. In an indefinitely liquid market, traders would

---

[3]Gang Hu, "Measures of Implicit Trading Costs and Buy-Sell Asymmetry," *Journal of Financial Markets* 12, no. 3 (2009): 418–437.
[4]Private communication RAS Asset Management.

be able to perform very large transactions directly at the quoted bid-ask prices. In reality, particularly for larger orders, the market requires traders to pay more than the ask when buying, and to receive less than the bid when selling. As we discussed previously, this percentage degradation of the bid-ask prices experienced when executing trades is the market impact cost.

The market impact cost varies with transaction size: the larger the trade size the larger the impact cost. Impact costs are not constant in time, but vary throughout the day as traders change the limit orders that they have in the limit order book. A *limit order* is a conditional order; it is executed only if the limit price or a better price can be obtained. For example, a buy limit order of a security XYZ at $60 indicates that the assets may be purchased only at $60 or lower. Therefore, a limit order is very different from a *market order*, which is an unconditional order to execute at the current best price available in the market (guarantees execution, not price). With a limit order, a trader can improve the execution price relative to the market order price, but the execution is neither certain nor immediate (guarantees price, not execution).

Notably, there are many different limit order types available such as pegging orders, discretionary limit orders, immediate or cancel order (IOC) orders, and fleeting orders. For example, fleeting orders are those limit orders that are canceled within two seconds of submission. Hasbrouck and Saar find that fleeting limit orders are much closer substitutes for market orders than for traditional limit orders.[5] This suggests that the role of limit orders has changed from the traditional view of being liquidity suppliers to being substitutes for market orders.

At any given instant, the list of orders sitting in the limit order book embodies the liquidity that exists at a particular point in time. By observing the entire limit order book, impact costs can be calculated for different transaction sizes. The limit order book reveals the prevailing supply and demand in the market.[6] Therefore, in a pure limit order market, we can obtain a measure of liquidity by aggregating limit buy orders (representing the demand) and limit sell orders (representing the supply).[7]

---

[5]Joel Hasbrouck and Gideon Saar, "Technology and Liquidity Provision: The Blurring of Traditional Definitions," *Journal of Financial Markets* 12, no. 2 (2008): 143–172.

[6]Note that even if it is possible to view the entire limit order book it does not give a *complete* picture of the liquidity in the market. This is because hidden and discretionary orders are not included. For a discussion on this topic, see Laura A. Tuttle, "Hidden Orders, Trading Costs and Information," working paper, Ohio State University, 2002.

[7]Ian Domowitz and Xiaoxin Wang, "Liquidity, Liquidity Commonality and Its Impact on Portfolio Theory," working paper, Smeal College of Business Administration, Pennsylvania State University, 2002; Thierry Foucault, Ohad Kadan, and

EXHIBIT 17.1   The Supply and Demand Schedule of a Security

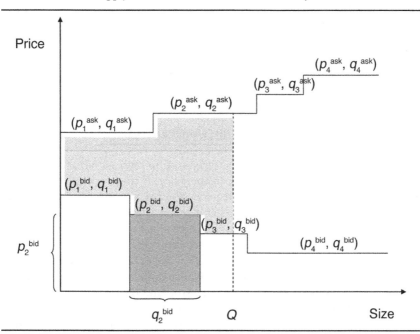

Source: Figure 1A in Ian Domowitz and Xiaoxin Wang, "Liquidity, Liquidity Commonality and Its Impact on Portfolio Theory," working paper, Smeal College of Business Administration, Pennsylvania State University, 2002, p. 38.

We start by sorting the bid and ask prices, $p_1^{bid},...,p_k^{bid}$ and $p_1^{ask},...,p_l^{ask}$, (from the most to the least competitive) and the corresponding order quantities $q_1^{bid},...,q_k^{bid}$ and $q_1^{ask},...,q_l^{ask}$. We then combine the sorted bid and ask prices into a supply and demand schedule according to Exhibit 17.1. For example, the block (p_2^{bid}, q_2^{bid}) represents the second best sell limit order with price p_2^{bid} and quantity q_2^{bid}.

We note that unless there is a gap between the bid (demand) and the ask (supply) sides, there will be a match between a seller and buyer, and a trade would occur. The larger the gap, the lower the liquidity and the market participants' desire to trade. For a trade of size Q, we can define its *liquidity* as the reciprocal of the area between the supply and demand curves up to Q (i.e., the "dotted" area in Exhibit 17.1).

However, few order books are publicly available and not all markets are pure limit order markets. In 2004, the New York Stock Exchange (NYSE)

Eugene Kandel, "Limit Order Book As a Market for Liquidity," *Review of Financial Studies* 18, no. 4 (2005): 1171–1217.

started selling information on its limit order book through its new system called the *NYSE OpenBook®*. The system provides an aggregated real-time view of the exchange's limit-order book for all NYSE-traded securities.[8]

In the absence of a fully transparent limit order book, expected market impact cost is the most practical and realistic measure of market liquidity. It is closer to the true cost of transacting faced by market participants as compared to other measures such as those based upon the bid-ask spread.

MARKET IMPACT MEASUREMENTS AND EMPIRICAL FINDINGS

The problem with measuring implicit transaction costs is that the true measure, which is the difference between the price of the stock in the absence of a money manager's trade and the execution price, is not observable. Furthermore, the execution price is dependent on supply and demand conditions at the margin. Thus, the execution price may be influenced by competitive traders who demand immediate execution or by other investors with similar motives for trading. This means that the execution price realized by an investor is the consequence of the structure of the market mechanism, the demand for liquidity by the marginal investor, and the competitive forces of investors with similar motivations for trading.

There are many ways to measure transaction costs. However, in general this cost is the difference between the execution price and some appropriate benchmark, a so-called *fair market benchmark*. The fair market benchmark of a security is the price that would have prevailed had the trade not taken place, the *no-trade price*. Since the no-trade price is not observable, it has to be estimated. Practitioners have identified three different basic approaches to measure the market impact:[9]

1. *Pre-trade measures* use prices occurring before or at the decision to trade as the benchmark, such as the opening price on the same-day or the closing price on the previous day.
2. *Post-trade measures* use prices occurring after the decision to trade as the benchmark, such as the closing price of the trading day or the opening price on the next day.

---

[8]NYSE and Securities Industry Automation Corporation, *NYSE OpenBook®*, Version 1.1 (New York: 2004).
[9]Bruce M. Collins and Frank J. Fabozzi, "A Methodology for Measuring Transaction Costs," *Financial Analysts Journal* 47, no. 2 (1991): 27–36; Louis K. C. Chan and Joseph Lakonishok, "Institutional Trades and Intraday Stock Price Behavior," *Journal of Financial Economics* 33, no. 2 (1993): 173–199; and Fabozzi and Grant, *Equity Portfolio Management*.

3. *Same-day* or *average measures* use average prices of a large number of trades during the day of the decision to trade, such as the *volume-weighted average price* (VWAP) calculated over all transactions in the security on the trade day.[10]

The volume-weighted average price is calculated as follows. Suppose that it was a trader's objective to purchase 10,000 shares of stock XYZ. After completion of the trade, the trade sheet showed that 4,000 shares were purchased at $80, another 4,000 at $81, and finally 2,000 at $82. In this case, the resulting VWAP is (4,000 × 80 + 4,000 × 81 + 2,000 × 82)/10,000 = $80.80.

We denote by χ the indicator function that takes on the value 1 or –1 if an order is a buy or sell order, respectively. Formally, we now express the three types of measures of *market impact* (*MI*) as follows

$$MI_{\text{pre}} = \left(\frac{p^{\text{ex}}}{p^{\text{pre}}} - 1 \right) \chi$$

$$MI_{\text{post}} = \left(\frac{p^{\text{ex}}}{p^{\text{post}}} - 1 \right) \chi$$

$$MI_{\text{VWAP}} = \left(\frac{\sum_{i=1}^{k} V_i \, p_i^{\text{ex}}}{\sum_{i=1}^{k} V_i} \Big/ p^{\text{pre}} - 1 \right) \chi$$

where p^{ex}, p^{pre}, and p^{post} denote the execution price, pre-trade price, and post-trade price of the stock, and k denotes the number of transactions in a particular security on the trade date. Using this definition, for a stock with market impact *MI* the resulting *market impact cost* for a trade of size *V*, *MIC*, is given by

$$MIC = MI \cdot V$$

It is also common to adjust market impact for general market movements. For example, the pre-trade market impact with market adjustment would take the form

$$MI_{\text{pre}} = \left(\frac{p^{\text{ex}}}{p^{\text{pre}}} - \frac{p_M^{\text{ex}}}{p_M^{\text{pre}}} \right) \chi$$

---

[10]Strictly speaking, VWAP is not the benchmark here but rather the transaction type.

where p_M^{ex} represent the value of the index at the time of the execution, and p_M^{pre} the price of the index at the time before the trade. Market adjusted market impact for the post-trade and same-day trade benchmarks are calculated in an analogous fashion.

The above three approaches to measure market impact are based upon measuring the fair market benchmark of stock at a point in time. Clearly, different definitions of market impact lead to different results. Which one should be used is a matter of preference and is dependent on the application at hand. For example, Elkins and McSherry, a financial consulting firm that provides customized trading costs and execution analysis, calculates a same-day benchmark price for each stock by taking the mean of the day's open, close, high, and low prices. The market impact is then computed as the percentage difference between the transaction price and this benchmark. However, in most cases VWAP and the Elkins McSherry approach lead to similar measurements.[11]

As we analyze a portfolio's return over time an important question to ask is whether we can attribute good/bad performance to investment profits/losses or to trading profits/losses. In other words, in order to better understand a portfolio's performance it can be useful to decompose investment decisions from order execution. This is the basic idea behind the *implementation shortfall approach*.[12]

In the implementation shortfall approach, we assume that there is a separation between investment and trading decisions. The portfolio manager makes decisions with respect to the investment strategy (i.e., what should be bought, sold, and held). Subsequently, these decisions are implemented by the traders.

By comparing the actual portfolio profit/loss (P/L) with the performance of a hypothetical *paper* portfolio in which all trades are made at hypothetical market prices, we can get an estimate of the implementation shortfall. For example, with a paper portfolio return of 6% and an actual portfolio return of 5%, the implementation shortfall is 1%.

There is considerable practical and academic interest in the measurement and analysis of international trading costs. Domowitz, Glen, and Madhavan[13] examine international equity trading costs across a broad sample of 42 countries using quarterly data from 1995 to 1998. They find that

[11]John Willoughby, "Executions Song," *Institutional Investor* 32, no. 11 (1998): 51–56; and Richard McSherry, "Global Trading Cost Analysis," mimeo, Elkins McSherry Co., Inc., 1998.

[12]André F. Perold, "The Implementation Shortfall: Paper versus Reality," *Journal of Portfolio Management* 14, no. 3 (1998): 4–9.

[13]Ian Domowitz, Jack Glen, and Ananth Madhavan, "International Equity Trading Costs: A Cross-Sectional and Time-Series Analysis," technical report, Pennsylvania

the mean total one-way trading cost is 69.81 basis points. However, there is an enormous variation in trading costs across countries. For example, in their study the highest was Korea with 196.85 basis points whereas the lowest was France with 29.85 basis points. Explicit costs are roughly two-thirds of total costs. However, one exception to this is the United States where the implicit costs are about 60% of the total costs.

Transaction costs in emerging markets are significantly higher than those in more developed markets. Domowitz, Glen, and Madhavan argue that this fact limits the gains of international diversification in these countries explaining in part the documented *home bias* of domestic investors.

In general, they find that transaction costs declined from the middle of 1997 to the end of 1998, with the exception of Eastern Europe. It is interesting to notice that this reduction in transaction costs happened despite the turmoil in the financial markets during this period. A few explanations that Domowitz et al. suggest are that (1) the increased institutional presence has resulted in a more competitive environment for brokers/dealers and other trading services; (2) technological innovation has led to a growth in the use of low-cost electronic crossing networks (ECNs) by institutional traders; and (3) soft dollar payments are now more common.

FORECASTING AND MODELING MARKET IMPACT

In this section, we describe a general methodology for constructing forecasting models for market impact. These types of models are very useful in predicting the resulting trading costs of specific trading strategies and in devising optimal trading approaches.

Explicit transaction costs are relatively straightforward to estimate and forecast. Therefore, our focus in this section is to develop a methodology for the implicit transaction costs, and more specifically, market impact costs. The methodology is a linear factor–based approach where market impact is the dependent variable. We distinguish between *trade-based* and *asset-based independent variables* or *forecasting factors*.

Trade-Based Factors

Some examples of trade-based factors include:

- Trade size
- Relative trade size

State University, International Finance Corp., University of Southern California, 1999.

- Price of market liquidity
- Type of trade (information or informationless trade)
- Efficiency and trading style of the investor
- Specific characteristics of the market or the exchange
- Time of trade submission and trade timing
- Order type

Probably the most important market impact forecasting variables are based on absolute or relative trade size. Absolute trade size is often measured in terms of the number of shares traded, or the dollar value of the trade. Relative trade size, on the other hand, can be calculated as number of shares traded divided by average daily volume, or number of shares traded divided by the total number of shares outstanding. Note that the former can be seen as an explanatory variable for the temporary market impact and the latter for the permanent market impact. In particular, we expect the temporary market impact to increase as the trade size to the average daily volume increases because a larger trade demands more liquidity.

Each type of investment style requires a different need for immediacy.[14] Technical trades often have to be traded at a faster pace in order to capitalize on some short-term signal and therefore exhibits higher market impact costs. In contrast, more traditional long-term value strategies can be traded more slowly. These types of strategies can in many cases even be liquidity providing, which might result in negative market impact costs.

Several studies show that there is a wide variation in equity transaction costs across different countries.[15] Markets and exchanges in each country are different, and so are the resulting market microstructures. Forecasting variables can be used to capture specific market characteristics such as liquidity, efficiency, and institutional features.

The particular timing of a trade can affect the market impact costs. For example, it appears that market impact costs are generally higher at the beginning of the month as compared to the end of it.[16] One of the reasons for this phenomenon is that many institutional investors tend to rebalance

---

[14]Donald B. Keim and Ananth Madhavan, "Transaction Costs and Investment Style: An Inter-Exchange Analysis of Institutional Equity Trades," *Journal of Financial Economics* 46, no. 3 (1997): 265–292.

[15]See Domowitz, Glen, and Madhavan, "Liquidity, Volatility, and Equity Trading Costs Across Countries and Over Time"; and Chiraphol N. Chiyachantana, Pankaj K. Jain, Christine Jiang, and Robert A. Wood, "International Evidence on Institutional Trading Behavior and Price Impact," *Journal of Finance* 59, no. 2 (2004): 869–895.

[16]F. Douglas Foster and S. Viswanathan, "A Theory of the Interday Variations in Volume, Variance, and Trading Costs in Securities Markets," *Review of Financial Studies* 3, no. 4 (1990): 593–624.

their portfolios at the beginning of the month. Because it is likely that many of these trades will be executed in the same stocks, this rebalancing pattern will induce an increase in market impact costs. The particular time of the day a trade takes place does also have an effect. Many informed institutional traders tend to trade at the market open as they want to capitalize on new information that appeared after the market close the day before.

As we discussed earlier in this chapter, market impact costs are asymmetric. In other words, buy and sell orders have significantly different market impact costs. Separate models for buy and sell orders can therefore be estimated. However, it is now more common to construct a model that includes dummy variables for different types of orders such as buy/sell orders, market orders, limit orders, and the like.

Asset-Based Factors

Some examples of asset-based factors are:

- Price momentum
- Price volatility
- Market capitalization
- Growth versus value
- Specific industry or sector characteristics

For a stock that is exhibiting positive price momentum, a buy order is liquidity demanding and it is, therefore, likely that it will have higher market impact cost than a sell order.

Generally, trades in high volatility stocks result in higher permanent price effects. It has been suggested by Chan and Lakonishok[17] and Smith et al.[18] that this is because trades have a tendency to contain more information when volatility is high. Another possibility is that higher volatility increases the probability of hitting and being able to execute at the liquidity providers' price. Consequently, liquidity suppliers display fewer shares at the best prices to mitigate adverse selection costs.

Large-cap stocks are more actively traded and therefore more liquid in comparison to small-cap stocks. As a result, market impact cost is normally lower for large caps.[19] However, if we measure market impact costs

---

[17]Louis K. C. Chan and Joseph Lakonishok, "Institutional Equity Trading Costs: NYSE versus Nasdaq," *Journal of Finance* 52, no. 2 (1997): 713–735.

[18]Brian F. Smith, D. Alasdair, S. Turnbull, and Robert W. White, "Upstairs Market for Principal and Agency Trades: Analysis of Adverse Information and Price Effects," *Journal of Finance* 56, no. 5 (2001): 1723–1746.

[19]Keim and Madhavan, "Transaction Costs and Investment Style"; and Laura Spierdijk, Theo Nijman, and Arthur van Soest, "Temporary and Persistent Price Effects

with respect to relative trade size (normalized by average daily volume, for instance), they are generally higher. Similarly, growth and value stocks have different market impact cost. One reason for that is related to the trading style. Growth stocks commonly exhibit momentum and high volatility. This attracts technical traders that are interested in capitalizing on short-term price swings. Value stocks are traded at a slower pace and holding periods tend to be slightly longer.

Different market sectors show different trading behaviors. For instance, Bikker and Spierdijk show that equity trades in the energy sector exhibit higher market impact costs than other comparable equities in nonenergy sectors.[20]

A Factor-Based Market Impact Model

One of the most common approaches in practice and in the literature in modeling market impact is through a linear factor model of the form:

$$MI_t = \alpha + \sum_{i=1}^{I} \beta_i x_i + \varepsilon_t$$

where α, β_i are the factor loadings and x_i are the factors. Frequently, the error term ε_t is assumed to be independently and identically distributed. Recall that the resulting market impact cost of a trade of (dollar) size V is then given by $MIC_t = MI_t \cdot V$. However, extensions of this model including conditional volatility specifications are also possible. By analyzing both the mean and the volatility of the market impact, we can better understand and manage the trade-off between the two. For example, Bikker and Spierdijk use a specification where the error terms are jointly and serially uncorrelated with mean zero, satisfying

$$\text{Var}(\varepsilon_t) = \exp\left(\gamma + \sum_{j=1}^{J} \delta_j z_j\right)$$

where γ, δ_j, and z_j are the volatility, factor loadings, and factors, respectively.

Although the market impact function is linear, this of course does not mean that the dependent variables have to be. In particular, the factors in

---

of Trades in Infrequently Traded Stocks," working paper, Tilburg University and Center, 2003.
[20]Jacob A. Bikker, Laura Spierdijk, and Pieter Jelle van der Sluis, "Market Impact Costs of Institutional Equity Trades," *Journal of International Money and Finance* 26, no. 6 (2007): 974–1000.

the previous specification can be nonlinear transformations of the descriptive variables.

Consider, for example, factors related to trade size (e.g., trade size and trade size to daily volume). It is well known that market impact is nonlinear in these trade size measures. One of the earliest studies in this regard was performed by Loeb,[21] who showed that for a large set of stocks the market impact is proportional to the square root of the trade size, resulting in a market impact cost proportional to $V^{3/2}$. Typically, a market impact function linear in trade size will underestimate the price impact of small- to medium-sized trades whereas larger trades will be overestimated.

Chen, Stanzl, and Watanabe suggest to model the nonlinear effects of trade size (dollar trade size V) in a market impact model by using the Box-Cox transformation;[22] that is,

$$MI(V_t) = \alpha_b + \beta_b \frac{V_t^{\lambda_b} - 1}{\lambda_b} + \varepsilon_t$$

where t and τ represent the time of transaction for the buys and the sells, respectively. In their specification, they assumed that ε_t and ε_τ are independent and identically distributed with mean zero and variance σ^2. The parameters α_b, β_b, λ_b, α_s, β_s, and λ_s were then estimated from market data by nonlinear least squares for each individual stock. We remark that λ_b, $\lambda_s \in [0,1]$ in order for the market impact for buys to be concave and for sells to be convex.

In their data sample (NYSE and Nasdaq trades between January 1993 and June 1993), Chen et al. report that for small companies the curvature parameters λ_b, λ_s are close to zero, whereas for larger companies they are not far away from 0.5. Observe that for $\lambda_b = \lambda_s = 1$ market impact is linear in the dollar trade size. Moreover, when $\lambda_b = \lambda_s = 0$ the impact function is logarithmic by the virtue of

$$\lim_{\lambda \to 0} \frac{V^\lambda - 1}{\lambda} = \ln(\lambda)$$

As just mentioned, market impact is also a function of the characteristics of the particular exchange where the securities are traded as well as of the trading style of the investor. These characteristics can also be included in

[21]Thomas F. Loeb, "Trading Costs: The Critical Link between Investment Information and Results," *Financial Analysts Journal* 39, no. 3 (1983): 39–44.
[22]Zhiwu Chen, Werner Stanzl, and Masahiro Watanabe, "Price Impact Costs and the Limit of Arbitrage," working paper, Yale School of Management, International Center for Finance, 2002.

the general specification outlined previously. For example, Keim and Madhavan proposed the following two different market impact specifications[23]

1. $MI = \alpha + \beta_1 \chi_{OTC} + \beta_2 \dfrac{1}{p} + \beta_3 |q| + \beta_4 |q|^2 + \beta_5 |q|^3 + \beta_6 \chi_{Up} + \varepsilon$

where

χ_{OTC} = a dummy variable equal to one if the stock is an OTC traded stock or zero otherwise.

p = the trade price.

q = the number of shares traded over the number of shares outstanding.

χ_{Up} = a dummy variable equal to one if the trade is done in the upstairs[24] market or zero otherwise.

2. $MI = \alpha + \beta_1 \chi_{Nasdaq} + \beta_2 q + \beta_3 \ln(MCap) + \beta_4 \dfrac{1}{p} + \beta_5 \chi_{Tech} + \beta_6 \chi_{Index} + \varepsilon$

where

χ_{Nasdaq} = a dummy variable equal to one if the stock is traded on Nasdaq or zero otherwise.

q = the number of shares traded over the number of shares outstanding.

$MCap$ = the market capitalization of the stock.

p = the trade price.

χ_{Tech} = a dummy variable equal to one if the trade is a short-term technical trade or zero otherwise.

χ_{Index} = a dummy variable equal to one if the trade is done for a portfolio that attempts to closely mimic the behavior of the underlying index or zero otherwise.

These two models provide good examples for how nonlinear transformations of the underlying dependent variables can be used along with dummy variables that describe specific market or trade characteristics.

---

[23]Donald B. Keim and Ananth Madhavan, "Transactions Costs and Investment Style: An Inter-Exchange Analysis of Institutional Equity Trades," *Journal of Financial Economics* 46, no. 3 (1997): 265–292; and Donald B. Keim and Ananth Madhavan, "The Upstairs Market for Large-Block Transactions: Analysis and Measurement of Price Effects," *Review of Financial Studies* 9, no. 1 (1996): 1–36.

[24]A securities transaction not executed on the exchange but completed directly by a broker in-house is referred to as an upstairs market transaction. Typically, the upstairs market consists of a network of trading desks of the major brokerages and institutional investors. The major purpose of the upstairs market is to facilitate large block and program trades.

Several vendors and broker-dealers such as MSCI Barra[25] and ITG[26] have developed commercially available market impact models. These are sophisticated multimarket models that rely upon specialized estimation techniques using intraday data or tick-by-tick transaction-based data. However, the general characteristics of these models are similar to the ones described in this section.

We emphasize that in the modeling of transaction costs it is important to factor in the objective of the trader or investor. For example, one market participant might trade just to take advantage of price movement and hence will only trade during favorable periods. His trading cost is different from an investor who has to rebalance a portfolio within a fixed time period and can therefore only partially use an opportunistic or liquidity searching strategy. In particular, this investor has to take into account the *risk of not completing* the transaction within a specified time period. Consequently, even if the market is not favorable, he may decide to transact a portion of the trade. The market impact models described previously assume that orders will be fully completed and ignore this point.

KEY POINTS

- Trading and execution are integral components of the investment process. A poorly executed trade can eat directly into portfolio returns because of transaction costs.
- Transaction costs are typically categorized in two dimensions: *fixed costs* versus *variable costs*, and *explicit costs* versus *implicit costs*.
- In the first dimension, fixed costs include commissions and fees. Bid-ask spreads, taxes, delay cost, price movement risk, market impact costs, timing risk, and opportunity cost are variable trading costs.
- In the second dimension, explicit costs include commissions, fees, bid-ask spreads, and taxes. Delay cost, price movement risk, market impact cost, timing risk, and opportunity cost are implicit transaction costs.
- Implicit costs make up the larger part of the total transaction costs. These costs are not observable and have to be estimated.
- Liquidity is created by agents transacting in the financial markets by buying and selling securities.

---

[25]Nicolo G. Torre and Mark J. Ferrari, "The Market Impact Model," Barra Research Insights.

[26]Investment Technology Group, Inc., "ITG ACE—Agency Cost Estimator: A Model Description," 2003, www.itginc.com.

- Liquidity and transaction costs are interrelated: In a highly liquid market, large transactions can be executed immediately without incurring high transaction costs.
- A limit order is an order to execute a trade only if the limit price or a better price can be obtained.
- A market order is an order to execute a trade at the current best price available in the market.
- In general, trading costs are measured as the difference between the execution price and some appropriate fair market benchmark. The fair market benchmark of a security is the price that would have prevailed had the trade not taken place.
- Typical forecasting models for market impact costs are based on a statistical factor approach where the independent variables are trade-based factors or asset-based factors.

QUESTIONS

1. Describe what market impact costs are.

2. Why is there market impact in the market?

3. a. How does a limit order differ from a market order?
   b. What are the advantages and disadvantages of a limit order?

4. a. What are the different approaches to measure market impact?
   b. What is meant by "VWAP" and how is it calculated?

5. What is implementation shortfall?

6. What types of explanatory variables are used in models for forecasting market impact?

CHAPTER 18

Equity Portfolio Selection
in Practice

Dessislava A. Pachamanova, Ph.D.
Associate Professor of Operations Research
Babson College

Frank J. Fabozzi, Ph.D., CFA, CPA
Professor of Finance
EDHEC Business School

An integrated investment process generally involves the following activities:[1]

1. An investor's objectives, preferences, and constraints are identified and specified to develop explicit investment policies.
2. Strategies are developed and implemented through the choice of optimal combinations of financial and real assets in the marketplace.
3. Market conditions, relative asset values, and the investor's circumstances are monitored.
4. Portfolio adjustments are made as appropriate to reflect significant changes in any or all of the relevant variables.

In this chapter, we focus on the second activity of the investment process, developing and implementing a portfolio strategy. The development of the portfolio strategy itself is typically done in two stages: First, funds are allocated among asset classes. Then, they are managed within the asset classes. The mean-variance framework is used at both stages, but in this

---

[1] See Chapter 1 in John L. Maginn and Donald L. Tuttle (eds.), *Managing Investment Portfolios: A Dynamic Process*, 2nd ed. (New York: Warren, Gorham & Lamont, 1990).

chapter, we discuss the second stage. Specifically, we introduce quantitative formulations of portfolio allocation problems used in equity portfolio management. Quantitative equity portfolio selection often involves extending the classical mean-variance framework as originally formulated by Harry Markowitz 60 years ago[2] or more advanced tail-risk portfolio allocation frameworks to include different constraints that take specific investment guidelines and institutional features into account.

We begin by providing a classification of the most common portfolio constraints used in practice. We then discuss extensions such as index tracking formulations, the inclusion of transaction costs, optimization of trades across multiple client accounts, and tax-aware strategies. We conclude with a review of methods for incorporating robustness in quantitative portfolio allocation procedures by using robust statistics, simulation, and robust optimization techniques.

PORTFOLIO CONSTRAINTS COMMONLY USED IN PRACTICE

Institutional features and investment policy specifications often lead to more complicated requirements than simple minimization of risk (whatever the definition of risk may be) or maximization of expected portfolio return. For instance, there can be constraints that limit the number of trades, the exposure to a specific industry, or the number of stocks to be kept in the portfolio. Some of these constraints are imposed by the clients, while others are imposed by regulators. For example, in the case of regulated investment companies, restrictions on asset allocation are set forth in the prospectus and may be changed only with the approval of the fund's board of directors. Pension funds must comply with Employee Retirement Income Security Act (ERISA) requirements. The objective of the portfolio optimization problem can also be modified to consider specifically the trade-off between risk and return, transactions costs, or taxes.

In this section, we take a single-period view of investing, in the sense that the goal of the portfolio allocation procedure will be to invest optimally over a single pre-determined period of interest, such as one month.[3] We use w_0 to denote the vector array of stock weights in the portfolio at the beginning of the period, and w to denote the weights at the end of the period (to be determined).

---

[2]Harry M. Markowitz, "Portfolio Theory," *Journal of Finance* 7, no. 1 (1952): 77–91.
[3]Multiperiod portfolio optimization models are still rarely used in practice, not because the value of multiperiod modeling is questioned, but because such models are often too intractable from a computational perspective.

Many investment companies, especially institutional investors, have a long investment horizon. However, in reality, they treat that horizon as a sequence of shorter period horizons. Risk budgets are often stated over a time period of a year, and return performance is monitored quarterly or monthly.

Long-Only (No Short Selling) Constraints

Many funds and institutional investors face restrictions or outright prohibitions on the amount of short selling they can do. When short selling is not allowed, the portfolio allocation optimization model contains the constraints $\mathbf{w} \geq 0$.

Holding Constraints

Diversification principles argue against investing a large proportion of the portfolio in a single asset, or having a large concentration of assets in a specific industry, sector, or country. Limits on the holdings of a specific stock can be imposed with the constraints

$$\mathbf{l} \leq \mathbf{w} \leq \mathbf{u}$$

where $\mathbf{l}$ and $\mathbf{u}$ are vectors of lower and upper bounds of the holdings of each stock in the portfolio.

Consider now a portfolio of 10 stocks. Suppose that the issuers of assets 1, 3, and 5 are in the same industry, and that we would like to limit the portfolio exposure to that industry to be at least 20% but at most 40%. To limit exposure to that industry, we add the constraint

$$0.20 \leq w_1 + w_3 + w_5 \leq 0.40$$

to the portfolio allocation optimization problem.

More generally, if we have a specific set of stocks I_j out of the investment universe I consisting of stocks in the same category (such as industry or country), we can write the constraint

$$L_j \leq \sum_{j \in I_j} w_j \leq U_j$$

In words, this constraint requires that the sum of all stock weights in the particular category of investments with indexes I_j is greater than or equal to a lower bound L_j and less than a maximum exposure of U_j.

Turnover Constraints

High portfolio turnover can result in large transaction costs that make portfolio rebalancing inefficient and costly. Thus, some portfolio managers limit the amount of turnover allowed when trading their portfolio. (Another way to control for transaction costs is to minimize them explicitly; we discuss the appropriate formulations later in this chapter.)

Most commonly, turnover constraints are imposed for each stock:

$$\left| w_i - w_{0,i} \right| \leq u_i$$

that is, the absolute magnitude of the difference between the final and the initial weight of stock i in the portfolio is restricted to be less than some upper bound u_i. Sometimes, a constraint is imposed to minimize the portfolio turnover as a whole:

$$\sum_{j \in I_i} \left| w_j - w_{0,j} \right| \leq U_i$$

that is, the total absolute difference between the initial and the final weights of the stocks in the portfolio is restricted to be less than or equal to an upper bound U_i. Under this constraint, some stock weights may deviate a lot more than others from their initial weights, but the total deviation is limited.

Turnover constraints are often imposed relative to the *average daily volume* (ADV) of a stock.[4] For example, we may want to restrict turnover to be no more than 5% of the ADV. (In the latter case, the upper bound u_i is set to a value equal to 5% of the ADV.) Modifications of these constraints, such as limiting turnover in a specific industry or sector, are also frequently applied.

Risk Factor Constraints

In practice, it is very common for quantitatively oriented portfolio managers to use *factor models* to control for risk exposures to different risk factors. Such risk factors could include the market return, size, and style. Let us assume that the return on stock i has a factor structure with K risk factors, that is, can be expressed through the equality

$$r_i = \alpha_i + \sum_{k=1}^{K} \beta_{ik} \cdot f_k + \varepsilon_i$$

---

[4]As the term intuitively implies, the ADV measures the total amount of a given asset traded in a day on average, where the average is taken over a prespecified time period.

The factors f_k are common to all securities. The coefficient β_{ik} in front of each factor f_k shows the sensitivity of the return on stock i to factor k. The value of α_i shows the expected excess return of the return on stock i, and ε_i is the idiosyncratic (called *nonsystematic*) part of the return of stock i. The coefficients α_i and β_{ik} are typically estimated by multiple regression analysis.

To limit the exposure of a portfolio of N stocks to the kth risk factor, we impose the constraint

$$\sum_{i=1}^{N} \beta_{ik} \cdot w_i \leq U_k$$

To understand this constraint, note that the total return on the portfolio can be written as

$$\sum_{i=1}^{N} w_i \cdot r_i = \sum_{i=1}^{N} w_i \cdot \left(\alpha_i + \sum_{k=1}^{K} \beta_{ik} \cdot f_k + \varepsilon_i \right)$$

$$= \sum_{i=1}^{N} w_i \cdot \alpha_i + \sum_{i=1}^{N} \left(w_i \cdot \left(\sum_{k=1}^{K} \beta_{ik} \cdot f_k \right) \right) + \sum_{i=1}^{N} w_i \cdot \varepsilon_i$$

The sensitivity of the portfolio to the different factors is represented by the second term, which can be also written as

$$\sum_{k=1}^{K} \left(\left(\sum_{i=1}^{N} w_i \cdot \beta_{ik} \right) \cdot f_k \right)$$

Therefore, the exposure to a particular factor k is the coefficient in front of f_k, that is,

$$\sum_{i=1}^{N} \beta_{ik} \cdot w_i$$

On an intuitive level, the sensitivity of the portfolio to a factor k will be larger the larger the presence of factor k in the portfolio through the exposure of the individual stocks. Thus, when we compute the total exposure of the portfolio to factor k, we need to take into consideration both how important this factor is for determining the return on each of the securities in the portfolio, and how much of each security we have in the portfolio.

A commonly used version of the maximum factor exposure constraint is

$$\sum_{i=1}^{N} \beta_{ik} \cdot w_i = 0$$

This constraint forces the portfolio optimization algorithm to find portfolio weights so that the overall risk exposure to factor k is 0, that is, so that the portfolio is neutral with respect to changes in factor k. Portfolio allocation strategies that claim to be "market neutral" typically employ this constraint, and the factor is, in fact, the return on the market.

Cardinality Constraints

Depending on the portfolio allocation model used, sometimes the optimization subroutine recommends holding small amounts of a large number of stocks, which can be costly when one takes into consideration the transaction costs incurred when acquiring these positions. Alternatively, a portfolio manager may be interested in limiting the number of stocks used to track a particular index. (We discuss index tracking later in this chapter.) To formulate the constraint on the number of stocks to be held in the portfolio (called *cardinality constraint*), we introduce binary variables, one for each of the N stocks in the portfolio. Let us call these binary variables $\delta_1, ..., \delta_N$. Variable δ_i will take value 1 if stock i is included in the portfolio, and 0 otherwise.

Suppose that out of the N stocks in the investment universe, we would like to include a maximum of K stocks in the final portfolio. K here is a positive integer, and is less than N. This constraint can be formulated as

$$\sum_{i=1}^{N} \delta_i \leq K$$

$$\delta_i \text{ binary}, i = 1,...,N$$

We need to make sure, however, that if a stock is not selected in the portfolio, then the binary variable that corresponds to that stock is set to 0, so that the stock is not counted as one of the K stocks left in the portfolio. When the portfolio weights are restricted to be nonnegative, this can be achieved by imposing the additional constraints

$$0 \leq w_i \leq \delta_i, i = 1,...,N$$

If the optimal weight for stock i turns out to be different from 0, then the binary variable δ_i associated with stock i is forced to take value 1, and stock i will be counted as one of the K stocks to be kept in the portfolio. If the optimal weight for stock i is 0, then the binary variable δ_i associated with stock i can be either 0 or 1, but that will not matter for all practical purposes, because the solver will set it to 0 if there are too many other attractive stocks that will be counted as the K stocks to be kept in the portfolio. At the same time, since the portfolio weights w_i are between 0 and 1, and δ_i is 0 or 1, the constraint $w_i \leq \delta_i$ does not restrict the values that the stock weight w_i can take.

The constraints are a little different if short sales are allowed, in which case the weights may be negative. We have

$$-M \cdot \delta_i \le w_i \le M \cdot \delta_i, \, i = 1,\ldots,N$$

where M is a "large" constant (large relative to the size of the inputs in the problem; so in this portfolio optimization application $M = 10$ can be considered "large"). You can observe that if the weight w_i is anything but 0, the value of the binary variable δ_i will be forced to be different from 0, that is, δ_i will need to be 1, since it can only take values 0 or 1.

Minimum Holding and Transaction-Size Constraints

Cardinality constraints are often used in conjunction with minimum holding and trading constraints. The latter set a minimum limit on the amount of a stock that can be held in the portfolio, or the amount of a stock that can be traded, effectively eliminating small trades. Both cardinality and minimum holding and trading constraints aim to reduce the amount of transaction costs.

Threshold constraints on the amount of stock i to be held in the portfolio can be imposed with the constraint

$$\left| w_i \right| \ge L_i \cdot \delta_i$$

where L_i is the smallest holding size allowed for stock i, and δ_i is a binary variable, analogous to the binary variables δ_i defined in the previous section—it equals 1 if stock i is included in the portfolio, and 0 otherwise. (All additional constraints relating δ_i and w_i described in the previous section still apply.)

Similarly, constraints can be imposed on the minimum trading amount for stock i. As we explained earlier in this section, the size of the trade for stock i is determined by the absolute value of the difference between the current weight of the stock, $w_{0,i}$, and the new weight w_i that will be found by the solver: $\left| w_i - w_{0,i} \right|$. The minimum trading size constraint formulation is

$$\left| w_i - w_{0,i} \right| \ge L_i^{\text{trade}} \cdot \delta_i$$

where L_i^{trade} is the smallest trading size allowed for stock i.

Adding binary variables to an optimization problem makes the problem more difficult for the solver and can increase the computation time substantially. That is why, in practice, portfolio managers often omit minimum holding and transaction-size constraints from the optimization problem formulation, selecting instead to eliminate weights and/or trades that appear too small manually, after the optimal portfolio is determined by the optimization solver. It is important to realize, however, that modifying the optimal solution for the simpler portfolio allocation problem—the optimal solution in this case is the weights and trades for the different stocks—by eliminating small positions manually does not necessarily produce that optimal solution to an optimization problem that contained the minimum holding and transaction-size constraints from the beginning. In fact, there can be pathological cases in which the solution is very different from the true optimal solution. However, for most cases in practice, the small manual adjustments to the optimal portfolio allocation do not cause tremendous discrepancies or inconsistencies.

Round Lot Constraints

So far, we have assumed that stocks are infinitely divisible, meaning we can trade and invest in fractions of stocks, bonds, and the like. This is, of course, not true. In reality, securities are traded in multiples of minimum transaction lots, or *rounds* (e.g., 100 or 500 shares).

In order to represent the condition that securities should be traded in rounds, we need to introduce additional decision variables (let us call them z_i, $i = 1,...,N$) that are integer and will correspond to the number of lots of a particular security that will be purchased. Each z_i will then be linked to the corresponding portfolio weight w_i through the equality

$$w_i = z_i \cdot f_i, i = 1, ..., N$$

where f_i is measured in dollars, and is a fraction of the total amount to be invested. For example, suppose there are a total of $100 million to be invested, and stock i trades at $50 in round lots of 100. Then

$$f_i = \frac{50 \cdot 100}{100,000,000} = 5 \cdot 10^{-7}$$

All remaining constraints in the portfolio allocation can be expressed through the weights w_i, as usual. However, we also need to specify for the solver that the decision variables z_i are integer.

An issue with imposing round lot constraints is that the budget constraint

$$\mathbf{w}'\iota = 1$$

which is, in fact,

$$\sum_{i=1}^{N} z_i \cdot f_i = 1$$

may not be satisfied exactly. One possibility to handle this problem is to relax the budget constraint. For example, we can state the constraint as

$$\mathbf{w}'\iota \le 1$$

or, equivalently,

$$\sum_{i=1}^{N} z_i \cdot f_i \le 1$$

This will ensure that we do not go over budget.

If our objective is stated as expected return maximization, the optimization solver will attempt to make this constraint as tight as possible, that is, we will end up using up as much of the budget as we can. Depending on the objective function and the other constraints in the formulation, however, this may not always happen. We can try to force the solver to minimize the slack in the budget constraint by introducing a pair of nonnegative decision variables (let us call them ε^+ and ε^-) that account for the amount that is "overinvested" or "underinvested." These variables will pick up the slack left over because of the inability to round the amounts for the different investments. Namely, we impose the constraints

$$\sum_{i=1}^{N} z_i \cdot f_i + \varepsilon^- - \varepsilon^+ = 1$$
$$\varepsilon^- \ge 0, \varepsilon^+ \ge 0$$

and subtract the following term from the objective function:

$$\lambda_{rl} \cdot (\varepsilon^- + \varepsilon^+)$$

where λ_{rl} is a penalty term associated with the amount of over- or underinvestment the portfolio manager is willing to tolerate (selected by the portfolio manager). In the final solution, the violation of the budget constraint will be minimized. Note, however, that this formulation technically allows for the budget to be overinvested.

Note that the optimal portfolio allocation we obtain after solving this optimization problem will not be the same as the allocation we would obtain if we solve an optimization problem without round lot constraints, and then round the amounts to fit the lots that can be traded in the market.

Cardinality constraints, minimum holding and trading constraints, and especially round lot constraints, require more sophisticated binary and integer programming solvers, and are difficult problems to solve in the case of large portfolios.

BENCHMARK EXPOSURE AND TRACKING ERROR MINIMIZATION

Expected portfolio return maximization under the mean-variance framework or other risk measure minimization are examples of *active investment strategies*, that is, strategies that identify a universe of attractive investments, and ignore inferior investments opportunities. A different approach, referred to as a *passive investment strategy*, argues that in the absence of any superior forecasting ability, investors might as well resign themselves to the fact that they cannot beat the market. From a theoretical perspective, the analytics of portfolio theory tell them to hold a broadly diversified portfolio anyway. Many mutual funds are managed relative to a particular benchmark or stock universe, such as the S&P 500 or the Russell 1000. The portfolio allocation models are then formulated in such a way that the tracking error relative to the benchmark is kept small.

Standard Definition of Tracking Error

To incorporate a passive investment strategy, we can change the objective function of the portfolio allocation problem so that instead of minimizing a portfolio risk measure, we minimize the tracking error with respect to a benchmark that represents the market, such as the Russell 3000, or the S&P 500. Such strategies are often referred to as *indexing*. The *tracking error* can be defined in different ways. However, practitioners typically mean a specific definition: the variance (or standard deviation) of the difference between the portfolio return, $\mathbf{w}'\tilde{\mathbf{r}}$, and the return on the benchmark, $\mathbf{w}_b'\tilde{\mathbf{r}}$. Mathematically, the tracking error (TE) can be expressed as

$$
\begin{aligned}
TE &= Var(\mathbf{w}'\tilde{\mathbf{r}} - \mathbf{w}_b'\tilde{\mathbf{r}}) \\
&= Var\big((\mathbf{w} - \mathbf{w}_b)'\tilde{\mathbf{r}}\big) \\
&= (\mathbf{w} - \mathbf{w}_b)'\, Var\big(\tilde{\mathbf{r}}\big)\,(\mathbf{w} - \mathbf{w}_b) \\
&= (\mathbf{w} - \mathbf{w}_b)'\, \Sigma\, (\mathbf{w} - \mathbf{w}_b)
\end{aligned}
$$

where Σ is the covariance matrix of the stock returns. One can observe that the formula is very similar to the formula for the portfolio variance;

however, the portfolio weights in the formula for the variance are replaced by differences between the weights of the stocks in the portfolio and the weights of the stocks in the index.

Why do we need to optimize portfolio weights in order to track a benchmark, when technically the most effective way to track a benchmark is by investing the portfolio in the stocks in the benchmark portfolio in the same proportions as the proportions of these securities in the benchmark? The problem with this approach is that, especially with large benchmarks like the Russell 3000, the transaction costs of a proportional investment and the subsequent rebalancing of the portfolio can be prohibitive (that is, dramatically adversely impact the performance of the portfolio relative to the benchmark). Furthermore, in practice securities are not infinitely divisible, so investing a portfolio of a limited size in the same proportions as the composition of the benchmark will still not achieve zero tracking error. Thus, the optimal formulation is to require that the portfolio follows the benchmark as closely as possible.

While indexing has become an essential part of many portfolio strategies, most portfolio managers cannot resist the temptation to identify at least some securities that will outperform others. Hence, restrictions on the tracking error are often imposed as a constraint, while the objective function is something different than minimizing the tracking error. The tracking error constraint takes the form

$$(\mathbf{w} - \mathbf{w}_b)' \, \mathbf{\Sigma} \, (\mathbf{w} - \mathbf{w}_b) \le \sigma^2_{TE}$$

where σ^2_{TE} is a limit (imposed by the investor) on the amount of tracking error the investor is willing to tolerate. This is a quadratic constraint, which is convex and computationally tractable, but requires specialized optimization software.

Alternative Ways of Defining Tracking Error

There are alternative ways in which tracking-error type constraints can be imposed. For example, we may require that the absolute deviations of the portfolio weights ($\mathbf{w}$) from the index weights ($\mathbf{w}_b$) are less than or equal to a given vector array of upper bounds $\mathbf{u}$:

$$|\mathbf{w} - \mathbf{w}_b| \le \mathbf{u}$$

where the absolute values $|.|$ for the vector differences are taken componentwise, that is, for pairs of corresponding elements from the two vector arrays. These constraints can be stated as linear constraints by rewriting them as

$$\mathbf{w} - \mathbf{w}_b \le \mathbf{u}$$
$$-(\mathbf{w} - \mathbf{w}_b) \le \mathbf{u}$$

Similarly, we can require that for stocks within a specific industry (whose indexes in the portfolio belong to a subset I_j of the investment universe I), the total tracking error is less than a given upper bound U_j:

$$\sum_{j \in I_j} (w_j - w_{b,j}) \le U_j$$

Finally, tracking error can be expressed through risk measures other than the absolute deviations or the variance of the deviations from the benchmark. Rockafellar and Uryasev[5] suggest using Conditional Value-at-Risk (CVaR)[6] to manage the tracking error. (Using CVaR as a risk measure results in computationally tractable optimization formulations for portfolio allocation, as long as the data are presented in the form of scenarios.[7]) We provide below a formulation that is somewhat different from Rockafellar and Uryasev, but preserves the main idea.

Suppose that we are given S scenarios for the return of a benchmark portfolio (or an instrument we are trying to replicate), b_s, $s = 1, ..., S$. These scenarios can be generated by simulation, or taken from historical data. We also have N stocks with returns $r_i^{(s)}$ ($i = 1, ..., N$, $s = 1, ..., S$) in each scenario. The value of the portfolio in scenario s is

$$\sum_{i=1}^{N} r_i^{(s)} \cdot w_i$$

or, equivalently, $(\mathbf{r}^{(s)})'\mathbf{w}$, where $\mathbf{r}^{(s)}$ is the vector of returns for the N stocks in scenario s. Consider the differences between the return on the benchmark and the return on the portfolio,

$$b_s - (\mathbf{r}^{(s)})'\mathbf{w} = -((\mathbf{r}^{(s)})'\mathbf{w} - b_s)$$

If this difference is positive, we have a loss; if the difference is negative, we have a gain; both gains and losses are computed relative to the benchmark.

---

[5] R. Tyrell Rockafellar and Stanislav Uryasev, "Optimization of Conditional Value at Risk," *Journal of Risk* 2, no. 3 (2000): 21–41.

[6] *Conditional Value-at-Risk* measures the average loss that can happen with probability less than some small probability, that is, the average loss in the tail of the distribution of portfolio losses.

[7] Another computationally tractable situation for minimizing CVaR is when the data are normally distributed. In that case, minimizing CVaR is equivalent to minimizing the standard deviation of the portfolio.

Rationally, the portfolio manager should not worry about differences that are negative; the only cause for concern would be if the portfolio underperforms the benchmark, which would result in a positive difference. Thus, it is not necessarily to limit the variance of the deviations of the portfolio returns from the benchmark, which penalizes for positive and negative deviations equally. Instead, we can impose a limit on the amount of loss we are willing to tolerate in terms of the CVaR of the distribution of losses relative to the benchmark.

The tracking error constraint in terms of the CVaR can be stated as the following set of constraints:[8]

$$\xi + \frac{1}{[\varepsilon \cdot S]} \cdot \sum_{s=1}^{S} y_s \leq U_{TE}$$

$$y_s \geq -\left((\mathbf{r}^{(s)})' \mathbf{w} - b_s \right) - \xi, \quad s = 1, \ldots, S$$

$$y_s \geq 0, \quad s = 1, \ldots, S$$

where U_{TE} is the upper bound on the negative deviations.

This formulation of tracking error is appealing in two ways. First, it treats positive and negative deviations relative to the benchmark differently, which agrees with the strategy of an investor seeking to maximize returns overall. Second, it results in a linear set of constraints, which are easy to handle computationally, in contrast to the first formulation of the tracking error constraint in this section, which results in a quadratic constraint.

Actual vs. Predicted Tracking Error

The tracking error calculation in practice is often backward-looking. For example, in computing the covariance matrix Σ in the standard tracking error definition as the variance of the deviations of the portfolio returns from the index, or in selecting the scenarios used in the CVaR-type tracking error constraint in the previous section, we may use historical data. The tracking error calculated in this manner is called the *ex post tracking error*, *backward-looking error*, or *actual tracking error*.

The problem with using the actual tracking error for assessing future performance relative to a benchmark is that the actual tracking error does not reflect the effect of the portfolio manager's current decisions on the future active returns and hence the tracking error that may be realized in

---

[8]For a more detailed explanation of CVaR and a derivation of the optimization formulation, see Chapters 8 and 9 in Dessislava A. Pachamanova and Frank J. Fabozzi, *Simulation and Optimization in Finance: Modeling with MATLAB, @RISK, and VBA* (Hoboken, NJ: John Wiley & Sons, 2010).

the future. The actual tracking error has little predictive value and can be misleading regarding portfolio risk.

Portfolio managers need forward-looking estimates of tracking error to reflect future portfolio performance more accurately. In practice, this is accomplished by using the services of a commercial vendor that has a multifactor risk model that has identified and defined the risks associated with the benchmark, or by building such a model in-house. Statistical analysis of historical return data for the stocks in the benchmark are used to obtain the risk factors and to quantify the risks. Using the manager's current portfolio holdings, the portfolio's current exposure to the various risk factors can be calculated and compared to the benchmark's exposures to the risk factors. From the differential factor exposures and the risks of the factors, a *forward-looking tracking error* for the portfolio can be computed. This tracking error is also referred to as *ex ante tracking error* or *predicted tracking error*.

There is no guarantee that the predicted tracking error will match exactly the tracking error realized over the future time period of interest. However, this calculation of the tracking error has its use in risk control and portfolio construction. By performing a simulation analysis on the factors that enter the calculation, the manager can evaluate the potential performance of portfolio strategies relative to the benchmark and eliminate those that result in tracking errors beyond the client-imposed tolerance for risk. The actual tracking error, on the other hand, is useful for assessing actual performance relative to a benchmark.

INCORPORATING TRANSACTION COSTS

Transaction costs can be generally divided into two categories: explicit (such as bid-ask spreads, commissions and fees), and implicit (such as price movement risk costs[9] and market impact costs[10]).

The typical portfolio allocation models are built on top of one or several forecasting models for expected returns and risk. Small changes in these forecasts can result in reallocations that would not occur if transaction costs are taken into account. In practice, the effect of transaction costs on portfolio performance is far from insignificant. If transaction costs are not taken

---

[9]*Price movement risk costs* are the costs resulting from the potential for a change in market price between the time the decision to trade is made and the time the trade is actually executed.

[10]*Market impact cost* is the effect a trader has on the market price of an asset when it sells or buys the asset. It is the extent to which the price moves up or down in response to the trader's actions. For example, a trader who tries to sell a large number of shares of a particular stock may drive down the stock's market price.

into consideration in allocation and rebalancing decisions, they can lead to poor portfolio performance.

This section describes some common transaction cost models for portfolio rebalancing. We use the mean-variance framework as the basis for describing the different approaches. However, it is straightforward to extend the transaction cost models into other portfolio allocation frameworks.

The earliest, and most widely used, model for transaction costs is the mean-variance risk-aversion formulation with transaction costs.[11] The optimization problem has the following objective function:

$$\max_{\mathbf{w}} \quad \mathbf{w}'\boldsymbol{\mu} - \lambda \cdot \mathbf{w}'\Sigma\mathbf{w} - \lambda_{TC} \cdot TC$$

where TC is a transaction cost penalty function, and λ_{TC} is the transaction cost aversion parameter. In other words, the objective is to maximize the expected portfolio return less the cost of risk and transaction costs. We can imagine that, as the transaction costs increase, at some point it becomes optimal to keep the current portfolio rather than to rebalance. Variations of this formulation exist. For example, it is common to maximize expected portfolio return minus transaction costs and impose limits on the risk as a constraint (i.e., to move the second term in the objective function in the constraints).

Transaction costs models can involve complicated nonlinear functions. Although software exists for general nonlinear optimization problems, the computational time required for solving such problems is often too long for realistic investment applications, and the quality of the solution is not guaranteed. In practice, an observed complicated nonlinear transaction costs function is often approximated with a computationally tractable function that is assumed to be separable in the portfolio weights, that is, it is often assumed that the transaction costs for each individual stock are independent

---

[11]Versions of this model have been suggested in Gerald Pogue, "An Extension of the Markowitz Portfolio Selection Model to Include Variable Transactions Costs, Short Sales, Leverage Policies, and Taxes," *Journal of Finance* 25, no. 5 (1970): 1005–1027; John Schreiner, "Portfolio Revision: A Turnover-Constrained Approach," *Financial Management* 9, no. 1 (1980): 67–75; Christopher J. Adcock and Nigel Meade, "A Simple Algorithm to Incorporate Transaction Costs in Quadratic Optimization," *European Journal of Operational Research* 79, no. 1 (1994): 85–94; Miguel S. Lobo, Maryam Fazel, and Stephen Boyd, "Portfolio Optimization with Linear and Fixed Transaction Costs and Bounds on Risk," *Annals of Operations Research* 152, no. 1 (2007): 376–394; and John E. Mitchell and Stephen Braun, "Rebalancing an Investment Portfolio in the Presence of Convex Transaction Costs," technical report, Department of Mathematical Sciences, Rensselaer Polytechnic Institute, 2004.

of the transaction costs for another stock. For the rest of this section, we denote the individual cost function for stock i by TC_i.

Next, we explain several widely used models for the transaction cost function.

Linear Transaction Costs

Let us start simple. Suppose that the transaction costs are proportional, that is, they are a percentage c_i of the transaction size $|t| = |w_i - w_{0,i}|$.[12] Then, the portfolio allocation problem with transaction costs can be written simply as

$$\max_{\mathbf{w}} \ \mathbf{w}'\boldsymbol{\mu} - \lambda \cdot \mathbf{w}'\Sigma\mathbf{w} - \lambda_{TC} \cdot \sum_{i=1}^{N} c_i \cdot |w_i - w_{0,i}|$$

The problem can be made solver-friendly by replacing the absolute value terms with new decision variables y_i, and adding two sets of constraints. Hence, we rewrite the objective function as

$$\max_{\mathbf{w},y} \ \mathbf{w}'\boldsymbol{\mu} - \lambda \cdot \mathbf{w}'\Sigma\mathbf{w} - \lambda_{TC} \cdot \sum_{i=1}^{N} c_i \cdot y_i$$

and add the constraints

$$y_i \geq w_i - w_{0,i}$$
$$y_i \geq -(w_i - w_{0,i})$$

This preserves the quadratic optimization problem formulation, a formulation that can be passed to quadratic optimization solvers such as Excel Solver and MATLAB's quadprog function, because the constraints are linear expressions, and the objective function contains only linear and quadratic terms.

In the optimal solution, the optimization solver will in fact set the value for y_i to $|w_i - w_{0,i}|$. This is because this is a maximization problem and y_i occurs with a negative sign in the objective function, so the solver will try to set y_i to the minimum value possible. That minimum value will be the maximum of $(w_i - w_{0,i})$ or $-(w_i - w_{0,i})$, which is in fact the absolute value $|w_i - w_{0,i}|$.

---

[12]Here we are thinking of w_i as the portfolio weights, but in fact it may be more intuitive to think of the transaction costs as a percentage of amount traded. It is easy to go back and forth between portfolio weights and portfolio amounts by simply multiplying w_i by the total amount in the portfolio. In fact, we can switch the whole portfolio optimization formulation around, and write it in terms of allocation of dollars, instead of weights. We just need to replace the vector of weights $\mathbf{w}$ by a vector $\mathbf{x}$ of dollar holdings.

Piecewise-Linear Transaction Costs

Taking the model in the previous section a step further, we can introduce piecewise-linear approximations to transaction cost function models. This kind of function is more realistic than the linear cost function, especially for large trades. As the trading size increases, it becomes increasingly more costly to trade because of the market impact of the trade.

An example of a piecewise-linear function of transaction costs for a trade of size t of a particular security is illustrated in Exhibit 18.1. The transaction cost function in the graph assumes that the rate of increase of transaction costs (reflected in the slope of the function) changes at certain threshold points. For example, it is smaller in the range 0% to 15% of daily volume than in the range 15% to 40% of daily volume (or some other trading volume index). Mathematically, the transaction cost function in Exhibit 18.1 can be expressed as

$$TC(t)$$
$$= \begin{cases} s_1 t, & 0 \le t \le 0.15 \cdot \text{Vol} \\ s_1(0.15 \cdot \text{Vol}) + s_2(t - 0.15 \cdot \text{Vol}), & 0.15 \cdot \text{Vol} \le t \le 0.40 \cdot \text{Vol} \\ s_1(0.15 \cdot \text{Vol}) + s_2(0.25 \cdot \text{Vol}) + s_3(t - 0.40 \cdot \text{Vol}), & 0.40 \cdot \text{Vol} \le t \le 0.50 \cdot \text{Vol} \end{cases}$$

where s_1, s_2, s_3 are the slopes of the three linear segments on the graph. (They are given data.)

EXHIBIT 18.1   Example of Modeling Transaction Costs (TC) as a Piecewise-Linear Function of Trade Size t

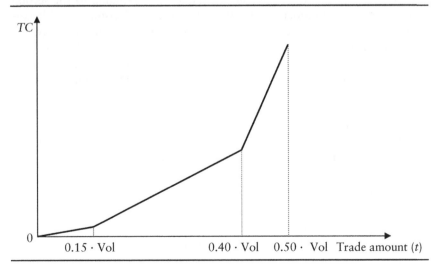

To include piecewise-linear functions for transaction costs in the objective function of a mean-variance (or any general mean-risk) portfolio optimization problem, we need to introduce new decision variables that correspond to the number of pieces in the piecewise-linear approximation of the transaction cost function (in this case, there are three linear segments, so we introduce variables z_1, z_2, z_3). We write the penalty term in the objective function for an individual stock as:[13]

$$\lambda_{TC} \cdot \left(s_1 \cdot z_1 + s_2 \cdot z_2 + s_3 \cdot z_3\right)$$

If there are N stocks in the portfolio, the total transaction cost will be the sum of the transaction costs for each individual stock, that is, the penalty term that involves transaction costs in the objective function becomes

$$-\lambda_{TC} \sum_{i=1}^{N} \left(s_{1,i} \cdot z_{1,i} + s_{2,i} \cdot z_{2,i} + s_{3,i} \cdot z_{3,i}\right)$$

In addition, we specify the following constraints on the new decision variables:

$$0 \le z_{1,i} \le 0.15 \cdot \text{Vol}_i$$
$$0 \le z_{2,i} \le 0.25 \cdot \text{Vol}_i$$
$$0 \le z_{3,i} \le 0.10 \cdot \text{Vol}_i$$

Note that because of the increasing slopes of the linear segments and the goal of making that term as small as possible in the objective function, the optimizer will never set the decision variable corresponding to the second segment, $z_{2,i}$, to a number greater than 0 unless the decision variable corresponding to the first segment, $z_{1,i}$, is at its upper bound. Similarly, the optimizer would never set $z_{3,i}$ to a number greater than 0 unless both $z_{1,i}$ and $z_{2,i}$ are at their upper bounds. So, this set of constraints allows us to compute the amount of transaction costs incurred in the trading of stock i as $z_{1,i} + z_{2,i} + z_{3,i}$.

Of course, we also need to link the amount of transaction costs incurred in the trading of stock i to the optimal portfolio allocation. This can be done by adding a few more variables and constraints. We introduce variables y_i, one for each stock in the portfolio, that would represent the amount traded (but not the direction of the trade), and would be nonnegative. Then, we require that

---

[13]See, for example, Dimitris Bertsimas, Christopher Darnell, and Robert Soucy, "Portfolio Construction through Mixed-Integer Programming at Grantham, Mayo, Van Otterloo and Company," *Interfaces* 29, no. 1 (1999): 49–66.

$$y_i = z_{1,i} + z_{2,i} + z_{3,i} \text{ for each stock } i,$$

and also that y_i equals the change in the portfolio position of stock i. The latter condition can be imposed by writing the constraint

$$y_i = \left| w_i - w_{0,i} \right|$$

where $w_{0,i}$ and w_i are the initial and the final amount of stock i in the portfolio, respectively.[14]

Despite their apparent complexity, piecewise-linear approximations for transaction costs are very solver-friendly, and save time (relative to nonlinear models) in the actual portfolio optimization. Although modeling transaction costs this way requires introducing new decision variables and constraints, the increase in the dimension of the portfolio optimization problem does not affect significantly the running time or the performance of the optimization solver, because the problem formulation is easy from a computational perspective.

Quadratic Transaction Costs

The transaction cost function is often parameterized as a quadratic function of the form

$$TC_i(t) = c_i \cdot \left| t \right| + d_i \cdot \left| t \right|^2$$

The coefficients c_i and d_i are calibrated from data, such as fitting a quadratic function to an observed pattern of transaction costs realized for trading a particular stock under normal conditions.

Including this function in the objective function of the portfolio optimization problem results in a quadratic program that can be solved with widely available quadratic optimization software.

Fixed Transaction Costs

In some cases, we need to model fixed transaction costs. Those are costs that are incurred independently of the amount traded. To include such costs in the portfolio optimization problem, we need to introduce binary variables

---

[14]As we explained earlier, this constraint can be written in an equivalent, more optimization solver-friendly form, namely,

$$y_i \geq w_i - w_{0,i}$$
$$y_i \geq -\left(w_i - w_{0,i} \right)$$

δ_1, ..., δ_N corresponding to each stock, where δ_i equals 0 if the amount traded of stock i is 0, and 1 otherwise. The idea is similar to the idea we used to model the requirement that only a given number of stocks can be included in the portfolio.

Suppose the fixed transaction cost is a_i for stock i. Then, the transaction cost function is

$$TC_i = a_i \cdot \delta_i$$

The objective function formulation is then

$$\max_{\mathbf{w}, \delta} \; \mathbf{w}'\boldsymbol{\mu} - \lambda \cdot \mathbf{w}'\Sigma\mathbf{w} - \lambda_{TC} \cdot \sum_{i=1}^{N} a_i \cdot \delta_i$$

and we need to add the following constraints to make sure that the binary variables are linked to the trades $|w_i - w_{0,i}|$:

$$|w_i - w_{0,i}| \le M \cdot \delta_i, \; i = 1,...,N,$$
$$\delta_i \text{ binary}$$

where M is a "large" constant. When the trading size $|w_i - w_{0,i}|$ is nonzero, δ_i will be forced to be 1. When the trading size is 0, then δ_i can be either 0 or 1, but the optimizer will set it to 0, since it will try to make its value the minimum possible in the objective function.

Of course, combinations of different trading cost models can be used in practice. For example, if the trade involves both a fixed and a variable quadratic transaction cost, then we could use a transaction cost function of the kind

$$TC_i(t) = a_i \cdot \delta_i + c_i \cdot |t| + d_i \cdot |t|^2$$

The important takeaway from this section is that when transaction costs are included in the portfolio rebalancing problem, the result is a reduced amount of trading and rebalancing, and a different portfolio allocation than the one that would be obtained if transaction costs are not taken into consideration.

INCORPORATING TAXES

When stocks in a portfolio appreciate or depreciate in value, *capital gains* (respectively, *losses*) accumulate. When stocks are sold, investors pay taxes on the realized net capital gains. The taxes are computed as a percentage of the difference between the current market value of the stocks and their tax basis, where the *tax basis* is the price at which the stocks were bought originally.[15] The percentage is less for long-term capital gains (when stocks have been held for more than a year) than it is for short-term capital gains (when stocks have been held for less than a year).[16] Since shares of the same stock could have been bought at different points in time (in different *lots*), selling one lot of the stock as opposed to another could incur a different amount of tax. In addition to capital gains taxes, investors who are not exempt from taxes owe taxes on the dividends paid on stocks in their portfolios. Those dividends are historically taxed at a higher rate than capital gains, and after 2010 will be taxed as income, i.e., at the investor's personal tax rate. The tax liability of a particular portfolio therefore depends on the timing of the execution of trades, on the tax basis of the portfolio, on the accumulated short-term and long-term capital gains, and on the tax bracket of the investor.

Over two-thirds of marketable portfolio assets in the United States are held by individuals, insurance and holding companies who pay taxes on their returns. (Exceptions are, for example, pension funds, which do not pay taxes year-to-year.) Studies have indicated that taxes are the greatest expense investors face—greater than commissions and investment management fees. To gain some intuition about the effect of taxes on the income of an investor over the investor's lifetime, consider a portfolio that has a capital appreciation of 6.00% per year. After 30 years, $1,000 invested in that portfolio will turn into $1,000 \cdot (1 + 0.06)^{30} = \$5,743.49$. Now suppose that the capital gains are realized each year, and a tax of 35% is paid on the gains (the remainder is reinvested). After 30 years, $1,000 invested in the portfolio will turn into $1,000 \cdot (1+(1 - 0.35) \cdot 0.06)^{30} = \$3,151.13$, about half of the amount without taxes even when the tax is about one third of the capital gains. In fact, in order to provide the same return as the portfolio with no taxes, the portfolio with annual realized capital gains would need to generate a capital appreciation of 9.23% per year! One can imagine that the same logic would make benchmark tracking and performance measurement very difficult on an after-tax basis.

As investors have become more aware of the dramatic impact of taxes on their returns, there is increasing pressure on portfolio managers to include tax considerations in their portfolio rebalancing decisions and to report after-tax performance. Consequently, the demand for computationally efficient and quantitatively rigorous methods for taking taxes into

---

[15]The computation of the tax basis is different for stocks and bonds. For bonds, there are special tax rules, and the original price is not the tax basis.

[16]The exact rates vary depending on the current version of the tax code, but the main idea behind the preferential treatment of long-term gains to short-term gains is to encourage long-term capital investments and fund entrepreneurial activity.

consideration in portfolio allocation decisions has grown in recent years. The complexity of the problem of incorporating taxes, however, is considerable, both from a theoretical and practical perspective:

1. The presence of tax liabilities changes the interpretation of even fundamental portfolio performance summary measures such as market value and risk. Thus, well-established methods for evaluating portfolio performance on a pretax basis do not work well in the case of tax-aware portfolio optimization. For example, in traditional portfolio management a loss is associated with risk, and is therefore minimized whenever possible. However, in the presence of taxes, losses may be less damaging, because they can be used to offset capital gains and reduce the tax burden of portfolio rebalancing strategies. Benchmarking is also not obvious in the presence of taxes: two portfolios that have exactly the same current holdings are not equivalent if the holdings have a different tax basis.[17]
2. Tax considerations are too complex to implement in a nonautomated fashion; at the same time, their automatic inclusion in portfolio rebalancing algorithms requires the ability to solve very difficult, large-scale optimization problems.
3. The best approach for portfolio management with tax considerations is optimization problem formulations that look at return forecasts over several time periods (such as, until the end of the year) before recommending new portfolio weights. However, the latter multiperiod *view* of the portfolio optimization problem is very difficult to handle computationally—the dimension of the optimization problem; that is, the number of variables and constraints, increases exponentially with the number of time periods under considerations.

We need to emphasize that while many of the techniques described in the previous sections of this chapter are widely known, there are no standard practices for tax-aware portfolio management that appear to be established. Different asset management firms interpret tax-aware portfolio allocation and approach the problem differently. To some firms, minimizing turnover,[18] such as, by investing in index funds, or selecting strategies that

---

[17]See David M. Stein, "Measuring and Evaluating Portfolio Performance after Taxes," *Journal of Portfolio Management* 24, no. 2 (1998): 117–124.
[18]See Apelfeld, Roberto, Gordon Fowler and James Gordon, "Tax-Aware Equity Investing," *Journal of Portfolio Management* 22, no. 2 (1996): 18–28. These authors show that a manager can outperform on an after-tax basis with high turnover as well, as long as the turnover does not result in net capital gains taxes. (There are other issues with high turnover, however, such as higher transaction costs that may result in a lower overall portfolio return.)

minimize the portfolio dividend yield[19] qualify as tax-aware portfolio strategies. Other asset management firms employ complex optimization algorithms that incorporate tax considerations directly in portfolio rebalancing decisions, so that they can keep up with the considerable burden of keeping track of thousands of managed accounts and their tax preferences. The fact is, even using simple rules of thumb, such as always selling stocks from the oldest lots after rebalancing the portfolio with classical portfolio optimization routines, can have a positive effect on after-tax portfolio returns. The latter strategy minimizes the likelihood that short-term gains will be incurred, which in turn reduces taxes, because short-term capital gains are taxed at a higher rate than long-term capital gains.

Apelfeld, Fowler, and Gordon suggest a tax-aware portfolio rebalancing framework that incorporates taxes directly into the portfolio optimization process.[20] The main idea of the approach is to treat different lots of the same stock as different securities and then penalize for taxes as if they were different transaction costs associated with the sale of each lot. (This means, for example, that Microsoft stock bought on Date 1 is treated as a different security from Microsoft stock bought on Date 2.) Many tax-aware quantitative investment strategies employ versions of this approach, but there are a few issues to beware when using it in practice:

- The first one is a general problem for all tax-aware approaches when they are used in the context of active portfolio management. For a portfolio manager who handles thousands of different accounts with different tax exposures, it is virtually impossible to pay attention to the tax cost incurred by each individual investor. While the tax-aware method described above minimizes the overall tax burden by reducing the amount of realized short-term sales, it has no provisions for differentiating between investors in different tax brackets because it is difficult to think of each trade as divided between all investors, and adjusted for each individual investor's tax circumstances. This issue is so intractable, that in practice it is not really brought under consideration.
- The dimension of the problem can become unmanageable very quickly. For example, a portfolio of 1,000 securities, each of which has 10 different lots, is equivalent to a portfolio of 10,000 securities when each lot is treated as a different security. Every time a new purchase is realized, a new security is added to the portfolio, since a new lot is created.

---

[19]Dividends are taxed as regular income, that is, at a higher rate than capital gains, so minimizing the portfolio dividend yield should theoretically result in a lower tax burden for the investor.

[20]See Apelfeld, Fowler, and Gordon, "Tax-Aware Equity Investing."

One needs to exercise care and "clean up" lots that have been sold and therefore have holdings of zero each time the portfolio is rebalanced.

■ Practitioners typically use factor models for forecasting returns and estimating risk. One of the assumptions when measuring portfolio risk through factor models is that the specific risk of a particular security is uncorrelated with the specific risk of other securities. (The only risk they share is the risk expressed through the factors in the factor model.) This assumption clearly does not hold when different "securities" are in fact different lots of the same stock.

DiBartolomeo describes a modification to the model used by North-field Information Service's portfolio management software that eliminates the last two problems.[21] Instead of treating each lot as a separate security, the software imposes a piecewise linear transaction costs (see Exhibit 18.1) where the break points on the horizontal axis correspond to the current size of different lots of the same security. The portfolio rebalancing algorithm goes through several iterations for the portfolio weights, and at each iteration, only the shares in the highest cost basis tax lot can be traded. Other shares of the same stock can be traded in subsequent iterations of the algorithm, with their appropriate tax costs attached.

The approaches we described so far take into consideration the short-term or long-term nature of capital gains but do not incorporate the ability the offset capital gains and losses accumulated over the year. This is an inherent limitation of single-period portfolio rebalancing approaches and is a strong argument in favor of adopting more realistic multiperiod portfolio optimization approaches. The rebalancing of the portfolio at each point in time should be made not only by considering the immediate consequences for the market value of the portfolio, but also the opportunity to correct for tax liabilities by realizing other capital gains or losses by the end of the taxable year. The scarce theoretical literature on multiperiod tax-aware portfolio optimization contains some characterizations of optimal portfolio strategies under numerous simplifying assumptions.[22] However, even under

---

[21]Dan DiBartolomeo, "Recent Advances in Management of Taxable Portfolios," working paper, Northfield Information Services, 2000.

[22]See George Constantinides, "Capital Market Equilibrium with Personal Taxes," *Econometrica* 51, no. 3 (1983): 611–636; Robert M. Dammon and Chester S. Spatt, "The Optimal Trading and Pricing of Securities with Asymmetric Capital Gains Tax-es and Transaction Costs," *Review of Financial Studies* 9, no. 3 (1996): 921–952; Robert M. Dammon, Chester S. Spatt, and Harold H. Zhang, "Optimal Consumption and Investment with Capital Gains Taxes," *Review of Financial Studies* 14, no. 3 (2001): 583–617; and Robert M. Dammon, Chester S. Spatt, and Harold H. Zhang, "Optimal Asset Location and Allocation with Taxable and Tax-Deferred Investing," *Journal of Finance* 59, no. 3 (2004): 999–1037.

such simplifying assumptions, the dimension of the problem grows exponentially with the number of stocks in a portfolio, and it is difficult to come up with computationally viable algorithms for portfolios of realistic size.

MULTI-ACCOUNT OPTIMIZATION

Portfolio managers who handle multiple accounts face an important practical issue. When individual clients' portfolios are managed, portfolio managers incorporate their clients' preferences and constraints. However, on any given trading day, the necessary trades for multiple diverse accounts are pooled and executed simultaneously. Moreover, typically trades may not be crossed, that is, it is not simply permissible to transfer an asset that should be sold on behalf of one client into the account of another client for whom the asset should be bought.[23] The trades should be executed in the market. Thus, each client's trades implicitly impact the results for the other clients: The *market impact* of the combined trades may be such that the benefits sought for individual accounts through trading are lost due to increased overall transaction costs. A robust multi-account management process should ensure accurate accounting and fair distribution of transaction costs among the individual accounts.

One possibility to handle the effect of trading in multiple accounts is to use an iterative process, in which at each iteration the market impact of the trades in previous iterations is taken into account.[24] More precisely, single clients' accounts are optimized as usual, and once the optimal allocations are obtained, the portfolio manager aggregates the trades and computes the actual marginal transaction costs based on the aggregate level of trading. The portfolio manager then reoptimizes individual accounts using these marginal transaction costs, and aggregates the resulting trades again to compute new marginal transaction costs, and so on. The advantage of this approach is that little needs to be changed in the way individual accounts are typically handled, so the existing single-account optimization and management infrastructure can be reused. The disadvantage is that most

---

[23]The Securities and Exchange Commission (SEC) in general prohibits cross-trading but does provide exemptions if prior to the execution of the cross trade the asset manager can demonstrate to the SEC that a particular cross trade benefits both parties. Similarly, Section 406(b)(3) of the Employee Retirement Income Security Act of 1974 (ERISA) forbids cross-trading, but there is new cross-trading exemption in Section 408(b)(19) adopted in the Pension Protection Act of 2006.

[24]Arlen Khodadadi, Reha Tutuncu, and Peter Zangari, "Optimization and Quantitative Investment Management," *Journal of Asset Management* 7, no. 2 (2006): 83–92.

generally, this iterative approach does not guarantee a convergence (or its convergence may be slow) to a "fair equilibrium," in which clients' portfolios receive an unbiased treatment with respect to the size and the constraint structure of their accounts.[25] The latter equilibrium is the one that would be attained if all clients traded independently and competitively in the market for liquidity, and is thus the correct and fair solution to the aggregate trading problem.

An alternative and more comprehensive approach is to optimize trades across all accounts simultaneously. O'Cinneide, Scherer, and Xu[26] describe such a model and show that it attains the fair equilibrium we mentioned previously.[27] Assume that client k's utility function is given by u_k, and is in the form of a dollar return penalized for risk. Assume also that a transaction cost model τ gives the cost of trading in dollars, and that τ is a convex increasing function.[28] Its exact form will depend on the details of how trading is implemented. Let $\mathbf{t}$ be the vector of trades. It will typically have the form $\left(t_1^+,...,t_N^+,t_1^-,...,t_N^-\right)$, that is, it will specify the aggregate buys t_i^+ and the aggregate sells t_i^- for each asset $i = 1, ..., N$, but it may also incorporate information about how the trade could be carried out.[29]

The multi-account optimization problem can be formulated as

$$\max_{\mathbf{w}_1,...,\mathbf{w}_K,\mathbf{t}} \quad E[u_1(\mathbf{w}_1)]+...+E[u_K(\mathbf{w}_K)]-\tau(\mathbf{t})$$

$$\text{s.t.} \quad \mathbf{w}_k \in C_k, k=1,...,K$$

where $\mathbf{w}_k$ is the N-dimensional vector of asset holdings (or weights) of client k, and C_k is the collection of constraints on the portfolio structure of client k. The objective can be interpreted as maximization of net expected utility,

[25]The iterative procedure is known to converge to the equilibrium, however, under special conditions. See Colm O'Cinneide, Bernd Scherer, and Xiaodong Xu, "Pooling Trades in a Quantitative Investment Process," *Journal of Portfolio Management* 32, no. 3 (2006): 33–43.

[26]O'Cinneide, Scherer, and Xu, "Pooling Trades in a Quantitative Investment Process."

[27]The issue of considering transaction costs in multi-account optimization has been discussed by others as well. See, for example, Bertsimas, Darnell, and Soucy, "Portfolio Construction through Mixed-Integer Programming at Grantham, Mayo, Van Otterloo and Company."

[28]As we mentioned earlier in this chapter, realistic transaction costs are in fact described by nonlinear functions, because costs per share traded typically increase with the size of the trade due to market impact.

[29]For example, if asset i is a euro-pound forward, then a trade in that asset can also be implemented as a euro-dollar forward plus a dollar-forward, so there will be two additional assets in the aggregate trade vector $\mathbf{t}$.

that is, as maximization of the expected dollar return penalized for risk and net of transaction costs.

The problem can be simplified by making some reasonable assumptions. For example, it can be assumed that the transaction cost function τ is additive across different assets, that is, trades in one asset do not influence trading costs in another. In such a case, the trading cost function can be split into more manageable terms, that is,

$$\tau(\mathbf{t}) = \sum_{i=1}^{N} \tau_i(t_i^+, t_i^-)$$

where $\tau_i(t_i^+, t_i^-)$ is the cost of trading asset i as a function of the aggregate buys and sells of that asset. Splitting the terms $\tau_i(t_i^+, t_i^-)$ further into separate costs of buying and selling, however, is not a reasonable assumption, because simultaneous buying and selling of an asset tends to have an offsetting effect on its price.

To formulate the problem completely, let $\mathbf{w}_k^0$ be the vector of original holdings (or weights) of client k's portfolio, $\mathbf{w}_k$ be the vector of decision variables for the optimal holdings (or weights) of client k's portfolio, and $\eta_{k,i}$ be constants that convert the holdings (or weight) of each asset i in client i's portfolio $w_{k,i}$ to dollars, that is, $\eta_{k,i} w_{k,i}$ is client k's dollar holdings of asset i.[30] We also introduce new variables $\mathbf{w}_k^+$ to represent the an upper bound on the weight of each asset client k will buy:

$$w_{k,i} - w_{k,i}^0 \le w_{k,i}^+, \quad i = 1, \dots, N, \, k = 1, \dots, K$$

The aggregate amount of asset i bought for all clients can then be computed as

$$t_i^+ = \sum_{k=1}^{K} \eta_{k,i} \cdot w_{k,i}^+$$

The aggregate amount of asset i sold for all clients can be easily expressed by noticing that the difference between the amounts bought and sold of each asset is exactly equal to the total amount of trades needed to get from the original position $w_{k,i}^0$ to the final position $w_{k,i}$ of that asset:[31]

---

[30]Note that $\eta_{k,i}$ equals 1 if $w_{k,i}$ is the actual dollar holdings.

[31]Note that, similarly to $\mathbf{w}_k^+$, we could introduce additional sell variables $\mathbf{w}_k^-$, but this is not necessary. By expressing aggregate sales through aggregate buys and total trades, we reduce the dimension of the optimization problem, because there are fewer decision variables. This would make a difference for the speed of obtaining a solution, especially in the case of large portfolios and complicated representation of transaction costs.

$$t_i^+ - t_i^- = \sum_{k=1}^{K} \eta_{k,i} \cdot \left(w_{k,i} - w_{k,i}^0 \right)$$

Here t_i^+ and t_i^- are nonnegative variables.

The multi-account optimization problem then takes the form

$$\max_{\mathbf{w}_1,\ldots,\mathbf{w}_K,\mathbf{t}^+,\mathbf{t}^-} \quad E[u_1(\mathbf{w}_1)] + \ldots + E[u_K(\mathbf{w}_K)] - \sum_{i=1}^{N} \tau_i(t_i^+, t_i^-)$$

$$\text{s.t.} \quad \mathbf{w}_k \in C_k, k = 1,\ldots,K$$

$$w_{k,i} - w_{k,i}^0 \leq w_{k,i}^+, \quad i = 1,\ldots,N, k = 1,\ldots,K$$

$$t_i^+ = \sum_{k=1}^{K} \eta_{k,i} w_{k,i}^+, \quad i = 1,\ldots,N$$

$$t_i^+ - t_i^- = \sum_{k=1}^{K} \eta_{k,i} \cdot \left(w_{k,i} - w_{k,i}^0 \right), \quad i = 1,\ldots,N$$

$$t_i^+ \geq 0, t_i^- \geq 0, w_{k,i}^+ \geq 0, \quad i = 1,\ldots,N, \quad k = 1,\ldots,K$$

O'Cinneide, Scherer, and Xu studied the behavior of the model in simulated experiments with a simple model for the transaction cost function, namely one in which

$$\tau(t) = \theta \cdot t^\gamma$$

where t is the trade size, and θ and γ are constants satisfying $\theta \geq 0$ and $\gamma \geq 1$.[32] θ and γ are specified in advance and calibrated to fit observed trading costs in the market. The transaction costs for each client k can therefore be expressed as

$$\tau_k = \theta \sum_{i=1}^{N} \left| w_{k,i} - w_{k,i}^0 \right|^\gamma$$

O'Cinneide, Scherer and Xu observed that key portfolio performance measures, such as the information ratio (IR),[33] turnover, and total transaction costs, change under this model relative to the traditional approach. Not surprisingly, the turnover and the net information ratios of the portfolios obtained with multi-account optimization are lower than those obtained with single-account optimization under the assumption that accounts are traded separately, while transaction costs are higher. These results are in

---

[32]Note that $\gamma = 1$ defines linear transaction costs. For linear transaction costs, multi-account optimization produces the same allocation as single-account optimization, because linear transaction costs assume that an increased aggregate amount of trading does not have an impact on prices.

[33]The information ratio is the ratio of (annualized) portfolio residual return (alpha) to (annualized) portfolio residual risk, where risk is defined as standard deviation.

fact more realistic, and are a better representation of the post-optimization performance of multiple client accounts in practice.

ROBUST PARAMETER ESTIMATION

The most commonly used approach for estimating security expected returns, covariances, and other parameters that are inputs to portfolio optimization models is to calculate the sample analogues from historical data. These are sample estimates for the parameters we need. It is important to remember that when we rely on historical data for estimation purposes, we in fact assume that the past provides a good representation of the future.

It is well-known, however, that expected returns exhibit significant time variation (referred to as *nonstationarity*). They are impacted by changes in markets and economic conditions, such as interest rates the political environment, consumer confidence, and the business cycles of different industry sectors and geographical regions. Consequently, extrapolated historical returns are often poor forecasts of future returns.

Similarly, the covariance matrix is unstable over time. Moreover, sample estimates of covariances for portfolios with thousands stocks are notoriously unreliable, because we need large data sets to estimate them, and such large data sets of relevant data are difficult to procure. Estimates of the covariance matrix based on *factor models* are often used to reduce the number of statistical estimates needed from a limited set of data.

In practice, portfolio managers often alter historical estimates of different parameters subjectively or objectively, based on their expectations and forecasting models for future trends. They also use statistical methods for finding estimators that are less sensitive to outliers and other sampling errors, such as Bayesian and shrinkage estimators. A complete review of advanced statistical estimation topics is beyond the scope of this chapter. We provide a brief overview of the most widely used concepts.[34]

Shrinkage is a form of averaging different estimators. The shrinkage estimator typically consists of three components: (1) an estimator with little or no structure (like the sample mean); (2) an estimator with a lot of structure (the shrinkage target); and (3) a coefficient that reflects the shrinkage intensity. Probably the most well-known estimator for expected returns in the financial literature was proposed by Jorion.[35] The shrinkage target in

---

[34]For further details, see Chapters 6, 7, and 8 in Frank J. Fabozzi, Petter N. Kolm, Dessislava A. Pachamanova, and Sergio Focardi, *Robust Portfolio Optimization and Management* (Hoboken, NJ: John Wiley & Sons, 2007).

[35]Philippe Jorion, "Bayes-Stein Estimator for Portfolio Analysis," *Journal of Financial and Quantitative Analysis* 21, no. 3 (1986): 279–292.

Jorion's model is a vector array with the return on the minimum variance portfolio, and the shrinkage intensity is determined from a specific formula.[36] Shrinkage estimators are used for estimates of the covariance matrix of returns as well[37]), although equally weighted *portfolios of covariance matrix estimators* have been shown to be equally effective as shrinkage estimators as well.[38]

Bayesian estimation approaches, named after the English mathematician Thomas Bayes, are based on subjective interpretations of the probability that a particular event will occur. A probability distribution, called the *prior distribution,* is used to represent the investor's knowledge about the probability before any data are observed. After more information is gathered (e.g., data are observed), a formula (known as *Bayes' rule*) is used to compute the new probability distribution, called the *posterior distribution.*

In the portfolio parameter estimation context, a posterior distribution of expected returns is derived by combining the forecast from the empirical data with a prior distribution. One of the most well-known examples of the application of the Bayesian framework in this context is the *Black-Litterman model,*[39] which produces an estimate of future expected returns by combining the market equilibrium returns (i.e., returns that are derived from pricing models and observable data) with the investor's subjective views. The investor's views are expressed as absolute or relative deviations from the equilibrium together with confidence levels of the views (as measured by the standard deviation of the views).

The ability to incorporate exogenous insight, such as a portfolio manager's opinion, into quantitative forecasting models is important; this insight may be the most valuable input to the model. The Bayesian framework provides a mechanism for forecasting systems to use both important traditional information sources such as proprietary market data, and subjective external information sources such as analyst's forecasts.

It is important to realize that regardless of how sophisticated the estimation and forecasting methods are, they are always subject to estimation

---

[36]See Chapter 8 (p. 217) in Fabozzi, Kolm, Pachamanova, and Focardi, *Robust Portfolio Optimization and Management.*

[37]See, for example, Oliver Ledoit and Michael Wolf, "Improved Estimation of the Covariance Matrix of Stock Returns with an Application to Portfolio Selection," *Journal of Empirical Finance* 10, no. 5 (2003): 603–621.

[38]For an overview of such models, see David Disatnik and Simon Benninga, "Shrinking the Covariance Matrix—Simpler is Better," *Journal of Portfolio Management* 33, no. 4 (2007): 56–63.

[39]For a step-by-step description of the Black-Litterman model, see Chapter 8 in Fabozzi, Kolm, Pachamanova, and Focardi, *Robust Portfolio Optimization and Management.*

error. What makes matters worse, however, is that different estimation errors can accumulate over the different activities of the portfolio management process, resulting in large aggregate errors at the final stage. It is therefore critical that the inputs evaluated at each stage are reliable and robust, so that the aggregate impact of estimation errors is minimized.

PORTFOLIO RESAMPLING

Robust parameter estimation is only one part of ensuring that the quantitative portfolio management process as a whole is reliable. It has been observed that portfolio allocation schemes are very sensitive to small changes in the inputs that go into the optimizer. In particular, a well-known study by Black and Litterman[40] demonstrated that in the case of mean-variance optimization, small changes in the inputs for expected returns had a substantial impact on the portfolio composition. "Optimal" portfolios constructed under conditions of uncertainty can have extreme or nonintuitive weights for some stocks.

With advances in computational capabilities and new research in the area of optimization under uncertainty, practitioners in recent years have been able to incorporate considerations for uncertainty not only at the estimation, but also at the portfolio optimization stage. Methods for taking into consideration inaccuracies in the inputs to the portfolio optimization problem include simulation (resampling) and robust optimization. We explain portfolio resampling in this section, and robust portfolio optimization in the following section.

A logical approach to making portfolio allocation more robust with respect to changes in the input parameters is to generate different scenarios for the values these parameters can take, and find weights that remain stable for small changes in the input parameters. This method is referred to as *portfolio resampling*.[41] To illustrate the resampling technique, we explain how it is applied to portfolio mean-variance optimization.

Suppose that have initial estimates for the expected stock returns, $\hat{\mu}$, and covariance matrix $\hat{\Sigma}$, for the N stocks in the portfolio. (We use "hat" to denote a statistical estimate.)

---

[40]See Fisher Black and Robert Litterman, "Global Portfolio Optimization," *Financial Analysts Journal* 48, no. 5 (1992): 28–43.

[41]See Richard O. Michaud, *Efficient Asset Management: A Practical Guide to Stock Portfolio Optimization and Asset Allocation* (Oxford: Oxford University Press, 1998); Jorion, "Bayes-Stein Estimator for Portfolio Analysis"; and Bernd Scherer, "Portfolio Resampling: Review and Critique," *Financial Analysts Journal* 58, no. 6 (2002): 98–109.

1. We simulate S samples of N returns from a multivariate normal distribution with mean $\hat{\mu}$ and covariance matrix $\hat{\Sigma}$.
2. We use the S samples we generated in (1) to compute S new estimates of vectors of expected returns $\hat{\mu}_1, ..., \hat{\mu}_S$ and covariance matrices $\hat{\Sigma}_1, ..., \hat{\Sigma}_S$.
3. We solve S portfolio optimization problems, one for each estimated pair of expected returns and covariances $(\hat{\mu}_s, \hat{\Sigma}_s)$, and save the weights for the N stocks in a vector array $\mathbf{w}^{(s)}$, where $s = 1, ..., S$. (The optimization problem itself could be any of the standard mean-variance formulations: maximize expected return subject to constraints on risk, minimize risk subject to constraints on the expected return, or maximize the utility function.)
4. To find the final portfolio weights, we average out the weight for each stock over the S weights found for that stock in each of the S optimization problems. In other words,

$$\mathbf{w} = \frac{1}{S} \sum_{s=1}^{S} \mathbf{w}^{(s)}$$

For example, stock i in the portfolio has final weight

$$w_i = \frac{w_i^{(1)} + \cdots + w_i^{(S)}}{S}$$

5. Perhaps even more valuable than the average estimate of the weights obtained from the simulation and optimization iterations is the probability distribution we obtain for the portfolio weights. If we plot the weights for each stock obtained over the S iterations, $w_i^{(1)}, ..., w_i^{(S)}$, we can get a sense for how variable this stock weight is in the portfolio. A large standard deviation computed from the distribution of portfolio weight i will be an indication that the original portfolio weight was not very precise due to estimation error.

An important question, of course, is how large is "large enough." Do we have evidence that the portfolios we obtained through resampling are statistically different from one another? We can evaluate that by using a test statistic. For example, it can be shown that the test statistic

$$d(\mathbf{w}^*, \mathbf{w}) = (\mathbf{w}^* - \mathbf{w})' \Sigma (\mathbf{w}^* - \mathbf{w})$$

follows a chi-square (χ^2) distribution with degrees of freedom equal to the number of securities in the portfolio. If the value of this statistic is statistically "large," then there will be evidence that the portfolio weights $\mathbf{w}'$ and $\mathbf{w}$ are statistically different. This is an important insight for the portfolio manager, and its applications extend beyond just resampling. Let us provide some intuition as to why.

Suppose that we are considering rebalancing our current portfolio. Given our forecasts of expected returns and risk, we could calculate a set of new portfolios through the resampling procedure. Using the test statistic above, we determine whether the new set of portfolio weights are statistically different from our current weights and, therefore, whether it would be worthwhile to rebalance or not. If we decide that it is worthwhile to rebalance, we could choose any of the resampled portfolios that are statistically different from our current portfolio. Which one should we choose? A natural choice would be to select the portfolio that would lead to the lowest transaction costs. The idea of determining statistically equivalent portfolios, therefore, has much wider implications than the ones illustrated in the context of resampling.

Resampling has its drawbacks:

- Since the resampled portfolio is calculated through a simulation procedure in which a portfolio optimization problem needs to be solved at each step, the approach is computationally cumbersome, especially for large portfolios. There is a trade-off between the number of resampling steps and the accuracy of estimation of the effect of errors on the portfolio composition.
- Due to the averaging in the calculation of the final portfolio weights, it is highly likely that all stocks will end up with nonzero weights. This has implications for the amount of transaction costs that will be incurred if the final portfolio is to be attained. One possibility is to include constraints that limit both the turnover and the number of stocks with nonzero weights. As we saw earlier, however, the formulation of such constraints adds another level of complexity to the optimization problem, and will slow down the resampling procedure.
- Since the averaging process happens *after* the optimization problems are solved, the final weights may not actually satisfy some of the constraints in the optimization formulation. In general, only convex (such as linear) constraints are guaranteed to be satisfied by the averaged final weights. Turnover constraints, for example, may not be satisfied. This is a serious limitation of the resampling approach for practical applications.

Despite these limitations, resampling has advantages, and presents a good alternative to using only point estimates of inputs to the optimization problem.

ROBUST PORTFOLIO OPTIMIZATION

Another way in which uncertainty about the inputs can be modeled is by incorporating it directly into the optimization process. Robust optimization is an intuitive and efficient way to deal with uncertainty. Robust portfolio optimization does not use the traditional forecasts, such as expected returns and stock covariances, but rather uncertainty sets containing these point estimates. An example of such an uncertainty set is a confidence interval around the forecast for each expected return (alpha). This uncertainty shape looks like a "box" in the space of the input parameters. (See Exhibit 18.2(A).) We can also formulate advanced uncertainty sets that incorporate more knowledge about the estimation error. For instance, a widely used uncertainty set is the ellipsoidal uncertainty set, which takes into consideration the covariance structure of the estimation errors. (See Exhibit 18.2(B).) We will see examples of both uncertainty sets in this section.

The robust optimization procedure for portfolio allocation is as follows. First, we specify the uncertainty sets around the input parameters in the problem. Then, we ask what the optimal portfolio allocation is when the input parameters take the worst possible value inside these uncertainty sets. In effect, we solve an inner problem which determines the worst possible realization of the uncertain parameters over the uncertainty set before we solve the original problem of optimal portfolio allocation.

Let us give a specific example of how the robust optimization framework can be applied in the portfolio optimization context. Consider the utility function formulation of the mean-variance portfolio allocation problem:

$$\max_{\mathbf{w}} \quad \mathbf{w}'\boldsymbol{\mu} - \lambda \cdot \mathbf{w}'\Sigma\mathbf{w}$$

$$\text{s.t.} \quad \mathbf{w}'\iota = 1$$

Suppose that we have estimates $\hat{\boldsymbol{\mu}}$ and $\hat{\Sigma}$ of the vector of expected returns and the covariance matrix. Instead of the estimate $\hat{\boldsymbol{\mu}}$, however, we will consider a set of vectors $\boldsymbol{\mu}$ that are "close" to $\hat{\boldsymbol{\mu}}$. We define the box uncertainty set:

$$U_\delta(\hat{\boldsymbol{\mu}}) = \left\{ \boldsymbol{\mu} \mid \left| \mu_i - \hat{\mu}_i \right| \leq \delta_i, i = 1, \ldots, N \right\}$$

In words, the set $U_\delta(\hat{\boldsymbol{\mu}})$ contains all vectors $\boldsymbol{\mu} = (\mu_1, \ldots, \mu_N)$ such that each component μ_i is in the interval $[\hat{\mu}_i - \delta_i, \hat{\mu}_i + \delta_i]$. We then solve the following problem:

$$\max_{\mathbf{w}} \quad \left\{ \min_{\boldsymbol{\mu} \in U_\delta(\hat{\boldsymbol{\mu}})} \left\{ \boldsymbol{\mu}'\mathbf{w} \right\} - \lambda \cdot \mathbf{w}'\Sigma\mathbf{w} \right\}$$

$$\text{s.t.} \quad \mathbf{w}'\iota = 1$$

EXHIBIT 18.2

A. Box Uncertainty Set in Three Dimensions

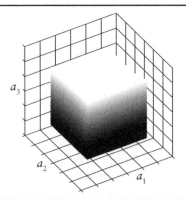

B. Ellipsoidal Uncertainty Set in Three Dimensions

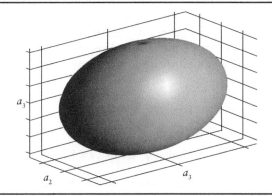

This is called the *robust counterpart* of the original problem. It is a max-min problem that searches for the optimal portfolio weights when the estimates of the uncertain returns take their worst-case values within the prespecified uncertainty set in the sense that the value of the objective function is the worst it can be over all possible values for the expected returns in the uncertainty set.

It can be shown[42] that the max-min problem above is equivalent to the following problem:

---

[42]For derivation, see, for example, Chapter 12 in Fabozzi, Kolm, Pachamanova, and Focardi, *Robust Portfolio Optimization and Management* or Chapter 9 in Pachamanova and Fabozzi, *Simulation and Optimization in Finance.*

$$\max_{\mathbf{w}} \quad \mathbf{w}'\boldsymbol{\mu} - \boldsymbol{\delta}'|\mathbf{w}| - \lambda \cdot \mathbf{w}'\Sigma\mathbf{w}$$

$$\text{s.t.} \quad \mathbf{w}'\iota = 1$$

where $|\mathbf{w}|$ denotes the absolute value of the entries of the vector of weights $\mathbf{w}$. To gain some intuition, notice that if the weight of stock i in the portfolio is negative, the worst-case expected return for stock i is $\mu_i + \delta_i$ (we lose the largest amount possible). If the weight of stock i in the portfolio is positive, then the worst-case expected return for stock i is $\mu_i - \delta_i$ (we gain the smallest amount possible). Observe that $\mu_i w_i - \delta_i |w_i|$ equals $(\mu_i - \delta_i)w_i$ if the weight w_i is positive and $(\mu_i + \delta_i)w_i$ if the weight w_i is negative. Hence, the mathematical expression in the objective agrees with our intuition: It minimizes the worst-case expected portfolio return. In this robust version of the mean-variance formulation, stocks whose mean return estimates are less accurate (i.e., have a larger estimation error δ_i) are therefore penalized in the objective function and will tend to have a smaller weight in the optimal portfolio allocation.

This optimization problem has the same computational complexity as the nonrobust mean-variance formulation—namely, it can be stated as a quadratic optimization problem. The latter can be achieved by using a standard trick that allows us to get rid of the absolute values for the weights. The idea is to introduce an N-dimensional vector of additional variables ψ to replace the absolute values $|\mathbf{w}|$, and to write an equivalent version of the optimization problem,

$$\max_{\mathbf{w},\psi} \quad \mathbf{w}'\hat{\boldsymbol{\mu}} - \boldsymbol{\delta}'\psi - \lambda \cdot \mathbf{w}'\Sigma\mathbf{w}$$

$$\text{s.t.} \quad \mathbf{w}'\iota = 1$$

$$\psi_i \geq w_i \; ; \; \psi_i \geq -w_i \, , i = 1, \dots, N$$

Therefore, incorporating considerations about the uncertainty in the estimates of the expected returns in this example has virtually no computational cost.

We can view the effect of this particular "robustification" of the mean-variance portfolio optimization formulation in two different ways. On the one hand, we can see that the values of the expected returns for the different stocks have been adjusted downwards in the objective function of the optimization problem. That is, the robust optimization model "shrinks" the expected return of stocks with large estimation error, i.e., in this case the robust formulation is related to statistical shrinkage methods, which we introduced earlier in this chapter. On the other hand, we can interpret the additional term in the objective function as a "risk-like" term that represents penalty for estimation error. The size of the penalty is determined by the investor's aversion to estimation risk, and is reflected in the magnitude of the deltas.

More complicated specifications for uncertainty sets have more involved mathematical representations, but can still be selected so that they preserve an easy computational structure for the robust optimization problem. For example, we can use the ellipsoidal uncertainty set from Exhibit 18.2(B), which can be expressed mathematically as

$$ U_\delta(\hat{\mu}) = \left\{ \mu \,\middle|\, (\mu - \hat{\mu})' \, \Sigma_\mu^{-1} (\mu - \hat{\mu}) \le \delta^2 \right\} $$

Here Σ_δ is the covariance matrix of estimation errors for the vector of expected returns μ. This uncertainty set represents the requirement that the sum of squares (scaled by the inverse of the covariance matrix of estimation errors) between all elements in the set and the point estimates $\hat{\mu}_1, \hat{\mu}_2, ..., \hat{\mu}_N$ can be no larger than δ^2. We note that this uncertainty set cannot be interpreted as individual confidence intervals around each point estimate. Instead, it captures the idea of a joint confidence region. In practical applications, the covariance matrix of estimation errors is often assumed to be diagonal. In the latter case, the set contains all vectors of expected returns that are within a certain number of standard deviations from the point estimate of the vector of expected returns, and the resulting robust portfolio optimization problem would protect the investor if the vector of expected returns is within that range.

It can be shown that the robust counterpart of the mean-variance portfolio optimization problem with an ellipsoidal uncertainty set for the expected return estimates is the following optimization problem formulation:

$$ \max_{\mathbf{w}} \quad \mathbf{w}'\mu - \lambda \cdot \mathbf{w}'\Sigma\mathbf{w} - \delta \cdot \sqrt{\mathbf{w}'\Sigma_\mu \mathbf{w}} $$
$$ \text{s.t.} \quad \mathbf{w}'\iota = 1 $$

This is a second-order cone optimization problem, and requires specialized software to solve, but the methods for solving it are very efficient.

Similarly, to the case of the robust counterpart with a box uncertainty set, we can interpret the extra term in the objective function

$$ \left(\delta \cdot \sqrt{\mathbf{w}'\Sigma_\mu \mathbf{w}} \right) $$

as the penalty for estimation risk, where δ incorporates the degree of the investor's aversion to estimation risk. Note, by the way, that the covariance matrix in the estimation error penalty term, Σ_μ, is not necessarily the same as the covariance matrix of returns Σ. In fact, it is not immediately obvious how Σ_μ can be estimated from data. Σ_μ is the covariance matrix of the errors in the estimation of the expected (average) returns. Thus, if a portfolio manager forecasts 5% active return over the next time period, but gets 1%, he cannot argue that there was a 4% error in his expected return—the actual error would consist of both an estimation error in the expected return and the inherent volatility in actual realized returns. In fact, critics of the approach have argued that the realized returns typically have large stochastic components that dwarf the expected returns. For that reason, estimating Σ_μ from data is very hard, if not impossible.[43]

Several approximate methods for estimating Σ_μ have been found to work well in practice. For example, it has been observed that simpler estimation approaches, such as using just the diagonal matrix containing the variances of the estimates (as opposed to the complete error covariance matrix), often provide most of the benefit in robust portfolio optimization.[44] In addition, standard approaches for estimating expected returns, such as Bayesian statistics and regression-based methods, can produce estimates for the estimation error covariance matrix in the process of generating the estimates themselves.[45]

Among practitioners, the notion of robust portfolio optimization is often equated with the robust mean-variance model we discussed in this section, with the box or the ellipsoidal uncertainty sets for the expected stock returns. While robust optimization applications often involve one form or another of this model, the actual scope of robust optimization can be much broader. We note that the term *robust optimization* refers to the technique of incorporating information about uncertainty sets for the parameters in the optimization model and not to the specific definitions of uncertainty sets or the choice of parameters to model as uncertain. For example, we can use the robust optimization methodology to incorporate considerations for uncertainty in the estimate of the covariance matrix in addition to the uncertainty in expected returns and obtain a different robust portfolio allocation formulation. Robust optimization can be applied also to portfolio allocation models that are different from the mean-variance framework, such as Sharpe ratio optimization and value-at-risk optimization.[46] Finally, robust optimization

---

[43]See Jyh-Huei Lee, Dan Stefek, and Alexander Zhelenyak, "Robust Portfolio Optimization—A Closer Look," report, *MSCI Barra Research Insights*, June 2006.

[44]See Robert Stubbs and Pamela Vance, "Computing Return Estimation Error Matrices for Robust Optimization," report, Axioma, 2005.

[45]For a more in-depth coverage of the topic of estimating input parameters for robust optimization formulations, see Chapter 12 in Fabozzi, Kolm, Pachamanova, and Focardi *Robust Portfolio Optimization and Management*.

[46]See, for example, Donald Goldfarb and Garud Iyengar, "Robust Portfolio Selection Problems," *Mathematics of Operations Research* 28, no. 1 (2003): 1–38; and Karthik Natarajan, Dessislava Pachamanova, and Melvyn Sim, "Incorporating Asymmetric Distributional Information in Robust Value-at-Risk Optimization," *Management Science* 54, no. 3 (2008): 573–585.

has the potential to provide a computationally efficient way to handle portfolio optimization over multiple stages—a problem for which so far there have been few satisfactory solutions.[47] There are numerous useful robust formulations, but a complete review is beyond the scope of this chapter.[48]

Is implementing robust optimization formulations worthwhile? Some tests with simulated and real market data indicate that robust optimization, when inaccuracy is assumed in the expected return estimates, outperforms classical mean-variance optimization in terms of total excess return a large percentage (70%–80%) of the time.[49] Other tests have not been as conclusive.[50] The factor that accounts for much of the difference is how the uncertainty in parameters is modeled. Therefore, finding a suitable degree of robustness and appropriate definitions of uncertainty sets can have a significant impact on portfolio performance.

Independent tests by practitioners and academics using both simulated and market data appear to confirm that robust optimization generally results in more stable portfolio weights, that is, that it eliminates the extreme corner solutions resulting from traditional mean-variance optimization. This fact has implications for portfolio rebalancing in the presence of transaction costs and taxes, as transaction costs and taxes can add substantial expenses when the portfolio is rebalanced. Depending on the particular robust formulations employed, robust mean-variance optimization also appears to improve worst-case portfolio performance, and results in smoother and more consistent portfolio returns. Finally, by preventing large swings in positions, robust optimization typically makes better use of the turnover budget and risk constraints.

Robust optimization, however, is not a panacea. By using robust portfolio optimization formulations, investors are likely to trade off the optimality of their portfolio allocation in cases in which nature behaves as they predicted for protection against the risk of inaccurate estimation. Therefore, investors using the technique should not expect to do better than classical

---

[47]See Aharon Ben-Tal, Tamar Margalit, and Arkadi Nemirovski, "Robust Modeling of Multi-Stage Portfolio Problems," in *High-Performance Optimization*, edited by H. Frenk, K. Roos, T. Terlaky, and S. Zhang (Dordrecht: Kluwer Academic Publishers, 2000), pp. 303–328; and Dimitris Bertsimas and Dessislava Pachamanova, "Robust Multiperiod Portfolio Management with Transaction Costs," *Computers and Operations Research* 35, no. 1, special issue on Applications of Operations Research in Finance (2008): 3–17.

[48]For further details, see Fabozzi, Kolm, Pachamanova, and Focardi (2007).

[49]See Sebastian Ceria and Robert Stubbs, "Incorporating Estimation Errors into Portfolio Selection: Robust Portfolio Construction," *Journal of Asset Management* 7, no. 2 (2006): 109–127.

[50]See Lee, Stefek, and Zhelenyak "Robust Portfolio Optimization—A Closer Look."

portfolio optimization when estimation errors have little impact, or when typical scenarios occur. They should, however, expect insurance in scenarios in which their estimates deviate from the actual realized values by up to the amount they have prespecified in the modeling process.

KEY POINTS

- Commonly used constraints in practice include long-only (no short-selling) constraints, turnover constraints, holding constraints, risk factor constraints, and tracking error constraints. These constraints can be handled in a straightforward way by the same type of optimization algorithms used for solving the classical mean-variance portfolio allocation problem.
- Minimum holding constraints, transaction-size constraints, cardinality constraints and round-lot constraints are also widely used in practice, but their nature is such that they require binary and integer modeling, which necessitates the use of mixed-integer and other specialized optimization solvers.
- Transaction costs can easily be incorporated in standard portfolio allocation models. Typical functions for representing transaction costs include linear, piecewise linear, and quadratic.
- Taxes can have a dramatic effect on portfolio returns; however, it is difficult to incorporate them into the classical portfolio optimization framework. Their importance to the individual investor is a strong argument for taking a multiperiod view of investments, but the computational burden of multiperiod portfolio optimization formulations with taxes is extremely high.
- For investment managers who handle multiple accounts, increased transaction costs because of the market impact of simultaneous trades can be an important practical issue and should be taken into consideration when individual clients' portfolio allocation decisions are made to ensure fairness across accounts.
- As the use of quantitative techniques has become widespread in the investment industry, the consideration of estimation risk and model risk has grown in importance. Methods for robust statistical estimation of parameters include shrinkage and Bayesian techniques.
- Portfolio resampling is a technique that uses simulation generate multiple scenarios for possible values of the input parameters in the portfolio optimization problem, and aims to determine portfolio weights that remain stable with respect to small changes in model parameters.

■ Robust portfolio optimization incorporates uncertainty directly into the optimization process. The uncertain parameters in the optimization problem are assumed to vary in prespecified uncertainty sets that are selected subjectively or based on data.

QUESTIONS

1. What are the most common constraints encountered in optimal portfolio allocation in practice?

2. State the standard definition of tracking error and discuss why other definitions of tracking error may be used.

3. How are transaction costs typically incorporated in portfolio allocation models?

4. Give an example of how the presence of taxes changes the concept of risk in portfolio optimization.

5. A limitation in the implementation of the mean-variance model for portfolio optimization is that one of the critical inputs in the model, the sample covariance matrix, is subject to considerable estimation risk. This can skew the optimizer towards suggesting extreme weights for some of the stocks in the portfolio and lead to poor performance. Explain what approaches can be used to deal with the problem.

CHAPTER 19

Portfolio Construction and Extreme Risk

Jennifer Bender, Ph.D.
Vice President
MSCI

Jyh-Huei Lee
Vice President
MSCI

Dan Stefek, Ph.D.
Managing Director
MSCI

The events of the last few years have refocused attention on risk—particularly the risk of extreme losses. Fortunately, researchers have recently developed new models and analytics for understanding and managing extreme risk. In this chapter, we look at using such tools to enhance portfolio construction. Our goal is to adapt mean-variance optimization to produce active portfolios with less exposure to extreme losses than normal optimized portfolios. We do so by constraining the shortfall beta of the optimal portfolio. Shortfall beta measures the sensitivity of a portfolio to periods of extreme stress.

The empirical study we present illustrates the possible benefits of constraining shortfall beta. Using three common alpha signals, we compare portfolios constructed using optimization with and without a shortfall constraint. Interestingly, portfolios with shortfall constraints tend to fare better during turbulent periods and outperformed their mean variance counterparts over the period from January 1994 through June 2009. This is true even after we prevent the portfolio from timing the benchmark by requiring its beta to be one. While this study does not account for many of the costs and constraints managers face, the results are intriguing.

MEASURES OF EXTREME LOSS

In portfolio management, a common measure of risk is the standard deviation of return, also known as *volatility*. Volatility reflects the typical range of returns that a manager might expect to see. Researchers, including Bertsimas[1] and Goldberg and Hayes,[2] have encouraged investors to supplement volatility with measures of extreme risk that more clearly portray the depth of potential losses. The magnitude of extreme losses may not be apparent even from the best volatility forecasts.

One measure of extreme risk is *expected shortfall*, or simply, *shortfall*. Shortfall is a measure of the expected loss over a given horizon, which in our study we define as one day. It represents how much a portfolio is expected to lose on a bad day. Loss can be measured either in terms of the value of the portfolio or the return of the portfolio. Focusing on return, we define the loss of a portfolio P to be: $L_p = -r_p$; thus, L_p measures the magnitude of the loss.

A more precise definition of the expected shortfall ES_p, of portfolio P, is

$$ES_p = E[L_p | L_p > VaR_p] \qquad (19.1)$$

Here, VaR_p denotes the portfolio's Value at Risk. The portfolio suffers a return worse than VaR_p or less, no more than 5% of the time.[3] Thus, shortfall is the expected size of the loss, given that the loss is among the 5% worst losses the portfolio experiences.

It is useful to understand how an asset's return is likely to respond when a portfolio sustains extreme losses. Does it tend to fall more or less than the portfolio, or not at all? Just as beta describes this behavior on average, shortfall beta captures this behavior during periods of extreme loss.

The shortfall beta, β, of asset i with respect to portfolio P can be written as

$$\beta_{S,i} = \frac{E[L_i | L_p > VaR_p]}{ES_p} \qquad (19.2)$$

where L_i is the loss to asset i.

---

[1]Dimitris Bertsimas, Geoffrey J. Lauprete, and Alexander Samarov, "Shortfall as a Risk Measure: Properties, Optimization and Applications," *Journal of Economic Dynamics and Control* 28, no. 7 (2004): 1353–1381.
[2]Lisa Goldberg, and Michael Hayes, "The Long View of Financial Risk," report, *MSCI Barra Research Insight* (2009).
[3]VaR can be computed at other likelihoods of loss as well. For example, The portfolio suffers a return worse than VaR_p at 1% or less no more than 1% of the time.

To estimate the beta of an asset, we first compute the expected shortfall of the portfolio and the expected shortfall of the asset. To do this, we simulate returns to the asset (or portfolio) using its current exposures and a history of daily factor returns over the last four years, ignoring the specific return. We then compute the sample shortfall. The methodology is similar to that developed by Goldberg and Hayes[4] and outlined in *Barra Extreme Risk Analytics Guide*[5]; however there a longer period to estimate shortfall is used. Further details are provided in the appendix to this chapter.

CONSTRAINING SHORTFALL

The standard active management, mean-variance optimization problem trades off risk against return. To limit the portfolio's exposure to extreme losses, we may constrain the shortfall beta of the portfolio. This is done by adding a single constraint, giving us what we will call the *shortfall-constrained* optimization problem:

$$\text{Maximize } h'\alpha - \frac{\lambda}{2}(h - h_B)'\Sigma(h - h_B)$$

subject to: $h'e = 1$ Full investment

              $h'\beta_S \leq S$ Shortfall beta bound   (19.3)

where h are the portfolio weights, α is the vector of alphas, Σ is the covariance matrix, and λ is the risk aversion parameter. The term β_S is the vector of asset-level shortfall betas ($\beta_{S,i}$) with respect to the benchmark portfolio and S is the maximum portfolio shortfall beta permitted.[6]

PERFORMANCE

We compare the performance of standard and shortfall constrained optimization in an empirical study, using three different alpha signals: relative strength, predicted earnings-to-price ratio (E/P), and cash plowback. For each signal, we create an optimal portfolio that has a forecast active risk of

---

[4]Lisa Goldberg, and Michael Hayes, "Barra Extreme Risk," report, MSCI Barra Research Conference 2010.
[5]MSCI Barra, *Barra Extreme Risk Analytics Guide* (New York: 2010).
[6]Prior research has also shown how shortfall can be directly included in the objective function; see Bertsimas, Lauprete, and Samarov, "Shortfall as a Risk Measure: Properties, Optimization and Applications." This approach deserves separate consideration, however, and we save this topic for a future study.

4%. We use the MSCI US Prime Market 750 Index as both the universe and benchmark, and the Barra Short-Term US Equity Model (USE3S) as the risk model. We rebalance the portfolios monthly over the test period from January 1994 to May 2009. When constraining shortfall beta, we set the upper bound to 0.9 to produce portfolios with less sensitivity to extreme market losses. We also relax the long-only constraint, allowing up to 5% shorting of individual stocks.

In portfolio optimization, imposing constraints tends to alter the ex-ante active risk that the optimal portfolio achieves for a fixed level of risk aversion. To ensure that any differences between shortfall and standard optimization are not simply due to differing levels of aggressiveness, we require each portfolio to have the same forecast active risk of 4%.

Exhibit 19.1 shows the cumulative difference in returns obtained using shortfall constrained optimization and standard optimization. We see that constraining shortfall beta improves performance for most signals during two main turbulent periods—the middle of 2000 through the middle of 2002 and late 2007 through 2008. On the other hand, standard optimization performs better in the few years before the bursting of the Internet bubble.

Exhibit 19.2 analyzes the results by time period. Again, the shortfall constraint tends to improve the performance of the strategies in periods where the market is down (January 2000–December 2002 and January

EXHIBIT 19.1 Cumulative Gains from Constraining Shortfall Beta Constraint

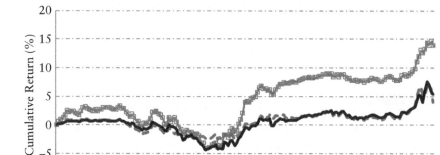

---

[a]Difference between mean variance optimization with shortfall constraint and mean-optimization without constraint.

EXHIBIT 19.2 Constraining on Shortfall Betas (base case): Information Ratios

	Relative Strength		Predicted E/P		Cash Plowback	
	Mean-Variance (MV)	MV with Shortfall	Mean-Variance (MV)	MV with Shortfall	Mean-Variance (MV)	MV with Shortfall
Jan. 1994–May 2009	0.33	0.51	0.77	0.83	0.64	0.73
By subperiod						
Jan. 1994–Dec. 1999	0.53	0.49	0.57	0.52	0.78	0.66
Jan. 2000–Dec. 2002	0.22	0.81	1.38	1.57	1.24	1.64
Jan. 2003–Dec. 2006	0.39	0.50	1.25	1.29	0.22	0.30
Jan. 2007–May 2009	–0.23	0.22	0.07	0.26	0.23	0.54

2007–May 2009). In the other periods, there are small or mixed differences in performance between the two optimization approaches.

The contrast in performance may be due, in part, to the differences in the betas of mean variance and shortfall constrained portfolios. Shortfall constrained portfolios tend to have lower betas. For the momentum strategy, the betas for shortfall constrained portfolios were 0.07 lower than their mean-variance counterparts, on average. These differences are not surprising since the average correlation between the betas and the shortfall betas of the MSCI US Prime Market 750 Index stocks is 0.92 over our analysis period. Constraining shortfall beta indirectly constrains beta.

IMPOSING BENCHMARK NEUTRALITY

To separate the effects of beta and shortfall beta, we rerun the optimizations, this time requiring the beta of all portfolios to be one. Specifically, we add the constraint: $h'\beta = 1$ to the problem in (19.3) where β is a vector of betas with respect to the MSCI US Prime Market 750 Index. This is of particular interest to managers who do not time the benchmark.

Exhibits 19.3 and 19.4 show that the benefits of constraining shortfall beta are even greater than before. As before, shortfall constrained optimization outperforms standard optimization over the entire period. It also outperforms during the Internet meltdown and to some extent over the more recent turbulent period, particularly for the relative strength strategy. Lastly, we see that by removing the benchmark timing implicit in shortfall optimization, we eliminate its underperformance during the Internet bubble.

Does constraining shortfall help protect against sharp daily losses? To address this question, we examine the realized shortfall of each portfolio

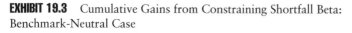

EXHIBIT 19.3 Cumulative Gains from Constraining Shortfall Beta: Benchmark-Neutral Case

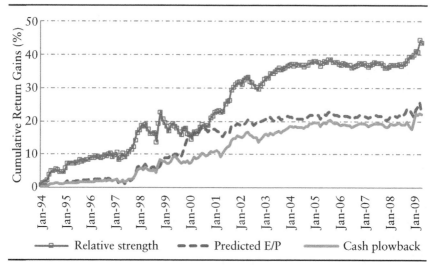

EXHIBIT 19.4 Constraining on Shortfall Betas: Benchmark-Neutral Case— Information Ratios

	Relative Strength		Predicted E/P		Cash Plowback	
	Mean-Variance (MV)	MV with Shortfall	Mean-Variance (MV)	MV with Shortfall	Mean-Variance (MV)	MV with Shortfall
Jan. 1994–May 2009	0.34	0.93	0.78	1.10	0.64	0.92
By subperiod						
Jan. 1994–Dec. 1999	0.54	1.11	0.57	1.01	0.76	0.95
Jan. 2000–Dec. 2002	0.27	1.28	1.38	1.84	1.27	1.85
Jan. 2003–Dec. 2006	0.36	0.70	1.26	1.37	0.21	0.46
Jan. 2007–May 2009	−0.21	0.32	0.12	0.20	0.27	0.54

by computing the average return of its 5% worst outcomes—the "bad days." Exhibit 19.5 shows the realized shortfall for nonoverlapping three year periods. Shortfall constrained portfolios have lower realized losses over each period, even though they have the same ex ante active risk as standard mean-variance portfolios. The difference in shortfall was greatest over the more volatile periods. We also find similar results at the yearly level.

EXHIBIT 19.5 Comparison of Realized Shortfall: Benchmark-Neutral Case

	Relative Strength		Predicted E/P		Cash Plowback	
	Mean-Variance (MV)	MV with Shortfall	Mean-Variance (MV)	MV with Shortfall	Mean-Variance (MV)	MV with Shortfall
Jan. 1994–Dec. 1996	1.57	1.50	1.53	1.50	1.48	1.46
Jan. 1997–Dec. 1999	2.77	2.72	2.69	2.63	2.69	2.67
Jan. 2000–Dec. 2002	3.22	3.09	3.25	3.15	3.18	3.12
Jan. 2003–Dec. 2005	1.94	1.90	1.79	1.78	1.77	1.74
Jan. 2006–Dec. 2008	4.58	4.31	4.52	4.30	4.24	4.10

ANALYSIS

How does constraining shortfall beta as shown above improve performance? The shortfall constraint forces the manager to adopt certain positions to limit the exposure to extreme losses. To better understand this, we decompose the active portfolio into positions due to the manager's alpha and positions taken to satisfy individual constraints. This decomposition is based on the portfolio optimality conditions.[7]

We can express the active portfolio as the sum of four component portfolios:

$$
h_A = \underbrace{\frac{\Sigma^{-1}\alpha}{\lambda}}_{h_{\text{Alpha}}} - \pi_I \underbrace{\frac{\Sigma^{-1}e}{\lambda}}_{h_{\text{Full investment}}} - \pi_\beta \underbrace{\frac{\Sigma^{-1}\beta}{\lambda}}_{h_{\text{Beta neutrality}}} - \pi_S \underbrace{\frac{\Sigma^{-1}\beta_S}{\lambda}}_{h_{\text{Shortfall beta}}} \tag{19.4}
$$

---

[7]The decomposition shown in the paper is based on the portfolio optimality conditions. For the shortfall constrained problem, these conditions are

$$
\underbrace{\alpha - \lambda\Sigma h_A}_{\substack{\text{Marginal} \\ \text{contribution to utility} \\ \text{(without constraints)}}} - \underbrace{\pi_I e - \pi_B \beta - \pi_s \beta_S}_{\text{Marginal cost of constraints}} = 0
$$

where h_A represents the active holdings and $\pi_I, \pi_\beta, \pi_{B_S}$ are the shadow prices of the full investment, beta and shortfall beta constraints, respectively. The shadow price of a constraint tells us how much utility changes as we increase the bound on the constraint. By multiplying both sides of the above equation by Σ^{-1}/λ and rearranging terms, we can express the optimized portfolio's holdings as a sum of individual component portfolios as in equation (19.4). This is discussed further in Jennifer Bender, Jyh-Huei Lee, and Dan Stefek, "Decomposing the Impact of Portfolio Constraints," *MSCI Barra Research Insights* (2009).

where h_A represents the active holdings and $\pi_I, \pi_\beta, \pi_{B_S}$ are the shadow prices[8] of the full investment, beta and shortfall beta constraints, respectively. Equation (19.4) shows the portfolio can be decomposed into the positions due to the manager's alpha (h_{Alpha}) and the positions taken to satisfy the three constraints—$h_{Full\ investment}, h_{Beta\ neutrality},$ and $h_{Shortfall\ beta}$.

The alpha portfolio is the portfolio in which the manager would invest in the absence of constraints. Each constraint portfolio—full investment, beta neutrality, and shortfall beta—contains the additional positions needed to satisfy that constraint in a way that maximizes portfolio utility. We define the *return due to each of these sources as the return of the corresponding portfolio.*

Exhibit 19.6 shows a return decomposition for the relative strength strategy implemented with standard mean variance optimization. The active return comes almost entirely from the alpha. Requiring the portfolio to be beta neutral and fully invested has little effect on performance.

Exhibit 19.7 shows the same breakdown for shortfall constrained optimization. The contribution from alpha is very similar to that obtained with mean-variance optimization. Once again, the full investment constraint has little impact on return. However, in this case, we constrain the shortfall beta while keeping the portfolio beta one. The "net shortfall beta portfolio,"

EXHIBIT 19.6 Return Decomposition for Standard Mean-Variance Optimization

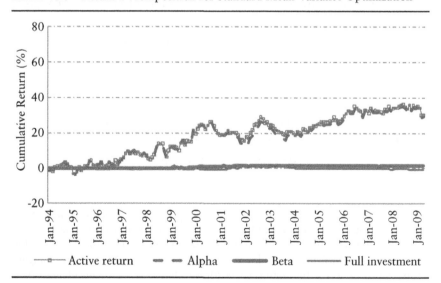

---

[8]The shadow price of a constraint tells us how much utility changes as we increase the bound on the constraint.

EXHIBIT 19.7 Return Decomposition for Shortfall Constrained Mean-Variance Optimization

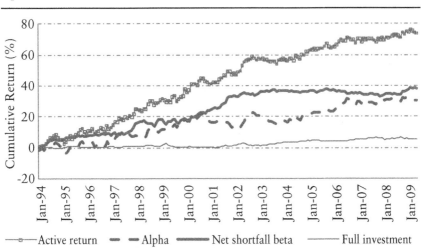

defined as the sum of the two constraint portfolios, $h_{\text{Beta neutrality}}$ and $h_{\text{Shortfall beta}}$, reflects this stipulation. As Exhibit 19.7 shows, that decision is a significant source of return, contributing roughly as much as the alpha.

Next, we take a closer look at the impact of constraining shortfall. The contribution of the net shortfall beta portfolio to the active return depends on two things. It depends on the size of the investment in this portfolio. It also depends on how well this portfolio performs. To disentangle these two effects, we note that we can split any component portfolio into two terms:

$$h_C = \underbrace{\sum_i \left| h_{C,i} \right|}_{\text{Weight}} \cdot \underbrace{\frac{h}{\sum_i \left| h_{C,i} \right|}}_{\substack{\text{Normalized} \\ \text{portfolio}}} \tag{19.5}$$

The first term tells us the size of the investment. The second term, the normalized portfolio, is a portfolio whose return is independent of the size of the investment.

The net shortfall beta portfolio's performance on a normalized basis is reported in Exhibit 19.8. We see that it performs well during our backtesting period, especially during the dot.com meltdown and again during the recent financial crisis. So the return from constraining shortfall beta comes, in part, from the strong performance of this portfolio.

EXHIBIT 19.8   Performance of the Normalized Net Shortfall Beta Portfolio

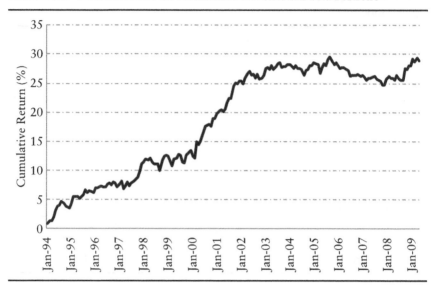

What about the size of the net shortfall beta portfolio? That is, what fraction of the portfolio weight is devoted to limiting extreme losses? To examine this, we define the relative weight of a component as:

$$w_C = \frac{\sum_i \left|b_{C,i}\right|}{\sum_C \sum_i \left|b_{C,i}\right|} = \frac{\text{Weight of component}}{\text{Total weight of all components}} \qquad (19.6)$$

The evolution of these weights is shown in Exhibit 19.9. Most of the time, the largest weight is devoted to alpha. However, during periods of market stress, the portfolio may place as much or even greater weight on insuring against losses than it does on pursuing alpha. This occurs around the Russian crisis of 1998 and during the more recent market plunge in the fall of 2008. So the shortfall beta constraint also seems to help by shifting the active portfolio toward the shortfall beta portfolio during periods of stress.

Our simple empirical examples suggest that constraining shortfall beta may offer some downside protection in turbulent periods without sacrificing performance over longer periods. Several questions still remain, including how to effectively capture the information in shortfall beta in the presence of additional constraints and execution costs.

EXHIBIT 19.9 Evolution of the Relative Weights of the Component Portfolios

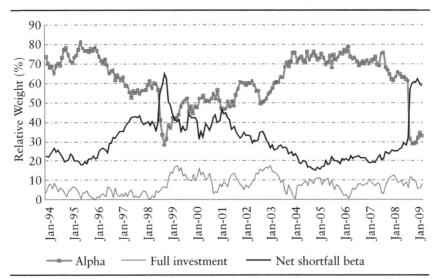

KEY POINTS

- Extreme risk can be incorporated into portfolio construction by constraining the shortfall beta of the optimal portfolio. Shortfall beta measures the relationship of a portfolio to a benchmark during periods of extreme stress. It is analogous to standard "beta" but differs in its focus on the left tail. We refer to this as the "shortfall constrained" optimization problem.
- Empirically, using three common alpha signals, shortfall constrained optimization outperformed mean-variance optimization. Constraining shortfall beta offered some downside protection in turbulent periods without sacrificing performance over longer periods.
- Decomposing an active portfolio into a portfolio due to the alpha and portfolios corresponding to each of the constraints allows one to attribute the active return to the alpha and the constraints.
- We find that the portfolio representing the net shortfall beta performed well over the historical period, especially during the Internet meltdown and again during the recent financial crisis. Moreover, during these stressful periods, the shortfall beta constraint shifts the active portfolio toward the shortfall beta portfolio. The two effects combine to drive the incremental gains we see in implementing the constraint.

APPENDIX: CONSTRUCTING OUT-OF-SAMPLE SHORTFALL BETAS

To compute shortfall betas as of a given month, we first simulate a distribution of future, daily portfolio returns using daily historical factor returns from the MSCI Barra Short-Term US Equity Model (USE3S). For each forecast date, we use the factor returns corresponding to the previous 1,000 days.

Since factor volatility is nonstationary, we adjust the historical factor returns to reflect the level of volatility as of the forecast date. There are a few ways to do this. One simple way is to scale the past individual factor return, $f_{t,i}$, by the ratio of its volatility as of the forecast month, T, to its volatility at time t; that is

$$f_{t,i}^* = \frac{\sigma_{f_{T,i}}}{\sigma_{f_{t,i}}} f_{t,i}$$

Another approach uses the entire covariance matrix to rescale the factor returns. Let F_t be the factor covariance matrix at t and f_t a vector of factor returns at t. Applying the Cholesky decomposition, we have $F_t = L_t L_t^T$. Then, the scaled factor return f_t^* is[9]

$$f_t^* = L_T L_t^{-1} f_t \tag{19.7}$$

After we have 1,000 scaled factor returns describing the distribution of future factor returns, we use the portfolio's current factor exposures X_T together with those factor returns to estimate the distribution of future asset or portfolio returns, that is,

$$r_t^* = X_T f_t^* \quad \text{for } t = 1 \text{ to } 1{,}000 \tag{19.8}$$

where $r_1^* \dots r_{1,000}^*$ represents the distribution of future returns. We ignore the specific returns in generating scenario returns.[10]

In the main analysis, we forecast the distribution of the MSCI US Prime Market 750 Index every month. Using the distribution, we can calculate the expected shortfall for the index portfolio as well as the marginal contribution of each asset to this shortfall, which along with its weight in the index, forms its shortfall beta.

---

[9]Another way to scale factor returns is by the square root of the factor covariance matrix $F_t^{1/2}$. In a separate study, we find that there is little difference between the results of this approach or from applying the Cholesky decomposition.

[10]Another choice is to assume a distribution for the specific return and simulate scenarios from the distribution.

QUESTIONS

1. There are different ways of computing the expected shortfall of a portfolio. A common approach is to use historical asset returns to simulate the portfolio return distribution. In the study presented in this chapter, why did the authors use a factor model and the associated factor return history to simulate a portfolio's historical return distribution?

2. Discuss the difference between beta and shortfall beta.

3. By constraining shortfall beta, one tends to lower the standard beta of the portfolio, since the two are strongly correlated. Is the outperformance of shortfall constrained optimization for the findings reported in this chapter simply due to its lower beta, especially during the turbulent periods?

4. Does constraining shortfall help protect against sharp daily losses?

5. Can you provide any insight into why shortfall constrained optimization performed better than mean-variance optimization in the empirical study?

CHAPTER 20

Working with High-Frequency Data

Irene Aldridge
Managing Partner
ABLE Alpha Trading

This chapter examines issues surrounding equity portfolio management in *high-frequency trading* (HFT). The chapter shows that HFT strategies by their nature use a different population of data and the traditional methods of data analyses need to be adjusted accordingly. In particular, the chapter considers the idiosyncrasies and opportunities that high-frequency data bring, and how the data compare with the low-frequency data, wherever appropriate. The chapter also parses through the topics of volume, bid-ask-bounce and time-spacing inherent in the high-frequency data, as well as the decay of correlations between securities observed at high-frequencies.

WHAT IS HIGH-FREQUENCY DATA?

High-frequency data, also known as "tick data," is a record of live market activity. Every time a customer, a dealer, or another entity posts a so-called limit order to buy s units of a specific security with ticker X at price q, a bid quote $q^b_{t_b}$ is logged at time t_b to buy $s^b_{t_b}$ units of X. (Market orders are incorporated into tick data in a different way as discussed below.) When the newly arrived bid quote $q^b_{t_b}$ has the highest price relative to all other previously arrived bid quotes in force, $q^b_{t_b}$ becomes known as "the best bid" available at time t_b. Similarly, when a trading entity posts a limit order to sell s units of X at price q, an ask quote $q^a_{t_a}$ is logged at time t_a to sell $s^a_{t_a}$ units of X. If the latest $q^a_{t_a}$ is lower than all other available ask quotes for security X, $q^a_{t_a}$ becomes known as "the best ask" at time t_a.

What happens to quotes from the moment they arrive largely depends on the venue where the orders are posted. Best bids and asks posted directly on an exchange will be broadcast to all exchange participants and other parties tracking quote data. In situations when the new best bid exceeds the best ask already in force on the exchange, $q_{t_b}^b \geq q_{t_a}^a$, most exchanges will immediately "match" such quotes, executing a trade at the preexisting best ask, $q_{t_a}^a$ at time t_b. Conversely, should the newly arrived best ask fall below the current best bid, $q_{t_a}^a \leq q_{t_b}^b$, the trade is executed at the preexisting best bid, $q_{t_b}^b$ at time t_a.

Most dark pools match bids and asks "crossing the spread," but may not broadcast the newly arrived quotes (hence the mysterious moniker, the "dark pools"). Similarly, quotes destined for the interdealer networks may or may not be disseminated to other market participants, depending on the venue.

Market orders contribute to high-frequency data in the form of "last trade" information. Unlike a limit order that is an order to buy a specified quantity of a security at a certain price, a market order is an order to buy a specified quantity of a security at the best price available at the moment the order is "posted" on the trading venue. As such, market orders are executed immediately at the best available bid or best ask prices, with each market buy order executed at the best ask and each market sell matched with the best bid, and the transaction is recorded in the quote data as the "last trade price" and the "last trade size."

A large market order may need to be matched with one or several best quotes, generating several "last trade" data points. For example, if the newly arrived market buy order is smaller in size than that of the best ask, the best ask quote may still remain in force on most trading venues; but the best ask size will be reduced to reflect that the portion of the best ask quote has been matched with the market order. When the size of the incoming market buy order is bigger than the size of the corresponding best ask, the market order consumes the best ask in its entirety, and then proceeds to be matched sequentially with the next available best ask until the size of the market order is fulfilled. The remaining lowest-priced ask quote becomes the best ask available on the trading venue.

Most limit and market orders are placed in so-called "lot sizes": increments of certain number of units, known as a *lot*. In foreign exchange, a standard trading lot today is US$5 million, a considerable reduction from a minimum of $25 million entertained by high-profile brokers just a few years ago. On equity exchanges, a lot can be as low as one share, but dark pools may still enforce a 100-share minimum requirement for orders. An order for the amount, other than an integer increment of a lot size, is called "an odd lot."

Small limit and market "odd lot" orders posted through a broker-dealer may be aggregated, or "packaged," by the broker-dealer into larger-size orders in order to obtain volume discounts at the orders' execution venue. In the process, the brokers may "sit" on quotes without transmitting them to an executing venue, delaying execution of customers' orders.

HOW IS HIGH-FREQUENCY DATA RECORDED?

The highest-frequency data is a collection of sequential "ticks," arrivals of the latest quote, trade, price, order size and volume information. Tick data usually has the following properties:

- A timestamp
- A financial security identification code
- An indicator of what information it carries:
  - Bid price
  - Ask price
  - Available bid size
  - Available ask size
  - Last trade price
  - Last trade size
- Security-specific data, such as implied volatility for options
- The market value information, such as the actual numerical value of the price, available volume, or size

A timestamp records the date and time at which the quote originated. It may be the time at which the exchange or the broker-dealer released the quote, or the time when the trading system has received the quote. At the time this article is written, the standard "round-trip" travel time of an order quote from the ordering customer to the exchange and back to the customer with the acknowledgement of order receipt is 15 milliseconds or less in New York. Brokers have been known to be fired by their customers if they are unable to process orders at this now standard speed. Sophisticated quotation systems, therefore, include milliseconds and even microseconds as part of their timestamps.

Another part of the quote is an identifier of the financial security. In equities, the identification code can be a ticker, or, for tickers simultaneously traded on multiple exchanges, a ticker followed by the exchange symbol. For futures, the identification code can consist of the underlying security, futures expiration date, and exchange code.

The last trade price shows the price at which the last trade in the security cleared. Last trade price can differ from the bid and ask. The differences can arise when a customer posts a favorable limit order that is immediately matched by the broker without broadcasting the customer's quote. Last trade size shows the actual size of the last executed trade.

The best bid is the highest price available for sale of the security in the market. The best ask is the lowest price entered for buying the security at any particular time. In addition to the best bid and best ask, quotation systems may disseminate "market depth" information: the bid and ask quotes entered posted on the trading venue at prices worse than the best bid and ask, as well as aggregate order sizes corresponding to each bid and ask recorded on the trading venue's "books." Market depth information is sometimes referred to as the Level II data, and may be disseminated as the premium subscription service only. In contrast, the best bid, best ask, last trade price and size information ("Level I data") is often available for a small nominal fee.

Exhibit 20.1(A) and (B) illustrate a 30-second log of Level I high-frequency data recorded by NYSE Arca for SPDR S&P 500 ETF (ticker SPY) from 14:00:16:400 to 14:02:00:000 GMT on November 9, 2009. Exhibit 20.1(A) shows quote data: best bid, best ask, and last trade information, while (B) displays corresponding position sizes (best bid size, best ask size, and last trade size).

PROPERTIES OF HIGH-FREQUENCY DATA

High-frequency securities data have been studied for many years. Yet it is still something of a novelty to many academics and practitioners. Unlike

EXHIBIT 20.1 Level I High-Frequency Data Recorded by NYSE Arca for SPDR S&P 500 ETF (ticker SPY) from 14:00:16:400 to 14:02:00:000 GMT on November 9, 2009

A. HF Data for S&P 500 ETF Recorded from 14:00:16:400 to 14:02:00:000 GMT: Best Bid, Best Ask and Last Trade Data

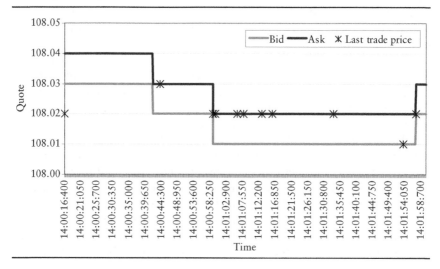

EXHIBIT 20.1 (Continued)

B. HF Data for S&P 500 ETF Recorded from 14:00:16:400 to 14:02:00:000 GMT: Bid Size, Ask Size and Last Trade Size

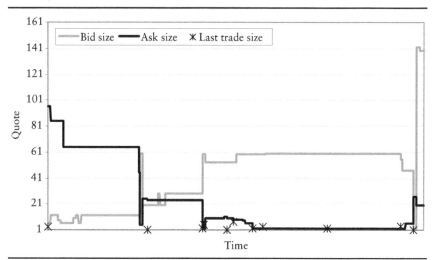

daily or monthly data sets commonly used in much of financial research and related applications, high-frequency data has distinct properties, which simultaneously can be advantageous and intimidating to researchers. Exhibit 20.2 summarizes the properties of high-frequency data. Each property, its advantages and disadvantages are discussed in detail later in the article.

HIGH-FREQUENCY DATA ARE VOLUMINOUS

The nearly two-minute sample of tick data for SPDR S&P 500 ETF (ticker SPY) shown in Exhibit 20.1 contained over 100 observations of Level I data: best bid quotes and sizes, best ask quotes and sizes, and last trade prices and sizes. Exhibit 20.3 summarizes the breakdown of the data points provided by NYSE Arca for SPY from 14:00:16:400 to 14:02:00:000 GMT on November 9, 2009, and SPY throughout the day on November 9, 2009. Other Level I data omitted from Exhibit 20.3 include cumulative daily trade volume for SPY. The number of quotes observed on November 9, 2009, for SPY alone would comprise over 160 years of daily open, high, low, close and volume data points, assuming an average of 252 trading days per year.

EXHIBIT 20.2 Summary of Properties of High-Frequency Data

Property of HF Data	Description	Pros	Cons
Voluminous	Each day of high-frequency data contains the number of observations equivalent to 30 years of daily data.	Large numbers of observations carry lots of information.	High-frequency data are difficult to handle manually.
Subject to bid-ask bounce	Unlike traditional data based on just closing prices, tick data carries additional supply and demand information in the form of bid and ask prices and offering sizes.	Bid and ask quotes can carry valuable information about impending market moves, can be harnessed to researcher's advantage.	Bid and ask quotes are separated by a spread. Continuous movement from bid to ask and back introduces a jump process, difficult to deal with through many conventional models.
Irregularly spaced in time	Arrival of tick data is asynchronous.	Durations between data arrivals carry information.	Most traditional models require regularly spaced data; need to convert high-frequency data to some regular intervals, or "bars" of data. Converted data is often sparse (populated with zero returns), once again making traditional econometric inferences difficult.

EXHIBIT 20.3 Summary Statistics for SPY Level I Quotes on November 9, 2009

Quote type	SPY, 14:00:16:400 to 14:02:00:000 GMT	SPY, all day
Best bid quote	4 (3%)	5,467 (3%)
Best bid size	36 (29%)	38,948 (19%)
Best ask quote	4 (3%)	4,998 (2%)
Best ask size	35 (28%)	38,721 (19%)
Last trade price	6 (5%)	9,803 (5%)
Last trade size	20 (16%)	27,750 (14%)
Total	125	203,792

HIGH-FREQUENCY DATA ARE SUBJECT TO BID-ASK BOUNCE

In addition to trade price and volume data long available in low-frequency formats, high-frequency data comprise bid and ask quotes and the associated order sizes. Bid and ask data arrive asynchronously and introduce noise in the quote process.

The difference between the bid quote and the ask quote at any given time is known as the bid-ask spread. The bid-ask spread is the cost of instantaneously buying and selling the security. The higher the bid-ask spread, the higher a gain the security must produce in order to cover the spread along with other transaction costs. Most low-frequency price changes are large enough to make the bid-ask spread negligible in comparison. In tick data, on the other hand, incremental price changes can be comparable or smaller than the bid-ask spread.

Bid-ask spreads usually vary throughout the day. As an illustration, Exhibit 20.4 shows the average bid-ask spreads observed on SPY in April 2010. It shows the spreads during both the normal market hours and during so-called before and after-hours trading sessions. The before- and after-hours trading sessions are often accompanied by a thinner trading volume. As a result, the average spread increases significantly during trading hours when the market is quiet, as Exhibit 20.4 illustrates.

EXHIBIT 20.4   Average Bid-Ask Spreads on NYSE-Traded SPY for Different Hours of the Day during April 2010

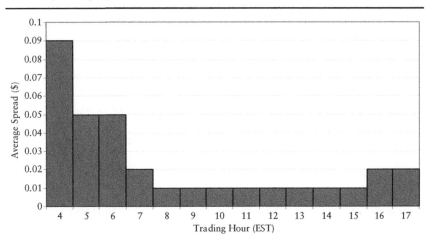

Bid-ask spreads also increase during periods of market uncertainty or instability. Higher spreads comprise higher costs for traders seeking to reverse their positions instantaneously. As a consequence, the profitability of high-frequency trading strategies decreases during the times of widened spreads.

While tick data carries information about market dynamics, it is also distorted by the same processes that make the data so valuable in the first place. Dacorogna, Gencay, Muller, Olsen, and Pictet report that sequential trade price bounces between the bid and ask quotes during market execution of orders introduce significant distortions into estimation of high-frequency parameters.[1] Corsi, Zumbach, Muller, and Dacorogna, for example, show that the bid-ask bounce introduces a considerable bias into volatility estimates. The authors calculate that the bid-ask bounce on average results in –40% negative first-order autocorrelation of tick data.[2] They as well as Voev and Lunde[3] propose to remedy the bias by filtering the data from the bid-ask noise prior to estimation.

[1]Dacorogna, Gencay, Muller, Olsen, and Pictet, *An Introduction to High-Frequency Finance.*

[2]Fulvio Corsi, Gilles Zumbach, Ulrich Müller, and Michael Dacorogna, M. "Consistent High-Precision Volatility from High-Frequency Data," *Economics Notes* 30, no. 2 (2001): 183–204.

[3]Valeri Voev and Asger Lunde, "Integrated Covariance Estimation Using High-Frequency Data in the Presence of Noise," *Journal of Financial Econometrics* 5, no. 1 (2007): 68–104.

To use standard econometric techniques in the presence of the bid-ask bounce, many practitioners convert the tick data to *midquote format*: the simple average of the latest bid and ask quotes. The midquote is used to approximate the price level at which the market is theoretically willing to trade if buyers and sellers agreed to meet each other half-way on the price spectrum. Mathematically, the midquote can be expressed as follows:

$$\hat{q}_{t_m}^m = \frac{1}{2}\left(q_{t_a}^a + q_{t_b}^b\right) \tag{20.1}$$

where

$$t_m = \begin{cases} t_a, \text{if } t_a \geq t_b \\ t_b, \text{otherwise} \end{cases}$$

The latter condition for t_m reflects the continuous updating of the midquote estimate: $\hat{q}_{t_m}^m$ is updated whenever the latest best bid, $q_{t_b}^b$, or best ask quote, $q_{t_a}^a$, arrives, at t_b or t_a respectively.

Another way to sample tick quotes into a cohesive data series is by weighing the latest best bid and best ask quotes by their accompanying order sizes:

$$\tilde{q}_t^s = \frac{q_{t_b}^b s_{t_a}^a + q_{t_a}^a s_{t_b}^b}{s_{t_a}^a + s_{t_b}^b} \tag{20.2}$$

where $q_{t_b}^b$ and $s_{t_b}^b$ is the best bid quote and the best bid available size recorded at time t_b (when $q_{t_b}^b$ became the best bid), and $q_{t_a}^a$ and $s_{t_a}^a$ is the best bid quote and the best bid available size recorded at time t_a.

Exhibit 20.5 (A), (B), and (C) compares the histograms of simple returns computed from midquote (A), size-weighted midquote (B) and trade-price (C) processes for SPDR S&P 500 ETF data recorded as they arrive throughout November 9, 2009. The data neglect the time difference between the adjacent quotes, treating each sequential quote as an independent observation. Exhibit 20.6 contrasts the quantile distribution plots of the same data sets with the quantiles of a standard normal distribution.

As Exhibits 20.5 and 20.6 show, the basic midquote distribution is constrained by the minimum "step size": the minimum changes in the midquote can occur at half-tick increments (at present, the minimum tick size is $0.01 in equities). The size-weighted midquote forms the most continuous distribution among the three distributions discussed. Exhibit 20.6 confirms this notion further and also illustrates the fat tails present in all three types of data distributions.

EXHIBIT 20.5 Histograms of Simple Returns Computed from Midquote (A), Size-Weighted Midquote (B), and Trade-Price (C) Processes for SPDR S&P 500 ETF Data Recorded as They Arrive throughout November 9, 2009

A. Midquote Simple Returns

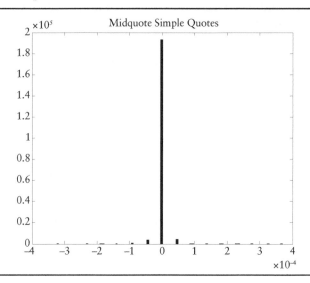

B. Size-Weighted (SW) Midquote Simple Returns

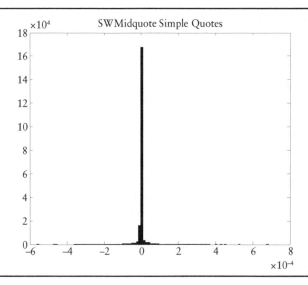

EXHIBIT 20.5 (Continued)
C. Last Trade Price Simple Returns

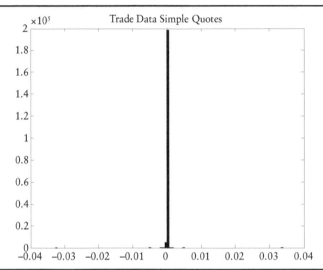

EXHIBIT 20.6 Quantile Plots of Simple Returns of Midquote (A), Size-Weighted Midquote (B), and Trade-Price (C) Processes for SPDR S&P 500 ETF Data Recorded as They Arrive throughout November 9, 2009

A. Midquote Returns

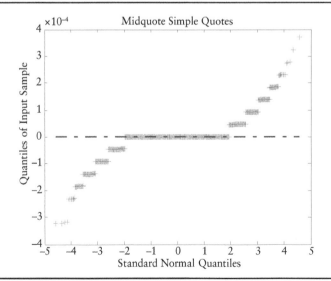

EXHIBIT 20.6 (Continued)

B. Size-Weighted Midquote Returns

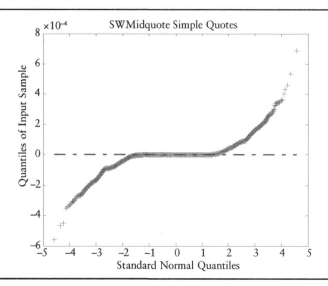

C. Trade Price Returns

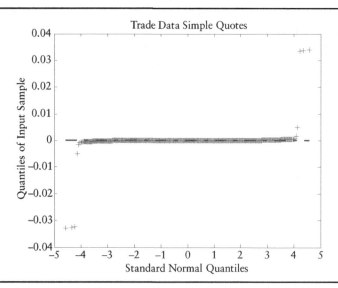

In addition to real-time adjustments to bid-ask data, researchers deploy forecasting techniques to estimate the impending bid-ask spread and adjust for it in models ahead of time. Future realizations of the bid-ask spread can be estimated using the model suggested by Roll,[4] where the price of an asset at time t, p_t, is assumed to equal an unobservable fundamental value, m_t, offset by a value equal to half of the bid-ask spread, s. The price offset is positive when the next market order is a buy, and negative when the trade is a sell, as shown in equation (20.3):

$$p_t = m_t + \frac{s}{2}I_t \qquad (20.3)$$

where

$$I_t = \begin{cases} 1, & \text{Market buy at ask} \\ -1, & \text{Market sell at bid} \end{cases}$$

If either a buy or a sell order can arrive next with equal probability, then $E[I_t] = 0$, and $E[\Delta p_t] = 0$, absent changes in the fundamental asset value, m_t. The covariance of subsequent price changes, however, is different from 0:

$$\text{cov}\left[\Delta p_t, \Delta p_{t+1}\right] = E\left[\Delta p_t \Delta p_{t+1}\right] = -\frac{s^2}{4} \qquad (20.4)$$

As a result, the future expected spread can be estimated as follows:

$$E\left[s\right] = 2\sqrt{-\text{cov}\left[\Delta p_t, \Delta p_{t+1}\right]} \text{ whenever } \text{cov}\left[\Delta p_t, \Delta p_{t+1}\right] < 0$$

Numerous extensions of Roll's model have been developed to account for contemporary market conditions along with numerous other variables. Hasbrouck provides a good summary of the models.[5]

HIGH-FREQUENCY DATA ARE IRREGULARLY SPACED IN TIME

Most modern computational techniques have been developed to work with regularly spaced data, presented in monthly, weekly, daily, hourly, or other consistent intervals. The traditional reliance of researchers on fixed time intervals is due to:

---

[4]Richard R. Roll, "A Simple Implicit Measure of the Effective Bid-Ask Spread in an Efficient Market," *Journal of Finance* 39, no. 4 (1984): 1127–1240.
[5]Joel Hasbrouck, *Empirical Market Microstructure: The Institutions, Economics, and Econometrics of Securities Trading* (New York: Oxford University Press, 2007).

- Relative availability of daily data (newspapers have published daily quotes since the 1920s).
- Relative ease of processing regularly spaced data.
- An outdated view, as noted by Goodhart and O'Hara[6] that "whatever drove security prices and returns, it probably did not vary significantly over short time intervals."

In contrast, high-frequency observations are separated by varying time intervals. One way to overcome the irregularities in the data are to sample it at certain predetermined periods of time—for example, every hour or minute. For example, if the data is to be converted from tick data to minute "bars," then under the traditional approach, the bid or ask price for any given minute would be determined as the last quote that arrived during that particular minute. If no quotes arrived during a certain minute, then the previous minute's last tick would be taken as the current minute's quote, and so on. Exhibit 20.7(A) illustrates this idea. This approach implicitly assumes that in the absence of new quotes, the prices stay constant, which does not have to be the case.

Dacorogna, Gencay, Muller, Olsen, and Pictet propose a potentially more precise way to sample quotes—linear time-weighted interpolation between adjacent quotes.[7] At the core of the interpolation technique is an assumption that at any given time, unobserved quotes lie on a straight line that connects two neighboring observed quotes. Exhibit 20.7(B) illustrates linear interpolation sampling.

As shown in Exhibit 20.7(A) and (B), the two quote-sampling methods produce quite different results.

Mathematically, the two sampling methods can be expressed as follows:

$$\text{Quote sampling using last tick: } \hat{q}_t = q_{t,last} \qquad (20.5)$$

Quote sampling using linear interpolation:

$$\hat{q}_t = q_{t,last} + (q_{t,next} - q_{t,last})\frac{t - t_{last}}{t_{next} - t_{last}} \qquad (20.6)$$

where $\hat{q}_t$ is the resulting sampled quote, t is the desired sampling time (start of a new minute, for example), t_{last} is the timestamp of the last observed quote prior to the sampling time t, $q_{t,last}$ is the value of the last quote prior to

---

[6]Charles Goodhart and Maureen O'Hara, "High Frequency Data in Financial Markets: Issues and Applications," *Journal of Empirical Finance* 4, nos. 2 and 3 (1997): 80–81.
[7]Dacorogna, Gencay, Muller, Olsen, and Pictet, *An Introduction to High-Frequency Finance*.

EXHIBIT 20.7 Data-Sampling Methodologies

A. Quote Sampling Using Closing Prices for the Desired Time Frequency

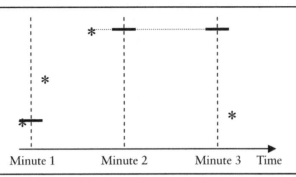

B. Quote Sampling Using the Interpolation Method for the Desired Time Frequency

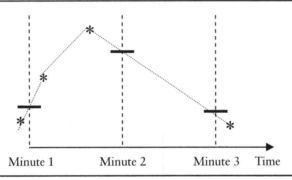

the sampling time t, t_{next} is the timestamp of the first observed quote after the sampling time t, and $q_{t,next}$ is the value of the first quote after the sampling time t.

Exhibits 20.8 and 20.9 compare histograms of the midquote data sampled as last tick and interpolated, at frequencies of 200 ms and 15s. Exhibit 20.10 compares quantile plots of last tick and interpolated distributions. As Exhibits 20.8 and 20.9 show, oft-sampled distributions are sparse, that is, contain more 0 returns than distributions sampled at lower frequencies. At the same time, returns computed from interpolated quotes are more continuous than last tick quotes, as Exhibit 20.10 illustrates.

Instead of manipulating the interquote intervals into the convenient regularly spaced formats, several researchers have studied whether the time distance between subsequent quote arrivals itself carries information. For example, most researchers agree that intertrade intervals carry information

EXHIBIT 20.8   Midquote "Last Tick" Quotes Sampled at 200 ms (top) and 15 s
Intervals

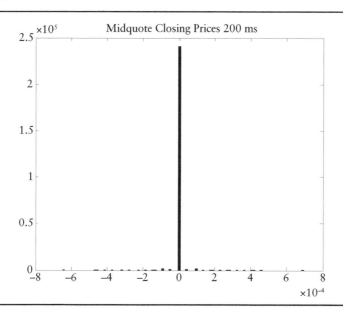

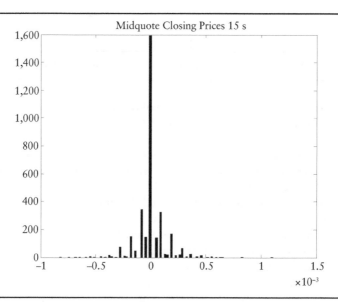

EXHIBIT 20.9 Midquote "Time-Interpolated Quotes" Sampled at 200 ms (Top) and 15 s Intervals

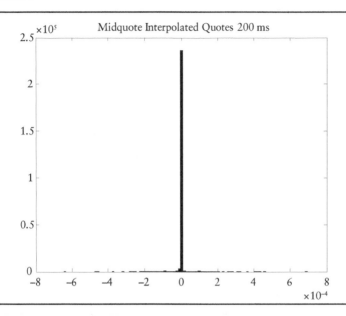

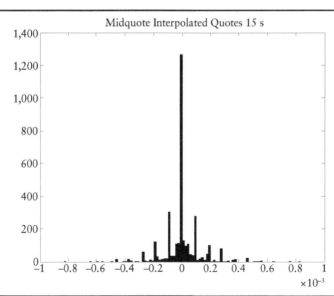

EXHIBIT 20.10   Quantile Plots: Last Tick Quotes vs. Interpolated Midquotes
Sampled at 200 ms

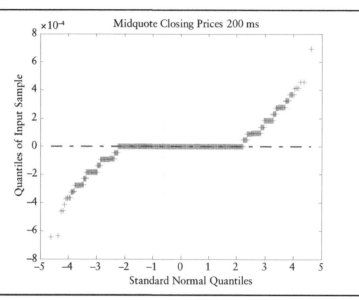

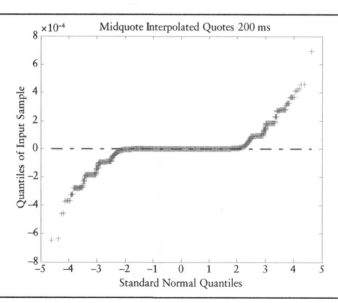

on securities for which short sales are disallowed; the lower the intertrade duration, the more likely the yet-to-be-observed good news and the higher the impending price change.

Duration models are used to estimate the factors affecting the time between any two sequential ticks. Such models are known as *quote processes* and *trade processes*, respectively. Duration models are also used to measure the time elapsed between price changes of a prespecified size, as well as the time interval between predetermined trade volume increments. The models working with fixed price are known as *price processes*; the models estimating variation in duration of fixed volume increments are known as *volume processes*.

Durations are often modeled using Poisson processes that assume that sequential events, like quote arrivals, occur independently of one another. The number of arrivals between any two time points t and $(t + \tau)$ is assumed to have a Poisson distribution. In a Poisson process, λ arrivals occur per unit time. In other words, the arrivals occur at an average rate of $(1/\lambda)$. The average arrival rate may be assumed to hold constant, or it may vary with time. If the average arrival rate is constant, the probability of observing exactly k arrivals between times t and $(t + \tau)$ is

$$P[(N(t + \tau) - N(t)) = k] = \frac{1}{k!} e^{-\lambda \tau} (\lambda \tau)^k, \quad k = 0, 1, 2, \ldots \quad (20.7)$$

Diamond and Verrecchia[8] and Easley and O'Hara[9] were the first to suggest that the duration between subsequent ticks carries information. Their models posit that in the presence of short-sale constraints, intertrade duration can indicate the presence of good news; in markets of securities where short selling is disallowed, the shorter the intertrade duration, the higher is the likelihood of unobserved good news. The reverse also holds: in markets with limited short selling and normal liquidity levels, the longer the duration between subsequent trade arrivals, the higher the probability of yet-unobserved bad news. A complete absence of trades, however, indicates a lack of news.

Easley and O'Hara further point out that trades that are separated by a time interval have a much different information content than trades occurring in close proximity. One of the implications of their analysis is that the entire price sequence conveys information and should be used in its entirety whenever possible, strengthening the argument for high-frequency trading.

---

[8]Douglas W. Diamond and Robert E. Verrecchia, "Constraints on Short-Selling and Asset Price Adjustment to Private Information," *Journal of Financial Economics* 18, no. 2 (1987): 277–311.
[9]David Easley and Maureen O'Hara, "Time and the Process of Security Price Adjustment," *Journal of Finance* 47, no. 2 (1992): 557–605.

EXHIBIT 20.11   Hourly Distributions of Intertrade Duration Observed on May 13, 2009 for S&P 500 Depository Receipts ETF (SPY)

Hour (ET)	No. of Trades	Intertrade Duration (milliseconds)				
		Average	Median	Std. Dev.	Skewness	Kurtosis
4–5 AM	170	19074.58	5998	47985.39	8.430986	91.11571
5–6 AM	306	11556.95	4781.5	18567.83	3.687372	21.92054
6–7 AM	288	12606.81	4251	20524.15	3.208992	16.64422
7–8 AM	514	7096.512	2995	11706.72	4.288352	29.86546
8–9 AM	767	4690.699	1997	7110.478	3.775796	23.56566
9–10 AM	1089	2113.328	1934	24702.9	3.5185	24.6587
10–11 AM	1421	2531.204	1373	3409.889	3.959082	28.53834
11–12 PM	1145	3148.547	1526	4323.262	3.240606	17.24866
12–1 PM	749	4798.666	1882	7272.774	2.961139	13.63373
1–2 PM	982	3668.247	1739.5	5032.795	2.879833	13.82796
2–3 PM	1056	3408.969	1556	4867.061	3.691909	23.90667
3–4 PM	1721	2094.206	1004	2684.231	2.9568	15.03321
4–5 PM	423	8473.593	1500	24718.41	7.264483	69.82157
5–6 PM	47	73579.23	30763	113747.8	2.281743	7.870699
6–7 PM	3	1077663	19241	1849464	0.707025	1.5

Exhibit 20.11 shows summary statistics for a duration measure computed on all trades recorded for S&P 500 Depository Receipts ETF (SPY) on May 13, 2009. As the table illustrates, the average inter-trade duration was the longest outside of regular market hours, and the shortest during the hour preceding the market close (3–4 P.M. ET).

The variation in duration between subsequent trades may be due to several other causes. While the lack of trading may be due to a lack of new information, trading inactivity may also be due to low levels of liquidity, trading halts on exchanges, and strategic motivations of traders. Foucault, Kadan, and Kandel consider that patiently providing liquidity using limit orders may itself be a profitable trading strategy, as liquidity providers should be compensated for their waiting.[10] The compensation usually comes in the form of a bid-ask spread and is a function of the waiting time until the order limit is "hit" by liquidity takers; lower intertrade durations induce

---

[10]Thierry Foucault, Ohad Kadan, and Eugene Kandel, "Limit Order Book as a Market for Liquidity," *Review of Financial Studies* 18, no. 4 (2005): 1171–1217.

lower spreads. However, Dufour and Engle[11] and Saar and Hasbrouck[12] find that spreads are actually higher when traders observe short durations, contrasting the time-based limit order compensation hypothesis.

In addition to durations between subsequent trades and quotes, researchers have also been modeling durations between fixed changes in security prices and volumes. The time interval between subsequent price changes of a specified magnitude is known as price duration. Price duration has been shown to decrease with increases in volatility. Similarly, the time interval between subsequent volume changes of a prespecified size is known as the volume duration. Volume duration has been shown to decrease with increases in liquidity.

The information content of quote, trade, price, and volume durations introduces biases into the estimation process, however. If the available information determines the time between subsequent trades, time itself ceases to be an independent variable, introducing substantial endogeneity bias into estimation. As a result, traditional estimates of variance of transaction prices are too high in comparison with the true variance of the price series.

EQUITY CORRELATIONS DECAY AT HIGH FREQUENCIES

Both the variable intertrade duration and the bid-ask bounce have been held responsible for yet another phenomenon in high-frequency data: the decaying correlation of equity returns. This property of high-frequency data is known as the *Epps effect*.[13]

The Epps effect can be vividly illustrated on any liquid pair of financial instruments. Exhibits 20.12 and 20.13 show the Epps effect on the returns of a pair of ETFs: SPY and EFA. The two securities were chosen mostly due to their high liquidity, which in turns enables granular high-frequency analysis. SPY, offered by the State Street Global Advisors, is an ETF designed to mimic S&P 500 and boasts a market capitalization of over US$75 billion at the time this Chapter is written. EFA is a Morgan Stanley-run ETF that tracks MSCI EAFE Index of large foreign equities. EFA presently has a market capitalization of over US$30 billion. Both securities trade on the New York Stock Exchange (NYSE) alongside common equities.

Exhibits 20.12 and 20.13 compare correlations of the returns of two securities sampled on November 9, 2009, at 45-second, 15-second, 1-second,

---

[11]Alfonso Dufour and Robert F. Engle, "Time and the Price Impact of a Trade," *Journal of Finance* 55, no. 6 (2000): 2467–2498.

[12]Joel Hasbrouck and Gideon Saar, "Limit orders and Volatility in a Hybrid Market: The Island ECN," working paper, New York University, 2002.

[13]T. Wake Epps, "Comovements in Stock Prices in the Very Short Run," *Journal of the American Statistical Association* 74, no. 366 (June 1979): 291–298.

EXHIBIT 20.12   Empirical Correlations of SPY and EFA Computed Using
"Last Tick" Sampled at Different Frequencies

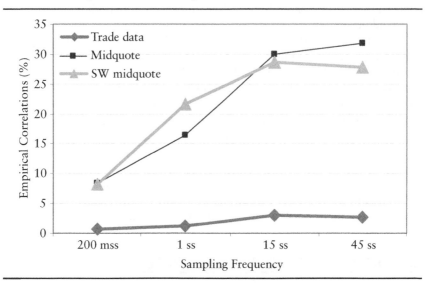

EXHIBIT 20.13   Empirical Correlations of SPY and EFA Computed Using
Interpolated Quotes Sampled at Different Frequencies

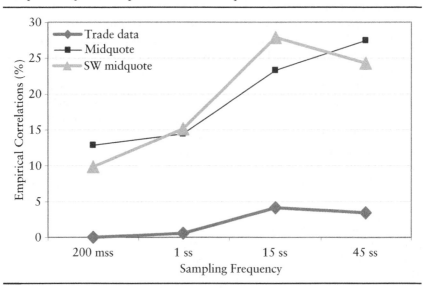

and 200-millisecond intervals. The returns were computed from two types of quotes: (1) "last tick" data at the end of each time interval; and (2) interpolated and sampled at the end of each time interval. Furthermore, the quotes were computed from trade data, simple bid-ask average and size-weighted bid-ask average, as discussed earlier in this chapter.

Interpolated quotes for trade data exhibit higher correlations than last tick trade data. However, the opposite is true for midquote and size-weighted midquote correlation estimates, where interpolated sampling actually delivers lower correlations than last tick quote sampling.

Overall, simple midquotes and size-weighted midquotes register a significantly higher correlation than trade data. This potentially signals that the quotes are much more attuned to broader market moves than are trade data, the latter more influenced by investors' beliefs and behavior, rather than broader market conditions. Yet even quote correlations decay to zero as the sampling frequency increases.

Several models have been proposed to account for the Epps effect. Zhang[14] and Zhang, Mykland, and Aït-Sahalia,[15] for example, suggest sampling "remedies" for the Epps effect observed on last tick trading data of any two securities. Large develops a stochastic volatility model that fits last tick sampling on midquote data.[16]

KEY POINTS

- High-frequency data are different from daily- or lower-frequency data. Whereas low-frequency data typically comprise regularly spaced open, high, low, close, and volume information for a given financial security recorded during a specific period of time, high-frequency data include bid and ask quotes, sizes, and latest trade characteristics that are recorded sequentially at irregular time intervals.
- The differences affect trading strategy modeling, introducing new opportunities and pitfalls for researchers. Numerous data points allow researchers to deduce statistically significant inferences on even short samples of high-frequency data.

---

[14]Lan Zhang, "Estimating Covariation: Epps Effect, Microstructure Noise," *Journal of Econometrics* 160, no. 1 (2011): 33–47.

[15]Lan Zhang, Per Mykland, and Yacine Aït-Sahalia, "A Tale of Two Timescales: Determining Integrated Volatility with Noisy High-Frequency Data," *Journal of the American Statistical Association* 100, no. 472 (2005): 1394–1411.

[16]Jeremy Large, "Accounting for the Epps Effect: Realized Covariation, Cointegration and Common Factors," working paper, Oxford-Man Institute of Quantitative Finance, 2007.

- Different sampling approaches have been developed to convert high-frequency data into a more regular format better familiar to researchers; nevertheless, diverse sampling methodologies result in data sets with drastically dissimilar statistical properties.
- The short-term dynamics among equities are also significantly different from those at lower frequencies, creating new frontiers in portfolio management research.

QUESTIONS

1. What properties of high-frequency data affect portfolio management strategies?

2. How does the volume of high-frequency data impact estimation of optimal portfolio allocation?

3. How does the bid-ask bounce factor into the high-frequency portfolio allocation decisions?

4. How does irregular spacing in time influence high-frequency portfolio allocation?

5. How can different data sampling methodologies affect high-frequency portfolio allocation decisions?

CHAPTER 21

Statistical Arbitrage

Brian J. Jacobsen, Ph.D., J.D., CFA, CFP®
Chief Portfolio Strategist
Wells Fargo Funds Management, LLC
and
Associate Professor
Wisconsin Lutheran College

A mantra of investing is, "Buy low and sell high." If one can simultaneously execute both sides of the transaction—the buying and the selling—without any commitment of capital, pure arbitrage exists (also known as *riskless arbitrage*). The activity of arbitrage tends to be self-exhausting: buying a lower priced good creates demand for it and drives up its price; while selling a higher priced good increases supply and drives down its price.

Why add "statistical" to arbitrage? Because statistical arbitrage relationships are much more prevalent than pure arbitrage opportunities. *Statistical arbitrage* strategies are based on the idea that we do not know with certainty what the future holds; so we can only make probabilistic statements about what may occur. Statistical arbitrage also refers to the use of statistics in identifying arbitrage opportunities.

Statistical arbitrage strategies are subject to myriad risks, but the most important one is model risk. Model risk refers to whether or not a model of the price process of a security is accurate (i.e., whether it conforms to reality). With an accurate model of security pricing, the identification and exploitation of statistical arbitrage opportunities becomes a relatively easy task. Making sure those models are indeed accurate is the golden key to investing.

Some additional, real-world problems with implementing a profitable statistical arbitrage strategy are in limitations on short selling, margin constraints, and timing issues. Not every security is available for short selling. For example, short selling a mutual fund is not possible—unless it is an exchange-traded fund. Also, whether a security can be sold short depends on the ability to obtain it from a security lender. Sometimes, the government will restrict the ability of investors to short sell and security lenders may change collateral requirements for borrowing a security.

An additional problem associated with shorting a security is that the investor might have to give back the security before he or she wants to. One cannot indefinitely short a security; and most of the time the security has to be returned on a moment's notice. This adds an additional dimension of risk—the risk of the early termination of the arbitrage positions.

Margin requirements can also limit one's ability to implement a statistical arbitrage strategy. Ideally, an equity would never fall below the maintenance margin level, but realistically, it might be subject to a margin call.

A great model can be constructed, but it can be grossly unprofitable with poor execution. As Robert Burns wrote in his 1785 poem "The Mouse," "The best laid schemes of Mice and Men often go awry." This is very true in investing since many things can come between a good idea and a profitable execution. For example, there could be a delay in getting the data to recognize an arbitrage opportunity, or a delay in acting on the opportunity (logging on to submit an order), or in how long it takes for the transaction to fill. Most arbitrage opportunities are only noticed after the opportunity has gone. Clearly, this is why institutional, and not individual, investors tend to dominate the arbitrage scene. Engaging in arbitrage is a full-time job that requires a large investment in information, processing, and execution technologies.

In this chapter, we first go through some rather simple models of statistical arbitrage—pairs trading and correlation trading. Then, we will move on to a more general method based on modeling the long-run relationships and short-run dynamics of the pricing processes. There are practical limitations to the use of statistical arbitrage that we do not incorporate in the models in this chapter: margin requirements, execution lags, and transaction costs, among others. All these things can give rise to the appearance of an arbitrage opportunity when, in fact, there was no opportunity because of the practical constraints.

Statistical arbitrage is an evolving field since the statistical tools at our disposal are constantly expanding. An additional source of dynamics in this area is in the feedback effects created by traders who use statistical arbitrage strategies: exploiting one opportunity forecloses that opportunity and creates new ones. All the models that are developed will become antiquated quickly, so the models themselves always need to be updated.

PAIRS TRADING

One of the earliest, and still most commonly used, forms of statistical arbitrage is in *pairs trading*. Pairs trading has been around since listed exchanges have opened, and it serves as the basis for most trading strategies. Pairs trading is a strategy that simultaneously buys one security and sells another to profit from the "spread" between the two.[1] The investor hopes that the asset he or she bought goes up relative to the asset that was sold short. What matters is the relative movement of prices, not the absolute movement of prices: One can have both prices go down as long as the one that is shorted goes down faster than the one you are long. Properly constructed, this can be a "market neutral" strategy. A market neutral strategy is when the profitability of a strategy is independent of the level of prices and only dependent on the relative price movements of the assets.

A trading opportunity usually arises as a result of some event that disrupts the normal relationship between the prices of the assets. For example, an announced merger or acquisition can dramatically alter the price of a security. In this case, a "merger arb" strategy can be used to speculate on the likelihood of the announced transaction closing. Another example is when there is a macroeconomic event that may affect one security's price more than another. This can happen with "global macro" strategies that invest on the basis of political changes or changes in global factors. Generally speaking, pairs trading opportunities can be "event driven" as the opportunities arise as a result of some event.

Really, all investing can be thought of as a generalization of pairs trading if we allow one of the assets to be cash. By investing in a security, you are hoping that the security price will go up relative to holding your funds in cash. By selling a security short, the investor is hoping that the security price will go down relative to holding funds in cash. The trick is in identifying the pairs, finding the right portfolio positions to take, and executing the trades. The ability to measure and manage the risk of the strategy is also vitally important. For example, it is important to track in real-time whether the strategy is working. If it is not working, it is important to identify why it is not working and if the strategy should be abandoned.

Correlation Trading

Closely related to pairs trading is *correlation trading*. Whereas pairs trading can be used in an "event-driven" portfolio; correlation trading is based on

[1]Douglas Ehrman, "Pairs Trading: New Look at an Old Strategy," *Futures* 33, no. 6 (May 2004): 32–34; and Ron McEwan, "A Simplified Approach to Pairs Trading," *Futures* 32, no. 15 (December 2003): 34–37.

the statistical relationship between security prices. An event-driven portfolio is one where the investor hopes to profit from the occurrence of some particular event—perhaps an earnings announcement, a large contract being signed, a political event, a merger, and so on. A typical event-driven pair trade would be a strategy where the investor bet that one firm would acquire another firm, but the acquiring firm would overpay. The investor could sell short the bidder's security and go long the target's security. If the investor is correct and there is an acquisition, and the bidder's share price goes down while the target's share price goes up, the investor has successfully executed an event-driven pair trade. With this type of strategy, there was not necessarily a statistical reason for the relationship between the security prices, but there was a fundamental reason for the relationship—the "event" linked the security prices. Obviously, the risk is that you are wrong and there is no acquisition announcement.

Correlation trading is typical where you have firms that are in the same industry and they are subject to the same macroeconomic forces. There may be a historical relationship—the correlation—between the security prices. If there is some current deviation from the historical average correlation, one can posit that this is a temporary divergence and there should be a reversion to the mean. One problem with using a typical correlation coefficient in measuring the relationship between two security prices is that it is difficult to perform significance tests. In other words, is the deviation from the normal relationship a statistical fluke, or not?

To perform a standard t-test on whether the correlation coefficient between two variables is nonzero requires that the two variables be normally distributed random variables. Since prices cannot go below zero, the assumption of normality is not generally very good. Three alternatives present themselves: (1) Use the empirical distribution to perform the significance test; (2) transform the prices into returns that might be "closer" to normal than the actual prices; or (3) use a nonparametric test like the Spearman rank correlation (explained in this section).

Using the empirical distribution to perform a significance test is useful if there is a lot of data on the securities and the data can be partitioned into a calibration set and a test set. The calibration set would be used for calculating the correlation coefficient between the security prices and finding the residuals from fitting a straight line to the data (see the subsection Linear Regression Methods). The residuals from the regression analysis can be formed into a relative frequency histogram, which can serve as the assumed distribution of the residuals of the data in the test set.

Transforming the prices into returns is attractive, but the added complication is in finding the correct portfolio positions to take (i.e., how many shares to buy or sell). Since securities trade in integer units, using the prices explicitly shows what size of position to take in each security.

The third option seems to be the most commonly used by traders. The Spearman rank correlation is useful when you want to see whether an increase in one variable is related to an increase or decrease in another variable. The null hypothesis (the hypothesis that there is no—or "null"— relationship) is that the ranks of one variable do not have covariance with the ranks of another. In order to perform this test, one must first convert the prices into ranks (the highest rank is coded as 1) and measure the correlation between the ranks. When there is a tie for a rank, the average rank is assigned to both variables (e.g., if two are tied for the highest price, the value 1.5 is assigned to both). By regressing one variable's rank on the other, a standard test of significance of the coefficient of determination (the R-squared) is used to asses whether the ranks have covariance.

The actual value of the Spearman rank correlation is not useful; but what is useful is in determining whether two security prices have covariance. This method does not help in finding optimal position sizes, so that is why it is one of the less sophisticated statistical arbitrage methods.

Examples of Pairs Trading

Below we presented three examples of pairs trading.

Constant Relative Price Process Model

The simplest model of security prices is to say that the relative price process reverts to a constant. In other words, one must assert that the ratio of one security's price to another security's price is independent of time, and any deviation from the historical average price ratio is an arbitrage opportunity. For example, if there is security A and security B, with prices A_t and B_t, with t representing the time of the observation, the relative price ratio,

$$P_t = \frac{A_t}{B_t}$$

can be assumed to eventually revert to its historical average $\bar{P}$. So, any deviation from this relationship should be short-lived and provides an arbitrage opportunity.

For example, if P_t should approach $\bar{P}$, then the theoretically correct price for security A is $\hat{A}_t = \bar{P}B_t$. If $A_t - \hat{A}_t > 0$ (i.e., $(P_t - \bar{P}) > 0$), then security A is overpriced relative to security B. To exploit this opportunity, security A needs to be sold short with the proceeds being used to purchase security B. If $A_t - \hat{A}_t < 0$, then security A is underpriced relative to security B, and security B should be shorted with the proceeds used to purchase security A.

If security A at time 0 is the over-priced security, ignoring things like margin requirements, "haircuts," and transaction costs, then selling it short will yield $^\$A_0$. Investing this in security B gives you

$$\frac{A_0}{B_0}$$

shares of B (assuming simultaneous execution). If the relative prices converge to the historical average at time T, and also assuming security B's price does not go to zero, then one share of A will need to be covered at a price of $A_T = \bar{P}B_T$. By selling the position in B one gets

$$\frac{A_0}{B_0} B_T$$

The return on this is

$$\left(\frac{A_0}{B_0} B_T - A_T \right) = \left(\frac{A_0}{B_0} B_T - \bar{P}B_T \right) = \left(P_0 - \bar{P} \right) B_T$$

which, by assumption, is positive. With no money down the result is a positive payoff. So, why stop at one share? Why not a million ... or more?

If you want to perform statistical tests on whether there indeed exists an arbitrage opportunity, some assumption needs to be made about the relationship between P_t and $\bar{P}$. One assumption might be that the difference, $P_t - \bar{P}$, follows a normal distribution that is independent of t.

Practically speaking, who is to say that the relative prices *will* converge to the postulated value $\bar{P}$? Perhaps there is some fundamental reason why the price relationship has changed. Additionally, how long will it take to converge? (See this chapter's discussion about cointegration and how to measure the rate of convergence.) Can one keep the short position open long enough? If security A actually goes up in price relative to B, the investor might be subject to a margin call; or, the person who lent security A to the investor might want it back. Plus, we have ignored transaction and financing costs. These are all practical limitations to this strategy. Without further assumptions about the price processes it is impossible to perform hypothesis tests about the extent of mispricing and the adequacy of the assumed relative price that it is postulated the prices should converge to.

Linear Regression-Based Model

A slightly more sophisticated method than the constant relative price process model is to use the tools of linear regression, either on the prices or on the returns (e.g., daily returns). If $\{A_t\} = \{A_1, A_2, ..., A_T\}$ and $\{B_t\} = \{B_1, B_2, ...,$ $B_T\}$ represent the set of observed prices (or returns) on the two securities for a number of time periods, then one can postulate a linear relationship exists between the prices (or returns). The population regression function might take the form of $A_t = \alpha + \beta B_t + \varepsilon_t$, where α and β are population parameters and ε_t is a noise term that has a particular distribution.

Taking a sample of price observations means one can approximate the population parameters with sample statistics. A popular method of doing this is through ordinary least squares. For the sample, one can postulate the relationship $A_t = a + bB_t + e_t$, where a and b are the coefficients to be estimated and the e_t's are the residuals from the regression. Ordinary least squares picks a and b such that the sum of squared residuals is minimized.

The predicted value of A_t, given B_t is $\hat{A}_t = \hat{a} + \hat{b}B_t$ with the coefficients given by the following system of equations:

$$
\left.
\begin{aligned}
\bar{A} &= \left(\frac{\sum\limits_{t=1}^{T} A_t}{T} \right) \\[2ex]
\bar{B} &= \left(\frac{\sum\limits_{t=1}^{T} B_t}{T} \right) \\[2ex]
\hat{a} &= \bar{A} - \hat{b}\bar{B} \\[2ex]
\hat{b} &= \frac{\sum\limits_{t=1}^{T}\left[\left(A_t - \bar{A}\right)\left(B_t - \bar{B}\right)\right]}{\sum\limits_{t=1}^{T}\left[\left(B_t - \bar{B}\right)^2\right]}
\end{aligned}
\right\}
\tag{21.1}
$$

If the process that you are measuring is the price process—as opposed to the return process, then the statistical arbitrage situation is similar as before: Find the theoretically correct value of A relative to B and buy low and sell high. The theoretically correct value for A is $\hat{A}_t = \hat{a} + \hat{b}B_t$. If, at $t = 1$, $A_1 > \hat{A}_1$, then security A should be sold short with the proceeds purchasing security B. The outlay at $t = 1$ is zero, and if the price relationship converges to the theoretically correct relationship at time T, the payoff at time T is

$$
\left(\frac{A_1}{B_1} B_T - A_T \right)
$$

Again, this assumes that the mispricing has corrected by time T. It is important to remember that mispricings can get worse before they get better and they can persist for a while.

In order for there to be a statistical arbitrage opportunity, we need to test whether the estimated relationships are statistically significant. This is the realm of hypothesis testing. To perform the hypotheses tests we need to assume something about the underlying processes. A useful, but perhaps inaccurate, assumption is to assume that $\varepsilon_t = A_t - \alpha - \beta B_t$ follows a normal distribution with a mean of zero and variance that does not change over time. A t-test, under the null hypotheses that the actual parameter values are zero, can be applied to $\hat{a}$ and $\hat{b}$ if we calculate the standard error of each estimate. The standard error of each estimate (se_a and se_b, respectively) is related to the standard deviation of the residuals ($\hat{\sigma}$).

$$\hat{\sigma} = \sqrt{\frac{\sum_{t=1}^{T} e_t^2}{T-2}}$$

$$se_a = \hat{\sigma}\sqrt{\frac{\sum_{t=1}^{T} B_t^2}{T\sum_{t=1}^{T}(B_t - \overline{B})^2}}$$

$$se_b = \frac{\hat{\sigma}}{\sqrt{\sum_{t=1}^{T}(B_t - \overline{B})^2}} \tag{21.2}$$

The t-values for $\hat{a}$ and $\hat{b}$ are then

$$t_a = \frac{\hat{a}}{se_a} \text{ and } t_b = \frac{\hat{b}}{se_b}$$

respectively, with $T-2$ degrees of freedom. As a general rule, if the absolute values of the t-values are greater than 1.65, then the estimates are statistically different from zero at the 10% level of significance, which is good.

If, instead of using the price process you are measuring the return process (e.g., daily or hourly returns), then the setup is very similar to a single factor model of security returns. If the regressor (the independent variable on the right-hand side of the equation) and regressand (the dependent variable on the left-hand side of the equation) are returns instead of prices, then the interpretation of $\hat{a}$ is that it is the excess return you earn on security A over security B. The interpretation of b is that it is a measure of the sensitivity of security A's returns to security B's returns.

Correlated Residuals Model

Another method used in practice is to measure the Spearman rank correlation between the residuals of the price processes when a straight line is fitted to each price process. In this case, each price process would be regressed on time (t) to find the residuals, and the Spearman rank correlation coefficient would be measured between the residuals. If the residuals are highly correlated, those securities become candidates for pairs trading.

To illustrate, given the price process of A and B, one can then run the following two regressions (21.3).

$$\left. \begin{aligned} A_t &= c_A + d_A t + e_t^A \\ B_t &= c_B + d_B t + e_t^B \end{aligned} \right\} \tag{21.3}$$

The residuals are then converted into ranks, r_t^A, r_t^B, where r stands for the rank of the respective residual (1 being the highest residual). The Spearman rank correlation (S) then measures the correlation coefficient between the two ranks which is given by equation (21.4).

$$\bar{r}_A = \frac{\sum\limits_{t=1}^{T} r_t^A}{T}, \bar{r}_B = \frac{\sum\limits_{t=1}^{T} r_t^B}{T}$$

$$S = \frac{\sum\limits_{t=1}^{T} \left(r_t^A - \bar{r}_A \right)\left(r_t^B - \bar{r}_B \right)}{\sqrt{\left(\sum\limits_{t=1}^{T} \left(r_t^A - \bar{r}_A \right)^2 \right)\left(\sum\limits_{t=1}^{T} \left(r_t^B - \bar{r}_B \right)^2 \right)}} \tag{21.4}$$

To see if S is statistically different from zero, a standard student's t-test can be performed where the t-statistic is given by equation (21.5).

$$t = \frac{S\sqrt{T-2}}{\sqrt{1-S^2}} \tag{21.5}$$

A t-table can be consulted to decide whether S is statistically different from zero with $T - 2$ degrees of freedom. Ideally, we would like S to be negative and close to negative 1. That would mean that when security A is overpriced, security B tends to be underpriced. If S is positive, then they tend to be overpriced simultaneously and underpriced simultaneously. If anything, this method serves as a good starting point for identifying candidates for pairs trading.

So far we have looked at some rather basic examples of statistical arbitrage. One challenge common to the preceding methods is in statistically testing the hypothesis that there indeed does exist a statistical arbitrage opportunity. When modeling the price process, one needs to make assumptions about how the error term behaves—what the properties of the probability distribution are and whether the distribution changes over time. Often times, the data in a financial time series will violate assumptions behind the use of a normal distribution for statistical tests. A slightly more sophisticated method based on cointegration analysis is presented next.

Cointegration and Error Correction Modeling

Cointegration analysis shows which securities move together in the long-term. This can be augmented with an error-correction model to show how the long-run relationship is approached when the security prices are out of line with their cointegrated (i.e., long-term) relationship. This method promises to be useful in statistical arbitrage applications: not only does it show what relative prices of securities should be, but it also illuminates the short-run dynamics of how equilibrium should be restored, along with how long it will take.

The relationship between cointegration and arbitrage is not new. Bondarenko[2] and Hogan, Jarrow, Teo, and Warachka[3] all defined statistical arbitrage as an attempt to exploit the long horizon trading opportunities revealed by cointegration relationships. One of the most inviting presentations of the concept of cointegration is contained in Dickey, Jansen, and Thornton.[4] They applied cointegration analysis to monetary theory, but the idea is easily extended into asset pricing theory.[5]

A lot of statistical arbitrage methods based on cointegration are applied to individual securities and the stock indicator series that they belong to. For example, if security ABC is part of index XYZ, then the cointegrating relationship can be examined between the two. This method has also been used to reveal arbitrage opportunities between futures and spot markets.[6] Statistical macroeconomic arbitrage has also been used, which is based on

[2]Oleg Bondarenko, "Statistical Arbitrage and Securities Prices," *Review of Financial Studies* 16, no. 3 (2003): 875–919.
[3]Steven Hogan, Robert Jarrow, Melvyn Teo, and Mitch Warachka, "Testing Market Efficiency Using Statistical Arbitrage with Applications to Momentum and Value Strategies," *Journal of Financial Economics* 73 no. 3 (2004): 525–565.
[4]David Dickey, Dennis Jansen, and Daniel Thornton, "A Primer On Cointegration with an Application to Money and Income," *Federal Reserve Bank of St. Louis*, March/April 1991, pp. 58–78.
[5]George Wang and Jot Yau, "A Time Series Approach to Testing for Market Linkage: Unit Root and Cointegration Test," *Journal of Futures Markets* 14, no. 4 (1994): 457–474.
[6]Carol Alexander and Anca Dimitriu, "Indexing and Statistical Arbitrage," *Journal of Portfolio Management* 31, no. 2 (2005): 50–53.

trying to take advantage of long-run relationships between macroeconomic factors (e.g., inflation) and security prices.[7]

One of the most compelling reasons for using cointegration analysis is because standard linear regression is based on the idea that there is a finite mean or variance for a process. The concept of a "mean" or a "variance" becomes meaningless if the time series has what is called a "unit root." If the time series has a unit root, that variable's use in regression analysis can give spurious results, showing a relationship among the levels of the variables without any real relationship existing. Additionally, the parameter estimates can be inconsistent. The only time variables that follow a unit-root process can be used meaningfully in regression analysis is if the variables are cointegrated.

A variable that has a unit root is also said to be "non-stationary," and "integrated of order one," (denoted by I(1)) if first differencing the variable eliminates the unit root. If individual time series are I(1), they may be cointegrated where there exists one or more linear combinations of the variables that are stationary, even though the individual variables are not stationary. Essentially, two variables that are cointegrated never move "too far away" from each other. A lack of a cointegrating relationship suggests there is no long-run link between the variables. One of the more famous analogies to describe a cointegrating relationship is when a person walks a dog: They never get too far away from each other due to the leash that connects them, though their dynamics can be quite different.

A time series, $\{p_t\}$, has a unit root if it follows a process like $p_t = \delta + \pi p_{t-1} + e_t$, with $\pi = 1$. This is what is typically known as a random walk and can be rewritten as $\Delta p_t = \delta + (\pi - 1) p_{t-1} + e_t$ where $\Delta p_t = p_t - p_{t-1}$. Dickey and Fuller, have shown that if this follows a unit root, then $\pi = 1$. If $\delta \neq 0$, then it has a unit root with a drift.[8]

The traditional t-test can be used to test the null hypothesis that the series has a unit root. A series, $\{p_t\}$, is said to be integrated of order one if the first difference, Δp_t, is stationary, but the level is not stationary.

Cointegration is a long-term relationship between two time series that are both integrated of order one, but a linear combination of the two series is stationary. If there exists two time series, $\{(A_t, B_t)\}$, a linear relationship that is stationary can be represented as $A_t - \chi B_t = \varepsilon_t$.

[7]John Tatom, "Stock Prices, Inflation and Monetary Policy," *Business Economics* 37 no. 4 (2002): 7–19; and Eugene Canjels, Gauri Prakash-Canjels, and Alan Taylor, "Measuring Market Integration: Foreign Exchange Arbitrage and the Gold Standard, 1879–1913," *Review of Economics and Statistics* 86, no. 4 (2004): 868–882.
[8]David Dickey and Wayne Fuller, "Distribution of the Estimators for Autoregressive Time Series with a Unit Root," *Journal of the American Statistical Association* 74, no. 366 (1979), pp. 423–431.

To be stationary, and for χ to be what is called the "cointegrating factor," ε_t must have a constant (i.e., independent of time) mean, variance, and autocovariance.

The simplest error correction model, which captures the short-run dynamics of how the long-run equilibrium relationship is restored, is given as follows:

$$\begin{bmatrix} \Delta A_t \\ \Delta B_t \end{bmatrix} = \begin{bmatrix} \alpha_1 \\ \alpha_2 \end{bmatrix} + \begin{bmatrix} \beta_{1,1} & \beta_{1,2} \\ \beta_{2,1} & \beta_{2,2} \end{bmatrix} \begin{bmatrix} \Delta A_{t-1} \\ \Delta B_{t-1} \end{bmatrix} + \begin{bmatrix} \theta_1 \\ \theta_2 \end{bmatrix} (A_{t-1} - \chi B_{t-1}) + \begin{bmatrix} \upsilon_t^1 \\ \upsilon_t^2 \end{bmatrix} \quad (21.6)$$

This is a system of equations that relate the changes in the variables (denoted by Δ) to the previous changes in those same variables and the deviation from the long-run relationship $(A_{t-1} - \chi B_{t-1})$.

If

$$\begin{bmatrix} \upsilon_t^1 \\ \upsilon_t^2 \end{bmatrix}$$

is bivariate-normally distributed, the vector

$$\begin{bmatrix} \theta_1 \\ \theta_2 \end{bmatrix}$$

represents how the preceding disequilibrium is corrected. The reciprocal of each coefficient can be interpreted as how many time periods it takes for the disequilibrium to be corrected. The longer it takes for the disequilibrium to be corrected, the harder it might be to exploit the arbitrage opportunity.

Those securities with a cointegrating relationship have a long-run equilibrium relationship between their prices. Any deviation from this equilibrium should be corrected over time, which means an investment strategy can be based on identifying the disequilibrium, shorting the overpriced security and going long the underpriced security. An error correction model can even identify how long this mispricing is likely to persist.

GENERAL MODELS

Let us generalize the idea of statistical arbitrage. Imagine that there are two price processes (realistic processes will be stochastic), $A(t, x_t, z_t)$ and $B(t, y_t, z_t)$. The arguments can be thought of as time (t), a unique factor to A and B (x and y, respectively), and a common factor (z). If you let $w_{A,t}$ and $w_{B,t}$ represent the number of shares invested in each, and these numbers need not be constant, then a statistical arbitrage opportunity exists if there is a zero cost position that never (i.e., for all t) becomes negative.

The initial position, at time zero, is given by $w_{A,0}A(0,x_0,z_0) + w_{B,0}B(0,y_0,z_0)$. This must be equal to zero in order to be a zero cost position to establish.

At any time after the position has been established, the value of the position must be greater than or equal to zero, represented by $w_{A,t}A(t,x_t,z_t) + w_{B,t}B(t,y_t,z_t)$.

The portfolio positions, $w_{A,t}$ and $w_{B,t}$, evolve according to the relationship that the strategy is "self-funding," or "self-financing." This simply means that when a position is established at time t, the portfolio is adjusted at $t + 1$ only with the proceeds from having held the portfolio positions from time t. This can be represented by the equation

$$w_{A,t}A\left(t+1,x_{t+1},z_{t+1}\right) + w_{B,t}B\left(t+1,y_{t+1},z_{t+1}\right)$$
$$= w_{A,t+1}A\left(t+1,x_{t+1},z_{t+1}\right) + w_{B,t+1}B\left(t+1,y_{t+1},z_{t+1}\right)$$

At the terminal time, T, the portfolio value must be greater than zero to yield a profit, $w_{A,T-1}A(T,x_T,z_T) + w_{B,T-1}B(T,y_T,z_T) > 0$. The reason we use $w_{A,T-1}$ and $w_{B,T-1}$ in the terminal portfolio value is that the position is established at time $T-1$ and held to time T.

One can think of the preceding as a system of equations where the weights need to be found such that initially it costs nothing to establish the position, there is never a possibility of a margin call (the portfolio's value must always be nonnegative), and on the terminal date the portfolio's value is strictly positive. There is also the constraint that the trading strategy must be self-financing, with the weights not having intraperiod changes: The weights are chosen at the beginning of the period and the value of the portfolio at the end of one period must be the same as the value of the portfolio at the beginning of the next period.

The preceding describes a dynamic programming problem. The objective function can be to maximize the terminal value of the portfolio, denoted by $\max w_{A,T-1}A\left(T,x_T,z_T\right) + w_{B,T-1}B\left(T,y_T,z_T\right)$, where one selects the two sequences $\{w_{A,0},w_{A,1},...,w_{A,T-1}\}$ and $\{w_{B,0},w_{B,1},...,w_{B,T-1}\}$.

If the price processes are stochastic, then this becomes a stochastic, dynamic programming problem subject to an informational constraint where we try to maximize the expected value of the portfolio at time T with only knowledge up to the present ($t < T$). The decision variables are the weights at each time step from $t = 0$ to $t = T - 1$.

The preceding is the general framework. Everything beyond that is a special case of the preceding: what are the unique and common factors, what are the models of the price processes, and are the weights constants or can they vary? Specific implementation requires modeling the price processes. So we are back where we started—the biggest risk in statistical arbitrage is model risk: Does the model of the price process comport to reality and will it persist over the investment horizon?

KEY POINTS

- Riskless arbitrage is when there is a guaranteed positive payoff without the commitment of any capital. Statistical arbitrage is when the positive payoff is not guaranteed, but can be expressed as a probability. Statistical arbitrage also refers to the use of statistics to identify possible arbitrage opportunities.
- The biggest risk associated with statistical arbitrage is "model risk," where the model of the world is not consistent with reality.
- Pairs trading is a fundamental type of statistical arbitrage. The question is, "What security is mispriced relative to the other security?" Once the mispricing is identified, then it is a matter of implementing the trade: buy the relatively underpriced security and short the relatively overpriced security. By doing this, one can create a "market neutral" portfolio where the profit is determined by the relative mispricing, not by the general level of the security prices.
- Cointegration analysis illuminates the long-run relationship between security prices. An error correction model shows how the deviations from the long-run relationship correct over time. This is perhaps one of the more interesting areas of statistical arbitrage research since it can be used to estimate the length of time a long or short position needs to be maintained to yield a profit.
- It is possible to create a completely general model of statistical arbitrage through stochastic, dynamic optimization. This involves creating a model of the price processes, subject to the constraint that the initial cost of the portfolio is zero and that the portfolio is self-financing.

QUESTIONS

1. What is the difference between "pure arbitrage" and "statistical arbitrage"?

2. What is the difference between a relative return strategy and an absolute return strategy?

3. Why is a t-test important when estimating a statistical arbitrage model?

4. How are cointegration and error correction models related?

5. What is meant by a "self-financing" strategy?

About the Web Site

This book is accompanied by a web site, www.wiley.com/go/equity valuationandportfoliomanagement.

The web site supplements the materials in the book by offering the solutions to the questions at the end of each chapter.

To receive these free benefits, you will need to follow two simple steps:

1. Enter the following URL in your browser's address bar:

   www.wiley.com/go/equityvaluationandportfoliomanagement.

2. Follow the instructions on the web site to register using your personal e-mail address. You will need a password from this book to complete the registration process. The password is: finance321.

Index

Abnormal earnings valuation, 55–57
Accumulated unamortized R&D account, addition, 57
Active equity strategies, 202
enhancement, 162
Active global portfolios
construction process, 416–419
country-neutral stock selection, 417–418
country selection, 418–419
empirical results, 420–422
naive stock selection, 416–417
Active investment strategies, examples, 450
Active management, 151–156
methods, 376–385
modeling, 385–392
Active management, labor-intensive methods, 153
Active/passive portfolio, tracking error, 254
Active return
attribution, 268
calculation, 252, 253e
data, 253e
Actual tracking error, 453
predicted tracking error, contrast, 453–454
Adaptive market hypothesis, 232
Adaptive modeling techniques, 217–218
Adaptive models, usage, 217–218
Adjusted R-square, increase, 240
After-tax interest expense, 41
After-tax performance, report, 461–462
After-tax ROC, 42
Aggregates, trading, 393–394
Alpha, 256–257
assignment, 331
calculation, 253e
data, 253e
factor, 309
models, 265
portfolio, 490
production, 225
repair portfolio

excess returns, 409e
outperformance, 410e
repair process, function, 408–411
sources, 22
American Depositary Receipts (ADRs), 110
Annualized return-to-volatility, increase, 406–407
Annual net payments, calculation, 83–84
Anti-franchise firms, 72
extreme, 74–75
money, loss, 74
Anti-franchise growth, examples, 95–96
Arbitrage
cointegration, relationship, 530
opportunity, recognition, 522
Arbitrage Pricing Theory (APT), 200
factors, 377
ARCH-GARCH model, volatility estimate, 192
Artificial intelligence, 239
Asian financial crisis (1997), 271
Asset-based factors, 433, 435–436
examples, 435
Asset class
performance, summary, 140e
performance, variation, 137–139
returns, 138e
Assets
aggregate amount, 467–468
allocation, importance, 226–227
management, 205
managers, models, 216
pricing models, 377
style performance, summary, 140e
turnover ratio, 29
Asset-specific returns, 300
Asymmetric market impact costs, 427
Attribution analysis, 256
forms, 365
Autoregressive model
absence, 201
impact, 235
Average daily volume (ADV), 444

Backtesting, 328–330
in-sample/out-of-sample methodologies, understanding, 329–330
process, 271
Backward-looking tracking error, 453–454
forward-looking tracking error, contrast, 255–256
Bad company growth, 50–51, 52
Balance sheet data, 27e
Band acceptance, 96–97
Barclays Capital Global Risk Model, availability, 340
Barra Extreme Risk Analytics Guide, 485
Barra Short-Term US Equity Model (USE3S), 486
Basic EVA, 40–42
Batting average, 14
determination, 15e
Bayesian estimation approaches, 470
Behavioral modeling, 201
Belief persistence, 202
Benchmark
exposure, 450–454
neutrality, imposition, 487–489
portfolio
market cap/style, comparison, 258–259
performance, contrast, 453
return, 452
sector deviation, 259
total risk, 353e
Benchmark-neutral case, realized shortfall (comparison), 489e
Benchmark-replicating portfolio, pure active portfolio (combination), 376
Benchmark stocks, tracking error (contrast), 258e
Beta, 257, 260–261
tracking error, comparison, 261e
Bets, position concentration/size, 4
Better Not Take the Chance/What the Heck paradox, 154

Bid-ask bounce, presence, 505
Bid-ask data, real-time adjustments, 509
Bid-ask spreads, 454–455
  increase, 504
  variation, 503
Bimodal patterns, 112
Binary variable, stocks (relationship), 446
Black, Fischer, 243–244
Black-Litterman model, 470
Bloomberg, data vendor, 112
Book-to-price ratio (B/P), 177–178, 266, 344
  naive returns, 178e
  pure returns, 178e
Book value
  calculation, example, 118
  measures, 113
Bottom-up managers, trends forecast, 255
Box-Cox transformation, usage, 437
Box uncertainty, 475e
  set, 477–478
Buffett, Warren, 74
Building factors, 274–275

Calendarization, 120
Capital Asset Pricing Model (CAPM), 37, 377
  FSR, contrast, 38e
  tests, 292
Capital cost, 97
Capital gains
  accumulation, 460–461
  offsetting, 464
  short-term/long-term characteristics, 464
Capital growth, EVA spread (contrast), 52e
Capital investments, usage, 94–95
Capital losses, accumulation, 460–461
Capital structure
  change, impact, 45e
  pricing implications, 46
  viewpoint, 45
Capital turnover ratio (S/C), 44
Cardinality constraints, 446–447
Cash flow-based valuations, exposure (maintenance), 322
Cash flow return on investment (CFROI), 39, 48–49
  calculation process, 49e
Cash plowback, 485–486
Characteristic
  batting average, determination, 15e
  combination, 18
  information coefficient, determination, 13e

information ratio, determination, 15e
  quintile spread, determination, 12e
  weightings, 18e
  weights, determination, 17
Characteristic testing, 10, 14–16
  flow, 11e
  quantitative research metrics, 11–14
Chartered Financial Analysts Institute, 205
Chi-square distribution, 472–473
Classification and regression tree (CART), advantage, 202
Classification variables, 346–347
Clients
  needs, meeting, 160
  risk-return goals/investment results, 168
Coca-Cola
  case study, 60–68
  integrated traditional analysis, 60–68
  JLG equity analysis template, 62e–68e
  traditional/value-based analysis, 58
  Value Line Report, 61e
  VBM analysis, 60–68
Cognitive errors, 153–155
Cointegration
  analysis, usage, 531
  arbitrage, relationship, 530
  error correction modeling, 530–532
  usage, 203
Commodities, lead, 137–138
Common factors, 32
  usage, 35–36
Company
  analysis, VBM (approach), 38–39
  characteristics, building factors, 274–275
  fair value, 122
  growth characteristics, 50–51
  investor focus, 3
  performance, IRR-based measure, 48
Company-specific risk premium, 48
Comparable companies, analysis, 110
Comparable firms
  bimodal patterns, 112
  geography/clientele, impact, 109–110
  multimodal patterns, 112
  number, 108
  sector/industry characteristics, 110–111
  selection, basis, 108–112

technology/intra-industry diversity, 111–112
Comparables (forecasted fundamentals), 32
  contrast, 34–35
Compustat Point-In-Time database, 333–336
  usage, 291
Compustat US database, templates, 279
Conditional value-at-risk (CVaR)
  risk measure, 452
  usage, 226
Confirmation bias, 154–155
Conglomerates
  central control, counterargument, 121
  discount, application, 120
Consistency, measures, 14–16
  information, usage, 14, 16
Constant earnings growth, example, 88e
Constant relative price process model, 525–526
Consumer staples, consumer discretionary portfolio (contrast), 356e
Contribution to TEV (CTEV), 359
Core equity market, dissection, 149
Corelike holding, creation, 156
Corporate debt policy, ROE (impact), 31e
Corporate executive investment/disinvestment behavior, 202
Correlated residuals model, 528–530
Correlation
  measurement, 16
  review, 17e
  trading, 523–525
Cost of equity, estimation, 47–48
Counterparty risk, presence, 220
Country equity indexes, opportunities, 387–388
Country membership
  explanatory power, 415e
  stock returns, 414–416
Country-neutral stock selection, 417–418
Country noise, 420
  loading, 421–422
  naive stock selection portfolio, usage, 422–423
Country risk, 413
Country selection, 418–419
  alpha, 422
  calculation usage, 420
  portfolio, holdings, 419
Country-specific exposures, 383
Country-specific fundamental factors model, 383

Covariance construction, risk
models, 268
Covariance matrix, 342
BARRA estimate, usage, 417, 420
decomposition, 340–341
estimators, weighted portfolios, 470
Credit risk, presence, 220
Credit Suisse/HOLT (CS/HOLT), 38
Cross-sectional averages, 283
Cross-sectional characteristics, 268
Cross-sectional factor-based
models/trading strategies, 291
Cross-sectional factor models, 345e
advantage, 344–345
econometric considerations,
301–303
measurement problems, 301
multicollinearity, 303
residuals, variation, 302–303
Cross-sectional OLS, 304
Cross-sectional regressions
performing, 304
running, 419
usage, 417
Cumulative monthly excess
returns, measurement, 178
Cumulative quintile spread
return, 16
Cyclicality, incorporation,
139–142

Dark pools, 498
Data
accounting principles, 280
acquisition/processing, 270
backfilling, 275–276
biases, 278–279
collection, 19
errors, 282
integrity, 275–278
issues, 279–280
restatements, 275–276
sampling methodologies, 511e
usage, 275–283
Data driven approach, statistical
methods (usage), 318–319
Data set
limitation, 469
outliers, 273
overmining, 241
Data snooping (data mining), 237
control, 238
Data vendors
impact, 239
projections, 112
Debt/credit (D/C), 46
Debt-equity ratio, 48
Debt-interest-tax subsidy, 38
Decomposition, steps, 419

Depositary receipts, usage, 110
Derivatives markets, chaos
(impact), 220
Despair phase (equity market
phase), 128
economic environment, dete-
rioration, 135
equity volatility, increase, 136–137
investor concern, 134
risk averse investor, bond
ownership, 137
unemployment, increase, 137
Diagonal matrix, usage, 478
Discount dividend model (DDM), 71
Discounted cash flow (DCF)
approach, 55–56
analyst preference, 122–123
methods, usage, 105
models, 27
relative valuation, comparison,
121–123
Discretionary limit orders, 428
Disentangling, 176–184
effects, 178–179
usage, 181–183
Distribution percentiles, 283
Dividend discount model (DDM)
stock valuation model, 386–387
usage, 126–127
value
estimates, correlation, 176
one-standard-deviation
exposure, 181–182
Dividend growth rate, 387
Dividend payout ratio (DPR), 35
Dividends, measures, 113
Dividend yield, 26
factor, suitability, 294
Dodd, David, 266
Downside risk, 134
Dramatic underperformance,
probability (increase), 259–260
Drivers, statistical analysis, 32
Dupont formula, 28
Dupont model, after-tax/pretax
versions, 29
Durability, rarity, 402e
Dynamic factor approaches, 375
Dynamic factor strategies, port-
folio management strategies
(contrast), 378
Dynamic modeling, 22

Earnings
dissipation, 210
growth, example, 88
growth factor, 307
returns, linkage, 126–132
revisions factors, cross-sectional distributions, 284

valuation/economic cycle,
relationship, 125–126
Earnings before income and
taxes (EBIT), 28–29, 41
Earnings before interest, taxes,
depreciation, and amortization
(EBITDA), 32
Earnings before interest taxes,
depreciation, and amortization
to enterprise value (EBITDA/
EV) factor, 277–278
basis, 295–296
cross-sectional values, histograms, 285e
data, analysis (example), 284
information coefficients, horizons, 307e
initiation, 306–307
performance, positive level, 313
Earnings growth rate (EGR), 35
Earnings per share (EPS) growth
rate, 27
Earnings per share to book value
(EPS/BV) ratio, 50
Earnings-to-price ratio (E/P),
485–486
Econometric models (financial
models), 193
Economic analysis, principles, 235
Economic cycle, valuation/earn-
ings (relationship), 125–126
Economic laws, validation precision, 234
Economic profit, 243e
guarantee, absence (statistical
significance), 242–243
Economic profit, measurement, 57
Economics, motivation, 237
Economic theories, significance, 235
Economic value added (EVA), 39–40
basic EVA, 40–42
calculation, 40
expression, 48
momentum
assessment, 51
role, 50–52
popularity, 40
spread, 42, 44
capital growth, contrast, 52e
value/capital ratio, contrast,
55e
three-part calculation, 43e
usage, financial significance, 40
valuation considerations, 52–57
Economy
human artifact, 234–235
phases, relationship, 132–137
recovery, 135
Economy-wide debt load, ROE
(variation), 32

Econophysics
  framework, 235–238
  impact, 235
  increase, 233–235
  information, 238
  model (estimation), methodol-
    ogy (selection), 239–246
  trial-and-error process, 238
EFA computation, empirical cor-
  relation, 518e
Efficient markets hypothesis, 373
Efficient portfolio, concept, 246
Electronic crossing networks
  (ECNs), 433
Ellipsoidal uncertainty, 475e
Emerging markets, transaction
  costs, 433
Employee Retirement Income
  Security Act (ERISA) requirements, compliance, 443
Endowment effect, 154
Engineered management, 157–160
  approaches, quantitative meth-
    ods (usage), 158
  discipline, 159
  opportunities, expansion,
    160–163
Engineering, impact, 159
Enterprise value, capital structure change (impact), 45e
Epps effect, 517, 519
Equal-weighted stock baskets,
  usage, 418
Equity
  architecture, 167–168
  correlations decay, high fre-
    quencies, 517–519
  cost, estimation, 47–48
  funds, net flows (impact), 213
  indexes, return contributions,
    368e
  multiplier (leverage), 28–39
  research reports, 274
  returns, 137
  risk factor models, 342–350
    model estimation, 344–346
Equity analysis, 171
  relative value methods, 105
  value-based metrics (VBM)
    approach, 36, 39–40
Equity investment, 1–2
  approaches, 151e
  comparison, 159e
  processes, 218
Equity market
  architectural building blocks,
    148–151
  relationship, 148e
  cycles, 127–128
  global size, trading (impact), 427

phases, 127–128
  dates/returns, 142–145
  derivation, 129e
  diagram, 128e
  premium, 160
  rate, example, 100
  return, 162
Equity portfolio management
  architecture, 147
  building blocks, 148–151
  derivatives, usage, 220
  dynamic factor approaches, 373
Equity portfolio models, role
  (change), 199
Equity portfolio selection, 441
Equity-risk buildup model, 47e
Equity risk models
  applications, 350–370
  factor-based scenario analysis,
    366–370
  factor model-based attribu-
    tion, 365
  factors, incorporation, 343–344
  performance attribution, 365–366
  return decomposition, 365
  style analysis, 365
Equity risk premium (ERP), 126,
  139, 141
  measures, 142
Error correction
  model, 532
  modeling, cointegration (rela-
    tionship), 530–532
Estimated returns, predictive
  power (improvement), 181–183
Estimation, 224
  errors, 220, 474
    covariance matrix, inverse, 477
    prediction errors, trade-offs, 240
  returns, 245e
Estimators, averaging, 469–470
Europe
  average earnings growth, 131e
  P/E expansion, 131e
  phases, dates/returns, 144e
  return, 131e
European market participants,
  global perception, 192
Event-driven portfolio, 523–524
Event studies, 265
Ex ante economic justification,
  development, 237
Ex ante expected return model,
  establishment, 244
Ex ante tracking error, 256, 454
Excess return, residual risk
  (trade-offs), 164–165
Exchange-traded funds (ETFs),
  394, 522
  quant product access, 213

Exogenous insight, incorpora-
  tion, 470
Expected returns
  estimation model, 243–244
  maximization, 449
  time variation, 469
Expected shortfall (shortfall), 484
Expected stock return (ER), 37
Explanatory variables
  determination, 240
  marginal contribution, 241e
Explicit transaction costs, 433
Ex post tracking error, 453
Extended Dupont formula,
  28–29, 36–37
Extreme loss, measures, 484–485
Extreme risk, portfolio construc-
  tion (relationship), 483
Extreme value theory (EVT),
  195–196

Factor-based equity portfolio
  construction/analysis, 265
Factor-based market impact
  model, 436–439
Factor-based scenario analysis,
  366–370
Factor-based strategies, risk
  models (interaction), 330
Factor-based trading, 266–269
  data driven approach, 318–319
  factor model approach, 319–320
  factor selection, importance,
    322–328
  heuristic approach, 320–321
  model construction, impor-
    tance, 322–328
  optimization approach, 321–322
Factor-based trading strategies, 265
  development, 269–270
  evaluation/backtesting/imple-
    mentation, 270
  example, 323–328
  factor weights, 325e
  framework/building blocks,
    269–270
  model construction method-
    ologies, 317–328
Factor mimicking portfolio
  (FMP), 293
Factor-mimicking portfolio,
  construction, 354–355
Factor model-based analysis, performance attribution, 365–366
Factor model-based attribution, 365
Factors
  adjustment, methods, 280–282
  analysis, 270
    framework, IC basis, 305
  categories, 268

classification variables, 346–347
competition, 403–405
construction, Compustat
    Point-In-Time/IBES data-
    bases (usage), 291
data analysis, 283–287
data driven approach, 318–319
definitions, 333–336,
    398e–399e
development, 269–270, 273
durability, rarity, 402e
evolution, 408e
exposures, 356e
    examples, 380–385
    regions/countries/industries/
        sectors, 381–383
    style/size, 380–381
firm characteristics, 347–348
incorporation, 343–344
information coefficients, 314e
loadings, 437
    standardization, 348–349
macroeconomic factors, 383–384
macroeconomic variables, 348
microeconomic factors, 384–385
monthly returns, rolling
    24-month correlations, 318e
negative values, 285e
number, usage, 405–407, 406e
orthogonalization, usage,
    281–282
past performance, 404e
performance evaluation, 310–317
performance variation, 315, 317
persistence, structural changes,
    407
portfolios, 308–310
    optimization-based
        approach, 309–310
positive values, 285e
premiums, evaluation (cross-sec-
    tional methods), 292–300
properties, 273
quantitative manager usage, 266
realized returns, 305–306
revisions, example, 284
risk assessment, information
    coefficient (usage), 306
rolling 24-month mean
    returns, 317e
selection
    importance, 322–328
    quantitative measures, 349
    reasons, 407–408
sources, 273–274
standardization, usage, 280–281
summary, 267e
time-series setting, 348
trading strategy, backtesting,
    330–331

transformation, usage, 282
types, 346–349
usage, 268
volatility, nonstationary char-
    acteristic, 494
weighting strategy, dynamic
    nature, 411e
Factors models, 300–310
    approach, 308–309, 319–320
    asset pricing models, relation-
        ship, 377
    basis, 469
    considerations, 349
    contemporaneous specifica-
        tion, 300–301
    control usage, 444–445
    cumulative return, 327e
    results, summary, 326e
    usage, 194, 464
Factor-specific returns, 300
Factors returns
    covariance matrix, 324
    examples, 368e, 369e
    history, 400e–401e
    K vector, 308–309
    realization pattern, variation,
        307–308
Facts, human insight (balance), 6
FactSet, data vendor, 112
Fair equilibrium, 466
Fair market benchmark, 430
Fair value, company worth, 122
Fama-Macbeth (FM) regression,
    303–304
    monthly coefficients, time
        series average, 315, 316e
    usage, 309
Fama-Macbeth (FM) unbiased
    standard errors, 303
Feasible generalized least squares
    (FGLS), 302
Financial data, consistency, 275–276
Financial databases, concern, 276
Financial integration, level, 343
Financial leverage multiplier, 28
Financial metric, usage, 39
Financial modeling, objection,
    191–192
Financial models (econometric
    models), 193
Financial risk, considerations,
    31–32
Financial security, identifier, 499
Firm characteristics, 347–348
Firms
    number, 108
    relative value, assessment, 109
    value, market cap (contrast), 114
First-order autocorrelation, cor-
    rection, 303

Fixed costs, variable costs (con-
    trast), 426
Fixed franchise spread, 83
Fixed time intervals, reliance,
    509–510
Fixed transaction costs, 459–460
Fleeting orders, 428
Forecasted fundamentals (com-
    parables), 32
Forecast horizon, momentum
    models (contrast), 389
Forecasting
    factors, 433
    models, usage, 268
    technique, 385–386
Foreign exchange (FX), total
    return portion, 367–368
Fortune 50 company, diversifica-
    tion, 79e
Forward-looking tracking error, 454
    backward-looking tracking
        error, contrast, 255–256
Franchise employee, impact, 97–98
Franchise factor (FF), 84
Franchise factor model (FFM), 71
    assumptions, impact, 72
    background, 72–75
    basic model, formulation, 81–85
    formulation, 84
    investment return, 73–74
    market forecasts, absence, 77
    P/E orbits, relationship, 93–94
    usage, 85
Franchise labor, 97–101
    ambiguity, 99
    claims, effects, 99e
Franchise-level margins, assur-
    ance, 97
Franchise ride, enjoyment, 97
Franchise spread, 83
Franchise value (FV), 72–73
    bubbles, 94, 96
    consumption, 94–95
    decay, 94–96
    FV-driven firm, challenge, 79
    growth, 94–96
Free cash flow to equity, usage,
    117–118
Friedman, Milton, 234
Full automation, progress, 218–219
Full optimization, 218
Full risk analysis, 6
Fundamental analysis, 195
Fundamental evaluation errors,
    82–83
Fundamental factors, portfolio man-
    ager exposure limitation, 357
Fundamental investors
    company/characteristic focus, 3
    narrow/broad focus, 4

Fundamental investors (*Cont.*)
past/future approach, contrast, 4–5
quantitative investors
contrast, 2–7
information, viewing, 2e
process differences, 5e
risk, perspective, 4
Fundamental quants, quality, 208
Fundamental risk, 271
Fundamental stock return (FSR), 36–38
calculation, 36
CAPM, contrast, 38e
Fundamental valuation-based methods, 386–388
Fundamental variables, usage, 182
Future earnings, estimates, 107
Future franchise labor, 98
Future profits, franchise labor (effects), 99
Future stock return, variance, 301
Future value (FV), 26–27

Gambler's fallacy, 154
Generalized autoregressive conditional heteroscedasticity (GARCH), 405
Generalized least squares (GLS), 302
Genetic algorithms, 239
G factor, 85
Global equity portfolios, unintended country bets (avoidance), 413
Global equity risk model, structure, 343
Global financial crisis (2007-2009), modeling, 226–228
Global Industry Classification Standard (GICS)
indexes, return series, 347
level 1, 359
usage, 110–111
Good company growth, 50–51
Good stocks, 52–53
identification, 53–54
Gordon model, 387
Graham, Benjamin, 266
Great Recession (2007), 75–79
Growth
calculations, 336
opportunities, present value (PV), 83–84
potential, P/E expression, 77
sources, 94
Growth phase (equity market phase), 128
commodity lead, 137–138
economy, recovery, 135

investor volatility, 134
Growth stocks
investment, 173
underweighting, 149

Haircuts, 526
Heteroskedasticity-consistent standard errors, 302
Hidden Markov models, 218
High-frequency data (tick data)
availability, increase, 227
bid-ask bounce, 503–509
conversion, midquote format, 505
explanation, 497–498
level I high-frequency data, NYSE Arca, 500e–501e
market dynamics information, 504
properties, 499, 500–501
summary, 502e
recordation, process, 499–500
spacing, irregularity, 509–517
usage, 497
volume, 501
High-frequency strategies, 265
High-frequency trading (HFT), 22–23, 497
diffusion, 227
High-growth stocks, P/E orbits, 87–90
High momentum stocks, performance, 354
Historical risk-adjusted IC, usage, 322
Holding constraints, 443
Holding period return, calculation, 86
Hope phase (equity market phase), 128
downside risk, 134
economic indicators, decline, 135
equities, returns, 137
real bond yield, decline, 137
unemployment, increase, 137
HSBC CCF, EVT applicability, 195
Human creativity, complement, 235
Human judgments, replacement, 233
Hyper-franchise firms, 72
extreme, 74–75
opportunities, 96

IBES database, 333–336
usage, 291
Idiosyncratic risk, 349–350, 392
exposures, 364e
Idiosyncratic stock returns, covariance matrix, 342
Idiosyncratic TEV, 352–353
increase, 357–358

Immediate or cancel order (IOC)
orders, 428
Imperfect substitution, 426
Implementation risk, 272
Implementation shortfall approach, 432
Implied growth rate, calculation, 56–57
Income statement
data, 27e
usage, 29
Index, tracking, 352–353
Index-based portfolio management strategies, usage, 373
Index returns, 367e, 369e
Industry characteristics, 110–111
Industry-specific multiples, 115
Information availability, 215
Information coefficient (IC), 12–14, 304–308
calculation, 13, 305
correlations, 314e
determination, 13e
example, 306–308
horizons, 307e
impact, 233
methodology, advantages, 306
unconditional correlation coefficients, 315
usage, 306
Information ratio (IR), 14, 16, 256–257
attribution, 268
benchmark-neutral case, shortfall beta constraint, 488e
calculation, 186, 253e, 257
data, 253e
determination, 15e
increase, 164
manager, 165, 167
shortfall betas, constraint, 487e
usage, 299
In-house software, usage, 215
Initial growth rates, 92e
Initial P/E, representation, 89
In-sample methodology, understanding, 329–330
In-sample tests, out-of-sample tests (trade-offs), 330
Insights, breadth/goodness, 152e
Institute for Supply Management (ISM) survey, 135
Integrated of order one, 531
Interest
pre-determined period, 442
risk-free rate, 38
Internal rate of return (IRR), IRR-based company performance measure, 48

International Business Machines (IBM), Value Line Report, 70e
Interpolated midquotes, last tick quotes (contrast), 514e
Interpolated quotes, trade data, 519
Interquote intervals, manipulation, 511, 515
Intertek European
  study (2003), 189–197
  study (2006), 197–205
    challenges, 204
    equity portfolio models, role (change), 199
    findings, 197–198
    industry evaluation, 200–203
    modeling methodologies, 200–203
    optimization, 203
    survey participants, 198
  study (2007), 205–224
    entry barriers, 222–224
    fund flows, 212–214
    model-driven investment strategies, impact, 206–207
    oversight/overlay, 214–216
    performance improvement, 211–212
    performance issues, 207–211
    quantitative process, 214–216
    quant process, implementation, 217–219
    quant process, implementation reasons, 220–222
    risk management, 219–220
    survey participants, 223
Intertek Group, model performance evaluation, 189–190
Intertemporal models (Merton), 225
Intertrade duration, distributions, 516e
Intraday data, availability (increase), 227
Intra-industry diversity, 111–112
Intratrade duration, impact, 515
Inventory effects, 426
Investable opportunities, PV, 83
Investment
  characteristic, investor focus, 3
  culture, 223
  decisions, exogenous events (impact), 215
  facts, human insight (balance), 6
  full risk analysis, 6
  fundamental/quantitative approach, combination (benefits), 6e
  growth, example, 89e
  management, objective, 167–168

process, integration, 441
quantamental approach, 7
return-risk level, achievement, 152
return-risk ratio, 152e
single-period view, 442
strategy
  defining, 269
  process, 236e
  style, immediacy, 434
Investors
  give-up, measurement, 165
  low-P/E stocks search, 185
  risk, risk/return change, 164e
  risk aversion, overestimation, 166e
Isolated TEV, 360, 360e
Iterative process, 465–466

JLG equity analysis template, 58, 62e–68e

Large-cap blend portfolio, 258
Large-cap growth, 147, 149
  stocks, large-cap value (contrast), 150e
Large-cap growth stocks, large-cap value stocks (contrast), 149
Large-cap stocks
  active trading, 435–436
  small-cap stocks, contrast, 149, 150e
Large-cap value, 147, 149
  underweighting, 149
Largest value added, 244–245
Last in, last out (LIFO) inventory, 57
Last tick quotes, interpolated midquotes (contrast), 514e
Last trade data points, 498
Last trade information, 498
Last trade price simple returns, 507e
Law of one alpha, 175
Least risky equity, 48
Leibowitz, Marty, 74
Leverage, 28–29
  debt, ROE (relationship), 31
  ROE, relationship, 29–31
Levered firm net operating profit after tax (LNOPAT), 40
Limit order (conditional order), 428
Linear regression, statistical inference (impact), 302
Linear regression-based model, 526–528
Linear transaction costs, 456
Liquidity
  concession, 426
  insufficiency, 210
  risk, 272
  transaction costs, relationship, 427–430

Loading, standardization, 348–349
Long-only constraints, 443
Long-run valuation levels, estimate, 115
Long-short balance, impact, 161–162
Long-short portfolios, 161–163
  construction, 354
  cumulative returns, 312–313, 312e
  monthly returns, statistics, 310, 311e
  monthly returns, unconditional correlation coefficients, 311e, 312
Long-short quantitative managed funds, problems, 213
Long-short strategies, 220
Long-Term Capital Management (LTCM), collapse, 198–199
Long-term value strategies, trading, 434
Look-ahead bias, avoidance, 276
Loss aversion, 154
Lots, usage, 461, 498
Low-growth stocks, P/E orbits, 90
Low-tracking error portfolio, risk aversion, 331

Machine learning techniques, 238
Macro-benchmarked ERP, 141e
Macroeconomic factors, 383–384
Macroeconomic influences, 268
Macroeconomic shocks, forecast response, 183e
Macroeconomic variables, 348
Macro valuation, 78
Macro variables (market implied ERP), univariate regressions (R^2), 142e
Manager skill, risk/return change, 164e
Margin requirements, 522, 526
Marketable portfolio assets, holding, 461
Market capitalization, 292
  firm value, contrast, 114
Market credibility, 223
Market depth information, dissemination, 500
Market efficiency, model-driven investment strategies (impact), 206–207
Market factors, 346
Market impact
  forecasting/modeling, 433–439
  function, linearity, 436–437
  specifications, proposals, 438
Market impact costs, 425–427, 454

Market impact costs (*Cont.*)
asymmetric characteristic, 427
modeling, 425
variation, 428
Market impact measurements
approaches, 430–431
empirical findings, 430–433
implementation shortfall
approach, 432
post-trade measures, 430
pre-trade measures, 430
same-day/average measures, 431
Market impact models
availability, 439
factor-based market impact
model, 436–438
trade size, nonlinear effects, 437
Market implied ERP, univariate
regressions (R²), 142e
Market indexes, 251
phases, 127–128
Market inefficiencies, capture, 232
Market-neutral long-short
portfolios
security selection return/equity
market return, 162
usage, 162
Market neutral strategy, 523
Market portfolio, tracking error
(relationship), 261
Market price, impact, 2
Market risk, 132e
Market sentiment, 194
Market timing strategies, 153
Market value, calculation, 81–82
Market value added (MVA), 39, 54
Market volatility, 257, 259–260
Markit Economics Purchas-
ing Managers Survey (PMI),
manufacturing activity
indexes, 135
Markowitz, Harry, 195–196
Max-min problem, 475–476
Mean-variance optimization,
return decomposition, 490e
Mean-variance portfolio alloca-
tion, utility function formula-
tion, 474
Mean-variance portfolio
optimization formulation,
robustification, 476
Mean-variance portfolio opti-
mization problem, ellipsoidal
uncertainty set, 477
Median absolute deviation,
116–117
Methodology selection, 239–246
Metrics, estimates, 107
Metrics, ROE/FSR (direct relationship), 36–37

Microcap stocks, relative valua-
tion, 108
Microeconomic factors, 384–385
Midcap industrial firm, example, 81e
Midquote simple returns, 506e
Midquote last tick quotes, 512e
Midquote time-interpolated
quotes, 513e
Minimum holding constraints,
447–448
Misspecification risk, 271–272
Model biases, analysis, 225
Model creation, 10, 16–18
components, 16
correlation review, 17e
Model diffusion, 225
Model-driven investment strategies, impact, 206–207
Modeling, 385–392
methods, 201–202
technique, 200–201
technology, advances, 239
Model risk, 192, 271–272
mitigation, 193
Model selection, methodology
(selection), 239–246
Modigliani and Miller (MM)
theory, 45
Momentum
appearance, report, 201
calculations, 336
coefficient, observation, 242–243
exhibition, 242–243
factor, volatility, 313
meaning, 194
modeling, 200
models, forecast horizon (contrast), 389
portfolio, long/short sides
(positions), 355e
strategies, 388–389
timing, 390e
valuation strategies, combination, 390–391
trading strategy, 242
usage, 389
Momentum-based methods, 388–389
Monitoring, quantitative investment process, 9, 21–22
Monotonic relation (MR) test, 300
Month-ahead return-to-volatility
ratio, 406
Monthly information coefficients, unconditional correlation coefficients, 314e, 315
Monthly stock returns, country
membership (explanatory
power), 415e
MSCI US Prime Market 750
Index, 486

Multi-account optimization,
465–469
Multicollinearity, 301, 303
Multifactor equity risk models
applications, 339
motivation, 340–342
Multifactor models, usage,
358–365
Multifactor risk models, goals, 341
Multimodal patterns, 112
Multiple accounts, iterative
process, 465–466
Multiple models, usage, 193
Multiple regression, 35
Multiples
calculation, 83
low/negative numbers, involve-
ment, 119
Multistage RI model, usage, 55–56
Multistep estimation process,
usage, 345–346

Naive portfolio, study, 419–420
Naive returns, 177–178
opportunities, hiding, 179e
Naive stock selection, 416–417
portfolio, impact, 422–423
strategy
problems, 421–422
regressions, 418
Net debt, calculation, 114
Net market weights (NMW), 359e
expression, 364
Net operating profit after tax
(NOPAT), 30
expression, 41–42
Net present value (NPV), 53–54
Net property, plant and equip-
ment (NPPE), 44
Net shortfall beta portfolio,
impact, 491
Net short-term operating assets, 44
Neural networks, 239
New businesses, capital invest-
ments (usage), 94–95
Newey-West corrections, 302
New York Stock Exchange (NYSE)
limit order book, 429–430
NYSE OpenBook, 430
NYSE-Traded SPY, bid-ask
spreads, 504e
Nikkei 225, performance, 78
Nikkei Index, investment (cumu-
lative value), 77e
Noise reduction, 177–179
Noise trader risk, 271
Nonbenchmark stocks, tracking
error (contrast), 259e
Nondiversifiable risk premium,
48

Nondividend-paying stock, 172
  grouping, 294
Nonquantitative funds, flows
  (Lipper tracking), 213–214
Nonrobust mean-variance for-
  mulation, 476
  computation, complexity, 476
Nonstationarity, 469
Nontrending markets, impact, 210
Normalized net shortfall beta
  portfolio, performance, 492e
No-trade price, 430
Numerator, selection, 114

Objective function formulation, 460
Observation, term, 234
On-board employees, right-on-
  point experience, 98
120-20 portfolios, 163–164
130-30 portfolios, 163–164
130-30-type strategies/scalability,
  220
One-month-ahead values, forecast, 405
One-step regression, usage, 345
Operating expenses, reduction, 42
Operating profit, focus, 29
Opportunity cost, 426
Optimal portfolios, construction, 471
Optimal sector view portfolio, factor
  exposures/contributions, 358e
Optimal tracking portfolio,
  stocks position, 353e
Optimism phase (equity market
  phase), 129
  built-up value, impact, 134
  economy limits, tests, 135
Optimization, 203, 224
  analytical solution, 309–310
  computation, complexity, 476
  problem
    binary variables, addition,
      447–448
    solution, 323
  running, 405–406
  techniques, usage, 161–162
Optimization-based approach,
  309–310
Ordinary least squares (OLS),
  302–303
Orthogonalization, usage, 281–282
Outliers, 273
  detection/management, 282–283
  trimming/winsorization, 282–283
Out-of-sample methodology,
  understanding, 329–330
Out-of-sample shortfall betas,
  construction, 494–495
Out-of-sample tests, 409

in-sample tests, trade-offs, 330
Overmining, 241
Over-valued stocks, 54

Pairs trading, 523–532
  constant relative price process
    model, 525–526
  correlated residuals model,
    528–530
  examples, 525–530
  linear regression-based model,
    526–528
Paper portfolio, 432
Passive investment strategy, 450
Passive management, 156–157
  approaches, style subset selec-
    tion, 157
  breadth, 157
Passive portfolios
  discipline, 156–157
  management strategies, usage,
    373
Pass-through inflation, 82
Patent protection, 96–97
Payoffs set, 391–392
Payoff values, 392
Pegging orders, 428
Perfect estimation/prediction,
  returns, 245e
Performance
  attribution, 21–22, 365–366
    process, congruency, 185
  decay, 205
    problem, 225
  exploitation, 210
Persistence, exhibition, 242–243
Physical securities, 393
Piecewise-linear transaction
  costs, 457–459
  inclusion, 458
POINT Factor-Based Scenario
  Analysis Tool, 366
POINT risk model outputs, 354–355
POINT U.S. equity risk model, 356
Poisson processes, usage, 515
Pooled time-series cross-sectional
  OLS, 304
Population regression function, 527
Portfolio allocation
  robust optimization procedure, 474
  schemes, 471
Portfolio constraints
  cardinality constraints, 446–447
  holding constraints, 443
  long-only constraints, 443
  minimum holding constraints,
    447–448
  risk factor constraints, 444–446
  round lot constraints, 448–450
  threshold constraints, 447

transaction-size constraints,
    447–448
  turnover constraints, 444
  usage, 442–450
Portfolio construction, 155–156,
  184–185
  approaches, 351–358
  constraints, portfolio manager
    usage, 328–329
  data collection, 19
  extreme risk, relationship, 483
  factor-mimicking portfolio,
    construction, 354–355
  forward-looking tracking
    error, usage, 256
  guidelines, 155
  implementation, 392–394
  optimization, 203
  passive management, usage, 156
  phase
    data collection steps, 19e
    security weights, creation, 20e
    steps, 18e
  process, robustness, 329
  qualitative approach, 351
  quantitative investment pro-
    cess, 9, 18–21
  quantitative optimization-
    based approach, 351
  risk models, 268
  sector views, implementation,
    356–358
  security weights, creation, 19–20
  sorting, 293
  trade, 19, 20–21
Portfolio management, 217
  dynamic factor approaches, 375
  funnel chart, 379e
  strategies, dynamic factor
    strategies (contrast), 378
  tax considerations, 462
Portfolio performance
  clarity, 6
  impact, 451
  measures, 468–469
Portfolio return, 311e
  calculation, 292–293
  decomposition, 382–383
  impact, 278–279
  maximization, optimization
    goal, 159
  range, 252
Portfolio risk, 196
  analysis, multifactor models
    (usage), 358–365
  factor exposures, 355
  level, 21
  net market weights, 359e
  risk contributions, 359e
  small-cap exposure, impact, 339

Portfolios
  beta, 257, 260–261
  creation, contrast, 5–6
  engineering, 158–160
  evaluation, 184–185
  formation strategies, 218
  idiosyncratic TEV, increase, 357–358
  integrity, absence, 159
  managers
    investment process, 350–351
    tracking errors, forward-looking estimates, 454
  market cap/style, benchmark (comparison), 258–259
  optimization, 474–478, 486
    algorithm, 445–446
  positions, 533
  rebalancing
    decisions, 461–462
    transaction cost models, 455
  resampling, 471–473
    disadvantage, 473
  risk-return profiles, 155
  securities, combination, 376
  selection, approaches, 254–255
  sensitivity, 445
  sets, 292–300
  standard deviation, 251–252
  stocks, number, 257–258
  structure, constraints, 466–467
  tracking error
    calculation, 254
    determination, 252
    increase, 261
  trading, 184–185
  turnover, summary statistics, 326e
  volatility, 251–252
    estimation, 342
  weights, optimization, 451
Portfolio sorts, 292–300
  average returns, 296e, 297e, 298e
  EBITDA/EV factor, basis, 295–296, 296e
  factor values, 296e
  inference, robustness (increase), 300
  information ratios (IR), usage, 299
  methodology, advantages/disadvantages, 295
  research, 299–300
  revisions factor, basis, 296–298
  share repurchase factor basis, 298–299
  sorting methodology, selection, 293–295
Post-trade measures, 430
Predicted tracking error, 256, 454

actual tracking error, contrast, 453–455
Prediction
  errors, estimation (trade-off), 240
  model, sequential testing, 246
  returns, 245e
  sample period, 246e
  testing, 245–246
Predictive power (improvement), disentangling (usage), 181–183
Present value (PV), 26–27
  sum, 83–84
Pretax operating margin, 29
Pretax ROA, 29
Pre-trade market impact, 431
Pre-trade measures, 430
Price-book ratio, basis, 55
Price multiples (price relatives), 32–36
  common factors, usage, 35–36
  comparables, forecasted fundamentals (contrast), 34–35
  drivers, usage, 35–36
  measurement, multifactor approach (usage), 35–36
  multiples, 33–34
  usage, 32–34
Price processes, 515
  measurement, 527–528
  model-driven investment strategies, impact, 206–207
Price return
  calculation, 86–87, 93
  components, 93–94
Prices, returns transformation, 524
Price-to-book multiple ratio, usage, 34
Price-to-book value ratio, 26
Price-to-cash flow ratio, 26
Price-to-earnings (P/E) collapse, 96
Price-to-earnings (P/E) forward, 86
Price-to-earnings (P/E) multiple, 126–127
  changes, 127
  cyclical fluctuation, 127
  cyclical/lower frequency movements, 127e
Price-to-earnings (P/E) myopia, 85–91
Price-to-earnings (P/E) orbits
  background, 72–75
  constant earnings growth, 88e
  depiction, 89
  franchise factor model, relationship, 93–94
  high-growth stocks, 89–90
  historical data observations, 75–80
  low-growth stocks, 90
  modeling, franchise factor approach, 71

tracing, 92–93
Price-to-earnings (P/E) path, decline, 96
Price-to-earnings (P/E) ratio, 16, 266
  assumption, 80
  calculation, 113
  contribution, 73
  cross-sectional regression, 35
  earnings growth rate, 32–34, 33e
  escalation/decline, smooth path, 80
  examination, 2–3
  factor, 404–405
  maintenance, 72, 79
  stability, fallacy, 85–91
  trading, 119
  usage, 34
Price to Earnings to Growth (PEG) ratio, 33
Price-to-revenue ratio, 26
Pride in Ownership syndrome, 154
Program trading, impact, 227
Prospective P/E ratio, calculation, 85–86
Pure active portfolio, benchmark-replicating portfolio (combination), 376
Pure returns
  opportunities, 180e
  response, 182
  volatility, decrease, 181e
Pure stock selection, 420

Q-type competition
  franchise valuation, 96–97
  implication, 97
Quadratic transaction costs, 459
Qualitative information, quantitative information (integration), 196–197
Quality factors, 335
Quantamental investment approach, 7
Quantile plots, 514e
Quantitative-driven equity investment processes, 218
Quantitative equity investment, challenges, 224–226
Quantitative equity investment, process
  characterization, 232–233
  implementation, 220
  phases, 9e
Quantitative equity management impact, 204
  usage, survey studies, 189
Quantitative equity models
  correlation, 194
  factors/sentiment, 194

momentum, 194
multiple models, usage, 193
performance, improvement, 191–192
role, increase, 190–191
switching, criteria, 193
Quantitative equity research, 231
Quantitative funds, flows (Lipper tracking), 213–214
Quantitative information, qualitative information (integration), 196–197
Quantitative investment process
challenges, 217
phases, 9
Quantitative investment trends, 22–23
Quantitative investors
characteristic testing, 10
company/characteristic focus, 3
fundamental investors
contrast, 2–7
information, viewing, 2e
process differences, 5e
model creation, 10
narrow/broad focus, 4
past/future approach, contrast, 4–5
risk, perspective, 4
stock selection process, 7–8
Quantitative outputs, interpretation, 216
Quantitative products, performance, 208
Quantitative research
competition, 241–242
process, 236e
Quantitative stock selection model, 7–9
Quantitative strategies, performance, 204
Quant performance, 209
Quants
advantage, 221
automation, impact, 218
data sources, 209
factors, usage, 210–211
full automation, progress, 218–219
funds, performance (problems), 207
impact, 233
investment space, 222
management
cost-benefit analysis, 222
styles, 223
models, usage, 216
performance, decays, 217–218
processes, 206–207
impact, 221

implementation, 217–219
products, 223
access, 213
Quarterly earning reports (10-Qs), 274
Quintile returns, 11–12
Quintile spread
determination, 12e
information coefficient, usage, 13
Quote processes, 515
Quote sampling, linear interpolation (usage), 510

Random walk
absence, 201
test, 246
Realized earnings growth, 86
Realized P/E, 86
Realized shortfall, comparison (benchmark-neutral case), 489e
Real price performance, 129
Real Required Return (RRR), 133
change, 133e
Recursive out-of-sample test, 329
Regime-shifting models, 218
Regional equity risk model, structure, 343
Regression
analysis, 200
parameters (sensitivities), 35
usage, 211–212
Regulatory regimes, regional differences (impact), 109–110
Relative valuation
adjustment, 139
analysis, calendarization, 120
approaches, focus, 107–108
cyclicality, incorporation, 139–142
data sources, 107–108
discounted cash flow (DCF), comparison, 121–123
principles, 106–115
results, example, 116e
Relative valuation methods
basis, 106
example, 115–123
analysis, 117–119
financial theory, assumptions, 121
focus, 122
issues, 119–123
sum-of-the-parts analysis, 120–121
usage, 106
Relative value, assessment, 109
Relative weight
defining, 492
evolution, 493e
Required return, 36–38

Resampling, 471–473
disadvantages, 473
Research, quantitative investment process, 9–18
characteristic testing, 11e
steps, 10e
Residual income (RI), 39, 50
forecasting, 51e
implied growth rate, calculation, 56–57
valuation, 53, 55–57
explanation, 56e
Residual returns, 308–309
Residual risk
excess return, trade-offs, 164–165
level, optimum, 163–164
Residual ROC, 42
Residuals
correlated residuals model, 528–530
time series, mean/standard errors, 304
variation, 302–303
Return-generating process, 242
Return on assets (ROA), 28–29
leverage, relationship, 31
Return on capital (ROC), 39
decomposition, 44
Return on equity (ROE)
achievement, 112
calculation, 30
example, 117–118
equity-risk buildup model, 47e
example, 100
extended Dupont formula, 28–29
impact, 31e
leverage, relationship, 29–31
Returns
attribution model, 391–392
computation, histograms, 506e
contribution, 244–245
decomposition, 365, 490
distribution, cycle valuation, 125
effects
measurement, 176–177
multivariate regression, 176
tangled web formation, 177e
estimated moments, impact, 279
pure returns, opportunities, 180e
revelation, 179–181
sacrifice, 166e
self-referentiality, 206
variables, relationship, 184
Return-to-volatility ratio, 406
Revenue growth, 42
price-revenue multiple, combination, 26
Revenues
estimates, 107
increase, inability, 190–191

Revisions example, 284
Revisions factors, 296–298
  cross-sectional values, histo-
    grams, 286e
  cumulative return, 313
  factor values, 297e
Risk
  contributions, 359e
  measurement, risk models, 268
  measures, sector analysis, 360,
    360e
  models, 219
    covariance matrix, usage,
      366–367
    factor-based strategies,
      interaction, 330
  perspective, 4
  quantitative manager aware-
    ness, 209–210
  source, 343
  variables, relationship, 184
Risk-adjusted discount rate, 82
Risk-adjusted return, attribution, 244
Risk averse investor, bond ownership, 137
Risk-averse investors, style
  subsets (usage), 163
Risk-based optimization exercise,
  351–352
Risk control, 246–247
  client demand, 191
  expected returns estimation,
    impact, 247
  forward-looking tracking
    error, usage, 256
  improvement, 162
Risk factor constraints, 444–446
Risk-free return, 377
RiskLab, 195
Riskless arbitrage, 521
Risk management, 21, 195–196,
  219–220
  importance, 339
  models, 219–220
  practice, performing, 247
Risk-return profiles, 163
Robust counterpart, 475
  box uncertainty set, 477–478
Robustification, 476
Robust optimization
  independent tests, 479
  problem, computational struc-
    ture, 477
  term, usage, 478–479
Robust parameter estimation,
  469–471
Robust portfolio optimization,
  474–480
  box uncertainty, 475

ellipsoidal uncertainty, 475e
  formulations, 479–480
  max-min problem, 475–476
  robust mean-variance model,
    equivalence, 478
Round lot constraints, 448–450
Rounds (minimum transaction
  lots), 448
R-square, increase, 240
Russell 1000
  alpha assignation, 331
  companies, EBITDA/EV factor
    ranking, 278e
  stocks, 277
    EBITDA/EV, 408–409
Russell 1000 Value Index, 75–76
  investment, example, 76e
Russell 3000, proxy, 148

Sales growth characteristic,
  assessment, 3
Same-day measures (average
  measures), 431
Sample period, 246e
Scenario analysis, usage, 351
Scientific methodology, 234
Second-order cone problem, 477
Sector characteristics, 110–111
Sector deviation, 257, 259
Sector risk, 413
Sector-risk premium, 48
Sector views, implementation,
  356–357
Securities
  bid/ask prices, 429
  selection, 378–379
  selection return, 162
  supply/demand schedule, 429e
  trading, 437–438
  value, assignation, 1–2
  weights, creation, 19–20, 20e
Securities analysis, 151–152
Securities market line (SML),
  37–38
Segmented market, integrated
  approach, 172–176
Sell-side firm modeling, 220
Sell-side reports, 274
Sensitivities, 341–342
Serial correlation, occurs, 302
Share repurchases factors, 295
  basis, 298–299
  cross-sectional distribution,
    284, 287
  cross-sectional values, histo-
    grams, 288e, 289e
  cumulative return, 313
  factor values, 298e
Sharpe capital asset pricing
  model, 377

Sharpe ratio
  maximization, 405
  optimization, 478–479
Sharpe technique, portfolio
  attribution tool, 374–375
Shortfall (expected shortfall), 484
  beta constraint, 485, 487e
  analysis, 489–493
    benchmark-neutral case, 488e
    cumulative gains, 486e
  constrained mean-variance
    optimization, return
    decomposition, 491e
  constrained optimization,
    breakdown, 490
  constraining, 485
  out-of-sample shortfall betas,
    construction, 494–495
  performance, 485–487
Short-sale constraints, presence,
  515
Short selling, 161
Shrinkage, 469–470
  estimators, 470
Simple returns, quantile plots, 507e
Size-related attributes, pure
  cumulative monthly excess
    returns, 180
Size-related variables, 179e, 180e
  monthly returns, 180e
Size-weighted (SW) midquote
  returns, 508e
Size-weighted (SW) midquote
  simple returns, 506e
Slopes, time series (mean/stan-
  dard errors), 304
Small capitalization, pure
  returns, 180–181
Small-cap stocks, 147, 150e
  large-cap stocks, contrast, 149
  price-to-earnings ratio, 176
Spearman rank coefficient, 305
Split-sample method, 329
SPY computation, empirical cor-
  relations, 518e
SPY Level I quotes, summary
  statistics, 503e
Stabilizing growth rate, 90–91
Stable P/E, 90–91
Standard deviation, 251–252
Standardization, usage, 280–281
Standard mean-variance optimiza-
  tion, return decomposition, 490e
Standard & Poor's 500 (S&P500
  Index), 75–76
  broad-based equity index, 148
  investment, example, 76e
  stocks, return, 244–245
  tracking error, benchmark
    stocks (contrast), 258e

tracking portfolio, contrast, 362e–363e
tracking portfolio, TEV, 359
Standard & Poor's Industrials, 52e, 55e
Starting P/Es, example, 92e
Statement of Financial Accounting Standards No. 85 (SFAS No. 85), 280
State-space models, 218
Statistical arbitrage, 265, 521
  examples, 527–528
  models, 532–534
  opportunity, 528
Statistical factors, 268, 348–349
  models, 345e
Statistical significance, 243e
  economic profit, 242
Stern, Joel, 39
Stewart III, G. Bennett, 39
Stock market
  balkanization, 173
  complexity, 171–172
  profit, 186–187
  crash (1987), 271
  decline, 135
  framework, coherence, 174–176
  segmentation, 173
  segments, 174
  unified approach, advantages, 174
Stock returns, 414–416
  country membership, explanatory power, 415e
  covariance matrix, 450–451
  cross-sectional variation, 414–415
  determination, 3
  riskiness, volatility measurement, 340–341
  variables, relationship, 184
Stocks
  analysis, price multiples (usage), 32–34
  binary variable, relationship, 446
  capitalization level, 172
  characteristics, impact, 278
  defining, 174
  differentiation, characteristic (usage), 11
  earnings growth, 172–173
  optimal weight, 446
  portfolio management, tracking error (relationship), 251
  price, calculation, 32
  price behavior, variables (inclusion), 183
  price efficiency, 161
  profitability, return (average), 12
  quantitative investor selection methodology, 7–8

risks, anticipation, 158
scoring process, 409e
turnover, 407
types, 172–173
valuation, model, 386–387
value, information sources (impact), 2e
Stock selection, 265
  characteristics, identification, 17
  factor competition approach, 397
    problem, 397–403
    solution, 403–407
  model
    characteristics, display, 20, 20e
    characteristic weightings, 18e
    example, 8e
  portfolios, components (weights), 421e
  quantitative characteristic, 159
Stock-specific risk, 413
Stock-specific sentiment, 194
Structured products, creation, 221
Style analysis, 365
Style rotation
  advantage, 160
  problem, 208
Style subsets
  performance, forecast, 160–161
  selection, 157
  usage, 163
Summary statistics, 336, 336e
Sum-of-the-parts analysis, 120–121
Super-skilled employees, impact, 97–98
Surplus rate of return on capital, 42
Survivorship bias, 276–277
  performance comparison, 239
  sample selection, 238–239
Sustainable growth rate, 36
Swap contracts, 394
Systematic beta, 360, 360e
Systematic co-movement, 361
Systematic risk, sensitivity, 260
Systematic TEV, 352–353
Systemic risk, awareness, 227–228

Tangible value (TV), 72–73, 81–82
  calculation, 93
Target capital structure, 45–46
Targeted annual turnover, 410
Tax-adjusted operating earnings, 30, 41
Tax-aware portfolio rebalancing framework, usage, 463
Tax-aware quantitative investment strategies, usage, 463
Taxes
  considerations, complexity, 462
  incorporation, 460–465
  laws, impact, 172

liabilities, presence, 462
tax-aware approaches, 463–464
Technical factors, portfolio manager exposure limitation, 357
Technology bubble (2000), 271
Technology diversity, 111–112
Telecommunications, media, and technology (TMT) bubble, 195
Terminal-phase effect, valuation impact, 96–97
Test statistic, usage, 472
Thomson Reuters, data vendor, 112
Three Mile Island, industry-related events, 178
Threshold constraints, 447
Time series, unit root, 531
Time-series averages, 283
Time-series models, 345e
Time-varying payoffs, incorporation, 392
Top-down managers, value (addition), 255
Total error volatility (TEV), 352–361
  contribution, 354–355
  elasticity, 360, 360e
  liquidation effect, 360, 360e
Total P/E, sum, 73
Total return
  foreign exchange, portion, 367–368
  report, 332e
Total stock return, systematic/idiosyncratic components, 341
Total TEV, factors, 361
Total tracking error volatility (total TEV), 352
Tracking error (TE)
  attribution, 268
  benchmark stocks, contrast, 258
  beta, comparison, 261e
  components, 254–255
  constraint, 453
  contrast, 255–256, 453–455
  control, 247
  definition, 251–254
    alternatives, 451–453
  determinants, 257–261
  determination, 252, 306
  formulation, 453
  forward-looking estimate, portfolio manager usage, 255–256, 454
  increase, 259–260
  marginal contribution, 261–262
  market portfolio, relationship, 261
  minimization, 450–454

Tracking error (*Cont.*)
  nonbenchmark stocks, contrast, 259e
  shortfall, comparison, 260e
  standard definition, 450–451
  stock portfolio management, relationship, 251
Tracking portfolio
  factor exposures/contributions, 362e–363e
  stocks position, 353e
Trade
  duration, variation, 516–517
  market impact, 465
  market impact cost, 431
  portfolio construction process step, 20–21
  price returns, 508e
  processes, 515
Trade-based factors, 433–435
Trade-based independent variables, asset-based independent variables (contrast), 433
Trading cost function, split, 467
Trading idea, defining, 269
Trading strategies
  assessment, information coefficients (usage), 306
  factor model basis, 301
  risk, 271–272
  success, 272–273
Traditional management
  insights, 153
  reliance, 155
Traditional metrics, overview, 25–32
Transaction costs (TC), 526
  fixed transaction costs, 459–460
  function, 460
  incorporation, 454–460
  linear transaction costs, 456
  liquidity, relationship, 427–430
  modeling, example, 457e
  models, 455–456
  penalty function, 455
  piecewise-linear transaction costs, 457–459
  quadratic transaction costs, 459
Transaction-size constraints, 447–448
Transformations, application, 282
Trend-based strategies, usage, 389
Trend-sensitive methods, 388–389
Trimming, 282–283

t-test
  performing, 524
  usage, 531
Turnover constraints, 444
Two-phase growth, starting P/Es, 92e
Two-phase growth model
  going-forward version, 91
  terminal earnings level assumption, 97
Two-phase P/E orbits, 91–96
Two-stage RI model, usage, 55–56

Underperformance, probability (increase), 259–260
United Kingdom
  average earnings growth, 131e
  P/E expansion, 131e
  phases, dates/returns, 145e
  return, 131e
United States
  average earnings growth, 130e
  equity market phases, derivation, 129e
  macro-benchmarked ERP, 141e
  macroeconomic backdrop, 136e
  market implied ERP, 141e
  phases, dates/returns, 143e
  price-to-earnings (P/E) expansion, 130e
  return, phase, 130e
Univariate regressions (R^2), 142e
Upper bounds, vector array, 451–452
U.S. equity styles, 33e

Valuation
  analysis, adjustment, 139
  earnings/economic cycle, relationship, 125–126
  strategies, momentum strategies (combination), 390–391
Valuation-based trading strategies, 388–389
Valuation measures, 16
Valuation multiples
  numerator, selection, 114
  selection, 113–115
Value
  creation, 57
  portfolio, 167–168
  strategies, 389–391
  timing, 390e
Value-at-risk (VaR), 484
  optimization, 478–479

Value-based analysis, case study, 60–68
Value-based metrics (VBM)
  approach, usage, 36
  background, 39–40
  information, 57–58
  overview, 39–58
Value-based models, 194–195
  performance, problem, 195
Value-capital ratio (V/C), 53–54
Value/capital ratio, EVA spread (contrast), 55e
Value factors, 334
  country-level timing, 387–388
Value investor, defensive posture, 182
Value Line Report, 61e, 70e
Value-related variables, monthly returns (market sensitivities), 182e
Variable costs, fixed costs (contrast), 426
Variables
  returns, relationship, 184
  risk, relationship, 184
  short-term overreaction, 183–184
  simultaneous analysis, 177
  stock returns, relationship, 184
Vector arrays, 451–452, 472
  Jorion model, 469–470
VIX index, 348
Volatility, 251–252
  estimate, ARCH-GARCH usage, 192
  term, usage, 484
Volume processes, 515
Volume-weighted average price (VWAP), 431

Wall Street analyst reports (sell-side reports/equity research reports), 274
Weighted average cost of capital (WACC), 39, 41–42, 53–54
  issues, 45–49
  reduction, 42
Wilshire 5000, proxy, 148
Winsorization, 282–283
Worldscope Global database, templates, 279

Zero-cost factor trading strategy, 293
Z-scores
  calculation, 408–409
  example, 368e, 369e
  multiplication, 409

Answers

CHAPTER 1

1. Ways that a quantitative investor's process may differ from a fundamental investor's process include

   - A quantitative investor creates an investment thesis for a characteristic while a fundamental investor creates an investment thesis for a company or industry.
   - A quantitative investor tends to have more holdings (smaller positions), while a fundamental investor tends to have fewer holdings (larger positions).
   - A quantitative investor discusses performance of certain characteristics they believe in, while a fundamental investor discusses performance of particular stocks or sectors.
   - A quantitative investor focuses more on understanding portfolio level risks, while a fundamental investor focuses more on understanding company specific risks.

2. A combined approach will offer breadth and depth in analysis, facts paired with human judgment, past and future perspectives on a company, and a more well-rounded view of risk and performance of the portfolio.

3. The IC is a better metric when a quantitative investor is considering owning a greater number of stocks in the portfolio. The reason is that the IC looks at the relationships across all of the stocks in the group. The quintile return is better suited for portfolios with more concentrated positions in fewer stocks since it measures fewer stocks at the extremes.

4. Quantitative investors create stock selection models for universes (i.e. small caps, small-cap value, and large-cap growth) or sectors/industries (i.e. technology, financials, materials, or consumer electronics).

5. Data come from many different sources, such as company fundamental data, pricing data, economic data, and other data (specialized data

sources). Recently, quantitative investors have been placing greater emphasis on specialized data sources such as industry specific data as well as alternative sources like news flow for companies through web-based search engines.

CHAPTER 2

1.

	2010	2011		2014
Revenue growth		0.0642		0.0808
Cash flow growth		0.0865		0.1135
EPS growth		0.1022		0.1323

IBM's prospective growth rates are "favorable."

2.

ROE: 5-factor Dupont:	
Tax burden [NI/PBT= $(1-t)$]	0.74
Interest burden[a] [PBT/EBIT]	1.07
OPM [EBIT/Sales]	0.193
Asset turnover	1.160
Equity multiplier	2.692
ROE: 5-factor Dupont	0.478

[a]Interest burden net of non-operating income/expense items.

IBM's estimated ROE for 2011 is quite attractive, due to favorable operating margins and asset turns and apparently judicious use of leverage (equity multiplier).

3.

D. Fundamental Stock Return	2011
FSR = DY + PBR × ROE	
Dividend yield (DPS/Stock price)	0.020
Dividend payout ratio (DPS/EPS)	0.222
PRB (plowback ratio)	0.778
FSR	0.3927

CAPM	0.0925
FSR spread	0.3002
FSR > CAPM (?)	Yes

IBM plots well above the SML (based on the Value Line beta of 0.85, risk-free rate of 5% and market risk premium of 5%).

4.

EVA = NOPAT – $WACC

B. Estimating NOPAT (basic)

NOPAT = EBIT × (1 – *t*) = [*S* – COGS – SGA – Depr] × (1 – *t*)
= [*S* × OM – Depr] × (1 – *t*)

Where: OM = EBITD/Sales

Year	2011
Sales	101500
Operating margin (EBITD/Sales)	0.24
EBITD	24360
Depreciation	4800
EBIT	19560
Tax rate	0.35
NOPAT	12714

C. Estimating $WACC (dollar cost of capital)

Note: $WACC = WACC × Capital

and:

WACC = *wd* × AT debt cost + *we* × cost of equity

WACC = *wd* × Pretax debt cost × (1 – *t*) + *we* × CAPM

Debt cost:

Pretax debt cost = Interest/LT debt

(Assumes bonds trading at "par")

| $Interest | 1050 |
| LT Debt | 21017 |

Pretax debt cost (minimum of 5%)   0.0500
AT Debt Cost = Pretax × (1 − t)

                                                    0.0325

Equity cost:
CAPM = RF + Beta × ERP

	RF	0.0500
	MRP	0.0500
	Beta	0.85
	CAPM	0.0925

EVA capital:
C = NWC + NPPE (assets approach)
C = Debt + Equity (financing approach)
(Can use EOY, BOY or average capital.)

	Year	2011
	LT Debt	26650
	Equity	32500
	Capital	59150

WACC = wd × AT debt cost + we × CAPM

	Debt weight	0.450549
	Equity weight	0.549451
	WACC	0.0655

$Capital cost = WACC × TC   3872

D. EVA and EVA Spread

Year	2011
EVA = NOPAT − $WACC	8842
Return on capital (ROC)	0.2149
WACC	0.0655
EVA spread	0.1495

Not surprisingly, IBM is a substantial wealth creator.

5.

EVA Momentum (determination of "good"/"bad" company growth)
Delta EVA = EVA Spread × Delta CapX

EVA Spread   0.1495

CapX Growth

Year	2010	2011		2014
Year relative	0	1		4
$CapX/Share	3	3.5		4.75
Shares	1240	1200		1100
$Gross CapX	3720	4200		5225
$Depreciation	4825	4800		5500
$Net CapX	–1105	–600		–275
$Net CapX growth		505		325
(Capital "catalyst")				
$-EVA Momentum:		75.4924		48.5842

[EVA spread × $Net CapX growth]   Good company growth if EVA momentum > 0

EVA Style (Grant and Abate):   International Business Machines (IBM)
Q1: Stagnant Company   Q2: Growth Creates Shareholder Value
Q2: Growth Creates Shareholder Value (Based on EVA spread and Cumulative
                                       Capital Catalyst)
Q3: Growth Destroys Shareholder
   Value
Q4: Positive Restructuring

IBM lies in EVA Style Quadrant #2: Growth creates shareholder value-hence a "good company" that knows how to rationalize capital not only in the present, but also for the future.

6. Open discussion leading to IBM stock recommendation:
Note: The instructor's assessment of Timeliness and Safety for IBM were as follows (as of Value Line report date):

Source:	"Timeliness"	"Safety"	
Value Line	2	1	
Analyst rating:	1	2	User assigned (Scale of 1 to 5):
(Grant and Fabozzi)			1 = High, 3 = Average, 5 = Low

CHAPTER 3

1. Under the given assumptions, both firms have the same P/E, the same P/E_{TV} and the same P/E_{FV}. The FV component of the P/E is calculated as the product of the Franchise Factor (FF) and the present value growth equivalent g. The growth equivalent measures the size of new investments relative to the book value of the firm. When both firms have the same g the dollar value of new investments will still vary. For example, if $g = 2$ the present value of future investments must be 2× the size of the current book value. For Firm D, that is $50 million, for Firm E that is $50 billion. Even if Firm E has a stronger franchise and market dominance, the $50 billion in new investments is an enormous challenge. If D is a relative young growth company $50 million is not necessarily easy but more within the realm of possibility. In the language of the FFM, it is more likely that the FV of Firm E will ultimately be revised downward.

2. FV is positive when the return on new investment is greater than the cost of capital. As new business opportunities fade, the FV approaches zero. The firm must be careful to not make investments that return less than the cost of capital and transition to and antifranchise firm with negative FV. When FV converges to zero, the firm will be a pure TV firm. Assuming a steady earnings stream E and cost of capital k, TV = E/k and P/E = $1/k$.

3. To maintain the firm's P/E the CEO must maintain the firm's FV. In a sense, this is a contradiction. Take the case of a new CEO of a growth firm where FV is much greater than TV. The CEO is expected to fulfill the firm's franchise promise, as embedded in FV. Each time an "expected" investment is made, some of the FV has been drawn down and the P/E will consequently drop. To maintain the P/E the CEO must "replenish" FV. This means searching for new markets and new products that heretofore were never visualized (or they would have already been included in FV). The size of new investments is always measured in comparison to the firm's current size. Each time the CEO makes an

anticipated investment, the firm grows and the base against which new investments are measured is larger. Thus, the more investments the CEO makes the more he must discover. CEO success, therefore, brings ever greater P/E challenges.

4. $P/E = 1/k + FF \times g$, $FF = (R - k)/rk$
$FF = (18\% - 9\%)/(15\% \times 9\%) = 6.67$ if $k = 9\%$
PV(Total investment of \$20 billion for 10 years at $k = 9\%$) = \$128.4 billion
$g = PV$/Economic book value $= 128.4/500 = 0.257$
$P/E = 1/9\% + 6.67 \times 0.257 = 12.8$

Results for various values of k and various investments:

Investment 1: \$20 billion/year for 20 years

k	1/k	FF	PV Investment	g	P/E
8%	12.5	8.33	196	0.393	15.8
9%	11.1	6.67	183	0.365	13.5
10%	10.0	5.33	170	0.341	11.8

Investment 2: \$30 billion/year for 20 years

k	1/k	FF	PV Investment	g	P/E
8%	12.5	8.33	295	0.589	17.4
9%	11.1	6.67	274	0.548	14.8
10%	10.0	5.33	255	0.511	12.7

Investment 3: \$40 billion/year for 20 years

k	1/k	FF	PV Investment	g	P/E
8%	12.5	8.33	393	0.785	19.0
9%	11.1	6.67	365	0.730	16.0
10%	10.0	5.33	341	0.681	13.6

5. Over the five-year period from 1995 to 2000, the price of Firm A grew by about 400% and for Firm B it grew about 2,000%. This growth came from both earnings growth and P/E growth. This means that the firms themselves were growing at an incredible rate and estimates of P/E were growing in lock-step with earnings growth. Implicitly, estimates of FV were increasingly dramatically. This type of growth is very hard (perhaps impossible) to maintain because it implies very high values of g. As these firms became mega-cap firms, the required dollar-value of new investment was implicitly viewed as impossible achieve. Therefore,

there was no place for FV to go but down. In the new millennium, there remained little reason to believe that substantial growth/investment opportunities, of the required dollar-size, were going to become available.

CHAPTER 4

1. Listed companies that are very small may have limited or no analyst coverage, and information for other comparable firms may not be available if those firms have not gone public. Conversely, listed companies that are very large may be dominant players, and thus trade at a premium reflecting their market position. Alternatively, large firms may be a conglomerate of numerous smaller entities, and there may be no other large or small firm producing an approximately equivalent blend of goods and services.

2. Most practitioners believe that companies are more likely to trade on forward-looking estimates than historical results. Investors typically care more about expected future performance than about past successes or disappointments.

3. Consensus numbers can be seen as reflecting the market's general opinion of a company's future prospects. Generally speaking, valuation multiples reflect consensus opinion, not the specific insights that any single individual may have.

4. Examples of industry-specific multiples might include revenue per available room for hotel chains, same-store sales for retailers, paid miles flown for airlines, or valuation by reserves for natural resource producers. Such data can provide insight into how the market is valuing individual firms' operating performance. However, it can be difficult to reconcile a company's operating performance with its financial results. Also, there may be little or no intuition about what might be a "reasonable" estimate for long-run valuation levels.

5. As the name suggests, a sum-of-the-parts analysis seeks to value each of a company's lines of business separately, by calculating a fair value based on the multiples for other firms engaged in such activities. A conglomerate discount reflects the fact that an investor is buying the whole company, and that the overall mix of industry exposures might not mimic the portfolio that the investor would have selected if it were possible instead to put money into individual companies. Conglomerate

discounts typically range between 5% and 15%, partly based on academic research into the effects of spin-offs.

CHAPTER 5

1. Interest rates, the equity risk premium, the payout ratio, and long-term earnings growth.

2. Earnings are the key driver, as valuation multiples tend to mean revert.

3. a. The ranking in terms of average real price returns are: Hope (highest), Optimism, Growth, Despair (lowest).
   b. Growth is the phase that offers the highest average real earnings growth.

4. The output gap.

5. Valuation multiples fluctuate over time and specifically the movements in the equity risk premium can be tied to the economic cycle. If you do not adjust for this when doing valuation, you are not taking into account that the cost of capital charged by the market varies over time. It is unrealistic to expect valuations to stay constant over the cycle and not adjust to changes in the cost of capital.

CHAPTER 6

1. It allows the investor to mix and match so as to pursue perceived return opportunities by overweighting various subsets. However, these may change as market and economic conditions change over time.

2. Traditional active management, with a focus on stock picking, provides in-depth examinations of portfolio candidates, but this may come at a price of reduced breadth of inquiry. Traditional management can cover a limited number of stocks in depth, but cannot cover a broad universe. Furthermore, traditional approaches are heavily reliant on human judgment and thus subject to cognitive errors. It is also difficult to translate the qualitative results of traditional research into inputs for portfolio construction. The resulting portfolios may lack rigor in terms of their adherence to style or other investment guidelines.

3. Passive portfolios can benefit from great breadth, as no in-depth analysis is undertaken. They are disciplined and not subject to cognitive biases. Management fees are generally less than for active traditional or

engineered approaches. A passive approach does not pursue or benefit from active returns (or risks); above-market returns are not achieved. Passive approaches may be used, however, to achieve active returns via selection of style subsets and rotation among them.

4. Engineered, or quantitative, approaches to investing are capable of dealing with and benefiting from as wide a selection universe as passive management. Depending on the level of sophistication it uses, engineered management can benefit from great depth of analysis, similar to that of traditional active management. With both breadth and depth, a manager can choose a focal point from which to frame the equity market, without loss of important framing information. The stock selection process results in numerical estimates (rather than the qualitative outcomes of traditional management), which are eminently suitable for portfolio construction via optimization. The quantitative nature of stock selection and portfolio construction imposes discipline on the resulting portfolios; there is little room for cognitive errors, and portfolios can be defined in terms of preset performance goals.

5. If not constrained to deliver benchmark-like returns, an engineered approach can offer even more leeway for potential performance. Style rotation shifts assets across style subsets as market and economic conditions change. Relaxing constraints on short sales allows for enhanced performance by eliminating constraints on the implementation of investment insights. No longer is a portfolio manager who desires to express negative views about a given stock constricted by a stock's weight in an index; with short selling, the manager can underweight the stock as much as risk considerations allow.

6. Critical factors are the investor's level of risk aversion and the manager's level of skill, as measured by information ratio. An investor who takes less than the optimal level of residual risk or who selects less than the best manager sacrifices potential return.

CHAPTER 7

1. It is not entirely random; it is possible to predict price movements, contrary to the assertions of the efficient market hypothesis. But it is difficult to do so; stock price behavior cannot be modeled by simple rules or screens or even by models such as the capital asset pricing model or arbitrage pricing theory. Stock price behavior is permeated by a web of interrelated return effects.

2. On the one hand, regulations, client guidelines, and investor tastes can segment the market into groupings such as value stocks, growth stocks, and large- and small-cap stocks. On the other hand, all stocks can be defined by the same fundamental parameters: All stocks lie on a continuum of size, growth, value, and the like. That the market is neither entirely segmented nor entirely integrated is another aspect of its complexity, and it is one that requires a unified approach that takes into account the behavior of stocks across the broadest possible selection universe, without losing sight of the significant differences that distinguish stocks in one market segment from those in another.

3. It provides a coherent framework for analysis; it benefits from the insights to be garnered from a wide and diverse range of securities; and it has both breadth and depth and is thus poised to take advantage of more opportunities than a more narrowly defined approach offers.

4. a. Disentangling is the simultaneous analysis of all variables relevant to stock price behavior. Such an analysis, undertaken via multivariate regression, takes into account and adjusts for interrelationships between variables. The end result is an estimate of the return to each variable separately, controlling for all related variables.

   b. Disentangling can reduce noise in return estimates because it distinguishes real effects from mere proxies. Disentangling can reveal hidden profit opportunities. Disentangling can result in estimates with more predictive power because it provides a clearer picture of the relationships between investor behavior, fundamental variables, and macroeconomic conditions.

   c. Regressing returns on various measures of value—specifically, high dividend discount model value, high book-to-price ratio, and high yield—indicates that DDM value tends to be procyclical whether measured separately or in disentangled form; stocks with high DDM value tend to rise more than the market in rising markets and fall more in falling markets. Return to high B/P, measured naively in a single-variable regression, appears to be anticyclical; thus high B/P stocks would appear to offer some defense against falling markets. When return to high B/P is measured in a multivariate regression, however, the disentangled return shows that B/P is not a defensive measure or an offensive measure; B/P in its pure, disentangled form is uncorrelated with broad market movements. Disentangling reveals that only high yield is truly countercyclical; stocks with high yields can be expected to lag the market in market upturns but to hold up relatively well during general market declines.

5. Congruence between stock selection and portfolio construction helps to ensure that the portfolio reflects all the profit opportunities and controls all the risks detected by the stock selection process. Congruence between performance attribution and stock selection processes enables the manager to monitor the results from the stock selection process so that performance evaluation can feed back to the research and stock selection process.

6. One measure of the success of an investment process is the resulting portfolio's information ratio, the ratio of the portfolio's annualized excess return to its annualized residual risk. The information ratio is a product of the quality of the investment insights going into the portfolio (as measured by the correlation between predicted and actual security returns) and the breadth of the insights incorporated into the portfolio (the number of independent insights upon which the investment decisions are based). A complex, unified approach can enhance both the number and the quality of investment insights.

CHAPTER 8

1. Assumptions about the functional form of dependencies between variables and on the distribution of noise are made for every model. Based on these assumptions, models are estimated and decisions made. The idea of estimating model risk is to estimate the distribution of errors that will be made if the model assumptions are violated.

2. Behavioral models try to capture phenomena such as departures from rationality on the part of investors (e.g., belief persistence), patterns in analyst estimates, and corporate executive investment/disinvestment behavior.

3. The greater use of optimization can be attributed to advances in large-scale optimization coupled with the ability to include constraints and robust methods for both estimation and optimization.

4. An investment process is said to be fundamental (or traditional) if it is performed by a human asset manager using information and judgment. A quantitative investment process is one where value-added decisions are made primarily in terms of quantitative outputs generated by computer-driven models following fixed rules. An investment process is said to be hybrid if it uses a combination of the two (e.g., a fundamental manager using a computer-driven stock-screening system to narrow his or her portfolio choices).

5. **a.** It is important in applying quantitative models that those models adapt to the changing environment that the portfolio manager faces. Adaptive modeling techniques are used for just this purpose since they can self-adapt to changing market conditions.

   b. Among the examples of adaptive modeling techniques are a class of models with hidden variables, including state-space models, hidden Markov models, or regime-shifting models. These models have one or more variables that represent different market conditions. The key challenge is estimation: the ability to identify regime shifts sufficiently early calls for a rich regime structure, but estimating a rich regime shifting model calls for a very large data sample—something rarely available to equity mangers.

6. Performance decay means the decline in performance attributable to the wider use of models.

7. The increasing availability of intraday (or high-frequency) data and modeling techniques based on optimizing the market impact of trades results in the much greater use of program trading and high-frequency trading. Program trading employs computer programs to reduce the market impact of large trades by subdividing a large trade into many small trades with optimal rules. This has created a flow of high-frequency trades which has, in turn, created trading opportunities for those able to make, at a very low cost, many small trades with very short holding periods. Holding periods for high-frequency trades are generally less than one day and can be as short as a few milliseconds.

CHAPTER 9

1. The primary source of decisions in a quantitative equity investment management process is the output obtained from computerized rules. In such a process, human intervention is limited to a control function that intervenes only exceptionally to modify decisions made by computers.

2. There are three key ways in which methodologies used in economics are different from those used in the physical sciences:

   - Economic laws are never validated with a high level of precision and, as a result, there is ample room for ambiguity.
   - The economy is a human artifact as well as an intelligent processor of information and therefore the economy cannot be viewed as a permanent physical object.

- With the advent of computers, human creativity is complemented and even replaced by a learning approach based on statistics and data mining.

3. The common objective of a quantitative process is to identify any persistent pattern in the data and, in finance, convert it into implementable and profitable investment strategies.

4. The process of how quantitative research is performed and converted into implementable trading strategies includes developing underlying economic theories, explaining actual returns, estimating expected returns, and formulating corresponding portfolios.

5. Data snooping—also referred to as data mining—is identifying seemingly significant but in fact spurious patterns in the data.

6. Any trading strategy applied to purely random data should yield no average profit. Of course, purely random fluctuations will produce profits and losses. However, because very long sequences of data can be simulated, a portfolio manager can test with high accuracy that a proposed model does not actually introduce artefacts that will not live up to a real-life test.

CHAPTER 10

1.

Monthly average (%)	0.0958
Monthly standard deviation (%)	0.4495
Alpha (annualized) (%)	1.15
Tracking error (TE) (%) (annualized standard deviation)	1.56
Information ratio	0.74 Alpha/TE

2.

	Standard Deviation Units	Range of Expected Active Return	
		Lower (%)	Upper (%)
67% confidence interval	1	−1	5
95% confidence interval	2	−4	8
99% confidence interval	3	−7	11

3. Percent of portfolio actively managed relative to S&P 500 = 10%
   Tracking error relative to S&P 500 = 12%
   Portfolio's tracking error relative to S&P 500 = 10% × 12% = 1.2%

4. Backward-tracking error reflects the portfolio manager's decisions during a prior time period with respect to portfolio positioning issues such as beta, sector allocations, style tilt, and stock selections. Consequently, the limitation of backward-looking tracking error is that it does not reflect the effect of current decisions by the portfolio manager on the future active returns and hence the future tracking error that may be realized. This type of tracking error will have little predictive value and can be misleading regarding portfolio risks going forward.

5. Forward-looking tracking error is computed in practice by using the services of a commercial vendor that has a model that has defined the risks associated with a benchmark index. This model is called a *multifactor risk model*. Based on historical return data of the stocks in the benchmark, statistical analysis of the variance and covariance of the returns is employed to obtain the risk factors and quantify their risks.

   The portfolio manager than applies the multifactor risk model to the portfolio's holdings in order to obtain the portfolio's current exposure to the various factors which are then compared to the benchmark's exposures to the factors. Forward-looking tracking error for the portfolio is then computed by applying the differential factor exposures and the risks of the factors.

6. The two reasons for this are (1) as the quarter progresses and the portfolio is rebalanced, the forward-looking tracking error estimate would change to reflect the new exposures and (2) the accuracy of the forward-looking tracking error depends on the extent of the stability in the variances and correlations that were used in the analysis.

7. a. The marginal contribution to tracking error indicators how a small change in a bet (holding all other bets constant) will change the tracking error.
   b. A negative marginal contribution to tracking error means an underweighting of a factor.
   c. A portfolio manager can use the marginal contributions when seeking to alter the portfolio tracking error. For example, if a portfolio manager wants to reduce the portfolio's tracking error, then she should reduce portfolio overweights in industries (or stocks) with the highest positive marginal contributions. Alternatively, the portfolio manager can reduce the underweights (that is, increase the overall weights) in industries (or stocks) with the most negative marginal

contributions. This approach is most effective in reducing the tracking error while minimizing the necessary turnover and the associated expenses.

CHAPTER 11

1. Investment strategies are subject to risk. These risks include fundamental risk, noise trader risk, horizon risk, model risk, implementation risk, funding risk, and liquidity risk.

   - *Fundamental risk* is the risk of suffering adverse fundamental news. This risk can be company specific or systemic.
   - *Noise trader risk* is the risk caused by investors who irrationally act on noise as if it were information.
   - *Horizon risk* is the idea that the forecasted value takes longer to be realized. As a consequence, the realized return may be lower than the target rate of return.
   - *Model risk* refers to the risk associated with making the wrong modeling assumptions and decisions. This includes the choice of variables, methodology, and context the model operates in.
   - *Implementation risk* is another risk faced by investors implementing trading strategies. For example, this risk category includes transaction costs, the availability of shorts and counterparty risk.
   - *Funding risk* occurs when the portfolio manager is no longer able to get the funding necessary to implement a trading strategy.
   - *Liquidity risk* is defined as the ability to trade quickly without significant price changes and the ability to trade large volumes without significant price changes.

2. Factor models are used throughout financial theory and in the financial industry. Some examples include models for forecasting returns, models for analytical support, asset pricing models, risk management models, and performance attribution models.

3. There are many data issues encountered when working with financial data. These issues distort the consistency of financial data and affect the availability of data.

   Consistency is affected by backfilling and restating data. Backfilling of data happens when data are first entered into a database at the current period and its historical data are also added. This process of backfilling data creates a selection bias because we now find historical data on this recently added company when previously it was unavailable.

Restatement of data occurs when historical data are overwritten with different data.

A number of issues arise that affects the availability of data in financial databases. First, some data items may only be available for a short period of time. Second, data items may be available for only a subset of the cross-section of the companies. A third issue is that a data item may simply not be available because it was not recorded at certain points in time. Fourth, different data items are sometimes combined. Fifth, certain data items are only available at certain periodicities. Sixth, data items may be inconsistently reported across different companies, sectors, or industries.

4. There are three main ways in which financial data are organized: time series, cross-sectional, and panel data. Time series data consist of information and variables collected over multiple time periods. Cross-sectional data consist of data collected at one point in time for many different companies (the cross-section of companies of interest). A panel data set consists of cross-sectional data collected at different points in time.

5. a. Outliers are observations that seem to be inconsistent with the other values in a data set.
   b. Financial data contain outliers for a number of reasons including data errors, measurement errors, or unusual events. Interpretation of data containing outliers may be misleading.

CHAPTER 12

1. a. The goal of the sorts test is to determine whether a factor earns a systematic premium.
   b. One application of the portfolio sort is the construction of a factor mimicking portfolio (FMP). An FMP is a long-short portfolio that goes long stocks with high values of a characteristic and short stocks with low values of a characteristic, in equal dollar amounts. An FMP is known as a zero-cost factor trading strategy.

2. Classical financial theory states that the average return of a stock is the payoff to investors for taking on risk. This risk-reward relationship is expressed through a factor model where the dependent variable is the stocks' returns and the independent factors are the exposures (characteristics) of that stocks. The factor model specification is contemporaneous if both left- and right-hand side variables (returns and factors) have the same time subscript, t. The factor model is a forecasting specification

where the time subscript of the return and the factors are t + h ($h \geq 1$) and t, respectively.

3. Three problems discussed in the chapter include estimation error, common variation in residuals, and multicollinearity.

   Sometimes the independent variables (factors) in the regression are not given explicitly and instead need to be estimated. Often, these factors are estimated with error. The estimation errors in the factors can have an impact on the inference from a factor model. This problem is commonly referred to as the "errors in variables problem."

   The residuals from a regression often contain a source of common variation. Sources of common variation in the residuals are heteroskedasticity and serial correlation.

   Heteroskedasticity occurs when the variance of the residual differs across observations and affects the statistical inference in a linear regression. In particular, the estimated standard errors will typically be underestimated and the t-statistics will therefore be inflated.

   Serial correlation occurs when consecutive residuals terms in a linear regression are correlated, violating the assumptions of regression theory. If the serial correlation is positive then the standard errors are underestimated and the t-statistics will be inflated.

   Multicollinearity occurs when two or more independent variables are highly correlated.

4. a. Factor portfolios are constructed to measure the information content of a factor. We evaluate the behavior of these factor portfolios to determine whether a factor earns a systematic premium. The objective of a factor is to mimic the return behavior of a factor and minimize the residual risk. Construction of factor portfolios requires holding both long and short positions.
   b. The two methodologies to build a factor portfolio are the factor model approach and the optimization approach.

5. An in-sample methodology refers to a backtesting methodology where the researcher uses the same data sample to specify, calibrate, and evaluate a model. An out-of-sample methodology is a backtesting methodology where the researcher uses a subset of the sample to specify and calibrate a model, and then evaluates the forecasting ability of the model on a different subset of data.

CHAPTER 13

1. The systematic risk of the stock is due to its exposure to the industry and size factors. Starting from the factor model formulation, the systematic return of each stock is given by $r_{\text{SYS}} = \beta \cdot F^{\text{IND}} + \ell \cdot F^{\text{SIZE}}$ and hence the systematic risk of the stock can be measured by

$$\sigma_{\text{SYS}} = \sqrt{\beta^2 \cdot \sigma_{\text{IND}}^2 + \ell^2 \cdot \sigma_{\text{SIZE}}^2 + 2 \cdot \beta \cdot \ell \cdot \rho_{\text{IND,SIZE}} \cdot \sigma_{\text{IND}} \cdot \sigma_{\text{SIZE}}}$$

Using this formula, the systematic risk is 7.36% and 7.21% for stock 1 and 2, respectively.

2. The total risk of each stock can be formulated as

$$\sigma_{\text{TOTAL}} = \sqrt{\sigma_{\text{SYS}}^2 + \sigma_{\text{IDIO}}^2}$$

There is no cross-term between the systematic and the idiosyncratic components in this formulation as we assume that they are uncorrelated in the framework of multi-factor risk models. Using this expression, the total risk of each security is $\sigma_{1,\text{TOTAL}} = 14.08\%$ and $\sigma_{2,\text{TOTAL}} = 8.77\%$. Even though the systematic risk of the two stocks are similar, their total risk turns out to be significantly different due to the large difference in their idiosyncratic risk.

3. The systematic return of the portfolio can be formulated as

$$r_{P,\text{SYS}} = w_1 \cdot r_{1,\text{SYS}} + w_2 \cdot r_{2,\text{SYS}}$$

where w_1 and w_2 are the weights, $r_{1,\text{SYS}}$ and $r_{2,\text{SYS}}$ are the systematic returns of each stock in the portfolio. These two stocks load onto different industry factors (as they belong to different industries) but they load onto the same size factor. Thus the systematic return of the portfolio can be formulated as

$$r_{P,\text{SYS}} = w_1 \cdot \beta_1 \cdot F^{\text{IND1}} + w_2 \cdot \beta_2 \cdot F^{\text{IND2}} + (w_1 \cdot \ell_1 + w_2 \cdot \ell_2) \cdot F^{\text{SIZE}}$$

Note that there are three components of the portfolio systematic return. Isolated risk of a portfolio coming from a risk factor can be measured as the product of the portfolio's loading to that factor and the volatility of the factor. From the previous equation, the loading of the portfolio to the first industry, second industry, and size factors are respectively: $w_1 \cdot \beta_1$, $w_2 \cdot \beta_2$, and $w_1 \cdot \ell_1 + w_2 \cdot \ell_2$.

As a result, isolated risk coming from the first industry factor is $\sigma_{\text{IND1}}^{\text{ISO}} = w_1 \cdot \beta_1 \cdot \sigma_{\text{IND1}} = 3.50\%$. Similarly, we find that $\sigma_{\text{IND2}}^{\text{ISO}} = 4.00\%$ and $\sigma_{\text{SIZE}}^{\text{ISO}} = 0.50\%$.

4. The systematic risk of the portfolio is a function of the isolated systematic risk coming from each factor and the correlations between these factors:

$$\sigma_{P,\text{SYS}} = \sqrt{\begin{array}{l} \left(\sigma_{\text{IND1}}^{\text{ISO}}\right)^2 + \left(\sigma_{\text{IND2}}^{\text{ISO}}\right)^2 + \left(\sigma_{\text{SIZE}}^{\text{ISO}}\right)^2 + 2\cdot\rho_{\text{IND1,IND2}}\cdot\sigma_{\text{IND1}}^{\text{ISO}}\cdot\sigma_{\text{IND2}}^{\text{ISO}} \\ + 2\cdot\rho_{\text{IND1,SIZE}}\cdot\sigma_{\text{IND1}}^{\text{ISO}}\cdot\sigma_{\text{SIZE}}^{\text{ISO}} + 2\cdot\rho_{\text{IND2,SIZE}}\cdot\sigma_{\text{IND2}}^{\text{ISO}}\cdot\sigma_{\text{SIZE}}^{\text{ISO}} \end{array}}$$

From this formula the systematic risk of the portfolio turns out to be 6.28%.

The idiosyncratic risk of the portfolio is computed using the assumption that the idiosyncratic returns of the two stocks are independent:

$$\sigma_{P,\text{IDIO}} = \sqrt{w_1^2 \cdot \sigma_{1,\text{IDIO}}^2 + w_2^2 \cdot \sigma_{2,\text{IDIO}}^2} = 6.50\%$$

Then the total risk of the portfolio can be computed as:

$$\sigma_{P,\text{TOTAL}} = \sqrt{\sigma_{P,\text{SYS}}^2 + \sigma_{P,\text{IDIO}}^2} = 9.04\%$$

Even though the total risk of the first stock is 14.08%, and it has a 50% weight in the portfolio, the portfolio risk is relatively close to that of the less risky stock—the second stock—(8.77%) due to the diversification effect across these two stocks. In the next question, we quantify this effect by looking into the correlation between the two stocks.

5. We can derive this from total portfolio risk and the risk of the individual stocks by the following:

$$\sigma_{P,\text{TOTAL}} = \sqrt{w_1^2 \cdot \sigma_{1,\text{TOTAL}}^2 + w_2^2 \cdot \sigma_{2,\text{TOTAL}}^2 + 2\cdot w_1 \cdot w_2 \cdot \rho_{1,2} \cdot \sigma_{1,\text{TOTAL}} \cdot \sigma_{2,\text{TOTAL}}}$$

The correlation comes out relatively low (0.21), hence the reason for the strong diversification effect observed in the previous question.

6. By using the expression in the previous question, these can be measured as

$$\sigma_1^{\text{CONT}} = \frac{w_1^2 \cdot \sigma_{1,\text{TOTAL}}^2 + w_1 \cdot w_2 \cdot \rho_{1,2} \cdot \sigma_{1,\text{TOTAL}} \cdot \sigma_{2,\text{TOTAL}}}{\sigma_{P,\text{TOTAL}}} = 6.20\%$$

$$\sigma_2^{\text{CONT}} = \frac{w_2^2 \cdot \sigma_{2,\text{TOTAL}}^2 + w_1 \cdot w_2 \cdot \rho_{1,2} \cdot \sigma_{1,\text{TOTAL}} \cdot \sigma_{2,\text{TOTAL}}}{\sigma_{P,\text{TOTAL}}} = 2.84\%$$

CHAPTER 14

1. Landmark studies on the determinants of portfolio performance were widely misinterpreted and viewed as evidence that asset allocation is more important than security selection. Combined with the growing popularity of returns-based style analysis, this led to the view that portfolios should be viewed as collections of asset classes, factors, and style exposures rather than collections of individual securities. This was followed by an increase in the availability of macro data and a decline in the cost of computing power, leading to an increased use of quantitative strategies and the adoption of dynamic factors models in portfolio management.

2. In almost any theoretical asset pricing model, the (excess) return of any security is a linear function of one or more factors (e.g., beta for the capital asset pricing model). The return of any portfolio is merely a linear combination of the returns of the constituent securities. Because any security can be written as a linear combination of factors, whether it is a single factor as in the case of the CAPM or a host of factors as in the APT, any portfolio of securities (which is a linear combination of the securities) may likewise be written as a linear combination of the factors.

3. When employing a factor-based portfolio management model, a portfolio manager is concerned more about factor exposure than idiosyncratic features of particular securities. Securities are included in a portfolio in order to capture the returns associated with their factor exposures rather than their idiosyncratic return. As a result, a portfolio built using a dynamic factor model will tend to hold more securities to ensure that the portfolio's return is driven less by the returns of individual securities and more by the factor exposure of the portfolio.

4. There is empirical support for the efficacy of both value and momentum strategies. These strategies have been successfully applied to stocks within particular markets and across markets (e.g., countries or sectors). Value strategies tend to trade early, while momentum strategies will always trade after turning points. Models incorporating a combination of valuation and momentum strategies are designed to remedy these problems, by allowing momentum to dominate when valuations have not yet reached an extreme position and valuations to dominate when momentum breaks down. Although it is rare in practice, the concurrence of valuation signals and momentum signals is a powerful indicator,

since both momentum and valuation have been shown to be predictive of future returns.

5. Investable versions of indexes are increasingly available to implement gain exposure to various market segments, including style categories, sectors, countries and geographic regions. Investing in these aggregates may be accomplished via futures contracts, swaps, and exchange-traded funds (ETFs). These vehicles allow a portfolio manager to gain exposure to a particular style, industry, sector, country, market capitalization segment, or other factor at an extremely low cost in a single trade.

CHAPTER 15

1. Factors and strategies can fail. The Alpha Repair process provides a systematic framework to remove failed factors and select winning factors in the investment process.

2. Return-to-volatility ratio as a zero interest rate version of the Sharpe ratio.

3. First, the size of the team of factors is kept small so that as similar factors compete for a spot, only the best ones survive the process. Second, the annualized return-to-volatility of selected factor portfolios increases with the number of factors used. But the annual return progressively declines from factor portfolios of size greater than three. The more factors used, the better the diversification and risk-adjusted return. The fewer factors used, the higher the annualized return. Three factors is a good compromise between these competing features.

4. No, for two reasons. First, the objective function will tend to swap factors that are correlated. The inferior factor in the portfolio will get replaced by a correlated contender that produces a superior result for the objective function. Consequently, the alpha of stocks is not dramatically affected. Second, we constrain stock turnover in the portfolio construction process.

5. No. A separate stock portfolio construction process is used after selecting the factors. The scores, that is, alphas, of stocks are only used as the input in this process. Using the monthly scores, portfolios are constructed to maximize alpha subject to a targeted tracking error relative to universe. The example we use in the chapter selects stock portfolios from the Russell 1000 universe, targeted to 100% per year turnover and a 600 bps tracking error.

CHAPTER 16

1. Building stock portfolios in a way that fails to explicitly control for country membership can result in significant misallocation of risk. In particular, country bets can dominate a portfolio that aims to represent skill in selecting individual stocks.

2. Ignoring country membership in constructing stock portfolios may result in two types of country bets—those consistent with a direct country selection strategy ("country selection bets") and those inconsistent with such a strategy ("country noise bets"). Both types of country bets are problematic. The country selection bets may provide alpha but present an obstacle to rigorous and accurate risk allocation. The country noise bets may be regarded as a zero-alpha, pure opportunity cost, and are therefore even worse.

3. Country noise bets arise because a country-agnostic stock selection process fails to recognize the following distinction. When countries are not equally represented in the sample of stocks, what is typical among countries will not be the same as what is typical among stocks. Avoiding country noise bets requires either (a) altogether segregating country bets from stock bets or (b) accounting for the differences in country representation. Either approach rests on incorporating country membership information into the stock selection process.

4. These issues are present in both developed and emerging markets, but are more pronounced in the latter. Lack of country neutralization can produce stock portfolios that are two-thirds driven by country bets in emerging markets and half driven by country bets in developed markets. In both regions, about half of these country bets are "noise" bets.

5. We recommend that managers get explicit about countries—either ensure that country deviations from benchmark are small and yield little tracking error, or manage country selection directly, potentially using the same philosophy as is used for stocks. Our recommendation applies for both quantitative and qualitative investment managers. (Note: There is evidence that many of the same alpha factors that work for selecting stocks also work for selecting countries. See Cliff S. Asness, John M. Liew, and Ross L. Stevens, "Parallels Between the Cross-Sectional Predictability of Stock and Country Returns," *Journal of Portfolio Management* 23, no. 3 (1997): 79–87. In addition, there is evidence that similar investment strategies work in both developed and emerging markets. See Michele Aghassi and Lars Nielsen, "Value

and Momentum Investing in Emerging and Developed Markets," AQR Capital Management Working Paper, 2011.)

CHAPTER 17

1. The market impact cost of a trade is the deviation of the transaction price from the price that would have prevailed had the trade not occurred. There are two different kinds of market impact costs: temporary and permanent.

2. Trading in the markets is not frictionless. The temporary market impact is of transitory nature and can be seen as the additional liquidity concession necessary for the liquidity provider to take the order, inventory effects (price effects due to broker/dealer inventory imbalances), or imperfect substitution (for example, price incentives to induce market participants to absorb the additional shares).

   The permanent market impact reflects the persistent price change that results as the market adjusts to the information content of the trade.

3. **a.** A limit order is a conditional order that is executed only if the limit price or a better price can be obtained. In contrast, a market order is an unconditional order to execute at the current best price available in the market (guarantees execution, not price).
   b. With a limit order a trader can improve the execution price relative to the market order price. The drawback, however, is that the execution is neither certain nor immediate (guarantees price, not execution).

4. **a.** The different approaches to measure market impact are pre-trade sales, post-trade sales, and same-day, or average, measures.
   b. VWAP stands for volume-weighted average price and is calculated over all transactions in the security on the trade day. It is a measure of market impact.

5. Implementation shortfall for a trade is the difference between the decision price and the final execution price (that may include commissions, taxes, etc.). This is sometimes referred to as *slippage*.

6. The explanatory or independent variables fall into two categories: trade-based factors and asset-based factors. The former include trade size, relative trade size, price of market liquidity, type of trade (information or informationless trade), investor's efficiency and trading style, specific characteristics of the market or the exchange, time of trade submission and trade timing, and order type. Asset-based factors include

price momentum, price volatility, market capitalization, style (growth versus value), and specific industry or sector characteristics.

CHAPTER 18

1. The specific constraints used in a portfolio allocation problem depend on the restrictions faced by the investment manager. Common constraints include long-only constraints that restrict short selling; holding constraints that set limits on the total concentration of assets in an industry, sector, or country; turnover constraints that restrict the amount of trading; risk factor constraints that limit the exposure of the portfolio to a risk factor such as the market; cardinality constraints that limit the number of assets in the portfolio; minimum holding or transaction size constraints that control the transaction costs associated with rebalancing the portfolio; round lot constraints that represent the condition that stocks and bonds cannot be traded in fractions; and tracking error constraints that restrict the deviation of the portfolio return from the return on a benchmark.

2. The most widely used definition of tracking error is as the variance of the difference between the portfolio return and the return on a benchmark. Other definitions include (a) the absolute value of the difference between the portfolio weights and the benchmark weights; and (b) the conditional value-at-risk for the difference between the portfolio returns and the benchmark returns. The three definitions are not equivalent, and may lead to very different portfolio allocations.

   The standard definition of tracking error is concerned with the variability of the overall portfolio returns around the benchmark returns. If, instead, the portfolio manager would like to limit the deviation of the portfolio weights from the benchmark weights directly, he may use the definition in (a). An advantage of (a) is also that the group of constraints through which it can be expressed as a condition is more solver-friendly, since the constraints are linear. One must keep in mind, however, that some benchmarks, such as the Russell 2000, are too large to be replicated exactly. Imposing a condition on the portfolio weights, rather than the overall portfolio return as in the standard case, is more restrictive.

   The variance penalizes for any deviation from the benchmark, and treats positive and negative deviations equally. If the portfolio manager is only concerned about situations in which the portfolio loses, not gains, relative to the benchmark, he may want to use a definition of tracking error that does not penalize for outperforming the benchmark, such as definition (b).

3. The most widely used models for portfolio allocation with transaction costs include a transaction cost–function term directly in the objective function. The transaction cost function is multiplied by a transaction cost–aversion parameter. The transaction cost function itself is typically assumed to be the sum of transaction cost functions for the individual stocks (that is, the transaction costs for the individual stocks are assumed to be independent). Each individual transaction cost function can be modeled as linear, piecewise-linear, quadratic, or more complex type of function.

4. Typically, a loss is associated with risk, and portfolio allocation schemes seek to minimize it. In the presence of tax liabilities, however, realizing a loss may be beneficial because it can be used to offset gains and reduce the overall tax burden.

5. To make the optimal portfolio allocation robust with respect to errors in input parameters such as the covariance matrix, one could (a) perform robust parameter estimation, (b) use portfolio resampling, (c) use robust optimization, or (d) use a combination of (a) and (c). In particular, in (a), one could use shrinkage to average out different estimators of the covariance matrix. In (b), the portfolio composition is recomputed for a set of possible covariance matrices, and the optimal weights obtained in the different cases are averaged out. In (c), an uncertainty set for the covariance matrix entries is specified, and the portfolio allocation that is optimal for the worst-case value of the covariance matrix within the uncertainty set is computed.

CHAPTER 19

1. There are practical issues with using historical asset returns. Some assets in the current portfolio may not have existed in the past. Even if they did exist, their characteristics may have changed significantly over time. The authors avoid this problem by using current portfolio factor exposures together with a history of factor returns to simulate the portfolio's historical return distribution. Using only the characteristics of the portfolio eliminates our need to worry about the consequences of assets dropping out of the portfolio during the simulation period.

2. Beta captures the average relationship between a stock, or a portfolio, and a market portfolio. In contrast, shortfall beta captures the relationship

between a stock, or a portfolio, and a market portfolio during a period of extreme stress. The cross-sectional correlation between beta and shortfall beta is high.

3. No. To test this, the authors constrained the beta of the shortfall optimized portfolio to be one. The performance was found to be even better.

4. The authors compared the average daily losses sustained by portfolios constructed with mean-variance and shortfall constrained optimization. The differences were small but consistent. Shortfall optimization performed better, especially during turbulent times.

5. The active portfolio can be decomposed into a portfolio due to the alpha and portfolios corresponding to each of the constraints. The portfolio representing the (net) shortfall beta performed well over the historical period. Moreover, during these stressful periods, the shortfall beta constraint shifts the active portfolio toward the shortfall beta portfolio. The two effects combine to drive the incremental gains the authors found in implementing the constraint.

CHAPTER 20

1. Unlike low-frequency data on which the classical portfolio management was developed, high-frequency data incorporates several idiosyncrasies that impact inputs into allocation frameworks. Specifically, high-frequency data is voluminous, subject to a bid-ask bounce, and is irregularly spaced in time.

2. A single day of high-frequency data of the lowest granularity (the so-called "tick data") contains as many observations as one hundred years of traditional daily data. While the quantities of high-frequency data make estimations more complex computationally, the data deliver higher statistical significance on shorter data samples.

3. The bid-ask bounce is a phenomenon describing the "bounce" of trading prices from the quoted bid to the ask, and back. The sequential price changes induced by the bid-ask bounce are prominent relative to short-term price changes caused by wider market movements or intrinsic equity values. The bounce is considered to be a "microstructure noise," creating an unwelcome discontinuity in data.

   Different quote sampling methodologies have been designed to mitigate the discretization of data induced by the bid-ask bounce. Yet, the bounce introduces biases into the computation of portfolio allocation parameters, such as empirical variance, complicating the search for the optimal solution.

4. The irregular (asynchronous) arrival of data introduces challenges to computations of contemporaneous correlations between any two securities, critical to classical portfolio allocation. In addition, both the bid-ask bounce and the irregular spacing induce the so-called Epps effect, under which the empirical correlations of equities decay at high frequencies.

5. Most researchers who have looked at the Epps effect to-date have only looked at trade data. Quote data shows smaller decay at high frequencies than does trade data. Overall, different data sampling methodologies appear to produce different information subsets that can be helpful in delivering more robust portfolio optimization solutions. This area is ripe for further study.

CHAPTER 21

1. Pure arbitrage opportunities are rare in that they are risk-free. Statistical arbitrage is based on modeling a price or return process and exploiting deviations from what the model says is a fair price. Both typically involve going long one security and going short another security, but statistical arbitrage involves uncertainty while pure arbitrage guarantees a profit.

2. Relative return strategies do not depend on the level of security prices or the direction of security prices. What matters is the relative movement of security prices. For example, if two security prices are going down, you can still profit by being short the security whose price is dropping faster and being long the security whose price is declining more slowly.

3. It is possible that the estimated relationship between two securities is spurious. A t-test is one way to test whether the coefficients estimated are statistically different from zero. The t-test can also give you a degree of confidence in the relationship to estimate probabilities of success.

4. A cointegrating relationship shows the long-run, equilibrium relationship between two variables. The error correction model shows the short-term dynamics of how the deviations from the cointegrating relationship return to equilibrium.

5. A self-financing strategy is one that requires no additional injections of capital to maintain the strategy. The portfolio positions can change over

time, so a self-financing constraint is one that means that only the proceeds from one period are used to establish the next period's positions.

Printed and bound by CPI Group (UK) Ltd, Croydon, CR0 4YY

23/04/2025

14660921-0005